ATLANTIC CANADA *A History*

Margaret R. Conrad • James K. Hiller • THIRD EDITION

OXFORD
UNIVERSITY PRESS

OXFORD
UNIVERSITY PRESS

Oxford University Press is a department of the University of Oxford.
It furthers the University's objective of excellence in research, scholarship,
and education by publishing worldwide. Oxford is a registered trade mark of
Oxford University Press in the UK and in certain other countries.

Published in Canada by
Oxford University Press
8 Sampson Mews, Suite 204,
Don Mills, Ontario M3C 0H5 Canada

www.oupcanada.com

Copyright © Oxford University Press Canada 2015

Library and Archives Canada Cataloguing in Publication

Conrad, Margaret, author
Atlantic Canada : a history / Margaret R. Conrad, James K. Hiller. — Third edition.

Includes bibliographical references and index.
ISBN 978-0-19-901326-5 (pbk.)

1. Atlantic Provinces—History—Textbooks. I. Hiller, J. K. (James K.), 1942–, author II. Title.

FC2005.C65 2015   971.5   C2015-900373-3

Oxford University Press is committed to our environment.
This book is printed on Forest Stewardship Council® certified paper
and comes from responsible sources.

Printed and bound in Canada

1 2 3 4 — 18 17 16 15

Table of Contents

List of Boxes   **iv**
Introduction: A Region in the Making   **vii**

Part I ❧ The Atlantic Region, 1500–1860
Chapter 1   Beginnings   **2**
Chapter 2   Aboriginal Peoples   **14**
Chapter 3   European Encounters, 1000–1598   **24**
Chapter 4   Colonial Experiments, 1598–1632   **37**
Chapter 5   Colonial Communities Take Root, 1632–1713   **50**
Chapter 6   Renegotiating the Atlantic Region, 1713–1763   **67**
Chapter 7   Community Formation, 1749–1815   **91**
Chapter 8   Maturing Colonial Societies, 1815–1860   **115**

Part II ❧ The Atlantic Region Since 1860
Chapter 9   Confronting Confederation, 1860–1873   **138**
Chapter 10   The Industrial Challenge, 1873–1901   **155**
Chapter 11   The Promise and Peril of a New Century, 1901–1919   **177**
Chapter 12   Between the Wars, 1919–1939   **200**
Chapter 13   The Emergence of Atlantic Canada, 1939–1949   **223**
Chapter 14   A Region Transformed, 1949–1975   **240**
Chapter 15   Atlantic Canada in the Global Village, 1975–2001   **261**
Chapter 16   Whither Tending? Atlantic Canada in the Twenty-First Century   **282**

Bibliographic Note   **291**
Notes   **292**
Index   **305**

List of Boxes

Biography

Klu'skap   18
John Cabot   29
Membertou   39
David and Sara Kirke   60
Joseph Broussard   83
Mikak   96
William Carson   131
Samuel Leonard Tilley   149

Alexander "Boss" Gibson   159
Edith Archibald   172
William Ford Coaker   183
Lucy Maud Montgomery   188
Mona Wilson and Public Health   207
Clarie Gillis Goes to Ottawa   228
Antonine Maillet   258
Elizabeth May   278

Document

The Capture of an Inuit Woman
    and Her Child, 1566   21
The Voyage of the *Grace* from
    Bristol, 1594   34
Planting a Colony in Ferryland, 1621   46
Building Dikes in Acadia, 1699   55
The Treaty of 1726   76
Edward Winslow's Plan for a "Gentlemanlike"
    Colony, 1783   106
Chief Joseph Malli Goes to London, 1842   120
The Prince Edward Island
    Land Commission, 1861   143

Joseph Howe on Confederation, 1865   148
The Royal Commission on Labour and
    Capital, 1889   161
Joining the Army, 1916   191
Lady Hope Simpson's Impressions of
    Newfoundlanders, 1935   213
Family Allowances and Public
    Schooling, 1946   232
The Progressive Conservatives Adopt the
    Atlantic Resolutions, 1957   243
The Constitution and Equalization,
    1982   265

Historical Focus

Oral History   17
L'Anse aux Meadows   27
Le Théâtre de Neptune in
    New France, 1606   41
Antoine Tecouenemac and the Conquest
    of Port-Royal   63
The Golden Age of Piracy, 1690–1730   71
Slavery in Louisbourg   73
Mapping the Region   93
The Black Loyalists   103
A Communications Revolution   123

British Financiers and Canadian
    Confederation   144
Acadian National Identity   170
Exploring Labrador   179
Beaumont Hamel   194
Newfoundland and Dominion Status   212
The Radio and Confederation   235
The Aboriginal Peoples of Newfoundland and
    Labrador and the Terms of Union   236
Africville   254
Neo-Nationalism in Newfoundland   273
Nunatsiavut   288

Setting the Context

The Americas in 1500   14
The Expansion of Europe   25
Ecological Exchanges   48
The Dutch Challenge   53
The Long Eighteenth Century   68
The American Revolution   97
The Industrial Age   116

The Atlantic Colonies in the Age of Industry   138
Causes of the Great War   190
The Interwar Economy   200
The World in Turmoil, 1939–49   223
The Postwar Liberal Consensus   240
The Information Age   261
11 September 2001   282

Introduction

A Region in the Making

*A*tlantic Canada: A History is designed to provide university students and general readers with a concise and up-to-date introduction to the region and its peoples. This third edition has been revised and expanded to place the region more broadly in its Atlantic and global contexts, while bringing the narrative further into the twenty-first century and reflecting recent scholarship.

In the precursor to this text, *Atlantic Canada: A Region in the Making* (2001), we noted the difficulty of writing a cohesive history of the space called Atlantic Canada. Although the concept of region has helped Canadians to come to terms with the physical, cultural, and historical differences in their enormous country, what constitutes a region is always fluid, subject to shifts in attitudes, communications systems, political regimes, population movements, and trade patterns.[1] Indeed, the term "Atlantic Canada" sits awkwardly with many scholars. A family resemblance among the four provinces is admitted, but Newfoundland and Labrador is often seen as a misfit. Writing in the 1980s, Alan Wilson concluded that, apart from fog and underdevelopment, the Maritime provinces of New Brunswick, Nova Scotia, and Prince Edward Island share very little with Newfoundland (Labrador only became part of the official name of the province in 2001).[2] In a much-admired two-volume history of the Atlantic region, Newfoundland is an integral part of the pre-1867 volume, but it is largely absent from the second volume until 1949, when it joined Confederation—as if it had been expelled from the regional fold for its failure, however brief, to conform to its apparently predetermined destiny.[3] Taking a political perspective in the late 1970s, J. Murray Beck could find no regional identity at all—only provincial ones.[4] Others have gone even further, claiming that identity exists primarily in Atlantic Canada's own untidy regionalisms. Mi'kma'ki, Acadie, Africadia, Cape Breton, and Labrador are only the most obvious examples of regions that exist within, across, and beyond provincial boundaries.

A shared location is obviously the cornerstone of any region, but even geography is an uncertain ally in the quest for definition. Consisting of islands, peninsulas, and fringes of the North American continent, the Atlantic region is not defined solely by its exposure to the North Atlantic. If it were, the Îles de la Madeleine, Saint-Pierre and Miquelon, the Gaspé, and even portions of the state of Maine would all be integral parts of Atlantic Canada; but political decisions have determined otherwise.

Although formal criteria relating to geography, history, and economic conditions can be used to define Atlantic Canada, it is above all the region's functional relation to the rest of the continent that now fixes its identity. This was not always the case. Nor has the region always been treated as a single geopolitical unit. Aboriginal peoples developed their own versions of local identities, which were disrupted with the invasion of Europeans beginning in the late fifteenth century. In the seventeenth and early eighteenth centuries the British and French empires carved overlapping spheres of influence in the Atlantic region, and between 1867 and 1873 the Maritime colonies (with varying degrees of reluctance) all became provinces of Canada, while Newfoundland resisted the modern continental drift.

The term "Maritime provinces" was coined before 1867, but "Atlantic Canada" and "Atlantic provinces" only came into common use after Newfoundland joined Confederation in 1949. Many observers make the mistake of labelling Newfoundland and Labrador as a Maritime province. It is not, and its differences from the Maritimes cannot be casually dismissed. In this volume we use the current political definition of Atlantic Canada—the sometimes controversial, often artificial boundaries marked on a map—but we do not argue for a quintessential Atlantic Canadian regional culture. Instead we chart formal and functional regional identities and consider the imagined sense of place that has evolved over time among a diverse population. From surviving documentary evidence, it is possible to glimpse regions of the mind in Atlantic Canada that have often had a greater impact on human motivation than more tangible political and economic structures.

These regions of the mind offer a curiously contradictory and often dated picture of Atlantic Canada. In the view of the literary scholar Janice Kulyk Keefer, one lens frames "white clapboard church in scarlet autumn dale, dories in the very shape of indolence nesting in placid harbours, the subtle rot of grey-shingled shacks in dense spruce groves"; another captures "senile, ruined faces, large families in two-roomed shacks."[5] Other writers have emphasized the Arcadian quality of the Atlantic landscape. Writing in 1912 from Leaskdale, Ontario, the popular writer Lucy Maud Montgomery conceded that her new home was "a very pretty country place [that] would be almost as pretty as Cavendish if it had the sea. . . . At times—generally in the winter twilight—I am very homesick and feel as if I would exchange all the kingdoms of the world and the glory thereof for a sunset ramble in Lover's Lane."[6]

Newfoundlanders have celebrated the outports in similar fashion, but flint-eyed critics such as Patrick O'Flaherty have shunned romanticism, noting the brutal geographical legacy that in Newfoundland and Labrador makes it impossible for "one generation to tame the environment for the benefit of the next."[7] O'Flaherty's comment may be less applicable to the Maritimes, where the landscape has been more receptive to human industry, but it touches on a problem that pollsters suggest is endemic in the region: a low sense of efficacy. Atlantic Canadians, past and present alike, have combined regional pride and relentless optimism with a Sisyphean resignation to the idea that it may well be their lot to strive rather than to succeed. The title of Edward MacDonald's history of twentieth-century Prince Edward Island—*If You're Stronghearted*—captures the essence of this ongoing struggle.[8]

Notions of failure and backwardness permeate scholarly and journalistic commentary on Atlantic Canada. "To be a scholar of Atlantic Canada," Ian McKay has observed, "is to wrestle, often at the very outset of one's inquiries, with a subtle, pervasive and durable language of disparagement and marginality."[9] The political scientist Barry Cooper, for example, has argued, as a matter of "fact," that "stagnation and decadence remain the most prominent features of pre-modern communal life to have survived into the present" in the Maritimes (by which he meant Atlantic Canada).[10] Although Cooper offers little evidence to back up his assertion, such comments serve to consolidate second-class citizenship.

Charges of conservatism and backwardness hold little weight. When Atlantic Canadians are accused of being more conservative than other North Americans, it is necessary to ask how this conservatism manifests itself. Those who favour the conservative stereotype point to the comparative reluctance of Atlantic Canadians to support radical political movements, a tendency among the region's artists and creative writers to cling to realism, and a commitment to the notion of "social good" in law and public policy. Scholars who dispute this view emphasize the region's leadership in the movement for responsible government; its early commitment to higher education for women; pitched battles between capital and labour; and the radical efforts of the region's governments to impose modernization through resettlement programs, sweeping municipal reform, and state-run enterprise. We contend that emphasizing radical departures serves the region no better than belabouring conservative stereotypes. The wiser course is to concede that Atlantic Canada is a complex region with a history long and deep enough to accommodate most academic prejudices.

It has even been suggested that some twentieth-century interpretations of the region's history may have helped to sell Atlantic Canada at a discount. In his provocative book *The Quest of the Folk*, Ian McKay has shown how, during the difficult interwar years (1919–39), Nova Scotians succumbed to the myth of a golden age when innocent fisherfolk lived in harmony with an idyllic rural landscape.[11] Romanticized notions of pre-industrial utopias have been common enough in Western societies, McKay argues, but they have proved particularly pernicious in Nova Scotia (and by implication across Atlantic Canada), reducing real people to static essences represented by stereotypical figures such as Glooscap, Rugged Fishermen, and Scottish Bagpipers. In Newfoundland, celebrations of outport life have been dangerously combined with a long-standing sense of victimization, and a parade of historical scapegoats—from the fishing admirals to Water Street merchants—used to explain relative backwardness and failure. In the early twenty-first century, fictional characters—Evangeline, Anne of Green Gables, La Sagouine, the Rowdyman—seem to loom larger on the region's historical landscape than do more complex realities.

Many scholars refuse to accept that Atlantic Canadians are constrained by historical determinism. In a recent study exploring how Canadians engage with the past in their everyday lives, the findings suggest that people in the Atlantic region are no more hobbled by their history than other Canadians, and that a coherent narrative of a community's evolution, such as the one that prevails among Acadians in New Brunswick, can serve as a source of optimism and empowerment.[12] Herb Wyile notes that even though it is depicted as "a haven from the consumerism, corporatization, and global competition that characterize our current milieu, Atlantic Canada has been palpably affected by these very trends, as recent writing in the region has underscored."[13] The title of his book on the subject—*Anne of Tim Hortons*—captures the essence of his conclusion that young women in the region today are more likely to be found in a popular coffee shop than in a green-gabled farmhouse.

What is clear is that, when they venture elsewhere, Atlantic Canadians often find that "folk" images work against them, the first impression being that they are quaint, eccentric rustics in a modern world of sophisticated go-getters. Gary Burrill argues that the idea of leaving home is inseparable from the Atlantic regional identity.[14] As the "light infantry of capital," Atlantic Canadians have sailed the oceans of the world and criss-crossed the continent in search of work and greener pastures. "Leaving" songs inspired by this phenomenon, such as "Prince Edward Island Adieu" and "Farewell to Nova Scotia," are now canonized in folklore, and the "Ode to Newfoundland" is sung with as much enthusiasm in the taverns of Toronto and Fort McMurray as in those of the province that so many of its sons and daughters have left. Such evidence of social cohesion notwithstanding, Atlantic Canadians have generally been quick to assimilate to other North American cultures and have left little permanent record of a distinctive legacy from a beloved homeland. This should come as no surprise. Despite their nostalgia for the "home place," Atlantic Canadians have been full participants in the creation of a shared continental culture in which they fit comfortably.

Identities are not inborn; they are learned. Moreover, they vary over time and are constrained by social and cultural factors. In his 1970s study of identity formation in Cape Breton, Stephen Ullman discovered that pride in the island (as opposed to pride in Nova Scotia or Canada) increased with age, was stronger among Mi'kmaq than Euro-Canadians, and was also more pronounced among the working than the middle class.[15] Had he included gender among his variables, he would likely have found that women and men also showed differing levels of regional awareness, reflecting their socialization to separate spheres. Marilyn Porter's work on outport Newfoundland suggests that family and community concerns among women may well have had some bearing on the findings of many quantitative studies purporting to measure regional or provincial traits.[16]

"Region" and "regionalism" are slippery concepts, reflecting shifting cultural and historical contexts rather than fixed and static "truths." It is also important to distinguish between the two terms. While the Atlantic "region" is easy to find on a map, "regionalism" implies a political stance, a consciousness of a shared outlook that can be summoned up when other structures—familial, communal, provincial, national, global—fail. It may manifest itself as friendliness in distant ports, but it has not been the stuff of political cohesion at home. Over the years, policy-makers desperate to find a quick fix for real or imagined ills have often called for a union of the Maritime or Atlantic provinces. That no such union has ever materialized suggests not only that there are other powerful identities in Atlantic Canada competing for dominance, but also that regionalism has limited value as a vehicle for common action.

It can nevertheless be documented that Atlantic Canadians share an angle of vision regarding the world. In large measure this common perspective derives from being economically poor and politically weak relative to much of the rest of North America. It might well be asked why 2.3 million people inhabiting a resource-rich area that is larger than most of the world's nation-states are not wallowing in wealth. Small countries off the edges of continents—among them Great Britain, Japan, and most Nordic nations—have proven that economic success is possible without vast hinterlands or favoured climates. What caused the Atlantic provinces to lag behind?

Fish, fur, timber, minerals, and agricultural land provided Atlantic Canadians with the material conditions for a degree of economic well-being, but the dispersal of these resources along an extensive North Atlantic coastline has also nurtured dependency and diversity. With no internal metropolitan centre to impose a homogenizing influence, Atlantic Canada has historically been loose-jointed and vulnerable to outside forces. In the "long eighteenth century" (1689–1815) the region became the site of a struggle between France and Great Britain for imperial domination. The losers in this contest were the Aboriginal peoples and Acadians—the region's first European settlers—who saw most of their lands taken over by immigrants from Europe and the Thirteen Colonies/United States. It was only in 1815 that the destructive influence of war receded, enabling colonial societies to develop in relative security.

In scholarly efforts to explain the region's relative backwardness in the Industrial Age, the blame is usually placed on the federal government and capitalist exploitation. E.R. Forbes and Donald Savoie have demonstrated convincingly that national policies have been deficient in addressing the needs of the Atlantic provinces.[17] This outcome, Sean Cadigan argues, is a result of dependency relationships in a capitalist society that "produced places that have enjoyed disproportionately economic benefits and concomitant power while other places have suffered disproportionately from exploitation."[18]

Ultimately, the Atlantic provinces present a puzzling paradox, observable in many areas of the modern world. A have-not region plagued by failed ventures and outmigration, it nevertheless has nurtured world-class entrepreneurs, including K.C. Irving, Frank Sobey, Harry Steele, Craig Dobbin, and Harrison McCain, who have remained committed to their communities.

Taking a slightly different perspective, Savoie has argued that community life in Atlantic Canada is richer than modern statistical analyses, based on narrow notions of economic well-being, suggest.[19] It is, after all, a moot point whether wage earners forced to spend most of their annual income on survival in more favoured regions of the continent are any better off than their counterparts in the Atlantic region, where the scale of living is smaller but may be equally rich in material and psychological well-being. Rosemary E. Ommer and Nancy J. Turner go further, suggesting that the practices developed in the region's informal rural economies may well serve as models for a world preoccupied by unrealistic visions of economic growth.[20]

David Alexander, who perhaps contributed more to the understanding of his adopted region than any scholar of his generation, suggested in 1980 that "a new notion of happiness" based on the idea of regional self-reliance was emerging.[21] This idea has not been realized, but the rising tide of globalism and threats of environmental and financial meltdown may well promote regional co-operation and reduced expectations.

Along with offering students an updated and concise history of Atlantic Canada, our primary goal in writing this book is to make this diverse region better known to its citizens. We also hope that it will appeal to readers who are unfamiliar with the region and its people. Making available a synthesis of the region's long and remarkable history may increase awareness and understanding, while helping Atlantic Canadians to develop a more accurate and assured sense of who they are.

Further Readings

Friesen, Gerald. 2005. "Space and Region in Canadian History," *Journal of the Canadian Historical Association 2005* New Series, 16: 1–22.

Hiller, James K. 2000. "Is Atlantic Canadian History Possible?" *Acadiensis* XXX, 1 (Autumn): 16–22.

McKay, Ian. 2000. "A Note on 'Region' in Writing the History of Atlantic Canada," *Acadiensis* XXIX, 2 (Spring): 89–101.

Widdis, Randy William, Margaret R. Conrad, Jean Barman, Bill Waiser, and Sean T. Cardigan. 2006. "Round Table on Re-Imagining Regions," *Acadiensis* XXXV, 2 (Spring): 127–68.

Historical Spotlight

Forbes, E.R. 1978. "In Search of a Post-Confederation Maritime Historiography," *Acadiensis* VIII, 1 (Autumn): 3–21.

Matthews, Keith. 2001. "Historical Fence Building: A Critique of the Historiography of Newfoundland," *Newfoundland Studies* 17, 2 (Spring): 143–65.

Recommended Websites

Atlantic Canada Portal
http://atlanticportal.hil.unb.ca

Dictionary of Canadian Biography
http://www.biographi.ca

Newfoundland and Labrador Heritage
http://www.heritage.nf.ca/home.html

Nova Scotia Archives
http://www.gov.ns.ca/archives/

Prince Edward Island Public Archives and Records Office
http://www.gov.pe.ca/archives

The Rooms Provincial Archives Division, Newfoundland and Labrador
http://www.therooms.ca/archives/

Provincial Archives of New Brunswick
http://archives.gnb.ca/Archives/Default.aspx?culture=en-CA

A Reader's Guide to the History of Newfoundland and Labrador to 1869
http://www2.grenfell.mun.ca/nfld_history/index.htm

Part I

The Atlantic Region, 1500–1860

In the late fifteenth century Christopher Columbus and John Cabot encountered the Americas. They were not the first Europeans to explore the western coasts of the Atlantic Ocean, but their voyages set in motion an extraordinary chain of events. Over the next three centuries Europeans traded with, plundered, and ultimately settled on the fringes of their "new world." The Aboriginal peoples who had been living in North America for millennia gradually accommodated the intruders, who brought with them not only valued trade goods but also devastating diseases, new flora and fauna, intermittent warfare, and a world view that often contrasted sharply with their own.

What is now Atlantic Canada was on the front line of these developments. The abundant fish and fur found in the region attracted both public and private investment, and soon European monarchs were vying for dominance of the entire continent. Although Britain ultimately triumphed over France in the Seven Years' War (1756–63), it soon lost 13 of its North American colonies, which declared their independence as the United States of America in 1776 and fought a war to make good on their intention. By the Treaty of Paris in 1783, most of the territory once claimed by France remained part of British North America. In this space, people from many backgrounds—Aboriginal, African, and European—created new colonial societies.

The French Revolutionary and Napoleonic wars, which raged between 1793 and 1815, stimulated economic growth and served as catalysts for the new political and social values sweeping across the North Atlantic world. By the mid-nineteenth century, the people living in the Atlantic region were beginning to forge their own destinies as part of an expanding British Empire that dominated global trade.

Chapter 1

Beginnings

In 1855, J. William Dawson, a native of Pictou County, Nova Scotia, published a book entitled *Acadian Geology*. In it he reflected on a time 350 million years earlier when "multitudes of large animals now extinct" inhabited the Maritimes and submerged tropical forests laid the foundations for the region's rich coal deposits. Dawson was a pioneer in the emerging fields of geology and paleontology, two of the sciences that, in the nineteenth century, were transforming everything people had hitherto believed about the planet Earth and its inhabitants. A strict Presbyterian, he refused to accept the theory of evolution expounded by his famous contemporary, Charles Darwin. Dawson nevertheless helped to advance new scientific ideas about the origins of Earth and the emergence of an "Atlantic region."

The Making of the Atlantic Region

In Dawson's time most people in British North America subscribed to a biblical interpretation of the origins of the universe. They believed that God had created Heaven and Earth in six days—some thought 4004 years before the birth of Christ—and placed Adam and Eve in the Garden of Eden, from which they were eventually expelled to populate an imperfect world. Aboriginal creation stories also attributed Earth's origins to powerful gods.

The implications of the scientific view of creation also took a leap of faith to grasp. In the 1830s, Abraham Gesner, another Nova Scotia-born scientist, discovered fossils in the Bay of Fundy region. These drew the attention of Charles Lyell, the British founder of modern geology. In 1852 Lyell and Dawson explored the cliffs around Joggins on Chignecto Bay, where they found the earliest reptilian remains discovered in North America to that time. These findings helped to confirm the view that Earth was much older than the Book of Genesis implied. The reptiles discovered in fossilized drowned forests around

"Reptiles of the Coal Period," an illustration from J. William Dawson, *The Geology of Nova Scotia, New Brunswick, and Prince Edward Island: or, Acadian Geology* (4th edition, London, 1891).

Joggins were the ancestors of the dinosaurs that dominated the region for nearly 200 million years until they suddenly became extinct—perhaps as the result of an asteroid hitting Earth—some 66 million years ago. In recognition of this wealth of geological history written in stone, the Joggins Fossil Cliffs were declared a UNESCO World Heritage Site in 2008.

Scientists now think that Earth is at least 4.5 billion years old, and explain the creation of continents and oceans in the framework of plate tectonics. According to this approach, continents are in constant movement, colliding and breaking apart as they float on the planet's soft, molten interior. When a supercontinent breaks apart into smaller continents, oceans form between them; when those continents collide, Earth's crust buckles to form mountain chains, and pieces of ocean crust, arcs of volcanic islands, and continental fragments litter the landscape. These redistributed elements are called "terranes." The Atlantic region represents a collage of such terranes, welded to each other over millions of years of continental movement.[1]

Labrador is part of the Canadian Shield. One of the oldest and most stable land forms in the world, the Shield is composed of ancient rocks such as those found at Saglek Bay, which date back some 3.6 billion years. The rest of the Atlantic region took shape at the centre of the supercontinent named Pangaea, which itself was formed around 350 million years ago when the collision of ancient continental plates created the Appalachian Mountains. Geological evidence of this event can be seen in the rugged landscape of Newfoundland's Gros Morne National Park, declared a World Heritage Site in 1987. The two plates that had formed Pangaea began separating about 200 million years ago, and the space between them was filled by an ever-expanding Atlantic Ocean. The terrain stretching from northern Africa to Scandinavia bears striking resemblances to the Atlantic shores of the Maritimes and Newfoundland because they were once part of the same land mass.

In the years since Pangaea divided and the North Atlantic continent began drifting northward, adjustments of Earth's crust and the forces of erosion have eaten away the once much higher

Table 1.1 Timeline

4.5 billion BCE*	Earth takes form.
350–200 million years BCE	Most of Earth's land masses are joined in supercontinent Pangaea, with its coal-forming swamps; fish and reptiles flourish.
200 million years BCE	Pangaea begins to break up, creating the Americas, Eurasia, and Africa.
66 million years BCE	Mass extinction of Earth's species, including the dinosaurs, perhaps as a result of the impact of an asteroid.
2 million–8000 BCE	Ice Age grips Earth.
18,000 BCE	Glaciers from the last Ice Age begin to melt.
8600 BCE	Approximate date of the Paleo-Indian site at Debert: the first known human habitation in the Atlantic region.
8000–500 BCE	Archaic cultures inhabit the Maritimes, Newfoundland, and Labrador.
2000 BCE	Paleo-Eskimos arrive in Labrador.
500 BCE	Woodland (Ceramic) cultures begin to dominate the Maritime region.
500 BCE–1300 CE	Dorset people arrive in Labrador and spread to the island of Newfoundland.
1450 CE	Thule culture arrives in Labrador.

* BCE means "before common era," the equivalent of BC ("before Christ").

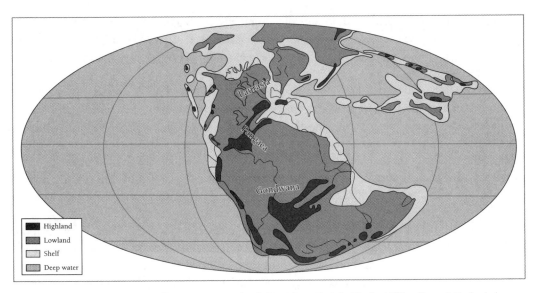

Global paleontology about 215 million years ago. Atlantic Geoscience Society, *The Last Billion Years: A Geological History of the Maritime Provinces* (Halifax: Nimbus Publishing, 2001), p. 126. Reprinted with permission from Nimbus Publishing Limited.

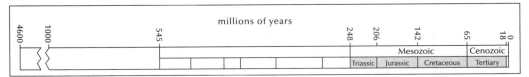

Paleontological timeline. Atlantic Geoscience Society. *The Last Billion Years: A Geological History of the Maritime Provinces* (Halifax: Nimbus Publishing, 2001), p. 126. Reprinted with permission from Nimbus Publishing Limited.

mountains of the Appalachian chain and built up the continental shelf, with its rich reserves of oil and natural gas. Water flowing from mountains along the coastal margins and the interior of the continent created the Gulf of St Lawrence, carved out the Cabot Strait and Strait of Belle Isle, and laid down the iron-rich sandstone deposits that are responsible for the red soils of Prince Edward Island.

The final shaping and scraping of the Atlantic landscape occurred during the last Ice Age, which gripped the continent from 2 million to 10,000 years ago. During the Wisconsinan glaciation (75,000–10,000 years ago), the Laurentide Ice Sheet gradually expanded to cover most of what is now Canada, including Labrador and the tip of Newfoundland's Northern Peninsula. The rest of Newfoundland and the Maritimes were covered by another ice cap, which formed part of the Appalachian Glacier Complex. Ice flowed over earlier river valleys, cut deep valleys and fiords, and dumped boulders, gravel, and fine sand throughout the region.

About 20,000 years ago the glaciers of the last Ice Age began to melt. The sea level rose, fell, and rose again as the ice retreated and the land rebounded from the weight of the glaciers. Prince Edward Island began as three islands and was later connected to the mainland by a land bridge. In periods when the sea level was low, sections of the continental shelf and much of what is now the undersea coast, including the Bay of Fundy, lay exposed. The Atlantic region took the geological form we recognize today as recently as 3,000 years ago.

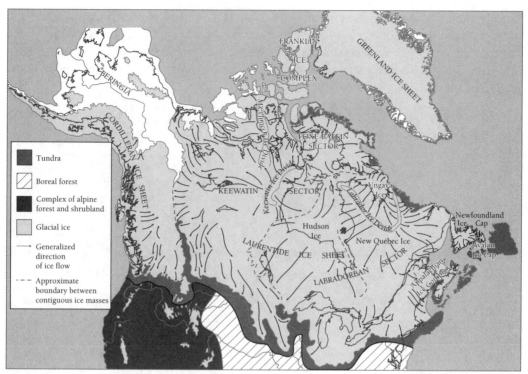

Plate 1, "The Last Ice Age" (Wisconsonian)," from *Historical Atlas of Canada I: From the Beginning to 1800*, by R. Cole Harris © University of Toronto Press, 1987.

Where Is Here?

What exactly is Atlantic Canada today? Geographic diversity rather than homogeneity is the region's most obvious feature. Extending more than 7 degrees of both longitude and latitude, Atlantic Canada contains 539,101 square kilometres of land and fresh water, and 16,000 kilometres of saltwater shoreline. At 1,652 metres, Mount Caubvick in Labrador's Torngat Mountains is the region's highest point, while no part of Prince Edward Island rises above 142 metres.

In western Newfoundland, New Brunswick, and Nova Scotia, the Appalachian range dominates the landscape. These mountains are so old that they have been eroded into stumps, the highest of which is Mount Carleton in New Brunswick (820 metres). In Cape Breton and Newfoundland the Appalachians rise steeply from the sea, helping to make the Cabot Trail and Gros Morne National Park two of the most spectacular tourist attractions in the world. Several millennia ago the Atlantic region was much larger than it is today, its ancient contours evident in the rough outlines of the continental shelf. Sable Island is now the only part of the former landscape that rises above sea level. The relative shallowness of the shelf has, until recently, provided a rich habitat for fish and still allows the extraction of undersea deposits of oil and natural gas.

Climate ranges widely in the region, from the subarctic conditions of northern Labrador to the temperate environment of southwestern Nova Scotia. Although weather is influenced primarily by continental systems moving eastwards, these are modified by the ocean, which gives Atlantic

Canada warmer winters and cooler summers than areas at similar latitudes farther west. Most of the region lacks the warming influence of the Gulf Stream that keeps Great Britain pleasantly mild compared to Newfoundland and Labrador, though the two regions are at roughly the same latitude. When the Gulf Stream meets the cold Labrador Current carrying ice from the north, it produces the fog for which the Grand Banks are infamous.

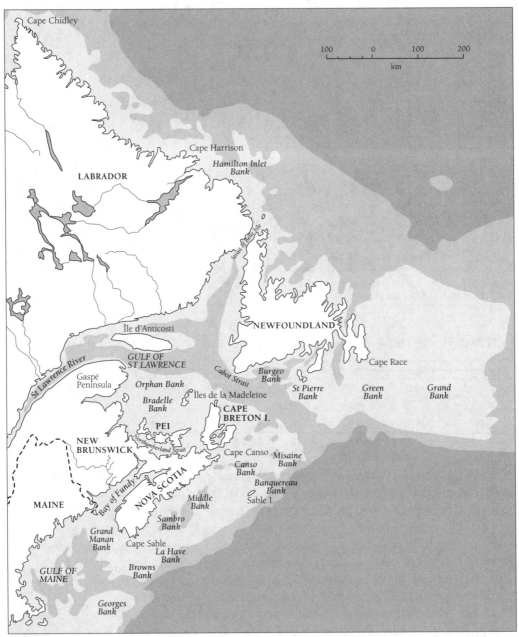

The continental shelf and fishing banks. Adapted from H.A. Innis, *The Cod Fisheries: The History of an International Economy* (New Haven: Yale University Press, 1940), p. 7.

Labrador makes up 54 per cent of the total land mass of the Atlantic region, but its rugged landscape has never supported a large population. By contrast, the rich soils of Prince Edward Island and the valleys of the St John and Annapolis–Cornwallis rivers invited settlement and continue to yield agricultural crops in modest abundance. Most of the region sustains a forest cover, much of it a mix of deciduous and coniferous trees. Over the past 500 years, the forests have been so thoroughly exploited that few old-growth stands are left. By contrast, the mineral wealth of the region, with the exceptions of the coal deposits in Nova Scotia and New Brunswick and the iron and nickel deposits in Labrador, has yet to be fully exploited.

The First Peoples

The early history of human habitation in the Atlantic region is difficult to determine because many areas of coastal settlement have sunk below sea level, and the region's acidic soils tend to destroy any organic materials that have not been submerged. As a result, there are few sites that offer evidence of continuous occupation over long stretches of time. Archaeological discoveries in recent years have enabled us to imagine the broad outlines of the region's early human history, but we may never know the full story.[2]

The earliest North American peoples are known as Paleo-Indians. Hunting large species such as mammoths, mastodons, and longhorn bison, they moved across the continent from the south and west as the retreating glaciers permitted, adapting their culture to changing climates, animal species, and vegetation. The oldest known remains of human settlement in the region were found in the 1960s near Debert, Nova Scotia. Dated to about 10,600 years ago, the site is believed to be a seasonal encampment near a caribou trail passing through the Cobequid Bay region. Other Paleo-Indian sites have been discovered at nearby Belmont and elsewhere in the Maritimes and southern Labrador.[3]

Three phases of Paleo-Indian culture—Clovis, Folsom, and Plano—have been identified. The chipped stone tools with fluted points recovered at the Debert–Belmont Complex suggest that the people who made them belonged to the Clovis culture.[4] Although these Paleo-Indians may have relied primarily on caribou for survival, their descendants pursued diverse hunting, fishing, and gathering subsistence strategies. In time these people made their way to the rich maritime life around the Strait of Belle Isle, where archaeological evidence dating back nearly 9,000 years has been found at Pinware Hill in southern Labrador.

The caribou hunters stopped going to Debert after a few hundred years. It is not clear why, but climate change may have been the cause. Sea levels are estimated to have been 60 metres below current levels 10,600 years ago; they rose dramatically for the next 5,000 years as the ice caps melted and then stabilized. With increasingly dense forests threatening their survival, the caribou may have moved away and the hunters followed; or the people may have adapted to the resources at hand, relying more on harp seals, walruses, and other marine life for their livelihood.

Paleo-Indian culture, based on chipped stone technology, gave way to a sequence of what are termed Archaic cultures, distinguished from their predecessors by their ground and polished stone tools. While it is believed that Archaic peoples inhabited the region from 10,000 to 2,500 years ago, very little is known about the first 5,000 years of their occupation. Because of evidence found near lakes and rivers and from drowned coastal sites, archaeologists now agree that the Early and Middle Archaic cultures identified in New England also lived in the Maritimes. Recent archaeological findings at Jemseg Crossing in New Brunswick reveal human occupation extending back 7,000 years or more. This is just one of the new sites currently under investigation that suggest we are on the verge of a more complex understanding of the region's "ancient" human history.[5]

By about 5,000 years ago, there were two distinct groups inhabiting the Atlantic region: the Interior Late Archaic and the Coastal Late Archaic. The former represented an eastern version of the Laurentian tradition that extended from the Great Lakes to the shores of what are now Maine and New Brunswick, while the latter marks a distinct phase in what the archaeologist James Tuck calls a Maritime Archaic tradition. With local variants, it extended from Maine to northern Labrador and from Newfoundland to the Gulf of St Lawrence, and reflects a continuous occupation of coastal areas from the Paleo-Indian period to European settlement.[6]

In Labrador and Newfoundland archaeologists have been able to document an unbroken Maritime Archaic tradition running from 7,500 to 3,500 years ago. Surviving artifacts from sites such as L'Anse Amour and Port au Choix indicate that the Northern Branch of that tradition— now referred to as the Labrador Archaic—spread from the Strait of Belle Isle along the coast of Labrador, eventually reaching Saglek and Ramah bays. The Southern Branch people occupied southern Labrador and were the first humans to colonize the island of Newfoundland, where they established themselves some 5,000 years ago (perhaps even earlier) and eventually spread along the entire coastline, with the possible exception of the Avalon Peninsula.

About 6,000 years ago, the Labrador Archaic moved away from southern Labrador and focused their activities between Hamilton Inlet and Nachvak. They also abandoned their traditional single-family dwellings for rectangular longhouses that could reach 80 metres in length and accommodate as many as 100 people. These structures suggest that the Archaic peoples came together in large groups at certain times of the year to quarry chert for sharp-edged tools, hunt caribou, and carry out elaborate mortuary rituals.

There is evidence that people belonging to the Broad Point (or Susquehanna) culture, first defined in the mid-Atlantic states of North America, moved into the southwestern extremes of the Maritimes in the late Archaic period. What makes them distinct, apart from the broad points of their tools, is that they cremated their dead and buried the ashes and bone fragments in pits. The Broad Point peoples seem not to have penetrated much beyond southwestern New Brunswick and the Yarmouth–Tusket region of Nova Scotia.

Whatever their specific traditions, all Archaic cultures depended—as had their Paleo-Indian predecessors—on some combination of fishing, hunting, and gathering. Their highly mobile communities consisted of a few related families numbering perhaps 50 people in all. Although they carved out territorial jurisdictions, there was probably significant interaction between the sea-based and interior peoples who shared the region's bounty. The discovery throughout the region of tools made of much-prized stone such as chert from Labrador or rhyolite from the island of Iona in Cape Breton suggest that Archaic peoples traded among themselves.[7]

Adapting their resources of stone and bone to the job at hand, the region's early inhabitants developed an impressive array of tools. Animals were butchered with stone knives and the skins dressed with bone scrapers. In the sea-based societies, toggling harpoons were used to spear seals and swordfish, which were then killed using lances tipped with bone and slate points. Ground and polished axes, adzes, and gouges were used to fashion wooden spear shafts, traps, dugout canoes, house frames, wooden bowls, and decorative objects. The bones of birds and small animals were crafted into fine needles and awls used to make shelters, clothing, footwear, and carrying bags.

Archaic peoples had highly developed spiritual beliefs, burying their dead, accompanied by red ochre, tools, weapons, and decorative objects, in cemeteries. If the surviving carved charms, tokens, and amulets are any indication, the Archaic peoples had great respect for the fish, sea birds, whales, and seals on which their survival depended. At Port au Choix, for example, some of the graves included the remains of a particular bird species, which may have served to identify family lines.

Climatic Change and Cultural Adaptation

Population movements and cultural evolution in the Maritimes appear to be linked to climatic change. About 3,500 years ago, rising sea levels and cooling temperatures encouraged greater reliance on shellfish and fur-bearing animals and the adoption of new practices and technologies. The Maritime Archaic culture as such disappeared. Absorbing influences and perhaps immigrants from the south and west, the Maritime peoples moved into the Woodland (or Ceramic) period, characterized in part by the use of clay pottery. Modern Mi'kmaq, Wolastoqiyik (Maliseet), and Passamaquoddy are almost certainly descended from the Woodland peoples.

The appearance of ceramics may be an indication that Archaic peoples borrowed technology from adjacent cultures in the New England and St Lawrence regions to meet changing circumstances. If this theory is accepted, it may also explain the Augustine and Oxbow burial mound sites found on the Miramichi River and at Skora, near Halifax. Similar to sites associated with the Adena in Ohio, they suggest either that people from the interior of the continent swept through the region 3,000 years ago or that Maritime Archaic people had learned new ways to inter their dead relatives, perhaps from a visiting spiritual leader.

Most Woodland sites are coastal or located on rivers where fish were abundant. From the available evidence, there seems to have been considerable continuity in the seasonal rhythms. Some communities in eastern New Brunswick, for example, made regular late-winter expeditions to Prince Edward Island to catch sea mammals. While most Aboriginal groups were highly mobile, the discovery of more than a hundred semi-subterranean pit-houses in the Passamaquoddy Bay area suggests that people living there were based in the same village for most of the year. These conical structures were framed with poles or saplings and covered with skins or sheets of bark and sometimes banked with a mixture of shells and soil, presumably to keep out the cold.

The peoples of southeastern New Brunswick developed somewhat different cultural patterns, but they shared with their neighbours the use of clay pots and a dependence on clams, quahogs, and other shellfish. Accumulations of discarded shells have been found throughout the region and offer valuable evidence about the evolution of Woodland material culture. A shell midden site at Sellar's Cove, on St Margaret's Bay in Nova Scotia, spans nearly the entire Woodland period and indicates that pottery techniques declined, perhaps because people were becoming more mobile. By the time of European contact, both the pottery and the semi-permanent dwellings along the coast had disappeared, for reasons that have yet to be explained.

Mobility was enhanced by the use of birchbark for making canoes, containers, and housing. Light and easily carried, canoes were used primarily for river and coastal travel, but also enabled the Woodland peoples to navigate the Northumberland Strait and the Strait of Canso. Whether they crossed the Cabot Strait before European contact is disputed. Watertight containers made from birchbark stitched with spruce roots and sealed with spruce gum were used to cook meat and fish in water brought to the boil by stones heated in the fire and placed in the pot. Poles covered with bark and lined with spruce bows served as mobile housing for people whose seasonal rounds

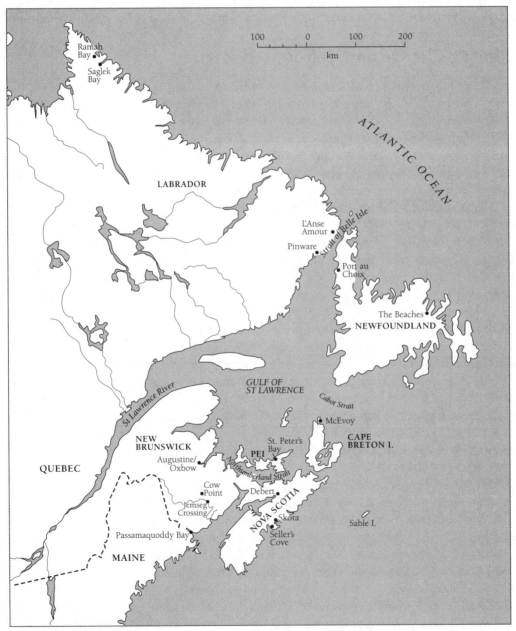

Major archaeological sites in the Atlantic region. Adapted from P.A. Buckner and J.G. Reid eds. *The Atlantic Region to Confederation* (Toronto: University of Toronto Press, 1994), p. 4.

required frequent migration. Snowshoes, which made it possible to speed along on top of the snow, increased the chances of success in the winter hunt.

Newfoundland and Labrador experienced the same climatic shift as the Maritimes, but received successive waves of immigrants from the north rather than the south and west.[8] The first of these, people known as Paleo-Eskimos, arrived in Labrador approximately 4,000 years ago, and their descendants later occupied regions of the island of Newfoundland abandoned by the Maritime Archaic. In turn, their culture was replaced about 2,000 years ago by the Late Paleo-Eskimo, usually called Dorset (after Cape Dorset on Baffin Island, where their culture was first identified). They disappeared from the island of Newfoundland by the ninth century and from Labrador by 1300. Skilled in crafting stone, bone, and ivory tools, the Dorset produced distinctive soapstone lamps and cooking vessels as well as whalebone "shoes" to protect the runners on their sleds, which they probably hauled themselves. Before the arrival of Europeans, the region's Aboriginal peoples had also adopted the bow and arrow, although the origins and timing of this innovation are uncertain.

The direct ancestors of the modern Labrador Inuit were the Thule, the last major group to arrive from the western Arctic. Adept at catching whales with their large toggling harpoons,

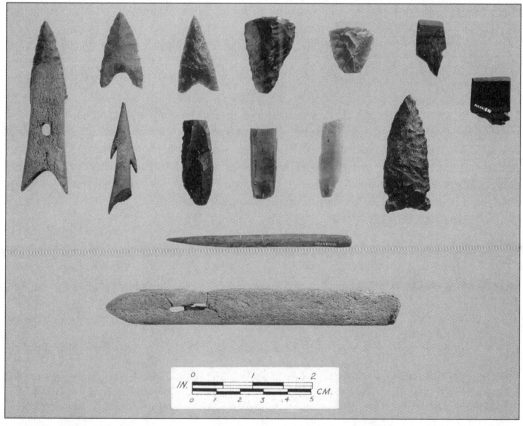

Dorset Paleo-Eskimo artifacts, 1,300 to 2,000 years old, from Port au Choix in northwestern Newfoundland. Clockwise from top left: a bone harpoon head tipped with a stone end-blade, two typical Dorset triangular end-blades, two end-scrapers, two ground nephrite engraving tools, a chipped-stone knife, three microblades, and a bone point. At the bottom is a segment of a whalebone sled-runner, and above that a stone awl. M.A.P. Renouf, Memorial University, St John's.

kayaks, and umiaks, they moved quickly across the High Arctic. Their success was facilitated by a warming trend, which reduced the sea ice and drew both bowhead and right whales into the northern waters. It has been suggested that the Thule's expansion into Labrador began when they lost contact with Norse settlements in Greenland and set out to find new sources of iron goods. Arriving in the north of Labrador in the fifteenth century, they reached Saglek by 1500 and soon after that encountered Europeans in the Strait of Belle Isle.

Since the material culture of the Thule has been well preserved, we know more about their lifeways than those of most early peoples in the region. Their typical house was an oval-shaped, semi-subterranean structure with three levels, entered through a tunnel leading to a slightly elevated flagstone floor. At the rear was a raised sleeping platform. A low earthen exterior wall supported a whalebone interior frame, which was covered with baleen and sod to create a domed roof. It seems likely that the Thule people also built igloos and trained dogs to pull their sleds. By 1500 the right whale was the mainstay of their diet, supplemented by other sea mammals, birds, fish, land animals, and wild berries.

The origins of the modern Labrador Innu are less well understood, but their immediate ancestors were almost certainly the Point Revenge people, active on the Quebec–Labrador peninsula from about 2,000 years ago. Part of a tradition known as Recent Indian, they spread to Newfoundland, where three phases of Recent Indian occupation have been identified. The last of these phases is associated with the Little Passage people, the direct ancestors of the Beothuk.

Conclusion

The history of the peoples of Atlantic Canada before European contact shifts constantly as new archaeological evidence emerges and gives rise to new theories. Many questions remain, but it is now possible to trace the main outlines of a human story that began with the arrival of Paleo-Indians more than 10,000 years ago. What we can say for certain is that the peoples living at the crossroads of the North Atlantic world have a long history of adapting to environmental change, developing new technologies, and interacting with new populations.

Further Readings

Atlantic Geoscience Society. 2001. *The Last Billion Years: A Geological History of the Maritime Provinces*. Halifax: Nimbus Publishing.

Colman-Sadd, S., and S.A. Scott. 2004. *Newfoundland and Labrador: Traveller's Guide to the Geology*. St John's: Government of Newfoundland and Labrador.

Davis, Stephen A. 1994. "Early Societies: Sequences of Change." Pp. 3–21 in Phillip A. Buckner and John G. Reid, eds. *The Atlantic Region to Confederation*. Toronto and Fredericton: University of Toronto and Acadiensis Press.

Erickson, Paul, and Jonathon Fowler, eds. 2013. *Underground New Brunswick: Stories of Archaeology*. Halifax: Nimbus.

———. 2010. *Underground Nova Scotia: Stories of Archaeology*. Halifax: Nimbus.

Meltzer, David J. 2009. *First Peoples in a New World: Colonizing Ice Age America*. Berkeley: University of California Press.

Rankin, Lisa. 2008. "Native Peoples from the Ice Age to the Extinction of the Beothuk." Pp. 1–22 in Newfoundland Historical Society. *Short History of Newfoundland and Labrador*. Portugal Cove–St Philip's: Boulder Publications.

Renouf, M.A.P., ed. 2011. *The Cultural Landscapes of Port au Choix: Precontact Hunter-gatherers of Northwestern Newfoundland*. New York: Springer.

Wright, James V. 1999. *A History of the Native People of Canada*. Vol. 2 (100 BC to AD 500). Ottawa: Canadian Museum of Civilization.

Historical Spotlight

Daniels, John D. 1992. "The Indian Population of North America in 1492," *William and Mary Quarterly*, 3rd series 49, 2 (April): 298–320.

Sanger, David. 2005. "Pre-European Dawnland: Archaeology of the Maritime Peninsula," in *New England and the Maritime Provinces: Connections and Comparisons*, ed. Stephen J. Hornsby and John G. Reid. Kingston and Montreal: McGill-Queen's University Press.

Recommended Websites

Gros Morne National Park
http://www.pc.gc.ca/pn-np/nl/grosmorne/index_e.asp

Joggins Fossil Cliffs
http://www.jogginsfossilcliffs.net/

Museum of Natural History
https://naturalhistory.novascotia.ca/

Newfoundland and Labrador Natural Environment
http://www.heritage.nf.ca/environment/ne_contents.html

NICHE: Network in Canadian History and Environment
http://niche-canada.org

Aboriginal Peoples

With the arrival of Europeans in the late fifteenth century, a much more detailed picture of Aboriginal societies begins to emerge. Europeans were intrigued by the "New World" they had found, and some of them wrote meticulous descriptions of the people they encountered. While the evidence was one-sided and must be treated with caution, it adds an important dimension to the information provided by the surviving material culture and oral traditions of the region's original inhabitants. Together, these sources reveal the contours of complex communities in which people were well-adapted to their environment.

Setting the Context

The Americas in 1500

When the Europeans began arriving in significant numbers 500 years ago, the Aboriginal population of the Americas was roughly the same as that of Western Europe.[1] Cities in what are now the southern United States, Mexico, and Central and South America were as large as any found across the Atlantic, and, as in Europe, empires rose and fell through war and conquest. The small populations on the frontiers of settlement had less elaborate institutional structures and often more co-operative social arrangements than those living in imperial centres.

All pre-contact peoples in the Americas shared a world view in which humans were part of a cosmological order that included all the inhabitants of the land, sea, and sky. The universe functioned harmoniously only when natural forces were in balance—a condition maintained by elaborate rituals. Before the arrival of Europeans, North Americans had calculated the movements of the sun and stars, and they understood a great deal about the medicinal properties of plants. While Aboriginal societies in New England and the Great Lakes region cultivated corn, beans, squash, and tobacco, the staple crops of the Mesoamerican civilizations, this was not likely the case in most of the area that is now Atlantic Canada. These products nevertheless made their way their way into the region by means of trade, and abundant land and ocean resources ensured a standard of living that was, for most of the region's inhabitants, as comfortable as that of other peoples who made northern North America their home.

Atlantic Canada's Aboriginal Peoples

At the time of European contact, what is now Atlantic Canada was home to several distinct cultures. The Labrador Inuit were the easternmost branch of a northern people living across the Arctic, while

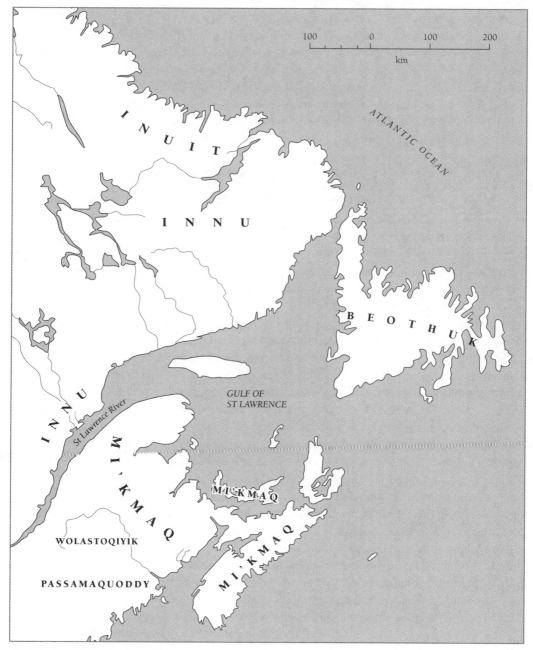

Aboriginal peoples in the sixteenth century.

the Mi'kmaq, Wolastoqiyik, Innu, and probably Beothuk belonged to the Algonkian language group, which occupied an extensive territory from the Atlantic to the Rockies.

The names that Europeans called these peoples were not necessarily the ones that they used themselves. It is highly unlikely, for example, that the people dwelling along what is now the St John River in New Brunswick called themselves "Maliseet." Meaning "broken (or slow) speakers," it was a term used by their Mi'kmaw neighbours, who spoke a different Algonkian dialect. Instead, they called themselves "Wolastoqiyik," referring to the "beautiful river" along which they lived; both terms are used today. "Mi'kmaq" began to replace the French term "Souriquois" in the late seventeenth century, and may be derived from "nikmaq" ("my kin"), which was used as a greeting.[2] Europeans initially referred to the Aboriginal people of Newfoundland simply as "savages," "natives," or "Indians," and did not adopt their own term, "Beothuk" ("the people"), until the early nineteenth century. Similarly, the peoples that Europeans initially called "Eskimos" and "Montagnais–Naskapi" used the terms "Inuit" and "Innu," both also meaning "people," for themselves.

The Mi'kmaq, Wolastoqiyik, and Passamaquoddy of the Maritimes

The Mi'kmaq in 1500 lived throughout what are now the Maritime provinces. While estimates of their numbers at the time of contact range from 3,500 to 200,000, most scholars now suggest a figure between 12,000 and 15,000.[3] The role that disease played in opening the Americas to European occupation has been the subject of much debate, but few scholars would deny that its impact was catastrophic. Summarizing decades of research, the geographer Cole Harris suggests that "a hundred years after the first epidemics reached a certain area it seldom had more than 10 per cent of its pre-epidemic population."[4]

The basic unit of Mi'kmaw society was the extended family, sometimes supplemented by a few unrelated individuals. Headed by a chief, or *sakamow*, this unit formed the summer village, which could number as many as 300 people but broke up into smaller groups for the winter. Summer was a time for Mi'kmaw leaders to consult one another on matters of common interest. By the eighteenth century, the Mi'kmaq were divided into seven districts, each governed by a chief who represented his district on a Grand Council. This form of political organization may have developed in response to European trade, but the significance of chiefs seems to have been deeply rooted in Mi'kmaw society.

Mi'kmaw men were skilled hunters, using dogs to help them track down their prey, which was then dispatched with spears and arrows. Fish were so plentiful that they were easy to catch with three-pronged spears, loosely woven nets, and weirs. When ducks and geese were migrating, hunters would float their canoes among the sleeping birds under cover of darkness, then light birchbark torches and use long poles to knock the confused birds down as they circled the lights. Similar pyrotechnics were used to catch salmon. Women gathered fiddleheads (the curled fronds of ferns) along with other greens, nuts, tubers, and wild fruit that added important nutrients to the otherwise high protein diet and were used in various medicinal remedies.[5] For most Aboriginal peoples, tobacco figured prominently in ceremonies and healing practices. The Mi'kmaq used a local leaf, perhaps from the willow, to produce a mild tobacco, but they also smoked pukeweed (*Lobelia inflata*) and tobacco obtained through trade with agricultural peoples to the southwest.

The moose played a central role in the Mi'kmaw economy. Its meat was eaten fresh and dried and its bones rendered a highly nutritious "butter" called *cacamos*. Moose skin was fashioned into clothing, moccasins, carrying bags, and snowshoe webbing. Antlers and bones became tools, weapons, and

Historical Focus

Oral History

To preserve the fire, especially in winter, we would entrust it to the care of our war-chief's women, who took turns to preserve the spark, using half-rotten pine wood covered with ash. Sometimes this fire lasted up to three moons. When it lasted the span of three moons, the fire became sacred and magical to us, and we showered with a thousand praises the chief's woman who had been the fire's guardian during the last days of the third moon. We would all gather together and, so that no member of the families which had camped there since the autumn should be absent, we sent out young men to fetch those who were missing. Then, when our numbers were complete, we would gather round and, without regard to age or rank, light our pipes at the fire. We would suck in the smoke and keep it in our mouths, and one by one we would puff it into the face of the woman who had last preserved the spark, telling her that she was worthy above all to share in the benign influence of the Father of Light, the Sun, because she had so skilfully preserved his emanations.[6]

This description of a Mi'kmaw cultural tradition, recorded in the 1740s on what is now Prince Edward Island, reveals detailed evidence about the problems posed for the region's indigenous peoples by a Maritime winter. Yet it leaves many unanswered questions. We have no way of knowing, for example, whether the practice described here was still current in the 1740s, or how widespread it may have been. Moreover, this account, attributed to Chief Arguimaut (L'kimu), was preserved for posterity by a Roman Catholic missionary, the Abbé Pierre Maillard, who may have brought his own biases to bear on what he heard. The Europeans who first came into contact with Aboriginals had a Christian world view, a sense of cultural superiority, and a gendered perspective that often led them to misinterpret—either deliberately or unconsciously—what they observed. The evidence of ethnographers is rarely accepted without scrutiny today, and we must not lose our critical perspective when we encounter a rare archival document. For all its seeming authenticity, this oral account must be treated like any other historical evidence: as the product of a particular time and place, with no greater claim to truth than any other kind of text.

needles; brains were used in tanning skins, shin bones were carved into dice, tendons served as thread, and hair was used in embroidery. While moose were killed throughout the year, they were most vulnerable in winter, when deep snow impeded their escape from hunters speeding along on snowshoes.

Europeans frequently commented on gender roles, courtship practices, and family relationships. According to Chrestien Le Clercq, a Récollet missionary living in the Gaspé region in the late seventeenth century, the Mi'kmaq were patriarchal, subordinating women and younger males to the authority of adult men. Le Clercq reported that polygamy was practised and that marriages were easily dissolved, especially when no children were involved. The method of carrying infants in cradleboards drew Le Clercq's particular attention. Both the cradleboard and the infant's clothing, he observed, were adorned with beadwork, porcupine quills, and painted designs, which he believed were used "to beautify it, and to render it just so much the finer in proportion as [the parents] love their children."[7] Men and women alike wore bracelets and necklaces made from shells and pierced their ears to hold carved pendants depicting birds, fish, and other animals. Like most Aboriginal peoples of the Americas, the Mi'kmaq painted their faces on special occasions and when going into battle.

By the time of European contact, the Mi'kmaq had a complex world view to explain their existence. They considered the sun and moon to be the ancestors of "People" who lived on Earth, which was part of a spiritual universe made up of Six Worlds. In addition to the Earth World, there were Worlds above and beneath the Earth, beneath the Water, and above the Sky, as well as the Ghost World where people went after death and a very few were able to visit while still living. The Mi'kmaw universe consisted of "power," which was manifested in people, animals, plants, and phenomena such as winds, weather, seasons, and directions. Not only could one form of power change into another—a person into a wolf, or a stone into a person—but the character or state of mind of the power force could also change, from good to evil, for instance, or strong to weak. This notion of power made for an unpredictable universe, but it encouraged people to acquire and use power responsibly through socially sanctioned behaviour.

People with special spiritual powers played a major role in articulating the Mi'kmaw sense of the world and the appropriate ways of living in it. Legends evoked spiritual truths, and signs representing spiritual phenomena, such as the sun, were often incorporated in the intricate designs adorning clothing, wigwams, and other material possessions. Believing that dreams and trances helped them to contact spirit powers, the Mi'kmaq developed various ways of achieving altered states of consciousness and paid close attention to the knowledge revealed in dreams.

The Wolastoqiyik, who lived in what is now southwestern New Brunswick and northeastern Maine, shared many characteristics with the Mi'kmaq. According to Mi'kmaw lore, the Wolastoqiyik

Biography Klu'skap

Klu'skap (or Glooscap) seems to have been a much-revered culture hero for the Mi'kmaq and for many Eastern Woodland peoples. Since the first documented reference to him dates only from the 1860s, after Christianity had been widely accepted, his role in the pre-contact period is unclear. He is variously represented as creator, teacher, and trickster, a person of greater power than any ordinary human being. In many accounts he had a grandmother, a younger brother or nephew, and a pair of dogs. After battling his evil twin brother, whom he turned to stone, and a frog monster, who on one occasion swallowed up the earth's water, Klu'skap set to work making "Mi'kma'ki" a "happy land for people."

Many prominent geological features in the Atlantic region, including Cape Blomidon and Kelly's Mountain, are associated with Klu'skap. According to one story, his favourite island was Abegweit (Prince Edward Island), which served as his pillow while he slept. Like the Christian God, he created a gendered social order, commanding men to hunt animals in the forest and women to cook them.[8] Klu'skap "was the friend and teacher of the Indians," Stephen Hood told the Baptist missionary and ethnographer Silas Rand, "all they knew of the arts he taught them. . . . He was always sober, grave, and good."[9] An ambiguous figure, Klu'skap clearly represented a time when his people reigned supreme in Mi'kma'ki.

were a breakaway tribe, but evidence suggests that their differences may have been rooted in deeper cultural patterns. For example, unlike the Mi'kmaq, the Wolastoqiyik grew corn in the early contact period, and may have done so before the arrival of Europeans.

Although Aboriginal oral history and early European records report conflict between the Wolastoqiyik and the Mi'kmaq, we have no way of knowing its extent in the pre-contact era. What is clear is that when the Mi'kmaq gained access to European weapons, they used their military advantage to expand their control over the Gaspé Peninsula and portions of the St John River watershed.[10] By the seventeenth century the Mi'kmaq were also scoring victories over Abenaki communities as far south as the Saco River in Maine.

The Passamaquoddy occupied portions of the north shore of the Bay of Fundy, the Gulf of Maine, and the St Croix River and its tributaries. Their seasonal rhythms were much like those of the Wolastoqiyik, whose language they shared.[11] With seafood as the mainstay of their diet, the Passamaquoddy

This engraving shows a Mi'kmaq marked with various symbols, including both a sun and crosses. "Homme Acadien," 1788–1796. Library and Archives Canada/Canadian Historical Prints and Watercolours collections/e010977229.

were skilled in catching such species as porpoises and pollock with their well-aimed spears. Their name is an anglicization of the Passamaquoddy word *peskotomuhkati*, meaning "pollock-spearer" or "those of the place where pollock are plentiful."

The Beothuk, Innu, and Inuit of Newfoundland and Labrador

At the time of contact, Newfoundland was home to the Beothuk, who were descended from the Recent Indians.[12] Their language was probably part of the Algonkian group, if a distant relative, although there has been speculation that it was an isolate. While it is difficult to determine population figures, their numbers appears to have been small, perhaps no more than 1,000. They were among the first Aboriginal peoples that Europeans encountered in North America, and it may have been their custom of painting themselves with red ochre that gave rise to the term "Red Indian."

The Beothuk were highly mobile and well adapted to their environment. For food and clothing, they depended mainly on caribou, which they hunted during fall migration, but marine resources such as seals, seabirds, fish, and shellfish were also essential for survival. Moving with the seasons, they travelled long distances in lightweight birchbark canoes and lived in easily assembled wigwams. Whether the Beothuk had encountered the Mi'kmaq before contact with Europeans is unlikely, but once they did, relations between the two groups seem to have been uneasy.

Although no Beothuk sites have been found on Newfoundland's Northern Peninsula, they were probably in contact with the Labrador Innu before Europeans arrived. By 1500, though, the Innu had come to depend more on the resources of the interior—principally caribou and freshwater fish, which they caught in the winter and spring—than their ancestors had, an adaptation probably motivated by the arrival of the Thule/Inuit. During the summer months they gathered on the coast in large groups to hunt whales, seals, and saltwater fish before breaking into small bands to winter in the interior.

Like other Aboriginal groups in the region, the Innu shared the rewards of a successful hunt and encouraged egalitarian values. Open displays of anger were discouraged, decisions were made through discussion and consensus, and conformity was promoted through joking and ridicule. Patience and good humour were considered important virtues. In contrast to Europeans, who practised a harsh discipline aimed largely at breaking a child's will, the Innu spared their children physical punishment. Europeans remarked that, although gender roles were clearly defined, Innu women appeared to be relatively independent and powerful. They dominated the life-sustaining lodge hearth, controlled the distribution of food, and readily abandoned husbands who proved inadequate providers.

The Labrador Inuit were primarily a coastal people, initially based north of Hamilton Inlet. By the mid-sixteenth century they had spread further south and ranged along the Quebec North Shore

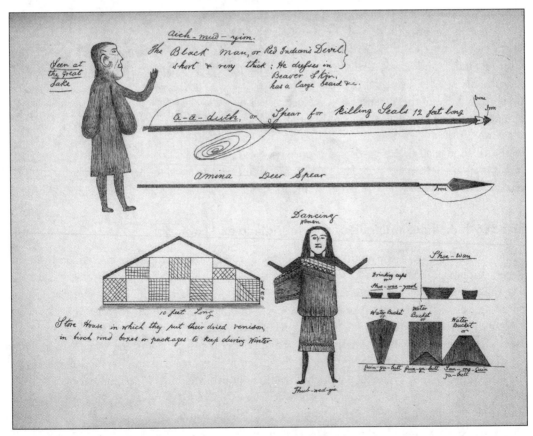

Before her death in 1829, Shanawdithit, the last surviving Beothuk on the island of Newfoundland, drew these images depicting aspects of her culture. Library and Archives Canada/Illustrated books, albums and scrapbooks collection/C028544.

as far east as Anticosti and Mingan. It is believed that there was continuous interaction between the southern and northern Inuit groups, and eventually European goods, which were highly valued, were traded all along the Labrador coast.

During the fall and winter the Inuit lived in semi-subterranean sod houses at the mouths of fiords. The men hunted whales and seals from their kayaks and umiaks until the sea froze, when they would hunt seals through the ice. In the spring some fished through lake ice, while others built snow houses on the outer islands, where they caught seals, fish, and mussels. In early summer everyone moved to the islands and lived in skin tents. In July the Inuit congregated at places where salmon were plentiful before beginning the inland caribou hunt.

The success of the hunt was assisted by shamans (*angakut*), who mediated between the human and spirit worlds. In 1772 the Moravian missionaries at Nain reported that a female shaman "fell into a trance, when her soul took a tour through the inland parts, where she saw a vast quantity of Rain Deer. Upon this the Esquimaux went to the inlet as directed by her, where they saw and got many deer."[13] Shamans also treated sickness, which was thought to be caused by evil spirits, and in general helped the Inuit to make sense of their lives and deaths.

One of the earliest European images of North America is a woodcut of an Inuit mother and daughter, probably from Labrador, who were captured by French fishermen and taken to Europe in 1566. The fact that the fishermen killed the woman's husband foreshadowed the hostile relations that quickly developed between Inuit and newcomers. Writing in the early seventeenth century, the French colonizer Samuel de Champlain noted that the Inuit were "very malicious . . . [attacking] fishermen, who in self defence arm small vessels to protect the boats which put to sea to fish cod."[14] In later years the French were slow to establish fishing and sealing stations on the Labrador coast, in part because of their fear of the Inuit.

Document

The Capture of an Inuit Woman and Her Child, 1566

Europeans frequently captured Aboriginal people and either forced them to work as slaves or put them on display as curiosities. The text accompanying this woodcut of an Inuit woman and child captured in 1566 on the Labrador coast reads (in part):

> In this year 1566 there arrived in Antwerp . . . a savage woman (a small person) together with her little daughter, and she is shaped and clothed as this picture shows, and was found in Nova Terra. . . . [T]his woman with her husband and little child were met by the French . . . and the husband was shot through his body with an arrow. However he would not surrender but took his stand bravely to defend himself. . . . Finally he was struck and wounded in his throat so severely that he fell to the ground and died from the wound. This man was 12 feet tall and had in twelve days killed eleven people with his own hand, French and Portuguese, in order to eat them. . . . [T]hen they took the woman with her child and brought her away; and none of the Frenchmen

Continued

could understand a single word of hers or speak with her at all. But she was taught enough in 8 months that it was known she had eaten many men. Her clothing is made of seal skins.

. . . The paint marks she has on her face are entirely blue [and] . . . cannot be taken off again. . . . Her body is yellow-brown. . . . The woman was 20 years old when she was captured . . . the child 7 years. Let us thank God the Almighty that He has enlightened us with His word so that we are not such savage people and man-eaters as are in this district, that this woman was captured and brought out of there, since she knows nothing of the true God, but lives almost more wickedly than the beasts. God grant that she be converted to acknowledge Him. Amen.[15]

Printed in Augsburg, Germany, in 1567, this woodcut is the first known European depiction of Inuit drawn from life. From W.C. Sturtevant, "The First Inuit Depiction by Europeans," *Etudes Inuit Studies* 4, 1–2 (1980): 47–9.

Conclusion

Every Aboriginal group in the Atlantic region would have had dramatic tales to tell once Europeans began to frequent their coasts in the early sixteenth century. In each case the encounter brought disease, death, and social and economic dislocation, even to those, such as the Mi'kmaq, who initially welcomed the Europeans and what they had to offer. The least affected were the most remote, the Inuit and northern Innu bands. Those who lived around the Gulf of St Lawrence bore the brunt of the first European efforts to explore, fish, trade, and spread the Christian faith.

Further Readings

Blair, Susan, ed. 2004. *Wolastoqiyik Ajemseg: The People of Beautiful River at Jemseg*, Vol. 2: *Archaeological Results*. Fredericton: Archaeological Services, Heritage Branch, Culture and Sports Secretariat.

Dickason, Olive Patricia, with David T. McNab. 2009. *Canada's First Nations: A History of Founding Peoples from Earliest Times*. 4th edn. Don Mills, ON: Oxford University Press.

Higgins, Jenny. 2009. "Pre-Contact Innu Land Use." Accessed 18 July 2014 at www.heritage.nl.ca/aboriginal/innu_land_use.html.

Johnston, A.J.B., and Jesse Francis. 2013. *Ni'n na L'nu: The Mi'kmaq of Prince Edward Island*. Charlottetown: Acorn Press.

McGhee, Robert. 1996. *Ancient People of the Arctic*. Vancouver: University of British Columbia Press.

Marshall, Ingeborg. 1996. *A History and Ethnography of the Beothuk*. Montreal: McGill-Queen's University Press.

Prins, Harald E.L. 1996. *The Mi'kmaq: Resistance, Accommodation, and Cultural Survival*. Fort Worth: Harcourt Brace College Publishers.

Rankin, Lisa K. 2009. "An Archaeological View of the Thule/Inuit Occupation of Labrador." www.mun.ca/labmetis/articles.html.

Ray, Arthur J. 2005. *I Have Lived Here Since the World Began: An Illustrated History of Canada's Native People*. Rev. edn. Toronto: Lester/Key Porter.

Stopp, Marianne P. 2002. "Reconsidering the Inuit Presence in Southern Labrador," *Etudes/Inuit/Studies* 26, 2: 71–106.

Historical Spotlight

Martijn, Charles A. 2003. "Early Mi'kmaq Presence in Southern Newfoundland: An Ethnohistorical Perspective, c. 1500–1763," *Newfoundland Studies* 19, 1 (Fall): 44–102.

Whitehead, Ruth Holmes.1988. "Introduction" to *Stories from the Six Worlds: Micmac Legends*. Halifax, Nimbus.

Recommended Websites

Aboriginal Peoples of Newfoundland and Labrador
http://www.heritage.nf.ca/aboriginal/default.html

Mi'kmaq-Maliseet Institute
http://www.unbf.ca/education/mmi/

Mi'kmaq Portraits Collection
http://museum.gov.ns.ca/mikmaq/

Passamaquoddy-Maliseet Language Portal
http://pmportal.org

Pepamuteiati Nitassinat [Innu Place Names]
http://www.innuplaces.ca/index.php?lang=en

Chapter 3

European Encounters, 1000–1598

When there were no people in this country but Indians, and before any others became known, a young woman had a singular dream. . . . A small island came floating in towards the land, with tall trees on it, and living beings. [The shaman] pondered the girl's dream but could make nothing of it. The next day an event occurred that explained all. What should they see but a singular little island, as they supposed, which had drifted near to the land and become stationary there. There were trees on it, and branches to the trees, on which a number of bears . . . were crawling about. . . . What was their surprise to find that these supposed bears were men.[1]

Josiah Jeremy's account of one Mi'kmaw community's first sighting of hirsute Europeans and their tall-masted sailing ships was recorded in the mid-nineteenth century. What encounter this story describes is impossible to determine, but one thing is clear: the meeting of two very different cultures marked the beginning of a new era for both.

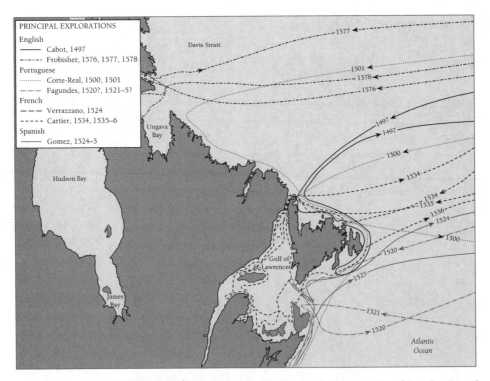

PRINCIPAL EXPLORATIONS
English
—— Cabot, 1497
------ Frobisher, 1576, 1577, 1578
Portuguese
·········· Corte-Real, 1500, 1501
—··—·· Fagundes, 1520?, 1521–5?
French
— — Verrazzano, 1524
----- Cartier, 1534, 1535–6
Spanish
—— Gomez, 1524–5

European exploration from 1497 to 1578. Adapted from R. Cole Harris, ed., *Historical Atlas of Canada I: From the Beginning to 1800* (Toronto: University of Toronto Press, 1987), Plate 19.

Setting the Context

The Expansion of Europe

During the second half of the fifteenth century, Europeans moved beyond the Mediterranean, which had hitherto been the centre of their trade, commerce, and culture. Emerging nation-states on the Atlantic littoral—Spain, Portugal, England, France, and the Netherlands—began to look for new opportunities and, in so doing, created an Atlantic world in which the Americas, Africa, and Europe became firmly interconnected.[2]

This reorientation towards the Atlantic was initially driven by commercial priorities. As the Middle East increasingly came under the control of hostile Islamic forces, Europeans searched for ways to trade directly with Asia. Developments in seagoing technology made a new sea route possible. With better ships and navigational devices, ambitious sailors, drawn by the lure of economic gain, became more willing to risk long-distance voyages. Another factor driving European exploration was rivalry among emerging nation-states. While monarchs generally respected one another's spheres of influence, each wanted to take the lead in staking claims to distant territories.

Overseas ventures were also part of a dramatic cultural awakening fuelled by the Renaissance, a rebirth of interest in the learning and cultural achievements of ancient Greece and Rome. Under the influence of Renaissance thinkers, Europeans began to ask troubling questions. Was the pope the final authority on matters religious and political? Could one reach Asia by sailing west? In the mid-1400s Johannes Gutenberg invented the mechanical printing press, which made it easier to disseminate new ideas, and Europe became a hotbed of intellectual ferment. It was in this context that the exploration of new frontiers, both geographic and intellectual, became a priority.

The Portuguese and the Spanish were the first to establish seaborne empires and were soon entrenched in Central and South America and the Far East. England, France, and the Netherlands followed. While nation-building, profit, and adventure were major spurs for imperialism, many European colonizers were also motivated by the religious rivalries unleased by the Reformation, which in the sixteenth century divided Europeans between Roman Catholicism and emerging Protestant denominations.

The expansion of Europe set people on the move in unprecedented numbers. Enslaved Africans, convicts, indentured servants, free labourers, religious refugees, and adventurers migrated to the frontiers of empire along with merchants eager to profit from new resources. Where Aboriginal peoples could be subdued, enslaved, displaced, or exterminated, European settlers occupied "vacant" lands for agriculture and resource extraction. The animals, plants, and diseases that they brought with them forever altered the ecology of the territories they exploited. By spreading their culture around the world, Europeans set in motion the processes of globalization, which continue to drive developments to the present day.

The Norse

The first Europeans to reach Atlantic Canada were the Norse. Their arrival in Labrador and Newfoundland more than 1,000 years ago marked the final stage in a migration that had begun

Table 3.1 Timeline

c. 1000	Greenland Norse reach northeastern America.
1492	Columbus reaches the Caribbean.
1497	John Cabot reaches Newfoundland.
1500	Gaspar Corte-Real reaches "Terra Verde."
1502	First known English fishing voyage to Newfoundland.
1504	First known French fishing voyage to Newfoundland.
1508–9	Sebastian Cabot looks for the northwest passage.
1520s	Basques enter the Newfoundland fishery.
1524	Giovanni da Verrazzano sails along the North American coast.
1524–5	Voyage of Estêvão Gomes along North America coast; possible Portuguese colony on Cape Breton.
1534	Jacques Cartier's first voyage to the Gulf of St Lawrence.
1550s	French develop offshore bank fishery; Basques develop whaling industry in Strait of Belle Isle.
1580s	English West Country ports begin to enter Newfoundland fishery; decline of Portuguese and Spanish fisheries.

several centuries earlier, when waves of Scandinavians spread across northern Europe and then sailed westward looking for land to settle.

Eirik the Red colonized southeastern Greenland from Iceland late in the tenth century. In 986, a merchant-shipowner named Bjarni Herjolfsson was blown off-course while travelling to the new settlement and found himself sailing along an unknown coastline. Although Bjarni did not explore the area, tales of his voyage were remembered, and a few years later, Leif Eiriksson retraced his route in reverse. According to Norse sagas, Leif found three lands. The first, which he called Helluland, consisted primarily of rock and ice, and was probably Baffin Island. The second, Markland, was flat, wooded, and almost certainly part of southern Labrador. Leif then reached a country with grassy meadows and well-stocked rivers that he called Vinland. The expedition wintered there before returning to Greenland.

Leif made several later expeditions, and others followed. The most ambitious of the known Norse ventures was headed by Thorfinn Karlsefni. He attempted to establish a settlement in Vinland but found it impossible to coexist with the local people, whom the Norse called Skraelings. After a few years Thorfinn retreated to Greenland, and the Norse eventually stopped travelling to Vinland. Whether this encounter had any impact in Europe is uncertain, but some scholars think that later explorers may well have heard rumours of lands to the west.

Europeans on the Move

The possibility of other transatlantic voyages before the late fifteenth century has generated a large literature of uneven quality. Some think that St Brendan set sail from Dingle Bay in Ireland with 17 monks in the sixth century and landed in America, possibly Newfoundland. Others claim that the Welsh Prince Madoc reached Florida in 1170, or that the Scottish Prince Henry Sinclair landed in Chedabucto Bay on 2 June 1398 (some say he buried the Holy Grail at Oak Island, on the southern shore of what is now Nova Scotia). The more plausible theories limit themselves to suggesting

Historical Focus

L'Anse aux Meadows

The location of Vinland has been debated since at least 1837. Various sites along the eastern seaboard of North America have been suggested, including Newfoundland's Northern Peninsula. In 1914 William A. Munn, a local merchant and amateur historian, identified L'Anse aux Meadows as the most likely site. Direct physical evidence of Norse occupation was discovered there by the Norwegian explorer Helge Ingstad in 1960. He and his wife, the archaeologist Anne Stine, supervised a team that conducted excavations at L'Anse aux Meadows between 1961 and 1968. Since 1978 it has been a World Heritage Site.

It seemed difficult at first to reconcile L'Anse aux Meadows (the name comes from the French *L'Anse aux Méduses*, "Jellyfish Cove") with some of the Norse accounts, especially the references to grapes. The consensus today is that Vinland was not a single place, but a region that encompassed the Gulf of St Lawrence. In this context, L'Anse aux Meadows was likely a base camp for exploration and the transshipment of goods—mainly lumber and wild grapes—found elsewhere. The Norse almost certainly visited the region that is now the Maritimes, and settlements might have been attempted at the harbours of the Miramichi and Margaree rivers.[3]

L'Anse aux Meadows differed in several important ways from other Norse sites. It was exposed to the sea and there is no evidence of livestock or other animals, nor of barns or byres. Of the nine buildings that have been excavated, eight were sod dwellings and the other was a small forge. The houses were designed for year-round habitation and could have accommodated between 70 and 90 people. Although women were present, most of the inhabitants were men. The main activities seem to have been carpentry, iron manufacture, and smithing—activities associated with boat repair and possibly boat building.

The base camp lasted from about 990 to 1050. Although the local people were unfriendly, it is improbable that their hostility put an end to the settlement. More likely, Vinland's resources were simply not important enough to make the long and difficult journey from Greenland worthwhile. Until the advent of the Little Ice Age in the fourteenth century forced a final retreat, the Norse continued to visit the northern reaches of North America, including Markland (Labrador).

that English vessels from Bristol and Portuguese vessels from the Azores may have reached North America sometime between 1450 and 1492.

The first to undertake the systematic exploration of the Atlantic were the Portuguese, who began probing south along the African coast in the second half of the fifteenth century. Their goal was to break the Italian monopoly on the lucrative spice trade by developing new sea routes to India and other parts of Asia. By the end of the century, when the Portuguese rounded the Cape of Good Hope and reached India, interest in the possibility of finding a route to Asia by sailing west was attracting interest throughout Europe.

Although Europeans had long speculated that the earth was round, they had good reasons not to try to prove it by venturing too far out to sea. The development of more seaworthy vessels and improvements in navigational instruments in the fifteenth century reduced the risks. Advances

Reconstructed Norse dwellings at L'Anse aux Meadows. Courtesy of Parks Canada. Photo: Chris Reardon.

that made it possible to establish a ship's position, set a course with reasonable accuracy, and sail for days without sighting land enabled the Genoa-born seaman Cristoforo Colombo (Christopher Columbus), sailing in the name of the Spanish Crown in 1492, to reach what he (and everyone else in Europe) thought was Asia, but was instead the Caribbean.

Five years later Zuan Caboto (John Cabot), commissioned by King Henry VII of England, also reached what was assumed to be Asia, where he raised a cross along with the banners of England and Venice. It is agreed that Cabot made a northerly landfall, but there has been considerable debate over its location—was it Cape Breton, Cape Bonavista, or some place in the Strait of Belle Isle? Today most scholars lean towards the last of these. Cabot likely sailed north along the Irish coast before turning west, and would have been capable of holding his latitude.

Cabot's voyage may have been just one of several that reached North America from Europe in the late fifteenth century, but it was singularly important. His report of the abundance of cod in the northwest Atlantic soon attracted substantial interest. Fishing vessels from western Europe followed in Cabot's wake, establishing the first permanent link with what is now Atlantic Canada.

The English were slow to follow up on Cabot's discoveries. Although there were a few more voyages to the west, Bristol merchants were generally more interested in trade than fishing. Moreover, English markets were adequately supplied by local and Icelandic fisheries and the major fishing ports were on the northeast coast—not the best starting point for transatlantic voyages. It was not until the second half of the sixteenth century that England began to take a renewed interest in what North America had to offer. Meanwhile, the non-Christian world had (with the

Biography *John Cabot*

Zuan Caboto was born somewhere in Italy around 1457. His family moved to Venice, where he became a Venetian citizen in or about 1476. He married a Venetian, and his sons were born there. Cabot made a living as a businessman and merchant, trading in hides, general merchandise, and property. He may also have been involved in construction, marine engineering, and trade with what we now call the Middle East—modern Lebanon, Syria, and Palestine—where spices arrived overland from the Far East. By the later 1480s, he had fled Venice to avoid creditors, and after some years in Spain and Portugal he turned up in England, promoting a voyage to Asia by sailing west across northern latitudes.

Cabot seems to have had little seafaring experience, but he may have sailed on Christopher Columbus's second voyage (1493–4), which would help to explain why King Henry VII was prepared to give a relatively obscure Venetian adventurer the letters patent he sought. Backed by Bristol merchants and Italian bankers, Cabot made his first voyage in a single vessel in 1496. That effort failed, but a second attempt, in 1497 in *The Matthew*, succeeded in reaching an American landfall. A third, larger expedition set out in 1498, but little is known about how it fared. It used to be thought that Cabot disappeared on this voyage, but recent evidence suggests that he may have survived. Cabot's second son, Sebastian, also went into the exploration business, and may have accompanied his father on the 1497 voyage. Until the twentieth century, John's accomplishments were often attributed to his son.[4]

pope's blessing) already been divided between Spain and Portugal by the Treaty of Tordesillas (1494), which drew a north–south line west of the Cape Verde Islands: territory west of the line was awarded to Spain and east of it to Portugal.

Cabot may have been trespassing, but his findings stimulated further exploration. Assuming that the "new" lands in the North Atlantic lay within his sphere, King Manoel of Portugal authorized a number of voyages by inhabitants of the Azores, sometimes in alliance with Bristol merchants. In 1499 João Fernandes, a small landowner or "labrador," reached Greenland, which as a result was called "Labrador" on some early maps. In the sixteenth century the name was transferred to the coast of North America, where it has remained. In 1500 Gaspar Corte-Real reached "Terra Verde"—probably Newfoundland. There he captured 60 of the local inhabitants, who were delivered to Lisbon. According to the Venetian ambassador, the captives were "tall, well-built" and would "make the best slaves I have ever seen."[5] The Corte-Reals were awarded a "captaincy" in eastern Newfoundland, and Gaspar returned to North America with three ships in 1501, but his vessel disappeared. A similar fate befell his brother Miguel in 1502. A third brother made a futile attempt to find them both in 1503.

Although these voyages provided cartographers with important information, it was not yet understood that the "new founde landes" were part of a new continent. Contemporary maps show the "discoveries" of Columbus, Cabot, and the Portuguese either as islands in the ocean or as extensions of Greenland and Asia. An important contribution to a better understanding of North American geography was made by Giovanni da Verrazzano. In 1524, on behalf of France's

King François I, he explored the coast between the Carolinas and Cape Breton, and possibly part of Newfoundland. His purpose had been to find a passage to Asia, but instead he ascertained the existence of a continuous North American coastline, part of which was now labelled "New France" on maps.[6] While most of the people Verrazzano met seemed to have had little previous contact with Europeans, the inhabitants of what was perhaps the coast of Maine had apparently become wary of foreigners: instead of boarding the ship to trade, they used ropes strung from ship to shore to exchange their merchandise.

Similar voyages along the North American coast were made in 1524–5 on behalf of Spain by Estêvão Gomes (who kidnapped a large number of Aboriginal people, probably on the Nova Scotian coast) and in 1527 by John Rut on behalf of Henry VIII of England. It is likely that the Portuguese navigator João Alvarez Fagundes, who in 1521 registered his discoveries from an earlier voyage to the Atlantic region, tried to establish a colony on Cape Breton Island in 1525. Designed to be self-supporting, it included ten families from the Azores and had the right to generate revenue through the manufacture of soap. Its failure has been attributed to the climate and the hostility of the local inhabitants.[7]

In 1534 François I commissioned Jacques Cartier to sail beyond Newfoundland to "discover certain islands and countries where it is said a great quantity of gold and other precious things are to be found." From a landfall near Bonavista, Cartier sailed through the Strait of Belle Isle and circumnavigated the Gulf of St Lawrence, thinking that it was an inland sea. He found the north shore of the gulf uninviting, but on sighting Prince Edward Island on a warm summer day he proclaimed it "the best-tempered region one can possibly see." He spent little time exploring it and seems not to have determined that it was an island. On his second voyage, in 1535, he found the entrance to the St Lawrence River. He and his men spent the winter of 1535–6 near present-day Quebec City, and in 1541–2 he participated in an unsuccessful attempt to establish a permanent European settlement there.

With Cartier's voyages the first phase in the European discovery of North America came to an end. The coastline from Mexico to Greenland had been explored, described, and mapped. For most of the explorers, who had no intention of staying, their voyages ended in disappointment. They found neither gold nor spices, and the Aboriginal peoples were sometimes hostile. Even a northwest passage to Asia eluded them, although for many years English explorers tried to find one. Nevertheless, the first generation of explorers had located a region that some Europeans thought potentially lucrative. John Cabot might not have found spices or precious metals, but he had located a rich new source of fish.

The Fishery

The northwest Atlantic fishery soon became exceedingly profitable.[8] In this period fishing employed more Europeans than any occupation other than agriculture. Fish was an important source of protein, was easy to preserve and transport, and often replaced meat on Roman Catholic fast days. In addition, work in the fishery served to train men for service at sea in time of war. The Atlantic region rapidly became a pole of European activity comparable to the Caribbean and the Gulf of Mexico. In the 1580s Spain sent about 100 ships and 4,000 or 5,000 men annually to Central America, while the Atlantic region attracted at least 400 European ships a year, carrying approximately 10,000 men and returning home with some 200,000 metric tonnes of cod.

At first the fishery was dominated by the French. The ports of northern and eastern France were well positioned for a transatlantic fishery, and domestic markets for North Sea cod were already in place before Cabot's voyage. Possibly as early as 1504, vessels from Channel ports in Brittany and Normandy fished regularly in Newfoundland waters. They were soon followed by fishermen from ports such as Bordeaux and La Rochelle, and after 1520 were joined by Basques from southern France and northern Spain. By the 1520s between 60 and 90 French vessels crossed the Atlantic each year to the region known variously as "the new found land," "terre neuve," or "terra de bacalhao."

The role of Portugal in the North Atlantic fishery of the 1500s is a subject of some debate. Certainly there was a Portuguese presence in the region, but whether it included a fishery of any significance is unclear. What we do know is that the Portuguese presence was intermittent, involving relatively few vessels, and was largely confined to the Avalon Peninsula, where Portuguese-derived place names line the shore south of St John's, among them Cape Spear (Cauo da espera), Ferryland (Farilham), and Cape Race (Capo raso). Overall, the Portuguese seem to have been more interested in the region's landward potential.

While the Portuguese apparently concentrated on Newfoundland, the French established a presence throughout the region. Bretons, Normans, and French Basques fished at Cape Breton and Gaspé. Later in the sixteenth century they moved along the coast of the Nova Scotia peninsula and into the Bay of Fundy. French and Spanish Basques often fished together off the Gaspé Peninsula, in the Gulf of St Lawrence, and in the Strait of Belle Isle. In Newfoundland, Bretons fished primarily on the northeast coast between Cape St John and Cape Bauld (le Petit Nord). French and Basque

A reconstructed Basque chalupa at Red Bay, Labrador. Crewed by six men and powered by either sails or oars, shallops such as this one were used for whaling in the Strait of Belle Isle. Courtesy of Parks Canada. Photo: Chris Reardon.

vessels alike used the island's south coast, from Trepassey to Fortune Bay (la Côte du Chapeau Rouge), and Placentia emerged as the centre of the northwest Atlantic fishery. These were at first shore-based fisheries, but later in the century France also began to exploit the offshore banks—first the Grand Banks, then those off southern Newfoundland and in the Gulf.

Basques whaling in the Strait of Belle Isle represented another form of economic diversification. They established stations on the Labrador coast between Cape Charles and the St Paul River, the most important at Red Bay (Butus, or Hable des Buttes), where archaeologists have excavated both the buildings and the wreck of the *San Juan*, a galleon that sank there in 1565. At the height of the industry, some 30 Basque ships employing about 2,500 men hunted right and bowhead whales annually. Although whalers sometimes remained in Labrador for the winter, such sojourns were usually involuntary, the result of delaying departure so long that the ships became icebound. Perhaps it was during one such enforced stay in Carroll's Cove (then known as Puerto Breton) that Joanes de Echaniz dictated his will—one of the earliest in Canada—on Christmas Eve 1584.

By the end of the sixteenth century the Iberian fishery was in decline. The Spanish government imposed new taxes and restrictions on trade and shipping, and inflation increased costs. Moreover, the war with England, which culminated in the disaster of the Spanish Armada in 1588, caused serious disruptions and financial losses. The fortunes of Portugal also declined after it was annexed by Spain in 1580. With the depletion of whale stocks off Labrador, perhaps due to overfishing and climate change associated to the Little Ice Age, Basque whalers moved elsewhere. Spanish Basques continued to fish in the Gulf and off southeastern Newfoundland throughout the seventeenth century, but in decreasing numbers. As a result, Iberia now needed to import significant quantities of fish.

In response, the French fleet expanded to as many as 500 vessels in the 1580s, and French fishermen began using the Gulf much more extensively than they had before, steadily moving farther west into the St Lawrence River. The same market opportunity caught the attention of ports in southwestern England (the West Country) such as Poole, Plymouth, and Dartmouth. Anthony Parkhurst, a merchant who first travelled to Newfoundland in 1574, estimated in 1578 that no more than 50 English vessels made the trip to the island each year; by the early seventeenth century that number had increased to at least 200.

Initially, English and French fishermen kept out of each other's way. Sailing from ports along the coast from Normandy to the Pyrenees, the French produced both a "wet" (or "green") cure, in which the fish were taken into the ship's hold and heavily salted or packed in brine, and a "dry" cure, in which the fish were split, lightly salted, and then dried on shore. Consumers in the north and east of France generally preferred green fish, but in response to demand from Spain, Portugal, and the Mediterranean, French Basques in particular produced dry-cured fish, which kept better in hot climates.

The English, sailing almost exclusively from West Country ports, produced only a dry cure. Ignoring the domestic market, they exchanged salt fish for bullion, fruits, wines, and other exotic Mediterranean goods. The production of dry cure fish demanded the building of seasonal fishing stations where the catch could be cleaned, salted, and dried. Increasingly, the English established themselves on the eastern shores of the Avalon Peninsula, gradually forcing out other nationalities and extending as far north as Bonavista. Newfoundland's "English Shore" was the first English foothold in what is now Canada.

By the end of the sixteenth century, pirates were also operating on the coasts of the Americas. They focused their efforts on the Caribbean where Spanish ships carrying bullion could be intercepted, but they sometimes raided fishing vessels and shore bases in the North Atlantic to secure supplies and conscript crew members. While a few of the buccaneers, such as Elizabeth I's courtier Francis Drake, were commissioned by their monarchs to cripple enemy shipping, others were genuine outlaws, who benefited from there being "no peace over the line" drawn in the western Atlantic by the Treaty of Tordesillas.[9]

Aboriginal–European Trade

No permanent, year-round European settlements took root in the Atlantic region in the sixteenth century. Since the fisheries were seasonal extensions of a European industry, dependent on a European workforce and European markets, there seemed little need for overseas colonies. One factor that helped to change this situation was the development of the fur trade. Aboriginal peoples were usually eager to barter with the newcomers, and casual trading was commonplace well before the 1530s.

By the time of Cartier's first voyage, the Mi'kmaq in the Gaspé region were familiar with the rituals of the fur trade. In July 1534 Cartier met a group of Mi'kmaq near the Baie des Chaleurs and noted that "As soon as they saw us they began to run away, making signs that they had come to barter with us; and held up some furs of small value, with which they clothe themselves." Cartier knew how to respond. "We likewise made signs to them that we wished them no harm, and sent two men on shore, to offer them some knives and other iron goods, and a red cap to give to their chief."[10] Basque whaling stations attracted Inuit, Innu, and St Lawrence Iroquoians, all of whom placed a high value on metal objects, especially knives, axes, and cooking pots. Aboriginal people sometimes pilfered metal items when Europeans were absent, but by mid-century the practice of trading furs for such goods had become well established. It was further stimulated after 1580 by the European demand for hats made of felted beaver fur.

Although fishers, whalers, and sailors traded on their own behalf, some French merchants began sending out vessels solely to buy furs along the coasts from Labrador to present-day New England. In 1583, for example, Étienne Bélanger of Rouen cruised from Cape Breton to Maine, collecting a valuable cargo of moose, deer, and seal pelts along with fine furs such as beaver, marten, and otter.[11] By the end of the sixteenth century, some outfitters combined fishing and fur-trading. There was little fur-trading in Newfoundland largely because there were few Native people to trade with.

Seasonal though it was, the European presence had profound consequences for the region's Aboriginal people. European diseases eventually infected even communities that had no direct contact with the newcomers, and populations diminished as a result. At the same time, the fur trade altered traditional subsistence patterns and created dependence on Europeans for foodstuffs, alcohol, and metal implements, including copper cooking pots, knives, and guns. The Inuit showed considerable hostility to Europeans and the Beothuk avoided contact, but relations with other Aboriginal groups in the Atlantic region were generally good.

The Basques seem to have got on well with the Innu. In the last decade of the sixteenth century, the West Country sea captain Richard Whitbourne reported that the Innu were "an ingenious and tractable people (being well used)," who worked in the whale fishery, helping to hunt and process the catch. In the Maritime region, the historian James Axtell reports that Aboriginals quickly became middlemen, "sailing in Basque shallops, wearing various items of European clothing . . . speaking

Document

The Voyage of the *Grace* from Bristol, 1594

In the 1590s, Bristol merchants became interested in the resources of the Gulf of St Lawrence, particularly whales and walrus. Several expeditions were sent, among them the *Grace*, Sylvester Wyet master, carrying a Basque pilot. The voyage was not very successful; the *Grace* failed to find whales and had to settle for cod instead.

> We departed with the aforesaid Barke manned with twelve men . . . from Bristoll the 4 of Aprill 1594, and fell with Cape D'Espere [Spear] on the coast of Newefoundland the nineteenth of May . . . [and sailed along the south coast of Newfoundland, and then north.]
>
> In this bay of Saint George, we found the wrackes of 2 great Biskayne [Basque] ships, which had bene cast away three yeeres before: where we had some seven or eight hundred Whale finnes, and some yron bolts and chaines. . . . Here we found the houses of the Savages, made of firre trees bound together in the top and set round like a Dovehouse, and covered with the barkes of firre trees, we found also some part of their victuals, which were Deeres flesh roasted upon wooden spits at the fire, & a dish made of a ryne of a tree, sowed together with the sinowes of the Deere, wherein the oile was of the Deere. There were also foules called Cormorants, which they had pluckt and made ready to have dressed, and there we found a wooden spoone of their making. And we discerned the tracks of the feete of some fortie or fiftie men, women and children.
>
> . . . [We then] shaped our course over to that lond Isle of Natiscotec [Anticosti]. . . . Here we . . . found wonderfull faire and great Cod fish. . . . And after wee had searched two dayes and a night for the Whales which were wounded which we had hoped to have found there, we returned backe to the Southwarde . . . and so came to the Bay of Placentia and arrived . . . among the fishermen of Saint John de Luz and of Sibiburo and of Biskay, which were to the number of three score and odd sayles . . . of whom we were very well used. . . . There the men of Saint John and Sibiburo men bestowed two pinnesses [pinaces] on us to make up our voyage with fish. Then wee departed over to the other side of the Bay . . . and fished so long, that in the ende the Savages came, and in the night, when our men were at rest, cut both our pinesse and our shippes boate away . . . yet it was our good fortune to . . . get them againe. Then for feare of a shrewder turne of the Savages, we departed . . . and arrived in Farrillon [Ferryland], and finding there two and twentie sayles of Englishmen, wee made up our fishing voyage to the full in that harborough . . . to our good content: and departing thence we arrived . . . in the river of Bristoll by the grace of God the 24 of September 1594.[12]

a half-Basque, half-Indian trade jargon," and bartering furs from as far south as the coast of Maine with French or Basque traders in the Gulf of St Lawrence and at Tadoussac.[13]

Conclusion

The European discovery of North America opened a period of encounter and exploration that gradually changed the way the world was perceived and experienced by Aboriginal people and Europeans alike. Fishing, fur-trading, and whaling ensured that the European presence would be permanent, even if it was largely seasonal in this period. Aboriginal peoples adapted in differing ways to the new arrivals, developing relationships that at first were not grossly imbalanced. This fluid, maritime world was the beginning of the modern Atlantic region and set in motion forces that would, over time, create a very different environment.

Further Readings

Bailey, Alfred G. 1969. *The Conflict of European and Eastern Algonkian Cultures, 1504–1700*. Toronto: University of Toronto Press.

Candow, James E., and Carol Corbin, eds. 1997. *How Deep Is the Ocean? Historical Essays on Canada's Atlantic Fishery*. Sydney: University College of Cape Breton Press.

Crosby, Alfred J. 1986. *Ecological Imperialism: The Biological Expansion of Europe, 900–1900*. Cambridge: Cambridge University Press.

Hunter, Douglas. 2012. *The Race to the New World: Christopher Columbus, John Cabot, and a Lost History of Discovery*. Vancouver/Toronto: Douglas and McIntyre.

Innis, Harold. 1940. *The Cod Fisheries: The History of an International Economy*. New Haven: Yale University Press.

Lewis-Simpson, Shannon, ed. 2003. *Vinland Revisited: The Norse World at the Turn of the First Millennium*. St John's: Historic Sites Association of Newfoundland and Labrador.

Pope, Peter E. 1997. *The Many Landfalls of John Cabot*. Toronto: University of Toronto Press.

Sawyer, P.H., ed. 2000. *The Oxford Illustrated History of the Vikings*. Oxford: Oxford University Press.

Starkey, David J., and James E, Candow, eds. 2006. *The North Atlantic Fisheries: Supply, Marketing and Consumption, 1560–1900*. Hull: Studia Atlantica Publications.

Wright, Ronald. 1993. *Stolen Continents: The New World Through Indian Eyes*. Toronto: Penguin.

Historical Spotlight

Codignola, Luca. 2005. "How Wide is the Atlantic Ocean? Larger and Larger," and John G. Reid, "How Wide is the Atlantic Ocean? Not Wide Enough," *Acadiensis* XXXIV, 2 (Spring): 74–80, 81–7.

Pope, Peter. 2003. "Comparisons: Atlantic Canada." In Daniel Vickers, ed., *A Companion to Colonial America*. Oxford: Blackwell, 489–507.

Recommended Websites

The Cabot Project
http://www.bristol.ac.uk/history/research/cabot.html

L'Anse aux Meadows Historic Site
http://www.pc.gc.ca/lhn-nhs/nl/meadows/index_e.asp

Newfoundland and Labrador Heritage: Exploration and Settlement
http://www.heritage.nf.ca/exploration/default.html

The Virtual Museum of Labrador
http://www.labradorvirtualmuseum.ca

The Virtual Museum Of New France
http://www.historymuseum.ca

Chapter 4

Colonial Experiments, 1598–1632

The success of Europeans in colonizing the Americas is one of the most significant developments in early modern history. Until recently, historians assumed that the outcome was predetermined by the supposed moral, technological, and institutional superiority of Europeans. Now it is recognized that, although their advanced technology and complex governance structures were advantages, the newcomers could not have colonized a strange new environment without learning how to survive in it. This knowledge was obtained partly through experience, but largely from the local inhabitants. Because the Europeans were unable to adapt quickly to the "New World," their colonization efforts in the sixteenth century failed and the small settlements established in the seventeenth century were unstable, subject to attacks from other Europeans, and dependent on the tolerance of Aboriginal inhabitants.

Early Colonizers

Early colonization efforts reflected the weakness of the European powers competing for ascendancy in the region—primarily France and England. In an effort to minimize the cost of their initiatives, the rulers of these emerging nation-states delegated colonization and governance to private individuals and companies. This approach, coupled with persistent international conflict, made the Atlantic region vulnerable to economic, political, and religious rivalries originating in Europe. With the Atlantic Ocean serving as much to link them to Europe as to distance them from it, the eastern margins of North America became a stage on which imperial characters acted out their competing roles.

Colonization efforts between 1578 and 1632 yielded some bold adventurers, high drama, and meagre results. In 1578 Queen Elizabeth I of England granted Sir Humphrey Gilbert—who dreamed of a colony in what is now Massachusetts—a patent to explore and occupy those parts of eastern North America not already taken by the Spanish. In 1583 Gilbert entered St John's harbour in search of food and other necessities. After convincing the captains of some 40 fishing vessels there that he was not a pirate, Gilbert was allowed to pass through the Narrows, where one of his ships ran anticlimactically aground. On 5 August he went ashore and formally claimed the land for the English Crown. He erected a pillar with the arms of England fixed to it, issued licences to non-English ships, and appropriated shore premises that he then leased back to those who were using them. Before it reached the mainland of North America, the expedition decided to return home. Gilbert, who was lost at sea on the way, was last seen sitting on deck, a book in his hand, shouting: "We are as neare to Heaven by sea as by land."[1] Historians once interpreted Gilbert's performance in St John's harbour as a significant event in the evolution of the first British Empire, but since neither his successors nor the English Crown followed up on his assertion of sovereignty, it meant little in practical terms.

Table 4.1   Timeline

1583	Sir Humphrey Gilbert claims Newfoundland for Elizabeth I.
1598	Marquis de la Roche attempts to establish a colony on Sable Island.
1604	Sieur de Monts attempts to establish a base at Sainte-Croix.
1605	De Monts and Samuel de Champlain establish Port-Royal.
1606	Champlain founds the Ordre de Bon Temps.
1610	London and Bristol Company founds colony at Cupids Cove; Membertou and his family baptized by a Roman Catholic priest at Port-Royal.
1613	Destruction of Saint-Sauveur and Port-Royal by Samuel Argall.
1621	Sir George Calvert founds the Colony of Avalon at Ferryland; James I of England grants "Nova Scotia" to Sir William Alexander.
1629	Colonies established on Cape Breton Island and at Port-Royal by Lord Ochiltree and William Alexander the younger.
1632	England recognizes French claim to Acadia in the Treaty of Saint-Germain-en-Laye.

It was not the English but the French who initiated European settlement of the Atlantic region. In 1598 Henri IV became king following a bloody civil war between Roman Catholics and Protestants (Huguenots) that had raged since 1562. Like other monarchs, he tried to restore his own treasury and the glory of his country through overseas ventures financed by private interests. Entrepreneurs were offered a monopoly of the fur trade in French-claimed territories if they would agree to transport settlers and support Christian missions among the local inhabitants. The first settlement attempt was made on Sable Island, where the Marquis de la Roche shipped 10 soldiers and 40 settlers from Rouen in 1598. By the spring of 1603, when the settlement was abandoned, only 11 were left.

The next, ultimately more successful, initiative was led by Pierre Du Gua, Sieur de Monts, a Huguenot who in 1603 was appointed viceroy in "la Cadie," Canada, and "autres terres de la Nouvelle France." In return for a 10-year fur-trade monopoly, de Monts agreed to sponsor at least 60 settlers annually and support efforts to convert Aboriginal people in the area to Christianity. The next year de Monts set out to establish a colony in "la Cadie." His entourage included two Roman Catholic priests, a Protestant minister, several noblemen, masons, and carpenters, a miner, a surgeon, and an apothecary. It also included Samuel de Champlain, a veteran of the religious wars and an enthusiastic proponent of European colonization.

After exploring the south coast of Nova Scotia and the Bay of Fundy (named "la Baie Française" by de Monts), the colonizers finally chose an island at the mouth of the St Croix River as the site for a settlement. The choice seems to have been dictated by a concern for military protection, but it proved disastrous. A harsh climate, lack of firewood, and inadequate provisions brought great hardship. By the spring, 35 of the 79 men who wintered on the island had died of scurvy. Most of those who survived returned to France in the spring, when de Monts arrived with more settlers and supplies. Among those determined to stay was Champlain.

Port-Royal

The French spent the summer of 1605 seeking a better settlement site. After exploring the coast as far as Cape Cod, they finally fixed on a sheltered basin on the south shore of the Bay of Fundy.[2] Natural military protection, good soil, and a temperate climate were not the only advantages that Port-Royal offered: the Mi'kmaq in the area under chief Membertou were prepared to tolerate the intruders. Having experienced a hostile reception from Aboriginal people in the Cape Cod region, the French recognized that friendship with the local inhabitants was a decided asset in any effort to establish a colony.

The would-be colonists established their new base on the north shore of what is now the Annapolis basin. More tightly constructed than the one at Sainte-Croix, their "habitation" included a "very fine cellar," so that cider and other supplies would not freeze as they had done the previous year. More importantly, the French planted gardens and made friends with the local Mi'kmaq, who were particularly fond of the fresh bread that the colonists made from corn flour ground with hand mills. Despite these improvements, a third of the 45 men who wintered at Port-Royal in 1605–6 succumbed to scurvy.

In the spring of 1606 Jean de Poutrincourt et de Saint-Just, who had been appointed lieutenant-governor of Acadia, arrived at Port-Royal with a group that included skilled workmen along with several aristocratic friends and relatives who would play important roles in the development of New France. These included his son, Charles de Biencourt; his cousin Louis Hébert, who was an apothecary and horticulturalist; another cousin, Claude de Saint-Etienne de La Tour, and his 14-year-old-son, Charles; and Marc Lescarbot, a lawyer from Paris who would later publish an account of the activities of this circle under the title *Histoire de la Nouvelle France* (1618). To reduce their dependence on supplies from France, the colonists planted wheat and built a gristmill. They also developed innovative responses to the challenges of survival. In 1606 Champlain founded the Ordre de Bon Temps, which obliged members to take turns providing game and fish for the table. The survival rate improved—only four people died of scurvy that winter.

Notwithstanding his success in establishing the colony, de Monts faced insurmountable challenges. His fur-trade monopoly was impossible to enforce and in 1607 it was revoked. Financial

Biography *Membertou*

Membertou, chief of the small band of Mi'kmaq in the Kespukwitk region in which Port-Royal was situated, impressed the colonizers on whose records we must rely for information about his life. Exceptionally tall, Membertou sported a beard (unusual for an Aboriginal man) and claimed to remember Cartier's visit in the 1530s. Historians are skeptical of this claim to such longevity. There can be no doubt, however, about his willingness to enter into an alliance with the French and his genuine affection for them (which seems to have been mutual).

On 24 June 1610 Membertou and 20 members of his family were baptized by the priest Jessé Fléché, becoming the first known Aboriginal converts to Roman Catholicism in New France. Membertou received the Christian name of the French King and thus appears as Henri Membertou in many historical accounts. Although his conversion was likely undertaken more in the spirit of alliance and friendship than of religious conviction, he nevertheless replaced the shamanic bag that he had worn around his neck with a cross, and as he was dying of dysentery in September 1611 he agreed to be buried in the French graveyard rather than with his ancestors.[3]

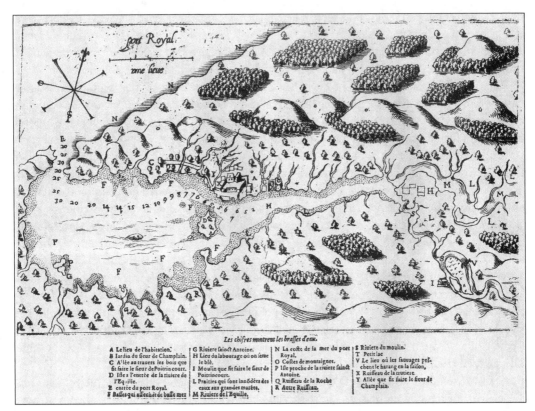

Champlain's map of the first Port-Royal. The habitation is flanked by a trout brook (X) and Champlain's garden (B). The wheat fields (H) would become the site of Fort Anne, and the mill is located on the Allain River (I). Library and Archives Canada/Champlain: la naissance de l'Amerique francaise/AMICUS 30597940/P.139/NL15325.

losses soon obliged him to order the abandonment of Port-Royal. De Monts and Champlain thereafter concentrated their efforts on the St Lawrence, establishing a base at Quebec in 1608. Poutrincourt remained committed to Acadia, and in 1610 he returned there with his son Charles de Biencourt and some 20 colonists, including the priest Jessé Fléché.

In short order Poutrincourt collected a shipload of furs and Fléché baptized Membertou and his family, demonstrating that the enterprise could be both financially and spiritually profitable. In Paris, Poutrincourt found a patron in the Marquise de Guercheville, whose support was tied to the condition that the Jesuits, who had become influential at the French court, would control missionary work in Acadia and become partners in the fur trade. While Poutrincourt remained in France to raise funds, young Biencourt returned to Port-Royal in May 1611 with 36 colonists and two Jesuit priests, Pierre Biard and Énemond Massé.

To further complicate matters, the English had established a colony at Jamestown in Virginia in 1607, and built Fort St George on the Kennebec River—the first moves in an effort to claim all territory between the 34th and 45th parallels. The Dutch were not far behind in the colonization sweepstakes, following up Henry Hudson's exploration, in 1609, of the river that now bears his name by issuing an exclusive patent in 1614 to the New Netherland Company for trade between the 40th and 45th parallels. Acadia/Mi'kma'ki now sat uncomfortably at the crossroads of competing European empires.

Historical Focus

Le Théâtre de Neptune in New France, 1606

Whatever their country of origin, the European explorers, traders, and colonizers who braved the difficult Atlantic crossing were men of the Renaissance and shared a cultural background centred on classical literature. They would have been familiar with the gods of Greece and Rome, among them Neptune, the god of the sea. Indeed, "yielding up the tribute to Neptune" was a polite way of describing sea-sickness.

One of the more memorable moments at Port-Royal occurred in November 1606 when Poutrincourt, Champlain, and their crew returned from two months of exploration along the Atlantic coast. As they anchored near the habitation, they were approached by "Father Neptune," complete with silvery locks and flowing beard, in a boat drawn by six "Tritons." The sea god, brandishing his trident, drew alongside Poutrincourt's longboat and addressed him in Alexandrine verse:

> Halt mighty Sagamo, no further fare!
> Look on a god who holds thee in his care.
> Thou knows't me not? I am of Saturn's line
> Brother to Pluto dark and Jove divine.

After outlining what had been achieved through his command of the oceans—adventure, trade, exotic goods—the explorers were reminded:

> If Man would taste the spice of fortune's savour
> He needs must seek the aid of Neptune's favour.
> For stay-at-homes who doze on kitchen settles
> Earn no more glory than their pots and kettles.[4]

Believed to have been the first theatrical piece, know as a masque, written by a European in North America, Le Théâtre de Neptune may not be exceptional as poetry, but its existence underlines the rich cultural life that the French brought with them to their "New World."

In Poutrincourt's absence, serious quarrels broke out between Biencourt and the Jesuits. The Marquise de Guercheville, who was determined to see the Jesuits prevail, obtained control over territories in Acadia outside Poutrincourt's jurisdiction and financed an expedition to move the Jesuits from Port-Royal to Saint-Sauveur, a new colony established opposite what is now known as Mount Desert Island on the Penobscot River in Maine. Shortly after their arrival, the settlement was attacked by Samuel Argall, an English sea captain and adventurer, who was subsequently commissioned by the Governor of Virginia, Sir Thomas Dale, to destroy all French settlements. In the autumn of 1613 Argall sacked the buildings at Saint-Sauveur and Sainte-Croix, and trashed everything at Port-Royal but the gristmill and barns. The colonists, who were on a hunting expedition at the time, sought shelter with the Mi'kmaq through the winter.

Returning the following year to find complete devastation, Poutrincourt and most of the colonists returned to France. Only Biencourt, his cousin Charles de Saint-Étienne de La Tour, and a few others stayed on. Backed by La Rochelle merchants, Biencourt and his partners built a successful business in fur and fish. They developed good relations with the Mi'kmaq and extended their activities into the harbours on the south shore of Acadia and at the mouth of the St John River.

Following Biencourt's death in 1623, the direction of the colony was entrusted to Charles de La Tour, who (like his father, Claude) continued to make Acadia his home. Charles married a Mi'kmaw woman (likely a chief's daughter) and their union, later blessed by a Récollet priest, produced three daughters. Two of them entered religious orders in France at a young age, suggesting that their mother had died; the elder, Antoinette, became renowned at court for her fine singing voice. A third daughter, Jeanne, married a Basque fur trader, Martin d'Aprendestiguy, who in 1672 was granted a seigneury on the St John River.[5]

Despite more than two decades of sustained effort by private interests sanctioned by the Crown, New France remained little more than a series of isolated trading posts: Charles de La Tour's bases at Cap-Sable on the south shore and Port-Royal were the principal French settlements in Acadia, while Quebec and Tadoussac anchored the St Lawrence colony known as Canada. None of these communities attracted many permanent settlers, and the military presence in the region consisted mostly of

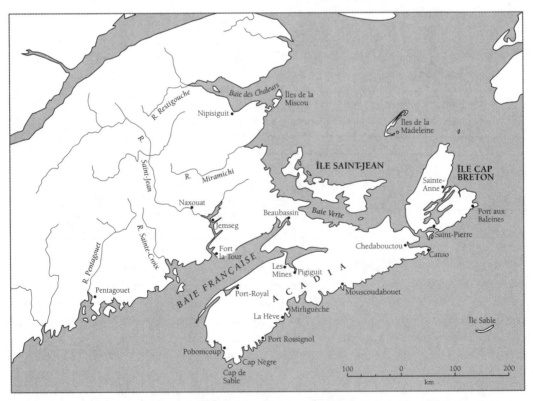

Acadian settlements in the seventeenth century. Adapted from J.G. Reid, *Acadia, Maine and New Scotland: Marginal Colonies in the Seventeenth Century* (Toronto: University of Toronto Press, 1981), pp. 191–4.

mercenaries employed by trading companies. If France was to best its rivals in staking claims in North America, a new approach was necessary. In 1627, Louis XIII, following the recommendation of his chief advisor, Cardinal Richelieu, established the Compagnie des Cent-Associés (Company of One Hundred Associates) to advance France's interests in North America. In 1628 the Cent-Associés dispatched four ships with supplies, soldiers, and 400 settlers, hoping to transform Canada and Acadia into thriving Roman Catholic colonies. Protestants would henceforth no longer be permitted to settle in New France.

Contested Terrain

By this time, French claims to Acadia were being directly challenged by England and Scotland. King James I of England (who was also James VI of Scotland) issued a charter to the Plymouth Council of New England (a joint stock company) in 1620, authorizing it to establish colonies between the 40th and 48th parallels. The next year, the king granted rights to the area, which now encompassed the Maritimes and Gaspé, to Sir William Alexander. In 1622 the Province of Maine, bounded by the Merrimack and Kennebec rivers, was awarded to Sir Fernando Gorges and John Mason. The English challenge to Acadia was confirmed in 1626 when a force from the Plymouth Colony, founded in 1620 by the Pilgrims (zealous Protestants who had separated from the Church of England), seized Claude de La Tour's trading post at Pentagouët on the Penobscot River.[6]

Alexander's early efforts to establish a colony in Nova Scotia—Latin for "New Scotland"—failed, but he persevered. In 1624 the king created 150 knights-baronet who, in return for payment, would each receive a title and a land grant of 30,000 acres (12,150 hectares). Modelled on English colonization practices in Ireland, the scheme attracted little interest except from the king, who wanted to develop closer relations between Scotland and England. His son Charles I, who ascended the throne in 1625, was equally eager to rule over a "Greater Britain."

The outbreak of war with France in 1627, part of the European conflict known as the Thirty Years' War (1618–48), prompted further English schemes to challenge French claims in North America. Commissioned by Charles I to remove the French from "Canida," David Kirke and his brothers intercepted the inaugural expedition of the Cent-Associés in 1628, occupied Tadoussac, and blockaded Quebec, which surrendered in 1629. Claude de La Tour, who had prevailed on the Cent-Associés to send resources to his son at Cap-Sable, was taken prisoner. At the king's urging, the Kirkes and Alexanders formed a company known as the Merchant Adventurers to Canada. They planned two Scottish colonies in Acadia, one at Port-Royal under the command of William Alexander the younger, and another more strategically located in Cape Breton under the direction of Sir James Stewart, Lord Ochiltree, supported by a £500 loan from the king.

The colonizers arrived in Cape Breton in July 1629, where they constructed a fortified base named Rosemar at Port-aux-Baleines, near the northeastern cape. Alexander moved on to Port-Royal, while Ochiltree patrolled the fisheries, levying duties and confiscating vessels found fishing without a licence.

The 60 settlers recruited for the Ochiltree colony included eight families of Brownists, a Puritan sect, who chose to live apart from the other settlers.[7] Internal divisions had little to do with the colony's failure. In September 1629 a French force dispatched to relieve the blockade of Quebec captured and destroyed Fort Rosemar. The inhabitants were then forced to build Fort Sainte-Anne at Grand Cibou for the French before being shipped back to Europe.

The younger Alexander had more success. Claude de La Tour—who had arrived in England as a prisoner but decided to become one of Alexander's knights-baronet and married a lady-in-waiting at the court—agreed to accompany the Scottish party to Port-Royal. There the 70 colonizers constructed Charlesfort (at the site of the present-day Fort Anne National Historic Park), planted gardens, and delighted in the rich soil and abundant wildlife. Shortly after their arrival, they entertained representatives from the Mi'kmaq and Wolastoqiyik, who appeared with presents, signalling their interest in trade and friendship. In the fall of 1629 the Mi'kmaw chief Segipt, his wife, and his son accompanied Claude de La Tour to England to be presented to the king.

On their return in 1630, La Tour tried to persuade his son Charles to join him on the English side—apparently under the threat of military force—but without success. Meanwhile, conditions at Charlesfort had become desperate. No more resilient in the face of a Maritime environment than their French counterparts, 30 of the colonists had died over the winter. Claude de La Tour obtained his son's permission to join him at Cap-Sable, and Charles, supported by the Cent-Associés, strengthened his base there and made plans to construct a fortified trading base (Sainte-Marie) at the mouth of the St John River. In 1631 the younger La Tour was appointed lieutenant-general of Acadia and a member of the Cent-Associés.

European diplomacy decided the fate of these ambitious initiatives. In March 1632, as part of the Treaty of Saint-Germain-en-Laye ending the war, King Charles agreed to restore Acadia and Canada to France in return for payment of his French queen's outstanding dowry, thus helping to fill his depleted coffers. When news of the peace treaty reached Charlesfort, its commander, Andrew Forrester, led a force across the Bay of Fundy to trash Fort Sainte-Marie. In compensation for his dashed hopes of New Scotland, Sir William Alexander was proclaimed the Earl of Stirling. His legacies include a name, a flag, and a coat of arms still used by the province of Nova Scotia.

The Newfoundland Plantations

The other, equally precarious node of European settlement in the region was Newfoundland's Avalon Peninsula. In 1610 the London and Bristol Company decided to establish a plantation at Cuper's Cove (soon better known as Cupids Cove) in Conception Bay. The investors hoped to develop a fur trade with the Beothuk and create a series of permanent settlements that would enable the company to control a substantial proportion of the Newfoundland fishery and trade. On behalf of the company, John Guy, a Bristol merchant, brought out 39 men in 1610, followed by 16 women in 1612. Cupids Cove became the first English settlement in what is now Canada.

Although the colony's early years were quite promising, problems soon developed. The settlement was harassed by the pirate Peter Easton; the soil and climate proved to be less favourable to agriculture than expected, and there was friction with the migratory fishermen. Since the settlers had little contact with the Beothuk, a fur trade failed to develop. These factors, added to internal dissension, led to the plantation's breakup. A few colonists remained in Cupids Cove, and some moved to Bristol's Hope (now Harbour Grace) and Carbonear, but most left Newfoundland behind them.

Cupids Cove may have been a business failure, but it sparked other initiatives. To recoup some of its investment, the London and Bristol Company began to sell tracts of land to other potential colonizers. The first of these was Sir William Vaughan, a Welsh lawyer and scholar who saw in overseas colonization a solution to social and economic problems at home. In 1616 he purchased the Avalon Peninsula south of a line from Caplin Bay (now Calvert) across to Placentia Bay, and called his land "New Cambriol." A flimsy settlement was established at Aquaforte, which Richard Whitbourne later moved to Renews. By 1621 the colony was finished. Vaughan sold off sections of his property to Sir George Calvert and Lord Falkland and retired to his library to write *The Golden Fleece* (1626), a fanciful book promoting the colonization of Newfoundland.

Although Falkland did nothing with his holdings, the wealthy and influential Calvert established a plantation at Ferryland in 1621. He called it the Colony of Avalon—a name derived from Arthurian legend, which in time was applied to the whole peninsula. Ferryland became one of the earliest permanent European settlements in North America and was among the best capitalized, with stone houses, a cobbled street, a quay, warehouses, and defences. Calvert, who became Lord Baltimore in 1625, viewed the colony as a business enterprise, but he also wanted Ferryland to be a haven of religious tolerance. A convert to Roman Catholicism, Baltimore allowed both Protestant and Catholic clergy to serve the colonists, who numbered more than 100 in the late 1620s.

Still, the colony failed to meet expectations. Baltimore was disheartened not only by the inhospitable climate but also by a slump in the fishery and the high cost of dealing with French privateers. After an interval in England, he departed for Maryland in 1632, leaving his Ferryland property (in which he had invested more than £20,000—$4 million today) in the hands of agents. By that time the village had dwindled to perhaps 30 people.

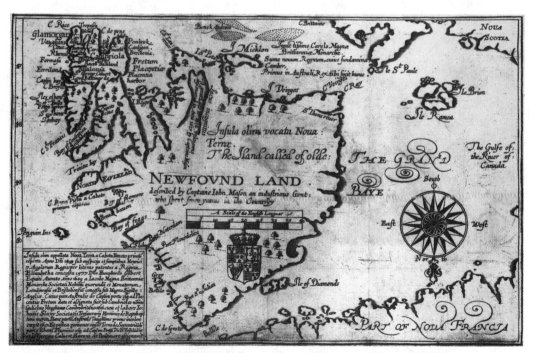

The John Mason Map, 1617. When Mason was appointed governor of the English colony at Cupids Cove in 1616, he was already familiar with Newfoundland. His map—the first English depiction of the island—constitutes an important piece of evidence for those who believe that John Cabot made his landfall at Cape Bonavista. On the left, just below the peninsula named "North Falkland" (now the Bonavista Peninsula), is the legend *C. Bona Vista a Cabato primum Reperta*. Library and Archives Canada, NMC-21046.

In the 1620s the total European winter population on the English Shore was probably no more than 200. A few "plantations" linked to West Country ports were established in Conception Bay and at St John's, the most important centres of the migratory fishery. A resident fishery was made possible when "sack" ships (large cargo vessels) entered the trade and began buying fish from the settlers. With conditions unfavourable for agriculture, the viability of settlement on the island of Newfoundland depended on imported foodstuffs until the mid-1700s, when locally grown potatoes became a dietary staple.

Document

Planting a Colony in Ferryland, 1621

On 26 August 1621, Edward Wynne wrote to his employer, Sir George Calvert, outlining his activities in planting a colony at Ferryland on the east coast of the Avalon Peninsula:

> The place whereon I have made choice to plant and build upon is . . . the fittest, the warmest, the most commodious of all about the harbour. As soon as the [Mansion] house and fortification is fitted and finished, I shall (God willing) prepare and fence in a proportion of seed ground and a garden, close by the house. It may please your Honour not to send out any cattle next year, because I cannot fodder for them so soon, before there be some quantity of corn [grain] growing, but it may please your honour to send some goats, a few tame conies [rabbits] for breed, as also pigs, geese, ducks and hens. I have some hens already. Some spades from London are necessary, if of the best making, also some good pick-axes, iron crows [crowbars], and a smith, and also such as can brew and bake.[8]

Like other European colonizers, Wynne was attempting to recreate the old world in the new, but the project proved more challenging than his optimistic letter implied. Baltimore himself spent part of 1627 and the winter of 1628–9 in Ferryland, before deciding "to shift to some other warmer climate of this new worlde." As he complained to King Charles I:

The Ferryland cross. This ornate iron cross, excavated at Lord Baltimore's Ferryland settlement, was once gilded and embedded with gems. James Tuck, Memorial University, St John's.

> . . . from the middest of October, to the middest of May there is a sad face of wynter upon all this land, both sea and land so frozen for the greatest part of the tyme as they are not penetrable, no plant or vegetable thing appearing out of the earth untill it be about the beginning of May nor fish in the sea besides the ayre is so intolerable cold as it is hardly to be endured.[9]

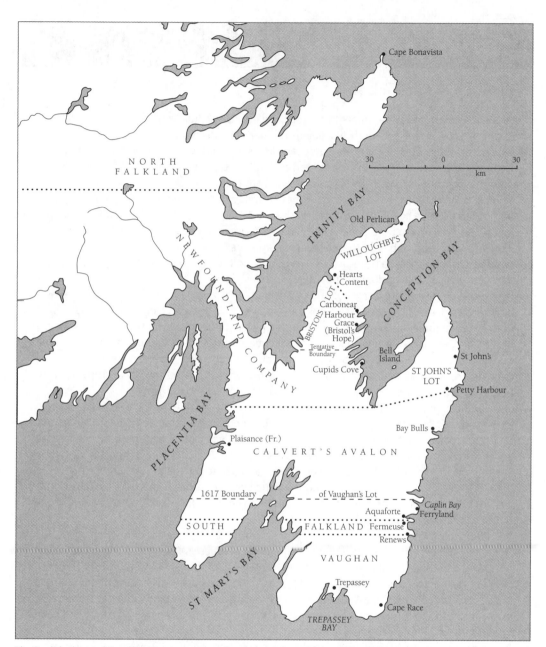

The English Shore of Newfoundland, seventeenth century. Adapted from Gillian Cell, ed., *Newfoundland Discovered: English Attempts at Colonisation, 1610–1630* (London: Hakluyt Society, 1982), p. 21.

Conclusion

Despite the difficulty of establishing stable colonies in the region, Europeans had staked out the Avalon Peninsula and the area surrounding the Bay of Fundy as potential sites for settlement by

Setting the Context

Ecological Exchanges

By the beginning of the seventeenth century, the environmental impact of European contact was well underway. Plant seeds (including the hardy dandelion) were among the early passengers on fishing vessels as were European diseases, which quickly took a toll among the Aboriginal population. Père Biard reported in 1612 that the Mi'kmaq "often complain that since the French mingle with and carry on trade with them, they are dying fast and the population is thinning out. . . . One by one the different coasts according as they have begun to traffic with us, have been more reduced by disease."[10] Within another century, bears, caribou, moose, and mice would be sharing the land with other four-legged European immigrants, including rats, cats, rabbits, cattle, sheep, pigs, and deer.

The sheer abundance of resources—fish, fowl, and fur in profusion, trees growing down to the shoreline, and pockets of potentially productive agricultural land—commended the region to European colonizers, but they were uncomfortable living in what to them was a howling "wilderness." As Ramsay Cook has pointed out, French colonizers in Acadia were determined to tame the North American landscape. Lescarbot, for example, took great pleasure "in digging and tilling my gardens, fencing them in against the gluttony of the swine, making terraces, preparing straight alleys, building storehouses, sowing wheat, rye, barley, oats, beans, peas, garden plants, and watering them. . . ."[11] In creating his European oasis, Lescarbot was participating in a crucial aspect of the colonization process.

The ecological exchange also worked in reverse. The Atlantic region was not as rich in exotic commodities as many other regions of the Americas, but it yielded objects of interest. De Monts took a number of curiosities to Paris in 1605, including a live female moose, moose antlers, a hummingbird, horseshoe crabs, bows "taller than a man," and a birchbark canoe. The four-year-old dauphin, the future Louis XIII, was taken to see the moose, and he marvelled at the speed of the canoe, paddled along the Seine by three sailors. Seeds of red maple, northeastern honeysuckle, and other indigenous flora also crossed the Atlantic to be planted in the public and private gardens so popular in France.

Europeans were notoriously careless of the abundance they found around them. When Sir Humphrey Gilbert arrived in Newfoundland in 1583, Stephen Parmenius, a young Hungarian poet who accompanied him, noted that they considered burning down the forests "so as to clear an open space for surveying the area." This ill-conceived plan was apparently abandoned after "some reliable person asserted that, when this had occurred by accident at some other settlement post, no fish had been seen for seven whole years, because the sea-water had been turned bitter by the turpentine that flowed down from the trees burning along the rivers."[12] By accident or by design, Europeans would make their mark on the North Atlantic landscape.

1632. They had learned by hard experience what was required to survive through the long winter months and knew that profits could be made in the fisheries and the fur trade. The region had also become a pawn in imperial rivalries. As Aboriginal populations declined, retreated, or made accommodations with the intruders, the way was paved for settler societies that would gradually transform the Atlantic region into a satellite of Western Europe.

Further Readings

Cell, Gillian, ed. 1982. *Newfoundland Discovered: English Attempts at Colonisation, 1610–1630*. London: Hakluyt Society.

Dunn, Brenda. 2000. *A History of Port-Royal/Annapolis Royal, 1605–1800*. Halifax: Nimbus.

Jones, Elizabeth. 1986. *Gentlemen and Jesuits: Quests for Glory and Adventure in the Early Days of New France*. Toronto: University of Toronto Press.

Nicholls, Andrew D. 2005. "'The purpois is honorabill, and may conduce to the good of our service': Lord Ochiltree and the Cape Breton Colony, 1629–1631." *Acadiensis* XXXIV, 2 (Spring): 109–23.

Pope, Peter E. 2004. *Fish into Wine: The Newfoundland Plantation in the Seventeenth Century*. Chapel Hill: University of North Carolina Press.

Reid, John G. 2008. "Sir William Alexander and North American Colonization" and "The 'Lost Colony' of New Scotland and its Successors to 1670." In *Essays on Northeastern North America: Seventeenth and Eighteenth Centuries*. Toronto: University of Toronto Press, 23–39 and 53–68.

Historical Spotlight

Cook, Ramsay. 1995. "1492 and All That: Making a Garden out of a Wilderness." Pp. 62–80 in Chad Gaffield and Pam Gaffield, eds. *Consuming Canada: Readings in Environmental History*. Toronto: Copp Clark.

Mancke, Elizabeth. 2005. "Spaces of Power in the Northeast." Pp. 32–49 in Stephen J. Hornsby and John G. Reid. eds. *New England and the Maritime Provinces: Connections and Comparisons*. Montreal: McGill-Queen's University Press.

Recommended Websites

Baccalieu Trail Archaeology
http://www.baccalieudigs.ca/

Cupids Legacy Centre
http://cupidslegacycentre.ca

Investigating Ferryland
http://www.heritage.nf.ca/avalon/arch/default.html

Port-Royal National Historic Site
http://www.pc.gc.ca/lhn-nhs/ns/portroyal/index_e.asp

Chapter 5

Colonial Communities Take Root, 1632–1713

Following the Treaty of Saint-Germain-en-Laye in 1632, the French government returned to the task of rebuilding its North American colonies. Most of its attention was focused on the St Lawrence, but efforts in Acadia and Newfoundland also bore fruit. By contrast, the English government showed little interest in sponsoring colonial endeavours of any kind north of New England, and some mercantile interests in England argued that Newfoundland should be cleared of all permanent settlers. Nevertheless, the Atlantic region figured prominently in English negotiating strategies during the Anglo–French wars that began in 1689—testimony not only to the significance of the fisheries, but also to the region's strategic location at the junction of competing imperial claims for control over northeastern North America.

Civil War in Acadia

The French government's new attitude towards Acadia became apparent when Cardinal Richelieu appointed his cousin Isaac de Razilly as the royal lieutenant-general in New France. A distinguished naval officer and an ardent Roman Catholic, he brought an energy and purpose to colonization matched only by his countryman in Canada, Samuel de Champlain. In September 1632 Razilly, with four ships carrying 300 soldiers, artisans, and labourers, and three Capuchin priests, arrived at the mouth of the La Hève River, a location better suited to his commercial interests than Port-Royal.

Thirty-six of the 200 people who wintered at La Hève died.[1] Undaunted, Razilly continued to lay the groundwork for a permanent French colony. One of his lieutenants, Nicolas Denys, engaged in fishing, lumbering, and fur-trading on Acadia's south shore, and another, Charles de Menou d'Aulnay, took possession of Pentagouët, which by treaty had reverted to France but was still occupied by New Englanders. Since Charles de La Tour also claimed jurisdiction over Acadia, some accommodation with him was necessary. Agreeing to share the profits from the fur trade, Razilly and La Tour dealt separately with the Cent-Associés and managed to get along. The French government also established the Compagnie du Cap-Breton in 1633 to exploit fish and fur from bases at Sainte-Anne and Saint-Pierre.[2]

Razilly's sudden death in early 1636 prompted many of his settlers to return to France. To replace them, his successor, Charles de Menou d'Aulnay, brought immigrants from his seigneury in Poitou. Because he believed that agriculture should be the colony's mainstay, he moved most of the settlers remaining at La Hève to the potentially more productive Port-Royal area. Families formed by marriages between the French and Mi'kmaq stayed at La Hève.

Table 5.1 Timeline

1632	Isaac de Razilly, lieutenant-general of New France, arrives in Acadia.
1634	English government issues the Western Charter to regulate the Newfoundland fishery.
1637	Commercial monopoly of the Newfoundland fish trade granted to Sir David Kirke and his business associates.
1640	Hostilities begin between Charles de Menou d'Aulnay and Charles de La Tour.
1645	D'Aulnay takes La Tour's fort on the St John River.
1651	Emmanuel Le Borgne seizes Port-Royal and attacks other settlements; La Tour appointed governor of Acadia.
1654	English force led by Robert Sedgwick attacks Acadia and imprisons La Tour.
1662	France establishes a colony and military base at Plaisance in Newfoundland.
1667	Acadia returned to France by the Treaty of Breda.
1670	Acadia declared a royal colony.
1672–4	Anglo-Dutch War.
1673	Dutch force attacks Ferryland and St John's.
1674	Dutch force attacks Jemseg.
1689–97	War of the League of Augsburg.
1690	Sir William Phips plunders Port-Royal.
1696–7	Pierre Le Moyne d'Iberville lifts the English blockade of the Bay of Fundy and attempts to drive the English out of Newfoundland.
1697	Treaty of Ryswick.
1699	"King William's Act" passed to govern the fishery and settlement at Newfoundland.
1702–13	War of the Spanish Succession.
1704, 1707	New Englanders attack Acadia.
1705, 1709	French attack English in Newfoundland.
1710	English force captures Port-Royal.
1713	Treaty of Utrecht; France recognizes British sovereignty over mainland Acadia, Newfoundland, and Hudson Bay.

D'Aulnay insisted on a monopoly of Acadia's resources and trade, refusing to accommodate La Tour's claims and forcing Denys to seek refuge in France. Defying the efforts of French bureaucrats to divide Acadia between them, La Tour, with the help of Aboriginal allies, attacked d'Aulnay's operations north of the Bay of Fundy, and in the summer of 1640 confronted him in a brief but bloody engagement at Port-Royal.[3] When d'Aulnay emerged the victor, La Tour sought assistance from the Massachusetts Bay Colony, founded in 1628. Its capital, Boston, was emerging as a substantial settlement with impressive resources at its disposal. La Tour eventually convinced the colony's Council to provide naval support to lift d'Aulnay's blockade of Fort La Tour at the mouth of the St John River and, in 1643, to make another attempt to capture Port-Royal. Both expeditions were unsuccessful.

Short of supplies, La Tour returned to Boston in January 1645, leaving his second wife, Françoise-Marie Jacqueline, in charge of the fort. Learning that his enemy's position was weak, d'Aulnay launched a winter campaign that culminated in the storming of Fort La Tour in April.

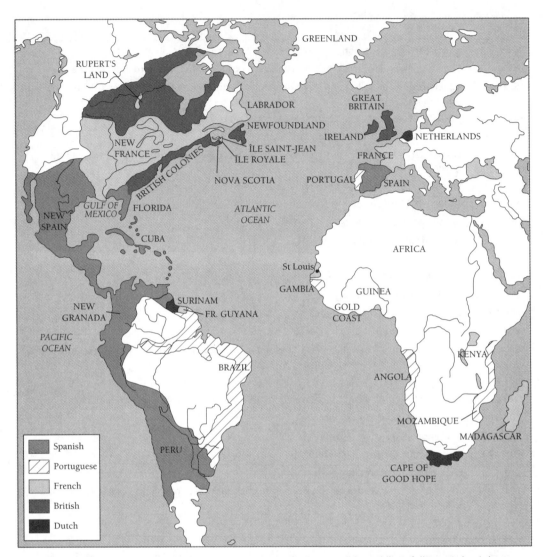

GREENLAND

RUPERT'S
LAND

LABRADOR

GREAT
BRITAIN

NEWFOUNDLAND

NEW
FRANCE

IRELAND

NETHERLANDS

ÎLE SAINT-JEAN
ÎLE ROYALE

FRANCE

BRITISH COLONIES

NOVA SCOTIA

PORTUGAL

SPAIN

GULF OF
MEXICO

FLORIDA

ATLANTIC
OCEAN

NEW
SPAIN

CUBA

AFRICA

St Louis

GAMBIA

GUINEA

NEW
GRANADA

SURINAM
FR. GUYANA

GOLD
COAST

PACIFIC
OCEAN

KENYA

BRAZIL

ANGOLA

MOZAMBIQUE

MADAGASCAR

PERU

CAPE OF
GOOD HOPE

Spanish
Portuguese
French
British
Dutch

The Atlantic World in 1715. Adapted from www.wwnorton.com/college/english/worldlit2e/full/maps/atlantic.htm

Françoise-Marie, who had valiantly led the defence, was forced to watch her surviving soldiers hanged. She died three weeks later in suspicious circumstances. With Acadia out of bounds, La Tour sought refuge in Quebec. Nicholas Denys, who had established a base at Miscou (in what is now northern New Brunswick) in 1645, was hounded out of Acadia a second time by d'Aulnay, who also captured the Compagnie du Cap-Breton's bases at Sainte-Anne and Saint-Pierre.

Acadia had not seen the last of La Tour. After d'Aulnay died in a boating accident in 1650, La Tour was reconfirmed as governor of Acadia in February 1651. Two years later, he consolidated his territorial interests by marrying d'Aulnay's widow, Jeanne Motin, becoming stepfather to her seven surviving children; they produced five more offspring. Denys also returned to Acadia, operating, with the support of the Cent-Associés, trading posts from Canso to the Gaspé. Denys and his family lived primarily in Saint-Pierre until their property was destroyed by fire in 1669. They relocated to Nispisquid, where Denys penned a remarkable two-volume description of Acadia in an effort to recoup his failing fortunes.[4]

Both La Tour and Denys were pursued by Emmanuel Le Borgne, an influential La Rochelle merchant who claimed jurisdiction over trade in Acadia as compensation for the extensive debts owed to him by d'Aulnay. A force dispatched by Le Borgne occupied Port-Royal in 1651, and Denys's trading posts were subjected to repeated raids. The situation took another dramatic turn in 1664, when an English expedition led by Major Robert Sedgwick from Massachusetts captured Fort La Tour, Port-Royal, and Pentagouët. While the settlers were allowed to stay, the Capuchins were expelled from Port-Royal, their new church and monastery were torched, and their superior was executed. Captured by Sedgwick, La Tour was taken to England where, in yet another twist on his family's ambiguous allegiances, he staked a claim to Acadia on the basis of his status, secured more than two decades earlier by his father Claude, as one of William Alexander's knights-baronet.

The republican government of Oliver Cromwell took the view that Acadia had reverted to its former identity as Nova Scotia. La Tour's claims were recognized, but on the condition that he pay the costs of Sedgwick's expedition. To do this, and to satisfy the substantial demands of his Boston creditors, La Tour sold his rights in Acadia to Sir Thomas Temple and William Crowne. La Tour then lived at Cap-Sable or Port-Royal, as his fancy dictated, until his death in 1666. The French government took a very different view of the situation, appointing Le Borgne governor of Acadia in 1657, while it was under English jurisdiction. In 1667 the Treaty of Breda returned Acadia to France, but it was not until 1669 that the English government forced a reluctant Temple to let the French assume control.

These destructive squabbles among rival claimants to Acadia reveal in the starkest way how the colony was used as a pawn in European corporate, family, monarchical, and religious power struggles. In this context, French bases in Acadia were badly mauled, investments were wantonly squandered, and settlement languished. This was not the case in most nearby colonial jurisdictions. By 1660 the English colonies along the Atlantic seaboard had a European population approaching 70,000; New Netherland, which in 1655 absorbed a short-lived Swedish colony along the Delaware River, was home to a multicultural community of 5,000 immigrants; and even ice-bound Canada boasted more than 3,000 souls. Acadia, meanwhile, could scarcely count 500 settlers.

Setting the Context

The Dutch Challenge

In this period all European nations were outdistanced in their quest for overseas trade by the United Provinces of the Netherlands, which had achieved independence from Spain in 1579. While other European nations were developing centralized monarchies, the Dutch established a republican government characterized by elected officials, religious toleration, and support for capitalist enterprise. By the mid-seventeenth century the Dutch merchant marine was larger than the combined mercantile fleets of England, France, and Spain. Other nations scrambled to catch up.

Continued

Beginning in the 1650s, England adopted a series of Navigation Acts that restricted trade within its empire to English-built ships, crewed primarily by English subjects; stipulated that valuable colonial commodities such as fish, rice, sugar, and tobacco could be shipped only to England; and required that European goods exported to English colonies be sent through English ports so that customs duties could be collected. This mercantilist policy had an immediate impact, more than doubling English shipping between 1640 and 1686.[5]

The Navigation Acts provoked three Anglo-Dutch wars between 1652 and 1674, with long-term implications for colonial North America. In 1664 an English expedition captured New Netherland, which was renamed New York. Its trading post at Fort Orange (renamed Albany) served as a major base for trade and military alliances with the Five Nations Confederacy, longtime enemies of the French and Algonkian peoples. Political troubles at home meant that France was slow off the mark in meeting the challenges posed by the Dutch and the English, but by the 1660s Louis XIV was poised to turn the tide of history to his advantage.

Acadia Redux

Following his 1661 decision to take the reins of government into his own hands, King Louis XIV began to intervene directly in matters relating to overseas colonization. Most French colonies were put under the control of a powerful bureaucratic regime with a governor supported by a standing army; a legal system based on the Custom of Paris; a seigneurial system of land distribution that concentrated wealth in the hands of an aristocratic elite; a Roman Catholic church closely allied to the state; and a closed mercantile trading system designed to advance France's economic interests. Distance, administrative inefficiencies, and the King's preoccupation with European affairs meant that North American colonies could often avoid some of the strict regulations imposed by officials based in Paris, but the colonies remained essential in the struggle for European ascendancy that Louis XIV's ambitions unleashed.

In 1670 Acadia was declared a royal colony like the others, with an administration subordinate to officials in Quebec. Canada received most of Louis XIV's attention and he had few resources, either financial or military, to spare for Acadia. Governor Hector d'Andigné de Grandfontaine established royal authority in the colony with only a handful of soldiers. The 60 settlers who accompanied him were joined by just 66 more (of whom only five were women) over the next 40 years.

Grandfontaine arranged for subordinates to take possession of the forts at Port-Royal, Cap-Sable, and Jemseg (established in 1659 by Temple) and set up his own headquarters farther south at Pentagouët. In 1674 a Dutch force razed both Pentagouët and Jemseg. After efforts to find a suitable location north of the Bay of Fundy, the administration moved back to Port-Royal in 1683. A company approved by the king in 1682 to exploit the sedentary fishery (the Compagnie de la pêche sédentaire de l'Acadie) built its base, Fort Saint-Louis, at Chedabuctou (now Guysborough), a site formerly occupied by Nicolas Denys. Lacking geopolitical cohesion and imperial interest, Acadia languished.

Despite these challenges, a small colonial society managed to take root in Acadia. With about 600 people in 1686, Port-Royal was the heart of French settlement. Other communities were developing at Pubnico (Pobomcoup), Cape Negro (Cap Nègre), Musquodoboit Harbour (Mouscoudabouet), and St Peter's (Saint-Pierre). In the 1670s and 1680s, young families moved

Document

Building Dikes in Acadia, 1699

One of the most enduring features of colonial Acadia was dikeland agriculture. The practice began in the Port-Royal area in the 1630s, introduced by *saulniers* (salt-marsh workers) from Poitou who knew how to drain and cultivate marshlands. As settlement spread, so did the construction of dikes, creating a landscape that still distinguishes the Bay of Fundy region. The marshland farms were highly productive, allowing the settlers to grow wheat and barley, along with fodder for livestock, and the salt produced in the drainage process was used to cure fish.

Dike-building represented a major engineering achievement. The Sieur de Dièreville, a French surgeon and writer who visited the colony in 1699, was clearly impressed by the labour-intensive process through which the marshland soil was reclaimed from the sea:

> To grow Wheat, the Marshes which are inundated by the Sea at high Tide, must be drained; these are called Lowlands & they are quite good, but what labour is needed to make them fit for cultivation! The ebb & flow of the Sea cannot easily be stopped, but the Acadians succeed in doing so by means of great Dikes called Aboteaux, & it is done in this way; five or six rows of large logs are driven whole into the ground at the points where the Tide enters the Marsh, & between each row other logs are laid, one on top of the other, & all the spaces between them are so carefully filled with well-pounded clay, that the water can no longer get through. In the centre of this construction, a Sluice is contrived in such a manner that the water on the Marshes flows out of its own accord, while that of the Sea is prevented from coming in. An undertaking of this nature, which can only be carried on at certain Seasons when the Tides do not rise so high, costs a great deal, & takes many days, but the abundant crop that is harvested in the second year, after the soil has been washed [of the salt] by Rain water compensates for all the expense. As these lands are owned by several Men, the work upon them is done in common.[6]

Acadians repairing dikes in the twentieth century. "Shadows of the Past" published by Albert County Historical Society Inc.

up the Bay of Fundy to Beaubassin and around the Minas Basin. Fifty-five seigneuries were granted in the colony in an effort to nurture local elites, who would be sustained by annual dues paid by tenants. Since so much land was available for the taking, most settlers resisted such feudal demands.

In the first half of the seventeenth century, Acadia was open to competing Roman Catholic missionaries, mainly Récollet, Jesuit, and Capuchin. Their presence reinforced the allegiance of French settlers to Roman Catholicism, and many Mi'kmaq and Wolastoqiyik eventually reconciled their beliefs with Christianity. After 1670 formal ecclesiastical structures were established. In 1676 Father Louis Petit was appointed vicar-general, subordinate to the Bishop of Quebec, who also appointed priests to the area. From 1701 to 1710, a sister of the Congregation of the Holy Cross conducted a school for young girls at Port-Royal. Legal and clerical records show that the clergy possessed considerable power and imposed strict, authoritarian injunctions relating to marriage and sexual conduct. In dealing with an illegitimate birth at Beaubassin in 1688, for example, the local priest ruled that the father of the child and 19 members of his family should be expelled from the community and their goods confiscated to compensate the woman's family for the outrage.

Because Acadians were few in number and their presence provided valued opportunities to trade, they got on reasonably well with their Aboriginal neighbours. Intermarriage decreased as settlement took root, but most communities served by unmarried French soldiers and traders included families of mixed heritage. According to Naomi Griffiths, Aboriginals in the eyes of the Acadians "were permanent neighbours, neither the middlemen in commercial enterprise nor a hostile force."[7] This symbiotic relationship was highly unusual in the story of European settlement in North America.

Marriages between Aboriginal women and French men played a significant role in cementing military alliances. Vincent de Saint-Castin, one of Grandfontaine's subordinates, returned to Pentagouët after the Dutch attack in 1674, charged with extending French influence among the Abenaki. Faced with an increasing number of English settlers in their territory, they welcomed his support during the war that erupted in 1675–6 between settlers in New England and their Aboriginal neighbours. Saint-Castin married Pidianske, the daughter of the Penobscot chief Madokawando, succeeded him as chief, and helped to bring the Abenaki, Penobscot, Passamaquoddy, Wolastoqiyik, and Mi'kmaq into an alliance—known as the Wabanaki ("Dawnland") Confederacy—to confront the aggressive New Englanders. While not a confederacy in the formal sense, it is a useful term to describe Aboriginal nations in the northeast of North America who usually allied themselves with the French to thwart the expansion of English settlement.

A more ambiguous relationship developed between the Acadians and the English colonists in Massachusetts. Although New Englanders were hostile to the French presence in the region, they fished along the Acadian coastline and traded with Acadian settlers, who exchanged furs and surplus agricultural produce for a variety of manufactured goods and foodstuffs. This clandestine trade continued after 1670, despite royal and clerical injunctions against it, making Acadia an economic satellite of New England.

By 1702 Port-Royal had a garrison of 200 soldiers. It offered limited protection and economic stimulus to the community while supplementing the small stable of prospective husbands and opening opportunities to the sons of Acadia's elite families. Often rough and rowdy, many of the soldiers suffered from mental illness, prompting one official to report that he had more need of an insane asylum than a barracks.[8] Most governors relied heavily on Aboriginal allies and the Acadian

These ink drawings of missionaries teaching Christianity to the Mi'kmaq were used to illustrate Chrestien Le Clercq's *Nouvelle Relation de la Gaspésie*, published in Paris in 1691.

militia, drawn from all able-bodied men between 16 and 60, for military protection. These auxiliary forces became a law unto themselves, adept at the terrorist practices common to what the French called *la petite guerre*—surprise attacks, taking captives and scalps, ritual executions, and torture—which inevitably were returned in kind.[9]

By the beginning of the eighteenth century, Acadia was home to about 1,500 people of European heritage and the gender balance was nearly equal. Thereafter, with little immigration, the population doubled every 20 years.[10] Well-adapted to their environment, Acadians were better nourished than most peasants in France and mercifully free of the plagues that periodically ravaged old-world communities. Few remained single, women married in their early twenties, and families were large. Over several generations, most of the inhabitants became related to each other, giving a society of varied origins the close-knit character of an extended family. A common language and religion further cemented an interdependence that was also encouraged by the political vacuum in the region. Learning to live both with their neighbours and with whatever regime was in power, the Acadians kept their own counsel. Frustrated French administrators accused them of being "republican" and lacking in deference and respect.

The English Shore

Acadia was a permanent French colony, and was viewed as such in Paris. The English attitude towards Newfoundland was not as clear-cut. Officials in London were not opposed to settlement, but they were preoccupied by the economic and naval value of the migratory fishery and provided neither local administration nor a military presence.

As a means of formalizing the rules and customs governing the English inshore fishery, the English government issued a Western Charter in 1634. It detailed how masters could claim fishing premises, known as "rooms," and empowered the fishing admirals (masters of migratory vessels who acquired authority by being the first to arrive in a given harbour) to settle disputes; it banned taverns, the dumping of ballast in harbours, stripping bark from trees ("rinding"), stealing, Sabbath-breaking, and the destruction of fishing stages and cookrooms. In the absence of penalty clauses—except for capital offences, which were to be tried in England—it proved to be a weak legal document and its provisions were often ignored.

In 1637 Charles I made a "Grant of Newfoundland" to Sir David Kirke and some aristocratic associates and acquiesced in Kirke's appropriation of the Ferryland plantation the following year. Known as the Company of Adventurers to Newfoundland, the patentees had been granted not property but the right to "the sole trade of Newfoundland, the Fishing excepted," with the power to tax French and Dutch vessels. The goal was to give English West Country merchants a monopoly of the fishery, while the patentees would monopolize the "sack" trade (from *vina de sacca*, wine for export) in association with a London business run by Kirke's brothers. David Kirke set himself up as a fish merchant in Ferryland and developed a profitable transatlantic trade in fish and wine. As governor he held courts and administered the southern Avalon Peninsula in a rough-and-ready way.

Kirke's career in Newfoundland ended in 1651 with the victory of Parliament in the English Civil War and the subsequent establishment of a republic. Since he was a royalist, Kirke's estates were sequestrated. Moreover, it seems that he had manipulated his operations to benefit his brothers rather than the other patentees. Recalled to face a suit brought by the Calverts, Kirke died in prison in 1654. The Ferryland plantation survived under the management of his widow, Lady Sara Kirke, while her sons developed their own plantations at Ferryland and Renews. In effect, the Kirkes functioned as a provincial gentry under the new governor, a merchant from Maine named John Treworgie, who served in Newfoundland from 1651 to 1660.

The West Country merchants who controlled the migratory fishery were concerned about the activities of Kirke and Treworgie, but they faced more serious challenges. Among them was an extensive bye-boat fishery, carried on by independent fishermen who bought passage to and from England annually and fished on their own account, leasing fishing rooms and bringing their own equipment. Bye-boat keepers worked closely with "planters," independent settlers who sold their fish to whoever would buy it, in defiance of the West Country merchants. By 1650 between 1,000 and 2,000 people had some sort of permanent attachment to Newfoundland, living in about 30 settlements along the English Shore, all linked to West Country ports. Around this core group of planters moved a much larger, shifting, and overwhelmingly male summer population that helped to produce salt fish and cod oil for export.

After the restoration of the monarchy in 1660, a West Country lobby argued that the growth of a settled population on the island, small as it was, threatened the viability of the migratory

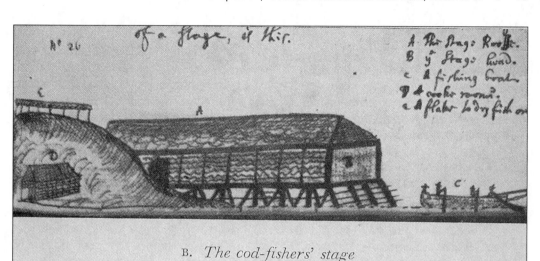

A Newfoundland fishing room, c. 1663, sketched by the surgeon James Yonge at either Renews or Fermeuse. The key reads: "A The Stage Roofe. B Ye Stage head. C A fishing boat. D A cooke room. E A flake to dry fish over." From F.N.L. Poynter, ed., *The Journal of James Yonge, 1647–1721, Plymouth Surgeon* (London: Green and Co., 1963).

fishery because planters pre-empted the best fishing locations and destroyed fishing stages. In addition, it was argued, settlement was not desirable since Newfoundland was "productive of no commodities as other Plantations, [n]or affords anything of food to keep men alive."[11] The government responded with an addition to the Western Charter in 1661 forbidding bye-boat fishing. Concerned by a decline in the migratory fishery, it also adopted an anti-settlement policy that was enshrined in a new charter issued in 1671. The naval commodore was instructed to encourage planters to leave the island.

In contrast, France placed a far higher value on the Newfoundland fisheries than on Acadia or even Canada. Determined to protect their interests in Newfoundland, the French established a formal colony on the island's southeast coast at Placentia in 1662. Theoretically subordinate (like Acadia) to Quebec, Plaisance was designed to serve as a base for the French fishing fleet, to monitor English activity on the Avalon Peninsula, and to protect the approaches to the Gulf. The community became home to a governor and other administrators, a military force, Roman Catholic priests, and, on its beach properties, bona fide settlers. By the end of the seventeenth century the resident population had reached approximately 200, swelled in season by *engagés* (labourers under contract) and the crews of trading and fishing ships coming from France. As in Acadia, there was a flourishing clandestine trade with New England.

Delayed by the Anglo–Dutch war of 1672–4, during which the Dutch attacked both Ferryland and St John's, the English government did not try to enforce its anti-settler policy until 1675. The naval commodore then sent to implement the order reported that the policy was both impractical and mistaken: "if the habitants are taken off and the French left solely in possession . . . they will in a short time invest themselves of the whole at least of Ferryland and St John's, where harbours are almost naturally fortified, to the disadvantage of the trade, if not the loss of all."[12]

In reality, the planters were an asset to the migratory fleet. They protected equipment, cut timber, crafted oars and boats, and provided hospitality. The government sensibly reconsidered

Biography | David and Sara Kirke

David Kirke was the tough, adventurous son of an English wine merchant. When war broke out between England and France in 1627, Kirke led a privateering expedition against the French in Canada. Largely a family affair, this effort was partly financed by his father and included David's four brothers. With the help of Innu allies, the Kirkes eventually managed to take Quebec from Champlain in 1629 and stayed there until 1632, when the Treaty of Saint-Germain-en-Laye obliged them to return it to France. Knighted for his achievements, David Kirke turned his attention to Newfoundland.

Kirke and his partners were interested in the sack trade, in which fish was collected at Newfoundland, freighted to southern Europe, and exchanged for wines and other Mediterranean commodities that were then sold in England. The need for a steady and adequate supply of fish persuaded Kirke and his wife, Sara, to take over the Ferryland plantation, where in 1650 they were joined by Lady Kirke's sister, Lady Frances Hopkins, and her children. Because the Hopkins family had sheltered Charles I while he was under house arrest in 1648, they were suspect to Oliver Cromwell's new parliamentary regime.

By 1654 the sisters were both widows. Despite their royalist affiliations, they survived the English Civil War and Interregnum with their properties intact. They did not go back to England but remained in Newfoundland to manage their substantial plantations—independent and, in local terms, wealthy. Although Frances Hopkins had a short-lived second marriage to an Acadian merchant, Alexandre Le Borgne de Belle-Isle, Sara did not remarry. Peter Pope suggests that, as heirs to large plantations, these women "had the least to gain and the most to lose from a new alliance" that would give control of the family wealth to a new husband. Both women died in Newfoundland in the early 1680s.[13]

its position, cancelled its instructions, and adopted a compromise: settlement in Newfoundland would be accepted and tolerated, but not encouraged. Eventually enshrined in the 1699 statute known as King William's Act, this policy remained on the books until 1824. There is an old and hardy myth that the British government opposed settlement in Newfoundland and made it illegal. In fact, until the 1660s the government supported settlement. Thereafter, British policy reflected the assumption that Newfoundland was an industry, not a colony.

The Impact of War, 1689–1713

Warfare dominated the final decades of Louis XIV's reign. Throughout the 1670s, he harassed the Dutch and tried to occupy their territories. The so-called Glorious Revolution, which put the Protestant ruler of the Netherlands, William of Orange, and his wife Mary (a Stuart) on the English throne in 1689, spelled disaster for Louis XIV's ambitions to expand French borders and to champion the cause of Roman Catholicism. William brought England into a defensive alliance with other European countries and the War of the League of Augsburg (also known as King William's War) quickly followed.

The Wabanaki Confederacy played a major role in how the conflict unfolded in North America. Its members were determined to defend their territory against New England expansion and also had long-standing animosity with the Iroquois (Haudenosaunee), who were now allied with the English. In August 1689, 1,500 Iroquois advanced on Montreal, while the Abenaki and their allies, led by Saint-Castin, launched a brutal attack on Pemaquid (Bristol, Maine). Governor-General Frontenac conducted winter raids along the New York and New England frontiers and sent assistance to the Wabanaki in their attacks on English bases in southern Maine. With Boston now in jeopardy, New Englanders struck back.

In 1690 a force commanded by Sir William Phips attacked French posts along the coast and plundered Port-Royal, taking the governor prisoner. The men in the community were forced to swear allegiance to the English Crown. Phips appointed a council of residents to act as a local government, and then tried, without success, to take Quebec. Fort Saint-Louis at Chedabuctou was an easier mark, falling to a force led by Captain Cyprian Southack, a naval officer, cartographer, and entrepreneur based in Boston. En route the expedition plundered La Hève.

When a French vessel from Cape Breton arrived at Port-Royal shortly after Phips's departure, the residents reaffirmed their allegiance to Louis XIV. Canadian-born Joseph Robineau de Villebon, the highest ranking official in the colony, then decamped to the north side of the Bay of Fundy, thereby missing a second sacking of Port-Royal by the outraged New Englanders. Establishing his headquarters at Jemseg in the vain hope of avoiding a seaborne assault, Villebon later moved up the St John River to Nashwaak. The audacity of French privateers, who operated out of Port-Royal with the help of local recruits, earned the town another drubbing by the English in 1693.

Military action resumed in the summer of 1696 when the Canadian-born naval captain Pierre Le Moyne d'Iberville lifted the English blockade of the St John River and, with the aid of Acadians and the Wabanaki Confederacy, captured the recently constructed Fort William Henry at Pemaquid. In retaliation, a force of New Englanders led by Benjamin Church pillaged Beaubassin and then besieged Fort Nashwaak. By that time Iberville and his Canadian, Acadian, and Wabanaki force had arrived in Newfoundland, where the Governor of Plaisance, Jacques-François de Brouillan, had already taken the English communities of Bay Bulls, Ferryland, and Fermeuse.

Iberville led his militia overland from Plaisance to meet Brouillan at Renews and then proceeded north, capturing and pillaging St John's. To encourage the surrender of the miserable inhabitants taking refuge in the town's only fortification—there was no military garrison—"the French took one William Drew, an Inhabitant a Prisoner and cutt all around his scalp and then by the strength of hand strip his skin from the forehead to the crowne and so sent him into the fortification, assuring the inhabitants that they would serve them all in like manner if they did not surrender."[14]

Brouillan returned to Plaisance while Iberville conducted a brutal winter campaign against the English settlements in Conception and Trinity bays, most of which he pillaged and burned. Although he failed to capture the people who had taken refuge on Carbonear Island, and was unable to reach Bonavista, his campaign was a brilliant success. In all, the French destroyed 36 settlements, killed about 200 people, took 700 prisoners, and captured 300 fishing vessels. Sir David Kirke's three surviving sons died as prisoners of war at Plaisance. One result of the campaign was that the planter gentry of the southern Avalon was almost entirely eliminated. It was, in effect, an English *dérangement*—a foretaste of what the British would inflict on the Acadians nearly 60 years later.

If the French had capitalized on this exercise in brutality, Newfoundland would have become a wholly French island, with important strategic and diplomatic consequences. Lacking the necessary resources, they failed to do so. Iberville retreated to Plaisance and was then sent to fight the English in Hudson Bay. Newfoundland's English population had suffered a severe blow, but planters were back on the English Shore in 1698, now protected, in theory at least, by a garrison in St John's and improved fortifications. The Treaty of Ryswick officially ended the war in 1697. In North America each side was awarded what it had held in 1689.

The next round began in 1702 with what is known as the War of the Spanish Succession or Queen Anne's War, after the reigning British monarch. (It was during Queen Anne's reign that the term "United Kingdom of Great Britain" came into common usage as a result of the terms of union of Scotland and England on 1 May 1707.) Before war was declared, French officials ordered Brouillan, who had been appointed commandant of Acadia in 1701, to move the colony's administrative centre back to Port-Royal. He strengthened the town's fortifications, summoned Aboriginal allies to supplement the reinforced garrison, and engaged a privateer to patrol the coastline. Acadians in the Bay of Fundy communities were obliged to work on fortifications and submit to levies on their wheat and cattle. When supplies of food and clothing ran short, Brouillan secured them from ever-obliging Boston merchants.

Brouillan and authorities in Canada were complicit in efforts to involve warriors from the Wabanaki Confederacy in brutal attacks on Wells, Saco, and Casco in the summer of 1703, and on Deerfield, Massachusetts, the following winter.[14] In retaliation, Massachusetts dispatched an expedition led by Benjamin Church, which sacked all major Acadian settlements except Port-Royal in 1704. Leaving a trail of broken dikes, burned homes, slaughtered cattle, and devastated crops, the New Englanders took 50 Acadian captives to Boston, most of them women and children to be exchanged for the equivalent English prisoners in Montreal and elsewhere.[16]

In June 1707 an army of 1,100 British officers, New England militia, and Aboriginal auxiliaries, led by Colonel John March and supported by 24 vessels, laid siege to Port-Royal. Severely outnumbered, the new governor, Daniel d'Auger de Subercase, ordered buildings in the line of fire to be burned and harboured more than 700 soldiers and civilians inside the fort. The siege was lifted with the help of an Abenaki militia, led by Saint-Castin's teenage son Bernard-Anselme. Before they returned home, March's forces destroyed what was left of the town outside the fort.

For the next two years Subercase relied on Acadian farmers, shipments from Canada, and, above all, privateers to keep Port-Royal supplied. One of the privateer vessels, under the command of Quebec-born Louis Denys de la Ronde, included Mi'kmaq and West Indians among the crew. They participated in the capture of St John's early in 1709 and eventually fetched up in Canada. In all, French privateers seized 35 vessels and took more than 300 prisoners in 1709, fuelling the resolve of New Englanders to rid themselves of the French menace once and for all.

Supported by a detachment of British marines and a company of grenadiers, General Francis Nicholson, a seasoned colonial administrator, led a force of 1,500 colonial troops and Iroquois allies in a bruising campaign against Port-Royal. After holding out for a week, Subercase and his small, demoralized garrison of 200 soldiers were forced to surrender. Articles of capitulation were signed on 2 October 1710 and Port-Royal, which had been passed back and forth between England and France several times over the previous century, was handed over for what turned out to be the last time.

In Newfoundland, settlers along the English Shore again suffered raids from Plaisance, which also served as a base for privateers. In 1705 Subercase and Jacques Testard de Montigny led a repeat performance of the 1697 raid, taking 1,200 prisoners and wreaking destruction as far north

Historical Focus

Antoine Tecouenemac and the Conquest of Port-Royal

At the time of the British capture of Port-Royal in October 1710, Antoine Tecouenemac was 16 years old, living in a territory he understood to be the land of the Mi'kmaq, or Mi'kma'ki. We know some of the details of his life because the missionary Antoine Gaulin conducted a census of seven villages inhabited by Mi'kmaq two years before the siege. Although Gaulin may have been interested in how many able-bodied Mi'kmaq might be recruited to defend the colony (240 men over the age of 15, he concluded), his census had little impact on French military strategy. Few Mi'kmaq bothered to answer Governor Subercase's plea for assistance.

The historian William Wicken draws on his knowledge of the seasonal rhythms of the Mi'kmaq to explain this outcome. Antoine, his parents, and his four siblings lived in the Cap-Sable area of southwestern Nova Scotia and were loosely associated with nearly 100 other Mi'kmaq in the region. During the winter months the family moved inland to hunt moose, caribou, and beaver; during the summer they frequented coastal areas. In the spring and fall they lived along rivers where migrating eels were plentiful. Since smoked eels were an important source of food for the winter months, Wicken concludes that few Mi'kmaq would have had time for warfare in early October, when the fall eel harvest was in progress.

Although largely oblivious to the capture of Port-Royal, Antoine and his family gradually felt its impact. The ongoing rivalry between the British and the French for control over Mi'kma'ki and the expansion of English settlement created an unstable situation on the northeastern frontier of North America that led to war from 1722 to 1725 between the Wabanaki Confederacy and the British. We do not know what role the Tecouenemac family played in the conflict—if, for example, they were among the nearly 60 Mi'kmaq and Wolastoqiyik who attacked Port-Royal in July 1724—but Antoine, his father, Paul, and his brother Philippe were among the 50 Mi'kmaq who signed a treaty ending the war, which explicitly acknowledged British jurisdiction over Europeans in the colony of Nova Scotia. As Wicken notes, in signing this treaty in 1726, they signified their conscious understanding of how their world had changed since 1710.[17]

as Bonavista. In 1709 French forces took Fort William at St John's, burned most of the town, and forced the inhabitants to pay a huge ransom. Again, the French found it impossible to secure their advantage. They withdrew to Plaisance, where they were blockaded by the British navy and suffered severe privation.

The Treaty of Utrecht

The treaty ending the War of the Spanish Succession is sometimes known as "the Peace of Utrecht" because it consisted not of a single document but of a complicated series of agreements signed in 1713 and 1714 involving Britain, France, Spain, the Netherlands, and other European countries.

At the heart of the settlement, which marked the end of Louis XIV's ambitions, was the concept of a European balance of power. This goal was most obvious in the provisions that effectively prohibited the union of the Crowns of France and Spain.

Great Britain was less concerned about balance in North America, where its aim was to contain French power. It refused to accept that the land between Hudson Bay and Hudson Strait (or the Labrador peninsula) was part of New France, and insisted that the French abandon any claim to the territory known as Rupert's Land, which had been granted to the London-based Hudson's Bay Company in 1670. Unwillingly, France eventually agreed to "restore" the territory between Hudson Bay and Hudson Strait to Britain. The question of how and where the boundary line should be drawn was left for future negotiation.

Acadia was partitioned, but with its landward boundary left undefined. Britain acquired the mainland, which again became Nova Scotia, and took possession of Port-Royal, renamed Annapolis Royal after the Queen. France retained the islands in the Gulf of St Lawrence, including Cape Breton Island and Île Saint-Jean, hoping that they would protect the route to Canada and serve as bases for the fisheries. Since the French placed great value on the northwest Atlantic fisheries, their recognition of British sovereignty over the island of Newfoundland and their agreement to abandon Plaisance were major concessions. French negotiators managed to extract permission for their migratory fishermen to make seasonal use of the Petit Nord, defined as extending from Cape Bonavista to Point Riche. Because the exact nature of the French fishing rights was not defined, this "Treaty Shore" became a long-standing source of dissension.

Conclusion

In retrospect, the Treaty of Utrecht marked the beginning of British dominance over France in North America, but this was hardly evident in 1713. The rivalry between Britain and France remained unresolved, and the two powers were left to share northeastern America. For the residents of the Atlantic region, who had received a severe mauling during the wars beginning in 1689, the future was uncertain. French settlers in Acadia had the choice of swearing allegiance to a Protestant monarch hostile to France or moving to French-controlled territory. For New Englanders, the prospect of the French re-establishing themselves anywhere in the Atlantic region was troubling. The relatively few Newfoundland settlers simply hoped for the best, but were well aware of the unwelcome presence of the French. Meanwhile, the Mi'kmaq, Wolastoqiyik, and Passamaquoddy found that their land had been given away to European powers without their knowledge, let alone their consent. The Treaty of Utrecht, in short, settled little and left much to be contested.

Further Readings

Bailey, A.G. 1969. *The Conflict of European and Eastern Algonkian Cultures, 1504–1700*, 2nd edn. Toronto: University of Toronto Press.

Baker, Emerson W., and John G. Reid. 1998. *The New England Knight: Sir William Phips, 1651–1695*. Toronto: University of Toronto Press.

Bannister, Jerry. 2003. *The Rule of the Admirals: Laws, Custom, and Naval Government, 1699–1832*. Toronto: University of Toronto Press.

Clark, Andrew Hill. 1968. *Acadia: The Geography of Early Nova Scotia to 1760*. Madison: University of Wisconsin Press.

Codignola, Luca. 1999. "Competing Networks: Roman Catholic Ecclesiastics in French North America, 1610-58." *Canadian Historical Review* 80, 4 (December): 539–84

Dunn, Brenda. 2004. *A History of Port-Royal/Annapolis Royal, 1605–1800*. Halifax: Nimbus.

———, Sally Ross, and Birgitta Wallace.1997. *Looking into Acadie: Three Illustrated Lectures*. Halifax, Nova Scotia Museum.

Griffiths, Naomi E.S. 2005. *From Migrant to Acadian: A North American Border People, 1604–1755*. Montreal and Kingston: McGill-Queen's University Press.

Handcock, Gordon. 1989. *"Soe longe as there comes noe women": Origins of English Settlement in Newfoundland*. St John's: Breakwater Press.

Kennedy, Gregory M.W. 2014. *Something of a Peasant Paradise? Comparing Rural Societies in Acadie and Loudunais, 1604–1755*. Montreal: McGill-Queen's University Press.

Landry, Nicholas. 2008. *Plaisance, Terre-Neuve, 1650–1713: Une colonie française en Amérique*. Sillery: Septentrion. *Newfoundland Studies*. 2003. Special issue, "The New Early Modern Newfoundland," 9:1, Part 2.

Pope, Peter E. 2004. *Fish into Wine: The Newfoundland Plantation in the Seventeenth Century*. Chapel Hill: University of North Carolina Press.

Pritchard, James. 2004. *In Search of Empire: The French in the Americas, 1670–1730*. Cambridge: Cambridge University Press.

Reid, John G. 1981. *Acadia, Maine, and New Scotland: Marginal Colonies in the Seventeenth Century*. Toronto: University of Toronto Press.

———. 2008. *Essays on Northeastern North America, Seventeenth and Eighteenth Centuries*. Toronto: University of Toronto Press.

———, et al. 2004. *The Conquest of Acadia, 1710: Imperial, Colonial and Aboriginal Constructions*. Toronto: University of Toronto Press.

Historical Spotlight

Basque, Maurice. 2004. "Family and Political Culture in Pre-Conquest Acadia," in John G. Reid et al., *The "Conquest" of Acadia, 1710: Imperial, Colonial and Aboriginal Constructions*. Toronto: University of Toronto Press.

Wallace, Birgitta. 1997. "An Archaeologist Discovers Early Acadia." Pp. 9–27 in *Looking Into Acadie: Three Illustrated Lectures*. Halifax: Nova Scotia Museum.

Recommended Websites

Acadian Museum of Prince Edward Island
http://museeacadien.org

European Migratory Fishery
http://www.heritage.nf.ca/exploration/efishery.html

History of Plaisance
http://www.heritage.nf.ca/exploration/placentia_text.html

Institut d'études acadiennes
http://www8.umoncton.ca/iea

La Société Promotion Grand-Pré
http://www.grand-pre.com

Musée acadien
http://www.umoncton.ca/umcm-maum/

Chapter 6

Renegotiating the Atlantic Region, 1713–1763

Fifty years separate the treaties of Utrecht (1713) and Paris (1763). The first confirmed Great Britain's acquisition of territory in the Atlantic region; the second signalled Britain's ascendancy. In the interim, the British and French continued to jockey for control, encouraged by ambitious colonial officials in Boston and Quebec. Caught between the two powers, Aboriginal people and Acadians suffered severely. As the equilibrium in the region gradually tipped toward the British, the area variously known as Mi'kma'ki, Acadia, or Nova Scotia took on global significance, becoming, John Reid argues, "a virtual laboratory for cultural and political realignments in the Atlantic world."[1]

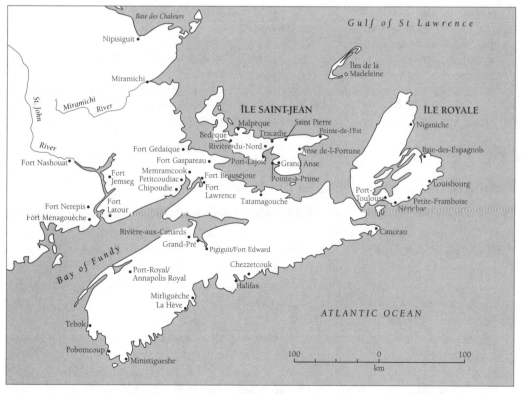

Major European Settlements in Nova Scotia, Île Royale, and Île Saint-Jean, 1755. Adapted from Jean Daigle, ed., *Acadia of the Maritimes* (Moncton, NB: Chaire d'études acadiennes, Université de Moncton, 1995), p. 33; and R. Cole Harris ed., *Historical Atlas of Canada I: From the Beginning to 1800* (Toronto: University of Toronto Press, 1987), Plate 30.

Setting the Context

The Long Eighteenth Century

What is now Atlantic Canada was part of a North Atlantic world that experienced a significant transformation during the "long" eighteenth century (from 1689 to 1815). Change was stimulated by scientific and technological advances and by an intellectual climate open to new ideas. As promoters of "enlightenment," intellectuals demanded a more modern, rational, secular, and critical approach to understanding the world. Books, newspapers, and pamphlets appeared in increasing numbers, and the highly influential French *Encyclopédie*, published between 1751 and 1772, offered a new way of mobilizing and accessing knowledge (much as *Wikipedia* does today). In the Age of Enlightenment, literacy became a required skill for anyone hoping to keep up with the times.

Embracing the idea of progress, merchants and professionals, who formed a powerful, literate, and increasingly prosperous middle class, began to promote liberal values such as free trade, separation of church and state, the rule of law, and representative political institutions. More egalitarian reforms, including women's rights and the abolition of slavery, were also in the air. Under assault from new ideas, old regimes based on authoritarian rule, state-supported churches, and hereditary privilege began to crumble.

The American Revolutionary War, which erupted in 1775, produced one of the world's great republican regimes. In France, republicanism triumphed briefly during a chaotic and bloody revolution beginning in 1789, but was brought to heel by Napoleon Bonaparte. He, in turn, was defeated in 1815 by an alliance of European powers determined to end French efforts to establish European dominance. Although aristocratic, ecclesiastical, and military interests mobilized in defence of the old order, the political firmament had been forever altered. This extraordinary period in the Atlantic region's history set the contours for its development to the present day.

Administrative Challenges in Nova Scotia

The acquisition of Nova Scotia in 1713 presented the British with an administrative dilemma. How were they to govern a colony with disputed borders, settlers who were primarily French Roman Catholics, and Aboriginal peoples allied with the enemy? These difficulties were compounded when France decided to construct a military base on Cape Breton Island. The imposing walled town of Louisbourg—designed to contain British power in North America, safeguard the approaches to the St Lawrence, and support the migratory fishery—made a major statement about French intentions in the region.

France also adopted an aggressive diplomatic position. Since the boundaries of Nova Scotia remained undefined, the French government claimed everything north of the Bay of Fundy (present-day New Brunswick), and even Canso (Grassy) Island. In Newfoundland, France argued that its fishing rights on the Treaty Shore were exclusive, while British authorities maintained that its citizens could fish there so long as they did not interfere with French operations. France also had a formidable fifth column in Nova Scotia. Under the terms of the Treaty of Utrecht, Roman

Catholic priests were permitted to minister to Aboriginals and Acadians in the colony. Two of the roughly two dozen priests who served in Nova Scotia during the early decades of British rule proved particularly effective as *agents-provocateurs*: Antoine Gaulin, appointed vicar-general in 1702, continued his ministry until 1732, and, Jean-Louis Le Loutre served mainland Mi'kmaq from his base at Shubenacadie beginning in 1738 and later from French posts at Beaubassin and Tatamagouche.

Great Britain initially had little interest in making its new North Atlantic possessions a major testing ground for imperial ascendancy. In the immediate aftermath of the war, the British government was preoccupied with the succession to the throne of George I, the first Hanoverian monarch. His rule was challenged by Jacobite uprisings in support of the claims of the Roman Catholic Stuarts. The struggle between supporters of constitutional monarchy, known as Whigs,

Table 6.1	Timeline
1713	Treaty of Utrecht signed.
1717	Richard Philipps appointed governor of Nova Scotia and Placentia.
1720	Louisbourg officially founded; Saint-Pierre establishes a colony on Île Saint-Jean.
1722–5	Wabanaki–New England War.
1726	British sign treaties with Mi'kmaq, Wolastoqiyik, and Passamaquoddy; French send a military detachment to Île Saint-Jean.
1729	Captain Henry Osborne appointed naval governor of Newfoundland.
1731	Acadians take a qualified oath of allegiance.
1735	Pierre-Antoine-Simon Maillard begins his mission on Île Royale.
1744–8	War of the Austrian Succession.
1745	Louisbourg captured.
1746	D'Anville Expedition.
1747	Battle of Grand Pré.
1748	Treaty of Aix-la-Chapelle.
1749	Founding of Halifax by the British; Mi'kmaq declare war on the British.
1750–3	"Foreign Protestants" arrive in Halifax.
1750	Construction of Fort Edward and Fort Lawrence.
1751	Construction of Fort Beauséjour.
1752	Treaty of Peace and Friendship with the Mi'kmaq.
1753	Lunenburg founded.
1755	Fort Beauséjour falls to the British.
1755–62	Expulsion of the Acadians.
1756–63	Seven Years' War.
1758	Louisbourg captured by the British.
1760	Battle of Restigouche.
1760–1	Mi'kmaq, Wolastoqiyik, and Passamaquoddy sign peace treaties with the British.
1762	French attack on St John's.
1763	Treaty of Paris; Royal Proclamation.

and their conservative opponents, called Tories, sometimes paralyzed administrative initiatives, with implications across the Atlantic.

In 1717 the British made a feeble attempt to mould the region into a coherent administrative unit by appointing Colonel Richard Philipps governor of Placentia and Nova Scotia. He lost his authority over Placentia in 1729 when the government of Newfoundland was reorganized but retained his Nova Scotia posting until 1749. Since Philipps rarely resided in the colony, his responsibilities were delegated to his subordinates. A small garrison of British and colonial soldiers, most of them stationed in Annapolis Royal, maintained order. Little consideration was given to establishing an elected assembly because only a few hundred Protestant residents would have been eligible to vote. While the Acadians were encouraged to take an oath of allegiance, most were reluctant to do so because it might require them to fight for a Protestant British monarch against France and its Aboriginal allies. The hostility of Aboriginal people, who refused to accept that any European power could grant their land away, cast a pall over all colonizing efforts.

Newfoundland

Despite a growing resident population, Newfoundland remained without a regular colonial administration of any kind. Inevitably, local problems became sufficiently serious to warrant something more than the often-ignored provisions of King William's Act, which empowered the fishing admirals to decide local disputes, with naval captains acting as appeal judges. This administrative structure, such as it was, disappeared altogether in winter. Eventually it was decided that the commodore of the naval squadron, which arrived in Newfoundland waters each spring, would double as governor and commander-in-chief.

The first migratory naval governor was Captain Henry Osborne, who in 1729 appointed magistrates and constables along the coast from Bonavista to Placentia. In summer these new authorities were supplemented by naval officers acting as surrogate magistrates. As a result, fishing admirals gradually disappeared as an independent force. Thus was born what Jerry Bannister has called a "naval state."[2] If the island did not fit the usual model of colonial development, neither was it—as has sometimes been assumed—a violent, anarchic frontier. Over time, local government in Newfoundland came to resemble county administration in England. A settler society continued to develop, untroubled by the kind of devastation inflicted during earlier wars.

Until the late 1720s the fisheries were generally poor, prompting the English to exploit the offshore banks, which became an increasingly important part of the overall fishery. The inshore failures may explain the fairly slow movement of the English fishery along the south coast, now abandoned by the French. Expansion on the northeast coast, into Bonavista and Notre Dame bays, was more vigorous, possibly because of the opportunities to diversify into furring, sealing, and salmon fishing. By the 1730s economic activity had picked up in all the bays as fish catches improved.

The number of winter inhabitants reached more than 7,000 in the 1750s (the summer population was more than twice as large). Half of the newcomers were immigrants from southeast Ireland. Before the 1720s Newfoundland's inhabitants had come mostly from the hinterlands of the English West Country ports involved in the fishery. The arrival of the Irish reflected not only domestic economic problems there but also the practice of West Country vessels stopping at

Waterford for provisions and fishing crews. About 1,000 Irish passengers came to Newfoundland annually; some decided to stay.

This change in the population troubled the British authorities, but they could do little about it. Indeed, it was in this period that the views held by the authorities and the merchants began to diverge. While the British government still regarded Newfoundland as a fishery and a nursery for mariners, merchants increasingly saw it as a place to make money—not just by fishing on their own account, but by supplying residents and bye-boatmen and purchasing their catches. A quasi-colonial society began to emerge, without any encouragement from the British government. Largely male (women made up less than a third of the population) and transient, this society was

Historical Focus

The Golden Age of Piracy, 1690-1730

Bartholomew Roberts with his ship and captured merchantmen in the background. From Captain Charles Johnson, *A General History of the Pyrates* (1724).

From the early seventeenth century, the waters of the Atlantic region swarmed not only with privateers officially sanctioned to capture enemy shipping, but also with pirates—outlaws

Continued

who terrorized merchant vessels and plundered seaports for their own benefit. The number of pirates ballooned after the War of the Spanish Succession as unemployed sailors were discharged from the British navy and wages for seamen plummeted. Although the Caribbean, West Africa, and the Indian Ocean attracted the most attention from pirates, the Atlantic region also offered worthy prizes, including fish, wine, bread, boats, bullion, and manpower. Moreover, the region's countless undefended harbours afforded refuge from storms and naval vessels trying to hunt them down. As many as 5,000 pirates infested North Atlantic waters during the Golden Age of Piracy, from 1690 to 1730.[3]

One of the most successful pirates in this period was Bartholomew Roberts. Ambitious and ruthless, he dressed lavishly, flew an array of menacing flags, and employed musicians to play for his pleasure and add dramatic emphasis during attacks. He began his career in 1719, focusing on West Africa and the Caribbean, but when the governors of Barbados and Martinique hired armed ships to capture him, Roberts sailed north. He fetched up at Canso in 1720, where he harassed New England fishing vessels, and then moved on to Trepassey, a harbour south of St John's. He met no resistance from the 22 terrified ship captains in the port, who readily yielded men and supplies under the threat of losing their ships. After bombarding the community, Roberts moved on to Cape Spear, looting fishing vessels along the way. He continued to enlarge both his wealth and his fleet in the busy shipping lanes around the Grand Banks before heading back to West Africa, where he died in battle with HMS *Swallow* in February 1722. His death marked the turning point in the Royal Navy's war against piracy.

Roberts captured more than 400 vessels during his short career, 55 of them off Nova Scotia and Newfoundland. After his death his exploits became the stuff of legend, earning him the posthumous nickname "Black Bart."

composed of British merchants at the apex, planters in the middle, and servants at the bottom. A middle class, in the usual sense of the term, was lacking.

Île Royale

Cape Breton was temporarily transformed by France's determination to challenge British ascendancy in the Atlantic region. To signal the island's new status, the name was changed to Île Royale and the ice-free port of Havre L'Anglois became the site of an imposing military base named in honour of the aging king. The residents of Plaisance began arriving in 1713, and in May 1720 Governor Saint-Ovide presided over a ceremony marking the official founding of Louisbourg. More than 4 million livres were spent building elaborate fortifications and another 16 million by 1753 to maintain the military stronghold.[4] Louisbourg quickly emerged as a major fishing port and commercial entrepôt, with a thriving trade that equalled Canada's in value. Well-positioned to nurture friendly relations with the Mi'kmaq, Louisbourg soon became a hub for subsidized trade, annual gift-giving, and missionary influence among France's most loyal North American allies.

The Treaty of Utrecht had given Acadians a choice: stay where they were and accept British rule, or move away. French authorities planned for them to settle on Île Royale and produce food for the residents of Louisbourg, but few Acadians were interested in leaving their well-established farms. In the two decades following the conquest, only 60 Acadian families moved to Île Royale.[5]

Most of them settled in outlying communities, such as Port Toulouse (formerly Saint-Pierre) and Port Dauphin (formerly Sainte-Anne).

As was the case in Acadia until 1710, the governor and other officials based at Louisbourg theoretically reported to authorities in Quebec, but in practice they communicated directly with France. The fishing proprietors (*habitants-pêcheurs*) from Plaisance initially dominated the island's economy and were well represented on the Superior Council. Sustained by subsidies from France, Récollets, Frères hospitaliers, and Soeurs de la Congrégation de Notre-Dame provided spiritual, medical, and educational services. From 1735 until his death in 1762, Pierre-Antoine-Simon Maillard was responsible for missionary activity and served as vicar-general beginning in 1740. Adept at learning Aboriginal languages, he established a mission at Île de la Sainte-Famille (Chapel Island), which became the site of annual celebrations and diplomacy.

By the 1740s Île Royale had a civilian population of more than 4,000, nearly two-thirds of whom lived in Louisbourg, the largest and most cosmopolitan community in the Atlantic region. Its residents included evacuees from Plaisance; French and Basque fishermen; a few Irish, Scots,

Historical Focus

Slavery in Louisbourg

Many Aboriginal societies used enslaved labour, but Europeans built whole economies in the Americas on the African slave trade. By 1750 more than 3.8 million Africans had been taken captive and shipped to the Americas. Enslavement soon became equated with skin colour, and racial stereotyping quickly followed.

The historian Kenneth Donovan has determined that more than 200 slaves lived on Île Royale between 1713 and 1760.[6] Although most of them were black—reflecting the close trading ties with the West Indies, where sugar, tobacco, indigo, and coffee plantations relied on African enslaved labour—nearly 10 per cent were Aboriginal. Most of these *Panis* or *sauvages* came from the colony of Canada, where they outnumbered slaves of African origin. Male slaves in Louisbourg worked as common labourers in the fishery, the military, and trade, or in artisan and service occupations; female slaves, who made up one-third of the enslaved population of Île Royale, were employed primarily as domestic servants.

In the French empire, slavery was theoretically regulated by the Code Noir. It obliged slave owners to house, feed, and clothe their slaves properly, to care for the aged and infirm, to encourage marriage, and to provide instruction in Roman Catholicism. Masters could whip their slaves, but not imprison or execute them without recourse to the courts. The Code also forbade the sexual exploitation of female slaves and the separation of pre-adolescent children from their parents. Since the Code Noir was not registered on Île Royale, the extent to which its provisions were followed is unclear.

Only six slaves in the colony achieved their freedom, one of whom was Marguerite Rose. After two decades in the service of an officer, she was freed in 1755 to marry an Aboriginal man, with whom she opened a tavern next door to her former owner. "Madam Rose negress" was able to secure credit in her own name for supplies of meat and rum.

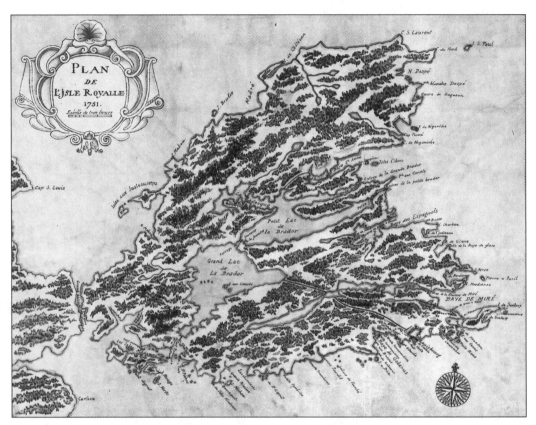

Map of Île Royale by Louis Franquet, 1751. This carefully labelled plan shows French settlement on the island before its final capture by the British in 1758. Library and Archives Canada/NMC-148.

and Spanish sojourners; and both Aboriginal and black slaves. The latter served the town's administrative and commercial elite, who lived comfortably, enhancing their standard of living by bilking the colonial treasury and trading discreetly with the English colonies.

About 700 troops were stationed on Île Royale. In addition to Troupes de la Marine, German and Swiss soldiers of the Karrer regiment were posted to Louisbourg. A few soldiers were also based at Port Toulouse, located on the strategic portage between the Atlantic and Bras d'Or Lake and within easy striking distance of Canso. Required to work long hours maintaining the fortifications, the lower ranks were well aware that they were being cheated by the officers who sold them alcohol, food, and other necessities at inflated prices. In the winter of 1744–5, tensions reached such a pitch that they took over the town, demanding better food, more firewood, and adequate uniforms.

Île Saint-Jean

Although Île Saint-Jean offered agricultural potential, it attracted little interest. Its forest-covered soils proved far less inviting to Acadians already established on their dikeland farms, and French authorities initially left development there to private interests. In 1719 the Comte de Saint-Pierre was granted the right to the cod fishery on Saint-Jean, Miscou, and the Îles de la Madeleine in return for sponsoring settlement. The following year his company sent out more than 250 colonists, who established themselves at coastal locations such as Port-la-Joye (near present-day Charlottetown) and Havre Saint-Pierre.

The venture was well conceived and designed to be permanent. Twenty married couples arrived in 1720, and the company supplied a midwife. To encourage family formation, the company recruited potential brides for unmarried workers and promised indentured servants that they would be released from their contracts if they married on Île Saint-Jean. Despite this careful planning, crop failures and competition from interlopers ultimately led to bankruptcy and the settlers moved away, some of them to Île Royale.

In 1726 the French government installed a detachment of 30 naval fusiliers in the dilapidated buildings formerly occupied by Saint-Pierre's company. Jean-Pierre Roma, an energetic Parisian merchant, established fishing operations on the island in the 1730s. Building roads to connect his base at Trois-Rivières (now Brudenell Point) with Havre Saint-Pierre and Port-la-Joye, he hoped to develop the colony into an important trading centre. He might well have succeeded if the War of the Austrian Succession had not intervened.

Imperial Rivalries and Aboriginal Strategies

After more than a century of interaction with the French, Aboriginal people in Nova Scotia had little interest in an alliance with the British, whose language and religion were foreign to them. The Mi'kmaq, in particular, were opposed to English encroachments on their territory. With a population of roughly 3,500 in 1713, the Mi'kmaq outnumbered the Acadians (2,000), let alone the British (about 400, including the garrison) and were clearly the dominant force in Nova Scotia both numerically and militarily.

After the conquest, the growing presence of New England fishermen and merchants in Nova Scotia made the Mi'kmaq nervous. Trade with New Englanders sometimes ended in violent altercations and confirmed the Mi'kmaq in their preference for trade with the French based on Île Royale, who were subsidized to trump their competitors. In 1719 Governor Saint-Ovide began meeting annually with the Mi'kmaq to shore up trade and military alliances. A Mi'kmaw force attacked Canso in the summer of 1720, touching off a confrontation that included a two-hour naval battle between New England fishermen and Mi'kmaq sailing on captured vessels.

This conflict merged into Abenaki resistance to English settlement in their territory. The result was a full-fledged "Indian War," which ranged along the New England–Nova Scotia frontier from 1722 to 1725. Known in New England as Dummer's War (after the acting governor), it was the first of two entirely local conflicts dominated by Aboriginal issues. Mi'kmaq and Wolastoqiyik captured 18 New England vessels trading in the Bay of Fundy in 1722 and harassed fishermen along the eastern shore of Nova Scotia. A small Aboriginal force attacked Annapolis Royal in July 1724, burning part of the town, killing a British soldier, and taking several captives, before retreating.

In December 1725 a peace agreement was reached in Boston with delegates from the Wabanaki Confederacy. Paul Mascarene, a Huguenot officer in the 40th Regiment, represented Nova Scotia. Because the agreement stipulated that each Aboriginal nation was obliged to ratify the treaty, 64 delegates representing the Mi'kmaq, Wolastoqiyik, and Passamaquoddy attended a ratification ceremony at Annapolis Royal in June 1726. The articles were read in English and French and then translated into Mi'kmaq and perhaps other Aboriginal languages. At the end of the ceremony,

Document

The Treaty of 1726

The Treaty of 1726 between the British and the Aboriginal peoples in Nova Scotia was subsequently violated by both sides. Although it was re-negotiated in 1760–1, Canadian courts have ruled that it was never superseded, and in the Constitution of 1982 it became the legal foundation for Aboriginal rights in the Maritimes. The treaty began with the articles of peace and outlined the rules that Aboriginal peoples would be obliged to follow in their relations with the British. It then detailed Britain's obligations. The documents read in part:

Article of Peace and Agreement: Annapolis Royal, 1726

Whereas His Majesty King George by the Concession of the Most Christian King made att the Treaty of Utrecht is become ye Rightfull Possessor of the Province of Nova Scotia or Acadia According to its ancient Boundaries, wee the Said Chiefs & Representatives of ye Penobscott, Norridgewalk, St. Johns, Cape Sables, & of the Other Indian Tribes Belonging to & Inhabiting within This His Majesties Province of Nova Scotia Or Acadia & New England do for our Selves & the said Tribes Wee represent acknowledge His Said Majesty King George's Jurisdiction & Dominion Over The Territories of the Said Province of Nova Scotia or Acadia & make our Submission to His said Majesty in as Ample a Manner as wee have formerly done to the Most Christian King.

That the Indians shall not molest any of His Majesty's Subjects or their Dependants in their Settlements already made or now fully to be made or in their carrying on their Trade or any other affairs within the said Province.

That if there Happens any Robbery or outrage Committed by any of our Indians the Tribe or Tribes they belong to shall Cause satisfaction to be made to ye partys Injured.

That the Indians shall not help to convey away any Soldiers belonging to His Majesty's forts, but on the contrary shall bring back any soldier they shall find endeavouring to run away.

That in case of any misunderstanding, Quarrel or Injury between the English and the Indians no private revenge shall be taken, but Application shall be made for redress according to His Majesty's Laws.

Lieutenant Governor Doucett entertained the delegates and offered them presents. When another delegation of Wolastoqiyik arrived in May 1627, the process was repeated. Since formal treaties were a British innovation, only time would tell whether they were worth the paper they were written on.

British Nova Scotia

Until 1749 the British presence in Nova Scotia was confined primarily to Annapolis Royal and Canso. The gap between British administrators and Acadians widened after the conquest, as many

That if there [be] any Prisoners amongst any of our aforesaid Tribes, wee faithfully promise that the said prisoners shall be releas'd & Carefully Conducted & delivered up to this Government or that of New England.

Reciprocal Promises Made by Captain John Doucett, 1726

Whereas the Chiefs of the Penobscott, Norridgewalk, St. Johns, Cape Sable Indians and of the other Indian Tribes & their Representatives Belonging to and Inhabiting within this his Majesty's Province of Nova Scotia Conforme to the Articles Stipulated by their Delegates . . . at Boston in New England The Fifteenth day of December one thousand Seven hundred & twenty five have come to this His Majesty's Fort of Annapolis Royal and Ratifyed said Articles and made their submission to his Majesty King George . . . and Acknowledged his said Majesty's Just title to this his said province of Nova Scotia or Acadia & promised to Live peaceably with all his Majestys Subjects & their Dependants & to performe what Further is Contained in the Severall articles of their Instruments. I do therefore in His Majesty's name for and in Behalf of this His said Government of Nova Scotia or Acadia Promise the Said Chiefs & their Respective Tribes all marks of Favour, Protection & Friendship.

And I do Further promise & in the absence of the honabl the Lt Govr of the Province in behalf of the this said Government, That the Said Indians shall not be Molested in their Persons, Hunting Fishing and Shooting & planting on their planting Ground nor in any other their Lawfull occasions, By his Majesty's Subjects or Their Descendants in the Exercise of their Religion Provided the Missionarys Residing amongst them have Leave from the Government for So Doing.

That if any Indians are Injured By any of his Majesty's Subjects or their Dependants They shall have Satisfaction and Reparation made to them According to His Majesty's Laws whereof the Indians shall have Benefit Equall with his Majesty's other Subjects.

That upon the Indians Bringing back any Soldier Endeavouring to run away from any of His Majesty's Forts or Garrisons, the Said Indians for this good Office Shall be hand-somely rewarded.

That as a Mark and token of a true Observation & Faithfull Performance of all and Every Article promised on his Majesty's part by the Government I have by and with the Advice of the Council for the said Government Releas'd and Sett att Liberty the Said Indian Prisoners.[7]

of the latter withdrew from the capital and the former felt that building estates in the countryside would make them vulnerable to attack. Closely tied to Boston (only a week away by sea) and London (a much longer voyage), the English residents of Nova Scotia introduced a variety of British institutions to sustain them in their anxious isolation.

By the 1740s Annapolis Royal was home to about 80 families, equally divided between Acadian and British. Administrators, merchants, and officers of the 40th Regiment and the Royal Artillery formed a tight little clique, bound together over time by marriage. If they were not on overseas leave, Church of England clergy ministered to soldiers and civilians alike. The Reverend Isaac Watt, acting garrison chaplain, was employed by the Society for the Propagation of the Gospel in 1728 to operate a school, which initially enrolled 50 students. In 1738 officers of the garrison established a lodge of the Masonic Order, the first of a range of social and philanthropic organizations that in the eighteenth century came to characterize British and, eventually, colonial culture.

Only three families were reported living permanently in Canso in 1729, but the population was much larger from May to November, when New England fishermen and traders (some of whom brought their families) were operating in the area. By 1736 the community had a Church of England chaplain, a chapel, and a school. Canso's most prominent citizen was Edward How, an Irish-born merchant who served as justice of the peace, sheriff, and militia captain. Like most merchants, How lived in the style appropriate to his class, with Chinese porcelain, fine furniture, and other goods acquired through illegal trade with Louisbourg.

Although Acadians resolved most of their problems among themselves, they relied on the court at Annapolis Royal to pronounce on prolonged disputes, most of them related to property rights. The court drew on the knowledge of representatives from Acadian villages, who functioned like justices of the peace but, as Roman Catholics, could not receive official appointments. Despite having no legal training, the British-appointed councillors believed that justice must be seen to be done, and in the view of the historian Thomas Garden Barnes, they rendered their decisions "with exceptional even-handedness."[8]

The major bone of contention between the Acadians and British administrators was the oath of allegiance. After two decades of futile efforts to extract an unqualified oath, British authorities lived uncomfortably with the accommodation reached by Governor Philipps in 1731, which included a verbal promise that Acadians could remain neutral and would not be forced to fight against France. A few ambitious families made the most of the situation. Marie Madeleine Maisonnat, for example, married the Huguenot officer William Winniett, who became prominent in the economic and political life of the colony. Similarly, Agathe de Saint-Étienne de La Tour married, in succession, two British officers stationed in Annapolis Royal. Her sons from the first marriage, Simon and John (baptized Jean-Baptiste) Bradstreet, both secured commissions in the British army. As defiant of authority as they had always been, Acadians living in Minas and Beaubassin cheekily drove their cattle to Tatamagouche for shipment to Louisbourg.

Naomi Griffiths has described the years between 1713 and 1744 as a "golden age" for Acadians in Nova Scotia, largely because it was a rare period of peace.[9] Family life flourished and opportunity beckoned as markets in New England and Île Royale expanded. By the mid-eighteenth century, more than 9,000 Acadians lived in mainland Nova Scotia and as many as 3,000 on Île Saint-Jean and Île Royale. They now saw themselves as a unique people, identifying with the region in which they were born. Even on Île Royale, they were viewed differently from more recent arrivals, though what identified them—accent, apparel, attitude—is impossible to determine.

The War of the Austrian Succession, 1744–8

The test of Acadian neutrality and Aboriginal alliances came in 1744, when France and Britain were drawn into the ongoing War of the Austrian Succession. In the early months of the war, "Bonnie" Prince Charlie's primarily Scottish army, supported and supplied by France, invaded England in an attempt to restore the Stuart dynasty. Although the army was routed at Culloden in April 1746, dealing with the rebellion meant that Britain had few resources to commit to North America. The slack was taken up by New Englanders, led by the purposeful governor of Massachusetts, William Shirley.[10]

As soon as news of the war reached Louisbourg, Governor Jean Baptiste-Louis Le Prévost Duquesnel authorized privateers to attack New England shipping and dispatched a force against Canso. The 87 soldiers stationed there were caught off guard and surrendered almost immediately in May 1744. Duquesnel then moved against Annapolis Royal, sending an advance force of some 300 Mi'kmaq and a few Acadians, mobilized by Le Loutre, to lay siege to the poorly defended capital. They retreated with the timely appearance of military reinforcements from New England. Paul Mascarene, appointed lieutenant-governor in 1744, might well have been obliged to surrender to a second assault later in the summer, but the siege was lifted when a company of New England rangers arrived.

In the early spring of 1745 Annapolis Royal was again under attack, this time by a Canadian expedition consisting of more than 600 Troupes de la Marine and Aboriginal auxiliaries. Before the siege could be resolved, the Canadians were summoned to Louisbourg, which was experiencing its first test as a military stronghold. A volunteer New England militia of 4,300 men, led by William Pepperrell and supported by a naval squadron of more than 100 British and colonial vessels under the command of British Commodore Peter Warren laid siege to Louisbourg early in May. After seven weeks under bombardment, Governor Louis Du Pont Duchambon surrendered on 17 June. The New Englanders also destroyed French installations on Île Saint-Jean, including Roma's base at Trois-Rivières.

In 1746 the French tried to seize the initiative in North America. They mobilized a mammoth expedition—more than 60 vessels carrying 11,000 soldiers and crew under the Duke d'Anville—to assist in the relief of Canada if it came under attack and, if not, to capture Louisbourg and Annapolis Royal. D'Anville planned to meet with a detachment of 700 Troupes de la Marine under Captain de Ramezay and 300 Aboriginal auxiliaries arriving from Canada. In anticipation of d'Anville's arrival, Ramezay's forces laid siege to Port-la-Joye and Annapolis Royal.

From the beginning things went terribly wrong. Adverse weather slowed the transatlantic crossing, during which typhus, typhoid, and scurvy took their toll. When the expedition finally found refuge in Chibouctou (now Halifax) harbour in September, three months after leaving France, it counted only 44 vessels. D'Anville died shortly after making landfall, and his successor tried to commit suicide. In October the tattered remnants of the squadron retreated to France without firing a shot against the enemy. Its major legacy in Nova Scotia was an outbreak of typhus, which the Mi'kmaq carried to their communities. It has been estimated that the disease killed from one-third to one-half of the Mi'kmaq. Acadians and Canadians were also affected, but their casualty rates are difficult to calculate.[11]

Its navy devastated, France could no longer support a military campaign in North America, but Ramezay and his Aboriginal allies, who had retreated to Beaubassin, were not deterred. Learning that Governor Shirley had sent 500 colonial militiamen to keep the Acadians under surveillance, Ramezay dispatched a force led by Louis Coulon de Villiers and Louis de la Corne on a classic winter guerrilla campaign. The troops made their way through heavy snow to Grand Pré, where the New Englanders were quartered in Acadian homes. Using information provided by sympathetic Acadians, the French surrounded the houses where the New Englanders were sleeping, killed 70, and forced the rest to surrender.

The "Massacre of Grand Pré," as the English called it, made the Acadian strategy of neutrality irrelevant. British administrators were now convinced that Acadians could be pressed into supplying both French and Aboriginals with billets, intelligence, and provisions. Whether their compliance was voluntary or extracted under duress was immaterial.

An Uneasy Peace, 1749–1755

The Treaty of Aix-la-Chapelle in 1748 temporarily averted reprisals between Britain and France. Each agreed to return what it had captured from the other, outraging the New Englanders who had spent blood and treasure on the capture of Louisbourg. Nevertheless, each side understood that the treaty represented a truce rather than a final settlement. In the Maritime region, the peace of 1748 would not last long.

French authorities moved quickly in 1749 to restore fortifications at Louisbourg and to accommodate a larger population. Fearing the ravages of another attack, many settlers who had formerly lived in outlying districts now sought refuge in the walled town. The garrison also expanded from 1,050 in 1749 to 2,100 in 1755. Meanwhile, the lower St John River and Chignecto areas were occupied by French troops and Canadian militia dispatched from Quebec.

To counter the threat posed by Louisbourg, the British government decided to build a fortified base on the south shore of the Nova Scotia peninsula. In June 1749 Lieutenant-General Edward Cornwallis led an expedition of more than 2,500 British soldiers, settlers, and labourers to the shores of Chebucto Bay. Halifax, named after the President of the Board of Trade, replaced Annapolis Royal as the capital, and was Britain's first serious attempt to colonize the territories acquired under the Treaty of Utrecht. Its founding marked a turning point in the history of the Atlantic region, signalling a new determination on the part of the British to control Nova Scotia.

In the early months of the town's development, more than a third of the immigrants left for Boston. They were replaced by a gaggle of merchants, labourers, and artisans from New England and elsewhere, eager to profit from government contracts and take advantage of the British decree that residents of Nova Scotia could not be sued for debts incurred outside the colony—a law that remained on the books until 1762. To attract Jewish merchants from Boston and New York, authorities ignored imperial proscriptions against the granting of royal favour, including free land, to Jews. The Jersey-born entrepreneur Joshua Mauger emerged as the most powerful merchant in Halifax, making his fortune from the West Indies trade, selling slaves, smuggling with Louisbourg, speculating in land, supplying the Navy, and manufacturing rum, over which he enjoyed a virtual monopoly.[12]

Sustained by Parliamentary grants, Halifax soon acquired civilian institutions. By the summer of 1750, a church had been constructed adjacent to the Grand Parade with timber shipped from Boston. Although built for the Church of England, St Paul's also served worshippers of other Protestant denominations until Mather's Meeting House, which initially catered mostly to New England and Scottish Congregationalists, opened in 1754. In year-round communication with the North Atlantic world, Haligonians were kept informed about the latest developments by their local newspaper, the *Halifax Gazette*, first published in March 1752 by New Englander John Bushell. It had few subscribers, but news spread quickly through the streets and taverns that served as the main conduits of information.

British efforts to assert dominance in the region included an immigration policy designed to swamp the resident population with loyal settlers. Between 1750 and 1753, nearly 2,500 German- and French-speaking Protestants (many of them from the Palatinate, Switzerland, and Montbéliard) arrived in Nova Scotia. Some of the "foreign Protestants" stayed in Halifax, but the majority settled along the south shore, where they founded the town of Lunenburg in 1753.

One of Cornwallis's first objectives was to reach an accommodation with the Aboriginal peoples living in the region. Although the Wolastoqiyik and Passamaquoddy were prepared to reaffirm the peace of 1726, the Mi'kmaq were in no mood to sign treaties. They attacked British ships at Beaubassin and Canso, and met French authorities at Port Toulouse in September 1749 to deter- mine how to deal with the British invasion. Abbé Maillard was on hand to help craft a declaration of war in both Mi'kmaq and French. Addressed to Cornwallis, it read in part:

> The place where you are, where you are building dwellings, where you are now building a fort . . .
> this land belongs to me. I have come from it as certainly as the grass, it is the very place of my birth
> and of my dwelling. . . . I swear, it is God who has given it to me to be my country for ever. . . .
> Show me where I, the Indian, will lodge? You drive me out; where do you want me to take refuge?[13]

The Mi'kmaq thus precipitated another war in Nova Scotia, sometimes called Le Loutre's War because of the priest's dogged persistence in challenging the British occupation. In July 1749 Le Loutre reported to his superiors: "As we cannot openly oppose the English ventures, I think we cannot do better than to incite the Indians to continue warring on the English." Ordered by the Ministry of Marine to move his mission from Shubenacadie to Beauséjour Ridge on the Isthmus of Chignecto where French forces were mobilizing, Le Loutre continued to create problems for the British from his new base of operations. Cornwallis viewed the troublesome priest as "a good for nothing scoundrel as ever lived."[14]

Well-schooled in methods of "pacifying" dissidents in Scotland after the Battle of Culloden, Cornwallis took a much tougher approach than his predecessors had to the Mi'kmaq and their pol- itical priests. He refused to declare war on the Mi'kmaq—to do that, he reasoned, "would be . . . to own them a free and Independent people"—but instead ordered British subjects to "take or destroy the savages commonly called Micmacks wherever they are found." He offered bounties "to be paid upon producing such savage taken or his scalp (as is the custom of America)" and put a price of £50 on Le Loutre's head.[15] Not surprisingly, attacks by Mi'kmaq and Acadian militants continued, encouraged by French authorities at Louisbourg and Quebec, who also paid for captives and scalps.

As tensions mounted, the Acadians were caught in the middle, pressed by both the British and the French to take sides. Shortly after his arrival, Cornwallis summoned representatives from Acadian communities to Halifax and demanded that their people take an unqualified oath of allegiance. The delegates could not commit to such a policy, fearing reprisals by the Mi'kmaq and French forces in the region. As subsequent developments confirmed, their caution was not misplaced.

In response to France's audacity in occupying disputed territory, inciting the Mi'kmaq to war, and attempting to elicit the active support of the Acadians, Cornwallis ordered the construction of Fort Edward at Pisiquid (Windsor) to keep an eye on the populous Minas settlements and dis- patched Lieutenant-Colonel Charles Lawrence to build a fort on the Isthmus of Chignecto. Despite stiff opposition from French forces, Fort Lawrence was completed in September 1750. The following year, the French built Fort Beauséjour across the Missaguash River from Fort Lawrence. Acadians from Beaubassin and elsewhere were urged to move to French-controlled territory, where they could establish farms to supply food to Île Royale, augment the colonial militia, and bolster French territorial claims. To force compliance, Le Loutre employed ruthless pressure tactics, withdrawing priests, abducting women and children, and destroying Acadian farms at Beaubassin. The golden age of Acadian life had come to an abrupt end.

Without the resources to conquer the Mi'kmaq, and unable to negotiate a settlement with them, Cornwallis returned to England in 1752. His successor, Peregrine Thompson Hopson, concluded a peace treaty with Jean-Baptiste Cope, chief of the Mi'kmaq around Shubenacadie, in September 1752, but raids, skirmishes, and reprisals continued. Le Loutre reported in 1753 that the extraordinary sum of 1,800 livres had been paid for 18 British scalps—grisly trophies that, along with enemy captives, had become a major source of wealth for guerilla fighters.

Following clashes with the French and their Aboriginal allies on the Ohio frontier in 1754, the British launched a four-pronged attack against the outer defences of New France: Fort Duquesne in the Ohio Valley, Fort Niagara in the Great Lakes region, Fort Frédéric on Lake Champlain, and Fort Beauséjour. The offensive failed on all fronts save one. A colonial militia of 2,500 men commanded by Colonel Robert Monckton captured Fort Beauséjour after a two-week siege. With only 160 regular soldiers and 300 militiamen, the French commander, Louis Du Pont Duchambon de Vergor, capitulated on 16 June 1755. Abbé Le Loutre managed to slip out of the fort and make his way to Quebec, but he was still a marked man. In September the ship carrying him to France was intercepted by the British, who held him prisoner until 1763.

The discovery that many of the French militiamen were Acadians had a major impact on British policy. Plans had been made to remove Acadians from the Chignecto region following the capture of Fort Beauséjour, but now the fate of the entire Acadian population, even those who had collaborated with the British, hung in the balance.

Le Grand Dérangement

In July 1755 the new governor, Charles Lawrence, offered Acadian delegates one last chance to take an unqualified oath of allegiance. When they refused, Lawrence and his council moved quickly to resolve the problem of the "neutral French" once and for all. Military commanders were instructed to seize Acadian men and boys and hold them in their communities, in forts, churches, and other makeshift prisons, until transports from Boston arrived. The prisoners and their families were then deported to the other British colonies in North America, taking only what they could carry. As they departed, soldiers burned Acadian homes, barns, churches, and crops and seized their cattle to pay the costs of what was by any measure an expensive operation.

The sorrows of the deportation did not end there. Since authorities in the receiving colonies had not been informed in advance, they offered little assistance, and some refused to accept their quotas of deportees. Many died of disease and misadventure. Of the 3,100 Acadians shipped from Île St-Jean in 1758, for example, 679 drowned at sea and another 970 died of other causes before reaching their destinations.[16]

Even the French living in Newfoundland were not spared. In August 1755 a British naval expedition was dispatched to the southwestern coast of the island, where it captured several French Basque ships and sent their crews north to Port au Choix to find passage home. The shore facilities and houses at five harbours between St George's Bay and Port aux Basques were burned and their 67 residents dumped on Île Royale, where they faced a second deportation.

By the time the expulsions ended in 1762, nearly 11,000 of approximately 14,000 Acadians had been deported. About 3,000 managed to hide until hostilities ended, of whom nearly 2,000 made their way to Quebec.

The Acadian diaspora had a remarkable reach. It took some to Louisiana, where their descendants, the Cajuns, still live; to Canada, where they quickly integrated into the colonial population; to the Îles de la Madeleine, Saint-Pierre, the West Indies, Great Britain, France, and even the Falkland Islands. Those who went to France felt like strangers and asked to be returned to North America. When the war ended, some of them got their wish. In 1764 Acadians who agreed to take an oath of allegiance were permitted to settle in their former homeland but not, for the most part, in the areas where they had once lived. New immigrants, many of them from New England, had already taken up their farmlands.

John Mack Faragher argues that the Acadian expulsion fits the United Nations definition of "ethnic cleansing," a term coined in the early 1990s in the context of

Table 6.2 Acadian Population in 1763	
Massachusetts	1,050
Connecticut	650
New York	250
Maryland	810
Pennsylvania	400
South Carolina	300
Georgia	200
Nova Scotia	1,250
St John River	100
Louisiana	300
England	850
France	3,500
Québec	2,000
St John's Island	300
Baie des Chaleurs	700
Total	**12,660**

Source: Adapted from R. Cole Harris, ed., *Historical Atlas of Canada*, vol. 1 (Toronto: University of Toronto Press, 1987), Plate 30.

Biography   *Joseph Broussard*

The Acadians did not submit meekly to their fate. One of the most notorious resisters was Joseph Broussard, known later in life as Beausoleil. Born in Port-Royal in 1702, Broussard was a rebel from an early age, embroiled in land disputes with his neighbours and, though married, named in a paternity suit. Fluent in Mi'kmaq, he participated in attacks on Annapolis Royal in 1724, on Grand Pré in 1747, and on British settlements in Nova Scotia during Le Loutre's War. At the siege of Fort Beauséjour, he led a militia unit outside the walls.

Captured and imprisoned in Fort Lawrence by the British, he managed to escape. Along with his brother Alexandre, who made his way back from imprisonment in South Carolina, and their seven sons, he helped to organize militia units that inflicted misery on British and colonial troops trying to establish control over the region. After the capture of Louisbourg and Quebec, Broussard and his comrades, now denied access to ammunition and food supplies, were forced to surrender. Broussard was imprisoned until the end of the war, when he and 600 of his fellow Acadians hired ships to take them to Saint-Domingue (Haiti). From there they moved to Louisiana in 1765. Shortly after his arrival, Broussard succumbed to the fevers common in southern climates. The town of Broussard was later named in honour of the man who had become an Acadian hero.[17]

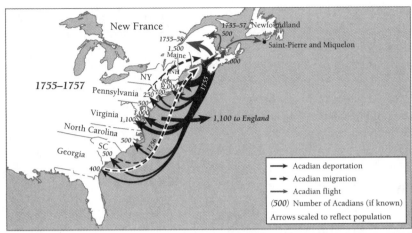

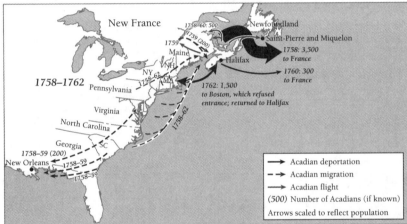

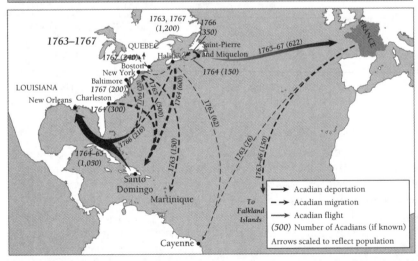

Acadian migrations, 1755–85. Adapted from R. Cole Harris, ed., *Historical Atlas of Canada, Vol.1, From the Beginning to 1800* (Toronto: University of Toronto Press, 1987), Plate 30. Available at www.umaine.edu/canam/ham/acadiansettlement.htm

the Balkan conflict.[18] While this conclusion has generated some debate, there is little disagreement about the impact of the expulsion on the Acadians. They had developed a sense of themselves as a separate people in North America by 1713, but the painful experience of the *grand dérangement* added new substance and cohesion to their identity. As the defining moment in their collective memory, it would long shape the cultural perceptions and political actions of their descendants, especially those living in the Maritimes and Louisiana, where Acadian culture continued to evolve.

Brutal as it was, the expulsion of the Acadians had the military impact that Lawrence had intended. The food supply problem reached crisis proportions in Louisbourg, where the authorities were overwhelmed by destitute Aboriginal allies and Acadian refugees. Even before warfare formally resumed in 1756, the French had lost the first round.

The Seven Years' War, 1756–63

Warfare in North America merged into a larger contest known as the Seven Years' War in 1756. This time France, Austria, and eventually Spain squared off against Great Britain and Prussia. Fought in Europe and European colonies around the world, the war permanently altered the balance of power in North America and put the Atlantic region on the front lines of the conflict.

In the midst of a temporary political crisis, the British government was slow to mobilize for war, but in the summer of 1757 the popular Whig leader William Pitt formed a coalition government and launched a comprehensive strategy that included a major thrust in North America. By that time three enormous French squadrons, loaded with war matériel, provisions, and troops, had eluded the British blockade and reached Louisbourg. The presence of the French fleet, under the command of the Comte Du Bois de la Motte, thwarted Britain's plan to attack Louisbourg in 1757. British warships cruised off Louisbourg beginning in August, but both fleets were badly mauled by a September hurricane. His ships battered and his forces laid low by typhus, Du Bois de la Motte retreated to France, and a Wabanaki force assembled for the defence of Louisbourg dispersed. Pitt, meanwhile, ordered eight ships of the line to winter in Halifax to prepare for an early start on a blockade of Louisbourg in the spring.

Their superior naval forces finally better organized, the British managed to delay or prevent the departure of two of the three French squadrons earmarked for the defence of Louisbourg in 1758. By the beginning of June Governor Augustin de Drucour, with a civilian population of about 4,000 and 8,500 soldiers, sailors, and militia, faced one of the largest military forces ever to campaign in North America: 27,000 British and colonial soldiers and sailors conveyed by 157 vessels under the command of Major General Jeffrey Amherst and Admiral Edward Boscawen. Also on board were several hundred women who, as wives, mistresses, cooks, cleaners, and caregivers, were an integral part of almost all military operations.

The British troops landed on 8 June, and a stiff bombardment soon reduced the town to ruins. Militia reinforcements from the mainland, among them Aboriginal people and Acadians, had little impact. On 26 July, with supplies of food and ammunition running short, Drucour agreed to terms of surrender. It has been calculated that 371 British and 93 French soldiers died in the battle; but if civilian and Aboriginal casualties are added, the losses were probably closely matched.[19] Both the military and civilian populations of Louisbourg were deported to France, in effect doubling the numbers of people expelled from the Atlantic region. To prevent Louisbourg from ever again becoming a centre of French power, the British demolished its fortifications.

"Britain's Glory or the Reduction of Cape Breton, By the Gallant Admiral Boscawen & General Amherst," engraving, 1758. News of the capture of Louisbourg was greeted with great rejoicing in Britain, where this engraving offered a visual representation of the bombardment of the fortified town. From Charles P. De Volpi, *Nova Scotia, A Pictorial Record* (Toronto: Longman Canada, 1974), Plate 6.

Amherst consolidated his victory by sending troops to Île Saint-Jean, the Gaspé, the Miramichi, and the St John River Valley to round up Acadians for deportation and destroy their settlements and those of their Aboriginal allies. To assist in the mopping-up operations along the St John River, Monckton employed a detachment of colonial rangers under Moses Hazen. Even Amherst, no stranger to military cruelty, was shocked when he learned of their ruthless behaviour. "I gave a Commission of Captain to Lieutenant Hazen as I thought he deserved it," he wrote. "I am sorry to say what I have since heard of that affair has sullied his merit with me, as I shall always disapprove of killing women and helpless children."[20]

A similarly brutal policy was carried out in the Baie des Chaleurs and Gaspésie by General James Wolfe, who had played a conspicuous role in the Louisbourg campaign. He subsequently commanded the army that captured Quebec in September 1759, dying in the battle that marked the end of the French Empire in North America. The last battle in the Maritime region was fought in July 1760 in the Baie des Chaleurs, where Commodore John Byron intercepted a small French expedition taking supplies to Montreal. The French retreated into the Restigouche River, where, aided by local Aboriginal people and Acadians, they mounted a fierce resistance but were ultimately defeated.

As French power collapsed, the Mi'kmaq, Wolastoqiyik, and Passamaquoddy made their accommodations with the British. They were encouraged to do so by Abbé Maillard and other priests

The destruction of Grimross (now Gagetown), watercolour by Thomas Davies. The artist was an officer in the army led by Colonel Robert Monckton that laid waste to Acadian and Aboriginal settlements along the St John River in 1758. Source:Thomas Davies, "A View of the Plundering and Burning of the City of Grimross, 1758," monochrome watercolour on laid paper, 36.9 x 53.5 cm, Purchased 1954, National Gallery of Canada, Ottawa, Photo © National Gallery of Canada.

in the region who feared for their survival in the face of severe deprivation. During 1760–1, all bands sent delegates to Halifax to sign formal treaties of "peace and friendship" with the governor and council, acknowledging "the jurisdiction and Dominion of His Majesty George the Second over the Territories of Nova Scotia or Accadia" and agreeing to submit "to His Majesty in the most perfect, ample, and solemn manner." The treaties promised what was most needed—government-operated trading posts—but reserved no lands for hunting and fishing. Governor Jonathan Belcher was instructed by the British government to draw up a proclamation forbidding encroachment on Aboriginal territory, which he obediently did, but he refused to publicize it because he was afraid it might encourage another round of attacks on the British settlements in the colony.

The final chapter in the Seven Years' War took place in Newfoundland. The French government devised a risky plan to disrupt the English fisheries by capturing St John's, raiding other settlements, and recruiting Irish Roman Catholics into French service. If successful, the expedition would reassert French claims to Newfoundland and its fisheries, and strengthen the French bargaining position in the looming treaty negotiations. In the spring of 1762, four vessels carrying 870 soldiers under the command of Charles-Henry d'Arsac de Ternay sailed from France and successfully evaded British blockades. Ternay's forces occupied St John's, Harbour Grace, Carbonear, and Trinity, and destroyed fishing premises and fishing vessels along the coast. A hastily assembled British force, recruited from New York and Nova Scotia, recaptured St John's. The last Anglo–French engagement to occur in the Atlantic region, it is remembered as the Battle of Signal Hill.

Peace and Reconstruction

In the Treaty of Paris, which formally ended the war in 1763, France gave up its North American empire to Great Britain. A major sticking point in the negotiations was French insistence on access to the Newfoundland fisheries. The final agreement renewed the French right to fish on the Treaty Shore and ceded Saint-Pierre and Miquelon to France, but on condition that the islands serve only as an unfortified shelter for French migratory fishing vessels. This was a minimal replacement for Île Royale, which French negotiators had fought hard to keep.

On 7 October 1763 the British government issued a proclamation outlining, in broad strokes, what it intended to do with its newly acquired territories. In the Atlantic region, Île Royale (renamed Cape Breton) and Île Saint-Jean (anglicized to the Island of St John) became part of Nova Scotia, while Anticosti Island, the Îles de la Madeleine, and "the Coast of Labrador" were placed "under the care and inspection" of the governor of Newfoundland, who had a naval squadron at his disposal and looked after the fisheries.

The proclamation also set out British policy regarding Aboriginal peoples. While no European settlement was permitted west of the Appalachian Mountains, Aboriginal people elsewhere were not to be "molested or disturbed" in the areas set aside for their hunting. All lands in the settled colonies not "ceded or purchased by Us" were to be "reserved to the said Indians," and no "private person" was authorized to buy Aboriginal land. Conceived with the western frontier in mind, these

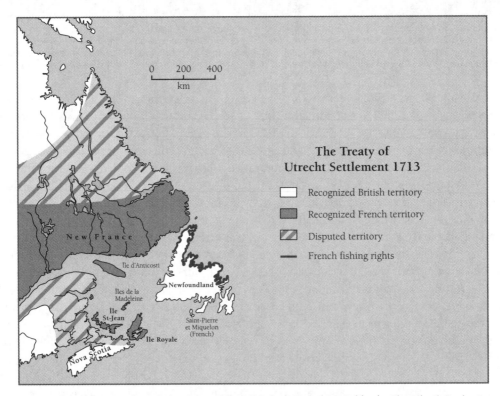

Eighteenth-century treaty boundaries. Adapted from P.A. Buckner and J.G. Reid, eds., *The Atlantic Region to Confederation* (Toronto: University of Toronto Press, 1994), p. 143.

policies were deliberately ignored by administrators in Nova Scotia, who were slow to establish reserves and only minimally involved in Aboriginal land transactions. Whether this aspect of the Royal Proclamation applied in Newfoundland and Labrador is unclear.

Conclusion

A half century of bitter rivalry between Great Britain and France ended in 1763 when, for the first time, all of what is now Atlantic Canada came under a single jurisdiction, to which Aboriginal people and returning Acadians had no option but to submit. The French presence was reduced to a seasonal fishery on the Newfoundland Treaty Shore and a base at Saint-Pierre and Miquelon. In this situation, the British government was eager to see the region—apart from Newfoundland and Labrador—settled, preferably by English-speaking Protestants.

Further Readings

Brebner, J.B. 1927. *New England's Outpost before the Conquest of Canada*. New York: Columbia University Press.

Brière, Jean-François. 1997. "The French Fishery in the Eighteenth Century," in *How Deep is the Ocean? Historical Essays on Canada's Atlantic Fishery*, ed. James E. Candow and Carol Corbin. Sydney, NS: University College of Cape Breton Press, 47–64.

Faragher, John Mack. 2005. *A Great and Noble Scheme: The Tragic Story of the Expulsion of the French Acadians from their American Homeland*. New York: W.W. Norton.

Godfrey, William G. 1982. *Pursuit of Profit and Preferment in Colonial North America: John Bradstreet's Quest*. Waterloo: Wilfrid Laurier Press.

Grenier, John. 2008. *The Far Reaches of Empire: War in Nova Scotia, 1710–1760*. Norman: University of Oklahoma Press

Head, C. Grant. 1976. *Eighteenth Century Newfoundland: A Geographer's Perspective*. Ottawa: Carleton University Press.

Humphries, Mark O. 2014. "A Calamity From Which No Relief Can Be Expected"; Empire, Authority and Civilian Responses to the French Occupation of Newfoundland, June–September, 1762." *Acadiensis* XLIII 1, 35–64.

Janzen, Olaf. 2008. "The 'Long' Eighteenth Century, 1697–1815," in Newfoundland Historical Society, *A Short History of Newfoundland and Labrador*. Portugal Cove–St Philip's: Bolder Publications, 50–76.

Jobb, Dean. 2005. *The Acadians: A People's Story of Exile and Triumph*. Mississauga: Wiley and Sons.

Johnston, A.J.B. 1984. *Religion in Life at Louisbourg*. Montreal: McGill-Queen's University Press.

———. 2001. *Control and Order in French Colonial Louisbourg, 1713–1758*. East Lansing: Michigan State University Press.

———. 2007. *Endgame 1758: The Promise, the Glory, and the Despair of Louisbourg's Last Decade*. Lincoln: University of Nebraska Press.

Landry, Nicolas. *La Cadie: frontière du Canada*. Québec: Septentrion, 2013.

Laxer, James. 2006. *The Acadians in Search of a Homeland*. Toronto: Doubleday Canada.

LeBlanc, Ronnie-Gilles, dir. 2005. *Du Grand Dérangement à la Déportation: nouvelles perspectives historiques*. Moncton: Chaire d'études acadiennes, Université de Moncton.

McNeil, John Robert. 1985. *Atlantic Empires of France and Spain, Louisbourg and Havana, 1700–1760*. Chapel Hill: University of North Carolina Press.

Moore, Christopher. 1982. *Louisbourg Portraits: Life in an Eighteenth-Century Garrison Town*. Toronto: Macmillan.

Newfoundland Studies (Special Issue) 17, 2 (Fall 2001).

Plank, Geoffrey. 2002. *An Unsettled Conquest: The British Campaign Against the Peoples of Acadia*. Philadelphia: University of Pennsylvania Press.

Rawlyk, George A. 1973. *Nova Scotia's Massachusetts: A Study of Massachusetts-Nova Scotia Relations*. Montreal: McGill-Queen's University Press.

Reid, John G., and Elizabeth Mancke. 2008. "From Global Processes to Continental Strategies: The Emergence of British North America to 1783," in *Canada and the British Empire*, ed. Phillip Buckner. Oxford: Oxford University Press.

Rudin, Ronald. 2009. *Remembering and Forgetting in Acadie: A Historian's Journey through Public Memory*. Toronto: University of Toronto Press.

Stanley, George F.G. 1968. *New France: The Last Phase, 1744–1760*. Toronto: McClelland and Stewart

Wicken, William C. 2002. *Mi'kmaq Treaties on Trial: History, Land, and Donald Marshall Junior*. Toronto: University of Toronto Press.

Historical Spotlight

Bannister, Jerry. 2001. "The Fishing Admirals in Eighteenth Century Newfoundland," *Newfoundland Studies* 17, 2: 166–219.

White, Stephen A. 2005. "The True Number of Acadians." Pp. 21–56 in Ronnie-Gilles LeBlanc, dir., *Du Grand Dérangement à la Déportation: nouvelles perspectives historiques* (Moncton: Chaire d'études acadiennes, Université de Moncton).

Recommended Websites

Acadian Heartland: The Records of British Government at Annapolis Royal, 1713–1749
http://novascotia.ca/archives/virtual/heartland/

The Fortress of Louisbourg
http://epe.lac-bac.gc.ca/100/205/301/ic/cdc/louisbourg/enghome.html

The English Fishery and Trade in the 18th Century
http://www.heritage.nf.ca/exploration/18fishery.html

Remembering Acadie
http://rememberingacadie.concordia.ca

Chapter 7

Community Formation, 1749–1815

B etween the founding of Halifax in 1749 and the end of the Napoleonic wars in 1815, the Atlantic region was redesigned. The expulsion of the Acadians and the razing of Louisbourg were major blows to the region's development, but these drastic actions ensured that British culture would prevail in the postwar reconstruction. Beginning in 1759, Nova Scotia became home to immigrants primarily from New England and Great Britain. St John's Island was proclaimed a separate colony in 1769 and also began attracting settlers. Following the American Revolutionary War (1775–83), nearly half of the 75,000 Loyalists who fled the newly independent United States of America settled in Nova Scotia, which was reduced in size in 1784 by the creation of two new colonies—New Brunswick and Cape Breton—to accommodate the refugees. With the arrival of the Loyalists, the uneasy equilibrium between Aboriginal people and the British in the Maritimes was swept away by the sheer force of numbers.[1] Newfoundland also increased in population, and during the French Revolutionary and Napoleonic Wars (1793–1815) became a settler society much like the others in the Atlantic region.

Immigration and Settlement

In this period Nova Scotia experienced unprecedented levels of immigration. Wartime conditions made it difficult to recruit settlers from overseas following the capture of Louisbourg, but New Englanders, whose sights had long been set on their northeastern frontier, were nearby. To encourage them to make the move, the Board of Trade, which was responsible for colonial policy, obliged a reluctant Governor Lawrence to call Nova Scotia's first elected assembly in 1758 and to issue proclamations outlining the rights that settlers would enjoy. These included two elected assembly representatives for each settled township, a judicial system similar to the one in New England, and freedom of worship for Protestant dissenters, with Calvinists, Lutherans, and Quakers specifically mentioned as having the right to be exempted from any taxes levied for the support of the "Established Church of England." As the ultimate incentive, settlers were to receive free land grants—100 acres (40 hectares) for each head of household, with an additional 50 for each family member and servant—which would be exempt from quitrents (taxes) for 10 years. Assistance was even provided to help some of the immigrants move to their new homes.

Their concerns addressed, nearly 8,000 New Englanders moved to Nova Scotia between 1759 and 1767. Known as "Planters," they settled in townships carved out for them on the south shore of Nova Scotia, in the Annapolis Valley, and in the Cobequid and Chignecto areas. In 1762 James Simonds, James White, and William Hazen—New England merchants associated with Joshua

Table 7.1   Timeline

1756–63	Seven Years' War.
1758–9	Governor Lawrence's Proclamations.
1759	New England Planters begin moving to Nova Scotia.
1763	Treaty of Paris; Royal Proclamation.
1763–7	James Cook surveys Newfoundland.
1764–8	Hugh Palliser serves as governor of Newfoundland.
1764	Samuel Holland surveys St John's Island; Acadians permitted to resettle in the Maritimes.
1767	St John's Island granted to British proprietors.
1769	St John's Island granted colonial status.
1770	George Cartwright builds a trading and fishing base in Labrador.
1771	Moravians establish a mission station at Nain, Labrador.
1772–4	Yorkshire settlers arrive in Nova Scotia.
1772	The *Hector* arrives in Pictou.
1773	Boston Tea Party.
1774–1809	Labrador under the jurisdiction of Quebec/Lower Canada.
1775–83	American Revolutionary War.
1775	American privateers begin to attack British shipping and ports.
1776	Rebels attack Fort Cumberland.
1778	Fort Howe constructed by the British.
1780	British convene assembly of Aboriginals on the St John River.
1783	Treaty of Paris.
1784	New Brunswick and Cape Breton Island established as separate colonies.
1789	French Revolution begins.
1791	Supreme Court established in Newfoundland.
1792	Black Loyalists depart for Sierra Leone.
1793–1815	French Revolutionary and Napoleonic Wars.
1798	St John's Island renamed Prince Edward Island.
1809	Labrador coast restored to jurisdiction of Newfoundland.
1812	War of 1812 begins.
1814	Treaty of Ghent ends the War of 1812.
1815	End of the Napoleonic wars.
1818	Anglo-American Convention.

Mauger—established their headquarters at Portland Point, near the mouth of the St John River. They developed a flourishing trade with Aboriginal people in the region and brought in labour to exploit the area's resources of fish, timber, and limestone. Further up the river, a group of farmers from Essex County, Massachusetts, squatted on land occupied by Acadians and Wolastoqiyik. Mauger, who was now living in London and in a good position to influence colonial policy, intervened to ensure that the newcomers prevailed. The grateful settlers named their community Maugerville.

Historical Focus

Mapping the Region

To support their imperial objectives, the British sponsored extensive exploration and mapping of the Atlantic region.[2] Captain James Cook, better known for his later work in the Pacific, charted part of the Gulf of St Lawrence and helped to prepare the map that enabled General James Wolfe to reach Quebec in 1759. After the war Cook became the naval surveyor for Newfoundland, and between 1763 and 1767 he charted the island's south and west coasts and the Strait of Belle Isle. A century later Cook's charts were still in use, as were those of his successor, Michael Lane, who completed the survey of Newfoundland and charted the south coast of Labrador. Local Mi'kmaq—who had moved to Newfoundland following the war—informed Cook about the island's river systems, which he included in the first accurate map of the entire island, published in collaboration with Lane in 1775.

During the same period, the army officer Samuel Holland carried out extensive surveys in the North Atlantic region. His report on St John's Island laid out counties, parishes, and townships; fixed the site of the projected capital, which he named Charlottetown in honour of the Queen; and gave a detailed account of the island's resources. Holland then moved on to the Îles de la Madeleine and Cape Breton, where he drew attention to the latter's deposits of coal, building stone, and gypsum. In the early 1770s, he helped to map the coast from the St John River to New York and conducted hydraulic surveys in Nova Scotia.

Between 1764 and 1773, Joseph F.W. DesBarres painstakingly charted the waters around the Nova Scotia peninsula, Sable Island, Cape Breton, and St John's Island. His maps and those of Holland, along with exquisite drawings by DesBarres, were published in his magnificent four-volume atlas, *The Atlantic Neptune* (1774–84), recognized in its day as a major cartographic achievement.

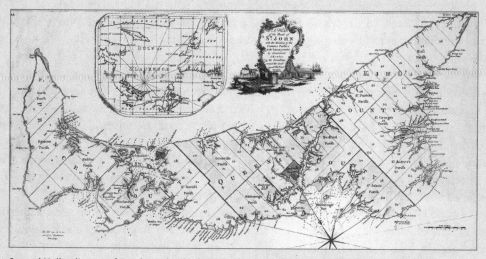

Samuel Holland's map of St John's Island. Library and Archives Canada, NMC-23350.

The largest group yet to settle in the Maritimes, the New England Planters added a distinctly "Yankee" flavour. They drew easily on the resources of their homeland, recruiting ministers for their Congregational churches, trading fish and farm produce in New England ports, and returning "home" periodically to visit family and friends. Although most Planters came with little capital, they were among the most fortunate of immigrants, making impressive progress in standards of living and institutional development in only one generation.

After the war Acadians became "planters" in their own right. They established communities in a number of locations, including Argyle and Clare in southwestern Nova Scotia, Île Madame and Cheticamp in Cape Breton, the northeastern areas of what would later become New Brunswick, and the western end of St John's Island. Scratching a hardscrabble existence from the inferior soil typical of the small land grants they received, they soon turned to fishing and became an indispensable labour force for the Jersey-based fishing companies that began operating in the Gaspé and Cape Breton in the 1760s. By 1800 the Atlantic region counted at least 8,000 francophones, and their numbers grew impressively with each generation.

In an attempt to populate the Maritime region on the cheap and at the same time promote a land-based social hierarchy, British authorities made large grants to "proprietors" on condition that they recruit Protestant settlers, improve their land, and pay quitrents to sustain the colonial administration. In a 17-day period in 1765, more than one million hectares of mainland Nova Scotia, much of it in the St John River area, were granted to speculators. Two years later, in an even more spectacular display of largesse, 64 of the 67 lots surveyed by Holland on St John's Island were granted to favourites of the king and court.

Most of the proprietors failed to meet the conditions of their grants, but a few tried. Alexander McNutt, who had planned to settle thousands of Ulster Protestants—some directly from Ireland and others from New Hampshire—on his enormous holdings, managed to bring a few hundred immigrants to communities such as Londonderry (Colchester County) and New Dublin (Lunenburg County). Near Windsor, Nova Scotia, two would-be aristocrats, Henry Denny Denson and J.F.W. DesBarres, employed tenant and enslaved labour to work their estates. Located on the Minas Basin, Windsor was fast becoming not only the country seat of the Halifax elite but also a commercial centre of some importance. In 1767 it hosted the region's first agricultural fair.

In 1765, 20 pacifist German Protestant families from Pennsylvania settled on the Petitcodiac River, becoming the founders of Hopewell, Hillsborough, and Moncton. The Philadelphia plantation, granted in 1765 to 14 proprietors in what became Pictou County, attracted a few settlers from Pennsylvania, but most of its founders arrived on board the *Hector* in 1773—the beginning of a substantial immigration from Scotland. Always alert to trading opportunities, Scottish merchants were drawn to the region specifically for its timber and fish. In 1765 William Davidson and his associates received a grant of 100,000 acres (40,500 hectares) on the Miramichi, where they developed a salmon fishery and eventually diversified into timber and shipbuilding.

Between 1772 and 1776 nearly 1,000 immigrants from Yorkshire, many of them Methodists, settled in the Chignecto area and elsewhere in Nova Scotia. Pushed out of England by high rents, land enclosure, and their own ambitions, they arrived with commercial and farming skills of a high order. Many of them had sufficient capital to purchase their farms outright, and they quickly brought them into efficient production.

Most of the unsettled proprietorial grants in Nova Scotia were eventually escheated (reverted to the Crown), but this was not the case on St John's Island. By having the island proclaimed a separate colony in 1769 and controlling its administration, the proprietors succeeded in frustrating all attempts to settle "the land question" in favour of freehold tenure. The colony thus became saddled with a proprietorial land system that was increasingly out of step with land-granting policies in other areas of North America.

Despite this handicap, the island managed to attract settlers. Many of the early immigrants were Scots, whose homeland was suffering severe political and economic upheaval. The first settlers, some 80 Scots recruited by Captain Robert Stewart for Lot 18, arrived on the *Arabella* in 1770. They were followed by indentured servants under contract to grow flax on the estates of Sir James Montgomery; Roman Catholic Highlanders under the direction of John MacDonald of Glenaladale; Protestants from Ulster; and Quakers from London. By 1775 the Island's 300 Acadian and Mi'kmaq residents were outnumbered by 1,200 new immigrants.

The year-round population of Newfoundland grew to more than 10,000 in the 1770s, in the same way as earlier in the century: slowly, informally, and without official encouragement. Sir Hugh Palliser, governor from 1764 to 1768, had tried to encourage the migratory fishery, but resident merchant establishments (both English and Irish) were increasingly supplanting non-residents as suppliers, shippers, wholesalers, and retailers. By the 1780s the island had more permanent than seasonal residents.

Eager to end clashes between the hard-pressed Beothuk and English fishermen on the island's northeast coast, Palliser commissioned Lieutenant John Cartwright to explore the Exploits River valley in 1768, but the Beothuk remained elusive. After 1763, Mi'kmaq moved to Newfoundland in increasing numbers, in part because of its proximity to the French Catholic presence on Saint-Pierre. Attempts were made to prevent them from visiting the French islands, but the Mi'kmaq eventually established a settlement at Bay d'Espoir (now Conne River reserve), which maintained connections across the channel. Another Mi'kmaq community took root at Bay St. George.

Palliser's efforts to promote a migratory fishery in southern Labrador were equally unsuccessful, given that fishermen needed year-round access to the coast's resources of cod, salmon, fur, and seals to make a living. A state of virtual warfare between fishermen and the Inuit, some of whom travelled from the north to the Strait of Belle Isle to trade whalebone and scavenge from fishing camps, led Palliser to accept a proposal from the highly disciplined Protestant sect commonly called the Moravians—officially the Unitas Fratrum (United Brethren)—to establish a mission in Labrador. Moravians who had served in Greenland understood Inuktitut, and therefore became valuable intermediaries in 1765 when Palliser tried to make an agreement with the Inuit at Chateau Bay. The first Moravian mission station, complete with a trading store, was built at Nain in 1771. Okak followed in 1776 and Hopedale (Hoffenthal) in 1782. The mission's presence made it unnecessary for the northern Inuit to trek to the Strait of Belle Isle, but the southern Inuit had to contend with a growing numbers of Europeans carrying infectious diseases.

Among the British and French-Canadian entrepreneurs who set their sights on Labrador in this period was John Cartwright's brother, Captain George Cartwright, who in 1770 established a fishing and trading base at Cape Charles and later moved to Sandwich Bay. A man of great energy, Cartwright published a lively account of his experiences in 1792. Labrador was placed under the jurisdiction of Quebec in 1774, but the governor of Newfoundland continued to supervise the mission stations and the fisheries in the region, which was formally restored to Newfoundland in 1809.

Biography Mikak

Born in Labrador around 1740, Mikak was a member of an Inuit band that frequented the south Labrador coast, trading with Europeans and often scavenging from their establishments. In 1767 trouble developed between her band and Europeans at Cape Charles. Marines from the blockhouse in Chateau Bay retaliated, and at least 24 men were killed in the ensuing skirmish, among them Mikak's husband. Taken captive—along with two other women and six children, including her son, Tutauk—Mikak spent the winter at Chateau Bay, where she and the second in command, Francis Lucas, each learned some words of the other's language.

Lucas took his captives to St John's in the summer of 1768. Impressed by Mikak, Governor Palliser arranged for Lucas to escort her to England with Tutauk and a boy named Karpik. In London Mikak was visited by the Moravian Jens Haven, whom she had met in 1765, and was lionized at court. The Dowager Princess of Wales gave her presents, including a fine dress, and John Russell, a fashionable artist, painted her portrait. She returned to Labrador in 1769.

Mikak was now a person of status among her own people, and this, together with her knowledge of English, made her a potentially important intermediary for Europeans. In 1770,

both Lucas and the Moravians sought her assistance, but the Moravians reached her first. With her new husband Tuglavina, Mikak helped them locate a suitable site for their mission. After the mission at Nain had been established in 1771, Mikak and Tuglavina drifted away from its influence. They separated in 1776, and she had a succession of other husbands. At one time she showed an interest in baptism, but in 1783 she left for south Labrador. In 1795 she became ill and returned to Nain, where she spent the last 10 days of her life. Tuglavina, now a convert, died there three years later.

Mikak's son Tutauk, who called himself Jonathan Palliser, moved back south. When a Methodist missionary met him in Hamilton Inlet in 1824, one of his wives was wearing Mikak's English dress. His descendants still live in Labrador.[3]

John Russell, "Esquimaux Lady," oil on canvas, 1769. Mikak is clothed in a dress given to her by the Dowager Princess of Wales. Völkerkundliche Sammlung der Universität Göttingen, Germany. Photographer: Harry Haase.

Revolution Rejected?

Historians have spent considerable energy exploring the reasons why Newfoundland, Nova Scotia, and St John's Island failed to join the American Revolution.[4] What caused them to remain in the British orbit?

In the case of Newfoundland, the reasons are clear. Without formal political institutions, Newfoundlanders had no way of entering into an alliance with the rebellious colonies even if they had wanted to—which they did not. Any sympathy they might have had for the American cause was quickly extinguished when, in retaliation against British regulations forbidding New Englanders from fishing in Newfoundland waters, the Americans imposed an embargo on trade with the island. This move caused widespread hardship for Newfoundlanders, who had come to depend on New

Setting the Context

The American Revolution

Following the Seven Years' War, imperial taxation, trade, and military policies led to tensions between Great Britain and 13 of its North American colonies. The Stamp Act (1765), which imposed a tax on printed documents, prompted the creation of local militias in disaffected ports. Calling themselves the Sons of Liberty, the militias began intimidating the colonial officials charged with implementing unpopular taxes and trade regulations. When self-styled "Patriots" disguised as Mohawks boarded three East India Company ships and dumped their cargo of tea into Boston harbour on 16 December 1773, British authorities responded with a series of measures known as the Coercive Acts. The aggrieved colonists dubbed them the Intolerable Acts. In addition to closing the port of Boston, the legislation suspended the Massachusetts legislature, restricted town meetings, and sent in troops under the command of General Thomas Gage.

To coordinate a response, all of Britain's North American colonies except Newfoundland, St John's Island, Nova Scotia, Quebec, and Georgia sent delegates to the First Continental Congress. Meeting in Philadelphia in September 1774, they demanded the repeal of the Coercive Acts. When Great Britain refused to back down, Patriot militias were placed on alert. The first shots in the American Revolutionary War were fired at Lexington, Massachusetts, in April 1775. The following September, a Second Continental Congress voted to raise an army under George Washington to defend "American liberty." In addition to driving the British out of Boston, the Patriots planned to capture Quebec. The invasion of Quebec, launched in the fall of 1775, failed miserably but Washington's army forced British troops to withdraw to Halifax in March 1776.

On 4 July 1776, the rebellious colonies declared their independence, and they fought a long and bitter war to make good their intentions. As one of the most dramatic developments in modern global history, the American Revolution redefined geopolitics and served as a catalyst for similar revolutionary movements elsewhere.[5] The Atlantic region was redefined in the vortex of this extraordinary historical moment.

England for foodstuffs and shipping in the West Indies trade. As a result of the war, the migratory fishery declined, the resident population fell, and misery ensued. American predators at sea made fishing hazardous, especially offshore. In the early years of the war, the poor state of the garrison and the reduced size of the naval squadron was a cause for concern, especially among the merchants whose investments were at risk. As the war dragged on, the British improved the fortifications at St John's and Placentia and reinforced the squadron. A local militia was created in 1778, later named the Royal Newfoundland Regiment, which became an army unit.

It is more difficult to explain why Nova Scotia resisted the continental drift. Its population was dominated by New Englanders, and many of its Scots- and Irish-born residents, along with most Aboriginal people and Acadians, harboured deep resentment against British authorities. In the run-up to the war, sympathy for the Patriot position, which cast King George III and his ministers as agents of tyranny, was widespread. Anthony Henry, the Montbéliard-born publisher of the *Halifax Gazette*, kept his readers informed about the resistance to the Stamp Act, championed its repeal, and lost his job as a result. According to the diarist Simeon Perkins, the good citizens of Liverpool, on the colony's south coast, erupted in two days of drunken celebration on learning of the act's withdrawal in 1766.

As battles raged in Massachusetts in the spring and summer of 1775, the merchant clique in Halifax hinted in communications with London that Nova Scotia might also succumb to rebellion if Governor Francis Legge persisted in his rigorous efforts to root out corruption. Tension in outlying regions escalated when the Halifax-dominated Assembly passed a militia bill and imposed a tax on land to support it. In response, "committees of safety" were established in Sunbury and Cumberland counties and in the Cobequid townships to mobilize opposition to the militia policy and to correspond with Patriot leaders in Massachusetts. Legge dispatched Captain John Stanton to the Annapolis Valley to gauge the mood of the people there, but his findings brought the governor little comfort. Their principles, he reported, were "Republican"; their greatest wish was that "the Rebels of New Hampshire and New England [might] invade this Province in the . . . Spring"; and their only fear was that "by mistake" they might join "the weaker Party & suffer [defeat] with them accordingly."[6]

Legge declared martial law in December 1775 and tried to mobilize rural militias for the defence of the capital, whose garrison had been depleted to support Gage's campaign in Boston. Few men in the townships responded to the call of duty, in part because their own communities were now under siege. In the autumn of 1775 the Continental Congress began licensing ship captains to plunder, burn, or sell at auction vessels taking munitions and supplies to British forces in Boston. The number of authorized privateer vessels cruising the Atlantic coast grew dramatically during the war, and ships sailing under the British flag became targets.[7] Even worse, freebooters out of Machias, Maine, cruised the Bay of Fundy in the summer of 1775, inspiring fear in coastal communities and trashing Fort Frederick at the mouth of the St John River. Halifax Harbour was sufficiently well protected to be spared attack, but Charlottetown was looted in November and the colony's acting governor, Phillips Callbeck, was taken prisoner. The war at sea quickly commanded the attention of everyone living in the Atlantic region.

In February 1776 the Council finally rescinded the unpopular militia legislation, and in May Legge sailed to London to answer charges levelled against him by his enemies in Halifax. The governor's departure removed the focus of grievance, and the administrator in his absence, Commodore Mariot Arbuthnot, encouraged harmony by fraternizing with members of the Assembly, visiting outlying communities, and refusing to take harsh measures even when they might have been war-ranted. In the summer of 1776, the Royal Fencible American Regiment, raised locally by Joseph Goreham to serve as a home guard, was installed at Fort Cumberland to keep an eye on troubling developments in the Chignecto region.

Nova Scotia's loyalism was reinforced by British legislation, passed in March 1775, excluding the rebellious colonies from the bank fisheries. As a result, a few New England fishermen and merchants moved to Nova Scotia ports, in effect becoming the colony's first Loyalist immigrants. Another 1,100 Loyalists arrived in Halifax in April 1776 aboard the ships that evacuated Gage's army from Boston. Although New York became the headquarters for the British military later in the summer, Halifax continued to play a supporting role in the transshipment of soldiers, prisoners, provisions, and war matériel. Had Halifax succumbed to the revolutionary spirit, the colony might well have been lost, but the mercantile community there thrived on government contracts and never seriously considered taking on the military establishment, even when it was represented by no more than 100 soldiers. Oceanic, commercial, and naval in its orientation, Halifax remained firmly fixed in the British Atlantic world.[8]

Nova Scotia in Question

The failure of the Quebec campaign, together with the British occupation of New York in the summer of 1776, discouraged Washington from invading Nova Scotia, but the threat of rebellion in outlying districts remained high. Within a week of the declaration of independence, the Massachusetts Council met with a delegation of Mi'kmaq and Wolastoqiyik in Watertown, on the outskirts of Boston, where they signed a treaty of "Alliance and Friendship." Washington hoped that Aboriginal allies would do his fighting in the northeast, but the delegates could not bind their people to such an agreement. Unwilling to commit themselves to either side, the Passamaquoddy and Mi'kmaq rejected the treaty, and the Wolastoqiyik were divided.

This response greatly disappointed Jonathan Allan and Jonathan Eddy, two dissident former members of the Assembly from the Chignecto area, who tried to organize an attack on Fort Cumberland. In the face of Aboriginal neutrality and Patriot inattention, Allan felt that the campaign should be postponed, but Eddy persevered. Gathering up what support he could muster in Machias, Passamaquoddy, and Maugerville, Eddy and his "army"—some 72 men, including 16 Wolastoqiyik—proceeded to their destination in canoes and whaleboats. Efforts to recruit locally brought Eddy more disappointment, netting 21 Acadians, 4 Mi'kmaq, and about 100 settlers from Chignecto, Cobequid, and Pictou. After a month-long siege, during which local inhabitants showing loyalist sympathies were harassed by Eddy's poorly disciplined recruits, the attackers were put on the run by a company of Royal Marines from Halifax on 27 November. Authorities moved quickly to suppress dissent. Nova Scotians in rebellious areas were required to take an oath of allegiance and a few prominent men perceived to be contravening wartime regulations and counselling sedition were hauled into court.

Eddy's campaign may have failed, but insurgents remained active. In May 1777 John Allan, now a colonel in the Continental Army with responsibility for "Eastern Indians," led about 100 men from Machias to the St John River, making his headquarters at the Wolastoqkew community of Aukpaque. This was meant to be the initial move in an invasion of 3,000 soldiers authorized by Congress, but the arrival of a contingent of Royal Fencibles from Halifax forced Allan's militia and his Aboriginal allies to retreat and the invasion to be called off. In November 1777 Fort Howe was constructed at the mouth of the St John River, and Nova Scotia's former lieutenant governor, Michael Francklin, was ordered to secure Aboriginal allegiance. This proved to be a daunting challenge. After the American victory at Saratoga in the fall of 1777, France (and ultimately Spain) joined the war on the side of the United States, renewing Aboriginal memories of happier alliances. A Wolastoqkew threat to Fort Howe in 1778 and sporadic Mi'kmaw attacks on settlers in the Miramichi area underscored the fragility of British control.

Determined to prevail, Francklin arranged a meeting at the mouth of the St John River early in the summer of 1780 to follow up on peace agreements concluded the previous year. He reported to have assembled "three hundred fighting men besides six hundred women and children" to meet with delegates from "the Ottawas, Hurons, Algonkins, Abenakis and other nations from Canada," who promised to wage war against any Mi'kmaq or Wolastoqiyik aligned with the Americans.[9] This intimidation tactic seemed to work, but it remained unclear which side Aboriginal people—or many settlers—would have supported if the United States and France had attacked Nova Scotia.

Fortunately for those responsible for keeping Nova Scotia in the imperial fold, a full-scale invasion failed to materialize, and continuing attacks by sea reduced support for the Patriots. Liverpool, Lunenburg, and Annapolis Royal were trashed in the course of the war, and even George Cartwright's trading posts in Sandwich Bay were plundered. In September 1777 the American naval commander John Paul Jones menaced the British coal mines at Spanish Harbour (now Sydney) and raided the fisheries at Île Madame and Canso, where he seized local seamen to fill vacancies among his crew. Captains of British naval vessels also tried to press Nova Scotia seamen into service, a practice that became legal in the colonies in 1775. After riots over impressment erupted in Halifax in 1779, press gangs were prohibited from operating on shore, but colonials remained vulnerable to capture from both sides while at sea.

Nova Scotia's western flank became more secure in June 1779, when a British force occupied Penobscot Bay, establishing a base at Castine. By that time most of the fighting had moved to the central and southern states. Various plans to invade the northern British colonies were rejected because they might have resulted in a renewed French presence in North America—a prospect that no Patriot would tolerate. French vessels nevertheless remained a menace to shipping until the end of the war. In July 1781, two French frigates engaged a British convoy of 18 vessels in a bruising encounter off Spanish Harbour.

It was in this worrisome context that an evangelical religious revival, led by Henry Alline, a charismatic itinerant preacher from Falmouth, gained momentum in Nova Scotia. Alline's "New Light" message that good Christians should pursue spiritual rather than military battles resonated especially among the New England Planters, who were also comforted by Alline's assertion that they had been rescued by God from the dark clouds hanging over their former homeland. Alline's ministry was short—he began preaching in 1776 and died in 1784—but he laid the foundations of an evangelical tradition that is still strong in many areas of the Maritimes. This tradition was reinforced by the ministry of William Black, Jr, who moved from Yorkshire to the Amherst area as a boy and began his long career as a Methodist preacher in 1781. His message was initially well received in communities settled by fellow Yorkshire immigrants, but he soon gained a wider following. With the American Revolution as their backdrop, Alline and Black helped many Nova Scotians assert their own notions of empowerment to sustain them in apocalyptic times.

The Spirit of 1783

After the victory of American and French forces at Yorktown, Virginia, in October 1781, the British abandoned their continental campaign to concentrate on challenges from France and Spain in the Caribbean, Europe, and India. Guerilla warfare continued on the frontier and in deeply divided communities everywhere in the North American colonies as diplomats in Paris tried to sort out the implications of the Patriot triumph. British negotiators, eager to prevent France from muddying the terms of peace, tended toward leniency, an approach that had significant implications for the Atlantic region.

In the Treaty of Paris (1783), Great Britain recognized the independence of the United States of America, leaving Newfoundland, Nova Scotia, St John's Island, Quebec, and the Hudson's Bay Company territory to form what was left of British North America. The British also agreed to an ill-defined boundary separating Nova Scotia from New England along the St Croix River, relinquishing much of the territory in Maine that their forces had occupied. In yet another significant concession, Americans were allowed to fish in the Gulf of St Lawrence, on the banks, and along the Newfoundland coast outside the French Treaty Shore, and were given the "liberty" to dry fish on the unsettled coasts of Nova Scotia, the Îles de la Madeleine, and Labrador. British negotiators gave some thought to offering free trade to the new United States of America, but the idea was rejected.

In a separate treaty with Britain, France obtained concessions in Newfoundland. The boundaries of the Treaty Shore were moved to Cape St John and Cape Ray, away from the areas where the English now fished, and an appended declaration, while avoiding the word "exclusive," in effect defined the shore as a French fishing zone. Saint-Pierre and Miquelon were returned to France without the deeply resented conditions of 1763, but it was agreed that the islands would never become "an object of jealousy," meaning that they would not be fortified.

The American Revolution was a defining moment in the history of the Atlantic region, firmly fixing it in the British Empire. While the war launched the United States on the road to democratic republicanism, it also inspired another experiment in North America, one characterized by constitutional monarchy, centralized government, and humanitarian ideals. Both were ultimately based on liberal principles and rule of law, but the second evolved in the context of an expanding British Empire, which hardly skipped a beat after the loss of the Thirteen Colonies. What separated the Atlantic region—and ultimately Canada—from the United States was not the rejection of liberalism—an ideology that continues to be debated and to evolve throughout the North Atlantic world—but loyalism.[10]

The Loyalists and Postwar Reconstruction

As a result of the American Revolution, the population of Nova Scotia more than doubled. Loyalists began moving to the British-controlled colony before hostilities had been officially declared, but most of them arrived between 1782 and 1784 on fleets departing from New York, Charleston, and Savannah, where refugees had gathered under British protection during the war. Still others found their way to Nova Scotia from Great Britain, Florida, the Bahamas, Jamaica, and other sites of refuge. As David Bell has argued, the Loyalists left the United States because they could not stay. Patriotic zeal in the wake of the war made it impossible for most Loyalists to recoup their losses or even return to their home communities for fear of violence, imprisonment, or death.[11]

The Loyalists represented a thick slice of North American society and greatly increased cultural diversity in the Maritimes. Along with a few elite families, the mix included farmers, labourers, and artisans, and a wide range of ethnic groups. Colonials of Dutch and Huguenot ancestry, free and enslaved African-Americans, and people who by religious conviction were pacifists swelled the Loyalist numbers. A significant proportion of the migrants were soldiers of all ranks. During the war about 19,000 men from the colonies fought in what were known as "Provincial" regiments. They became eligible for land grants in Nova Scotia, as did many of the regular British, Irish, Hessian, and Waldecker soldiers discharged from service when the war ended. Although the Loyalists had few good words for "Nova Scarcity," they were luckier than many refugee peoples. The British government supplied provisions and temporary shelter, compensated some of them for their losses, and provided most with free land.

The tsunami of Loyalist immigrants swamped the old colony of Nova Scotia and posed enormous administrative challenges. Arriving to take up his new post in the fall of 1782, Governor John Parr moved quickly to escheat unoccupied land and to carve out townships for the Loyalists, but bottle-necks inevitably occurred in arranging food, shelter, and land grants. Chaotic conditions generated much grumbling, some genuine hardship, and occasionally bitter conflict. Surveyor general Charles Morris, Jr, was especially hard-pressed, describing his experience in getting the Loyalists settled on their land as "next to Egyptian Slavery."[12]

Nearly 15,000 Loyalists landed at the mouth of the St John River, engulfing the tiny population already living there and founding the city of Saint John, which received its charter in 1785. Further up the river, Wolastoqiyik and Acadians were pushed off their land, the former onto reserves, most of the latter to Madawaska. Even more Loyalists—approximately 19,000—went to peninsular Nova Scotia. A majority of them settled in Shelburne, which for a time became the largest city in British North America. When it failed to develop into the prosperous trading port they had expected, most of the Loyalists drifted away. Some moved back to the United States when they judged it safe to do so. Others went to Quebec and still others to Halifax, Saint John, and the scores of smaller communities established by other Loyalists.

About 500 Loyalists settled in Cape Breton, created as a separate colony largely on the strength of Abraham Cuyler's unsuccessful scheme to attract 5,000 Loyalists from Quebec. A native of New York, Cuyler hoped to become governor of the new colony, but the position went instead to the now famous cartographer J.F.W. DesBarres. Early in the winter of 1784, DesBarres arrived at Spanish Harbour to establish the new capital—named, like its Australian counterpart, after Lord Sydney, President of the Board of Trade and Plantations. DesBarres recruited 120 settlers from England, who vied with the Loyalists in the capital for access to provisions and offices. The small number of the colony's inhabitants, many of them Roman Catholic Acadians and Mi'kmaq, provided an excuse for authorities to delay calling an assembly, leaving the appointed officials in Sydney to squabble among themselves. St John's Island also attracted about 500 Loyalists, most of them members of disbanded regiments. Although few Loyalists were interested in what Newfoundland had to offer, some were later attracted to opportunities in St John's, among them John Ryan and his son Michael, who moved from Saint John to establish the *Royal Gazette and Newfoundland Advertiser* in 1807.

New Brunswick attracted a significant number of elite Loyalists, who hoped to make the new colony "the envy of the American states," a model of order and hierarchy in contrast to the democratic anarchy they expected to engulf their neighbours to the south.[13] Concluding that the

Historical Focus

The Black Loyalists

During the war, the British encouraged slaves to leave their Patriot masters by promising them their freedom if they joined the British cause. At least 20,000 did so. In an effort to prevent black Loyalists from being re-enslaved by their aggrieved former masters, Sir Guy Carleton, who presided over the Loyalist evacuation, established a board made up of four British and three American commissioners to determine the legitimacy of black Loyalist claims. The names and demographic details of those appearing before the board in New York were recorded in "The Book of Negroes." Those who managed to establish their status were issued a certificate of freedom, most of them signed by Brigadier General Samuel Birch.

Of the more than 3,000 black Loyalists who settled in Nova Scotia, nearly half initially went to Shelburne. Driven to the opposite side of the harbour by white settlers, they founded Birchtown, where they struggled to farm the rocky soil allotted to them. Religion helped to sustain them in their difficult circumstances. Many of the Birchtown residents were Methodists under the pastoral care of Moses Wilkinson, a former slave who was blind from birth. A persuasive preacher, he inspired Boston King and John Ball to take up the ministry. More controversial was the Baptist David George. His impassioned preaching attracted some white as well as black settlers, but his Baptist message was too radical for more conventional Christians, even in Birchtown. (The Baptist insistence that religious belief should be a matter of "free will" and individual choice—exemplified in the practice of adult rather than infant baptism—was widely perceived as encouraging republicanism.) David George was repeatedly threatened with violence, as were many other blacks, both slave and free. In the summer of 1784 Shelburne erupted in a nasty race riot as disbanded soldiers attacked black labourers competing for wage-paying work.

Prejudice dogged black Loyalists wherever they went. Usually forced to live in segregated areas, they received smaller grants of land than white settlers—if they received any land at all—and were often denied provisions. Their communities, among them Brindley Town, Preston, and Little Tracadie, were defined by wretchedness. The Church of England established separate schools, staffed primarily by black teachers, but literacy remained secondary to survival. When wheat blight stuck Nova Scotia in 1791, the black settlers suffered terribly. Other than poverty and violent attacks, the biggest threat was re-enslavement, a fate experienced by a number of free men and women in Nova Scotia and New Brunswick.

The dream of a "promised land," where they could escape prejudice, own property, and live independently, had inspired black Loyalists to settle in Nova Scotia, but that dream turned into a nightmare for most of them. In 1792 nearly 1,200 black Loyalists, led by Thomas Peters, moved to Sierra Leone with the assistance of anti-slavery activists in Great Britain. Those who remained laid the foundations for a significant black population in the Maritime region. Despite continuing challenges, the black Loyalists left a legacy of literacy, religious conviction, and self-help in both the Maritimes and Sierra Leone, where the story of their particular war for independence remains an essential component of the collective historical memory.

Continued

In 1796 approximately 550 black freedom fighters from Jamaica, known as "Maroons," were deported to Nova Scotia after they had lost the most recent battle in their 140-year war against the British. They were immediately put to work building fortifications in Halifax, but within a few years they, too, had departed for Sierra Leone.

The more than 1,200 slaves who arrived with the Loyalist migration were denied the option of moving to Africa. With slavery under attack by humanitarians throughout the North Atlantic world, it gradually disappeared in the Atlantic region. The British Parliament abolished the slave trade in 1807, and an act to free slaves throughout the British Empire was passed in 1833 to take effect on 1 August 1834, henceforth celebrated as Emancipation Day.[14]

A black labourer in Shelburne, 1788; watercolour by William Booth. Library and Archives Canada/NAC-40162.

city of Saint John was both too crass and too close to the American border, Governor Thomas Carleton chose Fredericton—formerly Pointe-Sainte-Anne—as the capital of what he hoped would become a stable agricultural society led by a landholding gentry. Not surprisingly, the pretensions of the Loyalist elite were not well received by the mass of the refugees. In the 1785 election, some of the inhabitants of Saint John violently protested the condescension and corruption of the government based in Fredericton.

Loyalists were also politically active in Nova Scotia, where the smug Halifax elite were slow to offer the newcomers appointments to the Council and other high offices. Consequently, Loyalists became leading voices of the opposition in the Assembly. Governor Parr accused them of promoting republican principles—a common put-down for anyone challenging appointed officials. The Loyalists finally triumphed when Sir John Wentworth, the former governor of New Hampshire, replaced Parr in 1792. While the Loyalist elite in Halifax revelled in the court-like atmosphere surrounding the Wentworths, the pioneer experience had a levelling effect, and Loyalist roots counted for little in other parts of a colony where, after 1783, nearly everyone claimed to have supported the British cause.

View of Saint John, New Brunswick, 1814, by Joseph Brown Comingo. New Brunswick Museum, NB, Canada.1966.100A

In close contact with both Great Britain and the United States, the Loyalists contributed to the development of new cultural orientations. Elite families tried to maintain a high level of gentility, practising good manners, hosting fancy-dress balls, and establishing voluntary organizations devoted to sociability and intellectual improvement.[15] Throughout the settling-in process, they produced poems, essays, and sermons, wrote letters and kept diaries, and were avid readers of British fiction and advice books. In 1789, John Howe, a Loyalist from Massachusetts, and William Cochran, a Church of England clergyman and classical scholar, attempted to provide a forum for colonial writers. Their *Nova Scotia Magazine*, published in Halifax, lasted less than two years, but it ranks as the first literary journal in the British North American colonies. Although little is known about Lunenburg-born artist Joseph Brown Comingo, he worked extensively throughout Nova Scotia and New Brunswick, finding a market for his portraits and landscapes among those who could afford them.

Making Adjustments

In the wake of the American Revolution, the British government tried to strengthen the authority of the Crown and to create a hierarchical class system in the Maritime colonies. The Church of England was expected to play an important role in achieving these goals. In 1787 Charles Inglis, the former rector of Trinity Church in New York, was consecrated the first bishop of Nova Scotia, with jurisdiction over all the British North American colonies, including Newfoundland and Bermuda.

Document

Edward Winslow's Plan for a "Gentlemanlike" Colony, 1783

When the American Revolution began in 1775, 29-year-old Edward Winslow was a young man with great prospects. He was a Harvard graduate, a descendant of one of the founders of Massachusetts Bay colony, and the only son of a prominent New England family with valuable estates in the Plymouth area. In the tensions leading to the war, Edward actively supported the British cause, and during the war he was based in New York as muster master general of the colonial troops that fought alongside the British. The success of the Patriots left Edward and his family nearly destitute. Without the resources to establish themselves in England, Edward, his mistress Mary Simmonds, their three children, and their slaves moved to Nova Scotia early in 1783.

From the St John River on 7 July 1783, Winslow wrote the following letter to his friend Ward Chipman in New York. The letter reveals much about the attitudes of elite Loyalists faced with beginning life over again on the colonial frontier. Not surprisingly, Winslow and Chipman were strong advocates of a separate colony north of the Bay of Fundy where they might seek the government positions denied them in Halifax.

We have just begun our operations in the land way—the people who have arrived here are prodigiously pleased with the country—& I shall certainly soon be [possessed] of a good farm, and if we've our half pay I will be more than comfortable.—I have left those sweet little ones in as comfortable a place, as is in this province made so by my own exertions—I found a house & hired it for £6 a year & I've taken a lease for two years—I added two rooms—& a chimney & have now a spare bed-room at your service 'tis just on the bank of a most beautiful river immediately opposite the town of Annapolis.—I have left Thomson's William . . . . to superintend & Mother Silk & little George, we have plenty of poultry a good garden & such a variety of fish as you never saw & I have built a tolerable boat. So much for the family.

. . . I am determined at all events to distinguish myself by proposing a plan which affords the grandest field for speculation that ever offered.—take the general map of this province (even as it's now bounded) observe how detached this part is from the rest—how vastly extensive it is—notice the rivers—harbours &c. consider the numberless inconveniences that must arise—from [its] remoteness from the metropolis [Halifax] & the difficulty of communication.—Think what multitudes have & will come here—and then judge whether it must not from the nature of things—immediately become a separate government, & if it does it shall be the most Gentlemanlike one on earth. Suppose you & he go to England after being provided with the necessary facts—can you be better employed than in a solicitation of this kind—properly authorized. You know how Industrious I can be if I please—& you may rest assured that I will pursue this project with unremitted attention.—the people on the other side are already jealous—even the [Governor] fears it evidently. . . .[16]

The Society for the Propagation of the Gospel helped to pay the salaries of clergymen and the cost of building churches and schools. Inglis supported the founding of King's College in Windsor in 1788 as an exclusive institution for the sons of the Church of England elite, and the Provincial Academy of Arts and Sciences in Fredericton, which received its charter as the College of New Brunswick in 1800. Despite all its efforts, the Church of England in the Maritimes steadily lost adherents to the Baptists and Methodists, whose ministers promised ordinary people personal salvation and spiritual equality. Many of the sanctions against Roman Catholics, including laws that had excluded them from voting, acquiring land, and worshipping in public, were abolished in the Maritime colonies, but Catholics were still denied the right to sit in assemblies.

The American Revolution forced changes in customary trade patterns in the Atlantic region. Since the Navigation Acts curtailed legal trade with the United States and Americans had the right to fish in the region, clandestine trade became widespread. Although merchants in the colonies tried to replace New England in the triangular West Indies trade, they were initially bested by the Americans who now were free of imperial regulations and enthusiastically defied them. Newfoundlanders increasingly looked to other sources of foodstuffs, especially in the Maritimes and the Canadas. A shipbuilding industry grew on the island, and a Newfoundland-based fleet, managed largely by merchants recently arrived from Greenock, Scotland, traded to the mainland and Caribbean.

After the war, the winter population in Newfoundland recovered and began to grow steadily, with residents taking an increasing proportion of the total cod catch as migratory activity declined. The naval state continued, with the court system becoming more elaborate over time. A government house was built in the early 1780s, a supreme court was established in 1791, and civilians began to join naval officers as surrogate magistrates. It was a practical and reasonably effective system of government. The navy also contributed to religious life, since its chaplains were active on shore as well as on board their vessels, at least among Protestants. As in the Maritimes, the Church of England clergy were supported by the Society for the Propagation of the Gospel. Most immigrants from England belonged to the established church, but Protestant dissenters were gaining ground. Beginning in 1766 the Reverend Laurence Coughlan preached Methodism on the north shore of Conception Bay with considerable success, and in St John's dissenters attended John Jones's Congregational "Dissenting Church of Christ."

For the merchants in Newfoundland, both Protestant and Roman Catholic, the growing numbers of Irish represented a threat to public order, especially if they were under the influence of itinerant Irish priests, some of whom were politically radical. As a result, Irish merchants petitioned for the appointment of a bishop and agreed to pay his salary. A proclamation of 1784 established religious freedom in Newfoundland, and in the same year the conservative Father James O'Donnel arrived as prefect apostolic (he would become bishop in 1796) to bring some order to the Irish Roman Catholic community.

Between 1783 and 1803 nearly 17,000 Highland Scots immigrated to the Maritimes, most of them settling on St John's Island (renamed Prince Edward Island in 1798) and in Cape Breton and eastern Nova Scotia. One of the most ambitious settlement schemes was sponsored by the Earl of Selkirk, who in 1803 brought 800 Highlanders to the Orwell–Point Prim area of Prince Edward Island. On the Miramichi, a Scottish timber and shipbuilding company, Fraser and Thom, recruited Scottish labourers. Highlanders tended to be Gaelic-speaking Roman Catholics, whereas Lowland Scots were more likely to be English-speaking Presbyterians and to place strong emphasis

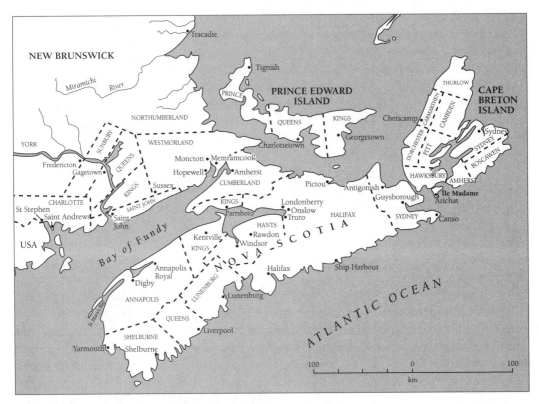

The Maritime colonies, c. 1800. Adapted from R. Cole Harris, ed., *Historical Atlas of Canada I: From the Beginning to 1800* (Toronto: University of Toronto Press, 1987), Plates 25 and 32.

on education. Two immigrant Presbyterian ministers, James MacGregor and Thomas McCulloch, helped to make Pictou, Nova Scotia, a religious and educational centre.

Like Scotland, Ireland was experiencing major social and economic upheavals. Conditions worsened when, in response to Irish unrest during the French Revolutionary War, the British Parliament passed the Act of Union in 1801, incorporating Ireland into Great Britain. Repression of Roman Catholics, along with periodic famines among a poor tenant population dependent on the potato for survival, contributed significantly to the stream of immigrants to the Atlantic region. While Irish Protestants quickly assimilated into the dominant culture, Roman Catholics remained distinct, separated by religion, history, and in many cases their Gaelic language. Irish Catholics swelled the population of southeastern Newfoundland outports, became tenant farmers on Prince Edward Island estates, cut New Brunswick forests, and worked as domestic servants. In the major port cities such as St John's, Halifax, and Saint John, the Irish quickly came to constitute a significant portion of the population. The desperate condition of many among them inspired their philanthropic compatriots to found a Charitable Irish Society in Halifax in 1776 and similar organizations in Saint John and St John's in the first decade of the nineteenth century.

For the Mi'kmaq and Wolastoqiyik these waves of migration represented another threat to their survival as more territory fell into private hands and competition for fish and game increased. Recognizing their vulnerability, Aboriginal leaders petitioned for land, sometimes successfully, but much of it was stolen by squatters who knew that the authorities would not take action against them. In 1783 Chief John Julien obtained a licence of occupation for 20,000 acres (8,100 hectares) on the Miramichi River. When the government finally got around to establishing the Eel Ground Reserve in 1808, it was half that size. No formal reserves were established on Prince Edward Island, but the Mi'kmaq eventually received permission from proprietor James Montgomery to live on the barren and rocky Lennox Island, off the north coast.

The French Revolutionary and Napoleonic Wars

Like earlier conflicts, the French Revolutionary and Napoleonic Wars had a profound and lasting impact on the Atlantic region. British demand for fish, foodstuffs, and timber skyrocketed, and, with alternative sources of supply cut off, the Atlantic colonies found ready markets for their resources. The Navigation Acts and the whole framework of mercantilist regulation that gave colonial producers preference in British markets over their foreign competitors further stimulated production. With the demand for primary resources high and money pouring in to pay for defence against a possible French attack, colonials found themselves in a privileged and profitable position.

For the most part free from invading armies, the Atlantic colonies were nevertheless vulnerable. The citizens of St John's organized a militia to supplement the garrison, the Royal Newfoundland Regiment was revived, and fortifications were strengthened. In September 1796 a French naval squadron—having sunk every British vessel it could find on the Grand Banks—attempted a raid on St John's. It withdrew when the harbour appeared to be effectively defended (it was not) to loot and burn Bay Bulls and Witless Bay instead. The French then descended on Saint-Pierre (in British hands since 1793) and southern Labrador. It proved to be the last of the many French raids on Newfoundland and its fisheries.

Fearing the influence of the Society of United Irishmen (which sought Irish independence) and French revolutionary ideas, British authorities questioned the loyalty of many of Newfoundland's Irish inhabitants. When 19 of the Newfoundland Regiment's soldiers attempted an uprising in 1800, using the United Irish cry of "Liberty or Death," they were rounded up—with Bishop O'Donnel's approval—and severely punished. Eight were executed.

As Great Britain's primary naval base in North America during the war, Halifax hummed with activity. Haligonians thrilled to the presence of the king's son, Prince Edward Augustus, and his French mistress, Julie de St-Laurent, who resided in the city from 1794 to 1800. As commander of the British forces in the Maritime region, Prince Edward attempted to improve Halifax's defences and to impose strict military discipline, which included parading the garrison every morning at 5 a.m. Struck by the miserable state of the town's public buildings, he was instrumental in the construction of three exquisite round structures: St George's Anglican Church, the Old Town Clock, and the Prince's Lodge Rotunda. In November 1798, British authorities approved the proposal to rename St John's Island after him.

For many years the British had reserved great stands of timber in North America to supply the Royal Navy. When Baltic resources were cut off by Napoleon, forests in the Maritimes came under intense exploitation. Exports of fir and pine from New Brunswick, Britain's pre-eminent "timber colony," increased more than twentyfold between 1805 and 1812.[17] Businessmen, many of them based in Greenock, brought their capital, labour, and technology to the shores of the Miramichi and St John rivers, and shipbuilding soon developed as a sideline of the timber trade. By 1815 New Brunswick's economy was dominated by forest-based industries.

During the two decades of war, vessels from the Maritimes began competing successfully with New Englanders in the carrying trade to the West Indies, where the sugar plantations represented a lucrative market. Halifax in particular emerged as a significant entrepôt for produce shipped under convoy to the Caribbean. The enhanced British naval and military presence in the region generated unprecedented market opportunities, increased the supply of hard currency, and opened careers in the army and navy to ambitious young men.

Newfoundland was transformed by the war with France. St John's acquired a mercantile society, a newspaper, a constabulary, and a fire brigade, and emerged as the capital of Newfoundland, now a colony in all but name and constitutional status. The long period of warfare nearly killed the English migratory fishery, and the bye-boatmen completely disappeared. As a result, the resident fishery expanded and the permanent population increased to more than 20,000. Although the settlers were not prosperous, they were adept at exploiting the island's potential. Locally grown potatoes joined fish as a staple of settler diets, and in the 1790s, for the first time, schooners from Conception Bay and other areas began to pursue the spring seal fishery. It rapidly became an important feature of the local economy, and in good years a lucrative one. Fish prices were low during the 1790s, but climbed thereafter. During the War of 1812, Newfoundland fish producers enjoyed a monopoly in Spain and Portugal, while continuing to supply the Italian and West Indian markets. Fish prices climbed to unprecedented levels, producing a few fortunes and attracting migrants, mainly from Ireland.

The War of 1812

The war with France led to friction between Great Britain and its former North American colonies. When the United States sought to remain neutral and trade with both sides, Britain insisted on a strict definition of the rights of neutral countries, one that could be backed up with sea power. President Thomas Jefferson responded in 1807 with an embargo on trade with all belligerents, a policy that not only hurt American exporters but also so threatened to cripple the British war effort. Britain retaliated by declaring Halifax, Shelburne, Saint John, and St Andrews to be "free ports"—a clever manoeuvre that served to keep the British army and navy supplied with American produce while making the designated ports thriving commercial centres.

Great Britain's impressment policies escalated tensions with the United States to the breaking point.[18] Determined to maintain its wartime complement of more than 100,000 sailors, the Royal Navy became notorious for sending press gangs into seaport towns at home and abroad and boarding vessels at sea to force sailors into service. Between 1793 and 1811, the British impressed more than 12,000 alleged deserters from American vessels. American outrage reached new heights in June 1807 when the British warship *Leopard* opened fire on the *USS Chesapeake* off the coast of Virginia, killing or wounding 24 men and capturing four alleged deserters, who were taken to Halifax for trial. Although all four of the prisoners had served in the British navy, only one was British-born. Jankin Ratford was hanged from the yardarm before the assembled fleet, while the other three remained in prison.

Tensions over impressment, the rights of neutral shipping on the high seas, and Aboriginal policy on the North American frontier finally prompted the United States to declare war against Great Britain in June 1812 and launch attacks against Upper and Lower Canada (present-day Ontario and Quebec).

The HMS *Shannon* leading its prize, the USS *Chesapeake*, into Halifax harbour, 6 June 1813. British pride received a major boost in June 1813, when HMS *Shannon* arrived in Halifax with the infamous USS *Chesapeake* in tow after a brief engagement off Boston harbour. The inscription on this print by Captain R.H. King, RN, reads in part: "As the ships entered the harbour, the men of war manned their yards in honour of the conquerors; the inhabitants crowded to the shore and lined the wharfs and buildings of the town. As they sailed past the assembled crowds, one burst of loud congratulations rose upon the air; but while the *Chesapeake* returned the cheering, an affecting silence distinguished the *Shannon*." J.G. Schetly, artist, 1813; NSA Documentary Art Collection: accession no. 1979-147 no 142.4. Nova Scotia Archives.

As during the Revolutionary War, the region's coasts swarmed with American privateers. Lacking a sizable navy, the United States commissioned more than 500 privateer vessels to attack British shipping. They inflicted considerable damage during the first year of the war, but the Royal Navy usually had the upper hand. With the Atlantic region relatively secure from attack because the leaders of the New England states refused to participate in the war, the 104th (New Brunswick) Regiment of Foot, based in Fredericton, was dispatched on a difficult 700-mile journey overland to Kingston, Upper Canada, in the winter of 1813 to be ready for the spring campaign against the Americans.

Between 1812 and 1814 the Vice Admiralty court in Halifax processed 714 "prizes" taken by Royal Navy vessels and local privateers. St John's also served as a base for prize ships and on one memorable occasion, 30 of them were roped together in the harbour. While historians still debate the military significance of privateering—Royal Navy ships made the majority of captures—there can be no doubt that it helped to line the pockets of ambitious merchants who bought the captured vessels at prize courts and sold their contents at immense profit. The *Liverpool Packet*, the most successful of the privateer vessels, is reputed to have captured enemy prizes worth $1.5 million, greatly enriching its owner, Enos Collins.

The tide of war turned in the summer of 1814. With Napoleon exiled to Elba, Great Britain focused its attention on North America. British troops and freed slaves led by Rear Admiral George

Cockburn attacked Washington in August, burning the White House and other public buildings. A month later, a British army under Sir John Coape Sherbrooke occupied part of the coast of present-day Maine, providing more opportunities for commercial profit. Indeed, the customs duties collected at Castine provided the initial funding of £7,000 for Dalhousie College, a non-denominational institution established in Halifax by Lieutenant-Governor Dalhousie in 1818. Napoleon's escape from Elba brought the War of 1812 to an abrupt end. By the Treaty of Ghent, signed 24 December 1814, both parties agreed to peace and the return of any captured territory. The Battle of Waterloo in June 1815 finally ended Napoleon's military exploits.

Although the war yielded no territorial gains, the Anglo-American Convention of 1818 redefined American fishing rights. Americans were no longer permitted to fish within three marine miles of the Nova Scotia coast, but were granted access to the inshore fisheries of Labrador and large portions of the west and south coasts of Newfoundland. It was not a final settlement, since disputes over the precise meaning of the convention continued for more than 90 years. The boundary of the French Shore, redefined in 1783, was confirmed as running from Cape St John on the northeast coast, around the Northern Peninsula, and down the west coast to Cape Ray; and Saint-Pierre and Miquelon were returned. These concessions remained the cause of persistent and at times bitter disagreements.

Conclusion

As the French Revolutionary and Napoleonic wars came to a weary end, the demand for colonial products declined and prices fell, but the contours of the Atlantic regional economy had been set. Newfoundland had found its niche in the rich fisheries off its shores; New Brunswick in the timber trade and shipbuilding; Prince Edward Island in wheat, root crops, and cattle. Nova Scotia had not only developed the most diversified economy (based on farm, fish, and forest resources) but was also carving a place for itself in the carrying trade to the West Indies and beyond. In every colony, British settlers and culture prevailed.

Further Readings

Brebner, J.B. 1969. *The Neutral Yankees of Nova Scotia* (1937). Toronto: McClelland and Stewart.
Bannister, Jerry. 2003. *The Rule of the Admirals: Laws, Custom, and Naval Government, 1699–1832*. Toronto: University of Toronto Press.
———, and Liam Riordan, eds. 2012. *The Loyal Atlantic: Remaking the British Atlantic in the Revolutionary Era*. Toronto: University of Toronto Press.
Bell, David. 2013. *Loyalist Rebellion in New Brunswick: A Defining Conflict for Canada's Political Culture*. Halifax: Formac.
Bitterman, Rusty. 2006. *Rural Protest on Prince Edward Island from British Colonization to the Escheat Movement*. Toronto: University of Toronto Press.

Bumsted, J.M. 1987. *Land, Settlement and Politics on Eighteenth-Century Prince Edward Island*. Montreal: McGill-Queen's University Press.

Cadigan, Sean T. 1995. *Hope and Deception in Conception Bay: Merchant-Settler Relations in Newfoundland, 1785–1855*. Toronto: University of Toronto Press.

Clarke, Ernest. 1995. *The Siege of Fort Cumberland, 1776: An Episode in the American Revolution*. Montreal: McGill-Queen's University Press.

Condon, Ann Gorman. 1984. *The Loyalist Dream for New Brunswick: The Envy of the American States*. Fredericton: New Ireland Press.

Conrad, Margaret. 1988. *They Planted Well: New England Planters in Maritime Canada*. Fredericton: Acadiensis Press.

Daigle, Jean, ed. 1995. *Acadia of the Maritimes: Thematic Studies*. Moncton, NB: Chaire d'études acadiennes, Université de Moncton.

Gwyn, Julian. 1998. *Excessive Expectations: Maritime Commerce and the Economic Development of Nova Scotia, 1740–1870*. Montreal: McGill-Queen's University Press.

———. 2003. *Frigates and Foremasts: The North American Squadron in Nova Scotia Waters, 1745–1815*. Vancouver: University of British Columbia Press.

Hornsby, Stephen J. 2005. *British Atlantic, American Frontier: Spaces of Power in Early Modern British America*. Hanover: University Press of New England.

Kert, Margaret. 1997. *Prize and Prejudice: Privateering and Naval Prize in Atlantic Canada in the War of 1812*. St John's: International Maritime Economic History Association.

MacKinnon, Neil. 1989. *This Unfriendly Soil: The Loyalist Experience in Nova Scotia, 1783–1791*. Montreal: McGill-Queen's University Press.

MacDonald, M.A. 1990. *Rebels and Royalists: The Lives and Material Culture of New Brunswick's Early English-Speaking Settlers, 1758–1783*. Fredericton: New Ireland Press.

Mancke, Elizabeth. 2004. *The Fault Lines of Empire: Political Differentiation in Massachusetts and Nova Scotia, ca. 1760–1830*. London: Routledge.

Nester, William R. 2014. *The French and Indian War and the Conquest of New France*. Norman: University of Oklahoma Press.

Rawlyk, George. 1968. *Revolution Rejected, 1775–1776*. Scarborough, ON: Prentice-Hall.

Ryan, Shannon. 2012. *A History of Newfoundland in the North Atlantic to 1818*. St. John's: Flanker Press, 2012

Walker, James. 1976, rep. 1992. *The Black Loyalists: The Search for a Promised Land in Nova Scotia and Sierra Leone, 1783–1870*. Toronto: University of Toronto Press.

Whitehead, Ruth Holmes. 2013. *Black Loyalists: Southern Settlers of Nova Scotia's First Free Black Communities*. Halifax: Nimbus.

Wicken, William C. 2012. *The Colonization of Mi'kmaw Memory and History, 1794–1928*. Toronto: University of Toronto Press.

Wright, Esther Clark. 1955. *The Loyalists of New Brunswick*. Wolfville, NS: Wright.

Historical Spotlight

Mercer, Keith. 2010. "Northern Exposure: Resistance to Naval Impressment in British North America, 1775–1815." *Canadian Historical Review* 91, 2 (June): 199–232.

Reid, John. 2004. "Pax Britannica or Pax Indigena? Planter Nova Scotia (1760–1782) and competing Strategies of Pacification." *Canadian Historical Review* 85, 4 (December 2004): 669–93.

Recommended Websites

Atlantic Canada Virtual Archives, "Black Loyalists in New Brunswick, 1783–1854"; "Edward Winslow Letters, 1783–1785"; "Loyalist Women in New Brunswick, 1783–1827"; "Contested Terrain: Aboriginal Land Petitions in New Brunswick, 1786–1878"
http://atlanticportal.hil.unb.ca/acva

Halifax Gazette—Canada's First Newspaper
http://www.novascotia.ca/archives/virtual/gazette

Island to Island: British Immigration to Prince Edward Island, 1763–1870
http://www.gov.pe.ca/cca/index.php3?number=1020743&lang=E

Newfoundland Government, 1730–1815
http://www.heritage.nf.ca/law/gov_1815.html

Nova Scotians in the Age of Slavery and Abolition
http://www.gov.ns.ca/archives/virtual/africanns/

Privateering in the War of 1812
http://www.eighteentwelve.ca/?q=eng/Topic/66/

The War of 1812 in Nova Scotia
http://museum.novascotia.ca/resources/nova-scotia-and-war-1812

Chapter 8

Maturing Colonial Societies, 1815–1860

Let the Frenchman delight in his vine-covered vales,
Let the Greek toast his old classic ground;
Here's the land where the bracing Northwester prevails,
And where jolly Blue Noses abound.[1]

As Joseph Howe's ode to "The Blue Noses" suggests, colonials in the Atlantic region in the first half of the nineteenth century were beginning to express a new confidence in themselves. Expansion in farming, fishing, forestry, and shipbuilding nurtured a prosperous commercial sector, while communities, large and small, sprouted newspapers, churches, schools, and colleges. When Great Britain dismantled the mercantile system in the 1840s, the Atlantic colonies quickly adjusted to free trade. They were also among the first in the British Empire to embrace a limited form of political autonomy known as "responsible government." For some, at least, this period would appear in retrospect as a golden age, when opportunities beckoned and anything seemed possible.

Setting the Context

The Industrial Age

In the early nineteenth century, the entire world felt the effects of the "great transformation" associated with the Industrial Revolution. Fundamental changes in technology and the organization of production not only encouraged new economic arrangements but also laid the groundwork for deep political, social, and intellectual changes that few could escape.[2] As the world's first industrial nation, Great Britain pioneered the application of steam power to machines and machines to production in agriculture, manufacturing, and transportation. The United States was quick to follow and became an industrial giant in its own right in the second half of the nineteenth century.

Mechanization transformed work processes, encouraging the division of labour into repetitive tasks and centralizing production in factories controlled by capitalists who could afford to finance such extensive operations. Labourers lost control of their work to supervisors, while factory owners, if they were successful, reaped profits. As they grew in numbers and wealth,

Continued

capitalists became adept at persuading governments to pass legislation to protect their interests. The communal management of land in the countryside, the guild control of industry in the towns, and the privilege of monopoly were all eventually pushed aside to facilitate the industrial system.

In Europe and the Americas, authoritarian governments and imperial regimes were either toppled or stripped of much of their power as nation-states increasingly came under the influence of the new middle class, which championed political structures that it could dominate. Uprisings in 1830 and again in 1848, many of them fuelled by nationalist and liberal sentiments, rocked European capitals and produced echoes around the world. In the *Communist Manifesto*, published in 1848, Friedrich Engels and Karl Marx urged the workers of the world to unite to throw off the chains of a capitalist system from which only a few benefited. Charles Dickens and Victor Hugo described the victims of the new world order in novels that found many sympathetic readers.

Industrial capitalism cut a wide swath in societies everywhere. It introduced a new ethic of materialism that challenged traditional spiritual values, encouraged the growth of cities at the expense of the countryside, and created a new class structure based on relationship to production rather than heredity. Even more fundamentally, it drove a wedge between the public world of work and the private realm of family and altered the relationship of human beings to their natural environment.

Industrialization also encouraged a new level of self-reliance and individualism. In the face of the limits on state action that were then assumed, voluntary associations emerged to press for a wide range of reforms—among them temperance, literacy, the abolition of slavery, the mitigation of poverty, and the prevention of cruelty to animals and children—and to sponsor religious missions both at home and overseas. Voluntarism in industrializing countries laid the foundations for a vigorous "civil society" where new ideas and practices could be discussed and promoted. Reform became the watchword of the industrial age, which encouraged social innovation and improvement.

People and Place

The international boundary between New Brunswick and the United States remained a source of tension. Although the St Croix River and "highlands" south of the St Lawrence River had been established as the border following the American Revolution, no one was certain which river was the St Croix and the highlands proved difficult to find. A boundary commission eventually agreed on the location of the St Croix River in 1798, when the site of Champlain's ill-fated settlement on an island in the river's mouth was discovered, but the territory on the upper St John River remained in dispute. In the late 1830s tensions over land and river rights in the Aroostook–Madawaska region erupted in violence, prompting Great Britain and the United States to seek a diplomatic resolution.

The boundary question was finally resolved in 1842 by the Webster–Ashburton Treaty, named after the principal negotiators. It ended the uncertainty over the boundary, but it disappointed New Brunswickers because it gave Americans navigation rights on the St John River and left a hump of American-controlled territory between New Brunswick and the united Canadas (formerly Lower Canada and Upper Canada). It also drew an international boundary through the middle of Madawaska Settlement, a primarily Acadian community whose interests were ignored in the negotiating process. In 1851 local inhabitants were further divided when Great Britain settled the boundary dispute between New Brunswick and Canada East (formerly Lower Canada), awarding Lake Témiscouta to the latter. Machias Seal Island and North Rock, two small islands located near Grand Manan, continue to keep the Maine–New Brunswick boundary dispute alive.[3]

Economic and political pressures in Great Britain encouraged emigration to the Atlantic region. Irish (both Protestant and Catholic), Scots, English, and a few Welsh immigrants filled up unsettled areas of the Maritimes. At 45 and 33 per cent respectively, Prince Edward Island and Nova Scotia had the highest proportions of people claiming Scottish ancestry. In Newfoundland emigrants from southeast Ireland moved to the Avalon Peninsula, and settlement began to spread along the south and northeast coasts. The Atlantic colonies no longer attracted many immigrants from the United States, with one exception. Following the War of 1812, 2,400 African-American slaves, offered their freedom if they deserted their owners to join the British cause, moved to the Maritimes. The majority of them settled in Preston and Hammonds Plains in Nova Scotia and Loch Lomond in New Brunswick.

Immigration slowed in the mid-nineteenth century and thereafter population growth depended primarily on natural increase. By 1861 nearly 800,000 people lived in the Atlantic region, up from 200,000 in 1815. Census figures record a mature and relatively stable pre-industrial society: the ratio of men to women was nearly equal, more than half the inhabitants were under the age of 18, and in all of the four colonies 80 per cent or more of the population was native-born. Families were large, averaging seven children, although this statistic masked differences in family size across class and culture. Like other areas of the Western world, the Atlantic region was beginning to reflect the impact of new values that favoured later marriage and smaller families, especially among members of the urban middle class.

Settlers came to the region seeking land and opportunity. Some found one or both, but others had a more difficult time. Like the black Loyalists before them, the African-American refugees faced bureaucratic delays in securing land, and their grants were invariably small and located in less desirable areas. Many settlers from Great Britain were ill-equipped to survive on what was at best marginal land. In remoter settlements only an overgrown graveyard testifies to the hardship and heartbreak that characterized the immigrant experience.

The most tragic episode by far was the arrival of thousands of destitute Irish fleeing the Great Famine that began with the failure of the potato crop in 1845. The Maritimes received only a small percentage of the more than 300,000 Irish who came to British North America between 1846 and 1851, and many of them quickly moved on, but they nevertheless represented a challenge to the port authorities whose job it was to process them. As many as 30,000 destitute and often disease-ridden refugees entered through Partridge Island, the quarantine station at the mouth of the St John River, while others fetched up in Chatham, Charlottetown, Halifax, St Andrews, and other ports connected to the North Atlantic carrying trade. Most of the good agricultural land in the region had been long taken up, and the destitute Irish had to be content with eking out a living either as labourers or as farmers on remote frontiers.

Clearing the land was a daunting task for most immigrants. Slashing and burning their way through the forests, they often set runaway fires that devastated huge areas. Walter Johnstone, a Scottish visitor to Prince Edward Island, remarked in 1820 that the burnt woods around the settlements formed "a scene the most ruinous, confused and disgusting the eye can possibly look upon."[4] In 1825 a fire on the Miramichi consumed more than 2 million hectares of forest and

Table 8.1   Timeline

1814–15	African-American refugees arrive in Nova Scotia and New Brunswick.
1818	John Young writes *Letters to Agricola*.
1820	Cape Breton re-annexed to Nova Scotia; Bank of New Brunswick founded.
1821–3	Thomas McCulloch writes *The Stepsure Letters*.
1822	William Cormack walks across Newfoundland.
1824	Newfoundland achieves colonial status; Julia Catherine Beckwith publishes *St Ursula's Convent*.
1825	Great Miramichi fire.
1826	General Mining Association receives a monopoly of Nova Scotia's mineral wealth.
1829	Death of Shanawdithit; Roman Catholic emancipation.
1832	Representative government adopted in Newfoundland.
1833	British Parliament passes the Act to Abolish Slavery in the British Empire, to take effect in 1834.
1839	The region's first railway line opens between Albion Mines and Pictou.
1840	Samuel Cunard inaugurates the first transatlantic steamship service.
1841	Webster–Ashburton Treaty.
1845	Great Irish famine begins.
1846	Great Britain adopts free trade.
1848	Nova Scotia becomes the first British colony to be granted responsible government. Other Atlantic colonies follow.
1849	Telegraph service comes to Nova Scotia and New Brunswick.
1852	Public schools established in Prince Edward Island.
1854	African United Baptist Association founded in Nova Scotia.
1854–66	Reciprocity Treaty with the United States.
1855	New Brunswick briefly adopts prohibition.
1858	General Mining Association's monopoly abolished.

killed 160 people. Animals also felt the impact of immigration. Moose were wantonly destroyed, primarily for their hides. As early as 1794, the Nova Scotia government passed a law to protect grouse and black duck, both facing extinction. By mid-century the great auk, a large flightless bird that Cartier had observed in vast numbers on the Funk Islands off Newfoundland in the sixteenth century, had become extinct.

A Dark Age for Aboriginal Peoples

Increasing European settlement drove Aboriginal people to new levels of desperation. Their numbers remained low in the first half of the nineteenth century as settler hostility, disease, and poor living conditions took their toll. By 1850 there were no more than 3,000 Mi'kmaq, Wolastoqiyik, and Passamaquoddy living in the Maritimes. Reduced in numbers and in morale, they found it difficult to prevent encroachment on reserve lands.

In the 1830s the Colonial Office began delegating responsibility for Aboriginal policy to the colonies. New Brunswick and Nova Scotia appointed men of considerable integrity—Joseph

"Indian Woman." Christianne Paul Morris, a Mi'kmaq from Halifax, made a good living from her needlework, quillwork, and splint baskets and developed an international reputation for her work. In 1860 her portrait, painted by William Gush, was presented to the Prince of Wales when he visited Halifax. This photograph is thought to show Morris with a miniature quillwork canoe and a small quilled box. W.D. O'Donnell, photographer, ca. 1864. NSA, W.D. O'Donnell Collection, Album 5, page 76. Nova Scotia Archives.

Howe and Abraham Gesner in Nova Scotia and Moses Perley in New Brunswick—as Indian Commissioners, but the story remained the same. In the late 1840s Gesner commented on the unjust exchange between Aboriginal people and newcomers: "in return for the lands for which they were the rightful owners, they have received loathsome diseases, alcoholic drink, the destruction of their game, and threatened extermination."[5]

Gesner's comment reflected a shift in attitude, at least at the official level, towards Aboriginal people. No longer a threat to European dominance, they became the subject of political, philanthropic, and ethnographic interest. In 1856 the Prince Edward Island government finally appointed an Indian commissioner, and with the assistance of the London-based Aborigines' Protection Society it purchased Lennox Island as a reserve in 1870. Although his evangelizing efforts had little impact, the Baptist missionary Silas Rand helped to preserve Mi'kmaq culture by collecting oral history and compiling a Mi'kmaq dictionary. Aboriginal crafts—quill boxes, woven baskets, brooms, and birchbark canoes, in particular—sold well at home and abroad and were sought out by discerning collectors.

Despite predictions to the contrary, the resilient Mi'kmaq, Wolastoqiyik, and Passamaquoddy managed to survive the European presence and adapt to the challenges that confronted them. The hard-pressed Beothuk, in contrast, faced extinction. The spread of commercial cod and salmon fisheries along Newfoundland's northeast coast in the later eighteenth century, and increased trapping, affected them in two ways. Conflict on the coast became more common and the Beothuk were forced to retreat further into the interior, away from the marine resources which had been an essential part of their diet. As a result, their health and living conditions declined. Efforts to make contact with them were often accompanied by violence. In 1819, for example, an expedition captured Demasduit (known to her captors as Mary March) at Red Indian Lake. During the encounter, her husband was killed and her child abandoned. Demasduit herself died of tuberculosis two years later. In 1823, a mother and two daughters were taken by a settler, but only the young Shanawdithit, the last known Beothuk, survived. She died of tuberculosis in 1829.

In the final year of her life, Shanawdithit lived in St John's under the care of William Cormack, president of the recently established "Boeothick Institution." She helped him to develop a Beothuk

Document

Chief Joseph Malli Goes to London, 1842

In 1842 Joseph Malli, Chief of the Mi'kmaq on the Restigouche River in New Brunswick, travelled to England in an effort to persuade the British government to stop incoming settlers from stealing Aboriginal property. His statement said in part:

> When the Superiority over the Territories in which we were born passed out of the hands of the French into those of the British, We—the Mic-Macs of the Restigouche River—were in possession of a Tract of Country, the quiet and undistinguished holding of which was secured to us by a written Deed.—The care of that Deed We entrusted to our Christian Priest.—He lost it. About 50 years ago a white man of the name of Mann came to us,—and asked our leave to build a Hut for him to sleep in when he came to fish—We said "No! If we allow you to build the Hut, you will keep Pigs and Sheep—We Indians have many Dogs—the Dogs will worry the Pigs & Sheep and bad consequences will spring up."—Mann did build his Hut, and we did not use force to expel him from our Reserve.—After some time Mann claimed a large Tract of our Reserve as his own.—We went and complained to the Governor.—The Governor sent three Commissioners [from Québec] to enquire into that Claim. I calculate that it must have been about eighteen years ago, in 1824, that these Commissioners were sent. . . . no portion of our own Lands have been restored to us, nor has any other land been allotted to us.—We remain without redress.[6]

vocabulary and drew pictures depicting the culture of her people as she had known it. Dr William Carson looked after her while she was sick, and described her as "tall and majestic, mild and tractable, but characteristically proud and cautious." After her death, Carson sent her skull and scalp to the Royal Society of Physicians in London—an action he would have thought prudent and responsible. The absent Beothuks continue to haunt the Newfoundland historical imagination.

The Labrador Middle Ground

The story was quite different in Labrador, where the Innu and Inuit outnumbered the small and widely scattered European population. By the 1860s a British "settler" population of some 1,600 lived along the coast from Blanc Sablon to Hamilton Inlet. Many of these people were the children or grandchildren of Aboriginal women and British fur traders and fishermen. In mid-century a clerical visitor remarked that "all the females are either Esquimaux, or mountaineer Indians, or descended from them." The settlers traded with Jersey and West Country firms established in south Labrador, with visiting traders, or with posts in Hamilton Inlet and Lake Melville operated by Quebec merchants. In 1837 these posts were purchased by the Hudson's Bay Company and became part of a chain of posts running through the interior to Ungava Bay, tapping the Innu fur trade. Continuing to lead a migratory life, the Innu travelled to the North Shore, Ungava Bay, or the Labrador coast to trade, and increasingly, to meet Roman Catholic priests. The Oblates of Mary Immaculate arrived in Canada East in the 1840s, and established a mission to the Innu on the North Shore.

North of Cape Harrison, the Moravians, with their mission stations and trading stores, were the most significant European presence. A new station was added at Hebron in 1830. After a religious revival in 1804–5, many Inuit were baptized and adapted their seasonal round so that they could

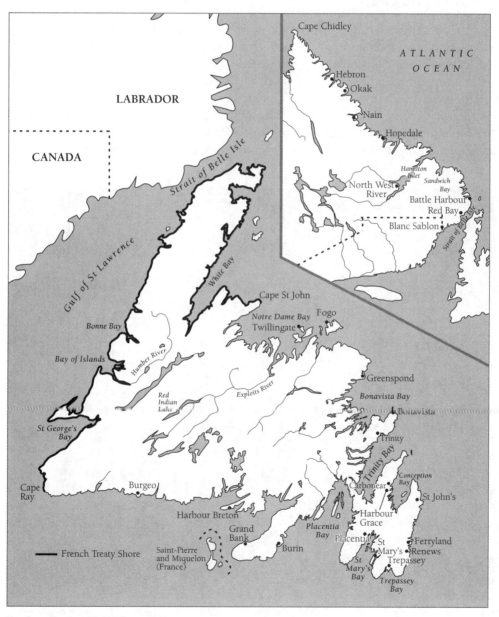

Newfoundland and Labrador, c. 1840.

spend much of the time between Christmas and Easter near the missionaries. The mission stations also provided schools—where children were taught in Inuktitut—and rudimentary medical care. The Hudson's Bay Company broke the Moravian trade monopoly after 1850, and during the early 1860s the isolation of northern Labrador was further disturbed by the arrival of migratory fishing schooners ("floaters") from Newfoundland each summer.

Colonial Economies

In the first half of the nineteenth century, settler society in the Atlantic region was buoyed by an increasingly productive commercial economy. A postwar recession caused hardship for rich and poor alike, but by the 1820s conditions began to improve. The colonial staples—fish, foodstuffs, and timber—found markets in an expanding global economy, while shipbuilding, financed by British and colonial capitalists, emerged as a major industry.

The success of the shipping and shipbuilding industries in the Atlantic region between 1850 and 1878 has become the stuff of legend and a source of local pride. In this period the four colonies accounted for as much as 72 per cent of the tonnage registered in British North America, which

Courtney Bay, New Brunswick, c. 1860. Many of the region's sailing ships were launched from this harbour, near East Saint John, including the famed *Marco Polo*. Provincial Archives of New Brunswick George Taylor fonds: P5-360.

Historical Focus

A Communications Revolution

In the mid-nineteenth century, people throughout the world were engulfed by a revolution in communications and transportation. Three new technologies—steamships, railways, and telegraph lines—quickened the pace of life and brought people in the Atlantic colonies and elsewhere closer together.

Although these technologies were pioneered in Great Britain and the United States, the Atlantic colonies contributed to their advancement. Halifax native Samuel Cunard was an early promoter of steamships, and in 1830 he joined forces with merchants in Quebec City to run a mail service between the two port cities. This consortium also sponsored the *Royal William*, which in 1833 made one of the first Atlantic crossings under steam, taking 25 days to make the trip from Pictou, Nova Scotia, to Gravesend, England. In 1839 Cunard succeeded in capturing the contract for mail delivery between Great Britain and North America. The first scheduled steamer arrived in Halifax on 17 July 1840, with Cunard on board, and then sailed to Boston, where the merchant prince of steam received an enthusiastic welcome.

By this time railways, the wonder of the age, were promising to overcome the limits of land-based travel and bring prosperity to those communities fortunate enough to be located near them. The General Mining Association built the region's first rail line in 1839 to carry coal from Albion Mines (now Stellarton) to Pictou harbour. Four years earlier, in one of the first railway ventures anywhere in the world, capitalists in St Andrews and Quebec City hatched a plan to build a line connecting the two cities. The project drew angry protests from Washington, which saw the initiative as pre-empting the still-disputed territory between New Brunswick and Maine. By the time the boundary was settled, other ambitious cities, including Saint John and Portland, Maine, had staked their claims to become the termini of continental railway lines. Construction on the St Andrews line finally began in 1847, but the project was abandoned in the backwoods of New Brunswick when its promoters ran out of money in 1863.

The electric telegraph was the e-mail of the nineteenth century, dramatically increasing the speed of communication. After successful testing by its American inventor Samuel Morse in 1844, telegraphic communication developed quickly. Frederic Newton Gisborne, a Montreal-based promoter, persuaded the Nova Scotia government in 1848 to construct a telegraph line from Halifax to Amherst as part of his plan to improve telegraph communications between the colonies. In his position as superintendent of the Nova Scotia's telegraph lines, he urged the extension of the telegraph to St John's. With the blessing of the Newfoundland government, Gisborne completed a remarkable survey of a route along the island's south coast, travelling with Mi'kmaq and white companions. In 1852 he connected New Brunswick and Prince Edward Island by the first undersea cable in North America. When his money ran out, he obtained financial backing from New York financier Cyrus W. Field to undertake an even more ambitious project: to lay an undersea cable across the Atlantic.[8]

Field organized the New York, Newfoundland, and London Telegraph Company, which completed the line between St John's and Cape Ray in 1856. In the same year the company laid a submarine cable under the Cabot Strait. Although the first attempt to lay an Atlantic cable, in 1858, failed, the second, in 1866, succeeded. Laid between Valencia, Ireland, and Heart's Content, Newfoundland, by the *Great Eastern*—an enormous iron vessel designed by I.K. Brunel—the cable made communication between the two continents almost instantaneous—at least for those who could afford to pay for it.

boasted the fourth largest merchant marine in the world, after Great Britain, the United States, and Norway. Ships such as the *Marco Polo*, built in Saint John in 1851, broke world speed records on the run to the Australian gold fields and made the region's shipbuilding skills famous.

Although Saint John was the largest shipbuilding centre, other communities, such as St Martins, Yarmouth, Windsor, Pictou, and Summerside became well known for their output of wooden vessels. Saint John, Charlottetown, and Halifax emerged as major trade entrepôts. By the 1860s Maritime vessels, operated in large part by foreign crews, were sailing all over the world, carrying cargoes at competitive prices. In the 1880s shipping barons in the Maritimes decided to invest their fortunes in railway and manufacturing ventures rather than in a steel- and steam-driven merchant marine—a decision that led to a rapid decline in both shipbuilding and the carrying trade.[7]

Newfoundland's economy was altogether more precarious. The end of the Napoleonic War precipitated a long and deep depression caused by short cod catches, market difficulties, the re-entry of France and the United States into the fisheries, and the expansion of the Nova Scotian fishing industry. To make matters worse, Newfoundlanders were driven off the French Treaty Shore, where they had fished during a French absence of more than 20 years. Although they then developed a migratory fishery on the Labrador coast, the season there was shorter and less certain. The increasing importance of the south coast herring fishery and the expansion of the seal fishery were more positive developments.

Schooners from St John's and other southeasterly ports had been involved in the spring seal hunt since the 1790s. The sealing fleet grew as investment in the industry increased, reaching a peak of nearly 400 vessels carrying some 14,000 men in the 1850s. Seal products represented one-third of the value of Newfoundland exports. Although sealskins were taken and exported, the main object of the hunt was the seal fat, which was rendered into oil and used for lighting and lubricants. The dramatic expansion proved to be a short-lived. Over-exploitation of the seal herds encouraged outfitters to turn to steam-powered vessels in the 1860s to increase yields and maintain profits. As a result, the industry became centralized in St John's and Conception Bay and the size of the fleet was reduced. Overall, sealing became steadily less important to the Newfoundland economy in the later nineteenth century, but it retained a considerable cultural significance.

The region's mineral resources also came under more intense exploitation in this period. Under a monopoly granted by the British Crown in 1826, the General Mining Association began developing Nova Scotia's coal resources in Cape Breton and Pictou County. The company brought in skilled miners and introduced modern technology, including steam-driven machinery and vessels. After its monopoly was abolished in 1858, investment in coal mining increased dramatically, stimulated by rising demand in the rapidly industrializing United States. In Albert County, New Brunswick, more than 230,000 tons of Albertite (solidified asphalt yielding oil and gas) were produced between 1850 and 1880. Gypsum and stone for building and grinding found markets, both locally and in the United States. The discovery of gold on Nova Scotia's south and eastern shores stimulated a gold rush that brought Prince Albert and other luminaries to Tangier Harbour, near Halifax, in 1861. By this time the iron works at Londonderry was turning out $40,000 of products annually.

Newfoundland's resources also attracted growing interest. In 1822 William Cormack walked across the island, the first European known to have done so. In 1839–40 the local government sponsored the first geological surveys, conducted by James Jukes. Copper was discovered in Notre Dame Bay in the late 1850s and copper mining started at Tilt Cove in 1864. In the same year the government established a permanent Geological Survey, which under its first director, Alexander Murray,

The Farmer's Bank of Rustico. In the early 1860s, Father George-Antoine Belcourt helped his fellow Prince Edward Island Acadians to establish a school and a banking co-operative to meet the challenges of the new industrial order. Public Archives and Records Office of Prince Edward Island, Acc. 2320/20-4.

and his assistant, James P. Howley, undertook systematic exploration of the island. Their optimistic reports had an important influence on public policy, raising the possibility that Newfoundland might become something more than a producer of salt fish and seal oil.

Stimulated by the opportunities of the industrial age, the region's mercantile elite were anything but narrow in their ambitions. Samuel Cunard laid the foundations for a globally successful steamship company from his Maritime base. Beginning with a clock-making business in St John's, Benjamin Bowring became the head of a highly profitable mercantile house with links to Liverpool, England. The most prominent entrepreneur in this period was Enos Collins. Having made a fortune in trade and privateering from his home town of Liverpool during the French Revolutionary and Napoleonic Wars, he went on to build a business empire based on trade and banking in Halifax. The founding of banking institutions, beginning with the Bank of New Brunswick in 1820 and the Halifax Banking Company in 1825, testified to the growth of the Maritime economy and the capacity of the region's entrepreneurs to mobilize capital for investment.

Economic growth in the Atlantic region was tied to the fortunes of the British Empire, but there were no special privileges after 1849, when Great Britain abandoned the last vestiges of colonial preference in trade and shipping. Although the dismantling of the old mercantile system helped to make the 1840s a "decade of tribulation,"[9] the transition proved less problematic than many had feared. Part of the reason was that Britain negotiated reciprocity (free trade) in primary products—fish, farm produce, minerals, and timber—with the United States in 1854. The Reciprocity Treaty remained in place until 1866 and, together with the high demand generated by the American Civil War (1861–5), stimulated colonial production and the carrying trade.

By mid-century the Industrial Revolution was beginning to transform production processes. Steam-driven machinery, the factory system, and conflicts between capital and labour were the hallmarks of a new age that demanded difficult adjustments for people accustomed to artisan production, kinship loyalties, and noblesse oblige. Saint John, flush with capital from the timber trade and the shipbuilding industry, emerged as the major industrial centre, with foundry, footwear, and clothing industries all surpassing shipbuilding in value by the 1860s. Halifax also developed an industrial base, specializing in food-processing industries such as brewing, baking, distilling, and sugar-refining. Milling was the most common industry in rural areas of the Maritimes. By 1871 Prince Edward Island alone boasted 500 carding, fulling, grist, dressing, saw, and shingle mills.

Most people lived at one remove from industrial discipline, their lives dominated by the seasonal rhythms of domestic production based on farming, fishing, and forestry—or in many cases all three. Most families continued to make their own cloth and clothing, to produce and preserve their own food, and to craft their own houses, barns, ploughs, carriages, horseshoes, furniture, soap, and candles. Surplus produce was bartered for the imported items—flour, molasses, sugar, tea, cloth, and metal utensils of various kinds—that stocked the shelves of local merchants. In turn, the merchants sold the products of farm and fishery in colonial towns and cities; to the men engaged in the region's fishing, shipping, and timber trades; or to markets in Europe, the United States, and the West Indies. In many communities, especially those centred on the fisheries, survival depended on a credit system in which merchants advanced supplies and paid for local products in goods rather than cash. This "truck system" encouraged dependence, but, as Sean Cadigan points out in his study of merchant–settler relationships in Conception Bay, it also enabled producers to participate, however minimally, in the market economy.[10]

Despite the growing complexity of the region's economy, poverty and destitution were common. The demand for foodstuffs outstripped the supply, and even farming families often had difficulty making ends meet. When crops or fisheries failed, as they sometimes did in all areas of the Atlantic region, disaster threatened. The potato blight hit the colonies in the late 1840s, creating hardship almost as severe as in Ireland and prompting at least one group of settlers in St Ann's, Cape Breton, led by the puritanical Reverend Norman McLeod, to search for greener pastures; they eventually fetched up in Waipu, New Zealand. Others shipped off to the United States, where jobs in the expanding industrial and service sectors and free homesteads on the western frontier offered hope for a better life.

By the 1830s most of the good farmland in the Maritimes had been taken up, and free land was largely a thing of the past. Not only recent immigrants but growing numbers of descendants of earlier settlers were therefore obliged to purchase property or take up marginal lands that yielded a meagre subsistence. Some of the poor squatted on Crown and Aboriginal reserves; others drifted to urban centres to find work. Given the small size and poor quality of their original grants, it is hardly surprising that blacks in Nova Scotia began moving to Halifax, where wage-paying jobs were more plentiful. They kept to themselves in an area on the Bedford Basin that soon became known as Africville.

Communities in Transition

Christian churches became firmly rooted throughout the Atlantic colonies in the first half of the nineteenth century. At a time when the family economy was the main source of security, churches often stepped in when the family could no longer find the wherewithal for survival. Church leaders also offered spiritual counsel in an age when human suffering was widely believed to be part of a divine plan.

Even before Roman Catholics were granted full civil rights in the British Empire in 1829, they had gained concessions in the Atlantic region. The ban on their holding public office was lifted first in Nova Scotia in 1823 for Lawrence Kavanagh, a Cape Breton merchant elected to the assembly. Newfoundland had its own Roman Catholic bishop by 1796, but Maritime Catholics remained under the jurisdiction of Quebec until 1817, when Edmund Burke was appointed bishop of Nova Scotia. Twelve years later, his jurisdiction was divided and separate bishops were appointed for New Brunswick and Prince Edward Island. These administrative changes marked the beginning of a new era in which a reinvigorated Catholic Church ministered to a growing constituency. By the mid-nineteenth century, more than 40 per cent of the populations of Newfoundland and Prince Edward Island, a third of New Brunswickers, and a quarter of Nova Scotians were Roman Catholics.

Evangelical churches—especially the Baptists and Methodists—generally took the lead in seeking converts and promoting moral rectitude, but all churches were swept up in the reforming spirit of the age. In the 1820s the temperance movement took root; it became so popular that New Brunswick briefly experimented with legislated prohibition in 1855. Most denominations established academies, Sunday schools, charity schools, orphanages, hospitals, shelters, and "houses of industry" where the unemployed inmates were encouraged to develop good work habits. Shunned by their white neighbours, black people in Nova Scotia found comfort in their own religious institutions. The spectacular growth of Baptist churches under the leadership of Richard Preston led to the establishment in 1854 of the African United Baptist Association, which was to become a linchpin in the black community's struggle for justice in a society riddled with racial prejudice.

Eager to spread the gospel to lost souls near and far, churches supported home and foreign missions and founded newspapers. The Maritime Baptists sent Richard Burpee to India in 1845 and in the following year the Presbyterian Church of Nova Scotia sponsored John Geddie's mission to the New Hebrides. Major religious denominations either published or supported newspapers sympathetic to their views. In St John's, for instance, *The Public Ledger* represented a Protestant perspective, while *The Newfoundlander* and *The Patriot* reflected Roman Catholic viewpoints. The first French-language newspaper in the region, the *Moniteur Acadien*, founded by Israël J.-D. Landry in 1867 in Shediac, New Brunswick, was closely aligned with the Roman Catholic hierarchy.

Reformers argued that sectarian tensions could be alleviated by the creation of a state-funded system of non-denominational public schools. In all the Atlantic colonies, their efforts were opposed not only by the Roman Catholic hierarchy but also by linguistic minorities, who feared the homogenizing tendencies of a state-supported school system. In 1852 Prince Edward Island became the first colony in the region to embrace public schools, but controversy quickly erupted over Bible reading in the classroom. While Protestants insisted that Bible-reading was essential to instilling Christian values, Roman Catholics staunchly resisted this practice because they associated independent Bible reading with Protestantism and feared that it would lead to proselytizing. They were ultimately placated by regulations that allowed students who found Bible reading offensive to be excused from attendance.

The Roman Catholic Cathedral in St John's, Newfoundland, engraving by A. Ruger, 1878. To the right of this imposing building are the Presentation and Mercy convents, to the left St Bonaventure's College. Consecrated in 1855, it overlooks the harbour and represents Bishop Michael Fleming's determination "to have a temple superior to any other in the island." Courtesy John FitzGerald.

In Newfoundland, efforts to introduce non-denominational public education in the 1830s were just as strongly opposed by the Church of England hierarchy as by its Roman Catholic counterpart. As a result, in 1842 the education grant was split between Protestants and Catholics.

Denominationalism prevailed in higher education throughout the Maritimes. The Church of England's exclusive control of King's College in Windsor and the College of New Brunswick in Fredericton inspired other denominations to establish their own institutions. In the mid-nineteenth century the foundations were laid for seven denominational colleges in the Maritimes: Acadia (Baptist); Mount Allison (Methodist); St Mary's, St Dunstan's, St Francis Xavier, Collège St-Joseph, and Mount Saint Vincent (all Roman Catholic). Dalhousie College, founded in 1818 as a non-denominational institution, became effectively Presbyterian when it finally began to offer classes in the 1860s. Prince of Wales College, established in Charlottetown in 1860, served mainly Protestant students.

Although clerics preached spiritual equality, church practices perpetuated worldly notions of hierarchy and prejudice. Many churches rented their pews, permitting the rich to pay for seating close to the pulpit. In some churches women were relegated to separate sections. People with black skin were almost always set apart. Protestants and Catholics had their own organizations, including the highly successful Orange Order, which championed the Protestant cause, sometimes provoking violence. On 12 July 1847, the 147th anniversary of the Battle of the Boyne, a confrontation between 300 Irish Catholics and an equal number of Protestants in Woodstock, New Brunswick, resulted in 10 deaths. Two years later, another bloody confrontation rocked the Catholic enclave of York Point in Saint John.

Violence was not confined to religious rivalries: it punctuated all aspects of colonial life. At election time, voting was conducted orally, with the result that polling stations often became scenes of violence and intimidation. Political tensions in Newfoundland were such that the conservative St John's newspaper editor Henry Winton had his ears cut off by masked opponents in 1835, and the Church of England archdeacon in the 1830s kept a pistol under his pillow. Mummering—a folk tradition associated with Christmas—became so menacing that in 1861 legislation made it illegal in St John's to appear in public wearing a mask or other disguise. In Prince Edward Island, tensions between tenants and their landlords (or their agents) often reached dangerous levels. Strikes by workers sometimes erupted in riots. Wife-beating was still legally sanctioned, and the foundation of discipline at home and at school was the adage "spare the rod and spoil the child." Cock fights and bear-baiting were popular pastimes.

Seaport towns were renowned for the violent and illegal activities that flourished along their waterfronts where an underworld of crimps (procurers of crewmen for sailing vessels), prostitutes, and greedy boardinghouse-keepers took advantage of the sailors in port. Like the British soldiers who were stationed in the region's major cities until mid-century, or the men confined to remote lumber camps throughout the long winters, sailors on board ship lived in an all-male environment, under repressive and often harsh conditions. Because colonial courts were likely to side with captains, sailors were notorious for various forms of resistance ranging from absence without leave to desertion, insubordination, and mutiny.

Middle-class citizens were concerned about violence and made concerted efforts to control it. City councils (in unincorporated areas, magistrates) appointed marshals and constables to keep the peace, swore in special deputies, and in extreme cases called on the military for help. By mid-century, full-time police forces were emerging in the larger urban areas. Legislation, backed by force, was imposed to control workers who dared to use strikes or intimidation to improve their wages and working conditions. By encouraging self-discipline, public schooling, and church attendance, reformers hoped to create a society in which the values of peaceful coexistence and civic virtue would be internalized, and force would no longer be required to maintain social control.

Colonial life was not all conflict and drudgery. In rural areas "bees" and "frolics" brought people together in communal bonhomie, and everywhere Sunday offered relief from weekday routines. Significant events on the Christian calendar, such as Christmas, Easter, and saints' days, provided opportunities for holidays and celebrations. In cities and towns, regimental bands, choral recitals, and singing schools flourished. Organized sport was still in its infancy, but racing, yachting, rowing, curling, and cricket clubs were becoming popular in urban centres. Hockey, also called "hurley" or "shinny," made inroads in Nova Scotia, though one commentator in 1864 argued that such a rowdy and dangerous game "ought to be sternly forbidden."[11] In St John's an annual regatta on Quidi Vidi Lake, begun in 1826, remains a highlight of the summer season.

Intellectual Awakenings

Educated people in the Atlantic region were full participants in the intellectual awakening of the nineteenth century. In a matter of weeks, ideas percolating in Boston, New York, Edinburgh, and London became topics of debate among colonial newspaper editors, college professors, and members of the urban elite. Ambitious colonials travelled to Great Britain and the United States for their education and returned home to practise or teach what they had learned. In the 1830s Mechanics' Institutes, founded in Scotland to disseminate scientific education among the artisan class, took root in the colonies, offering a broad range of literary, dramatic, and artistic activities.

Literacy was highly prized in the North Atlantic world and growing numbers of people struggled to master the arts of reading and writing. Not only were these skills valuable for religious and professional purposes; they also made it possible to read the books, magazines, and newspapers pouring off English-language presses. Newspaper editors emerged as influential political figures. In Nova Scotia, Joseph Howe, editor of the *Nova Scotian*, made his reputation by criticizing colonial magistrates and successfully defending himself in court in a much-publicized libel trial in 1835.

People in the Atlantic colonies read mostly British and American authors, but a few made their own contributions to the literary canon. Thomas McCulloch, the Presbyterian minister who founded Pictou Academy, wrote one of the first works of fiction produced in British North America. The *Stepsure Letters* (1821–3), which initially appeared in serial form in the *Acadian Recorder*, used gentle humour and satire to encourage more progressive attitudes. A similar approach was used by Judge Thomas Chandler Haliburton, who quickly achieved an international reputation with *The Clockmaker* (1836), in which he recounted the adventures of the clock-peddling Yankee salesman Sam Slick. In 1824 Julia Catherine Beckwith of Fredericton became the first native-born British North American novelist, with the publication of the little-read *St Ursula's Convent*, written when she was 17 years old. The Reverend R.T.S. Lowell's novel *The New Priest in Conception Bay* (1858)—the first to be set in a Newfoundland outport—captured a distinctive lifestyle and dialect. In an age that valued sensibility, romantic fiction and poetry were popular. The Halifax-born poet Mary Eliza Herbert began publishing the *Mayflower* in 1851. Devoted to those who wished "to roam awhile in the flowery field of romance—to hold communion with the Muses," it survived for only three issues and most of the contributions were from Herbert herself.

Before turning his hand to satire, Haliburton had written a two-volume history of Nova Scotia, published in 1829. The Reverend Lewis Anspach's *History of the Island of Newfoundland* (1819) and Peter Fisher's *First History of New Brunswick* (1825) appeared around the same time, reflecting a new preoccupation with the past. A growing interest in natural history inspired Nova Scotia artist Maria Morris to publish, in collaboration with pioneer naturalist Titus Smith, a book entitled *Wildflowers of Nova Scotia* in 1839. New England poet Henry Wadsworth Longfellow, who never set foot in the Maritimes, immortalized the deportation of the Acadians with his poem *Evangeline*, published in 1847.

These pioneering works documented a cultural maturity that also expressed itself in practical ways. In 1818 John Young, a Scottish merchant in Halifax writing under the name "Agricola," published a series of letters encouraging scientific methods in agriculture. His efforts, together with financial assistance from the government, led to the establishment of numerous agricultural societies in Nova Scotia. This fashion spread throughout the region, and by 1842 a society was founded in Newfoundland to encourage more effective use of the island's thin, acidic soils. Colonial inventors such as Charles Fenerty and Abraham Gesner devised ways to make paper out of wood rather than rags and kerosene from petroleum. In 1861, Gesner's *Practical Treatise on Coal, Petroleum and Other Distilled Oils* signalled the advent of the modern petroleum industry.

Political Awakenings

In the wake of the American Revolution, the British government had deliberately imposed constitutions on its remaining North American colonies that were designed to limit the democratic tendencies of elected assemblies. Power was weighted towards appointed elements: the governor, his council, and the judiciary. Assemblies—where they existed—were relatively powerless

Biography   William Carson

Born in 1770 in Kirkcudbright, Scotland, Carson studied at the University of Edinburgh's Medical Faculty in the late 1780s. It seems that he did not graduate, but this did not prevent him from claiming that he had done so, from practising medicine, or from calling himself "Dr." He practised in Birmingham until 1808, when he left for St John's, Newfoundland. His reasons for emigrating are not known, but Newfoundland was prospering at that time, and he may have seen opportunities there.

Carson had not been politically active in Britain, but once in St John's he started a career of almost ceaseless agitation. He was clearly influenced by British Whigs, such as Charles James Fox and Charles Grey, who stood for constitutional rights and reform, and against "secret influences." Thus Carson's first political pamphlets, published in 1812 and 1813, called for a civil governor and a legislative assembly to replace the naval state, which he regarded as autocratic and anachronistic.

Carson also promoted an interpretation of Newfoundland's past, drawn ultimately from John Reeves's 1793 *History*, which was to become the accepted orthodoxy. In his view, Newfoundlanders had been oppressed by the infamous West Country merchants who opposed settlement, denied them their just rights as British subjects, and deliberately retarded the economic development of the country. Naval governors were generally ignorant and guilty of illegal behaviour, while the naval surrogates lacked any sense of "the most common principles of law and justice." Not surprisingly, local authorities were outraged. Governor John Duckworth wanted to sue Carson for libel, but eventually settled for removing him as surgeon to the St John's Loyal Volunteers and refusing to pay his salary.

Initially Carson had few active supporters, but the severe economic depression that descended at the end of the Napoleonic Wars in 1815 created a climate in which a reform movement could develop. In 1820 he was joined by the Irish merchant Patrick Morris, and together they agitated for official colonial status, which was granted in 1824. Three years later Carson was appointed district surgeon. Governor Cochrane hoped the appointment would "keep the Doctor quiet," but it did no such thing, and Carson played a prominent role in a renewed campaign for the grant of a legislature, which the British government eventually conceded in 1832. Carson was defeated in the ensuing election, but found an assembly seat in December 1833, with the active support of the Roman Catholic bishop, Michael Fleming. For some time Carson had been cultivating support among the Irish Catholics in St John's, though he himself was a Presbyterian. This stance opened him to vicious attacks from the Protestant press, to which he replied in kind in the *Newfoundland Patriot*, a newspaper with which he was closely connected.

In 1834 Carson lost his position as district surgeon and had to resume his private medical practice, but he remained politically active, mounting a fierce and prolonged campaign against the conservative and obtuse chief justice, Henry John Boulton, which continued throughout Carson's controversial term as speaker of the House of Assembly, from 1837 to 1842. He died in 1843 at the age of 73. Although cantankerous and difficult, Carson undoubtedly played a key role in Newfoundland's political and constitutional development, while making significant contributions to health care and the development of agriculture.[12]

talking-shops, although their consent was needed to pass legislation relating to money bills. As a result, deadlocks were common.

Cape Breton and Newfoundland were still without elected assemblies in the early nineteenth century. Considered the birthright of all self-respecting Britons, representative government was denied to Cape Breton until it was united with the mainland in 1820. Thereafter, with two seats in the Nova Scotia assembly, Cape Breton had representative government, at least in theory, but little political clout. In Newfoundland the struggle for representative government was more protracted. After the end of the Napoleonic wars business and professional elites in St John's, led by Dr William Carson and Patrick Morris, began to demand formal recognition as a colony with representative government, security of land tenure, and the full range of British civil rights. Naval government no longer made sense, now that the English migratory fishery had died out and Newfoundland's economic and strategic importance to Britain had faded. Nevertheless, changing attitudes in London would take time and effort.

Arguing that the migratory fishery and naval government had stunted Newfoundland's development, the reformers drew attention to injustices such as the case of two Conception Bay fishermen who were flogged for contempt by order of the surrogate magistrates in 1820 and had their premises seized for debt. Finally, in 1824–5, circuit courts were instituted, King William's Act (under which Newfoundland had been governed as a naval state) was repealed, and Newfoundland became a Crown colony. Sir Thomas Cochrane became the colony's first civil governor in 1825 and appointed an executive council. After further reform agitation, representative government was established in 1832. Religious and ethnic divisions characterized Newfoundland politics and electoral violence erupted in some districts. In an attempt to calm the situation and prevent legislative problems, the Colonial Office instituted an experimental constitution that amalgamated the assembly and council in 1842, but it lasted only until 1848.

Meanwhile, the Maritime colonies were demanding not just representative but "responsible" government, in which the executive would be composed of members of the majority party in the assembly, to which it would be directly responsible. The most eloquent advocate of this reform was Nova Scotia's Joseph Howe, who in his famous letters to the Colonial Secretary, Lord John Russell in 1840, insisted that "every poor boy in Nova Scotia" should have "the same rights to honours and emoluments as he would have if he lived in Great Britain or the United States."

While Howe focused on the abuse of patronage, reformers in Prince Edward Island were animated by the "land question." By the late 1820s, more than half of the proprietors lived elsewhere, primarily in Great Britain. The absentee proprietors relied on agents to collect their rents and rarely set foot on the island. About one-third of the island's rural population consisted of small freeholders, who owned about one-fifth of the island's 1.4 million acres (567,000 hectares). The contrasting circumstances of tenants and freeholders made the former ready followers of William Cooper, who campaigned in an 1831 by-election on "Our country's freedom and farmers' rights." He won the contest handily and soon emerged as the articulate spokesman for escheat of all proprietary holdings. As the movement gained momentum, tenants refused to pay their rents and resisted landlords' efforts to collect arrears.

The Escheat Party won an overwhelming election victory in 1838, but the Colonial Office, reeling from the violence that had erupted in Upper and Lower Canada in 1837, refused to accept any legislation that undermined existing property rights. As Rusty Bittermann and Margaret McCallum argue, the temporary defeat of the movement did not end the struggle against proprietorship.

Instead, it "amplified, focused, and honed the conceptions and aspirations of much of the rural population, giving them a vision of a more just society and a historical, constitutional, and moral analysis that justified their efforts to realize that vision on Prince Edward Island."[13]

In New Brunswick, the central issue in political debates was the revenue from the selling, leasing, and licensing of Crown lands. Charles Simonds, a powerful Saint John timber baron and leader of the reform cause, managed to extract two important concessions from the Colonial Office in 1837: control over Crown land revenues (as long as the salaries of appointed administrators were guaranteed) and consultation with elected representatives in the appointment of the governor's executive councillors.

Great Britain finally abandoned its resistance to responsible government in settler colonies after the adoption of free trade in 1846 made it unnecessary to maintain a closed economic system. In 1847 Nova Scotia's lieutenant-governor, Sir John Harvey, was instructed to choose advisers from the party that had a majority in the assembly. Reformers were victorious in an election held later that year, and on 2 February 1848 a Liberal government under the leadership of James Boyle Uniacke became the first "responsible" administration in the British Empire. By 1855 all the remaining Atlantic colonies had followed Nova Scotia's lead. Still, this milestone in the region's political history did not mean that the colonies were fully independent: the Colonial Office still kept a watchful eye over defence, external affairs, legal matters, and constitutional amendment, and governors retained important discretionary powers.

Responsible government was a limited affair in other ways as well. In most places, property qualifications governed who could vote, while age, race, and gender further restricted voting privileges. Aboriginal people were disqualified by virtue of their poverty, but in Nova Scotia government formalized their disenfranchisement, explicitly denying the vote to them, along with paupers, in 1854. Women, no matter what their property status, were disfranchised by law in all the British North American colonies. Labrador was entirely ignored in the debate over political rights, as were the inhabitants of Newfoundland's French Treaty Shore.

In practice political power under responsible government was concentrated in the hands of the commercial and professional elites. They moved quickly to implement reforms, some of them liberal in intent. In Nova Scotia, the legislature repealed the law banning trade unions, revoked the special status of the Church of England, and put an end to the General Mining Association's monopoly over the colony's mineral resources. The New Brunswick assembly transformed King's College, a Church of England institution, into the secular University of New Brunswick, introduced the secret ballot at election time, and briefly adopted the prohibition of alcohol. In Prince Edward Island, Reform Party leaders George Coles and Edward Whelan failed to solve the land question—there was not enough money to buy out the landlords—but they managed to introduce the first Free Schools Act in the colonies and extend voting privileges to every man who performed four days of work on the colony's roads, a reform that enfranchised virtually all men between 21 and 60 years of age.

The first crisis that the Liberal government in Newfoundland faced after the implementation of responsible government concerned the French Treaty Shore. From the colony's perspective, an Anglo-French convention submitted to the legislature early in 1857 was a sellout because it effectively surrendered control of the Petit Nord and parts of the west coast to the French, allowed them access to bait on the south coast, and extended their fishing rights to Labrador. Outrage was fierce and universal, crossing party and denominational lines. The British ensign was flown half-mast and upside down, patriotic verses filled the newspapers, the support of other British North American colonies was enlisted, and strident protests went to London. Eventually, the British government withdrew the convention and gave an assurance that "the consent of the community" would be required for any "modification" of the colony's "maritime or territorial rights." This victory was long remembered as Newfoundland's own "Magna Carta."

Despite—or perhaps because of—the closed circle in which it operated, responsible government in the early years was a messy and muddled affair. Administrations were often unstable, with "loose fish" crossing the floor when they differed from their party on issues great or small. Bureaucratic processes were embryonic, patronage appointments commonplace, and alliances reflected religious affiliations—all to the detriment of good government. Governors continued to interfere in political matters, even though (like the British monarch) they were supposed to stand apart from the daily routine of political life and follow the recommendations of their executive advisers.

The historian Ian McKay has argued that the achievement of responsible government in British North America was an early step in what he calls the "project of liberal rule." Emphasizing individualism, rule of law, property rights, and civil liberties as key components of this ideology, liberalism gradually came to define the values of all political parties in the colonies, even those labelled "conservative."[14] There is no doubt that the ideals of freedom from traditional restraints galvanized many people to action, but historians disagree about the extent to which the liberal order prevailed in British North America either in the mid-nineteenth century or later. Jerry Bannister has noted that older aristocratic-loyalist notions have remained an essential feature of the Canadian story (a monarch is still the head of state, for example), and others have argued that communal values as expressed in families and among minorities complicated the embrace of liberalism. Nonetheless, those pushed to the sidelines by the proponents of liberalism appealed to some of the tenets of the same ideology in their struggle to improve their living conditions and to assert their rights as citizens.[15]

Conclusion

Despite the ambiguities and difficulties, the rituals of responsible government and a limited notion of political liberalism gradually took root in the Atlantic colonies. By the 1860s political parties had emerged in all the colonies, borrowing the names (and often the programs) of their Liberal and Conservative counterparts in Great Britain, and colonial leaders had begun to move beyond religious and ethnic allegiances to define new community goals. With political visions increasingly defined by industrial progress, public works, and material well-being, politicians even found themselves discussing a plan for colonial union.

Further Readings

Acheson, T.W. 1985. *Saint John: The Making of a Colonial Urban Community*. Toronto: University of Toronto Press.

Bittermann, Rusty. 2006. *Rural Protest on Prince Edward Island: From British Colonization to the Escheat Movement*. Toronto: University of Toronto Press.

————, and Margaret McCallum. 2008. *Lady Landlords of Prince Edward Island*. Toronto: University of Toronto Press.

Buckner, P.A. 1985. *The Transition to Responsible Government: British Policy in British North America, 1815–1850*. Westport, CT: Greenwood.

Greene, John P. 1999. *Between Damnation and Starvation: Priests and Merchants in Newfoundland Politics, 1745–1855*. Montreal: McGill-Queen's University Press.

Hiller, James K. 2008. "The Nineteenth Century, 1815–1914." Newfoundland Historical Society, *A Short History of Newfoundland and Labrador*. St John's: Boulder Publications.

Hornsby, Stephen. 1992. *Nineteenth-Century Cape Breton: A Historical Geography*. Montreal: McGill-Queen's University Press.

Keough, Willeen G. 2006. *The Slender Thread: Irish Women on the Southern Avalon, 1750–1860*. New York: Columbia University Press.

McCann, Phillip. 1994. *Schooling in a Fishing Society: Education and Economic Conditions in Newfoundland and Labrador 1836–1986*. St John's: Institute for Social Economic Research, Memorial University of Newfoundland.

Murphy, Terrence, and Cyril J. Byrne, eds. 1987. *Religion and Identity: The Experience of Irish and Scots Catholics in Atlantic Canada*. St John's: Jesperson Press.

Ryan, Shannon. 1994. *The Ice Hunters: A History of Newfoundland Sealing to 1914*. St John's: Breakwater Press.

Sager, Eric W., with Gerald E. Panting. 1990. *Maritime Capital: The Shipping Industry in Atlantic Canada, 1820–1914*. Montreal: McGill-Queen's University Press.

Samson, Daniel. 2008. *The Spirit of Industry and Improvement: Liberal Government and Rural-Industrial Society, Nova Scotia, 1790–1862*. Montreal: McGill-Queen's University Press.

See, Scott W. 1993. *Riots in New Brunswick: Orange Nativism and Social Violence in the 1840s*. Toronto: University of Toronto Press.

Whitfield, Harvey Amani. 2006. *Blacks on the Border: The Black Refugees in British North American, 1815–1860*. Burlington: University of Vermont Press.

Wynne, Graeme. 1981. *Timber Colony: A Historical Geography of Early Nineteenth Century New Brunswick*. Toronto: University of Toronto Press.

Historical Spotlight

Bittermann, Rusty, and Margaret McCallum. 2005. "When Private Rights Become Public Wrongs: Property and the State in Prince Edward Island in the 1830s." In *Despotic Dominion: Property Rights and British Settler Societies*, ed. John McLaren, A.R. Buck, and Nancy Wright. Vancouver: University of British Columbia Press.

Campbell, Gail. 1990. "The Most Restrictive Franchise in British North America? A Case Study," *Canadian Historical Review* 71, 2 (June): 159–88.

Recommended Websites

The Newfoundland Seal Fishery
http://www.heritage.nf.ca/society/seal.html

Irish Famine Migration to New Brunswick
http://archives.gnb.ca/Irish/IWDP/en/

The Labrador Inuit through Moravian Eyes
http://link.library.utoronto.ca/inuitmoravian

Part 2

The Atlantic Region Since 1860

In the nineteenth century, Britain's North American colonies struggled to find their place in a world being transformed by new industrial processes and new ideas about the origins of Earth and its peoples. Industrial development, liberalism, and materialism ultimately informed a new world view embraced by most people in the Atlantic region, who shared and incorporated as their own a broad North Atlantic culture.

While the Maritime colonies became part of the new Dominion of Canada between 1867 and 1873, Newfoundland resisted the continental drift. Nevertheless, they all felt the impact of the larger economic, social, and intellectual forces that shaped global developments in this period. Capitalist cycles of boom and bust, two world wars, and a deadly influenza pandemic in 1918 recognized no political boundaries. Despite determined efforts to meet the challenges facing them, the Atlantic region fell behind most other areas of North America in the race for industrial development, and its peoples increasingly looked elsewhere for opportunities.

When Newfoundland entered Confederation in 1949, it shared with its Maritime neighbours the distinction of being among the poorest provinces in Canada. Conditions in the region improved during the second half of the twentieth century, but new communication technologies and neo-liberal values privileging the market as the arbiter in all things brought more challenges to small states everywhere in "the global village."

Chapter 9

Confronting Confederation, 1860–1873

In 1867, Nova Scotia and New Brunswick were swept into Confederation with the Province of Canada. Prince Edward Island followed their lead in 1873, while Newfoundland remained independent. No matter what their political status, all the Atlantic colonies faced the same economic and social challenges. The new world order characterized by faster communications, galloping industrialization, and liberal political regimes demanded new values and smart strategies. If they could not keep up with the pace of change, the Atlantic colonies faced marginalization in a world where literacy, railroads, and factories stood supreme as the symbols of progress.

Setting the Context

The Atlantic Colonies in the Age of Industry

Following Great Britain's adoption of free trade and its acceptance of limited colonial self-government in the mid-nineteenth century, Atlantic colonists were preoccupied with adjusting to the new industrial order. Initially, the times were relatively good for undertaking bold initiatives. The British economy boomed for two decades after 1845, fuelled by expanding trade; the discovery of gold in California, Australia, British Columbia, and New Zealand; and the expansion of credit through banking and insurance companies, most of them connected to the great financial houses in London. The Crimean War in Europe (1854–6) and the Civil War in the United States (1861–5) further increased demand for colonial fish, foodstuffs, coal, and timber. As Great Britain consolidated its informal empire based on industrial supremacy, banking institutions, and free trade, the Atlantic colonies were well positioned on the edge of the North American continent to go along for the ride.

The 1860s were a critical decade for the Atlantic world. In 1861 the United States erupted in a civil war that pitted the industrialized North against the slave-owning, agrarian South. The war brought an end to slavery as an institution, but it failed to eradicate the racism that remained rampant in the United States and elsewhere. Meanwhile, nationalist movements achieved considerable success on both sides of the Atlantic. German and Italian states moved decisively along the road to nationhood, while the efforts of the French Emperor Napoleon III to establish an imperial regime in Mexico ended with the execution of the leader of his puppet government, Archduke Maximilian, by a Mexican firing squad in 1867. Even Great Britain had its hands full with Irish patriots both at home and in North America who were determined to dissolve the hated union imposed on their island in 1801.

It was in this tumultuous context that the union of most of the British North American colonies was achieved.

Whether in or out of Confederation, all four Atlantic colonies pursued industrial strategies with more or less enthusiasm and all four fell behind in the race for economic ascendancy. Without a metropolis that could compete with Montreal, Toronto, Boston, and New York, the Atlantic region became a source of willing workers who flocked to the other frontiers of opportunity. Out-migration reached significant proportions in the 1880s and continued until the 1930s Depression closed the doors of employment opportunity everywhere in North America. People in the Atlantic region were no strangers to hard times, which had engulfed the region from 1866 to 1896 and again in the 1920s. Nor were people in the region immune to the European conflicts that took a huge toll on lives in both the First and Second World Wars.

Big Dreams

The American Civil War convinced many colonial politicians that republicanism was flawed and that the colonies were better off under the British flag and parliamentary system. But staying the course proved difficult. Great Britain was trying to reduce its colonial commitments, and some people in the North, which emerged triumphant in 1865, were calling for the United States to take over all of North America. How could the small British colonies defend themselves against such a threat? The only defence, some argued, would be to beat the Americans at their own game. With the help of Great Britain, the colonies working together could perhaps build a transcontinental nation to rival their powerful neighbour.

Many supporters of British North American union were inspired by dreams of economic development. This was especially the case in the Province of Canada (after 1867, Ontario and Quebec), where industrial development and escape from a crippling railway debt were predicated on acquiring

Table 9.1	Timeline
1860	Prince Edward Island Land Commission appointed.
1861–5	American Civil War
1861	Trent Affair.
1862	Collapse of negotiations with the Canadians on plans to build an Intercolonial Railroad.
1864	Charlottetown and Quebec Conferences on Confederation; Tenant League founded.
1865	Pro-Confederation government defeated in New Brunswick.
1866	Fenian raid on New Brunswick; pro-Confederation government elected in New Brunswick; London Conference on Confederation.
1867	Confederation of New Brunswick, Nova Scotia, Ontario, and Quebec; secession movement begins in Nova Scotia.
1869	Anti-Confederates in Nova Scotia accept better terms; Newfoundland decisively rejects Confederation.
1871	Treaty of Washington.
1873	Prince Edward Island joins Confederation.

Rupert's Land—the vast territory controlled by the Hudson's Bay Company. The major impediment to the Canadian dream of a western empire was the political deadlock between the two populations that had been cobbled together by the British Parliament in 1840: largely French-speaking and Catholic in Canada East (formerly Lower Canada), English-speaking and Protestant in Canada West (formerly Upper Canada).

Following the collapse of yet another coalition government in the spring of 1864, a constitutional committee was established to seek a solution to the colony's political deadlock. Chaired by George Brown, editor of *The Globe* and leader of the Reform Party in Canada West, it recommended a federal union of all the British North American colonies. To see the project through to completion, a "Great Coalition" was established, which included Brown, the leaders of the Conservative-*Bleu* Party (John A. Macdonald from Canada West and George-Étienne Cartier from Canada East), and Alexander Galt, an early proponent of Confederation and spokesperson for the powerful business community of Montreal. It was a formidable alliance.

The Atlantic Colonies at the Crossroads

The Atlantic colonies initially had little interest in British North American union. Instead, they continued to focus their attention on the larger British Empire to which they were connected by sea—until railways began to dominate the agenda. Political and economic leaders in both Nova Scotia and New Brunswick envisioned their respective colonies taking advantage of their location to become the gateway to the continent. This goal seemed even more appealing when the American Civil War showed that, in the event of war between Great Britain and the United States, an ice-free Atlantic port linked to the St Lawrence by an all-British railway route would be essential to military and economic security.

Most people in the Atlantic region were more interested in the Civil War than in Confederation discussions. From the Confederate attack on Fort Sumter in April 1861 to Abraham Lincoln's assassination by John Wilkes Booth four years later, the news from the United States kept colonial tongues wagging. Close and longstanding cultural, economic, and kinship ties—according to the 1870 US Census, Maritimers and Newfoundlanders together formed the fourth-largest ethnic group in the republic—made the war a matter of personal interest for many colonials. Several thousand Maritimers, many of them working in the United States when war was declared, enlisted in the Union or Confederate armies. One of them, New Brunswick's Sara Emma Edmonds, posed as a man so that she could join the Union Army. She worked as a nurse, a spy, and a general's aid, and also saw combat.

As British possessions, the colonies were officially neutral, but there were supporters for both sides and growing fears that the war might escalate into another global conflict. The Confederacy hoped that Great Britain, which had a stake in the cotton and tobacco industries of the South, would formally support their cause. Throughout the war, military preparations in case of attack, and blockade running in waters off Nova Scotia and New Brunswick, brought the conflict home. Visits to Maritime ports by some 230 Union and 25 Confederate vessels were recorded during the war. In October 1863, two Yankee gunboats appeared on the coast of Prince Edward Island and were warmly received in Georgetown, perhaps because it was the hometown of one of the vessel's officers. Still, Nova Scotia's premier, Joseph Howe, was haunted by the spectre of invasion: "our cities would be captured, our fields laid to waste, our bridges blown up, our railways destroyed," he warned in December 1862.[1]

Howe's fears were not without justification. British-built warships purchased by the Confederacy, including the *Alabama*, the *Florida*, and the *Shenandoah*, sank more than 100 Northern vessels. In November 1861 war seemed imminent when a Northern warship seized the *Trent*, a British steamer, on the high seas and arrested two Confederate agents. They were eventually released, but tensions remained high. Despite plans to reduce its military commitments, Great Britain sent 15,000 troops to supplement the 3,000 soldiers already stationed in the colonies. Arriving in winter, they were obliged to march overland to Quebec City from New Brunswick—convincing proof of the need for a railway connecting the Maritimes to the Province of Canada.

When Joseph Howe assumed the premiership of Nova Scotia in 1860, he made railways one of his top priorities. His favourite project was a line linking Halifax to the St Lawrence, generally referred to as the Intercolonial Railway. As early as 1849, Howe had proposed such a line at a Halifax conference convened to address the implications of Great Britain's adoption of free trade on the colonies. Howe's railway projects, which managed only to link Halifax with Windsor and Pictou, fell far short of his larger goal and were the main reason that the provincial debt reached a total of $4.5 million in 1863. By that time, railway talks with representatives from Canada had collapsed. British capitalists had little enthusiasm for a railway project that required negotiations with a rabble of dysfunctional colonies, most of them teetering on the brink of bankruptcy.

Howe's government was defeated by the Conservatives in 1863. Under Charles Tupper, who assumed the premiership in 1864, the Conservatives continued to support public works and other progressive programs such as publicly funded schools. A medical doctor trained in Scotland, Tupper had represented Cumberland County since 1855. With substantial investments in his constituency's coal mines and a keen sense of its strategic location with regard to any railway built between Nova Scotia and points further west, Tupper was a great booster of enterprise both public and private. The Intercolonial held the promise of new markets in New Brunswick and Canada, but Nova Scotia lacked the financial resources to proceed. Under Tupper's government, the provincial debt quickly ballooned to $8 million. How long would Barings' Bank in London be willing to underwrite the colony's debt?

New Brunswickers were also caught up in the railway mania. Although the St Andrews and Quebec Railway Company ran out of money before achieving its objective, the idea of the Intercolonial Railway continued to find support among New Brunswick's political and business leaders. So, too, did the idea of a link to the United States. The Reciprocity Treaty created an intense interest in north–south lines of communication, and a promoter from Maine, Joseph Alfred Poor, seemed poised to help make the idea a reality. When Poor declared bankruptcy in 1855, New Brunswick pressed ahead with a line linking Shediac to Saint John and continued making plans to extend its ambitiously named European and North American railway into the United States.

In 1861 Reform Premier Charles Fisher, an active supporter of railway construction, was brought down by a conflict-of-interest scandal relating to the purchase of Crown lands. His successor, Leonard Tilley, was keen on the Intercolonial, but with a $5-million railway debt and annual revenues of only $600,000, New Brunswick could not move forward on its own. Without the support of the Canadians and financial assistance from Great Britain, neither of which was forthcoming, the project would never succeed.

Prince Edward Island was slow to jump on the railway-building bandwagon. As a result, its public debt in the 1860s remained under control. Islanders found export markets for their farm and fishery products in the United States under Reciprocity, and, like other Maritimers, boasted a healthy shipbuilding industry. Even the persistent land question seemed to be on the verge of resolution. Under the voluntary Land Purchase Act of 1853, Premier George Coles began using provincial funds to buy out some of the proprietors so that tenants could become landowners. Although the landlords and the Colonial Office resisted his efforts, by 1860 nearly 40 per cent of the island's residents were freeholders.

The increased accessibility of land under freehold tenure inevitably highlighted the hardships of those who continued to pay rents. In 1860 Conservative Premier Edward Palmer, himself a landlord, established the Prince Edward Island Land Commission to inquire into the issue. Joseph Howe, along with Halifax lawyer J.W. Ritchie and New Brunswick Liberal politician John Hamilton Gray, submitted a report that was sympathetic to tenant demands. It recommended that the tenants be given the right to purchase land from their landlords and to have arrears in payments prior to 1 May 1858 forgiven. In cases where tenants and landlords could not agree on a fair price for the land, it would be established by arbitration. The landlords were livid and the Colonial Office became nervous. Although Palmer's government passed legislation to implement the commission's recommendations, royal assent was withheld on a "technicality."

The rejection of the commissioners' award fuelled the resolve of the aggrieved tenants and their supporters to put an end to the colony's feudal landholding system once and for all. In 1864 a Tenant League was formed to support a tenant takeover of rented land, with rates of compensation for landlords to be set by the townships. Members vowed to withhold rent payments, and when soldiers tried to serve writs on those in arrears, violence ensued. With chaos looming, finding the resources to solve the land question became the central focus of Prince Edward Island administrators.

In Newfoundland, where Liberals were mainly Roman Catholic and Conservatives overwhelmingly Protestant, denominational tensions continued to characterize political life under responsible government. There were also tensions within the Liberal camp. After the 1861 election, a major riot in St John's involving rival Liberal factions resulted in troops firing on the crowd, killing three people and wounding twenty. This event prompted compromise. Religious leaders withdrew from

Table 9.2 Population of Eastern British North America, 1851–71

	1851	1861	1871
Ontario	952,004	1,396,091	1,620,851
Quebec	890,261	1,111,566	1,191,516
Nova Scotia	276,854	330,857	387,800
New Brunswick	193,800	252,047	285,594
Prince Edward Island	62,678*	80,857	94,021
Newfoundland†	—	122,638	146,536

* figure is from 1848
† Figures are from 1857 and 1869

Sources: "Series A 2-14. Population of Canada by province, census dates, 1851 to 1976," in *Historical Statistics of Canada*, 2nd edn., ed. F.H. Leacy (Ottawa: Minister of Supply and Services, 1983) and James Hiller, "Confederation Defeated: The Newfoundland Election of 1869," in James Hiller and Peter Neary, eds., *Newfoundland in the Nineteenth and Twentieth Centuries: Essays in Interpretation* (Toronto: University of Toronto Press, 1980).

Document

The Prince Edward Island Land Commission, 1861

In their report, submitted in 1861, the Prince Edward Island Land Commissioners included evidence from the hearings they had held throughout the colony. The document is thus an excellent source of information about the tensions between landlords and tenants on the Island. The following testimony by Nicolas Conroy, a Liberal member of the Island's assembly, described how new landlords such as Samuel Cunard became more efficient than their predecessors in ensuring payment of rents. Together with his son Edward, Cunard owned more than 190,000 acres (80,000 hectares), much of it acquired in the late 1830s.

In 1835, when I first settled in Tignish, no proprietors were recognized in Lots One and Two. There had been some competitors for proprietorship, but previous to that period, though the people were asked, and even pressed to pay rent, still they always refused. I was present when the first recognition of a proprietor took place on Lot Two. . . . Mr Peters, now Judge Peters, who was at the time agent for Mr Cunard, . . . desired me as I knew the people to accompany him . . . I did so. When we arrived, many of the inhabitants were assembled. Mr Peters told them, Mr Cunard was the proprietor of the Lot, and wished them to attorn to him as their landlord; but they refused, just as they had refused to attorn to Mr Hill, some years previous. They were free, and desired to remain so if possible. Mr Peters then spoke to them of the wealth and power of Mr Cunard in Halifax. He said he was an influential gentleman in that City, and to hold out against him would be preposterous. The better way was, to pay rents; he would protect them; and they would have an honorable gentleman for their landlord. After much coaxing, and half threatening they signed a paper which he wished them to subscribe. Some time after this Mr Peters and Mr Palmer came to some arrangement respecting Lot One. They accordingly sent word to the people, saying that they were coming to get them to take leases. The people met them, but unanimously refused to have anything to do with them. Messrs Peters and Palmer remained a week, and were on the eve of leaving, when, unfortunately, the people began to misunderstand each other—one thought the other was going to get his farm, and so forth, and the result was, all made a rush to the proprietor to attorn. I was present, I saw the rejoicing proprietors on that occasion. . . . The leases were for a term of 999 years, and at 1s sterling an acre. In addition to this, they signed notes of hand for £10, to be paid up the 25th March, then last past. Your Honors will remember that another year's rent was then nearly due, so that by the coming 25th of March, which was about one month hence, they were involved in £15 arrears. Now, some who signed those notes of hand, were very poor, and for them to make good their notes, was impossible. In the meantime, the proprietors pressed and threatened them, so that the greater number left their farms from sheer inability to pay these arrears. This I would call a real grievance.[2]

Historical Focus

British Financiers and Canadian Confederation

It has been long conceded that railway interests played a major role in promoting Confederation, but a recent study by Andrew Smith documents the extent to which London's financial district facilitated the process. Indeed, Smith argues that "Without the support of a small but influential group of investors, Confederation would not have occurred in 1867, if at all."[3]

By the early 1860s, crises in British North American investments, both in private ventures and in colonial administrations, threatened the survival of some of London's most important financial institutions, including Barings' Bank and Glyn, Mills, and Company. In particular, the financial troubles of Canada's Grand Trunk Railway Company compromised major investment houses and made the extension of the line from Quebec City to the ice-free ports of the Maritimes unlikely. At the same time, the American Civil War underscored the need for an all-British winter route connecting the eastern colonies. Financiers, always on the lookout for bigger projects, promoted the improbable scheme of recouping the Grand Trunk's fortunes by extending rails across the continent to the Pacific. Such a line would not only secure an alternative route to Asia, they argued, but also open up Rupert's Land—still under the monopoly control of the Hudson's Bay Company—to settlement and development.

At the suggestion of Joseph Howe, who was in London drumming up support for the Intercolonial Railway, men with financial interests in the colonies formed the British North American Association (BNAA) in December 1861. Its first objective was to lobby the British government in support of both the long-awaited Halifax–Quebec railway and the union of the colonies under one administration, which would make negotiations relating to development projects less complicated. The more conservative among them also saw union of the colonies as a means of implementing stiffer voting regulations as a means of reducing opposition to government spending from penny-pinching small producers in agriculture, forestry, and fisheries. In short order, the new lobby group had the ear of the Duke of Newcastle, Colonial Secretary from 1859 to 1864, who became an ardent champion of Confederation.

Most London financiers and businessmen had little interest in weakening the bonds that held the British Empire together. From their perspective a strong empire was good for trade and investment and a united British North America under a powerful central government would support Great Britain's global dominance. Significantly, the first clause in the British North America Act of 1867 declared that "the present and future prosperity of British North America will be promoted by a federal union under the crown of Great Britain."

It is a common misconception that Canada achieved independence in 1867; this was not so. Foreign affairs, military policy, and constitutional amendments still required British approval, and the Privy Council in London remained the final court of appeal in legal matters. Only with the passage of the Statute of Westminster in 1931 were Canada and other British Dominions granted the right to full political independence. Even then, most Dominions, including Canada, dragged their feet in exercising their new-found independence.

overt political activity, and the political elites gradually shaped an unwritten agreement whereby public patronage, and seats in the legislature and on the executive council, would be awarded to each denomination in proportion to its size. Premier Hugh Hoyles, a Conservative, signalled the new attitude by offering cabinet seats to a number of Roman Catholics. This denominational compromise was an important step, allowing the evolution of political parties based on factors other than religion.

The Road to Confederation

Charles Tupper inadvertently started the Confederation ball rolling by promoting the idea of Maritime Union. Discouraged both by the collapse of the negotiations with the Canadians on the Intercolonial project and by the general parochialism of colonial politics, he reasoned that the Maritime colonies would have more clout with British investors if they pooled their resources. Early in 1864 Maritime Union was debated in the Nova Scotia assembly, whose members agreed to send delegates to a conference on the subject. New Brunswick supported this initiative; Prince Edward Island ignored it.

The idea of Maritime Union would almost certainly have remained dormant if Canadian politicians had not been seeking solutions to the political stalemate in their legislature. On hearing of the developments in the "Lower provinces," the Canadians sought permission to attend the proposed Maritime Union conference. This galvanized plans for a meeting in Charlottetown in early September 1864. The location ensured the involvement of Islanders and was more convenient than other Maritime capitals for the Canadian delegates, many of whom arrived by boat. The meeting quickly expanded to include discussion of the Canadian proposal for a federation of all the British North America colonies. A month later, the delegates reassembled in Quebec to hammer out a detailed agreement. Joined by two representatives from Newfoundland (invited as afterthoughts), the delegates produced 69 resolutions, which became the basis of the British North America Act.

Since legislative union was unacceptable to most of the delegates, the agreement envisaged a federal system with two levels of jurisdiction: national and provincial. Members of the federal House of Commons were to be elected on the basis of population, giving the two sections of Canada, with their far greater numbers, overwhelming control. The appointed Senate was designed to provide a regional counter-balance, but was dominated by the Canadians because the Atlantic delegates failed to insist on equal provincial representation, settling instead for equal *regional* representation—the Maritimes, Quebec, and Ontario—with four additional seats to be allocated to Newfoundland if it decided to participate. Coupled with the agreement that senators would be appointed for life by the federal government, this structure ensured that, as Phillip Buckner puts it, "the Senate would have no moral authority to challenge the governing party in the House of Commons" and at the same time "limited its effectiveness as the guardian of regional interests."[4]

The federal government was assigned the most significant powers, including control over interprovincial trade and transportation; foreign policy and defence; criminal law; currency and banking; and Indian Affairs (Aboriginal people, not surprisingly, had no say in this decision). The federal government also controlled all the major sources of taxation. The provinces had jurisdiction over commerce within their borders, natural resources, civil law, municipal administration, education, and social services. Agriculture, immigration, and fisheries would be joint responsibilities.

The delegates to the Charlottetown Conference, September 1864.Library and Archives Canada/Credit: George P. Roberts/ National Archives of Canada fonds/C-000733.

It is highly unlikely that internal pressures alone would have produced a Confederation agreement. External forces were also important, especially the threat posed by the United States. As the Civil War came to an end, Secretary of State William Seward began making noises to the effect that it was the "manifest destiny" of the United States to control the whole continent. The purchase of Alaska from Russia in 1867 became the first step in the American thrust northward. The situation of the British North American colonies was further complicated by the Fenian Brotherhood, Irish nationalists whose leaders had concocted a scheme to invade British North America from American soil—a clever way, they thought, of provoking a war between Britain and the United States that might give Ireland a better chance of achieving independence.

Neither Great Britain nor the colonies wanted a war with the United States. Indeed, the Colonial Office saw British North American union as a way of reducing military commitments in North America. (By 1871 British troops had been withdrawn entirely except from Halifax, where they would remain until the early twentieth century.) To compound what was developing into a full-scale military crisis, Washington served notice in 1864 that it would terminate the Reciprocity Treaty in 1866, causing consternation among those who relied on American markets. Confederation suddenly looked more interesting.

Selling Confederation

Since none of the leaders who attended the 1864 conferences had a mandate to negotiate political union, they were obliged either to call elections or to have the Confederation agreement endorsed by their legislatures. The Quebec resolutions passed easily through the Canadian legislature, but the Atlantic colonies were less enthusiastic. Newfoundland's Premier Hoyles found little support for Confederation either in his party or in the colony at large. He therefore postponed a decision on the matter, though there was lively discussion in the press. Only 5 per cent of the island's trade was with British North America, and talk of railway building and military preparedness intensified well-founded fears that Newfoundland would be saddled with taxes from which it would receive little benefit. Among those of Irish descent, Confederation conjured up memories of Ireland's hated union with Great Britain and invoked fears that newly won rights with respect to schools and political patronage would be jeopardized.

In Prince Edward Island, Conservative Premier John Hamilton Gray also shelved the issue. His own party was divided on the Quebec resolutions, and few Islanders saw much advantage in a union that would give their colony only five seats in the Commons and do nothing to resolve the "land question." So contentious was the issue in Nova Scotia, where Joseph Howe emerged as the spokesman for the anti-Confederate cause, that Tupper was forced to delay introducing the Quebec resolutions in the legislature.

New Brunswick's Premier Tilley took a more direct route. In March 1865 he led his badly divided party to a resounding electoral defeat at the hands of anti-Confederates led by Albert J. Smith. Strong forces intervened, some intentionally, others fortuitously, to put the Confederation movement back on track. Smith's anti-Confederate government broke into factions, and Lieutenant-Governor Arthur Hamilton Gordon, in a high-handed manoeuvre that defied the principle of responsible government, forced another election in May 1866. This time Tilley, promising major revisions to the Quebec agreement, won a convincing victory. Support from Roman Catholic bishops and timber merchants, a timely invasion at Campobello Island by the Fenians (smartly dispersed by a naval force dispatched from Halifax), and money from the Canadians and their Grand Trunk railway allies all helped to bring about this reversal of fortunes. It would not be the last time that patronage rather than policy was used to legitimize Confederation in the Atlantic region.

In Nova Scotia as in New Brunswick, the office of lieutenant governor was used to advance the Confederation cause. Sir William Fenwick Williams, a native of Annapolis Royal and a hero of the Battle of Kars in the Crimean War, was appointed to the position in November 1865. By twisting the arms of enough politicians, he gave Tupper the support he needed to ensure that the legislature passed a resolution authorizing continued discussion of British North American union. Significantly, Tupper's resolution made no reference to the Quebec "scheme," which had been thoroughly discredited by the anti-Confederate forces in the colony.

The final negotiations were conducted in London in the fall of 1866. Although no substantive changes were made to the arrangements forged in Quebec in 1864, Tupper managed to secure a clause in the British North America Act providing for the "immediate" construction of the Intercolonial Railway "by the Government of Canada." The Maritime delegation also ceded to the federal government exclusive control over the fisheries—the final agreement provided only joint jurisdiction for agriculture and immigration—and export duties on coal. Despite a strong lobby from Halifax's Archbishop T.L. Connelly for a clause providing legal support for separate schools in the Maritimes, the delegates could not be moved, with the result that denominational schools were constitutionally recognized only in Ontario and Quebec.

Document

Joseph Howe on Confederation, 1865

In the winter of 1865, the Halifax *Chronicle* anonymously published Joseph Howe's "Botheration Letters," attacking the Quebec scheme for British North American union. Claiming that the Confederation proposal was "neither fish, flesh, nor good red herring," Howe outlined the reasons why the terms of union as embodied in the Quebec resolutions were inimical to the Maritime colonies. He summarized his objections in a letter to Earl Russell on 19 January 1865:

1. That by adopting the principle of Representation by population, the Maritime Provinces will be forever swamped by the Canadians.
2. That, if the Canadas, always in trouble of some sort, and two or three times in open rebellion, should repeat such eccentricities, we should be compromised, and our connexion with the Mother Country endangered.
3. Because the plan of double Legislatures, tried in Scotland and Ireland and swept away, is cumbersome and expensive, and cannot be carried out without raising our ad valorum duty, which is now only 10 percent to 20.
4. That, when we raise our duties to this point, for the benefit of 3,000,000 Canadians, we burthen our trade with the Mother country and with our British brethren in 50 other Colonies scattered all over the world.
5. That when the tariff is thus raised but £250,000 currency will be left for defence, a sum utterly inadequate for any such purpose while nothing is gained by weakening the unity of command and control now promised by Her Majesty's Government.[5]

Notwithstanding his failure to get major concessions from the Canadians, Tupper remained optimistic about the potential of Confederation to stimulate industrial development in Nova Scotia. In justifying the transfer to the federal government of the power to levy coal duties, he told the members of the Nova Scotia assembly in the spring of 1867 that "the possession of coal mines, together with other natural resources must, in the course of time, make Nova Scotia the great emporium for manufactures in British America." He went on to explain that in taking it out of the power of any legislature to double the amount of royalty, "we were giving a guarantee to capitalists who might come and invest their money in these coal mines."[6] In short, if Tupper had his way, Nova Scotia would be open for business.

With little debate, the British North America Act passed in the British Parliament in March 1867, and on 1 July 1867 Ontario, Quebec, New Brunswick, and Nova Scotia came together to form the Dominion of Canada. The *Morning Chronicle*, a Liberal newspaper in Halifax, marked the occasion with a black border of mourning, while the New Glasgow *Eastern Chronicle* carried a mock birth notice: "On Monday last, at 12:05 a.m. (premature) the Dominion of Canada—illegitimate. This prodigy is known as the infant monster Confederation."

Biography — Samuel Leonard Tilley

Samuel Leonard Tilley. Library and Archives Canada/Topley Studio fonds/PA-012632.

With the exception of John A. Macdonald, no one played a more prominent role in the early years of Confederation than Samuel Leonard Tilley, commonly known as Leonard. He was born in Gagetown, New Brunswick, in 1818, a descendant of Loyalists on both sides of his family. At the age of 13 he began an apprenticeship with a pharmacist in Saint John, and in 1838 he and his cousin Thomas Peters opened their own "Cheap Drug Store." A year later Tilley was so deeply moved by a sermon that religious conviction thereafter governed his life. He taught Sunday school, served as a warden in the Church of England, and embraced the temperance movement. In 1854 he reached the highest office of the Sons of Temperance when he was named Most Worthy Patriarch.

Elected to the New Brunswick assembly in 1850, Tilley became a major player in the movement for responsible government, which was fully achieved in 1854. As provincial secretary he was a moving spirit behind the 1855 Prohibition Bill, but opposition to it was so great that he was defeated in the election of 1856 and the measure was rescinded. Regaining his seat, along with his position as provincial secretary in 1857, he became premier of New Brunswick in 1861. With Joseph Howe, Tilley worked tirelessly to secure British and Canadian backing for the Intercolonial Railway. When the Canadians withdrew from the deal in 1862, he refused to give up the dream and pushed an enabling bill through the assembly.

By the summer of 1864 Tilley was convinced of the need "to bind together the Atlantic and Pacific by a continuous chain of settlements and a line of communications for that [was] the destiny of this country, and the race which inhabited it."[7] He fought two bitter elections in New Brunswick over the Confederation issue and was appointed minister of customs in John A. Macdonald's first cabinet.

An early proponent of tariff protection for New Brunswick's infant industries, Tilley twice drew the wrath of free traders in the Maritimes. The tariff structure that he introduced in December 1867 helped to fuel the secession movement in Nova Scotia, and as minister of finance Tilley introduced the 1879 tariff legislation that became the keystone of Macdonald's "National Policy." Tariff walls to protect Canadian industry would define the nation's economic strategy until the Canada–US Free Trade Agreement came into effect on 1 January 1989.

Nova Scotia's Secessionist Movement

Nova Scotians had good reason to feel they had been hoodwinked into joining the new union. Neither voters nor their elected representatives had given their approval to the proposals that ultimately became the basis for Confederation. Even worse, they felt that they had been literally "railroaded" into a bad bargain. Commercial elements in the colony were particularly wary of a political structure initiated by "Upper Canadians" who might pursue trade and tariff policies that would cripple their global ambitions.

Nova Scotia voters finally had their say at the polls in September 1867, and they made their views clear. Thirty-six of 38 seats in the provincial assembly were won by candidates running on anti-Confederate tickets, and only Tupper survived the federal contest in which anti-Confederates were elected to 18 of Nova Scotia's 19 seats in the House of Commons.

In 1868 Howe led a delegation to London seeking repeal of the union, but the British were not interested. This outcome pushed some Nova Scotia separatists to pursue union with the United States as an alternative to Confederation. In 1869 an Annexation League was formed, its support concentrated in southwestern Nova Scotia, which was virtually a suburb of Boston, and in Cape Breton, where coal interests were keen to restore access to American markets. At a meeting in the summer of 1869, the annexationists drew up a manifesto, which they circulated around the province. "Our only hope of commercial prosperity, material development and permanent peace," the petitioners argued, "lies in closer relations with the United States. Therefore be it resolved that every legitimate means should be used by members of this convention to sever our connection with Canada and to bring about a union on fair and equitable terms with the American Republic."[8]

Nova Scotia's opposition to Confederation represented more than wounded local pride. As constituted in 1867, the Dominion of Canada was little more than the united Canadas writ large, and was designed to serve the needs of the larger colony. The capital of the new nation was Ottawa, the former capital of the Canadas, and the civil service was Canadian in structure and personnel. With their small populations compared to Quebec and Ontario, the Maritime provinces could never dominate either the House of Commons or the cabinet table. Moreover, the financial arrangements established by the British North America Act were particularly disadvantageous to small provinces. By absorbing customs revenues, Ottawa took away the chief source of funds on which colonial admin-istrations had relied; the smaller colonies were given per capita grants, which proved inadequate.

Nova Scotians were not opposed to becoming part of a larger political entity. Imperial union, with colonial representation in London, was Howe's preferred option, while Maritime Union and annexation to the United States also had their supporters. What rankled was the obvious Canadian bias in the constitutional arrangements of 1867. This is not to say that the Maritime colonies would have fared better outside the Dominion of Canada: the fate of the Newfoundland government in the 1930s is often cited as proof that Confederation at least allowed the Maritimes a "shabby dignity" in hard times.[9] Nevertheless, most of the predictions of the anti-Confederates proved correct in that the Maritimes did indeed have difficulty making their way in the new political structure.

Faced with growing support for annexation at home, Howe—ever loyal to Britain—agreed in 1869 to an accommodation with Ottawa that gave seats in the federal cabinet to two anti-Confed-erates and promised the province a 10-year bridging subsidy of about $800,000, with additional compensation for those public buildings that were transferred to federal control. Largely because of the lingering separatist sentiment in Nova Scotia, Prime Minister John A. Macdonald authorized the immediate construction of the Intercolonial Railway.

Macdonald also tried to represent Nova Scotia's interests as a member of the British delegation that met with American representatives to settle various issues left over from the Civil War. At the top of his agenda was a new reciprocity treaty. Although protectionists in the United States prevented such a concession, Macdonald managed to ensure that the Treaty of Washington, signed in 1871, provided free entry for Canadian fish into the American market and compensation, to be determined by arbitration, for American access to Canadian inshore waters—terms that also applied to Newfoundland.

While Nova Scotians and Canadians generally had hoped for more from the Washington negotiations, they accepted what was on offer. Only two Nova Scotia MPs voted against the treaty, and in the federal election of 1872 two-thirds of the MPs from Nova Scotia supported Macdonald. Nevertheless, the province's continuing financial problems and the difficulties faced by both the primary and the commercial sectors guaranteed that anti-Confederation sentiment could easily be rekindled.

Courting the Islands

Determined to unite Canada from sea-to-sea, Macdonald managed to incorporate Rupert's Land into the new nation in 1869, and British Columbia fol-

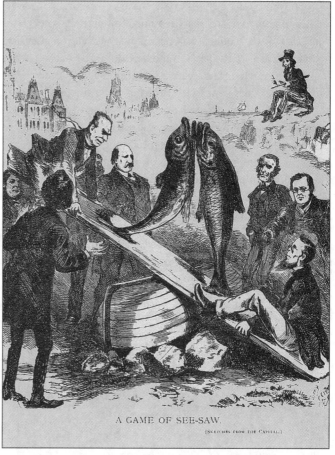

A GAME OF SEE-SAW.
[Sketches from the Capital.]

J.W. Bengough, "A Game of See-Saw," *Canadian Illustrated News*, 4 May 1872. In the 1872 election, Maritime opposition to Confederation was sufficiently muted to give the federal Conservatives a large majority of seats. One reason, this cartoon suggests, was Macdonald's success in gaining entry to American markets for Canadian fish. Courtesy of Chinook Multimedia, Edmonton.

lowed two years later. Newfoundland and Prince Edward Island continued to elude him.

Despite widespread opposition to the idea, Confederation remained on the political agenda of Newfoundland's Conservative premier, Frederic Carter, who perhaps doubted the colony's ability to prosper on its own. In March of 1869—an election year—he persuaded the assembly to accept draft union terms that were more generous than those proposed in the Quebec resolutions. He then went to Ottawa to negotiate the final document. Canada was prepared to offer a special annual grant of $150,000 in exchange for surrender of the island's Crown lands, and agreed that no export tax would be levied on its fish or other exports unless it applied to all provinces. To meet anti-Confederate claims that Newfoundlanders would be drafted into the Canadian militia and their bones left to bleach on the American border, the Canadian government agreed to encourage a local naval reserve and militia, and adjust its legislation appropriately. The terms passed the Canadian House of Commons on 10 June.

Buoyed by the best fishery in some years, having no overwhelming debt, and seeing little tangible or obvious advantage to be gained from union, voters remained unimpressed. Anti-Confederate forces, led by the eloquent and persuasive merchant Charles Fox Bennett—an energetic 76-year-old—won two-thirds of the seats in the assembly. The margin of victory was enough that Confederation would not re-emerge as a viable political issue until the 1940s. Most Newfoundlanders apparently believed that their country had the resources to support an independent future.[10]

Prince Edward Islanders, by contrast, eventually warmed to Macdonald's blandishments. The main issue in their 1867 election was not Confederation but the funding of denominational schools. Supported by a majority of Roman Catholic voters, the Liberals defeated the Conservatives. Once in office, however, they proved equally unwilling to embrace denominational funding. Consequently, they lost much of their support and in turn suffered defeat in the 1870 election. The triumphant Conservatives under James Pope, a leading businessman and supporter of Confederation, formed the new government in alliance with the Roman Catholic independents who had broken away from the Liberals.

An apostle of progress, Pope built a railway line that wound a serpentine route through many of the island's communities. Islanders soon found, as others had before them, that railway building was

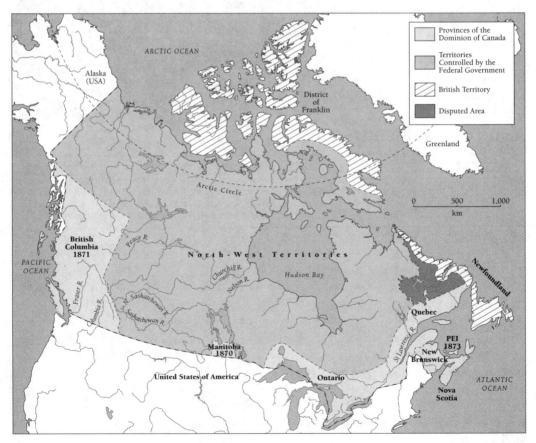

Canada in 1873.

hard on the pocketbook. Meanwhile, the land question remained unresolved. Although the Tenant League had collapsed in the autumn of 1865 (when confronted by two companies of British troops called in from Halifax), the historian Ian Robertson argues that it succeeded in convincing many landlords that the system was impossible to sustain.[11] In May 1865 Samuel Cunard and Laurence Sullivan, who together owned 20 per cent of the land in the colony, announced that they would be selling, not leasing, their land, and others began to follow their lead. If a general policy to manage the transition from leasehold to freehold remained elusive, that was only because the funding was lacking.

Pope argued that the answer was to let Ottawa come to the rescue. Although he lost the 1872 election, his successor, Robert Haythorne, continued building railway lines and chalking up debts. To alleviate a financial burden that was rapidly becoming untenable, Haythorne's government negotiated a Confederation agreement and took it to the electorate in March 1873. Pope then returned to power—not because he opposed Confederation but because he promised to drive a harder bargain with Ottawa. In the end he succeeded in securing most of the concessions that Islanders had wanted in 1864 and more besides. Prime Minister Macdonald agreed not only to assume the railway debt and help to buy out the remaining proprietors, but also to establish year-round communications with the mainland and give Islanders the six Commons seats that they demanded.

Conclusion

The debate over Confederation in the Atlantic region was defined to a striking degree by economic considerations. At the risk of oversimplification, it might be argued that anti-Confederates tended to look east and south—to the North Atlantic, Britain, the oceanic trades, and the promising American market—whereas supporters of Confederation looked west, seeing the future in economic integration with the central provinces and expansion to the Pacific. Both groups recognized the need to adjust to a world in which Britain had abandoned imperial protectionism for free trade, reduced its defence commitments, and accepted colonial demands for responsible government, and in which the Americans had retreated behind a wall of protectionism. These changes were compounded by the spread of new technologies, based on coal, iron, and steel, that threatened traditional industries based on wood and wind. In a time of flux, it seemed to many people in the Maritimes that political consolidation made sense. Newfoundlanders took much longer to accept that their future was as a North American, not a North Atlantic, country.

Further Readings

Bolger, Francis W.P. 1964. *Prince Edward Island and Confederation, 1863–1973*. Charlottetown: St Dunstan's.

Dallison, Robert L. 2006. *Turning Back the Fenians: New Brunswick's Last Colonial Campaign*. Fredericton: Goose Lane and New Brunswick Military Project, 2006.

Hiller, James K. 1993. "Newfoundland Confronts Canada, 1867–1949," in E.R. Forbes and D.A. Muise, eds, *The Atlantic Provinces in Confederation*. Fredericton/Toronto: Acadiensis Press/University of Toronto Press.

Marquis, Greg. 1998. *In Armageddon's Shadow: The Civil War and Canada's Maritime Provinces*. Montreal; McGill-Queen's University Press.

Martin, Ged, ed. 1990. *The Causes of Canadian Confederation*. Fredericton: Acadiensis Press.

Pryke, Kenneth G. 1978. *Nova Scotia and Confederation, 1864–74*. Toronto: University of Toronto Press.

Robertson, Ian Ross. 1996. *The Tenant League of Prince Edward Island, 1864–1867: Leasehold Tenure in the New World*. Toronto: University of Toronto Press.

Smith, Andrew. 2008. *British Businessmen and Canadian Confederation: Constitution Making in an Age of Anglo-Globalization*. Montreal: McGill-Queen's University Press.

Historical Spotlight

Buckner, Phillip A. 1990. "The Maritimes and Confederation: A Reassessment," in Ged Martin, ed., *The Causes of Canadian Confederation*. Fredericton: Acadiensis Press.

Hiller, James K. 1980. "Confederation Defeated: The Newfoundland Election of 1869," in James K. Hiller and Peter Neary, eds, *Newfoundland in the Nineteenth and Twentieth Centuries: Essays in Interpretation*. Toronto: University of Toronto Press.

Recommended Websites

Confederation
http://www.collectionscanada.gc.ca/confederation/index-e.html

Newfoundland and Canada, 1864–1948
http://www.heritage.nf.ca/law/confed.html and law/terms/html

Chapter 10

The Industrial Challenge, 1873–1901

The three Maritime provinces and Newfoundland had chosen separate political destinies, but in the last three decades of the nineteenth century they followed parallel paths. While the Maritime provinces worked out their positions within a federal state dominated by Ontario and Quebec, Newfoundland was obliged to deal with an imperial government that hoped the colony would soon see its error and join Canada. Relations with central governments, whether in Ottawa or London, were characterized by ambivalence and frustration. As they adjusted to the larger forces swirling around them, most Maritimers gradually became conscious of being Canadians, but, like Newfoundlanders, they were proud of their association with the ever-expanding British Empire. Imperial ties not only helped to balance the growing economic and cultural impact of the United States, but, also gave them a sense of power that they could never achieve on their own.

Industries in Transition

Located at the crossroads of American, British, and Canadian influences, individuals and governments in the Atlantic region faced major challenges in the fast-paced industrial age. Maritimers experienced a difficult transition from dependence on staple export trades to a more diversified economy. Under the leadership of Prime Minister John A. Macdonald, the Canadian government embarked on an ambitious "National Policy" that included building a transcontinental railway, developing the western territories, and imposing a high tariff on imported manufactured goods to give infant Canadian industries a chance to grow in the face of stiff competition from the United States. This framework initially seemed to work for the Maritimes, but over time it served to concentrate development in the St Lawrence–Great Lakes heartland. Newfoundlanders also attempted industrialization and diversification, but with limited success. The adjustment was made all the more difficult by an extended economic recession from 1873 to 1896, characterized by falling prices and low rates of economic growth.

Of the primary industries, agriculture—central to the economy of the Maritime provinces—did better than most. Output increased, if modestly, and specialization enabled some farmers to survive the loss of markets resulting from the end of reciprocity in 1866 and the decline of the Caribbean economies. While falling prices forced many farmers into subsistence agriculture, often in combination with lumbering and fishing, others specialized in livestock and dairy farming to supply growing urban centres, or focused on products for an elusive export market. Apple orchards proliferated, especially in Nova Scotia's Annapolis Valley, while potatoes became an important crop in Prince Edward Island and New Brunswick. With few commercial farms, Newfoundland relied heavily on imported livestock and foodstuffs, much of it from the Maritimes; Saint-Pierre provided a nearby market for Cape Breton produce.

The forest industry, a major engine of the New Brunswick economy, was badly damaged by the decline in British demand for both lumber and wooden ships. During the 1870s Saint John lost 29 per cent of its population as the unemployed and those with high ambitions drifted to opportunities in the United States. A disastrous fire on 20 June 1877, causing losses estimated at $27 million, was a further blow. Nevertheless, with sawmills aplenty, Saint John was Canada's leading lumber producer in the 1890s. Maritime lumbermen extended their activity to Newfoundland, first assaulting the pine forests of the Humber River valley and later establishing sawmills in the watersheds of rivers along the island's east coast.

All three Maritime provinces suffered as shipbuilding gradually declined into insignificance and the world's carrying trade came to be dominated by other seagoing nations. With iron (later steel) hulls and steam taking over the marine world, wooden sailing ships were increasingly confined to the coastal trades, fishing, and some long-distance freight routes. Shipbuilders in the Maritimes might well have attempted to build iron or steel vessels and maintain a competitive merchant marine, but the smart money tended towards consumer goods and heavy industries associated with

Table 10.1	Timeline
1875	Caraquet riots; Grace Annie Lockhart graduates from Mount Allison, the first woman to graduate from a university in the British Empire.
1876	Intercolonial Railway completed; Indian Act.
1877	Saint John fire.
1878	Scott Act.
1879	Protective tariff imposed under National Policy; Provincial Workmen's Association established.
1881	First Acadian National Convention.
1882	Nova Scotia Steel and Coal Company founded at New Glasgow.
1885	Treaty of Washington concessions regarding fisheries expire; Canadian Pacific Railway completed.
1886	Secession motion in Nova Scotia.
1890	Newfoundland attempts to negotiate reciprocity.
1891	Intercolonial Railway reaches Sydney and Yarmouth.
1892	St John's fire; Dr Wilfred Grenfell arrives in Labrador.
1893	Nova Scotia legislature rejects women's suffrage; Dominion Coal Company established at Glace Bay.
1894	Newfoundland bank crash.
1897	Newfoundland Railway completed.
1899	Triennial Band Council Elections Act.
1899–1902	South African War.
1900	Dominion Iron and Steel Company begins building steel mill at Sydney; Nova Scotia Steel and Coal Co. at Sydney Mines; Prince Edward Island becomes the first province in Canada to adopt prohibition.
1901	Bank of Nova Scotia moves headquarters to Toronto.

Victor Croucher, age five, with two prize codfish at Battle Harbour, Labrador, 1902. The Rooms Provincial Archives Division, VA 21-18/ R.E. Holloway.

railways. Although locally built cargo schooners remained in use until the 1940s, small-vessel fleets gradually contracted everywhere except in Newfoundland, where expansion continued until 1919.

The swarm of small Newfoundland schooners reflected that colony's continuing reliance on the cod and seal fisheries, and the absence of reasonable road and rail connections until the turn of the twentieth century. In the 1880s the fisheries represented 67 per cent of goods production, compared to 13 per cent in the Maritimes, and employed 85 per cent of the workforce. The Newfoundland economy was therefore especially vulnerable to falling international prices for salt cod and seal oil. Apart from the development of an offshore bank fishery in the 1880s, there was little fisheries diversification. The bank fishery was primarily a response to government restrictions on the sale of bait to foreign offshore fleets, particularly the French banking fleet, whose product competed with Newfoundland exports. Lobster canning, an industry initiated by Maritimers, became increasingly important, but salt cod remained the staple, tied to congested markets in southern Europe and the Caribbean.

With improvements in railway connections and refrigeration technology, Maritimers were well placed to meet the demand for fresh and frozen fish in the United States and central Canada. Federal bounties helped to stimulate the expansion of the fisheries until 1886, when the easy access to American fish markets provided by the Treaty of Washington expired. In response, many Nova

Scotian skippers and crew moved to Gloucester and other New England ports. As the demand for salt fish fell, businesses went bankrupt, among them Charles Robin and Company, the largest inshore cod firm in the Maritimes. The bank fisheries, centred in Lunenburg and adjacent ports, continued to be an important industry, but inshore fishers came to rely less on cod and more on salmon, sardines, oysters, and lobsters. In the 1880s and 1890s, a lobster canning boom energized ports throughout the region and provided seasonal jobs for women, who were hired as a cheap labour by cannery owners.[1]

An Industrial Revolution in the Maritimes

Coal, abundant in Cape Breton, northeastern Nova Scotia, and southern New Brunswick, was the key component in the efforts of Maritimers to join the Industrial Revolution. When the Reciprocity Treaty expired in 1866, the United States slapped prohibitive duties on imported coal. Maritime coal producers then turned their attention to markets in central Canada. The success of this strategy depended on the completion of a railway to the St Lawrence and the imposition of a protective tariff to keep out cheaper imports. By 1876 the Intercolonial Railway linked Halifax to Lévis, giving Maritime producers their long-desired year-round access to central Canadian markets. Extensions to Sydney and Yarmouth were in place by 1891.

The National Policy budget of 1879, which imposed high tariffs on imported manufactured goods, set off a binge of investment in secondary industries in the Maritimes. Two zones of development emerged. In the ports of Halifax, Saint John, and Yarmouth, imported staples such as cotton, spices, sugar, and tea were processed. In the corridor defined by the Intercolonial Railway, manufacturing was based on coal, iron, and steel. By 1885 Nova Scotia and New Brunswick supported eight cotton mills, three sugar refineries, two confectionaries, two rope works, and a glass factory.[2] Dartmouth, across the harbour from Halifax, sprouted a number of successful industries, including Starr Manufacturing, famous for its skates and hockey sticks, and Dartmouth Rope Works, which by 1890 was the largest manufacturer of binder twine in Canada. The Rope Works was part of a cluster of industries and financial institutions owned by William Stairs, Son and Morrow, the largest mercantile house in eastern Canada by the end of the century.

The National Policy tariff also included a hefty duty on imported coal. In this period, the Maritimes accounted for most of the coal produced in Canada, and shipments to the Quebec market increased dramatically. Since the region's producers were unable to supply much more than 10 per cent of the total demand, high-quality anthracite coal for domestic use came largely from the United States, as did the bituminous coal used by industries west of Montreal. Coal mines proliferated in Cape Breton, Inverness, Pictou, and Cumberland counties in Nova Scotia and, by the first decade of the twentieth century, in the Grand Lake area of New Brunswick as well.

With the development of a flourishing iron and steel industry, Nova Scotia's industrial pre-eminence seemed assured. Founded in Pictou County in 1882, Nova Scotia Steel and Coal became, for a time, Canada's leading producer of iron and steel products. Using iron ore from Bell Island, Newfoundland, the company integrated its operations at Sydney Mines in 1900. A second corporate success story began in 1893 with the creation of the Dominion Coal Company, spearheaded by Boston financier Henry M. Whitney. Six years later the company was granted a 99-year lease on all unassigned coal resources in Cape Breton in return for a royalty. Armed with this assurance,

Biography | *Alexander "Boss" Gibson*

Born in 1819 near St Andrews, New Brunswick, Alexander Gibson was the son of hard-working pioneer farmers. Gibson had a rudimentary education and then began work in the lumber business, in which he prospered. By the age of 30 he was an expert in the management of water-powered sawmills and the new technology of gang saws. A tall, powerful, and highly ambitious man, Gibson soon became a force to be reckoned with in his native province.

In the 1850s, in partnership with an American lumberman, he worked sawmills on the Lepreau River and in the 1860s he acquired mills and timber rights from the Scottish firm of Gilmour, Rankin, and Company on the Nashwaak River near Fredericton. Eventually controlling nearly 300,000 acres (120,000 hectares) of forest, Gibson shipped deals (squared "sticks" of spruce and pine) to Saint John and onward to Britain and the United States, where they were sawn into lumber. He also developed other enterprises, including a tannery, a leather factory, and a shipyard.

Like many entrepreneurs of his time, Gibson became involved in railway promotion. He was a director of the Fredericton Railway Company and later president of the New Brunswick Railway Company, which built a narrow-gauge railway, known as the "Gibson line," on the east bank of the St John River. The interchange with river traffic was located at the village of Gibson (at the mouth of the Nashwaak), where a roundhouse, machine shops, and a freight yard were established. He was also instrumental in building a railway line from Gibson to Chatham at the mouth of the Miramichi.

Gibson's most ambitious project was the building of a large cotton mill on the Nashwaak at Marysville, a community he named after his wife and their eldest daughter, who died in 1867. From the outset, Marysville was a company town, the creation of "Boss" Gibson, who at his own expense built a school, a store, a fine Methodist church—Gibson paid the minister and the organist, and forbade the sale of alcohol—and "a palatial residence" for his family on "Nob Hill." The cotton mill, which began production in 1885, was a magnificent structure, designed by a Boston firm to house 1,100 looms and 60,000 spindles. Around the mill Gibson built 53 two-storey brick tenements to house his workers.

At the height of his career Gibson employed up to 2,000 people in his various enterprises, but by the 1890s his lumber and leather companies were encountering difficulties. Cotton proved to be a highly competitive business, increasingly subject to central Canadian intervention. As Murray Young has written, "the Gibson enterprise was an old-fashioned family concern dependent on the banks for its working capital, with a patriarchal head who was contemptuous of banking rules and regulations and given to arbitrary decisions."[3] By the early twentieth century, Gibson was bankrupt. In a 1907 settlement, he retained only a pension and the lifetime use of his house. He died in 1913 at the age of 94. His cotton mill continued production, passing through various owners, until the 1970s. Now a suburb of Fredericton, Marysville is a national historic site and a striking monument to the early age of industrialization in the Maritimes.

Whitney incorporated the Dominion Iron and Steel Company and began construction of a primary steel mill at Sydney in 1900. Small rolling mills were established in Halifax and Saint John, as well as in Amherst, where in 1893 J. Rhodes, Curry, and Company built the first railway cars manufactured in Canada.[4]

Workers at the Intercolonial Railway shop in Moncton. Completed from Halifax to Lévis in 1876, the Intercolonial helped to make Moncton, the railway's eastern headquarters, a major distribution and manufacturing centre. Moncton Museum Collection.

The Intercolonial Railway and other lines built in this period were the keys to economic development in many Maritime communities.[5] Strategically located towns, including Moncton, Truro, Windsor, and Yarmouth, produced textiles, foundry goods, furniture, and processed foods that found markets near and far. Communities such as Chatham, Newcastle, Bathurst, Dalhousie, and Campbellton on New Brunswick's eastern shore experienced mini-booms when the railway was completed. On the surface at least, the Maritimes appeared to be making a successful transition to an industrial economy. Yet, as Table 10.2 shows, the gross value of production in the manufacturing sector increased by only 32 per cent between 1880 and 1900—about the same as forestry—and as a percentage of the total actually declined by 3 per cent. In 1901 manufacturing employed only 28 per

Table 10.2 Timeline Gross Value of Production ($000), Maritimes

	Agriculture	Forestry	Mining	Fishery	Manufacturing	Total
1880	41.9	13.3	3.1	14.9	42.6	115.9
1900	58.7	17.2	14.4	20.3	56.4	167.1
Change (%)	40.1	29.3	364.5	36.2	32.4	44.1

Percentage of Gross Value of Production, Maritimes					
	Agriculture	Forestry	Mining	Fishery	Manufacturing
1880	36	12	3	13	37
1900	51	10	9	12	34
Change	15	(–2)	6	(–1)	(–3)

Source: Table 4, Gross value of production: Maritimes (1935-9), from "Economic Growth in the Atlantic Region 1880–1940," in *Atlantic Canada and Confederation: Essays in Canadian Political Economy*, by David G. Alexander (compiled by Eric W. Sager, Lewis R. Fischer, and Stuart O. Pierson), © University of Toronto Press, 1983; published in association with Memorial University of Newfoundland.

cent of the workforce (47 per cent were in primary production and 25 per cent in services). Maritime factories tended to be smaller and less efficient than those in central Canada, which meant lower pay for workers and lower profits for owners. Handicapped by a relatively small local market, managerial inexperience, and a long recession, they fought an uphill battle against central Canadian competitors.

Soon, central Canadian interests swooped into the Maritimes to "rationalize" production and protect their profits. Dominion Cotton Mills and the Canadian Coloured Cotton Company, both of Montreal, took over the region's cotton mills, while Diamond Glass, also of Montreal, bought and eventually closed the three glassworks at Trenton. It was the same story in coal, sugar, and cordage. By 1895 only spices, confectionary—most notably Ganongs in St Stephens and Moirs in Halifax—and manufacturing related to iron, steel, and local staples remained under regional control. Small manufacturers and traditional trades were vulnerable to the marketing, through branch businesses, of goods produced elsewhere. With the completion of nationwide railway systems, mail-order companies such as the one run by Timothy Eaton in Toronto extended their reach to the most remote corners of the country.

Increasingly reluctant to invest in regional enterprises, Maritime banks looked for safer and more profitable places to do business. A clear sign of this shift was the Bank of Nova Scotia's decision to move its headquarters from Halifax to Toronto in 1901. Other regionally based banks quickly followed. By 1910 only three of the 13 banks which in 1900 had headquarters in the Maritimes remained rooted in the region.

Document

The Royal Commission on Labour and Capital, 1889

The Industrial Revolution was built on the backs of workers who initially had little say in the conditions of their employment. In 1886 the Canadian government responded to concerns about the exploitative nature of industrial capitalism by establishing a Royal Commission on Labour and Capital. The commissioners heard nearly 1,800 witnesses, many of them from Nova Scotia and New Brunswick.

The following testimony by Joseph Larkins, a young factory worker in Halifax, was published in the commission's 1889 report. It illustrates the common practice among entrepreneurs, pressured by stiff competition, of hiring children under 16 and paying them less than adults for doing the same work. Reformers demanded legislation to regulate the employment of children and provide compensation for workers injured on the job.

Q. How old are you? A. I am 11 years.
Q. What is the matter with your hand? A. It got hurt in the machinery.
Q. How? A. It got caught in the rollers.
Q. What rollers? A. The rollers of a cracker machine—a biscuit machine.
Q. How long were you working in the biscuit factory? A. About seven weeks.
Q. Was it part of your work to look after the machinery? A. No; I was taken in as a packer and was then put to work on the machinery.

Continued

Q. How much wages did they give you? A. A dollar a week first, and then a dollar and a quarter.

Q. How much do they give you now? A. Nothing at all.

Q. How long is it since you were hurt? A. Nine weeks Thursday.

Q. And have they not given you anything? A. No; except for the week when I was hurt.

Q. Did you ask for employment? A. My mother asked for a job for me, and they said I could get a job biscuit packing; then they changed me to where the machinery was.

Q. How long were you working at the machinery before you were hurt? A. I could not say.

Q. What were you doing at the machinery? A. I was brushing the dough off according as it came through.

Q. Are other boys your age employed in the concern? A. I could not say. There was a boy about the same size.

Q. Did you lose any fingers? A. I lost one.

Q. Did you lose any of the joints in the others? A. I think I will lose a second finger.

Q. Who paid the doctor? A. I could not say.

Q. Who took you to the doctor? A. A man who was there. The doctor put seven or eight stitches in. . . .⁶

Newfoundland's National Policy

Newfoundlanders were also caught up in dreams of new industries and diversification. Realizing that political independence had to be underpinned by a stronger economy, the government led by Sir William Whiteway in the late 1870s and early 1880s adopted a local version of the National Policy, trumpeted as the "Policy of Progress." The centrepiece was a railway across the island, designed—like the Canadian Pacific Railway (CPR)—to link the east and west coasts and stimulate the development of land-based industries. The first track was laid in 1881. Tariff policy was adjusted to protect small manufacturers in St John's. Convinced by Geological Survey reports that the island contained valuable natural resources in abundance, railway enthusiasts predicted rapid growth in agriculture, forest industries, and mining.

Another dimension of this policy was a determined attempt to gain unrestricted access to the resources of the French Treaty Shore. Having long claimed an exclusive right to fish between Cape St John and Cape Ray, the French maintained that settlement (and by implication economic development) on "their" Shore was illegal because it would interfere with the fishery. As a result, the growing numbers of settlers on the Shore were not represented in the legislature, had no local government, and were denied Crown land grants as well as mining and timber licences.

Although the French Shore fishery was declining as the bank fishery based at Saint-Pierre expanded, France refused to give up its privileges. The British government was wary of precipitating a diplomatic crisis with France, but Whiteway persevered. He managed to negotiate political representation, the appointment of magistrates, and qualified land grants, but the railway and ferry terminal had to be placed at Port-aux-Basques, just outside the Treaty Shore. As tensions between

Newfoundland, the Colonial Office, and France intensified, they were compounded by an arcane but passionately argued dispute over whether lobsters were fish within the meaning of the treaties and therefore a resource that France could catch and process. The argument was never resolved, but it helped to cement a self-conscious Newfoundland nationalism, which gained strength during the second half of the nineteenth century.

In the short term at least, the Policy of Progress failed to alter the island's economy in any significant way. Employment in secondary and service industries increased, but employment in primary industries fell by 20 per cent between 1874 and 1901. The economic imperialism of central Canada reached the island in 1890 when the railway project was taken over by Montreal-based contractor Robert G. Reid, who had close links with the CPR. Reid completed the line in 1897, and then negotiated a highly controversial contract by which he (and his successors) acquired control of the railway, much of the telegraph system, and extensive land grants—among other concessions. The contract was soon modified, but the accompanying political crisis redefined party alliances.

Reid was also associated with the Bank of Montreal. It became banker to the Newfoundland government after the crash of the colony's two private banks in December 1894 as a result of the prolonged recession, lack of oversight, and severe market competition in the salt fish trade. Like the Maritime provinces, Newfoundland lost control of its financial institutions—Canadian banks arrived in St John's a week after the crash—and its currency became tied to the Canadian dollar. In the mid-1890s mainland steel companies took over the huge deposits of iron ore at Bell Island in Conception Bay, shipping it to their blast furnaces at Cape Breton.[7]

People on the Move

In the last three decades of the nineteenth century, people throughout the Maritimes and Newfoundland were on the move from country to town and from the Atlantic region to other areas of North America. The lure of urban jobs in factories, service industries, and emerging professions such as engineering, medicine, and teaching drew young people like a magnet and was typical of wider North American trends. Since the Atlantic region lacked a major metropolis to absorb them, they became part of what contemporaries called "the exodus." New England was the main attraction, but there were few parts of North America where Maritimers and Newfoundlanders could not be found. With railways supplementing ships, migrants fetched up in communities on the Great Lakes, in farms on the interior plains, and everywhere on the west coast, including the Yukon following the discovery of gold at Bonanza Creek in 1896.

Out-migration was both a result and a cause of the region's shaky economic performance.[8] As early as the 1860s, the Maritimes began to suffer net migration losses, which reached a peak in the 1880s but continued at a significant rate until the 1930s. Between 1871 and 1881 the population grew by 13.5 per cent; thereafter growth dropped to 1.2 per cent between 1881 and 1891 and 1.5 per cent between 1891 and 1901. After 1891 the population of Prince Edward Island began to decline in absolute terms. In all, some 250,000 people left the Maritimes between 1871 and 1901. Women were more likely to leave than men, the young more likely than the middle-aged, anglophones more likely than francophones, and people living in rural areas more likely than urban dwellers. In the view of the historian Judith Fingard, the "exodus of the last quarter of the nineteenth century may have resulted in the decapitation of Maritime society."[9] The hemorrhage was not quite as severe in Newfoundland, but the trends were similar. In the 1880s the population grew by only 3 per cent, and for the first time more people left the colony than arrived from elsewhere. Most districts around Conception Bay and on the southeastern Avalon declined in absolute numbers.

The emphasis that scholars place on out-migration has masked the attention that policy-makers in this period paid to immigration. Attracting newcomers became a priority in Ottawa, which assumed responsibility for funding the immigrant bureaucracy, including quarantine facilities in Halifax, Saint John, and Quebec City. New Brunswick was particularly aggressive in seeking immigrants. In anticipation of the completion of the Intercolonial Railway, which opened new areas for settlement, the province implemented a generous land grants policy in 1872. More than 800 immigrants arrived that year, and the numbers reached a high of 3,714 in 1889.[10]

Although most immigrants to the Maritimes came from Great Britain, a few originated elsewhere. Danes, who began arriving in New Brunswick in 1872, named their community on the hilly upper reaches of the St John River New Denmark. On the outskirts of Sydney, the community around Whitney Pier would soon become one of the region's most multicultural communities, attracting workers from Poland, Ukraine, Croatia, Italy, and the Caribbean. Jews fleeing poverty and persecution in Europe gravitated to the region's cities, their numbers approaching 1,000 by the end of the century. The Maritimes also became a receiving area for "home children"—orphaned or destitute British youngsters who were shipped to "the colonies" to begin a new life, most of them as domestic servants or farm labourers. While most Asian immigrants to Canada settled in the west, nearly every town in the Maritimes had a Chinese laundry or restaurant after the Canadian Pacific Railway was completed in 1885. The first Chinese immigrants in St John's arrived in the mid-1890s. Both Canada and Newfoundland imposed a head tax on Chinese immigrants, making it difficult for men to bring family members to their new homeland.

Although the promotional literature promised a land of opportunity, many immigrants found only hardship, drudgery, and prejudice. Newcomers therefore often followed the same path as many from the region, moving on United States to find work and, for a few, great fame and fortune. Lazar Meir, for example—a 19-year-old Russian-born Jew—moved from Saint John to Boston in 1904, where he made a transition from dealing in scrap metal to the burgeoning movie business. As Louis B. Meyer, he became a founder of one of the world's great Hollywood film studios, Metro-Goldwyn-Meyer.

Aboriginals in the Age of Industry

Aboriginal people in the Maritimes were subject to the same pressures as their non-Aboriginal neighbours, but for them the barriers to modernization were often insurmountable. As cheap factory goods increasingly flooded the market, income from sales of hand-crafted items declined. Domestic and unskilled labour became the primary options for paid employment. In some areas, Aboriginal men earned good wages as guides for sports fishermen and hunters, who had access to natural resources from which Aboriginal people were increasingly excluded by game laws. A few found jobs in rapidly expanding urban centres, but for all practical purposes they were barred from industrial ventures by local prejudice, lack of capital, and the rigid provisions of the Indian Act.

Following Confederation, people living on reserves in Canada became "Status Indians" under the jurisdiction of the federal government. The Indian Act of 1876 consolidated nation-wide policies, with little concern for regional and cultural differences. Assuming that Aboriginal people were incapable of integrating into "civilized" society, the Act treated them as wards of the state. They could neither vote nor drink alcohol; they risked losing their Indian status if they pursued higher education or took up a profession; and Aboriginal women who married white men automatically lost their status, along with their ability to pass it on to their children. Freezing the Mi'kmaq, Wolastoqiyik, and Passamaquoddy in patriarchal, pre-industrial social and economic arrangements, the Indian Act made integration into the larger Maritime society all but impossible.

In 1899 the Canadian government passed legislation to replace the community appointment of Aboriginal leaders in eastern Canada with a system of band council elections to be held every three years. Officials in Ottawa saw this as a progressive move, but many bands in the Maritimes either ignored the new rules or found ways to get around them and maintain hereditary chiefdom. There was little that overworked and poorly paid superintendents could or would do in such cases.[11]

Newfoundland had neither reserves nor an equivalent to the Indian Act. The approximately 200 Mi'kmaq living there—mainly in the Conne River area—survived by working as guides and mail carriers, trapping, fishing, hunting caribou, and selling basketry. For most of the nineteenth century they had the island's interior largely to themselves, but the situation changed in the 1890s with the building of the railway, the subsequent development of forest industries, and the arrival of sport hunters.

In Labrador the Innu relied heavily on trapping furs, which they traded at North West River, Davis Inlet, and elsewhere. By the 1890s, however, white and mixed-heritage settlers living in Hamilton Inlet were encroaching on their hunting territory, causing angry confrontations. The Inuit population of about 1,000 was assumed to be on the way to either extinction or absorption into white society. With up to 1,200 Newfoundland fishing schooners arriving each summer, diet, clothing, and housing all began to change, and fishing for cod and char became the mainstay of the local Inuit economy. As contact with whites increased, Inuit proved susceptible to diseases such as measles and influenza brought from elsewhere. In 1893, several Inuit were put on display at the Columbian Exhibition in Chicago, where they were exposed to typhoid fever.

Lydia Campbell, the daughter of an English Hudson's Bay Company trapper and his Inuit wife, was well into her seventies when her memoirs were recorded and published in the 1890s. Reflecting on the changes she had witnessed in Labrador over the course of her life, she blamed alcohol for the decline in human health and lamented the over-exploitation of Labrador's fish and wildlife, which brought an end to the abundance she remembered as a child. "[I]t was a pretty sight to see a lot of birch canoes shining red in the sunshine. . . men steering the women paddling, the children singing or chatting [but] where are [they] now, hardly ever see a family now except in winter."[12]

Political Machinations

Inadequate federal subsidies meant that the Maritime provinces experienced severe financial problems. Prince Edward Island—which, unlike Nova Scotia and New Brunswick, lacked the resources to generate timber and mineral royalties—was particularly hard pressed. By 1900 the province relied on federal subsidies for 64.5 per cent of its provincial budget. The Island government therefore had little choice but to retrench, going so far as to abolish the secret ballot (which was more expensive than open voting) and introduce statutory road labour. At the same time, Islanders were preoccupied with Ottawa's failure to provide the "efficient and continuous communication" with the mainland promised by the Confederation agreement. In the mid-1880s, after making a direct appeal to the imperial government, they got a better ferry, although there was considerable local support for a tunnel under the Northumberland Strait.

In New Brunswick the economic recession of the mid-1880s exposed the weakness of the province's industrial base and underscored the steady decline of the once world-renowned shipbuilding industry. Discontent was manifested in a loose alliance of all political interests that coalesced under Andrew G. Blair in 1886 to become a powerful Liberal machine. Although Blair abolished the Legislative Council to save money—a popular measure—he was at a loss to bring prosperity to his province. The Macdonald government, preoccupied with a second uprising in the Northwest and the completion of the Canadian Pacific Railway, seemed deaf to Maritime demands, especially from provinces that persisted in electing Liberal governments.

Frustration with Ottawa led Nova Scotia's Liberal Premier, William S. Fielding, to introduce a motion in the legislature in 1886 calling for Maritime union as a preliminary to secession from Canada. New Brunswick and Prince Edward Island proved lukewarm to the idea, and even Nova Scotia voters effectively repudiated Fielding's proposal in the 1887 federal election, when Macdonald's Conservatives won a majority of Maritime seats. As a fallback position, Fielding took up two new causes: provincial rights and free trade with the United States. These policies were supported by a number of provinces with Liberal premiers, and also by the federal Liberal Party under its new leader Wilfrid Laurier. Blair and Fielding attended the first interprovincial conference in 1887—a harbinger of what would prove to be long-standing tensions between federal and provincial jurisdictions in Canada.[13]

Reciprocity was also popular in Newfoundland, where fish exporters faced heavy French and Norwegian competition in Europe and were interested in new markets in North America. Asserting its rights within the Empire, the Newfoundland government received permission to open talks with the United States government. When its representative, Robert Bond, and the American Secretary of State, James Blaine, concluded a draft reciprocity treaty in 1890, there was surprise in London, consternation in Ottawa, and outrage in Halifax. If Newfoundland was allowed to gain advantages outside Confederation that Nova Scotia could not obtain within it, secession might well become more than a threat. The treaty was swiftly killed by the British government—though whether the treaty would have survived the American Senate is questionable.

Humiliated and angry, the Newfoundland government retaliated by imposing extra duties on imports from Canada and by refusing to issue bait licences to fishermen from Nova Scotia. Canada countered with similar measures. In 1892 the two sides met in Halifax to discuss their differences, but nothing was resolved. The Newfoundlanders were unwilling to talk seriously about Confederation and the Canadian government maintained its objections to a separate Newfoundland reciprocity treaty. Since London and the courts had already ruled that Newfoundland could not discriminate against other British subjects, Canadians were confident that their interests would prevail.

Social Unrest

As in the past, political divisions prompted by economic concerns were complicated by issues of class, ethnicity, and religion. Labour unrest—a product of urbanization, industrialization, and new political ideas—became increasingly common. The centre of organized labour activity was the Nova Scotia coalfields, where repressive and unsafe corporate practices led to the formation of Canada's first industrial union, the Provincial Workmen's Association (PWA), in 1879.[14] A relatively conservative organization, the PWA sought to raise the status of miners to that of skilled tradesmen and lobbied for reforms in mining practices, but it did not challenge the industry's structure or promote collective bargaining. As a result, coal strikes were restricted to individual fields: Pictou in 1886–7, Springhill in 1890 and 1897, and Joggins in 1896. Nova Scotia's mines nevertheless saw some of the most protracted strikes in Canada in the late nineteenth century. Other sectors experienced strikes as well, including the Saint John and Halifax waterfronts, but the labour movement was too decentralized and scattered to have much overall impact.

Nova Scotia's coal mines had the dubious distinction of experiencing some of the continent's worst mining disasters. In 1891, 125 men and boys—some as young as 10 years of age—died in an explosion and fire in one Springhill colliery.[15] This tragedy underscored the dangers faced by coal workers and increased the demand for legislation to improve safety in the mines, to provide workman's compensation, and to make the employment of children in mines illegal.

If strikes reflected growing class divisions, prolonged debates over education revealed religious, ethnic, and linguistic cleavages. The basic question was how far public school systems should go to accommodate religious and cultural diversity. The Newfoundland solution, finalized in 1873, was to cut the education budget three ways, producing a denominational educational system with separate Roman Catholic, Church of England, and Methodist schools—a practice later expanded to include other denominations, including the Salvation Army. In Nova Scotia and Prince Edward Island, compromises were struck allowing Roman Catholic schools to operate with provincial funding.

Nova Scotia legislation in 1865 also made provision for separate schools for black children in areas where numbers warranted. As elsewhere, "separate" did not mean equal in funding and facilities. After a close vote in the legislature, the Education Act of 1884 stipulated that black children could not be barred from attending any school in their district. The upshot was that segregated schools were strengthened in areas such as Halifax, where there was a large black population, and weakened in areas with only a few black families.[16] Although most black youngsters had little hope of attending university, the colour bar was breached in Nova Scotia when James Johnston was admitted to Dalhousie Law School in 1898. Mary Matilda Winslow, who graduated from the University of New Brunswick in 1905, broke the colour bar for women.

In New Brunswick the funding of separate schools for Roman Catholics became a contentious issue in the wake of the Common Schools Act of 1871, which legislated a fully non-sectarian system. Outraged, Catholics refused to pay school assessments and appealed to Ottawa for disallowance. The federal government declined to intervene on the grounds that education was a provincial responsibility, and the courts ruled the act to be constitutional. Thus fortified, the provincial government went to the polls in 1874 and, emerging victorious, began legal actions against those refusing to pay school assessments.

Resistance was especially fierce among Acadians. Since only one Acadian child in six attended schools, there was little incentive to support schools of any kind, let alone schools that excluded Catholic teachings. Tensions culminated in the Caraquet riots of 1875, in which two people died. A compromise then emerged: where numbers warranted, Roman Catholics could be taught by members of religious orders and have religious instruction after school hours. For Acadians, the

Robert Harris, *The Meeting of the School Trustees*, 1885, oil on canvas, 102.2 x 126.5 cm. Only seven years old when his family migrated from Wales to Prince Edward Island, Robert Harris (1849–1919) became one of Canada's best-known artists. Scenes similar to the one depicted here must have been played out in a number of communities following the introduction of publicly funded schooling. By the end of the nineteenth century, many children under the age of 12 spent a significant proportion of their day in school, receiving their moral and academic training from young female teachers such as the one depicted here rather than their parents. National Art Gallery of Canada, Ottawa, Purchased 1886, #6. Photo © National Gallery of Canada.

availability of French-language instruction remained a serious problem, since New Brunswick, like the other provinces, insisted on the use of English in schools.

The schools dispute served as a rallying point for the scattered but increasingly self-conscious Acadian community, which by the 1870s numbered about 90,000, half of them in New Brunswick. Longfellow's poem *Evangeline* (1847), a love story set against the background of the deportation, had begun to circulate in French translation during the 1860s. Adopted for use in the Collège St-Joseph at Memramcook, the poem seemed to the growing Acadian elite to be "the poetic distillation of their history, the true legend of their past."[17] It became, in effect, a unifying narrative at a time when Acadians were trying to establish a collective identity.

At the first Acadian Congress, held in 1881 at Memramcook, the majority of delegates decided to adopt the Feast of the Assumption (15 August) as the Acadian national holiday rather than that of St-Jean-Baptiste, thus choosing distinctiveness over closer ties with Quebec. The 1884 convention at Miscouche adopted an Acadian flag—the French tricolour (which at that time was also used in

The original Acadian flag, 1884, conceived by Father Marcel-François Richard. Photo Léo Blanchard, Musée acadien, Université de Moncton.

Quebec), with a yellow star signifying devotion both to the Virgin Mary and to the papacy. "Ave Maris Stella" became the Acadian "national" hymn. The Société Nationale l'Assomption, founded in 1881 (now the Société Nationale de l'Acadie), provided leadership and continuity by promoting Acadian interests. Several newspapers appeared, among them *L'Évangeline* in 1887, and in the 1890s new colleges were established at Pointe de l'Église in Nova Scotia and Caraquet in New Brunswick.

More reluctant than anglophones to leave the region, Acadians also had a high fertility rate. Accordingly, their numbers increased both absolutely and as a percentage of the Maritime population. In New Brunswick, which lost 76,000 people to the United States during the last two decades of the nineteenth century, Acadians made up 24 per cent of the population by 1901, replacing the Irish as the largest Roman Catholic group. Not surprisingly, it was in this province that the issue of cultural uniformity—a sensitive issue throughout Canada—surfaced in the Maritimes.

At a time when a revived cult of Loyalism, with its strongly imperial overtones, was spreading among Protestant New Brunswickers, Herman H. Pitts used a difficult schools dispute in Bathurst to launch a determined campaign in favour of "equal rights." The same euphemism was used in Ontario to identify a movement designed to end "concessions" to Roman Catholics and francophones and to promote an evangelical Protestant reform agenda, which included, among other things, prohibition, Sabbath observance, and, eventually, limited female suffrage. A central (and divisive) figure during the 1890s, Pitts was ultimately rejected by an electorate that opted for accommodation over confrontation.

Historical Focus

Acadian National Identity

Between 1881 and 1890 Acadians met in three large congresses, one in each of the Maritime provinces: Memramcook, New Brunswick; Miscouche, Prince Edward Island; and Pointe de l'Église, Nova Scotia. The inspiration came from a meeting in Quebec City in 1880, when francophones from across North America were invited to a convention held on Saint-Jean-Baptiste Day. There was a special committee for Acadians, which was well attended. Joseph-Octave Arsenault, a prominent political leader in Prince Edward Island, encouraged Island Acadians to attend the Saint-Jean-Baptiste convention, in part because they were experiencing massive out-migration caused by a lack of available agricultural land.

Arsenault was aware of efforts in Quebec to open rural areas for group settlement and hoped that a similar approach might help to protect the Acadian "national" identity from the homogenizing tendencies of industrial cities. As he told a parish assembly:

It is here, under national banners, that we the Acadian people will find the strength and resources to gain respect for our rights which have been ignored for too long, and to preserve the integrity of our national character and the language we love and that our mothers taught us; in short, everything that is of concern to our nation: religion, education, science, industry, and colonization. He made us realize that we could benefit from joining our Canadian brothers to form one national family. Above all, the Honourable Arsenault emphasized the question of colonization. Since this issue is on the programme of the convention, it would be very much in our interest to be represented, if only to discuss a subject that concerns us so much; our properties are already too small and we shall soon be forced to seek settlements elsewhere for our children, and that will certainly be in Canada.[18]

The Pitts crusade was an unattractive feature of the reform movement that swept the region in the late nineteenth century: a mix of (usually Protestant) religion, imperialism, and faith in progress. Rooted in cities and churches, it addressed many of the problems associated with industrial development. The temperance movement was well established, and there had been widespread support in the Maritimes for the 1878 Scott Act, a federal measure that permitted municipalities to bar the sale of alcohol. Newfoundland had similar legislation, and organizations such as the Sons of Temperance and the Woman's Christian Temperance Union (WCTU) were active across the region.

Increasingly, reformers looked to the state to enact aspects of their program, a prospect not always welcomed by political leaders. They understood the potentially divisive nature of some issues on the "social gospel" agenda and were wary of the costs associated with extending the state's responsibilities. With pressure for prohibition mounting, the Canadian government held a referendum on the matter in 1898, but the turnout was low and Quebec was opposed, so Prime Minister Laurier dropped the idea. In 1900 Prince Edward Island became the first province to legislate prohibition, but the other provinces were slow to follow. In many communities, local-option legislation meant that prohibition was a fact of life, though it was easily circumvented.

While prohibition attracted the most attention, reformers were also concerned with public health, urban renewal, the treatment of children and animals, social and economic justice, and the rights of women. In the region's cities, reformers focused on young people, who were perceived as needing protection from the temptations that cities offered. The Young Men's Christian Association (YMCA), founded in England in 1844, appeared in St John's in 1854, and moved into the Maritimes after Confederation, the first Canadian building dedicated to "the Y" opening in Pictou in 1872. Two years earlier, the first Young Women's Christian Association (YWCA) in Canada had opened its doors in Saint John. The Edward Jost Mission, established in Halifax in the 1860s to address the needs of the urban poor, continued to grow as the city expanded. So too did the Children's Aid Society, another British initiative.

By the end of the nineteenth century, a new class of educated experts was at the forefront of progressive reform. Doctors, riding high on scientific discoveries, proved particularly successful in developing their professional status and harnessing it to social needs. Using provincial medical boards, over which they presided, to advance their monopolization of medical practice, they lobbied governments to curb the widespread reliance on patent medicines, home cures, and unlicensed practitioners, and to encourage improved sanitation, the gathering of vital statistics, and the incorporation of their expertise into the legal process. With the establishment of a Faculty of Medicine, which evolved into the Halifax Medical College in 1875, young men in the region no longer had to go abroad for their medical education. Young women, initially denied entry to the college, either studied elsewhere or, more likely, took up nursing, which emerged as a primarily female profession in this period. The first nursing schools in the region opened in Halifax, Saint John, and Charlottetown in the early 1890s, and in St John's in 1903. Together doctors and nurses, whose numbers grew impressively, formed a powerful alliance in demanding that governments support improved public health policies and sustain the ascendancy of professionals over unlicensed practitioners.[19]

A dramatic example of the social reform activism associated with the "muscular Christianity" of the era was the work of the tireless Dr Wilfred Grenfell. An English evangelical Christian, Grenfell was employed in 1892 by the Royal National Mission to Deep Sea Fishermen to investigate the condition of fishers engaged in the Labrador fishery. Grenfell found widespread poverty and a serious need for medical facilities, both for the fishermen and for the residents. Over the following years he raised money to build a network of hospitals, nursing stations, children's homes, and schools that eventually extended from Newfoundland's Northern Peninsula to Lake Melville in Labrador, with a headquarters at St Anthony. More than this, Grenfell attempted to reshape the economy and society of the region, arguing that poverty, ignorance, and malnutrition were the causes of most health problems. He encouraged the formation of co-operatives; promoted improvements in both hygiene and diet; started a sawmill and an industrial crafts program; tried to improve educational facilities; and, in the hope of providing a new source of food, clothing, and jobs, introduced reindeer (the experiment failed). In Newfoundland he was a controversial figure who offended church leaders by attacking denominational education, the mercantile establishment by alleging exploitation, and some politicians by arguing that the government was corrupt and incompetent. Nevertheless, his ceaseless energy and activism helped to improve health care and stimulated the emergence of a public health movement that initially focused on combatting a tuberculosis epidemic then sweeping the colony.

Middle-class women were often in the vanguard of reform movements, on behalf of themselves and others. By the end of the century, married women had gained rights relating to child custody, marital property, and the municipal franchise in the Maritimes, but women's right to vote at the provincial level was denied. In 1893 the Nova Scotia legislature narrowly passed a motion granting female suffrage, but it was quashed in committee by Attorney General J.W. Longley, who was appalled by the prospect that Nova Scotia might lead the nation in such a controversial measure. The WCTU petitioned the Newfoundland legislature in 1891 to allow women to vote on local liquor options—a modest request—but motions in support were narrowly defeated in the following two sessions.

As a result of the hard line taken by male legislators and their supporters, feminists turned to other reform causes and worked tirelessly behind the scenes to gain support for their enfranchisement. That many women opposed female suffrage was a great disappointment to liberal feminists, who sought equality for women in all aspects of the public sphere, including access to universities, the professions, and political office. Over time resistance to female suffrage slowly receded. The National Council of Women of Canada (NCWC), a coalition of women's organizations established in 1893, brought women

Biography *Edith Archibald*

Born in 1854 to a prominent family in St John's, Edith Archibald received her early education in New York and London. She briefly taught school in her father's home town of Truro and at the age of 20 married her second cousin Charles Archibald, a mining engineer who was the son of a senator with extensive coal-rich properties in Cape Breton. After 19 years at Cow Bay (now Port Morien), the Archibalds moved to Halifax in 1894, where Charles became president of the Bank of Nova Scotia. With servants to care for the household, which ultimately included four children, Edith Archibald had time for social activism.

In the 1880s she became involved in the WCTU at Cow Bay, leading its members on raids of illicit saloons and hosting "parlour meetings" to reach a wider audience. Her activism expanded after the move to Halifax. Surrounded by women of like mind, such as Agnes Dennis, Anna Leonowens, Amelia Ritchie, and Ritchie's three talented daughters, Mary, Eliza, and Ella, Archibald threw herself into a hectic round of volunteer activities. She served as president of the Maritime WCTU from 1892 to 1896, president of the Halifax Local Council of Women from 1896 to 1906, and president of the Halifax Victorian Order of Nurses from 1897 to 1901. During the First World War she became vice-president of the Nova Scotia Red Cross and chaired the department responsible for Canadian prisoners of war overseas.

Archibald never wavered in her support for female suffrage. In 1917 she led the delegation of women who persuaded Nova Scotia's Premier George Murray to support the suffrage bill, which finally passed in April 1918. She later chaired the Halifax Conservative Party's women's auxiliary. In addition to her voluntary activities, she published articles, pamphlets, songs, plays, and several books, including one about her father, *Life and Letters of Sir Edward Mortimer Archibald* (1924), and *The Token* (1930), a novel set in the aftermath of the American Civil War.[20] She died in 1936.

together around social reform and began to nudge its members in a more progressive direction. Female suffrage became a central plank in the NCWC platform at a meeting in Halifax in 1910.

With national and provincial governments under the thumb of powerful interests, progressive reformers turned to the promotion of honesty and efficiency at the municipal level, where many of their policies could be implemented. In 1912 Saint John replaced the old system of ward elections, which could be dominated by small cliques, with a commission-style council elected by all voters on a city-wide basis. St John's followed suit in 1914. Although this reform in municipal government was intended to usher in an era in which appointed experts would determine best practices, commission governments, too, were often open to private influence.

Close economic and ethnic ties in the region helped to ensure that many people were swept up in the rising tide of imperial sentiment that characterized the closing decades of the nineteenth century. In the 1880s New Brunswick's George Parkin, in his own words "the wandering evangelist of Empire," became a leader of the Imperial Federation Movement, designed to draw Great Britain and its colonies closer together. Portraits of Queen Victoria could be found in many homes, and her diamond jubilee was celebrated with enthusiasm across the region in 1897. The same year marked the 400th anniversary of Cabot's voyage. With Maritimers claiming Cape Breton as the first land sighted and Newfoundlanders Cape Bonavista, commemorative ceremonies were held at both Halifax and St John's. In each city traditions were invented and embellished, with speakers celebrating Cabot as the founder not only of their respective countries but also of the British Empire, of which they were proud members.

In 1899 imperialists became preoccupied with Great Britain's declaration of war on the two independent Boer (Dutch settler) republics in South Africa. The Canadian government agreed to equip and raise volunteers for the British army, and Newfoundland sent money to assist military widows and orphans. Maritimers were prominent among the 7,000 Canadians who fought in the South African War, which continued until 1902 and proved more bitter and protracted than anyone expected.

Family in the Industrial Age

Notwithstanding the challenges, the closing decades of the nineteenth century were heady times for many people in the Atlantic region. Advances in communications, new ideas about the universe, new ways of making a living and enjoying leisure time, higher levels of literacy, and the growth of cities were only a few of the modernizing trends that affected everyday life. By making decisions about where to work, what to believe, how long to stay in school, if and whom to marry, and whether to protest injustices, people of all ranks and cultures participated in the creation of a new social order that, not surprisingly, was similar in many ways to the one taking root elsewhere in the North Atlantic world. Long accustomed to being transatlantic citizens, they brought back new ideas from their travels and helped to modernize the places where they lived and worked.

The family remained the fundamental economic and social unit, but its general contours changed. As employment opportunities expanded, young people married later—on average, at age 25 or 26 for women and a couple of years later for men in the Maritimes—and more than 5 per cent never married at all. Later marriage and the increasing practice of birth control reduced the number of children in many households. So concerned was the Canadian government about the trend to smaller families that in 1892 it made the promotion of birth control and abortifacients an offence under the Criminal Code. Same-sex relationships were deemed to be unnatural and pro-scribed by law. For gays and lesbians this meant hiding sexual desires and in many cases leading unhappy, unfulfilled lives.

Legal sanctions on birth control had little impact on the general trends. In the early nineteenth century, married women of normal fertility could expect to have a child every two or three years, and completed families (in which both parents lived through the mother's child-bearing years) were large, averaging seven or eight children. By the end of the century that figure was cut nearly in half. Still, there were considerable variations across class and culture. Acadians married earlier and had larger families, a practice encouraged by the Roman Catholic Church. Scots, especially those of the Presbyterian persuasion, married later and had smaller families. Urban middle-class couples were more likely to limit the size of their families than rural and working-class couples, who tended to rely on their children for security in their old age.

Gender roles were also changing, and again the trends were most evident in the middle class. In rural pre-industrial societies, families were economic units, producing most of what they con-sumed. With the increase in manufactured products, the introduction of public schooling, and the tendency toward smaller families, much of what had been considered women's work moved outside the home. Middle-class men objected to the idea of their wives finding work outside the house-hold, lest it be thought that, as husbands, they were not good providers. The careful delineation of separate spheres meant that men dominated the public sphere and its expanding opportunities, while women were relegated to the private spheres of motherhood, domesticity, and good works. Thus women were denied access to higher education, the professions, the boardrooms, and pol-itical office. No sanctions, of course, were placed on women working in factories or as domestics in homes that could afford to employ household help.

Exclusionary policies in this period were an extension of the subordinate position that women in settler societies had occupied since colonial times. Under the provisions of British common law, which prevailed in the Atlantic region, husband and wife were treated as one person, with the sole right over property and children vested in the male head of household. Divorce was exceedingly rare and difficult to obtain, leaving women who were at the mercy of a cruel, despotic, or absent husband. Even in relatively harmonious families, it was difficult for a married woman to own property in her own right, and her husband could control any income she earned. In the latter half of the nineteenth century, values relating to women's rights and industrial development began to converge, but govern-ments dragged their feet in granting political equality for women, and most women were unable to take advantage of new legislation that advanced married women's rights over property and children.

The Atlantic region was not unique in its treatment of women in marriage or in its acceptance of the separate spheres ideology. Nor were women in the region slow to take up opportunities where they could be found. Women flocked to the new professions open to them, especially teaching, nursing, and clerical work. A study conducted in 1905 estimated that 75 per cent of the nurses working in Massachusetts came from Canada, most of them from the Maritimes. The same study noted that with incomes equal or better than those of the men they knew, "they refuse[d] to exchange single competence for the double poverty that must result in marriage." For this reason they remained single, a situation that worried many traditionalists.[21]

A few women from the region were at the forefront of efforts to break down barriers to their advancement in the public sphere. When Grace Annie Lockhart graduated from Mount Allison

University in 1875, she became the first woman in the British Empire to receive a university degree, and it was Maritime Baptist women who established the first female foreign missionary societies in Canada. While Acadia and Dalhousie quickly followed Mount Allison in opening their doors to women, Catholic colleges rejected co-education. Instead, the Roman Catholic Church encouraged separate educational facilities for women. The Congregation of Notre Dame, which established an academy for young women in Antigonish in 1883, began giving collegiate courses for women in affiliation with St Francis Xavier University (StFX) in 1894. Three years later, four young women received Bachelor of Arts degrees from StFX, the first degrees granted to women by a Catholic university in North America.

Conclusion

As the long recession began to lift in the late 1890s, the region was in some ways much changed from what it had been 30 years earlier. Farms, forests, and fisheries still underpinned life in the region, but a quarter of Maritimers now lived in towns; new industries had been established; mining and the service sector had expanded significantly; and the economy (in the Maritimes at least) no longer relied so extensively on the old staple trades. Political divisions and local rivalries remained deeply entrenched, but by the turn of the century transportation links were in place across the region: the Newfoundland railway was completed in 1897, and regular ferry service across the Cabot Strait began the next year. At the same time many people throughout the region shared common enthusiasms, whether for the Empire, for temperance, or for social reform. Despite bitter disputes over education, levels of literacy had improved, and a more sophisticated society was emerging. There were signs that not all was well—the control exercised by central Canadian banks and corporations was especially troubling—but there was some reason for optimism as the twentieth century dawned.

Further Readings

Alexander, David. 1983. *Atlantic Canada and Confederation: Essays in Canadian Political Economy*, comp. Eric W. Sager, Lewis R. Fischer, and Stuart O. Pierson. Toronto: University of Toronto Press.

Barman, Jean. 2003. *Sojourning Sisters: The Lives and Letters of Jessie and Annie McQueen*. Toronto: University of Toronto Press.

Beattie, Betsy. 2000. *Obligations and Opportunity: Single Maritime Women in Boston, 1870–1930*. Montreal: McGill-Queen's University Press.

Couturier, Jacques Paul, and Phyllis E. LeBlanc, dirs. 1996. *Économie et société en Acadie, 1850–1950*. Moncton: Éditions d'Acadie.

Fingard, Judith. 1989. *The Dark Side of Life in Victorian Halifax*. Porters Lake, NS: Pottersfield Press.

Forbes, E.R. 1989. *Challenging the Regional Stereotype: Essays on the 20th Century Maritimes*. Fredericton: Acadiensis Press.

Frank, David, and Gregory S. Kealey, eds. 1995. *Labour and Working-Class History in Atlantic Canada: A Reader*. St John's: Institute of Social and Economic Research.

Frost, James D. 2003. *Merchant Princes: Halifax's First Family of Finance, Ships, and Steel*. Halifax: Toronto: Lorimer.

Guildford, Janet, and Suzanne Morton, eds. 1994. *Separate Spheres: Women's Worlds in the 19th Century Maritimes*. Fredericton: Acadiensis Press.

Inwood, Kris, ed. 1993. *Farm, Factory and Fortune: New Studies in the Economic History of the Maritime Provinces*. Fredericton: Acadiensis Press.

Porter, Marilyn. 1993. *Place and Persistence in the Lives of Newfoundland Women*. Aldershot: Avebury.

Sager, Eric W., and Gerald E. Panting. 1990. *Maritime Capital: The Shipping Industry in Atlantic Canada, 1820–1914*. Montreal: McGill-Queen's University Press.

Walls, Martha Elizabeth. 2010. *No Need of a Chief for this Band: The Maritime Mi'kmaq and Federal Electoral Legislation, 1899–1951*. Vancouver: University of British Columbia Press.

Historical Spotlight

Alexander, David. 1978. "Economic Growth in the Atlantic Region, 1880 to 1940," *Acadiensis* VIII, 1 (Autumn): 47–76.

Parenteau, Bill. 1998. "Care, Control and Supervision: Native People in the Canadian Atlantic Salmon Fishery," *Canadian Historical Review* 69, 1 (March): 1–35.

Recommended Websites

Cape Breton Miners Museum
http://www.minersmuseum.com/

Grenfell Mission
http://www.heritage.nf.ca/society/grenfellmission.html

Labour History in New Brunswick
http://www.lhtnb.ca/00/en_welcome.cfm

The McQueen Family Letters, 1866–1934, Atlantic Canada Virtual Archives
http://atlanticportal.hil.unb.ca/acva

Newfoundland and Labrador Heritage: Industrialization and Diversification
http://www.heritage.nf.ca/society/industry.html

Saint John: An Industrial City in Transition
http://website.nbm-mnb.ca/Transition/English/index.asp

Chapter 11

The Promise and Peril of a New Century, 1901–1919

For almost two decades after 1900, many Atlantic Canadians thought they were living in an age of social and economic progress. Even the First World War, as devastating as it was, brought economic investment and the hope of a better future; but as it drew to a close, the mood shifted dramatically. Expectations of growth and security vanished in the face of the Spanish influenza epidemic, a wave of strikes, and the onset of a prolonged economic recession. Disillusionment and uncertainty, no strangers to the region, proved to be enduring features of the modern world.

The Busy East

At the turn of the twentieth century, optimism seemed warranted. Economic indicators were trending upward internationally and the effects were felt in both the Maritimes and Newfoundland. The populations of Nova Scotia and New Brunswick grew, if modestly—only Prince Edward Island experienced a net loss—and between 1900 and 1920 the gross value of production expanded in every sector except the fisheries. Agriculture was stimulated by strong demand for potatoes and apples in central Canada, in the rapidly developing West, and in expanding urban markets in the Atlantic region itself. Great Britain still imported apples and sawn lumber in large volumes, and demand for fashionable and rare "silver" fox pelts—black fur with pale outer guard hair—sparked a boom for breeders on Prince Edward Island. The annual output of coal increased from nearly 3 million short tons in the 1890s to 6.5 million in 1916. In this instance the regional market was all-important, much of the coal being consumed by new iron and steel industries. Products from the Maritimes were transported by an expanding complex of railways, a result of two new trans-continental lines granted charters by the Liberal government led by Sir Wilfrid Laurier. Although they—along with the Intercolonial—would soon face bankruptcy, the initial impact of the railway boom was to bring welcome investment and jobs.

The history of the fisheries in this period arguably represents a missed opportunity. By the turn of the century, consumers were moving from salted fish to fresh and frozen varieties. With the advent of steam trawlers, fishermen could catch larger volumes of fish and get them to market more efficiently. New Englanders moved most of their vessels from the Grand Banks to grounds closer to shore and rapidly developed a large trawler fleet. By 1908 the French had between 10 and 15 trawlers on the banks (which put into Sydney for ice and coal) in addition to their fleet of more than 200 sailing vessels. If fishermen in the Atlantic region hoped to compete for the common resource located on their very doorstep, they would have to modernize their practices.

Maritimers, especially Nova Scotians, proved cautious. While they were prepared to adopt the gasoline engine and the motor boat, invest in bait freezers (at Canso and Halifax, for example), and respond to the demand for fresh fish, there was strong opposition to trawlers from inshore fishermen and schooner owners. They feared—with good reason—damage to fish stocks and the dominance of large corporations. In 1915 trawlers were forbidden to fish within 12 nautical miles (22 km) of the coast. As a result, the Canadian trawler fleet grew slowly in comparison to its competitors, and the Atlantic fishery stagnated. Salt fish production declined from an annual average of 693,000 hundredweight (35,206,025 kg) early in the century to 448,000 hundredweight (22,759,450 kg) by 1914, in spite of rising prices. The value of Nova Scotia's fresh fish exports increased by almost 50 per cent between 1901 and 1911, but the total could have been even higher.

In St John's, merchants invested in steel-hulled steamers for sealing, passenger, and freight services and showed considerable interest in product diversification. They also experimented with steam trawling, but were at a comparative disadvantage because of their small domestic market and Newfoundland's distance from potential markets in Canada, the United States, and Europe. Inherently conservative, the Newfoundland Board of Trade opposed government intervention in the fishing industry and, given the relative economic prosperity of this period, there was little incentive to undertake radical change. Had the Canadian and Newfoundland governments been willing and able to emulate the American and French governments by actively encouraging the fishery, the story might have been very different.

Table 11.1	Timeline
1902	Sealers strike in St John's.
1904	The *entente cordiale* settles the Newfoundland French Shore dispute.
1906	Federal subsidies to provinces revised.
1907	Canada passes Lord's Day Act.
1908	William Coaker founds the Fishermen's Protective Union in Newfoundland; *Anne of Green Gables* published; automobiles prohibited on Prince Edward Island.
1909–11	Strikes in Nova Scotia's coal industry, including a 22-month strike by coal miners in Springhill.
1909	Formation through mergers of Dominion Steel Company; Glace Bay miners form local of United Mineworkers of America; the region's first pulp and paper mill opens at Grand Falls, Newfoundland; J.A.D. McCurdy becomes first person in the British Empire to fly an airplane.
1910	Prohibition legislated in Nova Scotia.
1911	International Court at The Hague rules on American fishing rights.
1912	Saint John adopts commission government.
1914	Outbreak of the Great War; Newfoundland sealing disasters.
1915	Agreement that no province should have fewer MPs than senators.
1916	Newfoundland Regiment decimated at Beaumont Hamel on 1 July; Number 2 Construction Battalion formed.
1917	Conscription imposed in Canada; explosion in Halifax Harbour.
1918	Prohibition across Canada; women's suffrage legislated in Canada and Nova Scotia; Great War ends on 11 November.
1918–19	Spanish influenza epidemic.
1919	Women's suffrage legislated in New Brunswick.

By contrast, the steel and coal industries seemed to be fulfilling the promise of the National Policy. Nova Scotia now accounted for 44 per cent of the pig iron and more than 80 per cent of the coal produced in Canada. Many communities along the Intercolonial route were transformed by new investment. In this period 60 per cent of the region's industrial workforce could be found between Moncton and Glace Bay. The population of Cape Breton County—the epicentre of coal and steel production—increased by 49 per cent between 1901 and 1911. "Busy Amherst," with factories producing textiles, boots and shoes, gas-boilers, and railway cars, was the poster child for industrial growth. Little wonder that a new regional business magazine, founded in 1910, was called the *Busy East of Canada*.

In Newfoundland, a short-lived sawmilling boom, fuelled by Maritime, American, and Scottish investors, followed the completion of the trans-island railway, but it soon became obvious that the colony's stands of good timber were limited and that its forests were best suited for the manufacture of wood pulp. That opportunity attracted the English newspaper tycoons Harold and Alfred Harmsworth, who reached an extraordinarily generous deal with the Newfoundland government in 1905. Their Anglo-Newfoundland Development Company was granted what amounted to a perpetual lease of timber lands in the Exploits River valley, with mineral and water power rights thrown in for good measure. In 1909 the region's first pulp and paper mill opened at Grand Falls. As the supporters of the Policy of Progress had hoped, the island had a new staple industry and the first settlement of any size in the interior. A century later, the mill, now owned by AbitibiBowater, closed amidst much controversy.

The natural resources of Labrador also attracted interest. In the 1890s a series of remarkable pioneering surveys, conducted by A.P. Low for the Geological Survey of Canada, confirmed the existence of huge iron ore deposits in the interior and the potential of the Grand (now the Churchill) Falls for hydroelectricity. Since these resources seemed too remote for development, attention focused instead on exploiting the Labrador forests. A grant of timber concessions on the Hamilton (Churchill) River to a Nova Scotia company in 1902 raised once again the long-standing question of who owned the Labrador interior.

Historical Focus

Exploring Labrador

The interior of Labrador was well known to the Innu and local Métis trappers, but it was the last frontier to be explored by outsiders. In the eighteenth century French traders had found interior routes between the North Shore and Hudson and James bays, and overland to Lake Melville and Hamilton Inlet, an area then known as "Esquimaux Bay." Similar journeys resumed in the 1830s, when the Hudson Bay Company decided to link its post at North West River in central Labrador with Fort Chimo, upriver from Ungava Bay. In 1838 John McLean travelled from Chimo to Lake Melville and back, and the following year became the first European, so far as is known, to see what is now Churchill Falls. Albert Low's surveys in the mid-1890s added significantly to formal geographical knowledge of the interior of Labrador, but much remained to be explored.

Continued

With Wilfred Grenfell's rise to prominence, Labrador became attractive to "manly" adventurers. It was relatively accessible and provided the prospect of remoteness, adversity, and the romance of "the North." Thus the young American Leonidas Hubbard, an editor at the outdoors magazine *Outlook*, decided to explore the river system connecting Lake Melville, Lake Michikamau, and Ungava Bay. He was accompanied by his friend Dillon Wallace, a New York lawyer, and George Elson, a Métis guide from James Bay. The Americans had little wilderness experience, and even Elson had never been to Labrador. Leaving North West River in mid-July 1903—late in the year for such an expedition—they soon found themselves in serious trouble. Hubbard died in camp in October, and Wallace was lucky to survive. Hubbard's body was eventually recovered and buried in New York.

Hubbard's wife Mina, born in Ontario in 1870, rejected Wallace's explanation of the tragedy, as set out in the draft of his book *The Lure of the Labrador Wild* (1905), and blamed him for her husband's death. Determined to complete her husband's journey, she hired George Elson and, most importantly, a local guide, and left North West River on the same day that Wallace set out on a similar mission. Using different routes, both reached Ungava Bay, but Mina Hubbard arrived six weeks earlier. This was a highly unusual achievement for a woman at that time. Hubbard and Wallace both published books about their Labrador journeys. Wallace became a writer and Mina Hubbard lived much of the rest of her life in England, where she died in 1956.[1]

In 1898 the Canadian government, without consulting Newfoundland, legislated a new northern boundary for the province of Quebec. The line was drawn westwards from the Eastmain River on James Bay to Hamilton Inlet until it met the coastal strip, which in Canada's opinion was all that Newfoundland rightfully controlled. The governments of Quebec and Canada thereupon began protesting against Newfoundland's issuance of timber licences in Labrador, since they applied to territory now claimed by Canada. By 1907 all parties had agreed to submit the question of where the boundary lay to the Judicial Committee of the Privy Council in London, the central question being what constituted "the coast of Labrador," the phrase used in the Proclamation of 1763. The decision was slow in coming, but eventually the Privy Council found in Newfoundland's favour.

Storm Clouds on the Industrial Horizon

By the beginning of the twentieth century there were signs that the gains made in the Maritimes' industrial sector under the National Policy were beginning to erode. The disappearance of the region's financial sector, severe competition from branch businesses, and further takeovers and mergers promoted by central Canadian interests took a heavy toll. When Rhodes, Curry in Amherst was amalgamated with two Montreal firms in 1909, it marked the beginning of the end for heavy industry in the region.

The coal and steel industries also fell victim to consolidation. In 1901 Henry M. Whitney sold his share of the Cape Breton-based Dominion Coal and Dominion Iron and Steel to Montreal interests, and in 1909 the company was amalgamated with the Cumberland Coal and Rail Company at Springhill to form the Dominion Steel Corporation. With close links to the Bank of Commerce and the Bank of Montreal, Dominion Steel controlled most of the Nova Scotia coalfields. The company also set its sights on the Nova Scotia Steel and Coal Company but it eluded them, at least for the moment.

Holding at least 179 directorships among them, the directors of Dominion Steel were the high priests of the Gilded Age in Canada. They lived in opulence in Montreal and Toronto and built elegant summer homes in communities such as St Andrews. Sir William Van Horne's estate on Minister's

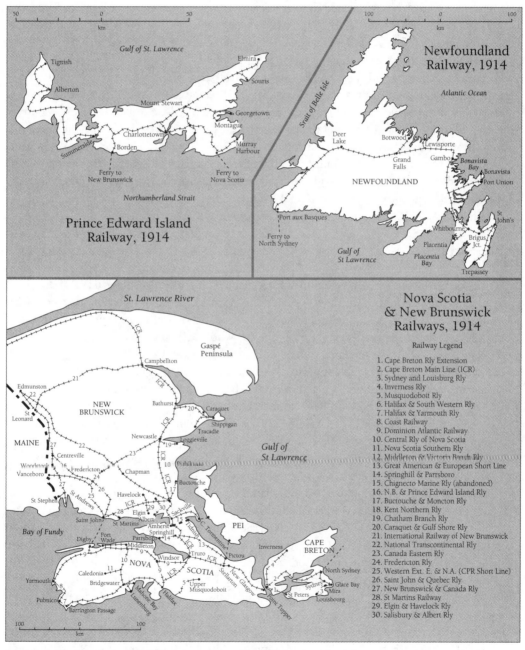

Railways in the Atlantic Region, 1914. Adapted from Shirley E. Woods, *Cinders and Saltwater: The Story of Atlantic Canada's Railways* (Halifax: Nimbus, 1992).

Island, New Brunswick, included a model farm and a swimming pool filled by the ocean tides twice a day. As David Frank points out, these men integrated the Nova Scotia coal and steel industries into the national economy, but in so doing they contributed to the crises that those industries faced at the end of the First World War.[2] Political and economic fragmentation and competition to attract investment meant that the region had no defence against either economic imperialism or dependency.

Distant company directors alone could not be blamed for the situation. Many of the deals that centralized Canadian finance and industry were masterminded by the financial wizard Max Aitken, who had followed the money from his home on the Miramichi to Calgary and then to Halifax, where he became the protégé of John Stairs, the leading industrialist and financier in the Maritimes. In 1903, Aitken was appointed president of Royal Securities, an investment bank created by Stairs to finance enterprises in the West Indies and Central America. In 1907 Aitken settled in Montreal, where he used Montreal Trust to take over Royal Securities and presided over a consolidation movement that transformed Canada's corporate sector. His crowning achievement was the creation in 1910 of the Canadian Cement Company and the Steel Company of Canada. Rich and powerful, Aitken moved to London, where he had marketed much of his speculative stock, became a member of the British Parliament, and bought himself the title of Lord Beaverbrook. From his place at the centre of the Empire, he continued to keep an eye on his Canadian interests.[3]

Labour Unrest

Industrial expansion was accompanied by unprecedented labour unrest. Between 1901 and 1914 there were 411 strikes in the Maritimes—evidence of a workforce that was becoming increasingly class-conscious, unionized, and radical as industrial giants played out their competitive advantage on the backs of labour. Workers often faced employers who had no particular attachment or loyalty to the region and who were prepared to fight employees with any weapons at their disposal, safe in the knowledge that they could count on the support of all levels of government.[4]

A particularly bitter dispute occurred in 1909, when Glace Bay miners, disillusioned with the Provincial Workmen's Association (PWA), formed a local of the United Mineworkers of America (UMW) led locally by Scottish-born James B. McLachlan. Dominion Steel refused to recognize the union, brought in strike breakers (Newfoundlanders among them) protected by troops obligingly provided by the federal government, and gradually wore the strikers down. The same happened at Springhill, where miners held out for 22 months in 1909–11.

Labour militancy also erupted in Newfoundland. Between 1901 and 1914 St John's experienced 120 strikes, mostly by unskilled workers. Bell Island miners, longshoremen, fish curers, and fishing crews struck as well, and in 1902 some 3,000 sealers refused to board the steamers in St John's harbour until the owners agreed to improvements in pay and conditions. Remarkably, 42 per cent of those strikes were successful, and 21 per cent ended in compromises.

With trade unions established in St John's and Grand Falls, William Coaker decided to organize rural "toilers," as he called them—fishermen, loggers, and sealers—in the Fishermen's Protective Union (FPU), launched in 1908. A populist who took his cue from Canadian farmers' movements, Coaker wanted economic, social, and political reforms that would ensure fair treatment for his members. The response was immediate and impressive except in predominantly Roman Catholic districts, which followed a conservative church hierarchy opposed to unions and class-based politics.

The union also became a political party, winning eight seats in the 1913 election. Serving as the official opposition in all but name, the FPU promoted an ambitious reform program with goals that ranged from government control of fish grading and marketing to non-denominational night schools.

Biography — William Ford Coaker

Born in St John's, Newfoundland, in 1871, William Coaker had a checkered career as an outport trader, telegraph operator, farmer, and minor office-holder until, in 1908, he formed the Fishermen's Protective Union (FPU) at Herring Neck in Notre Dame Bay. Its motto was *suum cuisque* ("to each his own"). Did a fisherman receive "his own," asked Coaker, when

> . . . he boards a coastal or bay steamer, as a steerage passenger and has to sleep like a dog, eat like a pig, and be treated like a serf? . . . does he receive his own at the seal fishery where he has to live like a brute, work like a dog and be paid like a nigger? Do they receive their own when they pay taxes to keep up five splendid colleges in St John's . . . while thousands of fishermen's children are growing up illiterate? Do they receive their own when forced to supply funds to maintain a hospital at St. John's while fishermen, their wives and daughters are dying daily in the outports for want of hospitals?[5]

Strenuous opposition from the Roman Catholic Church meant that the FPU became an almost exclusively Protestant organization, largely confined to the island's northeast coast. From the beginning, Coaker had planned to take the FPU into politics, its aims spelled out in the "Bonavista Platform" of 1912 and publicized in the union's newspaper, *The Fishermen's Advocate*. The platform was bold and comprehensive, calling for sweeping changes in the fishing industry, administrative and constitutional reform, free and compulsory education, a minimum wage, and other legislation that would benefit outport residents. In the 1913 election, Coaker and seven other FPU candidates won seats in the Assembly. At the same time, Coaker was president of the Fishermen's Union Trading Company, founded in 1911, which in 1918 relocated to the union's new town in Bonavista Bay, called Port Union.

In 1917 the Union party joined the wartime National Government, and Coaker became a minister without portfolio. He was immediately faced with the difficult and divisive issue of conscription, which was strenuously opposed by the union membership. He eventually decided to support both conscription and prohibition, moves that significantly damaged his standing and reputation among fishermen. The pre-war crusade was clearly over.

Coaker might have re-established his position had he been able to implement the fisheries reforms he had advocated for so long, but as minister of marine and fisheries between 1919 and 1923 he failed, largely as a result of the postwar economic crisis, political infighting, and opposition from others in the fish trade. He stayed out of politics between 1924 and 1928, became increasingly preoccupied with the union's commercial enterprises, and resigned as president of the FPU. He played only a minor role in the second administration of Sir Richard Squires, between 1928 and 1932, by which time he had become so disillusioned that he endorsed the idea of government by an elected commission. Coaker spent an increasing amount of time at a property he owned in Jamaica—a far cry from Herring Neck—and died in 1938.

Progressives in Action

By the end of the nineteenth century, labour organizers had joined professionals, church leaders, and women's rights activists in an impressive coalition to demand a growing list of reforms. Dubbed the "regenerators" by the historian Ramsay Cook, they were inspired by a vision of scientific expertise, efficient management, and government oversight that would transform capitalist society from a Darwinian competition for survival of the fittest to a Christian paradise on earth.[6]

Notwithstanding the hurdles, progressive reformers scored a number of successes. In response to intense pressure, the Canadian government passed the Lord's Day Act in 1907, which banned paid employment, shopping, and commercial leisure activities on Sundays. Buoyed by this victory, the Methodists and Presbyterians established the Moral and Social Reform Council of Canada (renamed the Social Service Council of Canada in 1913) to pursue a more ambitious agenda. In 1910 Nova Scotia (Halifax excepted) followed Prince Edward Island's lead a decade earlier by adopting prohibition. Its premier, George Murray, also introduced legislation to improve working conditions, provide compensation to workers injured on the job, and establish the Nova Scotia Agricultural College (1905) and the Nova Scotia Technical College (1909). While scientific education was generally reserved for men, governments also encouraged the expansion of Women's Institutes—first established in Ontario in 1897—to help women adjust to the new technologies that were transforming rural life both inside and outside the home.

Farmers in the Maritimes had followed North American trends in trying to mobilize their political clout. In the 1870s the Grange Movement swept through the region. It focused on improving agricultural education rather than direct political action and was soon eclipsed by the Patrons of Industry, which encouraged farmers to enter the political arena. Farmers established newspapers to promote their interests and pursued alternatives to the exploitative capitalist system, such as co-operatives, which were gaining popularity throughout Canada. By 1910, Maritime farmers had both the Co-operative Union of Canada and the Canadian Council of Agriculture to voice their concerns. Farmers did not always call for the same reforms, but they all agreed that high tariffs increased the cost of the imported machinery that was essential to operating a modern farm.

The impact of their lobbying efforts, which included a protest march of 1,000 farmers on Parliament Hill in 1910, induced the Laurier government to sign a free trade agreement with the United States in in 1911. It was negotiated by his finance minister, former Nova Scotia premier W.S. Fielding, who had moved from provincial to federal politics in 1896. Even in the Liberal Party, free trade had its critics, and it was greatly feared by industrialists who had grown wealthy behind high tariff walls. Supported by defecting Liberals and nervous business leaders, the Conservatives won the 1911 election, and free trade with the United States remained off the agenda. For the third time since Confederation, a Nova Scotian, Halifax lawyer Robert Borden, was the Conservative prime minister. Neither of his predecessors—John Thompson (1892–4) and Charles Tupper (1896)—had served in office long enough to make much of a difference in national policy with respect to the Maritimes. Could Borden do any better?

Politics in the Industrial Age

While Reformers wanted a progressive society, politicians were preoccupied by the challenge of finding money to pay for expanding government responsibilities. In 1906 Ottawa revised its subsidy policy, but the increases for the Maritimes were much lower than those granted to Quebec, Ontario, and British Columbia—a reflection of the region's diminished power and influence. In the redistributions of 1892 and 1903 the Maritimes lost eight seats in the House of Commons, and the reductions might have continued over the years had it not been agreed in 1915 that no province could have fewer MPs than senators. The meanness of this concession spoke volumes about the disadvantages faced by small provinces compared with giants like Ontario, Quebec, and Manitoba, each of which more than doubled its size in 1912 by absorbing huge, resource-rich sections of the Northwest Territories. In 1908 New Brunswick's Conservative Premier J.D. Hazen called for a "United Acadia" to counter the region's declining power position in Confederation, but there was little response.[7]

Even if Maritime politicians had managed to present a common front to Ottawa, it is unlikely that much could have been achieved. With the opening of the Prairies and continuing discontent in Quebec, the federal government's attention was invariably focused elsewhere. Prime Minister Borden was sensitive to the problems facing the Maritimes and occasionally used his power to achieve results—for example, he responded favourably to Prince Edward Island's demand for better winter ferry service—but, with national and international issues always at the forefront, he had little time to address the systemic problems facing the region.

As the Maritime provinces were being marginalized in Ottawa, Newfoundland remained a very junior player in London. Although recognized as one of the dominions, it carried less weight than the others, and the imperial government remained concerned about problems created by fisheries treaties for which it was ultimately responsible. Its decision to reach a rapprochement with France resulted in the 1904 *entente cordiale*, which included an agreement on France's part to give up the fishing rights it had enjoyed since the eighteenth century, although a French presence was not completely eliminated.

In 1902 Great Britain had smoothed the way to a compromise with France by granting Newfoundland permission, over Prime Minister Laurier's objections, to attempt to negotiate another reciprocity agreement with the United States. A draft treaty was arranged, but this time it was effectively killed in the US Senate. In response, the government of Sir Robert Bond in 1905 launched a campaign of harassment against American vessels engaged in the winter herring fishery in the Bay of Islands. The British government, in the process of settling outstanding disputes with the United States, swiftly intervened, unilaterally imposing a *modus vivendi* pending arbitration on the interpretation of the 1818 fisheries convention (which applied to Canadian as well as to Newfoundland waters) and forbidding by imperial order-in-council the seizure or arrest of any American vessel. Colonial protests against this heavy-handed treatment were rejected. The eventual arbitration at The Hague in 1911 largely upheld Great Britain's—that is, Canada's and Newfoundland's—arguments relating to American rights under the 1818 convention. The tribunal rejected American claims that the fishery should not be regulated by the coastal states, and made important recommendations concerning the delineation of the three-mile marine limit and the definition of bays.

These complicated diplomatic manoeuvrings had little to do with the everyday concerns of many Newfoundlanders, who found Bond's crusade irrelevant. In 1908 a highly unusual tied election precipitated a constitutional and political crisis. The governor, who favoured the opposition party led by Sir Edward Morris, allowed him to take over and hold a second election in May 1909. Given ice and weather conditions, spring elections were usually avoided, but Morris had no problem in winning a majority.

Cultural Currents

In this period technological innovations continued to make headlines and transform ways of doing things. Typewriters and telephones came into practical use, especially in business operations, while motor cars and even airplanes were promising to revolutionize transportation. For ordinary people the bicycle was the favoured new way of getting around, at least in the summer time. Better communications linked the region's creative writers to the larger English-speaking world, and sports teams were able to compete further afield.

Cape Breton made communication history in 1902 when Guglielmo Marconi's Wireless Telegraph Company began operating the first transatlantic link from Glace Bay, Nova Scotia. The previous year, Marconi had used kites flying from Signal Hill in St John's to pick up the first wireless signal sent across the Atlantic. The Newfoundland government was disappointed when he moved to Cape Breton, which was also the site of experiments in air flight. In February 1909 J.A.D. McCurdy and F.W. Baldwin, under the auspices of Alexander Graham Bell's Aerial Experiment Association, made the first controlled manned flight in the British Empire. With McCurdy at the controls, the *Silver Dart* soared over the ice of Lake Bras d'Or near Bell's home in Baddeck. By that time the invention of the telephone had made Bell a household name.

Reliable railway service made it possible for sports teams to compete on a regional basis in leagues designed to manage and promote competitive sports. By 1900 professional baseball teams, many

The Royals Baseball Club of Saint John, New Brunswick, Intermediate Champions, 1921. Sports teams were often closed to racial minorities. They therefore began forming their own baseball teams in the 1880s and by the turn of the century were hosting their own regional championships. Provincial Archives of New Brunswick Jason and Jessalyn Wright Collection: P338-2

of them on tour from the United States, drew large numbers of spectators. The Maritime Provinces Amateur Athletic Association (MPAAA) initially turned a blind eye when amateur teams strengthened their ranks with professional players. In 1907 the MPAAA took a more principled approach and put an end to the experiment with semi-professional baseball in the region. This prompted many teams to turn professional, beginning with the Socials and the Standards in Halifax in 1911. All efforts to put an end to the gambling and match "fixing" rampant in professional baseball proved fruitless.

Amateur sports remained popular, especially among those who shunned the corruption associated with professional teams. Since spectator sports did little to advance physical fitness, reformers emphasized individual participation. Bicycling and tennis emerged as popular pastimes among those who could afford the equipment, while organizations such as the YMCA and the YWCA made athletic facilities more widely accessible. Inevitably, children, who increasingly spent long hours sitting at school desks, became the focus of attention. In the wake of the South African War, youth organizations, first established in Great Britain, were founded to prepare youth for war and other emergencies. Boy Scouts and Girl Guides quickly took root in the Atlantic region and a Canadian organization, Canadian Girls in Training (CGIT), was established in 1915.

While women also became sports enthusiasts, their involvement troubled those who identified physical freedom and scandalous sporting attire for women with moral laxity. Opposition to female participation in competitive play was gradually reduced but not entirely overcome. In universities throughout the region, women formed teams to play basketball, field hockey, and ice hockey, but few female athletes could look forward to a professional career in their sport.

As in other areas of social life, many Maritime sportsmen made their reputations south of the border. Two black boxers from Nova Scotia, George Dixon and Sam Langford, won acclaim for their

Skating behind the college at Caraquet, New Brunswick. Hockey became an increasingly popular sport in the Maritimes in the second half of the nineteenth century. Provincial Archives of New Brunswick Fonds du père Jean-Marie Courtois, Eudistes: P38-109

successes in the boxing ring, following in the footsteps of George Godfrey from Charlottetown, recognized as the "first U.S. heavyweight champion" in the 1880s. Nat Butler, a native of Halifax who began his bicycle racing career in Boston, broke records at the Winter Velodrome in Paris in 1905. The Maritime region's best baseball players were quickly snapped up by American teams, and keeping up with the careers of local heroes provided plenty of copy for newspapers, which now included whole sections devoted to individual and team sports.

New opportunities also opened in arts and culture. In 1908 Prince Edward Island's Lucy Maud Montgomery launched a spectacular career with the publication of *Anne of Green Gables*. In these and subsequent works, she tapped into the growing demand for sentimental fiction about rural life and the values it was believed to represent. She was not the first Maritime writer to accomplish such a feat. In 1893 Margaret Marshall Saunders published *Beautiful Joe*, the story about an abused dog that was reputedly the first book by a Canadian to sell more than a million copies. Meanwhile, two Maritimers, Charles G.D. Roberts and his cousin Bliss Carman, were beginning to make names for themselves as "Confederation poets," so called because they had been born in the 1860s. By the beginning of the twentieth century, Prince Edward Island's Robert Harris was Canada's most

Biography | *Lucy Maud Montgomery*

Lucy Maud Montgomery (1874–1942) became one of North America's most popular authors following the publication of *Anne of Green Gables* in 1908. Public Archives and Records Office of Prince Edward Island, P0002563, Acc. 3110/1.

Lucy Maud Montgomery is one of Atlantic Canada's best-known authors. Born in 1874 in Prince Edward Island, she lost her mother at an early age and was raised by her grandparents in Cavendish. She was educated at Prince of Wales College and spent a year at Dalhousie University. Although she began making money from the publication of her poems and short stories in the 1890s, her fame derived from the 1908 publication of the novel *Anne of Green Gables*. The red-haired orphan girl sent to work on an Island farm won the hearts of readers all over the world.

In 1911, following the death of her grandmother, for whom she was the primary care-giver, Montgomery married the Reverend Ewan Macdonald. The couple moved to Ontario, where Ewan ministered in a number of Presbyterian churches. Between raising two sons, coping with her husband's debilitating depressions, and attending to the endless round of public duties demanded of a minister's wife, Montgomery continued to write. She produced 22 novels, including seven sequels to *Anne*, 450 poems, and 500 short stories. One of her most enduring legacies is "The Island Hymn," the unofficial anthem of Prince Edward Island. From 1889 to 1942 she kept a diary chronicling the darker aspects of her life. Selected diary entries have been published in five volumes that Montgomery fans have read no less avidly than her novels.[8]

renowned portrait artist, while his brother William, an architect, was producing some of the region's most elegant Gothic revival churches and Queen-Anne style homes.

In Newfoundland, Norman Duncan's stories sympathetically explored the lives of outport fishing families. Three literary periodicals began publication in St John's in the early years of the century, which was also a golden age for ballads and poetry—including the "Ode to Newfoundland" (1902), which became the unofficial national anthem. In 1909 a young E.J. Pratt produced his first published poem while a still a student at Victoria College in Toronto. "A poem on May examinations" was not of quite the same calibre as the poems that made up his first collection, *Newfoundland Verse*, which was released in 1923 to considerable acclaim.

Journalists and boosters were also hard at work, often at the behest of the railroads and the emerging tourism industry. They conjured up an image of Nova Scotia as Evangeline's Acadia, "a gently rolling and fertile land filled with Old World Charm."[9] So widespread was Evangeline's appeal in this period that she became the subject of Canada's first feature film in 1913. In Prince Edward Island, the prohibition of automobiles in 1908 helped to preserve the pastoral image so important to tourists, while fishing and hunting were heavily promoted elsewhere in the region. Much of the tourism literature sought to change the image of rural people from one of backward bumpkins to one of picturesque, stalwart "folk," living enviably simple lives. With an apparently straight face, the Reid Newfoundland Company assured potential tourists that "no people in the world maintains a more comfortable and contented existence than the Newfoundland fisherman."[10]

The reality was somewhat different. The loss of life in the Newfoundland seal fishery in the spring of 1914 was the highest in the history of that dangerous industry. On 31 March the SS *Southern Cross*, loaded with pelts taken in the Gulf, sank with its crew of 173 men in a storm, somewhere off Trepassey Bay. There was much speculation about what had happened, but since the ship had no radio and there were no survivors, certainty was impossible. It has been suggested that the captain wanted the distinction of being the first to return to port and so did not take shelter from the storm. On the same day the captain of the ageing SS *Newfoundland* ordered his crew to walk across the ice to the SS *Stephano*, which had signalled that it had found the "main patch" of seals. The difficult trek took more than four hours. Although the weather was fast deteriorating, Captain Abram Kean of the *Stephano* ordered the 132 men to get back on the ice, kill seals, and then return to the *Newfoundland*. They were engulfed by the storm and stranded for 53 hours, during which 78 men died; the bodies were carried back to St John's "stacked like cordwood." Kean, who continued taking seals, refused to accept any responsibility and was exonerated by an inquiry. In retrospect, these tragedies can be seen as local harbingers of the world crisis that was to erupt the following August.

Into the Abyss

A European crisis in the summer of 1914 developed into a war between Germany and Austria-Hungary on one side and the so-called "entente powers" of Great Britain, France, and Russia on the other. As members of the British Empire, Canada and Newfoundland were automatically involved. Although their governments could have refused to send troops overseas, such a response was never contemplated. In the Maritimes militia regiments were called out and headquarters staff in Halifax began a recruitment campaign, first to bring the regiments up to strength, and then to provide additional overseas drafts. Involving clergy, educators, and the press, the war effort soon became all-consuming.

Setting the Context

Causes of the Great War

The unexpected outbreak of war in Europe in the summer of 1914 sent shockwaves around the world. The reasons for what proved to be an unimaginable tragedy have been endlessly debated, as has the question of ultimate responsibility. Why did it happen and who was to blame?

It is accepted that tense and difficult relations between the major continental European powers, the Russian and Austro-Hungarian empires in particular, were of central importance. These tensions became increasingly focused on the Balkan region, where the two empires were competing to expand their spheres of influence as the Ottoman (Turkish) empire retreated from southeastern Europe. The activities of pro-Russian, anti-Austrian Slav nationalists complicated the situation. On 8 June 1914, the heir to the Austro-Hungarian Empire and his wife were assassinated in Sarajevo, the capital of Austrian-controlled Bosnia, by Slav terrorists based in Serbia. This outrage precipitated the chain of events that led to what was initially known as the Great War and, after 1939, as the First World War.

There had been previous Balkan crises, but this time generals, diplomats, and governments seemed to be unable or unwilling to prevent the tensions from escalating out of control. It was as though the European powers had accepted that a showdown was inevitable, and once troop mobilizations began, the process was difficult to stop. Assured of German support, Austria-Hungary declared war on Serbia on July 28, and Russia began to mobilize its forces in support of the latter. With a plan already in place to defeat France in the west before facing Russia in the east, Germany invaded France and Belgium on 2–3 August. Britain, its relations with Germany already strained, had guaranteed Belgium's neutrality, and declared war against Germany on 4 August when that neutrality was breached. This meant that the British Empire was automatically at war, and that a European conflict would become a world war.

Initially, both Canada and Newfoundland responded with enthusiasm. Imperial loyalty was central to each country's identity, and it was generally accepted that the "mother country" and the Empire had to be defended against "German aggression" and "Prussian militarism." It was also widely assumed that Britain and its allies would soon be victorious. The reality proved to be different. The war was, in the words of the historian Fritz Stern, "the first calamity of the twentieth century, the calamity from which all other calamities sprang."[11]

In Newfoundland, which had no militia and hence no militia department, the Newfoundland Regiment was raised—indeed, improvised—by the Patriotic Association of Newfoundland (NPA), founded in August 1914 by Governor Sir Walter Davidson in consultation with the prime minister, Sir Edward Morris. Composed mostly of prominent St John's men from a variety of political and religious backgrounds, the NPA functioned as the unofficial war ministry for three years, with a wide range of responsibilities. Its creation reflected a desire to place the war effort above political and denominational rivalries.

Voluntary enlistment rates in the Maritimes were higher than in Quebec and Saskatchewan, but lower than in other provinces. In Newfoundland the percentage of the population that volunteered

Document

Joining the Army, 1916

At the outset of the war, few could have imagined how many human lives it would take. Many young men simply wanted to be part of a great adventure that also offered a chance to make a better wage. In his memoir of the war, James Robert Johnston, who grew up on a farm in Notre Dame, near Moncton, recalls the context that prompted him to join the 145th Battalion in 1916:

> Little did I think when I bought a ticket for Moncton at Notre Dame on April 23, 1916, that I would be giving up civilian life for over three years. I had been down to Collingwood, NS, working in the lumber woods with my father for about three months and came home the first of April after the woods operation was completed. . . . I was getting restless, as about all the conversation these days was regarding enlisting, and, as I was eighteen now, knew that I would be in the army before too long.
>
> I went to Moncton on April 23 to collect the balance of my pay, which was twenty dollars. I was receiving twenty dollars a month in the woods, and that was six days a week from before daylight until after dark. The way I looked at things then was that if I only got twenty dollars in the woods and the army would pay me thirty-three, it should be a pretty good deal.
>
> I had planned on buying myself a new suit of clothes, but while walking down Main Street I met Tom Colbourne. We talked for awhile and decided we had better go down and enlist. We went in and signed all the papers, and after everything was fixed up, we found Tom had a finger off, so naturally he was turned down.
>
> They gave me a good once over, one of the biggest pair of brown army boots I had ever seen, and told me to come back in a couple of weeks. . . . In a way I dreaded going home, as I knew Mother was going to feel bad, and she certainly did. Dad said he knew I would be in the army shortly anyway, and was glad that I had guts enough to go, before being conscripted. I spent a couple of days around home, and my main worry was that the war would be over before I would get to Europe.[12]

A year later, Johnston experienced his baptism of fire at Vimy Ridge and then faced what he called the "hell" of Passchendaele. He was one of the lucky ones to survive the war, serving as a horse driver in the transport section of the Canadian Machine Gun Corps. When the war ended on 11 November 1918, he was en route to a leave in London. He finally arrived in Moncton in July 1919, where he had a happy homecoming. In retrospect, he played down any lasting scars left by his frequent brushes with death and his anxiety over his horses, whose hard work is lovingly described in his memoir. "I believe I came home as well physically as when I went away," Johnston concluded, "but my nerves were not too good and I remember a lot of nights I would get up and when no one else was around have to go for a long walk. After some time this seemed to wear off and I was soon back to a new life again."

was similar to that in the Maritimes, although high numbers of medical rejections reduced the proportion that actually served. In both Canada and Newfoundland, those living in rural areas were least likely to volunteer, and the rate was reduced further in the Maritimes by the importance of war-related industries such as coal mining, steel production, and agriculture. Including those compelled to enlist under conscription, implemented in Canada in 1917 and Newfoundland in 1918, some 72,500 men from the Atlantic region joined the allied army. Others served at sea, in the air, or in the forestry corps.

About 300 women from the Maritimes and 43 from Newfoundland went overseas as nurses. Among those travelling with the First Canadian Division in October 1914 was Pictou County's Margaret MacDonald, the matron in charge of 101 volunteer nurses who were the first women to become full-fledged members of the Canadian Expeditionary Force.

By 1916 the diminishing supply of new recruits gave ethnic minorities, who were initially not welcome, a chance to enlist for overseas service. Aboriginal men were, for the most part, integrated into existing units. On the Lennox Island reserve, 32 of the 64 eligible men enlisted, and 20 of them were eventually killed or wounded. John J. Sark, the son of the Lennox Island chief, returned home with an English bride. A nurse by training, Elsie Sark dedicated her life to improving conditions in her Island community, even though some of its members perceived her as a domineering "white lady."[13]

African-Canadians were not welcomed into the army. When 50 black men turned up at a recruiting office in Sydney, they were advised that "This is not for you fellows, this is a white man's war."[14] Still, black people in the Maritimes lobbied their MPs and found a champion of sorts in Prime Minister Borden. The Militia Council, with Borden presiding, agreed in April 1916 to form a black battalion. All the officers of the No. 2 Construction Battalion were white except for its Baptist chaplain, the Reverend William White. Because it was feared that the efficiency of white soldiers would be reduced if they were forced to fight alongside black recruits, the battalion was attached to the Canadian Forestry Corps and assigned to produce lumber for the trenches and coal mines. The battalion recruited across Canada and included 145 African-Americans who crossed the border to take part in the war before their own country entered it in April 1917.

Of those who went overseas, about 14 per cent of Canadians and 25 per cent of Newfoundlanders were killed. In town centres throughout the region, war memorials testify to the appalling death toll. A great blow was inflicted on the newly formed Newfoundland Regiment at Beaumont Hamel on 1 July 1916, the first day of the Battle of the Somme.

Women throughout the region, schooled for generations to embrace volunteer work, "did their bit" to support the war effort. In Newfoundland a Women's Patriotic Association (WPA) was formed at the outset of the war under the presidency of Lady Margaret Davidson. With branches throughout Newfoundland and Labrador, it attracted 15,000 members within a few months. By 1916 women and children of both sexes had produced, among other "comforts," 62,685 pairs of socks—an astonishing number, which achieved legendary status abroad. The WPA became involved with the Red Cross and health care, as well as general welfare issues, and raised money for a range of causes. Women in the Maritimes were also heavily engaged in war-related activities, often working through the Red Cross and the St John Ambulance. In Halifax, a busy port throughout the war, women's volunteer services were stretched to the limit.

The demands on the people of the Halifax area increased dramatically on 6 December 1917, when the French munitions ship *Mont Blanc*, loaded with TNT, collided with the Belgian relief ship

Imo in the city's harbour. The resulting explosion, the largest man-made blast before Hiroshima, levelled the city's North End, killing nearly 2,000 people, injuring 9,000, and leaving 22,000 without adequate shelter. Homes, factories, train stations, churches, and a great sweep of harbour facilities disappeared in the subsequent fires and the tidal wave that engulfed the city.

As word of the disaster spread, help poured in from across Canada and around the world. Massachusetts and Newfoundland were among the most generous "foreign" contributors to the devastated city, testimony to the close family ties connecting communities on the Atlantic coast. In Boston a Massachusetts–Halifax Relief Committee was established to collect donations, and, in conjunction with the American Red Cross, it dispatched a train equipped with medical personnel and supplies to the crippled city. Sir John Eaton, president of the T. Eaton Company, well known in the region for its mail-order catalogues, arrived in Halifax with his own train, food, sleeping car, and medical unit. In Eaton's supply depot, his staff handed out building materials and other necessities free of charge to anyone with a requisition from a pastor or relief committee official.

Prince Edward Island, home of the famous fictional orphan Anne Shirley, was particularly generous in offering to take the scores of orphaned children and the many more whose mothers and fathers, for various reasons, were unable to care for them. On 14 December authorities in

There are five memorial parks in France and Belgium commemorating the Royal Newfoundland Regiment. The most important is at Beaumont Hamel, where the Newfoundland government purchased 40 acres (16 hectares) of land, planted trees, and erected a bronze caribou (the regimental symbol) as a monument. All the parks have identical caribou sculptures. The Beaumont-Hamel site was officially dedicated on 27 June 1925, by Earl Haig, who had commanded the British armies. The Rooms Provincial Archives Division, NA 3106/Central Press Photos.

Historical Focus

Beaumont Hamel

The Allied war plan for 1916 called for a major offensive by French and British troops in the region of the Somme. By the end of June the preparations were complete and the offensive began at 7:30 a.m. on 1 July. In the Beaumont Hamel area, the plan called for a 5,000-metre advance led by the 86th and 87th Brigades, while the 88th (1st Essex and Newfoundland Regiments) was held in reserve. The plan proved to be irrelevant. Withering enemy fire caused the advance to falter, but the commanding general, mistaking German flares for a signal from the 87th Brigade that it had succeeded, ordered the 88th to move forward.

The Newfoundlanders went into battle at 9:15 a.m. It was all over in 30 minutes. Unprotected by artillery, they advanced into heavy fire concentrated on the gaps in the British wire from which they emerged. "The only visible sign that the men knew they were under this terrific fire," wrote one observer, "was that they all instinctively tucked their chins into an advanced shoulder as they had so often done when fighting their way home against a blizzard in some little outport in far off Newfoundland."[15] Most were cut down before they reached the British front line.

The Newfoundland Regiment at the front on 30 June had consisted of 25 officers and 776 non-commissioned officers and other ranks. After the battle, 233 were listed as killed, 477 as wounded or missing. For a small country this was a devastating loss.

Beginning in 1917, 1 July was observed as Memorial Day, Newfoundland's own national day of remembrance. Although the Regiment fought other battles, Beaumont Hamel became iconic. As an expression of the sterling qualities and imperial loyalty of Newfoundlanders, the failed offensive was transmuted into an occasion for solemn patriotic pride. Memorial Day is still observed today, coinciding (perhaps uneasily) with upbeat Canada Day celebrations.

Charlottetown sent a telegram announcing: "HAVE SIXTY PRIVATE HOMES FOR CHILDREN MOSTLY PROTESTANT/SOME FOR PERMANENT ADOPTION/REST WILLING TO HOME INDEFINITE TIME." They also offered to send a committee to take charge of transporting the children to their new Island homes.[16]

Nearly a month after the blast, the federal government established the Halifax Relief Commission to take charge of assistance, medical care, and reconstruction. Some $30 million, over half of it from Ottawa, was provided to help Halifax and its sister city, Dartmouth, which had also suffered from the blast, with their recovery.

The explosion exposed deeply rooted tensions in the metropolitan area. Class divisions were heightened when the Halifax Relief Commission used its extraordinary powers to determine wages and working conditions for the projects it sponsored, blithely ignoring agreements with the organized building trades in the city. The Mi'kmaq living along the Dartmouth side of the harbour at Turtle Cove, which took the full brunt of the blast, were offered free land if they agreed to relocate, but the promise was conveniently forgotten. The black community in Halifax was better organized under its religious and educational leaders to rebound from the calamity, but the levelling of the Nova Scotia Home for Coloured Children, which had just hired its first matron, was a great disappointment. The facility finally opened its doors in 1921.

The explosion also revealed the inadequacy of Halifax's public health services when, in the process of treating the victims, relief workers learned the extent of infant mortality and tuberculosis in the city. The Massachusetts–Halifax Relief Committee sent public health expert Dr Victor G. Heiser to investigate, but local officials felt threatened and resisted efforts to build the medical infrastructure that the city so badly needed.

The horror of the explosion brought the war closer to home and contributed to a growing mood of disillusionment. The mounting death toll overseas, rampant inflation, food restrictions, and a series of tawdry scandals further dampened enthusiasm for the war effort. Class and cultural divisions deepened after Prime Minister Robert Borden's Conservatives formed a Union government with some members of the badly split Liberals in 1917 and introduced compulsory military service for men between the ages of 20 and 35. Even the granting of suffrage to female relatives of men serving overseas—a major step in women's political emancipation—was tainted by the fact that it was crudely calculated to win votes in the "conscription" election of December 1917. Conscription was widely opposed in the Maritimes, and the majority of electors in both Prince Edward Island and Nova Scotia voted against the Union government, which nevertheless prevailed.

As the evidence of profiteering mounted and the gap between rich and poor grew, labour unrest increased. The Maritimes experienced more than 30 strikes in 1918 alone, and the Newfoundland Industrial Workers Association's 3,500 members successfully struck against the Reid Newfoundland Company in the spring of that year. Calls for the conscription of wealth as well as manpower grew louder. Farmers became disenchanted when the government reneged on its promise to exempt their sons from the draft, and fishing crews could not afford the loss of young men. Although Acadians were not as uniformly opposed to the war as Quebecers, they resented not only the anti-francophone tone of the conscription debate but also the heavy-handed tactics used against "deserters."

After the Halifax Explosion, December 1917. This photograph of women travelling downtown from Africville reveals the extent of the devastation along the waterfront. City of Toronto Archives, Fonds 1244, Item 2451.

In New Brunswick, one Acadian resister was seriously wounded and 26 others were taken to Saint John under military escort for resisting compulsory service.

The same factors led to a full-blown crisis in Newfoundland, where Morris manoeuvred the three political parties into a National Government and then promptly departed for London and a peerage, leaving his successors to bring in conscription. As unpopular in Newfoundland as in the Maritimes, conscription created tensions between urban and outlying districts. A militia department replaced the Patriotic Association in 1917 and, as in Canada, income and profits taxes made their first appearance. So too did prohibition, which was already more or less in place everywhere else in the region except Halifax. Ottawa imposed nationwide prohibition in 1918.

Social unrest and cultural tensions during the war emerged against a background of general economic prosperity. Although the fur-farming bubble burst and the overseas markets for apples temporarily collapsed, the steel industry expanded as many factories converted to munitions manufacturing; fisheries and agriculture generally did well; and lumbermen supplied pit props to British coal mines. The gains were undermined to some extent by inflation, rising freight rates, and a shortage of shipping, but the region's economic performance during the war still provided grounds for optimism, which government propaganda did its best to encourage. These were, as Ian McKay notes, the "last years of abundant hope."[17]

Postwar Challenges

The end of the war on 11 November 1918 was greeted with relief, if not jubilation. By that time people were preoccupied with the influenza pandemic that was raging throughout the Atlantic region. It was called the "Spanish flu" only because the press in Spain, which was not a combatant in the war, was the first to publish accounts of the disease. Recent research suggests that the virus entered Canada from the United States in September 1918 primarily with American soldiers on their way to battlefields in Europe. In the end, the pandemic killed nearly 50,000 Canadians and 100 million people worldwide.[18]

The impact of the flu was particularly devastating in northern Labrador, where the infection was carried by the Moravian mission ship *Harmony*. As many as a third of the Inuit in the area of the mission died between November 1918 and January 1919. The worst affected settlement was Okak: of a population of 263, only 56 women and children survived. According to one observer: "When the *Harmony* left Okak, people were beginning to fall sick. . . . Crews went off to their sealing places only to fall sick and die. . . . the dogs played havoc with the corpses." In nearby Sillutalik, 36 persons died, but only 18 remained to be buried. "The only visible remains of the others were a few bare skulls and a few shankbones lying around in the houses."[19]

As a result of the tragedy, Okak was abandoned. The Moravians, facing persistent economic difficulties, gradually reduced their activities, and in 1926 they handed over their trading stores to the Hudson's Bay Company.

New Brunswick was the only province in Canada with a Department of Health, established in October 1918 just as the pandemic descended. Determined to reform medical services, Health Minister Dr William F. Roberts and his Chief Medical Health Officer had their hands full with 35,000 influenza cases, but they demonstrated the advantages of centralized government administration. Within a year, boards of health chaired by medically trained health officers were established throughout the province.

These boards upheld regulations to control communicable diseases, promoted the improvement of sanitation regulations, and began health inspections of schools, all financed by the provincial government with the aid of a grant of $54,000 from the Rockefeller Foundation.[20]

Veterans returned home to perfunctory welcoming ceremonies and inadequate government help with the challenges of reintegration into a society that had been subjected to severe strain. Their discontent merged with a militant class-consciousness sparked by wartime injustices and fanned by the success of the 1917 Bolshevik Revolution in Russia. There were riots in Sydney and Halifax in which veterans played prominent roles, and in 1919–20 a wave of labour unrest swept the Maritimes, resulting in 93 strikes, including general strikes at Amherst and on the Miramichi. The recession that arrived in 1920 blunted the effectiveness and much of the militancy of the labour movement. There was no strike wave in Newfoundland, where problems in the Italian market brought the wartime fishery boom to a sudden end in the fall of 1918. Overextended fish merchants, pressed by their bankers, faced heavy losses and the possibility of a general market collapse.

The crisis was so acute and the political situation so unstable that attention was diverted from Newfoundland's humiliation at the Paris peace conference in 1919. During the war the Dominion (as it now called itself) had been represented in the Imperial War Cabinet and at the Imperial War Conference, but its fragile status was clearly exposed in the Paris negotiations. Manoeuvring between the United States' objections to separate dominion representation and the justifiable expectations of the dominions themselves, the British government decided to sacrifice the claims of the least influential dominion to obtain representation for the others. Thus Newfoundland was sidelined, excluded not only from the list of signatories of the Versailles Treaty but also from the list of original members of the League of Nations. There could not have been a clearer demonstration of Newfoundland's subordinate place in the imperial hierarchy.

While Newfoundland politics after 1918 became personal and factionalized, Maritime voters increasingly threw their support to new political parties. The comfortable give-and-take of political power between Liberals and Conservatives came to an end in the wake of the war with the emergence of Farmer and Labour parties in New Brunswick and Nova Scotia and the Progressive Party at the federal level. No one was certain what impact female suffrage would have on electoral politics when, in May 1918, women were granted the federal vote on the same basis as men. Nova Scotia had already passed similar legislation the previous month and Prince Edward Island followed suit in 1922. New Brunswick granted women the right to vote in 1919 but withheld the right to hold elected office until 1934. Newfoundland finally adopted the British model in 1925, extending the franchise to women over the age of 25.[21]

Conclusion

The Great War served as a catalyst for many changes, most notably an enhanced role for the state in the lives of its citizens. It also destroyed the confidence that had prevailed in the early twentieth century and caused many people to question the Victorian values on which they had been raised. Only time would tell if the political turmoil of 1919 was part of a new world order or just a brief, if troubling, interlude in the Atlantic region's long history. Two things were certain: the stakes in the industrial age were high and the competition keen. Unless the region could sustain economic growth and staunch the tide of out-migration, the prospects for the future would be bleak.

Further Readings

Bogaard, Paul A., ed. 1990. *Profiles of Science and Society in the Maritimes prior to 1914*. Fredericton: Acadiensis Press.

Cadigan, Sean. 2013. *Death on Two Fronts: National Tragedies and the Fate of Democracy in Newfoundland, 1914–34*. Toronto: Allen Lane.

Duley, Margot L. 1993. *Where Once Our Mothers Stood We Stand: Women's Suffrage in Newfoundland, 1890–1925*. Charlottetown: gynergy books.

Hiller, James, and Peter Neary, eds. 1994. *Twentieth Century Newfoundland: Explorations*. St John's: Breakwater Press.

Howell, Colin D. 1995. *Northern Sandlots: A Social History of Maritime Baseball*. Toronto: University of Toronto Press.

Kitz, Janet F. 1989. *Shattered City: The Halifax Explosion and the Road to Recovery*. Halifax: Nimbus.

MacDonald, Edward. 2000. *If You're Stronghearted: Prince Edward Island in the Twentieth Century*. Charlottetown: Prince Edward Island Museum and Heritage Foundation.

McDonald, Ian D.H. 1987. *"To Each His Own": William Coaker and the Fishermen's Protective Union in Newfoundland Politics, 1908–1925*. St John's: Institute of Social and Economic Research, Memorial University.

Mann, Susan. 2005. *Margaret Macdonald: Imperial Daughter*. Montreal: McGill-Queen's University Press.

Noel, S.J.R. 1971. *Politics in Newfoundland*. Toronto: University of Toronto Press.

Robertson, Ian Ross. 2008. *Sir Andrew Macphail: The Life and Legacy of a Man of Letters*. Montreal: McGill-Queen's University Press.

Ruffman, Alan, and Colin D. Howell, eds. 1994. *Ground Zero: A Reassessment of the 1917 Explosion in Halifax Harbour*. Halifax: Nimbus.

Rubio, Mary Henley. 2009. *Lucy Maud Montgomery: The Gift of Wings*. Toronto: Doubleday Canada.

Theobald, Andrew. 2008. *The Bitter Harvests of War: New Brunswick and the Conscription Crisis of 1917*. New Brunswick Military Heritage Series. Vol. 11. Fredericton: Goose Lane.

Historical Spotlight

Forbes, E.R. 1989. "Battles in Another War: Edith Archibald and the Halifax Feminist Movement," in *Challenging the Regional Stereotype: Essays on the 20th Century Maritimes*. Fredericton: Acadiensis Press.

MacKenzie, David. "Eastern Approaches: Maritime Canada and Newfoundland," in *Canada and the First World War: Essays in Honour of Robert Craig Brown*, ed. David MacKenzie. Toronto: University of Toronto Press, 2005.

Recommended Websites

Balls, Bats, and Boats: Sporting and Recreation in New Brunswick
http://website.nbm-mnb.ca/BBB/starte.asp

Canada and the First World War.
http://www.warmuseum.ca/firstworldwar/

The First World War
http://www.veterans.gc.ca/eng/remembrance/history/first-world-war

Fishermen's Protective Union
http://www.mun.ca/mha/fpu/index.html

Halifax Explosion
www.halifaxexplosion.org
http://maritimemuseum.novascotia.ca/what-see-do/halifax-explosion

Halifax Explosion: A Vision of Regeneration
http://www.gov.ns.ca/archives/virtual/explosion

Jack Turner's War [PEI soldier]
http://epe.lac-bac.gc.ca/100/205/301/ic/cdc/turner/default.htm

L.M. Montgomery Research Centre
http://www.lmmrc.ca

Newfoundland and the Great War
http://www.heritage.nf.ca/greatwar/articles/default.html

Chapter 12

Between the Wars, 1919–1939

Between the end of the First World War and the beginning of the Second, the Atlantic region fell further behind in the contest for economic success. The 1920s roared in many parts of North America but not in the Maritimes and Newfoundland, where a prolonged recession following the war was compounded by the Great Depression of the 1930s. Facing severe financial problems, all governments in the region had to turn to Ottawa or London for assistance. At the same time, mass consumer culture was sweeping across North America, making automobiles, household appliances, radios, and modern fashions the symbols of status and success. Prompted by the sheer scale of human misery and the desire for a better life, new movements and political parties offered solutions to this crisis of capitalism. Answers were slow in coming.

Setting the Context

The Interwar Economy

Following the Great War, the global economy became increasingly unstable and unpredictable. The reasons were complex. A central factor seems to have been the growing imbalance between a powerful, wealthy, and in some ways self-sufficient United States and the rest of the world. To protect its own burgeoning industrial sector, the United States continued to impose high tariffs on foreign goods, which impeded economic recovery elsewhere. None of the international financial institutions we know today existed in the interwar years, and the United States was reluctant to take over Britain's pre-war role as stabilizer of the world economy. As a result, what happened in an isolationist United States largely determined what happened on an international scale.[1]

This situation is clear in hindsight. At the time many policy-makers assumed that the world could return to the relatively stable pre-1914 financial and economic environment. They were mistaken. While the United States experienced a consumer-led boom in the 1920s, many other countries struggled with hyperinflation, debt, and falling prices for primary products. This set the stage for economic disaster. In October 1929 the New York stock market crashed, the result of madcap speculation and the overproduction of industrial goods for which there was insufficient global demand. Banks collapsed, loans dried up, trade contracted, and the capitalist world crumbled into a nightmare of high unemployment, financial insecurity, and political unrest. There was some recovery after 1932, but the "Great Depression" continued until the Second World War. In this context, extreme political movements flourished, most notably in Germany and Italy, where fascism gained support.

With an economy highly dependent on international trade, Canada was hard hit. Fishers and farmers suffered disproportionately, several provinces and Newfoundland faced bankruptcy, and new political parties emerged, among them Social Credit, the Co-operative Commonwealth Federation (the direct ancestor of the NDP), and the Reconstruction Party. As the Depression worsened, support for the Communist Party, founded in the wake of the Russian Revolution of 1917, increased to the point where the federal government imprisoned its leader, Tim Buck, from 1932 to 1934. At the same time, the Depression gradually stimulated new thinking about economic policy that would have a major impact on international affairs.

Economic Uncertainty

In the 1920s, poverty, unemployment, and labour unrest were endemic in the Maritimes and Newfoundland. Out-migration continued at alarming levels until job opportunities everywhere dried up with the onset of the Great Depression in 1929. Although the worst was over by 1933, except possibly in Newfoundland, recovery would be difficult.

Some sectors of the economy coped better than others. Between 1920 and 1939, the gross value of production in the Maritimes actually increased by 17.3 per cent and more than doubled in Newfoundland, but the overall figures disguise uneven experiences. Agriculture in the Maritimes struggled to modernize, and the Newfoundland fishery declined after 1919, while manufacturing took a hit from which it never recovered. While many other areas of North America were moving towards the production of mass consumer goods, the Atlantic region was unable to make the transition to a modern economy.

The fisheries that sustained many families, in whole or in part, continued to languish. European markets for salt fish were slow to recover after the war, demand for Canadian fish in the Caribbean and South America was weakening, and competition from Norway and Iceland was becoming more aggressive. In the Maritimes the production of salt fish, whether dried or green, collapsed, the extent of the decline reflected in the size of the Lunenburg fleet of saltbankers, which dropped from about 140 to 20 vessels between 1919 and 1939. Given the uncertainty of international markets for salt fish, it is little wonder that Maritime fishermen sought other ways of making a living. Newfoundland remained a serious competitor in the salt fish trade, increasing its low-priced exports to the West Indies and Brazil when European markets became unstable, but more lucrative markets proved elusive.

The United States, meanwhile, raised its tariffs and revoked the permission it had given Canadians to land fish in American ports. As a result, 1921 was the worst year for the Atlantic fishery in four decades. There was some recovery thereafter, largely in the fresh fish sector, which was stimulated by the expansion of fish processing firms. By the mid-1920s Nova Scotia boasted 11 trawlers, and Halifax was beginning to emerge as the centre of a modern industrial fishery. Yet resistance to modernization of the fishery remained strong among inshore fishermen and was reinforced when a 1927 royal commission on the fisheries (the Maclean Commission) recommended restrictions on steam trawling. By 1939 the trawler fleet had been reduced to three. Together, uncertain markets and resistance to change stunted the overall development of the Maritime fisheries. Instead of pursuing technological innovation, the industry continued to rely on cheap labour, to the detriment of both the well-being of the workers and the value of the catch, which sank to approximately what it had been in 1880.

The Newfoundland government met the fisheries crisis with an unprecedented dose of state intervention as prescribed by William Coaker, founder of the Fishermen's Protective Union and, from 1919, minister of fisheries. His aims were to regulate the marketing of salt fish and to end destructive competition between rival exporters. He failed to achieve his goals primarily because of poor markets, but also because he was regarded with suspicion by the "long-coated chaps" of St John's on account of his union affiliations and a perceived conflict of interest as president of the Union Trading Company, itself a major exporter. Moreover, merchants could not afford to hold fish until prices and markets improved, as Coaker's scheme essentially required; the banks were unhelpful; and the government lacked the financial resources to provide the trade with a cushion. As a result the "Coaker regulations" were short-lived. It was only in 1933, in the depths of the Depression, that a merchant-supported government finally created a Salt Codfish Board to control exports. Coaker turned his attention to finding alternative employment for poverty-stricken fishing families and enthusiastically supported plans (originally promoted by the Reid Newfoundland Company) to establish a second newsprint mill at Corner Brook, which began production in 1925—just as the postwar boom in paper prices ended.

Table 12.1	Timeline
1919–23	Intercolonial Railway integrated into Canadian National Railways.
1920	First Congress of Coloured Women of Canada held in Halifax.
1921	Scotia and Dominion Steel merge to form British Empire Steel Corp. (BESCO); launch of the *Bluenose*; W.F. Coaker's attempt to regulate the Newfoundland fishery fails.
1922	Cape Breton miners' strike; women in Prince Edward Island gain the right to vote.
1923	Cape Breton steelworkers' strike.
1925	Maritime Rights Election in Nova Scotia; Cape Breton miners' strike; Royal Commission on the Coal Mining Industry in Nova Scotia chaired by Sir Andrew Rae Duncan; newsprint mill opens at Corner Brook; women's suffrage legislated in Newfoundland.
1925–9	Prohibition ends in Newfoundland, Nova Scotia, and New Brunswick.
1926	Duncan Royal Commission on Maritime Claims; Moravians lease their trading stores in Labrador to Hudson's Bay Company.
1927	Maclean Royal Commission on the Fisheries of the Maritime Provinces; Labrador boundary defined by the Privy Council.
1928	Gabriel Sylliboy loses court case; Antigonish Movement launched.
1929	Great Depression begins; Persons Case.
1931	Statute of Westminster.
1933	Report of the Newfoundland (Amulree) Royal Commission.
1934	Responsible government suspended in Newfoundland.
1937	Nova Scotia Trade Union Act passed.
1939	Second World War begins.

Built by British interests, the Corner Brook mill was sold to International Power and Paper (IPP) in 1927, an American firm that was expanding in the Maritimes. IPP developed hydro power at Grand Falls in New Brunswick and built mills at Dalhousie and Bathurst. Other firms constructed pulp mills at Edmundston and Atholville in New Brunswick and at Liverpool, Nova Scotia. The pulp and paper mills partially made up for the decline in sawmilling, which faced a twofold challenge: rising costs for lumber production as the more accessible stands of trees disappeared, and stiff competition from Pacific coast producers, who could now ship through the recently completed Panama Canal to the east coast and Britain.

Agriculture also faced challenges. The apple industry recovered its coveted British market following the Great War and expanded production. In 1933 growers sold 82 per cent of their bumper crop of more than 8 million bushels (nearly half of the entire Canadian output) overseas. Since the competitive position of Maritime growers depended on price, not quality, they grew mainly medium-quality cooking apples, which were subject to stiff competition. By the 1930s apples from the United States, British Columbia, and New Zealand were making serious inroads in British markets and consumers everywhere were turning to the larger dessert varieties. Maritime producers would have to plant new orchards, develop new packing techniques, and improve their marketing skills or be left behind.

During the fashion-conscious 1920s, the demand for silver fox collars—a single pelt draped over the shoulder—soared. Prince Edward Island boasted 600 fox farms, and many farmers kept a few silver foxes to make extra income. Participation in the industry required deep pockets. In 1924 one especially fine breeding pair sold for $32,500. The industry began to decline in the 1930s as a result of poor economic conditions, changes in fashion, and competition from Scandinavia, but even in the depths of the Depression a single pelt sold for an all-time high of $2,600.[2]

With markets in the United States, the Caribbean, and South America, the potato industry in the Maritimes expanded. Prince Edward Island seed potatoes found a ready market, and acreage expanded at the expense of other types of farming. Although some Maritime farmers focused on dairy, chicken, and beef production for local consumption, most failed to specialize, and their operations gradually became unsustainable. As a proportion of total gross value of production in the Maritimes, agriculture fell from 34.3 per cent in 1920 to 27.8 per cent in 1939. Farm families needed other sources of income, and many farmers took seasonal jobs—if they could find them—to make ends meet. During the 1930s the family farm became a refuge for those who lost their jobs in the urban centres, but the general trend was clear. Young people who could abandon the rural life for jobs in cities, often outside the region, did so. In the 1920s the Maritimes' population increased by less than 1 per cent, and both Nova Scotia and Prince Edward Island experienced absolute declines.

Trouble was also brewing in the industrial belt that had grown along the Intercolonial route. Between 1919 and 1923, the railway was integrated into Canadian National Railways, a Crown corporation with scant sympathy for the people living in the eastern provinces. Freight rates—now determined outside the region—increased by 140 to 216 per cent, making it virtually impossible for Maritime producers to compete in the central Canadian market. With the end of railway expansion, the demand for rails and railway equipment contracted sharply. The iron and steel industry had difficulty adapting, hampered by lack of capital and the challenge of competing with central Canadian producers.

The result was a sudden downsizing. Between 1919 and 1921 the labour force employed in iron and steel declined by 85 per cent and in manufacturing generally by 40 per cent. This contraction in turn hurt the region's coal industry, since iron and steel had absorbed 25 per cent of its output. Nor was this the only problem faced by coal producers. The Quebec market had been lost during the war and would take time to regain. High freight rates and cheaper American imports effectively blocked sales west of Quebec, where hydro power and oil were gaining ground. For Maritime producers to compete, they would have to reduce their prices—but the costs of production in Cape Breton, where the shafts extended under the seabed, were higher than elsewhere because of the long distance to and from the coal face and the need for expensive ventilation and drainage systems.

Overall, the manufacturing sector was badly crippled in the early 1920s as plants closed or were consolidated into central Canadian companies. The net value of production declined from $325 million in 1920 to a low point of $192.5 million in 1924, and employment fell significantly below the levels of the 1890s. As S.A. Saunders pointed out as early as 1939, the Maritimes failed to make the transition from heavy industry geared to railway and nation-building to light industry producing consumer goods.[3] The consequences would be felt for the remainder of the twentieth century.

A significant contribution to the regional economy in the interwar years was the illicit liquor trade. It emerged as a by-product of prohibition, which remained in place in most Canadian provinces following the war and became federal law in the United States in 1920. With the fisheries languishing, many seagoing Maritimers were only too happy to make a living as "rum-runners." Typically, liquor from Europe, the Caribbean, and Canada was delivered to Saint-Pierre and Miquelon, where Maritime vessels picked it up and then legally carried it to "rum row," just outside the American 12-mile limit. There they would wait for a fast motor launch sent by one of the American crime syndicates that made fortunes smuggling it into the country.

The tidy income made by bootleggers was not lost on provincial administrations looking to finance public works and social services. One by one, governments in the Atlantic region abandoned prohibition and took control of liquor sales (and profits) themselves: Newfoundland in 1925, New Brunswick in 1927, and Nova Scotia in 1929. The US trade continued unabated until the American Congress finally gave up and repealed prohibition in 1933. Only Prince Edward Island held out until after the Second World War, making bootlegging a profitable occupation there.

Maritimers Take a Stand

Economic adversity prompted a variety of responses. In Nova Scotia members of the newly formed Labour Party entered a loose alliance with alienated farmers to win 11 seats in the 1920 provincial election, making the Farmer–Labour coalition the official opposition to the incumbent Liberals, who had held office since 1882. Later the same year the United Farmers did equally well in New Brunswick, where they had 141 locals and ran co-operatives. In Prince Edward Island fishermen became formally organized and, like the farmers, began to establish co-operatives.

Unions also rose to the challenge. Although the postwar recession blunted labour militancy, Cape Breton remained a battlefield. In 1921 Nova Scotia Steel and Coal merged with Dominion Iron and Steel to form the British Empire Steel Corporation (BESCO), with headquarters in Montreal. The following year BESCO announced a 37.5 per cent wage cut for miners. Already hit by plant closures and reductions in hours, the UMW local in Cape Breton called for "the complete overthrow of the

Lawren S. Harris, "Glace Bay." A member of the Group of Seven, Harris visited Cape Breton in 1921. This stark image of a miner's family appeared on the cover of the July 1925 issue of the *Canadian Forum*, which included an article on the strikebound island. Library and Archives Canada/C-110249. Reprinted with permission from Mr. Stewart Sheppard, Estate of Lawren S. Harris.

capitalist system" and went on strike. Alarmed by what was seen as an eruption of Bolshevism, authorities called in soldiers and special police to crush it. In 1923, when the troops returned to put down a steelworkers' strike, an unprovoked mounted charge through the Whitney Pier district of Sydney led coal miners to walk out in sympathy, and union leaders "Red" Dan Livingstone and J.B. McLachlan were arrested. Unrest continued to escalate. On 11 June 1925, another protracted and bitter strike by coal miners ended in the death of William Davis, a 37-year-old miner who was shot by the police. The date was later declared Davis Day, and it is still commemorated in Cape Breton.

By the mid-1920s all workers in the coal and steel industries had suffered severe wage cuts, and BESCO was on the edge of bankruptcy. It was cold comfort for the miners that a 1925 provincial royal commission on the coal industry found the size of the original wage cut unjustified. Chaired by British lawyer-industrialist Sir Andrew Rae Duncan, the commission criticized the company for bad faith and intransigence, but since neither the commission nor the provincial government was prepared to consider genuinely radical solutions, the tensions continued.

The rise of the Canadian west and the dominance of Ontario and Quebec underlined the increasing political marginalization of the Maritime provinces. Federal leaders were inevitably more sympathetic to the demands of the more powerful regions, tending to view the Maritimes as backward and their leaders as chronic grumblers with no good reason for complaint. Unable and sometimes unwilling to counter hostile and unsympathetic federal policies and attitudes, Maritime MPs exerted little influence on national policy.

In the 1921 federal election, voters in Nova Scotia and Prince Edward Island showed their hostility to the Conservatives, now led by Arthur Meighen, and elected only Liberals. New Brunswick showed some resistance to the trend, returning five Liberals, five Conservatives, and one Progressive. The Conservatives were defeated, but the new prime minister, William Lyon Mackenzie King, was held hostage by the spectacular success of 65 Progressive Party candidates, most of them from the badly alienated Prairie provinces and rural Ontario. He had little time to devote to the grievances of his Liberal backbenchers from the Maritimes.

After more than half a century of Confederation, Maritimers were no more reconciled to federal structures than they had been in 1867. Federal subsidies to all three provinces were parsimonious in comparison with the generous financial terms granted to Alberta and Saskatchewan when they achieved provincial status in 1905, and no compensation was given to other provinces for the huge chunks of Crown land (formerly Hudson's Bay Company territory) awarded to Manitoba, Ontario, and Quebec in 1912. Nor was Ottawa prepared to act on freight rates. Indeed, in 1922 it restored the Crow's Nest Pass rate, benefiting Prairie farmers and Ontario manufacturers, while allowing Intercolonial rates to increase dramatically.

An all-pervasive sense of injustice finally found political expression in the Maritime Rights movement. A genuinely regional phenomenon, the movement was dominated by professionals and businessmen hoping to shore up their unsteady ascendancy in troubled times, but was readily embraced by all classes and cultures. The Nova Scotia Conservatives, led by the industrialist E.N. Rhodes, fought the 1925 election under the Maritime Rights banner, winning 40 out of 43 seats. The Conservative premiers of New Brunswick and Prince Edward Island, J.B.M. Baxter and J.D. Stewart, respectively, were quick to climb on the bandwagon, although the frugal Islanders (who believed in minimal government and usually ran a budget surplus) never adopted Maritime Rights with the same enthusiasm as the other two provinces.

Maritime Rights campaigners made sufficient noise for even the prime minister to take notice. Needing support from the Maritime MPs to sustain his minority government, King reluctantly appointed a Royal Commission on Maritime Claims, chaired by the same Sir Andrew Duncan who had

This cartoon captured the spirit of the Maritime Rights movement that helped to define issues in both provincial and federal elections in Nova Scotia in 1925 and 1926. Donald McRitchie, "Let's Keep It at the Masthead," *Halifax Herald*, 2 May 1925.

investigated the problems in the coal industry. In a carefully worded report released in 1926, the commission recommended increased subsidies, lower freight rates, development of the harbours at Saint John and Halifax, a subsidy for the steel industry, and improved ferry service to Prince Edward Island—Duncan had been convinced of the need for the latter by his trip to Charlottetown. The report avoided any discussion of tariffs or special grants to ensure that services in the Maritime provinces would not fall behind those in the rest of the country.

Well-received in the Maritimes, the report met heavy opposition in Ottawa. The result was a compromise that, according to the historian E.R. Forbes, "changed Duncan's program for Maritime rehabilitation into a plan for Maritime pacification . . . to be achieved with the fewest possible concessions."[4] And it worked. Although the federal government refused to budge on the subsidy issue, Maritime Rights leaders gratefully accepted the Maritime Freight Rates Act (1927), the Dominion Fuel Act (1927), port development for Saint John and Halifax, and a new ferry for Prince Edward Island. With that, the movement petered out, but the resentment lingered.

Biography | *Mona Wilson and Public Health*

In the interwar years, governments in the Atlantic region were hard pressed to provide the level of health services that wealthier jurisdictions could afford. New Brunswick had a department of health, but most of the work of keeping people healthy tended to fall on nurses and voluntary associations such as the Red Cross. In Newfoundland, the staff of the Newfoundland Outport Nursing and Industrial Association (NONIA), formed in 1924, took modern ideas about health and nutrition to outport communities and encouraged the production of handicrafts to help pay for nursing services.

In Prince Edward Island, the dynamic Mona Wilson played a singular role in advancing public health. Born in Toronto in 1894, she was educated at Johns Hopkins University and served overseas with the American Army Nursing Corps in the First World War. She joined the American Red Cross in 1919 and served in Vladivostok and the Balkans. After studying for her Public Health diploma at the University of Toronto, she became Chief Red Cross Public Health Nurse for Prince Edward Island in 1923.

Wilson and her small staff introduced a variety of programs to serve the island's health needs. They implemented school medical inspections; established dental clinics, tuberculosis clinics, and camps for physically handicapped children; organized province-wide smallpox and diphtheria vaccinations; promoted the consumption of fruits, vegetables, and milk; and encouraged scrupulous hygiene. Through Junior Red Cross Clubs, children were taught that they should have a warm bath at least once a week, brush their teeth twice a day, cough or sneeze into a handkerchief, and sleep 10 hours a night with the window open.

When the province finally established a Department of Health in 1931, Wilson was appointed Provincial Director of Public Nursing. She held this position until her retirement in 1961, except during the Second World War, when she served as Red Cross Commissioner

Continued

for Newfoundland. Wilson's contributions to Island life include the establishment of the Girl Guides, the Zonta Club, and the Business and Professional Women's Club.[5]

Mona Wilson conducting a health inspection at the Charlottetown Model School in 1926. Public Archives and Records Office of Prince Edward Island, Acc. 2320/29-2.

Trouble in Newfoundland

Newfoundland's problems mirrored those experienced by the Maritimes, in part because it was now more closely linked to the mainland. The Bell Island iron ore mines, for instance, were in serious trouble because of the collapse of the market in Cape Breton. Although pulp and paper industries survived in Grand Falls and Corner Brook, the loggers producing the raw material were ill-treated and poorly paid. Major losses for fish exporters forced many businesses to declare bankruptcy between 1921 and 1923. Observers such as Joseph Smallwood (later to become the first provincial premier) recognized that outside St John's there were now two worlds: that of the long-established but old-fashioned salt fish industry, and that of the modern industrial centres created by newsprint, hydroelectricity, and mining, which seemed to represent the future.

The war had changed the nature of Newfoundland politics, complicating the government's efforts to respond to the economic crisis. With the collapse of the National Government in 1919, the three parties dissolved into factions and party labels lost their meaning. There was, however, a broad distinction between conservative St John's–based politicians, and those outside who were more populist and oriented toward the outports. Victory in the 1919 election went to a coalition between William Coaker's Unionists and the Liberal followers of Richard Squires. Like all interwar administrations, its freedom to address the crisis was limited by a public debt that had grown substantially during the war.

As unemployment mounted and emigration increased to between 1,000 and 1,500 people annually, there were demonstrations in St John's and, in 1921, mob scenes in the House of Assembly. The agreement to build the a paper mill at Corner Brook was a major achievement, but as part of the deal the government had to take over the operation of the dilapidated railway—yet another financial burden. If it had not done so, the Reid Newfoundland Company would have launched an array of expensive and time-consuming lawsuits.

Squires was re-elected in May 1923, but his government soon collapsed amid charges that he had taken kickbacks from the mining companies on Bell Island and had turned the Board of Liquor Control into a covert bootlegging operation with the profits from "private" sales going into his political account. The charges were largely substantiated by an independent inquiry. With Squires temporarily out of public life, the St John's-based Conservatives took over in June 1924, promising clean, stable, business-like government. They also belatedly enfranchised women, in 1925, and ended prohibition.

A piece of good fortune came in 1927, when the Judicial Committee of the Privy Council ruled that the western boundary between Newfoundland and Canada in the Labrador Peninsula should, for the most part, follow the height of land, but this bonanza meant little in the short term. When Newfoundland twice offered to sell the territory, neither Canada nor Quebec was interested in buying. For the moment Labrador remained a potential rather than an actual asset, its resources too remote for effective development. The Newfoundland government provided only minimal services, otherwise leaving Labrador in the hands of the Moravian and Grenfell missions and the Hudson's Bay Company, but this was scarcely a lasting solution.

First Nations in Difficult Times

The living conditions in most Maritime Aboriginal communities continued to deteriorate through the interwar years. Amendments to the Indian Act only made matters worse, permitting governments to relocate people from reserves near towns and cities with more than 8,000 residents and to expropriate reserve lands anywhere for roads, railroads, and other public purposes. These provisions were invoked in Nova Scotia to move Mi'kmaq from the Halifax and Sydney areas. Because they were distant from jobs and markets, the Mi'kmaq relied more than ever on hunting, fishing, and selling their crafts from door to door.

On numerous occasions the Mi'kmaq and Wolastoqiyik petitioned governments to acknowledge their rights to land and resources under treaties signed in the eighteenth century, but to no avail. In 1928 Grand Chief Gabriel Sylliboy, a Mi'kmaq living in Cape Breton, was tried for possessing pelts in contravention of the increasingly restrictive game laws imposed under the Lands and Forests Act. In court, Sylliboy argued that as a "Registered Indian" he was exempt from the provisions of the Act and that he had "by Treaty the right to hunt and trap at all times." Although he lost his case, Sylliboy represented a new spirit among First Nations in Canada, who had kept the memory of their ill-treatment alive and were now mobilizing to use the colonizer's institutions to make their case.[6]

In 1935 the Department of Indian Affairs hired Dr Thomas Robertson to study the conditions on Maritime reserves. Finding sub-standard housing, rampant tuberculosis, and poor nutrition, his report warned that the federal government was facing a much higher outlay for assistance if people living on reserves could not become self-supporting. "The opinion of the man on the street," he noted, "is that the Indian is lazy, useless and himself responsible for his present conditions. However, a study of the record of each individual shows that the great majority of the Indians are good workers and that his present condition is due to matters over which he has no control."[7]

Canadian authorities had long viewed education as one means of integrating Aboriginal children into mainstream society. To that end they established both day and residential schools on or near reserves. Most children in the Maritimes attended day schools, if they had any schooling at all, but one residential school was established at Shubenacadie in 1923, operated by the Sisters of Charity Vincent Saint Paul and the Missionary Oblates of Mary Immaculate. Its teachers tried to erase the language and traditions of young Mi'kmaq and Wolastoqiyik, instill Christian values, and develop practical skills, but harsh discipline and underfunded facilities brought only hardship, heartache, and misery. The school finally closed in 1967.

Germain Laksi played a major role in preserving the history of his people. Born in Maine in 1854 to Mi'kmaq parents originally from Nova Scotia, and trained in herbal medicine, he played the role of Dr Jerry Lonecloud in American medicine shows and then settled in Halifax, where in 1910 he began helping Harry Piers, curator of the Provincial Museum of Nova Scotia, to collect Mi'kmaw artifacts. From 1923 to 1929, Halifax reporter Clara Dennis conducted a series of interviews with Laksi about his life and Mi'kmaw culture. Together, the interviews and artifacts represent a rich historical legacy.[8]

The Great Depression

Conditions seemed to be improving in the late 1920s, but then the Great Depression arrived. Prices fell, markets collapsed, and unemployment climbed. The situation was exacerbated by the loss of emigration as a safety valve for the unemployed. The US border was closed to all newcomers looking for work, and Canada for the first time restricted the entry of immigrants from Newfoundland. In 1930 the Smoot–Hawley tariff closed the US market to most imports. By 1931 nearly 20 per cent of wage earners were unemployed. Although this figure was only slightly above the national average, the Maritime provinces had fewer resources than others to put into Ottawa's cost-shared relief programs.

The strain on all levels of government was extreme. By 1931 Guysborough County in Nova Scotia was facing bankruptcy, and several counties in northern New Brunswick were soon in the same position. Provincial governments were also in difficulty. Income per capita had fallen to 71 per cent of the Canadian average by 1933, revenues stagnated, and borrowing drove debt charges to impossible heights—more than 30 per cent of revenue in Nova Scotia and more than 50 per cent in New Brunswick. In 1933, 12 per cent of Maritimers were on direct relief, which in most cases paid only a pittance and was sometimes cut off in the summer. Prince Edward Island's rate of $1.93 per person per month (the same as Newfoundland's) was the second lowest in Canada. Given the level of the crisis, the resources of churches, charities, and the Red Cross proved woefully inadequate.

Fishermen, urban labourers, and the elderly were the worst hit. Strictly means-tested old-age pensions, which had been introduced in Newfoundland after 1909, arrived in the Maritime provinces between 1933 and 1936 at rates 20 to 40 per cent below the Canadian average. They were a convenient way to reduce relief rolls, but the result was widespread malnutrition, and near-starvation in some areas. Even so, Maritimers and Newfoundlanders found the time, energy, and resources to send aid to the Prairies, where the wheat economy had collapsed.[9]

The Depression precipitated the end of responsible government in Newfoundland. Squires had returned to power in 1928, but his government was soon engulfed by the economic collapse. Four years later, revenue had fallen by 21 per cent; spending had risen by 7 per cent; the debt had increased by 23 per cent; and servicing it now absorbed more than 60 per cent of government revenue. These bald figures represented an escalating economic and financial crisis: low prices for fish, poor catches, rising urban unemployment, a quarter of the population on the "dole" (which was centrally administered), and the necessity of borrowing to maintain the basic operations of the state, even after swingeing cuts in public expenditure. As bank loans became ever more difficult to arrange, another attempt was made to sell Labrador, this time for $110 million, but there were still no takers.

The atmosphere was especially tense in St John's, where the prime minister's opponents sensed blood and organized a march on the legislature on 5 April 1932. It turned into a violent riot, and Squires was lucky to escape unharmed. His party was virtually wiped out in the ensuing general election and the Conservatives assumed power. Having assessed the financial situation, they suggested what Squires had consistently refused: a partial default on debt payments. There seemed to be no other alternative.

Alarm bells rang in both London and Ottawa, where the possibility that a dominion might default on its debt was viewed with dismay. Newfoundland was given a proposition that it was not allowed to refuse: Canada and Britain would assist with the debt payments on condition that an

Crowds outside the Colonial Building, St John's, 5 April 1932. Accusations of corruption levelled against the prime minister, Sir Richard Squires, precipitated this demonstration, which turned into a riot. The Rooms Provincial Archives Division, A 19-23/E. Holloway.

Historical Focus

Newfoundland and Dominion Status

The concept of "dominion status" in the British Empire evolved between the mid-nineteenth century, when responsible government was first established in the colonies of settlement, and 1931, when the British Parliament passed the Statute of Westminster, granting dominions the freedom to exercise their independence in domestic and foreign affairs. Signifying autonomy under the British imperial umbrella, the term "dominion" was applied to the self-governing countries that made up what was then known as the British Commonwealth: Canada, Australia, New Zealand, South Africa, Newfoundland, and the Irish Free State. Although Canada was slow to take advantage of its new status, the groundwork was laid for cutting the remaining colonial ties with Great Britain.

Newfoundland proved to be a special case. Officially, it had the same status as its peers. Its prime ministers attended imperial conferences and, during the Great War, meetings of the Imperial War Cabinet and the Imperial War Conference. Its affairs were administered in London by the Dominions Office, even during the period from 1934 to 1949 when the country was governed by an appointed commission. However, unlike its theoretical equals, Newfoundland did not sign the Versailles Treaty in 1919 and was not a member of the League of Nations. It allowed its external affairs to be handled by the imperial government, and in 1931 decided, along with Australia and New Zealand, to postpone taking up the Statute's grant of autonomy. A British official noted that Newfoundland was unique as a "minor" type of dominion.[10] After 1934 Newfoundland can be best characterized as a dominion in suspension.

imperial royal commission investigate the situation and advise on what to do in the longer term. Chaired by Lord Amulree, the royal commission reported in October 1933. It placed the primary blame for the debt crisis not on the Depression, structural economic problems, or the cost of the war and the railway, but rather on "persistent extravagance and neglect of proper financial principles," "greed, graft and corruption," and general incompetence, along with various other shortcomings. Its central recommendation, fabricated by the Whitehall bureaucracy, was that the country's debt should be rescheduled and guaranteed by the British government. In return, Newfoundland would surrender responsible government and be administered by a British-appointed commission until such time as it was again "self-supporting."

Weary of persistent economic problems, disillusioned with the political elite, fearful of further violence and unrest, Newfoundlanders threw in the towel. Politicians and commentators thanked the British government for its intervention. "The political past of our country is dead and buried," said the mayor of St John's; "it is not my wish to revive it or refer to it." The legislature voted itself out of existence and the Commission of Government took office in February 1934. Chaired by a British-appointed governor, it consisted of three British civil servants (who held the more important portfolios of Finance, Public Utilities, and Natural Resources) and three Newfoundlanders. Although the surrender of responsible government was initially welcomed, it very soon came to be (and is still) seen as a humiliation, and the Amulree report's analysis as unfair and prejudiced.

Joining Canada might have been less of an indignity, but at the time there was little support for Confederation on the island and none at all in Ottawa.

Document

Lady Hope Simpson's Impressions of Newfoundlanders, 1935

The Commission of Government took office in Newfoundland in early 1934. Sir John Hope Simpson was appointed commissioner for natural resources, serving until 1936. In 1935 he and his wife Quita toured the south coast of the island on a coastal boat. The Hope Simpsons admitted that conditions varied from place to place, but in a letter to her son, Lady Hope Simpson offered her impressions of the poverty she encountered in two outports:

La Hune was our first port of call. . . . It is a most miserable place—so poor—so wretched. The children ran away like little wild animals & hid at our approach. We went into some of the houses. The people hardly stirred when we came in. . . . All looked dreadfully dirty, the men grey & unshaven, their clothing ragged & patched; the children many of them in a cotton nightgown with bare feet, the women often with nothing on under a cotton gown & the snow still lying down to the seashore in many places. . . .

They are a queer people. Wherever we go, we get a first impression of unfriend-liness. . . . But it has been our experience everywhere that all this apparent unfriend-liness is a sort of smokescreen of shyness, almost indeed a custom of the country. Very quickly it goes down before an assault, and before we leave the people are responsive & friendly. . . .

The most marked case was yesterday at Isle aux Morts. . . . On the wharf lounged about a dozen men, lying on a pile of planks. They let us approach without moving to greet us, as usual. . . . "Well, how are things with you here?" "Worse than ever before. Isn't that so, lads? Worse than ever before they are; and that's so." "But you've had good fishing this winter, haven't you?" "Yes, that's so, plenty of fish there be." "Yes, plenty fish," corroborated the crowd; then silence. We know what that means—low prices for their fish & high prices for their supplier & the merchant getting all the profits. The truck system is the ruin of the people.

The school was truly a dreadful place, great holes in the floor & a broken roof. But the crowd pushed in after us, & I suggested that the children make room for the men & [John] talked to them, asking them questions & making notes of their difficulties & telling them what the government is doing & suggesting what they could do. . . .

It always comes as a surprise to me when these children talk English—they seem such little foreigners—so wild & furtive. One little figure specially stands out in my memory—a girl child of about six with straight fair hair & delicate features, standing on the edge of a wharf seeing us off from Grey River—barelegged & barefooted in a grimy white nightgown, snow on the hillside behind her. I wanted to go back & wrap her in my coat & carry her into her house.[11]

Responses to Hard Times

Two strategies were adopted across the region to cope with the economic crisis. The first was to provide unemployed people with land and encourage them to become self-sufficient farmers. This program was most popular in New Brunswick, where the government opened new areas for pioneer settlement and provided minimal assistance. Acadians were particularly involved in the scheme, establishing a number of new communities in the northern part of the province. In Nova Scotia some 600 vacant farms were made available, but most of the beneficiaries were unemployed miners and their families. Lacking the necessary agricultural skills, many of them drifted away. The results were similarly disappointing in Newfoundland, where the Commission government created eight land settlements and relocated approximately 365 families.

The second, more famous and influential strategy was developed by the Extension Department of St Francis Xavier University under the direction of Father Moses Coady. The Antigonish Movement, as it came to be known, focused on self-help through adult education and the establishment of co-operatives to do everything from marketing fish to building houses. Although co-operatives were not new to the Maritimes, the Antigonish Movement provided a new impetus for this approach to economic development, especially in rural areas where the Roman Catholic Church was strong. By the end of 1939 Antigonish claimed involvement in 2,390 study clubs and 140 credit unions throughout all three Maritime provinces.[12]

The Newfoundland government established its own division of co-operatives in the mid-1930s, with Antigonish alumni as the director and field workers. There was considerable early success both in St John's and on the island's west coast. Less well-received was the commission's insistence that, to prevent beriberi, dole recipients should use brown rather than white flour. Unemployed marchers in St John's in 1935 responded with a banner reading "We work for our cash; we want money not cattle feed."[13]

The Antigonish Movement was inherently conservative. Its leaders had no interest in radical politics; indeed, it has been accused of being more romantic than realist, and of failing to involve industrial and urban workers. Other organizations were more willing to challenge the status quo. Until it was suppressed by the federal government in 1931, the Communist Party had some support in the Maritimes. The social-democratic Co-operative Commonwealth Federation (CCF) won both provincial and federal seats in industrial Cape Breton within a decade of its founding in 1932. In the 1935 federal election, the upstart Reconstruction Party, which split from the Conservatives, attracted followers in eastern Nova Scotia, where the Antigonish Movement had cultivated support for a "middle way." Even the Ku Klux Klan appeared, blaming Roman Catholics, blacks, and other minorities for the hard times.

The emergence of new parties did not substantially transform Maritime politics, nor did it bring meaningful change in federal–provincial relations. In Nova Scotia, Angus L. Macdonald's Liberal government, elected in 1933, appointed a royal commission on the impact of Canada's fiscal and trade policies on the province's economy. Chaired by J. Harry Jones, a British economist, the commission included Harold Innis, a rising Canadian academic star. While its 1934 report concluded that tariff policies, transportation costs, and industrial protectionism had contributed to Nova Scotia's relative economic decline, it underlined the inadequacy of existing subsidies and recommended that the federal government either base its provincial subsidies on need, or take responsibility for certain services. Real change had to await 1940 report of the Royal Commission on Dominion–Provincial Relations (the Rowell–Sirois Commission), which appeared in 1940. The increasing acceptance of Keynesian economic principles, which included support for government spending to offset capitalist boom and bust cycles, also had to wait until the Second World War. In the meantime, provincial governments had no option but to borrow money to pay for relief and essential services.

Widespread unemployment in the 1930s left unions on the defensive but also encouraged new departures. In the summer of 1932, dissidents from the United Mine Workers organized the Amalgamated Mine Workers of America (District 26), whose radical stance soon attracted the support of more than half of the coal miners in Nova Scotia. The steelworkers, encouraged by the US-based Committee for Industrial Organization (CIO), also became more militant. In 1936 they chose to support, by an overwhelming 90 per cent, a new CIO-inspired union led by Sylbie Barrett. When the Dominion Steel and Coal Corporation refused to bargain with the new organization, it looked as if the labour troubles of the 1920s would be repeated.

Facing an election in 1937, Premier Macdonald wanted to avoid a confrontation. Unlike Ontario's Liberal Premier Mitch Hepburn, who fought tooth and nail to keep the CIO out of the province, Macdonald decided to institutionalize collective bargaining and earn the support of workers. Following the lead of US President Franklin D. Roosevelt, who had made an accommodation with labour in the 1936 Wagner Act, the Nova Scotia legislature passed a Trade Union Act (1937) that compelled employers to recognize and bargain with the union chosen by a majority of their employees, and provided protection for union members. The Canadian Manufacturers' Association predictably denounced the legislation as empowering "foreign agents and agitators."

Nova Scotia was the first Canadian province to adopt labour legislation that would eventually become nationwide, with significant consequences. It encouraged the growth of unions and ushered in a new era of labour–employer relations that depended more on negotiations than on strikes to achieve better wages and working conditions. And, most importantly from the point of view of politicians who supported the new accommodation with labour, such legislation undermined the appeal of radical alternatives.

In Newfoundland, the Commission government was a caretaker regime subject to the supervision of the British government through the Dominions Office and the Treasury. London wanted to see progress, but at the same time insisted on economy and avoidance of controversy—there were to be no awkward questions in Parliament about Newfoundland. The Commission's achievements were real: it reorganized the civil service, reformed taxation, introduced improvements in health and education, and encouraged modernization and regulation in the fishing industry through the Newfoundland Fisheries Board. The newly formed Broadcasting Corporation of Newfoundland became its publicity arm. It also created the Newfoundland Ranger Force, whose members were to be at once policemen, administrators, and the government's eyes and ears in rural districts, including Labrador, where there was now for the first time an official government presence.

Valuable as such initiatives were, the Commission was cautious, and instead of confronting Newfoundland's basic problems effectively, it became concerned with the spread of unions and social unrest. Most Newfoundlanders could see little change in their economic circumstances, and the inflated expectations that had accompanied the Commission's inauguration were soon replaced by disillusion. The Commission was no more capable than its predecessors of balancing the budget, reducing the debt, or finding work for the unemployed. By the late 1930s it was widely unpopular.

In the Maritimes a slow recovery after 1933, fuelled in part by ambitious road-building programs, encouraged cautious optimism. Exports of lumber and apples were protected by the 1932 Ottawa agreements on imperial trade, an achievement of the New Brunswick–born Conservative Prime Minister R.B. Bennett. Thanks to government subventions and increased tariff protection, steel and coal production revived. The lobster and fresh fish industries expanded, as did dairy and poultry farming. In Newfoundland mining was the only sector to show any significant improvement, though newsprint maintained its position, as it did in the Maritimes. Yet prices remained low and markets uncertain, and employers drove wages as low as possible. In terms of national income per capita, the region continued to lag behind. In the late 1930s, average annual income in Newfoundland was approximately $150; in the Maritimes $248; and in Canada as a whole $360.

Mass Consumer Culture

To counter the general misery and mean-spiritedness of the period, many people found solace in the mass consumer culture that was transforming North American society. Radio, movies, mail-order catalogues, glossy magazines, automobiles, and modern conveniences exploded on the market in the interwar years, to dramatic effect. The Victorian era had attached great value to control, both internal and external. Self-discipline, self-denial, duty, religiosity, and sensitivity were preached from pulpits, taught in classrooms, and explored in novels and advice books. When these approaches failed, laws, prisons, and police ensured conformity. By the 1920s, pre-war values were giving way to self-fulfillment, secular pleasures, and sexuality.[14] Maritimers and Newfoundlanders were on the periphery of these changes, but they were no less attracted to the new ways of thinking.

Nothing was more symbolic of the modern age than the automobile. In the Maritimes, provincial governments spent the income from liquor taxes (and more) to build roads for the growing numbers of motorized vehicles. Garages to service cars and trucks proliferated, while blacksmiths found their clientele dwindling. By 1925 there were approximately 1,000 motor vehicles in Newfoundland, but the roads were atrocious even in St John's. Richard Squires reported in 1920 that he travelled with four spare tires and extra inner tubes, and that it was sometimes difficult to find gasoline. Beginning in the 1920s, new road-building programs were introduced, mostly on the Avalon Peninsula and around industrial towns.

The isolation of most rural communities was mitigated by radio, which arrived in the early 1920s. By the mid-1930s nearly 20 per cent of Maritimers owned a radio and roughly 7,000 radios had been purchased in Newfoundland. Families without electricity initially bought a "crystal" radio, which required only an antenna to pick up radio waves. These were soon replaced by battery-operated receivers whose sound was less likely to fade, though recharging could be a problem. Most of the early radio stations in the Maritimes were owned by newspaper publishers or appliance retailers, who sold advertising and dreams, often on easy instalment plans. In St John's the first radio stations were local and church-sponsored, but island-wide broadcasts began in 1935.

American stations and programming dominated early radio. In an effort to encourage home-grown content, the Bennett government established the Canadian Radio Broadcasting Commission in 1932, which was reorganized as the Canadian Broadcasting Corporation (CBC) four years later. The Broadcasting Corporation of Newfoundland (BCN, call letters VONF) was established in 1934 in part to promote the Commission's reconstruction agenda. Neither the CBC nor the BCN had a monopoly. Private broadcasters continued to operate, and the proliferation of radio studios offered opportunities for local talent. By 1934 Don Messer, a young fiddler from Harvey, New Brunswick, had organized a band—the New Brunswick Lumberjacks—that aired regularly on CHSJ Saint John. Messer moved to Charlottetown in 1939 where he organized the "Islanders." Together, they had a long career on CBC radio and television. Other Maritimers found opportunities in the United States. The most successful was Nova Scotia–born Wilf Carter, who performed as "Montana Slim" and was beamed into Atlantic homes from his studio in New York City. In his wake, Hank Snow, from Liverpool, Nova Scotia, gained a wide following in the Maritimes in the 1930s and became a regular at the Grand Ole Opry following the Second World War. While Nashville and New York dominated the burgeoning radio and record industries, they increased the audience for live bands, encouraging the establishment of dancehalls in communities throughout the Atlantic region.

After the First World War, movies became a favourite North American pastime. Hollywood and the movie business now defined the material desires—fashion, hairstyles, leisure pursuits, and romantic love—of mass consumer society. Magazines and comic books, most of them produced in the United States, also helped to establish standards of taste and behaviour. Beauty pageants for babies and young women that objectified their participants also became popular, offering fleeting fame and sometimes modest material rewards.

Those without pretensions to respectability found ways to get by in hard times. An ambitious young man might make moonshine, run a gambling den, or pimp for prostitutes; women could make money by selling their bodies. The problem of juvenile delinquency preoccupied many moral arbiters who demanded that working-class youth be prosecuted in courts designed for them, in the hope that this would prevent them from becoming hardened criminals. As for divorce, it was not available at all in Newfoundland, and was expensive and frowned on elsewhere; thus unhappy marriages were usually ended by either desertion or consensual separation. The judicial system continued to be unsympathetic to most women's accusations of battering and deaf to children's claims of abuse by relatives. As Suzanne Morton has documented, female single parents faced dismal prospects and their children enjoyed few educational opportunities, as their labour was needed to support the family. In 1931 Halifax, 25 per cent of all 15- to 19-year-olds were in school, but the figure was only 12 per cent for children of widows.[15]

With movies, radio, and popular literature promoting modern values, fears surfaced about the moral breakdown of society. Church leaders and social conservatives railed against drinking, smoking, swearing, gambling, and sex outside heterosexual marriage, but the tide of modernism was strong. Men could usually get away with violating traditional moral codes, but women still risked their reputations if they became sexually available "flappers." An unmarried woman who became pregnant lost all claim to respectability, and—if she could afford it—would pay well to keep her condition unknown. In East Chester, Nova Scotia, the Ideal Maternity Home, established in 1928, charged high fees to both the unwed women who stayed there until they gave birth and the would-be parents, many of them from the United States, who adopted the babies. A high percentage of the infants died, their bodies packed in empty butter boxes and hastily buried.[16] More benevolent maternity homes were also available, often run by organizations such as the Salvation Army, but most babies born outside marriage continued to be entrusted to other family members.

Although birth control would not be fully decriminalized until the 1960s, the injunctions against it seemed antiquated to growing numbers of people (though not to Roman Catholics and social conservatives), especially during the Depression when limiting family size became an essential survival strategy. At the same time, an influential eugenics movement sought to improve the basic population stock through birth control and sterilization—in essence arguing that people deemed "inferior" because of mental or physical defects should not be allowed to reproduce. The appalling example of Nazi Germany, whose leaders set out to eradicate the mentally ill and phys-ically disabled—along with Jews, Roma, homosexuals, and others who failed to meet the Aryan ideal—largely finished the eugenics movement, but it still has its followers.

Spurred by increased urbanization and a shorter work week, voluntary organizations prolif-erated. Churches and fraternal associations continued to provide men with opportunities to bond on the basis of religious, ethnic, or patriotic inclinations. New community-service organizations such as the Rotary Club, which had no ethnic or religious affiliation, had branches in most cities. In 1932 the increasingly well-organized black community in Halifax founded a Colored Citizen's Improvement League. Under the leadership of Halifax businessman Beresford Augustus Husbands, who served as its president until 1968, the League initiated campaigns against discriminatory practices in Nova Scotia and founded the Colored Education Association in 1938.

Women continued to be active in church auxiliaries and secular voluntary organizations such as Women's Institutes or their Newfoundland equivalents, the Jubilee Guilds. Branches of the Canadian Federation of University Women, founded in 1919, were established in the Maritimes to pursue social reform and charitable activities. In 1920 Halifax hosted the first Congress of Coloured Women in Canada, testimony to the growing numbers and organized activism of the city's black citizens. Following the Privy Council ruling on the Persons Case in 1929, in which Canadian women were deemed equal to men in rights and privileges as well as pains and penalties, the door was open for them to interpret their empowerment in the public sphere as part of a larger movement for human rights, which was gaining momentum internationally.

In 1925 all Canadian Methodists merged with most of the Congregationalists and Presbyterians to form the United Church. It was the culmination of a long-standing conviction in those churches that duplication, overlap, and resource inefficiencies had to be addressed if they were to continue to be effective and influential. Still, in the Maritimes a substantial minority of Presbyterians, many of whom were deeply rooted in their Scottish traditions, rejected the union and maintained the Presbyterian Church as a separate entity. Newfoundland's Methodists also joined the new church, but the small numbers of Congregationalists and Presbyterians refused to do so.

Culture and Tradition

Amid the difficulties of the period, an upsurge of romantic interest in the region's heritage and folklore helped to sustain notions of identity. The image of the mid-nineteenth century as a mythical Golden Age for the Maritimes became firmly embedded with the publication in 1924 of F.W. Wallace's *Wooden Ships and Iron Men*, which idealized the hardy mariners and fishing folk of the sea-bound coast. Billing Nova Scotia as "Canada's Ocean Playground" as early as 1929, local promoters excelled at inventing tradition. The *Bluenose*, designed as a banking schooner and racer, was launched at Lunenburg in March 1921. Only once defeated in races for the International Fishermen's Trophy, sponsored by the *Halifax Herald* and its purposeful publisher, William H. Dennis, the schooner entered local mythology as an enormously potent symbol and its image has been on the reverse of the Canadian dime since

1937. Nova Scotia's cultural elite, meanwhile, had discovered Peggy's Cove, located conveniently near Halifax. The region's "primary symbolic landscape," it epitomized the hardiness, simplicity, and virtues of the seafaring life, and the physical beauty of Nova Scotia's south shore.[17]

Prince Edward Islanders were not far behind Nova Scotians in promoting the virtues of their clean air and white sand beaches. As early as 1904, inhabitants of the "Garden Province" had organized "Old Home Week" as a way of luring out-migrants back for summer vacations. The trick was to convince other people that the island had something special to offer. In the first edition of the *Official Motoring Guide of Prince Edward Island*, published in 1929, the province was promoted as "preeminently a land of refreshing rest where the visitor can escape the rush and noise of everyday life."[18]

The new interest in the pre-industrial past also stimulated the study of folklore. Early in the 1930s, Helen Creighton embarked on a lifelong career collecting Maritime folk songs and stories. In Newfoundland, Gerald S. Doyle, Elisabeth Greenleaf, and Maud Karpeles similarly collected songs. Doyle, a successful businessman, made his immensely popular and influential collection available to the public at no cost.

However well the "cult of the folk" sold to tourists, the folk themselves were less than enthusiastic about becoming cultural artifacts. In 1927 Frank Parker Day, one of the Maritime literary group known as the "song fishermen," published *Rockbound*, a thinly disguised fictional account of the people of Ironbound, an island off the south shore of Nova Scotia. The Ironbounders felt that Day had misrepresented and betrayed them, and in a letter to the *Lunenburg Progress-Enterprise* protested that they were not the "ignorant, immoral and superstitious" people portrayed in the novel.[19]

Invented traditions were a standard feature of the developing tourist industry, which received government assistance throughout the region, mainly in the form of new roads. Major hotels were built in Halifax, Saint John, Charlottetown, Digby, Pictou, and St John's, while "cabins" appeared along well-travelled highways in the Maritimes. In Newfoundland the government-created Tourist and Publicity Commission trumpeted, in addition to the usual fins, furs, feathers, and scenery, what is now known as heritage tourism. In this it was following the example of Nova Scotia, where in the 1930s tourists were encouraged to visit the newly constructed Cabot Trail or the replica of an Acadian church at Grand Pré. Under Angus L. Macdonald's influence, Nova Scotians were urged to remember their Celtic heritage and in 1939 Cape Breton acquired its own Gaelic College at St Ann's. It was not long before "tartanism," complete with bagpipes, kilts, and crests, trumped all other local identities in the province.

The federal government played a critical role in transforming the Maritime landscape into a series of tourist destinations. With the founding of the Historic Sites and Monuments Board of Canada in 1919, historic places were rediscovered, many of them, such as Port Royal and Louisbourg, harking back to the French regime. After much lobbying by heritage enthusiasts, the Canadian government began a reconstruction of the Habitation at Port-Royal in 1939. Maritime boosters including William H. Dennis (appointed a Senator in 1932) eventually convinced the National Parks Branch, which focused primarily on dramatic western sites such as Banff and Jasper, to cast its eye eastward. If Maine could have Acadia National Park, why could the Atlantic region not also showcase its natural beauty? By 1936 plans were underway to expropriate land for Cape Breton Highlands National Park and Prince Edward Island National Park (the latter encompassing, after much controversy, both Green Gables and Dalvay by the Sea, another heritage dwelling).[20] Both parks included world-class golf courses designed by Stanley Thompson.

In this period, a modern art movement developed in the Maritimes that had an impact beyond the region's borders. It was orchestrated in large measure by US-born educator and arts activist Walter Abell, who was Professor of Fine Arts at Acadia University from 1928 to 1943. Supported by funds from the Carnegie Corporation, Abell taught courses and published widely on the importance of art; brought the region's artists together through the Maritime Arts Association established in 1935; founded *Maritime Art*, the first fine arts magazine in Canada, in 1940; and in 1941 played a leading role in the creation of the Federation of Canadian Artists. Abell introduced new ideas about modern and socially relevant art that were finding favour in New York and also inspiring distinguished artists such as Miller Brittain, Ted Campbell, Julia Crawford, and Jack Humphrey, who were members of a vibrant artistic community in Saint John in the 1930s. Although Abell eventually found Canada too small a canvas for his ambitions, he left a legacy as a "missionary for culture" that continued to percolate among artists who shared his vision of a more just and democratic society.[21]

Newfoundland's small cultural community was concentrated for the most part in St John's. Musical activities remained important, though there were fewer visiting performers. In addition, frequent lectures and debates, lively journalism and other writing—Smallwood having an important role—and amateur plays satisfied the thirst for cultural stimulation. During the 1930s, the talented Margaret Duley began writing locally placed novels, among them the highly praised *Highway to Valour* (1941). Another significant cultural development was the opening in 1925 of Memorial University College, which attained full university status in 1949. It was the country's first institution of higher education, and significantly non-denominational. Founded to commemorate the dead of the Great War, the college, for all its Britishness, helped to advance the local intellectual climate. One initiative was to start a travelling library program, which brought boxes of books to settlements that would otherwise have had no access to such resources.

In the early 1920s, an attempt to bring six of the major universities in the Maritimes into a federation stirred up controversy. Father Jimmy Tompkins enlisted the Carnegie Foundation in the idea as a way to help the small, cash-strapped universities meet the demands for new programs and better facilities. The Foundation agreed to provide $3 million to establish a federated university of the Maritime provinces, with outlying colleges becoming affiliates of Dalhousie University in Halifax. This recommendation raised hackles in outlying communities and the idea was quickly dropped. Only Kings College, whose campus had been destroyed by fire in 1920, moved to Halifax.[22]

Conclusion

The interwar years left an indelible mark on the Atlantic region. At a time when other areas of North America were making the transition, however unevenly, to mass consumer society, the Maritimes and Newfoundland lagged behind. Much would change with the outbreak of the Second World War, but the image of the Atlantic region as the "sick man" of Canada would continue to have an impact. Despite its many difficulties, the region embraced the modern age, its citizens determined to share in the higher standards of living that now seemed within their reach.

Further Readings

Brym, Robert J., and R. James Sacouman, eds. 1979. *Underdevelopment and Social Movements in Atlantic Canada*. Toronto: New Hogtown Press.

Cadigan, Sean. 2013. *Death on Two Fronts: National Tragedies and the Fate of Newfoundland Democracy, 1914–1934*. Toronto: Allen Lane.

Fizzard, Garfield, ed. 2000. *Amulree's Legacy: Truth, Lies and Consequences*. St John's: Newfoundland Historical Society.

Forbes, E.R. 1970. *The Maritime Rights Movement: 1919–1927: A Study in Canadian Regionalism*. Montreal: McGill-Queen's University Press.

Frank, David. 1999. *J.B. McLachlan: A Biography*. Toronto: Lorimer.

Guildford, Janet, and Suzanne Morton. 2010. *Making Up the State: Women in 20th-Century Atlantic Canada*. Fredericton: Acadiensis Press.

Journal of Canadian Art History XXVII (2006, Special Issue).

MacEachern, Alan. 2001. *Natural Selections: National Parks in Atlantic Canada, 1935–1970*. Montreal: McGill-Queen's University Press.

McKay, Ian. 1994. *The Quest of the Folk: Antimodernism and Cultural Selection in Twentieth-Century Nova Scotia*. Montreal: McGill-Queen's University Press.

———, and Robin Bates. 2010. *In the Province of History: The Making of a Public Past in Twentieth-Century Nova Scotia*. Montreal: McGill-Queens University Press.

Morton, Suzanne. 1995. *Ideal Surroundings: Domestic Life in a Working-Class Suburb in the 1920s*. Toronto: University of Toronto Press.

Neal, Rusty. 1999. *Brotherhood Economics: Women and Cooperatives in Nova Scotia*. Sydney: University of Cape Breton Press.

Neary, Peter. 1988. *Newfoundland and the North Atlantic World, 1929–1949*. Montreal: McGill-Queen's University Press.

Taylor, M. Brook. 2006. *A Camera on the Banks: Frederick William Wallace and the Fishermen of Nova Scotia*. Fredericton: Goose Lane.

Wicken, William C. 2012. *The Colonization of Mi'kmaw Memory and History, 1794–1928*. Toronto: University of Toronto Press.

Historical Spotlight

McKay, Ian. 1992. "Tartanism Triumphant: The Construction of Scottishness in Nova Scotia, 1933–1954," *Acadiensis* XXI, 2 (Spring): 5–47.

Overton, James. 1990. "Economic Crisis and the End of Democracy: Politics in Newfoundland during the Great Depression," *Labour/Le Travail* 26, 85–124.

Recommended Websites

The Bluenose: A Canadian Icon
http://www.gov.ns.ca/nsarm/virtual/bluenose

Canada's Ocean Playground: The Tourism Industry in Nova Scotia
http://www.gov.ns.ca/archives/virtual/tourism

The Coady International Institute
http://www.coady.stfx.ca

The Commission of Government
http://www.heritage.nf.ca/law/commission_gov.html

Chapter 13

The Emergence of Atlantic Canada, 1939–1949

The Second World War originated in the determination of Adolf Hitler's Nazi regime to undo by force what it saw as the humiliations imposed on Germany by the Treaty of Versailles in 1919. In an effort to establish Germany as the dominant European power, Hitler set out to annex bordering states, beginning with Austria and Czechoslovakia in 1938. Great Britain declared war against Germany on 3 September 1939, two days after the German invasion of Poland, which Great Britain and France had pledged to defend against Hitler's aggression. Although Newfoundland was automatically at war on the same day, Canada, emphasizing its new autonomous status, did not follow until 10 September.

The war brought more loss of life overseas and, closer to home, the threat of German seaborne attacks in the Gulf of St Lawrence and inshore waters. As was the case in the First World War, economic conditions improved because of military spending, but postwar readjustment would prove difficult. The reforms undertaken during and immediately after the war did little to change the structure of federal–provincial relationships, and no solutions were offered to the growing problems of regional disparity. For Newfoundland (and Labrador), the war precipitated fundamental political

Setting the Context

The World in Turmoil, 1939–49

The Second World War ushered in a new era for the Atlantic region, and indeed, for people around the globe. Not only did the war end the Depression, but it also marked the transition of world dominance from Great Britain to the United States, which had enormous implications for people everywhere, and especially for Canadians. Economic, military, and political ties between the United States and Canada were strengthened during the war, and in its aftermath Canada became a willing ally of the United States in its Cold War with the Soviet Union.

In 1945 Canada helped to establish the United Nations (UN), an international body, headquartered in New York, which was designed to keep the peace and to promote human rights. When the UN became hamstrung by posturing among the countries represented on the Security Council, Canada backed the creation in 1949 of the North Atlantic Treaty Organization (NATO), a military pact designed to protect the West from Soviet aggression. It was in this context that Newfoundland joined Confederation and the governments of the four Atlantic provinces began working to translate wartime prosperity, such as it was, into peacetime development.[1]

and constitutional changes. The suspended dominion became a Canadian province in 1949, and the term "Atlantic Provinces" came into use. Many citizens of the new province expected that joining Canada would solve their major economic problems. Only time would tell if they were right.

The Military Occupation

For the duration of the war, the Atlantic region was essentially a military base extending from Labrador to the American border. As the part of North America nearest to the European theatre of conflict, the region became an indispensable base for air and sea links to Great Britain. While there was investment in military infrastructure, especially in Newfoundland, the main permanent benefits of Canada's war effort went to Quebec and Ontario, where the industrial component was centralized. The federal government had little interest in using the opportunities presented by the war to promote regional development. From Ottawa's perspective, the role of the Maritimes and Newfoundland was simply to shield the industrial heartland and safeguard the necessary conduits to Europe.[2]

Approximately 47.5 per cent of the eligible male population joined one of the three branches of the military: the army, navy, or air force. Others served in the merchant navy, providing an essential workforce for wartime shipping. For the first time Canadian women were permitted to join the armed forces. They were incorporated into separate divisions, where they served primarily as clerks, cooks, nurses, and secretaries, though a few became mechanics, truck drivers, technicians, and spies. About 7,500 men and 860 women from Newfoundland and Labrador joined the British or Canadian forces, and several thousand more joined the Overseas Forestry Unit or crewed on merchant vessels. Unemployment disappeared as men and women from across the region either migrated to industrial jobs in central Canada or found work closer to home. Many of the local jobs involved building and strengthening military bases, not only in the Maritimes but also in Newfoundland and in Labrador, where the Canadian government assumed the responsibility for defence in association with the United States.

With their large harbours, Halifax and Sydney became the most important Canadian military bases on the east coast. All three armed services had detachments there and also at Saint John and Gaspé. The Royal Canadian Navy had additional bases at Shelburne and Cornwallis; the Royal Canadian Air Force (RCAF) at Greenwood, North Sydney, Chatham, Moncton, Yarmouth, Shelburne, Debert, Eastern Passage, Summerside, and Charlottetown; and the army at Debert, Edmundston, Sussex, Aldershot, and Little River. The Canadian government understood that Newfoundland would have to be included in its defence planning, and RCAF planes began to patrol the waters around the island, using the seaplane base at Botwood, which had served civilian aviation on transatlantic flights since 1937.

By June 1940 Canadian troops and aircraft were stationed at Gander, where the "Newfoundland Airport" had opened in early 1938. Both Botwood and Gander were also placed under Canadian control, along with the Newfoundland Militia (formed in 1939 for home defence and renamed the Newfoundland Regiment in 1943). Starting in 1941, the Canadians built another air base just north of St John's (now the city's international airport), and the next year began to construct naval facilities there. HMCS *Avalon*, with 3,600 personnel by 1943, became the Canadian navy's second largest base, with more than 100 destroyers, frigates, and corvettes. The Canadian government also constructed a huge new airfield at Goose Bay, Labrador, which was operational by the end of 1941. In total, the infrastructure established in Newfoundland and Labrador cost roughly $65 million.

Table 13.1	Timeline
1939–45	Second World War.
1940	Unemployment insurance legislation passed in Canada.
1941	Anglo-American Leased Bases Agreement signed; Canadian High Commission established in St John's.
1942–4	U-boats sink vessels in Gulf and approaches, including the ferry *Caribou*.
1942	Newfoundland government takes over the north Labrador trade.
1944	Maritime provinces conduct inquiries on reconstruction; Canada adopts family allowance legislation.
1945	End of the Second World War; riots in Halifax, Sydney, and New Waterford; formation of National Sea Products Ltd.
1946–8	National Convention debates Newfoundland's future.
1947	Maritime coal miners' strike.
1948	Newfoundland voters choose Confederation with Canada; UN Declaration of Human Rights.
1949	Newfoundland becomes a province; union-breaking in Halifax orchestrated by Hal Banks.

In September 1940 the British and American governments agreed in principle that, in return for 50 aging destroyers and other military equipment, Britain would allow the United States to lease sites for military bases in Newfoundland, Bermuda, and the Caribbean "freely and without consideration" for 99 years. The Leased Bases Agreement, finalized in June 1941, was unpopular in Newfoundland since it gave the United States virtual sovereignty over its facilities. Although the Commission government objected, it had little choice in the matter, especially after Britain's wartime leader, Winston Churchill, made an appeal to Newfoundlanders to accept the deal "for the sake of the Empire, of liberty and of the welfare of all mankind." The Americans built an army base at St John's, a naval and army base at Argentia, and an air base at Stephenville; leased part of St John's harbour; and stationed personnel at Gander, Goose Bay, and elsewhere. In 1943, at the height of the military occupation, 10,000 Americans and more than 6,000 Canadians were stationed in Newfoundland and Labrador—tangible proof of that country's strategic importance.

Another wartime initiative was Ferry Command, which delivered planes built in North America to Great Britain. Since surface shipping was too slow, and the ships were needed for other purposes, Lord Beaverbrook, as British minister of aircraft production, proposed that the planes be flown across the Atlantic. This was a controversial idea at a time when regular transatlantic flights were few and potentially dangerous, but Beaverbrook persevered. Based in Montreal, Ferry Command flew more than 9,000 planes to Britain from enlarged and newly created bases such as Goose Bay and Gander. Its success—only 100 planes were lost—laid the groundwork for regular civilian flights in the immediate postwar period, when most North American flights to and from Europe refuelled at Goose Bay and Gander.

The Battle of the St Lawrence and the Battle of the Atlantic gave people living in the Atlantic region a real sense of being on the front lines of the war. Between May 1942 and November 1944, German submarines sank 23 ships in the Gulf. In September and November 1942, four vessels were sunk at Bell Island with the loss of 69 lives, and in October the Newfoundland ferry *Caribou* was torpedoed 40 miles (64 km) off Port aux Basques with the loss of 137 passengers and crew. After a shaky start, Canadian aircraft and naval vessels succeeded in containing the U-boat threat. Stories of Germans landing in remote places along the region's long coastline circulated—the Germans managed to place an automatic weather station on the north Labrador coast—but by 1944 the region was safe from direct enemy attacks.

Allied forces depended on supplies from North America, making control of the Atlantic critical to the war effort. In the first 18 months of the war, German U-boats sank more than 61 million tons of shipping, much of which could not be quickly replaced. Protecting convoys of merchant vessels placed an immense strain on the Canadian navy and air force, which played a leading role in the Battle of the Atlantic. Since they began this mission almost from scratch, rapid expansion meant that officers and crews often lacked training and experience, and equipment was sometimes inadequate. Moreover, repair and refit capacity was limited, partly because skilled tradesmen were in short supply and more directly because the federal government decided to locate the major repair centre at Montreal—despite the danger posed by U-boats in the St Lawrence and the fact that the river was blocked to ocean-going vessels by ice for half the year. British and American authorities questioned the decision to no avail. By 1943 the Allies were more successful in protecting allied shipping, but the Battle of the Atlantic did not end until the war did. With

Bedford Basin, on the inner reaches of Halifax Harbour, offered shelter to merchant ships and their naval escorts assembling for the dangerous voyage across the North Atlantic during the Second World War. Library and Archives Canada/Department of National Defence fonds/PA-112993.

the loss of 3,500 merchant ships and 175 naval vessels, it turned out to be one of the longest and most deadly battles in naval history.

There was no enemy invasion of the North Atlantic coast, but Halifax again suffered a major explosion, this time as a result of its role as a munitions storage site. Fire and explosions racked the city for 24 hours in July 1945 after the munitions magazine, on the Dartmouth side of the Bedford Basin, caught fire. When Halifax residents north of Quinpool Road were ordered to evacuate their homes, many refused and instead lined the slopes of the harbour to watch the fireworks.

The Economic Impact of War

Notwithstanding Ottawa's bias toward central Canada, the war boosted the economy of the Maritimes. Steel production and processing at Sydney and Trenton revived and expanded, and shipyards were busy at Saint John, Halifax, Dartmouth, and Pictou. Newsprint production increased, and overall employment in manufacturing expanded by 25,000 (74 per cent). Even the cotton industry bounced back, and wool producers enjoyed a steady demand for their product, which was used in military uniforms.

The Halifax docks generally functioned well, thanks to a reorganization of labour and the imposition of a minimum wage that more than met the increase in the cost of living. In 1944, a three-month strike erupted when the Dominion Steel and Coal Corporation (DOSCO)–owned Halifax Shipyards Limited challenged the legality of the union dues check-off; the dispute was resolved in the union's favour. The war did little to reduce tensions in the coal industry, with its history of intense antagonism between workers and management. Vital as coal was to the war effort, production actually declined between 1941 and 1945, and serious labour unrest continued until 1943, when the federal government agreed to top up miners' wages. This decision reflected both poor government control of skilled labour and the inability (or unwillingness) of corporations and governments to find a permanent solution to the industry's problems. As miners quit their jobs to join the armed forces, labour was recruited from the Caribbean and elsewhere, but the number of coalface workers declined by 29 per cent during the war.

As urban-based industries expanded to meet wartime needs, they drew labour away from the rural economy at the very time when demand for farm, fish, and forest products increased sharply. Between 1939 and 1945 the total farm income for the Maritimes rose by 98 per cent (from $25 million to $49 million). Apple growers faced disaster when the British market was abruptly closed at the beginning of the war so that capital and shipping could be diverted to the military effort. At the request of growers and shippers, the federal government stepped in to help, establishing marketing boards to sell some of the vast surplus and to process the rest as juice, sauce, and pie filling. Processing accounted for nearly 80 per cent of the crop in 1942, up from 11.4 per cent in 1938, and growers continued to get good returns as they waited for overseas sales to resume once the war had ended. With men drawn into the military, women, who had been pushed out of the workforce during the Depression, once again found their labour in high demand, and in occupations traditionally dominated by men—at least as long as the war lasted.

The war helped to stimulate astonishing gains in the fisheries: the value of Maritime fish landings increased 230 per cent (from $8 million to $27 million), while the value of Newfoundland's salt fish exports quadrupled, from $4.1 million to $16.7 million, over the same period. In the

Biography | *Clarie Gillis Goes to Ottawa*

Clarence "Clarie" Gillis was born in 1895 in Londonderry, Nova Scotia. Nine years later, his family moved to Glace Bay, where his father worked in the mines and became a close associate of the union activist J.B. McLachlan. Because of this union activity, the Gillises were expelled from company housing and forced to spend a winter living in a tent. Blacklisted, the elder Gillis worked from 1910 to 1923 in the United States.

At the age of 14, with a grade 5 education, Clarie began his career as a miner in No. 2 colliery in Glace Bay. When war was declared, he volunteered for service overseas and was wounded three times. Back in Cape Breton, Gillis played an active role in the coal miners' struggle against the British Empire Steel Corporation (BESCO), supported the co-operative movement, and helped establish a local branch of the Canadian Legion.

In 1927 Gillis was elected president of the Phalen Local—known as the "Red Local"—of District 26 of the United Mine Workers of America (UMW). After a group broke away in 1932 to form the Amalgamated Mine Workers of Nova Scotia, he served as its vice-president, but by 1938 he was back in the UMW and deeply involved with the CCF. After decades of bitter internal struggle, Cape Breton miners were ready to bury their differences and put their weight behind a political party dedicated to serving the interests of working people.

District 26 was the first union to affiliate with the CCF at the national level, and in a provincial by-election in December 1939 a miner named Douglas Macdonald won the riding of Cape Breton Centre for the party—its first seat east of Ontario. In the federal election of the following year, Gillis won Cape Breton South and became the first miner to sit in the Canadian House of Commons. He was to hold the seat until the Diefenbaker landslide of 1958.[3]

Maritimes and Newfoundland alike, governments encouraged modernization, offering financial incentives for the construction of larger vessels (including trawlers and draggers) and freezing plants. The establishment of the giant National Sea Products Limited in 1945 marked the arrival of mechanized, industrial fishing. This trend was endorsed in an influential report produced in 1944 by Stewart Bates for Nova Scotia's royal commission on reconstruction. Soon to become federal deputy minister of fisheries, Bates argued that the future lay with fresh fish, trawlers, centralization, consolidation, and the North American market. The Newfoundland government made almost identical recommendations the same year.

The militarization of the region also created economic spinoffs. People had money to spend, even if rationing, shortages, and restrictive liquor laws limited what they could buy. Men and women in the armed services received regular salaries, and the construction of military bases created many jobs—about 20,000 in Newfoundland and Labrador alone in 1942. In the Maritimes, base development in communities such as Summerside, Greenwood, and Chatham generated economic growth and work for people in the surrounding area. Some bases became nuclei for new or vastly expanded towns, displacing rural families and communities. Farms belonging to francophones in St George's Bay were expropriated to make way for the Stephenville base, while at Argentia two villages were closed; their residents were moved a short distance away, along with their cemeteries.

The construction of the Goose Bay airfield is considered, with reason, to be the watershed dividing the old Labrador from the new. Labradorians, including Inuit and Innu, who arrived to build the base also established the town of Happy Valley—originally called "Refuge Cove" because there was no place to stay (as at other base sites, workers had to live in tents and shacks). Another significant change came about in 1942, when the Hudson's Bay Company decided to abandon the trading posts it had leased from the Moravians in 1926. Now the Newfoundland government had no choice but to take full responsibility for Labrador.

War and Society

The military presence was not an unmixed blessing for cities and towns still recovering from the Depression. The 65,000 residents of Halifax, Canada's main Atlantic port, were particularly hard pressed to make room for some 100,000 additional people, including military personnel, their families, and sundry camp followers. With many unpaved streets and a dilapidated water system, Halifax was a dismal place for many of the new arrivals: rents were high, living conditions often disgraceful, and hospitals and schools overstretched. The city had never been particularly open at the best of times, and the Depression had taken its toll on amenities such as restaurants and theatres. Thus it was left to volunteers to set up hostels and canteens and to arrange concerts. Conditions were similar in Sydney and Saint John, which were also required to host growing military and civilian populations. In St John's, a relatively small and old-fashioned city of 40,000, relations between townspeople and the Canadian and American forces were generally good, but there were similar social tensions. People in Newfoundland had to contend with serious price and rent inflation, pressure on local services, and the sudden influx of two foreign military entities with different entitlements and expectations. If the Americans are remembered as being especially popular, it may well be partly because of their superior glamour and spending power, but it helped that their delinquents were dealt with by their own military, rather than paraded through the local courts, as were Canadians in trouble with the law. It also helped that the United States sent its military dependents home after the Japanese attack on Pearl Harbor.

Ties with the mainland became closer during the war. The labour movement, which already had North American connections, became more influential, given the government's need to prevent strikes in key sectors. Imports came increasingly from North America, Trans-Canada Airlines began a service to St John's, and Newfoundlanders soon found themselves driving on the right rather than the left side of the road. It was at this time that the still-controversial epithet "Newfie" began to be used, almost certainly a Canadian coinage. Not surprisingly, discussion of Newfoundland's constitutional future continued at both official and popular levels, especially after the Commission government increased taxes in 1943. Taxation without representation became a sore point.

When the end of the war in Europe was announced on 8 May 1945, Halifax erupted in two days of rioting and looting. The immediate cause may have been the authorities' decision to close all shops, cafés, and liquor stores, which led frustrated revellers to break in and help themselves, but the violence spread, and the total damages amounted to more than $5 million. After the federal inquiry that followed, Rear-Admiral L.W. Murray was relieved of his commission for failing to control the men under his command, and 211 people (civilians as well as military personnel) were indicted for offences. Riots also erupted in Sydney and New Waterford, where the authorities followed the same heavy-handed strategy as those in Halifax.

War brides arriving in Canada at Pier 21. Many of the nearly 48,000 war brides and their 22,000 children arrived in Canada through Pier 21. While they were destined for communities all across Canada, many of them found homes in the Maritimes. Library and Archives Canada/Credit: Lieut. W.J. Hynes/Department of National Defence fonds/PA-147114

With such events serving as examples, some people argued that the war had weakened traditional morality and encouraged "licence." The reality was that attitudes towards alcohol, sex, and religion had been changing for some time; the war only accelerated the process. Bootleggers and prostitutes operated more openly than before, and casual liaisons between servicemen and local women became more common. In an era when "safe sex" was rarely discussed, the numbers of illegitimate children increased, and venereal disease became a growing cause for concern.

The war also strained marriages and family life. In some cases, husbands who were absent for long periods of time formed new relationships, as did wives left at home. Wartime circumstances encouraged hasty marriages—in Newfoundland alone, more than 900 women married servicemen from either the United States or Canada. Many servicemen from the region found brides in Europe. While war brides were no doubt eager to leave behind the wartime conditions prevailing in their homelands, some of them had difficulty adjusting to new families and cultures. Demands for easier and less costly divorces escalated following the war, but reforms were slow in coming. In Newfoundland, where divorce was a taboo subject, the courts eventually agreed to handle formal judicial separations—though not until 1948.

Whatever the fate of wartime marriages, they contributed to a "baby boom" that would last until the mid-1960s. Soon new schools would be needed for the swarms of children, but in the meantime

Maritime universities were obliged to handle a bubble of "mature students" whose tuitions were covered by the federal government as part of its comprehensive program to reintegrate veterans into civilian life. University administrators who tried to exercise control over men with military experience would do so at their peril.

Postwar Reconstruction

As the war wound down, Ottawa asked each province to take stock of its future. Nova Scotia appointed a Royal Commission on Provincial Development chaired by Robert McGregor Dawson, a political scientist at the University of Toronto. New Brunswick enlisted Norman A.M. Mackenzie, president of the University of New Brunswick, to chair a commission, while Prince Edward Island chose Dr J.E. Lattimer, chair of the Department of Agricultural Economics at Macdonald College, McGill University, to head its inquiry. All three commissions recognized that the prosperity brought by the war was transient, that the unequal distribution of wartime benefits had aggravated regional disparities, and that the economy remained dangerously vulnerable. Nevertheless, there was hope that a postwar slump could be avoided and a growing consensus that state intervention would help to prevent a postwar return to the desperate conditions of the 1930s.

In 1940 the Rowell–Sirois Commission on Dominion–Provincial Relations had recommended equalization payments and national standards in basic services, reflecting a new approach to federalism and to the poverty that co-existed with the wealth created by an industrial economy. The provinces balked at reforms that reduced their powers, but the war had changed attitudes in both the civilian population and the public service. Since the beginning of the war Ottawa had been seriously considering a national policy that would incorporate some welfare-state measures. Unemployment insurance was introduced in 1940 to cover industrial workers; in 1944 family allowances became the first in a series of universal programs; and in 1945 the Mackenzie King government proposed an ambitious federal reconstruction plan designed to address deficiencies in public works and social services.

Condemned by Ontario and Quebec as "state socialism," this approach was also opposed by Angus L. Macdonald, who regained the premiership of Nova Scotia in 1945 after a wartime stint as minister of national defence for naval services. Macdonald had witnessed at close range the extent to which federal politics was dominated by central Canadian interests, and he had no wish to strengthen Ottawa's hand. As a result of provincial opposition, the program was modified. In any event, it had never aimed to remedy uneven economic development or to give any special consideration to the Maritimes. The federal government had no desire to play an interventionist role and focused on cutting its losses. It shut down DOSCO's steel plate mill, for example, and when the British market remained closed to Canadian producers after the war, it paid farmers to uproot their apple trees.

The failure of governments to address regional needs in postwar reconstruction had disastrous results. By the late 1940s Pictou and Cape Breton counties had the highest unemployment rates in Canada, and employment in secondary manufacturing was fast declining. Unions, meanwhile, faced anti-communist hysteria and intimidation. Nowhere was this more obvious than on the Halifax waterfront, where in 1949 goon squads orchestrated by American labour leader Harold ("Hal") Banks used violence to break up the Communist-controlled Canadian Seamen's Union.

Document

Family Allowances and Public Schooling, 1946

After the establishment of public schooling in the mid-nineteenth century, education reformers in the Maritimes began demanding that attendance be compulsory. Poor families, who depended on the labour of their children to make ends meet, often found themselves in trouble with truant officers as schooling up to 12, 14, and then 16 years of age became mandatory. Attitudes changed when the federal government tied payment of family allowances to school attendance for children up to the age 16. In Prince Edward Island, François-E. Doiron, who monitored school attendance, noted in his 1946 report:

> The appointment of an Attendance Officer and the granting of Family Allowance, I believe, has been a forward step in education in this province. It is pleasing to note a very marked improvement in attendance in this inspectorate under the new system. In fact some of the schools are now overcrowded and hardly able to accommodate the increased number of pupils in attendance. It is true there are still some children of school age not going to school and trying to circumvent the work of the Attendance Officer, but as time goes on I believe the children will gradually become accustomed to attend regularly as they begin to realize that they cannot absent themselves from school with impunity as they have done in the past.[4]

The Canadian Fishermen and Fish Handlers' Union (CFFU), which launched a strike in December 1946, also faced intimidation tactics. The Nova Scotia government did not help matters: 10 years after demonstrating a progressive approach to unions, it introduced a Trade Union Act in early 1947 that weakened the position of organized labour.

For the three Liberal premiers in the Maritime provinces—Macdonald in Nova Scotia, J.B. McNair in New Brunswick, and "Farmer" Walter Jones in Prince Edward Island—the postwar picture looked bleak. Their provinces lagged behind most of the rest of the country in health and educational services, and their roads could no longer accommodate the growing traffic. Other parts of North America were beginning to take electricity and running water for granted, but many people in the Maritimes still lived without either. New Brunswick had the dubious distinctions of the highest illiteracy rate in Canada and a social welfare policy that was the brunt of widespread criticism. In Prince Edward Island, 405 of the 473 schools had only one room and 69 of those were beyond repair. As the North American economy began to improve, out-migration accelerated. There seemed to be no end to the dreary tale of economic decline.

Economic difficulties could not be ignored, but other issues began to dominate the political agenda. As a direct result of a war fought against the injustices of fascist regimes, human rights and social justice became part of the postwar political agenda. Individual Canadian provinces began passing human rights legislation—Ontario and Saskatchewan led the way—and the UN issued a Universal Declaration of Human Rights in 1948, which all members were urged to sign and implement. Legal scholar John Peters Humphrey, born in Hampton, New Brunswick, played a leading role in crafting the stirring words of the declaration which claimed basic human rights for all people. These included the right to life, liberty, and security; the right to freedom of speech, thought, and assembly; and the right to a standard of living adequate for health and well-being, including "food, clothing, housing and medical care and necessary social services, and the right to security in the event of unemployment, sickness, disability, widowhood, old age or other lack of livelihood." Article 2 stated that "Everyone is entitled to all the rights and freedoms set forth in this Declaration, without distinction of any kind, such as race, colour, sex, language, religion, political or other opinion, national or social origin, property, birth or other status."[5] In the aftermath of the war these ideas caught fire and gradually transformed social relations throughout the Western world.

The Maritimes were slow to pass human rights legislation, but they could not ignore the issue for long. The Nova Scotia Association for the Advancement of Coloured People (NSAACP) was founded in 1945. The following year Viola Desmond, a black beautician from Halifax, was fined and jailed overnight for "tax evasion" after refusing to sit in the balcony of a New Glasgow movie theatre as demanded by the owner. The NSAACP raised money to help her fight her conviction. Although the Nova Scotia Supreme Court refused to hear the case on a technicality, the incident generated so much negative publicity that racial discrimination came under closer scrutiny.

Aboriginal people in the postwar period also mobilized to resist their ill-treatment. In 1942 the Department of Indian Affairs, in a misguided attempt to save money, launched a program to concentrate Mi'kmaq in Nova Scotia at Escasoni in Cape Breton and Shubenacadie on the mainland. This program was largely fulfilled under the cloak of the war. When it was decided in 1945 to relocate the Wolastoqiyik living on reserves at Oromocto, St Mary's, and Woodstock to Kingsclear, resistance was fierce and attracted support from non-Aboriginal activists. The campaign against centralization took advantage of a travelling federal commission, which held hearings between 1946 and 1948 in advance of the 1951 revision of the Indian Act. Despite bureaucratic opposition, the Wolastoqiyik retained control of their valuable St John River reserves. The Mi'kmaq also had resistance on their agenda. In August 1945, 200 of their leaders met in Big Cove, New Brunswick, to consider nation-wide collaboration under the North American Indian Brotherhood. Clearly, Aboriginal rights could no longer be ignored.[6]

Newfoundland Joins Canada

The British government understood that Newfoundland's wartime prosperity was ephemeral and that the narrow base of its economy remained fundamentally unchanged. It also accepted that Commission government could not continue indefinitely, but feared—with reason—that a return to responsible government would mean another financial crisis, sooner or later, and another application for British help. To insure against that possibility, the Newfoundland government developed a $100-million reconstruction scheme, which was approved by the Dominions Office. When the British Treasury denied funding, an approach was made to Ottawa, where the reaction was equally negative. Instead, Canadian officials signalled that they would favour bringing Newfoundland into Canada, preferably without a prior return to responsible government. The reconstruction scheme was buried and in late 1945 the two governments quietly agreed that their objective would be Confederation—which British officials had always supported.

Ottawa was not enthusiastic about taking on what it saw as another "Maritime" province, but it now recognized that Canada had vital long-term interests in Newfoundland and in Labrador. The war had demonstrated the area's strategic importance for defence and aviation; the economic potential of Labrador was now well understood; and Ottawa feared that the large American military presence (sheltered by 99-year leases) might draw Newfoundland into Washington's orbit. Moreover, reports from the Canadian High Commission in St John's, established in 1941, suggested that Confederation might attract majority support. In December 1945 the British government announced that citizens of Newfoundland and Labrador (the latter having the franchise for the first time) would elect a national convention to recommend the constitutional options to be placed on a referendum ballot. It was a calculated risk in that the British and Canadian governments could only hope that opinion in Newfoundland would come to favour Confederation.

The convention sat from September 1946 to January 1948. From the beginning it contained a vocal Confederate minority, led by journalist, farmer, and broadcaster Joseph Smallwood and lawyer-turned-outport-businessman Gordon Bradley, who had been a member of the last Squires administration. Neither man was a member of the colonial elite, which was largely anti-Confederate. The convention's debates concerning the country's condition and prospects, broadcast by the government radio station, were closely followed. Delegations were sent to both London and Ottawa, where Smallwood and Bradley persuaded a reluctant federal government to formulate draft terms of union. Finally, after days of passionate discussion, Smallwood's motion to make Confederation an option was defeated, and the convention recommended that the referendum choice be between continuing with Commission government and returning to responsible government. The British government, determined to submit Confederation to the voters, overruled the convention and placed all three options on the ballot.

Anti-Confederates were outraged, but they were divided and lacked strong leadership. Smallwood and his allies stressed that Confederation would improve social security payments and services while reducing the cost of living. In his words, the referendum would give voters "the best chance that they EVER HAD to make Newfoundland a better place for themselves and their families." Who opposed these goals? "Water Street [merchants] . . . the rich and wealthy. . . the few fortunate, well-fed, well-clothed, well-housed people amongst us." Confederation was the cause of "the toiling masses" who wanted "a NEW Newfoundland."[7]

The referendum, held on 3 June 1948, failed to settle the issue: responsible government received 44.6 per cent of the vote, Confederation 41.1, and Commission government 14.3. A run-off vote was scheduled for 22 July. Although the Avalon Peninsula, including St John's, was strongly anti-Confederate,

Joseph Smallwood as "The Barrelman" on radio station VONF. Courtesy of the *Atlantic Guardian*, 1946, Archives and Manuscript Division, QEII Library, Memorial University, St John's.

the Confederates were confident that victory was within reach. In addition to stressing the economic benefits of Confederation, they deliberately played the sectarian card. Members of every Orange Lodge were reminded that many Roman Catholics—including members of religious orders, voting for the first time in history—opposed Confederation. Anti-Confederates were also viciously accused of disloyalty to Britain, while Confederation was presented as "British Union."

In the end, Confederation emerged with a majority of 4.6 per cent over responsible government. The geographical voting pattern was largely unchanged. What gave the Confederates the edge was their success in attracting most of those who had supported Commission government in the first referendum—voters described by one member of the St John's elite as "ignorant and avaricious outporters" who had "handed over [Newfoundland] to Canada as a free gift."[8] Although the victory was narrow in numerical terms, the Confederates won every district off the Avalon Peninsula and in Labrador, the equivalent of an electoral landslide. Three factors in particular contributed to the final result: the significant social and economic changes that had taken place in Newfoundland and Labrador since the early 1930s; genuine uncertainty about the wisdom of returning to independence; and the desire to benefit from the social programs offered by postwar federalism. Newfoundlanders and Labradorians had great hopes and expectations for their future as a province.

Historical Focus

The Radio and Confederation

Before he emerged as Newfoundland's Father of Confederation, "Joe" Smallwood had become a household name throughout Newfoundland as the popular host of *The Barrelman*, a radio show intended to make Newfoundland better known to Newfoundlanders (the show's title referred to the lookout stationed on the "barrel" or "crow's nest" of a sealing vessel). During the Second World War radios became more widely available, and listeners recognized themselves in Smallwood's folksy programs. Smallwood used the radio to great effect when the Confederation debates were being aired between 1946 and 1948. Here he explains the role he thought it played in clinching the outcome of the referendum:

> I had spent many years in broadcasting and I knew the magic of it. The sheer, sheer magic, especially in a place like Newfoundland with so many isolated people. Radio, I always contended, was invented by God especially for Newfoundland, and having done it for Newfoundland, He graciously allowed it to be used in other parts of the world. It was *meant* for Newfoundland. It was meant for remote and isolated people who never met, who never saw each other. Radio was a great unifying thing. I knew how to use it. I never let my mouth turn away from that microphone. Never. Many of the debaters at the Convention disdained the microphones. They wouldn't go near them with the result that my point of view was heard loud and clear in every home. The anti-Confederationists, disdaining radio as they did, were not heard. The result was that, when the referendum was held, Confederation passed by a narrow margin. I credit that margin to the use of radio.[9]

SHALL WE SAY GRACE

"Shall We Say Grace?" This cartoon from *The Confederate*, 20 May 1948, draws on memories of the Great Depression to emphasize the message that the wealthy elites supported a return to responsible government, which (allegedly) had only brought misery to the common people in the past.

During the negotiation of the final terms of union, fisheries administration became a bone of contention. That Newfoundland had to place its main industry under federal control caused some justifiable shaking of heads. Financial arrangements also caused some concern. Ottawa had originally insisted that Newfoundland be fitted into the 1867 mould, but eventually agreed to a special 12-year transitional grant and undertook, in Term 29, to establish within eight years a royal commission that would determine what additional assistance might be required to maintain adequate public services while keeping taxes comparable to those in the Maritime provinces. Although little was made of it at the time, it was significant that the benchmark for Newfoundland's success as Canada's tenth province under Term 29 was the standard of living in the Maritimes, not Canada as a whole. It is also significant that Aboriginal peoples disappeared from the text, the tacit decision being that their affairs would be administered by the provincial government, with the federal government supplying some of the necessary funds.

Historical Focus

The Aboriginal Peoples of Newfoundland and Labrador and the Terms of Union

The final draft of the terms of union between Newfoundland and Labrador and Canada made no mention of the new province's Aboriginal peoples, who were placed under provincial jurisdiction. How did this situation develop?

At the start of serious negotiations it was assumed on both sides that the federal government would, as elsewhere in Canada, take responsibility for Aboriginal peoples, but Canadian officials gradually changed their position. In 1948, a Newfoundland official suggested that to apply the Indian Act to Aboriginal people in Labrador would be a backward step—they would lose the right to vote, for example—and that it might be preferable for the provincial government to administer "Indian affairs" with federal subsidies. The Mi'kmaq on the island of Newfoundland were assumed to be part of the general population and were not even mentioned.

On the Canadian side there was no enthusiasm for taking on responsibility for more indigenous peoples. Indeed, the federal government had recently tried to avoid taking responsibility for the

By the end of 1948 the terms of union were settled, and Newfoundland became Canada's tenth province on 31 March 1949. Smallwood served as its first premier and Bradley as its first representative in the federal cabinet. The ceremonies were subdued. In the Maritimes, Newfoundland's entry into Confederation was generally well received. At Mount Saint Vincent Ladies' College in Halifax, the union prompted a pageant to welcome Newfoundland students as Canadians. According to the account in the Antigonish *Casket*: "The infant country was depicted through its long struggle for independence, with Great Britain, Canada and the United States always ready to hold out an invited hand. The hard choice being made, the new province was welcomed by Mother Canada who called in the nine provinces to extend individual welcomes, bring their gifts, and witness the crowning of Newfoundland as a tenth province."[10]

Others saw economic and political advantages to be gained by Newfoundland's entry into Confederation. One of the first and most ardent proponents of union was A. Neil McLean, a New Brunswick Senator and fishing magnate who had invested in a modern fish-packing plant near Corner Brook and was eager to see a canal built across the Isthmus of Chignecto to facilitate communications within the region. Prince Edward Island Premier Walter Jones, who had spent considerable effort enhancing agricultural trade with Newfoundland, correctly predicted that greater volumes of PEI beef and vegetables would soon reach kitchen tables in Newfoundland. Although Nova Scotia Premier Angus L. Macdonald's enthusiasm was more muted, even he welcomed the new province, which would add weight to his argument for a causeway connecting Cape Breton to the Nova Scotia mainland. A few commentators saw the possibility of closer collaboration—perhaps union—among the four jurisdictions to mount a more effective campaign for better treatment from Ottawa, but none of the Maritime premiers (Liberals all) were prepared to go too far down that road, at least not then.

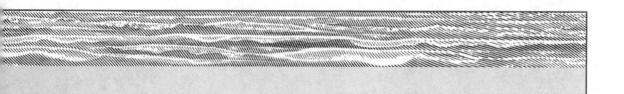

Quebec Inuit. The Newfoundland proposal would not only save money, but avoid the difficulties implicit in adapting the Indian Act to the different circumstances prevailing in Newfoundland and in Labrador, where there were no equivalents to Canadian legislation, no treaties, and no reserves, and where Aboriginal people were already enfranchised. Additional (and less convincing) justifications included the small numbers of Aboriginal people and the extent of racial mixing and absorption, which was exaggerated. The Newfoundland proposal was accepted and Aboriginal peoples disappeared from the terms of union. The details of the federal–provincial relationship in this area were not settled until 1954.

It has been argued that this arrangement allowed the federal government to evade its constitutional responsibilities to the Aboriginal peoples of Newfoundland and Labrador, and that they have been significantly disadvantaged as a result. Certainly, they have not been treated on an equal footing with their counterparts elsewhere in Canada.[11]

Conclusion

In 1949 a new region was born. Instead of becoming a fourth "Maritime province," Newfoundland inspired new labels: "Atlantic Provinces" and, by the 1960s, "Atlantic Canada." These were convenient terms for Ottawa to describe a space that had no effective regional identity and whose provinces often followed separate, at times conflicting, agendas. Although cushioned now by a kinder, gentler federalism, optimistic about the future, and part of a prosperous country, "Atlantic Canada" had to accept that it would function in a world where the centralization of political and economic power was irreversible.

Further Readings

Blake, Raymond B. 1994. *Canadians at Last: Canada Integrates Newfoundland as a Province*. Toronto: University of Toronto Press.

Christie, Carl. 1995. *Ocean Bridge: The History of RAF Ferry Command*. Toronto: University of Toronto Press.

Granatstein, J.L., and Peter Neary, eds. 1995. *The Good Fight: Canadians and World War II*. Toronto: Copp, Clark.

Gwyn, Richard. 1972. *Smallwood: The Unlikely Revolutionary*. 2nd edn. Toronto: McClelland and Stewart.

Henderson, T. Stephen. 2007. *Angus L. Macdonald: A Provincial Liberal*. Toronto: University of Toronto Press.

High, Steven, ed. 2010. *Occupied St. John's. A Social History of a City at War, 1939–1945*. Montreal: McGill-Queen's University Press.

Hiller, James K. 1998. *Confederation: Deciding Newfoundland's Future, 1934–1949*. St John's: Newfoundland Historical Society.

Jarratt, Melynda. 2008. *Captured Hearts: New Brunswick's War Brides*. Fredericton: Goose Lane and New Brunswick Military Heritage Project.

MacKenzie, David. 1986. *Inside the Atlantic Triangle: Canada and the Entrance of Newfoundland into Confederation, 1939–1949*. Toronto: University of Toronto Press.

Milner, Marc. 1985. *North Atlantic Run: The Royal Navy and the Battle for Convoys*. Toronto: University of Toronto Press.

———. 1994. *The U-Boat Hunters: The Royal Canadian Navy and the Offensive against Germany's Submarines*. Toronto: University of Toronto Press.

Neary, Peter. 1988. *Newfoundland and the North Atlantic World, 1929–1949*. Montreal: McGill-Queen's University Press.

Sarty, Roger. 2001. *The Battle of the Atlantic: The Royal Canadian Navy's Greatest Campaign, 1939–1945*. Ottawa: CEF Books.

———. 2012. *War in the St Lawrence: The Forgotten U-Boat Battles on Canada's Shores*. Toronto: Allen Lane

Slumkoski, Corey. 2011. *Inventing Atlantic Canada: Regionalism and the Maritime Reaction to Newfoundland's Entry into Canadian Confederation*. Toronto: University of Toronto Press.

Tennyson, Brian, and Roger Sarty. 1997. *The Maritime Defence of Canada*. Toronto: Canadian Institute for Strategic Studies.

Webb, Jeff A. 2008. *The Voice of Newfoundland. A Social History of the Broadcasting Corporation of Newfoundland, 1939–1949*. Toronto: University of Toronto Press.

Historical Spotlight

Forbes, E.R. 1989. "Consolidating Disparity: The Maritimes and Industrialization during the Second World War." In *Challenging the Regional Stereotype: Essays on the 20th Century Maritimes.* Fredericton: Acadiensis Press.

High, Steven. 2002. "From Outport to Outport Base: The American Occupation of Stephenville, 1940–1945." *Newfoundland Studies* 18, 1 (Spring): 84–113.

Recommended Websites

Canadian War Brides
http://www.canadianwarbrides.com/

Canadian War Museum
http://www.warmuseum.ca/education

"An East Coast Port": Halifax in Wartime, 1939–1945
http://www.gov.ns.ca/archives/virtual/eastcoastport

Newfoundland and Labrador Heritage
The Second World War, 1939–1945
http://www.heritage.nf.ca/law/wwii.html

Newfoundland and Canada, 1864–1949
http://www.heritage.nf.ca/law/confed.html

Pier 21
http://www.pier21.ca

The Second World War
http://www.veterans.gc.ca/eng/remembrance/history/second-world-war

Chapter 14

A Region Transformed, 1949–1975

Scarred by two world wars and the Depression of the 1930s, Atlantic Canadians longed for a better future. The onset of the Cold War seemed to offer an opportunity to achieve this goal. With policy-makers in the Western world eager to prove the merits of capitalism over communism, and the United Nations championing human rights, governments at all levels shaped a new liberal order that was designed to benefit a broad social spectrum. In Canada the federal government's commitment to economic planning and social welfare encouraged efforts to pursue regional development. The result was an economic and social transformation of the region. Although the

Setting the Context

The Postwar Liberal Consensus

From 1945 to 1975 Canadians embraced what is often described as the "postwar liberal consensus." Liberalism had initially meant freedom from state intervention and freedom of trade, speech, and worship. The new postwar liberalism confirmed these goals, but also emphasized freedom from want. In this context, state intervention was considered essential to achieve greater social equality.

The term "welfare state" is often used to describe policies designed to ensure, as a matter of right, basic well-being and social opportunities for all citizens. In pursuing these goals, governments introduced unemployment insurance, farm subsidies, minimum wage legislation, and regional development strategies, along with universal programs such as public education, medical insurance, family allowances, and old age pensions. Opponents of the welfare state rarely attacked spending on education or infrastructure, but they argued that social assistance and unemployment insurance programs robbed people of initiative, cost too much, and led to inefficiencies in the operation of free market economies.

In the postwar period, two economists, the University of Chicago's Milton Friedman and the Canadian-born Harvard professor John Kenneth Galbraith, debated these perspectives in both scholarly and popular media. Friedman's ideas, which championed unfettered free market principles, had limited appeal during the postwar boom, but they attracted a significant following in business circles. When the global economy began to stumble in the 1970s, Galbraith's Keynesian approach was discredited and "less government" became the mantra of the so-called neo-liberals, who became increasingly influential.[1]

oil crisis of the 1970s ended this expansive period, the three decades following the Second World War left a legacy of interregional co-operation, institutional development, and claims to entitlement that to a considerable extent still inform public policy.

The Atlantic Revolution

During the immediate postwar years, conditions in the Atlantic region worsened in comparison with those in most other areas of North America, which were experiencing unprecedented economic growth and social progress. Per capita income in the Maritimes in 1945 was 24 per cent below the Canadian average, increasing to 33 per cent in 1955. Newfoundland was the poorest province, its per capita income 55 per cent below the national average. In studies of health and welfare programs, the Atlantic region was invariably singled out as lagging behind the rest of the country. Victorian poorhouses still served as the repositories of last resort for destitute, mentally ill, and physically disabled Maritimers, while a high proportion of the region's population lived without modern amenities such as electricity, indoor plumbing, and telephones.

As in the 1920s, business interests played a critical role in the postwar version of regional protest. In 1951 the Maritime Provinces Board of Trade established an office in Moncton and began an aggressive campaign to encourage regional co-operation. The board sponsored a meeting with Atlantic premiers in 1953; a year later it helped to create the Atlantic Provinces Economic Council (APEC), designed to spearhead development efforts. R. Whidden Ganong, the chocolate manufacturer from St Stephen, New Brunswick, served as its first president, and 25 directors, seven from each of the Maritime provinces and four from Newfoundland, were elected to the first Board.

The Atlantic premiers were also keen to pursue regional economic development. Having promised Newfoundlanders that Confederation would usher in a new era, Premier Joseph Smallwood began a whirlwind of activity, recruiting entrepreneurs from Europe, and badgering "Uncle Ottawa" for financial aid. To improve his political position, he persuaded J.W. Pickersgill to run for the federal riding of Bonavista–Twillingate in 1953. As a former assistant both to Mackenzie King and to his successor, Louis St Laurent, the Manitoba-born Pickersgill was well placed to manipulate the levers of federal power. In New Brunswick, Progressive Conservative Premier Hugh John Flemming pursued an energetic program to develop "power for industry." He was outraged when the St Laurent government refused assistance for the Beechwood power project on the St John River while pouring money into the construction of the St Lawrence Seaway, which brought improved transportation and large-scale power development to central Canada. Prince Edward Island's Liberal Premier Alexander Matheson was similarly offended when Ottawa insisted that his province return $1.4 million mistakenly remitted in per capita grants at a time when it was giving considerable sums to the developing world. In Nova Scotia, the death of Angus L. Macdonald in 1954 opened the way for a more interventionist approach under Robert L. Stanfield, who led a Progressive Conservative government from 1956 to 1967. When the Atlantic premiers met in Fredericton in July 1956, Flemming presented a list of proposals that his fellow premiers agreed to support: federal subsidies based on need; assistance for resource development; and fiscal, tariff, and transportation policies that would help to stimulate regional economic growth.

By this time the federal Liberal government, blessed with treasury surpluses, was willing to accommodate what the historian W.S. MacNutt described as an "Atlantic Revolution."[2] Legislation

Table 14.1	Timeline
1951	Maritime Provinces Board of Trade establishes an office in Moncton.
1954	Atlantic Provinces Economic Council founded; resettlement program begins in Newfoundland.
1955	Canso Causeway opened.
1956	Ottawa passes equalization legislation; Conference of Atlantic Premiers.
1957	Report of the Royal Commission on Canada's Economic Prospects submitted; Industrial Estates Limited established by the Nova Scotia government.
1958	Ottawa approves Atlantic Provinces Adjustment Grants.
1959	Loggers' strike in Newfoundland.
1960	Aboriginal people granted the right to vote on the same terms as other Canadians.
1962	Atlantic Development Board established; Halifax City Council decides to relocate residents of Africville.
1964	Byrne Report advocates municipal reform in New Brunswick.
1967	Cape Breton Development Corporation created.
1968	BRINCO signs deal to sell Churchill Falls power to Hydro-Québec.
1969	New Brunswick declared officially bilingual; Prince Edward Island development plan signed; Black United Front founded; White Paper on Indian Policy; Department of Regional Economic Expansion created.
1970	Deutsch Report recommends Maritime Union; Report of the Royal Commission on the Status of Women.
1971	Council of Maritime Premiers founded.
1972	Parti Acadien founded; Smallwood resigns as premier of Newfoundland.
1974–5	Strike by Newfoundland trawler crews.

introduced in 1956 provided for equalization payments to the poorer provinces. The following year, there were concessions on freight rates and power development, and, at Pickersgill's insistence, seasonal fishery workers became eligible for unemployment insurance. Ottawa's decision in 1955 to appoint the Royal Commission on Canada's Economic Prospects, chaired by Toronto accountant Walter Gordon, played into the regional agenda. The preliminary report, released in January 1957, singled out the Atlantic provinces as deserving "positive and comprehensive" attention. A proposal to offer assistance in moving people from the region to growth centres elsewhere received well-deserved derision and was deleted from the final document.

The Progressive Conservatives under John Diefenbaker also proved sensitive to regional concerns. During the 1957 election campaign, the party's candidates developed a series of "Atlantic Resolutions" based on Flemming's proposals and the recommendations of the Gordon Commission. Diefenbaker squeaked through to victory, and, in his cabinet, ministers from the Atlantic and Western provinces outnumbered those from Quebec and Ontario for the first time in Canadian history. Several policies favourable to Atlantic Canada were implemented before the next election in March 1958. With a $25-million Atlantic Provinces Adjustment Grant, a $29.5-million loan to the Beechwood power development, subventions for coal, and aid to thermal power development, 25 Progressive Conservatives from the region were smiling when the Diefenbaker government won by a landslide.

Only Newfoundland failed to follow the regional trend, awarding just two of its seven seats to the Progressive Conservatives. Since 1949 Smallwood had generally stood at one remove from the "Atlantic front" in the hope that the province's status as the most recent member of Confederation would serve him better than the politics of regionalism. This strategy backfired. Smallwood had expected an annual grant of $15 million under Term 29 of the Terms of Union, but in July 1958 the royal commission on the matter, chaired by former New Brunswick premier John B. McNair, recommended $8 million in perpetuity. The Diefenbaker government accepted McNair's recommendation as to the amount, but refused to make payments beyond 1962. A bitter confrontation erupted. The province

Robert Chambers, "The Order of Good Cheer—circa 1960," *Atlantic Advocate*, September 1960. This cartoon reflects the optimism that circulated in the region as the "Atlantic Revolution," led by the region's premiers, got under way. Courtesy of the Chambers family.

Document

The Progressive Conservatives Adopt the Atlantic Resolutions, 1957

The son of a Baptist minister from Woodstock, New Brunswick, Dalton Camp played a major role as a Progressive Conservative Party organizer in the postwar years. In his book *Gentlemen, Players and Politicians* he described how the Atlantic Resolutions—the basis for the party's national platform in the June 1957 election—took shape. Several candidates from the Atlantic provinces, including two from Newfoundland, met in a Moncton hotel on 11 May. Along with New Brunswick organizer Kenneth Carson, Camp retreated to an upstairs room while candidates pondered their strategies downstairs. After describing how George Nowlan, the only Progressive Conservative to have won a Nova Scotia seat in the 1953 election, "commuted from the downstairs meeting to our upstairs room, offering encouragement, topping off our glasses, and refilling his own," Camp continues:

Continued

When we had had drafted a resolution to our common satisfaction, Nowlan would bear it downstairs, and place it before candidates who cheerfully and promptly gave their consent. After the resolutions had been completed and approved, we drafted the preamble:

> We, the Progressive Conservative Candidates from the 31 federal constituencies in the Atlantic provinces, believe the just demands of the Atlantic Community for recognition of their economic problems and special needs urgently require more united and forceful representation in the Parliament of Canada.
>
> In keeping with the growing co-operative spirit of the people of the Atlantic community, which has already led to the creation of APEC and the Conference of Atlantic Premiers, we are resolved to stand together in support of these measures which will help to overcome the historic disabilities which have limited and even denied opportunity to this area. We believe our young people have the right to opportunity at home and we are convinced that only by united action by all individuals and all levels of government and the constructive efforts of private organizations, can this right be made real.
>
> We believe that all those who live in this Atlantic community are entitled to the benefits of opportunity and security which shall be no more, but certainly no less, than all Canadians have the right to enjoy.

Amendments and changes were few. Bill Browne, representing the unknown and isolated Tory party in Newfoundland, asked only that his province be specifically mentioned in the manifesto and this was cheerfully agreed. But apart from that the words remained largely as they were when George Nowlan brought them from our hotel room to the meeting below.[3]

Camp continued to play a major role in the affairs of the Progressive Conservative Party and was central in persuading Robert Stanfield to challenge John Diefenbaker for the national party leadership in 1967.

eventually settled with the Liberal government of Lester Pearson for McNair's recommendation, and in 1996 Premier Brian Peckford negotiated a lump sum payment to cover a 20-year period.

In the short run, the row over Term 29 was a useful diversion for Smallwood, who was facing criticism for his belligerent suppression of a loggers' strike in central Newfoundland in 1959. The strike had begun after loggers working for the Anglo-Newfoundland Development Company at Grand Falls, dissatisfied with the inadequate wages and working conditions negotiated by the Newfoundland Lumbermen's Association, turned to the more aggressive International Woodworkers of America (IWA). As the situation became increasingly tense, Smallwood asked for RCMP reinforcements. Diefenbaker refused, and Smallwood responded by sending in the Newfoundland Constabulary, which lacked experience in such situations. When a constable died in a confrontation with loggers at Badger, Smallwood used the death to turn public opinion against the union, claiming that it was riddled with communists, gangsters, and outsiders. The legislature decertified the IWA and created a new, more conciliatory union. Although widely condemned for his handling of the strike, Smallwood survived. It was now clear that if forced to choose, his government would side with corporate interests rather than labour.

The Atlantic provinces benefited from a succession of minority governments in Ottawa between 1962 and 1968. In the dying days of the Diefenbaker administration, the Atlantic Development Board (ADB) was established to orchestrate investment in the region. When the Liberal Party under Lester Pearson formed a minority government after the 1963 election, it expanded the functions of the ADB and endowed it with funds. Other federal programs were tailored to meet the region's needs. After Pierre Elliott Trudeau became prime minister in 1968, his government replaced the ADB with the Department of Regional Economic Expansion (DREE), which applied regional development principles to the entire country.

Planning in the Provinces

Spurred by infusions of federal money, politicians and planners in the Atlantic provinces and Ottawa embarked on ambitious programs. Development agencies were created to attract industrial investment and blueprints for social change multiplied impressively. Newfoundland had the farthest to go and went the fastest. Tapping into the cash surplus of $40.2 million bequeathed by the Commission government, Smallwood induced European firms to invest in 16 new industries between 1950 and 1956. Few of these industries survived for any length of time, and the program both exhausted the surplus and helped to triple the provincial debt. It was perhaps unfortunate that Smallwood had decided to recruit—on the recommendation of the powerful federal cabinet minister C.D. Howe—the Latvian economist Alfred Valdmanis as director of economic development. He spent money extravagantly and in 1954 was convicted of fraud and extortion.

The best prospects for resource development appeared to be in Labrador, with which Smallwood was increasingly obsessed. Western Labrador was opened to development in 1954 with the completion of the Quebec, North Shore, and Labrador Railway to Sept-Îles. The first iron mines were located on the Quebec side of the border, but in the 1960s new mines were developed on the Labrador side, along with new towns: Labrador City in 1962 and Wabush in 1964.

Smallwood was intent on exploiting the hydro potential of Labrador's Grand or Hamilton Falls (renamed Churchill Falls in 1965). In the early 1950s the province leased the falls to the British Newfoundland Corporation (BRINCO), a consortium put together by the Rothschilds on Smallwood's initiative, with Winston Churchill's blessing. Since Quebec would not allow transmission lines to carry power across its territory to customers in Ontario and the United States, and the federal government would not intervene, BRINCO's subsidiary, the Hamilton Falls Power Company (HFPCo), was obliged from the outset to agree in principle to a long-term low-price deal with Hydro-Québec.

In the protracted bargaining that eventually led to the 1968 power contract, Hydro-Québec took advantage of its position to drive a hard bargain. BRINCO and HFPCo (from 1965 the Churchill Falls Labrador Co.) were in financial difficulties, Hydro-Québec was the sole customer, and it was represented on HFPCo's board, having inherited the stake held before 1962 by a private Quebec power producer. Not only did Hydro-Québec obtain cheap power for 40 years, but it also insisted upon automatic renewal at the same mill rate for a further 25 years. A rate of 2.2 mills per kilowatt hour was cheap in 1968; in 2007 it was described as "unbelievably low," and it will amount to a virtual giveaway when the renewal clause comes into effect in 2016.[4]

Quebec has been reaping windfall profits from Churchill Falls since the mid-1970s, when energy prices began to rise steeply. Newfoundland's persistent attempts to challenge the contract have failed, and it seems that Quebec will continue to collect a great deal of money from Churchill Falls until at least 2041. This debacle haunts the people of Newfoundland and Labrador. Although Smallwood has taken much of the blame for making a bad deal, the provincial government was not directly involved in the negotiations, and he was presented with a fait accompli in 1968. Nor were the Innu either consulted or compensated, even though they lost a large amount of their traditional territory to the Smallwood Reservoir.

Churchill Falls was not the only controversial project promoted by the Smallwood administration. In 1954, as part of its diversification and modernization program, the government began to encourage the people living in small and remote outports to move to larger communities. A joint federal–provincial resettlement program followed in 1965. Between 1954 and 1970, approximately 30,000 people from 250 communities were relocated. This was a spectacular exercise in social engineering and has since been widely criticized. Yet the program was not without its supporters, and there is evidence that more women than men saw its advantages. Those who moved enjoyed better public services, including education, medical care, electricity, and roads, but the "growth centres" often failed to provide the expected jobs, even in the fishery, which was becoming mechanized

Malcolm Rogers's house, moored off the beach at Dover, Bonavista Bay, waiting for high tide so it can be hauled ashore. It had been floated from Fox Island as part of Newfoundland's outport resettlement program in the 1960s. Library and Archives Canada/Credit: B. Brooks/National Film Board fonds/PA-154123.

and capital-intensive. It is also clear that abandoning a deeply rooted way of life left many former outport residents with a profound sense of loss.

Smallwood was not alone among the Atlantic premiers in exercising state powers in controversial ways. In New Brunswick a young Louis J. Robichaud led his Liberal Party to victory in June 1960 and appointed a cabinet in which the majority of members were francophones. Determined to improve conditions in the poor rural municipalities where most Acadians lived, Robichaud established the Royal Commission on Municipal Finance and Taxation, chaired by Edward G. Byrne. Its 1964 report documented the inequalities that characterized New Brunswick municipalities and recommended sweeping changes. This was a green light for massive reform in the province's municipal government.

For his "Programme of Equal Opportunity" to succeed, Robichaud needed a civil service with the capacity to implement it. He therefore imported administrators from Saskatchewan, where the defeat of the CCF government in 1964 had freed up a significant pool of talent. The most important member of the so-called "Saskatchewan mafia" was Donald Tansley, whose motto was "Process Is the Policy." As deputy minister of finance, Tansley played a critical role in persuading Robichaud's cabinet to embrace controversial new policies, including unionization of significant sectors of the civil service.[5]

Many anglophones complained that Robichaud's administration represented a "French takeover," but they could not stop the transformation of New Brunswick's political landscape. The centralization of health and educational services, the establishment of a francophone university in Moncton in 1963, and the decision in 1969 to declare New Brunswick a bilingual province—the only one in Canada—underscored the growing power of the francophone minority both in New Brunswick and in Canada as a whole. Although Robichaud lost the 1970 election to the Progressive Conservatives under Richard Hatfield, the latter refused to turn back the clock. The new political and cultural realities were there to stay.

Prince Edward Island also joined the Atlantic Revolution. In 1969 Liberal Premier Alexander Campbell agreed to a 15-year Comprehensive Development Plan that promised an investment of $725 million ($255 million from Ottawa) to help restructure farming and fishing, improve infrastructure, and diversify the economy, with a particular focus on tourism. The agreement recognized that Prince Edward Islanders needed help if they were to maintain adequate services without sinking further into debt. By 1971 the island had slipped below Newfoundland as the poorest province in Canada and its per capita debt was higher than that of any other Atlantic province. Even so, many Islanders were offended by the apparent arrogance of the planners. Del Gallagher, a New Brunswicker who spearheaded the development program, was particularly unpopular, and jokes about "Gallagher's Island," in reference to a popular American television series, became commonplace.[6]

In Nova Scotia the Progressive Conservatives under Robert Stanfield embraced the entrepreneurial spirit of the Atlantic Revolution. The affluent son of a Truro clothing manufacturer, he was disciplined, purposeful, and progressive in his approach to politics. In 1957 his government created Industrial Estates Limited to promote investment, and by the early 1960s two Swedish firms, Volvo and Stora Forest, had been persuaded to locate in Nova Scotia. Michelin Tire arrived in the 1970s and became one of the province's largest employers, with plants in Bridgewater, Granton, and Waterville. By that time Stanfield had moved to Ottawa, where he served as leader of the Progressive Conservative Party from 1967 to 1976.

The crisis in the coal and steel industries spurred further government intervention. With oil and gas rapidly replacing coal and the demand for steel rails shrinking, Nova Scotia's industrial base collapsed. Following the recommendations of the 1960 Royal Commission on Coal, chaired by Chief Justice Ivan Rand—a native of Moncton—the federal government set out to develop alternative industries on Cape Breton Island, where hardship was most acute. Money was pumped into Cape Breton Highlands National Park and the rebuilding of the fortress of Louisbourg, but those initiatives absorbed only a fraction of the island's unemployed workers. Cape Bretoners left in droves for jobs on the mainland, their departure facilitated by the completion of the Canso Causeway in 1955. To mitigate both human distress and unpleasant political repercussions, Ottawa created the Cape Breton Development Corporation (DEVCO) in 1967, which purchased and operated the mines, while the province established the Sydney Steel Corporation (SYSCO), which bought the steel mill. If anyone could salvage the situation, it was Tom Kent, the progressive British-born advisor to Prime Minister Pearson, who was despatched to Cape Breton to serve as president of DEVCO and later of the Steel Corporation. Kent faced an uphill battle.

The push for economic development had positive and negative aspects. With government assistance, Halifax, Port Hawkesbury, and Saint John became superports and a few homegrown entrepreneurs emerged—among them R.A. Jodrey, K.C. Irving, the McCain brothers, Frank Sobey, and Harry Steele. At the same time, there was a price to pay for governments that jumped on the corporate bandwagon. To keep their investors happy, both Newfoundland and Nova Scotia passed restrictive labour legislation (Nova Scotia's became known as the "Michelin bill"). K.C. Irving moved to Bermuda to avoid paying Canadian taxes even though his oil, transportation, and media empires benefited greatly from government assistance.

Eager to support economic development, political leaders backed a series of "white elephants." Clairtone Sound and the Point Tupper Heavy Water plant were serious embarrassments for the Stanfield government and Hatfield's image was tarnished when the Bricklin gull-wing sports car on which he had pinned his industrial hopes proved unviable. Throughout the region, government-assisted food- and fish-processing operations appeared and disappeared with unnerving regularity. Ever a gambler on the next big project, Smallwood made a deal with the American John Shaheen to build an oil refinery and petrochemical plant at Come By Chance. This move prompted two of his most ambitious ministers, John Crosbie and Clyde Wells, to leave his cabinet in May 1968. In the federal election a month later, six of the province's seven seats were won by Conservatives, and three years later a revived Progressive Conservative Party, led by Frank Moores and including Crosbie, defeated Smallwood's Liberal government in a cliff-hanger election.

Although politicians liked to conjure up visions of an "Atlantic Community," the provinces often disagreed on how to achieve regional development. Prince Edward Island felt cheated when the Atlantic Provinces Adjustment Grant was divided on a 30:30:30:10 ratio, and each province had its own ideas about which capital projects should have priority if and when Ottawa could be induced to provide funding. By the early 1970s Labradorians were starting to resent what they perceived as their exploitation by a provincial government that otherwise ignored their region. The New Labrador Party was formed in time for the 1971 provincial election, in which it proved to be the spoiler (it dissolved in 1975), and a Labrador flag was created in 1974. Cape Bretoners, experiencing deindustrialization at an alarming rate, resented a Halifax-based government that increasingly seemed to favour the provincial mainland.

In 1964 Robichaud had added yet another controversial project to the mix: union of the Atlantic provinces. His francophone supporters might well have opposed such a move, but it was popular in Ottawa, which was growing impatient with the region's proliferating demands. At Robichaud's urging, the three Maritime premiers—Smallwood remained detached—established a commission in 1968 to study the issue. It was chaired by Queen's University professor John Deutsch, who recommended unification in his 1970 report. Not surprisingly, this advice was ignored. The commission's most important outcome was the creation of the Council of Maritime Premiers, established in 1971.

Social Adjustments

While political and business elites manoeuvred and negotiated, ordinary Atlantic Canadians were living the postwar revolution in their daily lives. The impact of economic restructuring is reflected in the statistics. During the 1950s alone, the numbers of people working in agriculture dropped by 49 per cent, in fishing and trapping by 37 per cent, in forestry by 24 per cent, and in mining by 22 per cent. The exit from primary pursuits continued through the 1960s. Each sector had its own cycle, but all were reshaped to meet the demands of an increasingly bureaucratized, centralized, mechanized, and, ultimately, computerized world.

Long an endangered species, the family farm survived only by adopting corporate practices. Quotas, marketing boards, and national standards spelled the end of part-time farming for any purpose other than personal interest. One in five people in the Maritimes lived on a farm in 1951; only one in 50 did so three decades later. Apple growers in the Annapolis Valley, faced with the permanent closure of the British market, were encouraged by generous government subsidies to convert their acreage to mixed crops for a regional market. Most of them got out of farming altogether.

In Prince Edward Island, the National Farmers Union and the Brothers and Sisters of Cornelius Howatt—named after the island's most famous nineteenth-century anti-Confederate—staged a protest against development policies that they believed had contributed to the decline of family farming: at the height of the 1971 tourist season they jammed the highway between Charlottetown and Borden with their tractors. Their action had no effect on the general trend. Between 1951 and 1981 the proportion of Islanders employed in farming dropped from nearly 50 per cent to less than 10 per cent, and the number of farms from 10,137 to 3,154.

The story was the same in forestry, where mechanization made it possible to process more trees with fewer workers. Milling for the construction industry continued to thrive in New Brunswick, but even there, as elsewhere in the region, the major product was pulpwood. By the 1980s the 19 pulp-and-paper operations in Atlantic Canada all depended on foreign markets, and the competition among them was intense. In the absence of tough environmental laws, companies were tempted to cut and run rather than follow the costly practices required to ensure a sustainable industry. A side effect was a monoculture of softwood trees that invited periodic spruce budworm infestations and what turned out to be unhealthy spraying programs.

In mining, restructuring produced mixed results. A growing demand for base metals such as lead, zinc, copper, and iron produced a mining boom in northern New Brunswick and western Labrador. The most dramatic new frontier was offshore oil and natural gas, to which multinational investors were attracted by generous tax incentives. On the down side, the steady decline of the coal industry meant hard times for many communities. Mine disasters in Springhill in 1956 and

1958 tragically underlined the inadequacy of safety measures in antiquated mines. The fluorspar industry on the Burin Peninsula appeared to be a success story, but the discovery that radon gas caused cancer among the miners, plus cheaper ore from Mexico, led to the mine's closure in 1977.

In the fisheries, modernization and expansion were setting the stage for a dramatic collapse. In the early 1950s Europeans began sending freezer trawlers to the bank fishery, signalling a major transition in the region's oldest primary industry. With the emphasis on the offshore banks and fresh or frozen fish, and overwhelmingly on the American market, salt fish production declined, while a record 810,000 tonnes of groundfish, such as cod, halibut, haddock, and sole, were taken in 1968. Eager to tap a resource on its own doorstep, the Canadian government declared a 9-mile limit in 1964, a 12-mile limit in 1970, then a 200-mile limit in 1977, and encouraged massive investment. The numbers of people engaged in the fisheries began to rise for the first time in more than a century. Government policies created overcapacity, while failing to regulate the exploitation of a resource that was a mainstay to the regional economy.

The expansion of employment in the fisheries notwithstanding, most of the jobs created in this period were in the trade and service sectors, and often tied to state spending. By the early 1960s government employment accounted for more than 100,000 jobs in the Atlantic region—more than forestry and mining combined. The Department of Defence, its budgets fattened by spending associated with the Korean War (1950–3) and the Cold War, employed 41,000 Atlantic Canadians in 1961. Military bases were given a new lease on life, and several new ones were established, among them CFB Gagetown in New Brunswick. While Nova Scotia led the region in dependence on defence jobs—more than 11 per cent of its labour force was employed in defence in 1961—all four Atlantic provinces benefited economically from the federal government's decision to locate more than one-quarter of the nation's armed forces on the east coast.

Many Atlantic Canadians had difficulty making the transition from primary to tertiary industries. Those displaced from farming, forestry, and mining often lacked the skills required for the available jobs and were obliged to find work outside the region. Increasingly, skilled employment went to qualified immigrants. Employment in areas traditionally dominated by women—clerical, teaching, nursing, and social work—expanded rapidly. As more women entered the paid workforce, their subordinate positions and unfair wage scales were called into question, as were gender relations within the family. Aboriginal, Acadian, and African minorities, protested their unequal access to economic opportunities.

The human costs of economic transformation were alleviated in part by federal government intervention in the form of welfare-state policies: universal family allowances (1944), old-age pensions (1951), hospital insurance (1957), Canada pension (1965), social assistance (1966), and Medicare (1968). Unemployment insurance (now employment insurance) expanded in the postwar period to cover a growing number of Canadian workers, including the seasonally unemployed. For those who had never had much disposable income, these programs often meant the difference between dignified subsistence and destitution.

Seeing formal education as the key to success in the new economy, political leaders focused energy and funds on educational infrastructure. School enrolments in Atlantic Canada grew from 338,364 in 1950 to 485,051 in 1959, with most of the baby boomers attending large, new consolidated institutions. Vocational schools proliferated, and higher education was transformed. In the 1940s most universities were small, private operations, often with religious affiliations, but by 1970

Atlantic Canada boasted an impressive network of state-funded universities and a total enrolment of 15,820 students, up from just 5,811 a decade before. The Maritime Provinces Higher Education Commission was established in 1974 to control escalating costs and duplication of programs, but university enrolments and budgets continued to rise, making higher education one of the most important industries in the region.

Despite its poor economic prospects, the Atlantic region continued to attract immigrants in the postwar period. War brides, most of them British, and their children were followed by refugees and displaced persons from Europe and domestic workers from the Caribbean. After Canada's immigration laws were liberalized in the 1960s, people from all over the world began arriving in the region. American "draft dodgers" from the Vietnam War (1965–75) slipped across the border and many of them put down roots. With the exception of the Dutch, who tended to take up farming, most immigrants settled in urban centres. The expansion of the medical profession under Medicare attracted immigrant doctors and nurses. Until the 1970s, professors for the region's universities were recruited primarily in Great Britain and the United States.

People's Politics

Businessmen, politicians, and bureaucrats were not the only ones changing the face of Atlantic Canada. Ordinary people also had an impact. In the early years of the Cold War, movements for social reform still faced major challenges. The United States was enthusiastic about rooting out "subversives," and Canadian authorities were prepared to follow suit, purging the civil service, trade unions, universities, voluntary organizations, and the media of anyone deemed too radical. In the 1960s the public mood began to change. Civil rights and liberation movements flourishing in the United States quickly took root in the Atlantic region, aided by the popular medium of television, which broadcast how American protesters were disrupting the status quo.[7]

The labour movement revived, its fortunes reflecting changes in the workforce. From a high of 32 per cent in 1953, union membership dropped to 21 per cent in the early 1960s, but rose again as white-collar workers—teachers, nurses, and government employees—began signing union cards. Workers in what remained of the primary industries also organized more aggressively. By the 1980s Newfoundland had the highest proportion of organized labour in the region—37 per cent—primarily because of a 1971 decision to grant collective bargaining rights in the fishery. The Newfoundland Fishermen, Food, and Allied Workers, under its feisty leader Richard Cashin, fought two successful actions: a strike at Burgeo in 1971 and a massive work stoppage by trawler crews in 1974–5. In Canso a protracted strike led by the United Fishermen and Allied Workers' Union in 1970 won concessions in prices and berthing facilities, only to be challenged by the Canadian Food and Allied Workers Union, which was determined to represent all workers associated with the fisheries.

The tendency of business and government to treat workers as just another natural resource helped to build support for the New Democratic Party (NDP). Created in 1961 through a marriage of the old CCF and organized labour, the NDP gradually gained strength in the Maritimes under its popular first leader, former Saskatchewan premier Tommy Douglas. Support came initially from Cape Breton but soon spread elsewhere as white-collar workers, most notably in Halifax, began reconsidering their traditional political allegiances. At the national level, the NDP's 31 seats proved critical in the close 1972 election, which gave the Liberals a two-seat majority over the Progressive Conservatives.

By the early 1970s Labour was clearly a force to be reckoned with. When Nigadoo Mines near Bathurst, New Brunswick, announced in January 1972 that it was suspending operations and putting 300 employees out of work, there was an angry outburst from locals, who organized a "Day of Concern." Attended by Jean Marchand (the minister responsible for DREE), Premier Hatfield, and the leaders of both federal and provincial opposition parties, it sparked the creation of a $10-million temporary make-work program. Together, the protest and the response it received were testimony to a political climate which accepted that all levels of government had a responsibility to address poverty and unemployment.

The Day of Concern also reflected complex developments in New Brunswick's francophone community. While not all francophones in the Maritimes were descended from pre-deportation

Student unrest hit the Atlantic region in the 1960s and nowhere more dramatically than at the Université de Moncton, where students boycotted classes for 10 days in February 1968 to protest fee increases. Then, with the silent blessing of university presidents in the region, they led a province-wide "sit-in" at government offices in Fredericton. UM-008453, Centre d'études acadiennes Anselme-Chiasson, Université de Moncton.

Acadians, most identified with the deeply rooted Acadian heritage. The commemoration of the deportation in 1955 reinvigorated efforts to improve the status of Acadians in the region, especially in New Brunswick, where one-third of the population identified as francophone. When the election of an Acadian premier in New Brunswick in 1960 coincided with the beginning of the Quiet Revolution in Quebec, the pressure for change was intense.

Many working-class and younger francophones became critical of the gradualist approach taken by their leaders. In 1968 the refusal of Moncton's mayor, Leonard Jones, to consider making the municipality bilingual precipitated a confrontation between the city council and students from the Université de Moncton. Student unrest flared again in January 1972 after a showing of the National Film Board's *L'Acadie, l'Acadie* and, together with the Nigadoo mine closures, inspired the creation of the Parti Acadien. Although its goal was to politicize francophones rather than to win seats, it fielded candidates in provincial elections between 1974 and 1984 and made headlines with its call for a francophone province—"Acadie"—in northeastern New Brunswick. Premier Hatfield's implementation of sections of the Official Languages Act helped to defuse some of the anger while confirming the province's bilingual status.

Fewer in number than their New Brunswick counterparts, francophones in Nova Scotia and Prince Edward Island had more reason to be concerned about cultural survival. Some 90 per cent of people of French heritage in New Brunswick claimed French as their mother tongue in 1960, but only 45 per cent did so in Nova Scotia and Prince Edward Island. In 1967 francophones in Nova Scotia formed the Fédération Acadienne de la Nouvelle-Écosse, and the Société Saint-Thomas-d'Aquin, established in Prince Edward Island in 1919, took on a more active political role. PEI's legislature became officially bilingual in 1968, and all four provinces gradually made concessions in the area of French-language schooling. Francophone groups in Newfoundland and in Labrador began organizing in the early 1970s, forming the Fédération francophone de Terre-Neuve et du Labrador in 1973. With Moncton serving as the capital of the larger regional "Acadie," French-language radio, television, arts, and cultural expression flourished.

As issues of human rights and social justice became part of the political agenda, members of the black minority stepped up their protests against their second-class status. The Nova Scotia government—prompted by a 1954 US Supreme Court decision declaring separate educational facilities to be inherently unequal—quietly dropped a clause in the education act sanctioning separate black schools. The last segregated school was closed in the early 1960s. New Brunswick's smaller black community formed its own Association for the Advancement of Coloured People in 1959. In the 1960s all provinces in the region passed human rights legislation and established monitoring agencies. A federal Bill of Rights was passed in 1960, but it lacked the teeth necessary to force compliance.

Encouraged by the Black Power movement in the United States and galvanized by the decision of Halifax city council to demolish the community of Africville, blacks in Nova Scotia stepped up their efforts to fight discrimination and crippling poverty. The Black United Front (BUF) was founded in Halifax in 1968–9, after a visit to the city by Stokeley Carmichael and other leaders of the Black Panthers. Along with long-time activists such as the Reverend Pearly Oliver and his wife Pearleen, a younger generation, which included Gus Wedderburn, Burnley "Rocky" Jones, and Jules Oliver, sprang into action. This time politicians took notice. Working with grants from the federal and provincial governments, BUF leaders sponsored workshops and projects designed to help African Nova Scotians increase both their self-esteem and their material well-being. The Black Cultural Society, established in 1977, accomplished a major goal in 1983 with the opening of the Black Cultural Centre in Dartmouth.

Like Africville, many black communities near urban centres elsewhere in the Maritimes disappeared in the twentieth century, the result of out-migration and galloping development. The black population of Charlottetown's Bog district, for instance, began to decline in the early twentieth century, and in the 1960s a provincial government building was located on the site that in 1881 had been home to nearly 200 black Islanders. New Brunswick's black population was also reduced by outmigration, much of it to nearby American communities such as Bangor and Boston.[8]

As in earlier periods, black people often found their prospects better elsewhere than in their native region. One example was the Fredericton-born Willie O'Ree, who in 1958 became the

Historical Focus

Africville

The plight of blacks in Nova Scotia came to international attention when the city of Halifax decided to demolish Africville. Located on the shores of Bedford Basin, Africville had been home to Halifax's black population since the mid-nineteenth century. Shamefully neglected, the community existed without water and sewage services; there was no garbage collection, and in the 1950s a municipal dump was located nearby. A serious fire in December 1947 drew attention to the lack of a water supply, but the city authorities did nothing.

In 1962 the city council decided to relocate the residents and use the site for industrial development. The residents, who were not consulted about this decision, erupted in protest. Their plight soon caught the attention of human rights activists throughout North America, and became the subject of commentary on the CBC and in *Maclean's*. Aaron Carvery, the last resident to reach a settlement, was invited to City Hall in December 1969 and shown a "suitcase full of money tied up in neat bundles"—$14,000—as an inducement to move.[9] He eventually received an apology for this outrageous attempt at bribery, but the city pressed on with its plans. Most whites and a few blacks argued that urban renewal was a necessary prelude to a better future for all Haligonians.

Although residents of Africville were compensated for their property and offered alternative housing, they resented their shabby treatment. The use of garbage trucks instead of moving vans to relocate some members of the community seemed to symbolize the city's attitude. The residents also feared the loss of community, but, if anything, the destruction of Africville galvanized a collective spirit. Because of the prolonged struggle, Africville has been immortalized in books, films, and songs. Every year a picnic is held on the site of the former community, part of which is now a park.

Africville was declared a national historic site in 2002 and in 2010 the Halifax Council ratified an official apology for the eviction. As part of a $4.5 million compensation package, a trust was established to build a museum and a replica of the community church on the Africville site.

first—and until 1986 the only—black player in the National Hockey League. Although blind in one eye (as a result of being hit by a puck), he was an exceptional left-winger and played in the junior leagues in Kitchener and Quebec City before being recruited to the Boston Bruins' farm team. He played in two Bruins' games in 1958 and for much of the 1961 season.

Aboriginal people also became more activist. After three centuries of decline, their numbers in the region had begun to increase, reaching 18,000 by 1981. Revisions to the Indian Act in 1951 eliminated some of its more repugnant features and granted women the right to vote in band elections. In 1960 Status Indians were enfranchised. Ottawa's desire to abolish both the Indian Act and Indian status, articulated in a controversial 1969 White Paper, provoked a national effort to redress long-standing grievances and to resist assimilation. By this time, the Union of New Brunswick Indians (1967) and Union of Nova Scotia Indians (1969) had been established.

Canadian courts played a singular role in obliging politicians to take a new approach to Aboriginal rights. In a landmark decision relating to the Nisga'a in British Columbia, the Supreme Court ruled in 1973 that Aboriginal title existed before European colonization. This led the Trudeau government to concede that Ottawa was required to negotiate comprehensive land claims with Aboriginal peoples not already covered by treaties, a ruling that applied to all First Nations in the Atlantic region. While it would take some time to enshrine land and other rights in the Canadian constitution, and even longer to establish these rights through legal action, a new era had dawned in the history of Atlantic Canada's Aboriginal peoples.

In Labrador, more funds were invested in Aboriginal health, education, and housing. In the late 1950s, however, the provincial government decided, in concert with the Grenfell and Moravian missions, to close the northern Inuit settlements of Nutak and Hebron and move their residents to communities farther south. Neither the people who were to be relocated nor the people who were to receive them were consulted. As the Labrador Inuit Association has put it: "The government told [us] that our social and economic welfare would be improved. Instead, a social, cultural and economic disintegration occurred, the effects of which can be felt to this day."[10] In 2005 Premier Danny Williams issued a formal apology on behalf of the government for the way the decision was made and the difficulties that the people and their descendants experienced as a result of the move.

The consequences of relocation were perhaps even more devastating for the semi-nomadic Innu who in the 1960s were settled at Sheshatshiu and Davis Inlet. Arguably, no Aboriginal group in the region suffered more in this period. The distress that accompanied the collapse of the fur trade was compounded by high rates of tuberculosis and the loss of traditional lands—without any compensation—to mining operations in western Labrador, military installations at Goose Bay, and the Churchill Falls project. In 1973 both the Labrador Inuit Association and the Federation of Newfoundland and Labrador Indians were formed. The latter soon split into island and Labrador components, and in 1990 the Labrador Innu adopted the name Innu Nation.

In the Atlantic provinces as across North America, some of the most dramatic developments in the postwar period involved the changing status of women. Women flocked to jobs in the paid labour force and began entering university in unprecedented numbers. With the plummeting birth rate, escalating divorce rate, and the increasing incidence of single motherhood, traditionalists made dire predictions about the future of the family. Most women now had no more than two children, if they had any at all, and increasingly both parents worked outside the home. Spurred by the changes in their lives, Atlantic Canadian women joined their counterparts throughout North

America in breaking down the barriers to achieving equality. By the late 1960s, married women were eligible for civil service jobs that had previously been denied them, and quotas restricting women's entry into law, medical, and engineering schools had disappeared, as had the use of all-male juries in the court system.

The achievement of Helena Squires, who became the region's first elected female politician when she sat in the Newfoundland House of Assembly between 1930 and 1932, was finally matched in Nova Scotia when former Kentville mayor Gladys Porter was elected to the legislature in 1960. In 1953 Muriel McQueen Fergusson, Fredericton's first female "alderman," was named to the Senate, and in 1972 she became its first female speaker. The Royal Commission on the Status of Women, which reported in 1970, eventually prompted provincial governments to establish commissions and advisory councils to address women's issues, to legislate equal pay and a fairer division of marital property upon divorce, and to fund women's centres and shelters.

Another issue that stimulated regional action was world peace. In 1960 Halifax became one of the first cities in Canada to form a branch of the Voice of Women, an organization devoted to peace and disarmament. Three years earlier, Pugwash, Nova Scotia, had been the site of a unique effort to put an end to the nuclear madness that defined the Cold War. Twenty-two scientists from around the world, including the United States and the Soviet Union, converged on the summer home of the Nova Scotia–born industrialist Cyrus Eaton to discuss nuclear disarmament. In 1995 the Pugwash Conference on Science and World Affairs, which had met periodically since 1957, was awarded the Nobel Peace Prize for its efforts on behalf of world peace.

Environmental issues also became increasingly important. In the 1950s, fish and game associations in New Brunswick called attention to the decline of salmon populations caused by the use of DDT to control the spruce budworm that competed with pulp and paper companies for softwood. Scientists soon began making connections between insecticides and ecological integrity generally, but the provincial government and Forest Protection Limited, the company formed to conduct the spraying, remained committed to the program. In 1962 the issue received international attention when Rachel Carson, in her ground-breaking book *Silent Spring*, singled out the "rivers of death" created in New Brunswick by aerial pesticide spraying.

In 1969 groups opposed to the spraying program established the Conservation Council of New Brunswick, one of the first environmental organizations in Canada to take a stand against governments that refused to consider what increasingly seemed to be prudent policies. The Hatfield government passed a Pesticides Control Act in 1973 but protests continued, especially after scientists discovered a link between pesticides and Reye's syndrome. In Nova Scotia, the "budworm battles" heated up when Elizabeth May, who had immigrated to Cape Breton from the United States with her family in 1972, led a similar campaign beginning in 1975.[11]

At the same time, animal rights groups mounted a high-profile attack on the seal hunt, arguing in particular that the clubbing of seal pups was cruel and unnecessary. Greenpeace, an activist environmental organization founded in the early 1970s, joined in, bringing French movie star Brigitte Bardot to the ice floes in 1977 and calling for boycotts of seal products in Europe and the United States. Newfoundlanders were outraged both by the threat that the anti-sealing campaign posed to the rural economy and by what they saw as an unwarranted, condescending, and insulting attack on a distinct culture. Among the responses was a theatre production entitled *They Club Seals, Don't They?* by the Mummers' Troupe in St John's, which toured Canada.

Cultural Awakenings

For many Atlantic Canadians in this period, and especially for the baby boomers who came of age in the 1960s, life was defined as much by popular culture as by political developments. Elders were alarmed by what they saw as rampant hedonism, but there was little they could do to stem the tide of mass consumer culture. Standoffs between teachers and students over the length of boys' hair (too long) and girls' skirts (too short) became common, as did debates between parents and their teenage children over pre-marital sex and the volume settings on transistor radios and record players. In many recreational settings, the scent of marijuana smoke wafted gently on the air. It was the age of sex, drugs, and rock 'n roll.

The sexual revolution was sustained in large measure by the introduction of the birth control pill in the early 1960s. Even though the dissemination of birth control remained illegal, doctors prescribed the pill, women embraced it, and the average size of families almost instantly declined. The legal proscription against birth control was finally dropped from the Criminal Code in 1969, in an omnibus bill that also reformed the laws relating to homosexual relations and abortion. Gays and lesbians began "coming out of the closet," the official rates of abortion increased dramatically, and (the divorce law having been reformed the previous year) divorce rates skyrocketed.

With improvements in education, nation-wide radio and television broadcasting, and federal support for Canadian content, Atlantic Canadians experienced a cultural awakening.

In 1944 the Nova Scotia-born contralto Portia White (1910–68), who had already won national acclaim, made her New York debut. She later toured the United States, Europe, and the Caribbean. Library and Archives Canada/Yousuf Karsh fonds/PA-192783

Anne Murray rose to international fame in 1969 with "Snowbird," composed by Prince Edward Island's Gene MacLellan. Carroll Baker won numerous Juno Awards, Stompin' Tom Connors became a Canadian icon, and although Stan Rogers grew up in Ontario, many of his songs were inspired by his Maritime roots. Edith Butler introduced Acadian folk songs to international audiences and, along with Prince Edward Island's Angèle Arsenault, composed new songs documenting the Acadian perspective on the world. In their wake came a whole host of Acadian singers and songwriters. The success of Portia White, a gifted contralto who performed at New York's Carnegie Hall in 1944, set the stage for a better reception for the region's black musicians.

Local traditions also flourished with the boom in popular culture, in particular Celtic music, which had deep roots in much of the region. In the 1970s two Cape Bretoners, John Allan Cameron and Rita McNeil, embarked on life-long careers in music. They were soon followed by, among others, the Barra MacNeils, the Rankin Family, Ashley MacIsaac, Scott MacMillan, and Natalie MacMaster.[12] From Newfoundland, the Wonderful Grand Band, Figgy Duff, and Rawlins Cross became well known throughout the region and beyond. With the production of his first album, *Discovery* (1972), Newfoundland's Ron Hynes, a member of The Wonderful Grand Band, emerged as one of Canada's most talented singer-songwriters.

The opening of Fredericton's Beaverbrook Art Gallery in 1959 was a highlight for the Canadian arts community in this period. Financially supported by its generous namesake, the Beaverbrook and other galleries also benefited from grants awarded by the Canada Council. Founded by the federal government in 1957, the Canada Council was endowed with funds from the windfall estate taxes of two Maritime-born entrepreneurs, Isaac Walton Killam and Sir James Dunn. Canada Council grants also supported the founding of Halifax's Neptune Theatre, opened in 1963, and the Confederation Centre of the Arts (home of the Charlottetown Festival) opened the following year, during the centennial of the Charlottetown Conference. Theatre New Brunswick followed in 1968. The previous year, a large Arts and Culture Centre opened in St John's, which showcased an increasingly important Newfoundland art scene and provided a forum for local theatre. The success of the comedy groups CODCO and the Mummers' Troupe, based in a former downtown union hall, laid the groundwork for more ambitious ventures later in the century.

In the postwar period a new cultural maturity was being reflected in the regionally grounded work of poets and novelists such as Milton Acorn, Ernest Buckler, Harold Horwood, Percy Janes, Antonine Maillet, Alden Nowlan, and Ted Russell. Regional themes also inspired filmmakers.

Biography *Antonine Maillet*

Born in Bouctouche, New Brunswick, in 1929, Antonine Maillet gained international acclaim by giving an imaginative voice to Acadians in Atlantic Canada. Her plays, short stories, and novels were inspired by her Acadian roots, which offered plenty of drama for her creative genius.

Although her writing career began in the late 1950s, the research she conducted for her 1970 PhD dissertation in literature at Laval University deepened the quality of her work. Published in 1971 as *Rabelais et les traditions populaires en Acadie*, it catalogued more than 500 archaic phrases and figures of speech from sixteenth-century French that were still used in the Acadian communities. She brought this knowledge to *La Sagouine* (1971), a series of humorous monologues presented by an old Acadian washerwoman. The play highlighted the unique Acadian dialect and was performed in both French and English throughout North America and Europe by Viola Léger.

In 1972 Maillet followed up this success with the fantastic tale of *Don L'Orignal* (1972), which won the Governor General's Award for Fiction (French). Her 1979 epic novel *Pélagie-la Charette*, chronicling the story of the 10-year odyssey of a group of Acadians returning to their homeland 15 years after their expulsion, won her the prestigious French Prix Goncourt. Now living in Montreal, Maillet represents the best of the Acadian cultural revival that continues to inspire extraordinary talent.[14]

Don Shebib's award-winning film *Goin' Down the Road* (1970) exposed the plight of working-class Maritimers in Ontario,[13] and Gordon Pinsent's *John and the Missus* (1974) was a gripping portrayal of outport resettlement in Newfoundland.

In this period, Alex Colville and his students at Mount Allison University, including Christopher Pratt, Mary Pratt, and Tom Forrestall, developed representational art in a direction that has come to be called "Atlantic realism." New Brunswick artists such as Miller Brittain often portrayed the harsher side of Maritime life as did David Blackwood, who gained widespread acclaim for his images of the seal hunt and other aspects of traditional life on Newfoundland's northeast coast. In Prince Edward Island, artists such as Erica Rutherford revealed new ways of looking at the Island's landscape. By the end of the twentieth century, Aboriginal artists who had long been excluded from formal channels of art education and marketing in the region began to exhibit their work, among them Ned Bear, Shirley Bear, Teresa Marshall, Leonard Paul, Jonathan Sark, Alan Syliboy, and Gilbert Hay. The region's self-taught folk artists, including Maud Lewis, Joseph Norris, Arch Williams, and Joseph Cullen, added yet another dimension of locally rooted artistic expression.

Conclusion

In the period from 1949 to 1975, Atlantic Canadians experienced significant economic and social change. The majority of people now lived in urban centres and no longer made a living in primary industries; minorities were empowered to protest their subordination; and formal training came to be seen as the key to making a decent living. At the same time, many of the old economic and social patterns remained in place. Out-migration was slowing but not halted, economic stagnation was confronted but not vanquished, and "have-not" status was still an ever-present reality. What *was* striking about the period, in retrospect, was the conviction that progress was possible. The closing years of the twentieth century would test the convictions of even the most determined optimist.

Further Readings

Acadiensis XXXV, 2 (Spring 2006), special issue on Atlantic Canada since 1939.

Bickerton, James P. 1990. *Nova Scotia, Ottawa, and the Politics of Regional Development.* Toronto: University of Toronto Press.

Conrad, Margaret. 1988. *George Nowlan: Maritime Conservative in Maritime Politics.* Toronto: University of Toronto Press.

Fingard, Judith, and Janet Guildford, eds. 2005. *Mothers of the Municipality: Women, Work, and Social Policy In Post-1945 Halifax.* Toronto: University of Toronto Press.

Fleming, Berkeley. 1988. *Beyond Anger and Longing: Community and Development in Atlantic Canada.* Sackville and Fredericton: Centre for Canadian Studies, Mount Allison University and Acadiensis Press.

Kent, Peter C. 2012. *Inventing Academic Freedom: The 1968 Strax Affair at the University of New Brunswick.* Halifax: Formac.

MacDonald, Edward. 2000. *If You're Stronghearted: Prince Edward Island in the Twentieth Century.* Charlottetown: Prince Edward Island Museum and Heritage Foundation.

Overton, James. 1996. *Making A World of Difference: Essays on Tourism, Culture and Development in Newfoundland.* St John's: Institute of Social and Economic Research.

Pachai, Bridglal. 2007. *The Nova Scotia Black Experience Through the Ages.* Halifax: Nimbus.

Smitheram, Verner, David Milne, and Satadal Dasgupta, eds. 1982. *The Garden Transformed: Prince Edward Island, 1945–1980.* Charlottetown: Ragweed Press.

Stanley, Della M.M. 1984. *Louis Robichaud: A Decade of Power.* Halifax: Nimbus Publishing.

Wright, Miriam. 2001. *A Fishery for Modern Times: The State and Industrialization of the Newfoundland Fishery, 1934–1968.* Don Mills: Oxford University Press.

Historical Spotlight

Edward MacDonald, "A Landscape . . . with Figures: Tourism and Environment in Prince Edward Island," *Acadiensis* XXXX, 1 (Winter/Spring 2011): 70–85.

Morton, Suzanne. 2005. "Managing the Unmarried Mother "Problem": Halifax Maternity Homes," in *Mothers of the Municipality: Women, Work and Social Policy in Post-1945*, ed. Judith Fingard and Janet Guildford. *Halifax.* Toronto: University of Toronto Press, 110–140.

Recommended Websites

Black Cultural Centre for Nova Scotia
http://www.bccns.com

Churchill Falls
http://www.heritage.nf.ca/law/cfimpacts.html

Thinkers Lodge (Pugwash Conference)
http://thinkerslodge.org/about/national-historic-site

Chapter 15

Atlantic Canada in the Global Village, 1975–2001

In 1973 a global oil crisis precipitated by the Organization of Petroleum Exporting Countries (OPEC) brought an end to the postwar boom. Oil prices rose sharply, throwing industrial economies into a tailspin. Faced with rising government deficits and "stagflation"—a combination of runaway inflation, slow economic growth, and high unemployment—Ottawa imposed wage and price controls in 1975. Long alarmed by the degree of state intervention justified by Keynesian economic principles, many in the corporate sector and on the political right now urged the adoption of neo-liberal policies to address the economic crisis—lower taxes, smaller government, privatization, deregulation, and free trade. As policy-makers began to focus on "restructuring" to accommodate the new reality, assistance to the poor, the unemployed, and outlying regions was increasingly questioned. Atlantic Canadians seemed to have no option but to adjust to "globalization," the code word for imposing free-market principles not merely on international trade relations, but also on the internal affairs of nations everywhere.[1]

Setting the Context

The Information Age

The closing decades of the twentieth century brought dramatic changes in information and communications technologies. With satellites, high-speed computers, and the Internet connecting people around the world in seconds by the end of the 1990s, the pace of change accelerated. Finding information was facilitated by the World Wide Web, a system of hyperlinked documents accessed via the Internet. In the 1990s web search engines such as Yahoo! and Google made knowledge easier to access, and "virtual" networks facilitated collaboration across vast distances. In this context it became essential to engage the new communications technologies or be left behind.[2]

As historians were quick to point out, this communications breakthrough was only the latest in a process of global integration set in motion 500 years earlier, when Europeans began using new technologies to extend their power. The invention of the printing press in the mid-fifteenth century and the development of more seaworthy vessels made possible a new stage in the compression of time and space that is the defining feature of globalization. In the eighteenth century, printed texts in the form of pamphlets, books, and newspapers became

Continued

essential tools in the pursuit of power and in supporting the activities of ever-expanding bureaucratic states and businesses. In the nineteenth century, railways, steamships, the telegraph, and the telephone further reduced the time it took to "spread the word."

By the end of the twentieth century the world had become what the Canadian communications theorist Marshall McLuhan called a "global village." Events anywhere could be communicated instantaneously by radio, television, and, increasingly, the Internet. As Atlantic Canadians felt the impact of the "Information Age," they faced new challenges no less daunting than those that had accompanied the Industrial Revolution in the nineteenth century.

Launching the Neo-Liberal Order

The elections of Margaret Thatcher in Great Britain (1979), Ronald Reagan in the United States (1980), and Brian Mulroney in Canada (1984) marked the arrival of a neo-liberal order in the Western world that was reinforced in 1989 by the collapse of communism in Eastern Europe. Neo-liberals in Canada—represented most directly by the Business Council on National Issues, founded in 1976—hammered home the message that lower taxes, fewer regulations, and greater power for private interests were more effective for the national economy than government "handouts"— though many companies in the private sector were happy to take them. The Atlantic region offered empirical evidence that unfettered free enterprise did little to counter regional underdevelopment, but neo-liberals were deaf to arguments that contradicted their theories.[3]

The neo-liberal turn in Canada was launched in a typically bureaucratic way. In 1982 Prime Minister Pierre Elliott Trudeau appointed a Royal Commission on the Economic Union and Development Prospects for Canada, chaired by the former Liberal Finance Minister Donald Macdonald. The commission's report, submitted in 1985, was strongly influenced by neo-liberal thinking, supporting demands for a more "flexible" economy that could adjust to global trends and new technologies. In addition to recommending free trade with the United States, the commission called for an end to universal welfare state programs and raised the possibility of a guaranteed minimum annual income to mitigate the pain of restructuring, though this suggestion was quickly abandoned. The principle of regional equity did not generate much interest among the commissioners.

The Mulroney government, which came to office in 1984 with an overwhelming majority, including 25 of the Atlantic region's 32 seats, moved quickly to implement the commission's recommendations. A comprehensive free trade agreement with the United States was concluded in the autumn of 1987 and a hard-fought federal election, held a year later, was essentially a referendum on what had become a highly contentious issue. Although the Progressive Conservatives received only 43 per cent of the popular vote, Canadians opposed to free trade split their votes between the Liberals and the NDP. The agreement went into effect in January 1989 and in 1994 was extended to Mexico, in accordance with the North American Free Trade Agreement (NAFTA) signed in 1992. No longer sheltered by tariff walls, many Canadian companies moved their operations to countries offering lower wage scales and fewer regulations.

The Atlantic premiers made no coordinated effort to influence the Macdonald Commission's deliberations or the way its recommendations were implemented. In the 1988 federal election, the

Bruce MacKinnon, "Oh Please, Oh Please," 1992. As this award-winning cartoon, published in the *Halifax Herald*, suggests, regional fortunes were increasingly tied to those of the United States following the Free Trade agreements of 1989 and 1992. Republished with permission from The Halifax Herald Limited.

popular vote in Atlantic Canada favoured the Liberals, though not by a wide margin. The Progressive Conservative Party received more than 40 per cent of the votes in all four provinces and 12 of the region's 32 seats. Since all but 6 constituencies in Western Canada and 12 in Quebec were won by the Progressive Conservatives, there would be no turning back on free trade.

Ottawa's attention, meanwhile, was increasingly preoccupied by Quebec and the western provinces. In 1976 René Levesque led the Parti Québécois to power, with the goal of achieving independence for Quebec. The sovereignty referendum of 1980 focused attention across Canada on the possibility of the breakup of the country and compelled Ottawa to try to address Quebec's concerns. At the same time, a new phase of "Western alienation" erupted in the context of the oil crisis, and was exacerbated by the Trudeau government's implementation of the National Energy Program (NEP) in 1982. Designed to establish lower-than-world prices for oil in Canada, to increase Canadian ownership of the resource, and to sustain federal revenues in the face of crippling deficits, the NEP set off a fire-storm in the Western provinces, which would have to bear much of the financial burden.

Outraged by this and other policies that seemed to favour central Canada, Progressive Conservatives in the west embraced their own regionally oriented party led by Preston Manning, the son of a former premier of Alberta. Founded in 1987, the Reform Party quickly attracted so much support, especially in Alberta and British Columbia, that in the 1993 election it effectively supplanted the Progressive Conservatives in Ottawa. Staunch proponents of the neo-liberal agenda, Reformers were outspoken in their criticism of big government. The new Liberal government led by Jean Chrétien was obliged to pay attention.

Table 15.1 Timeline

1973	Global oil crisis ends postwar boom.
1976	Parti Québécois wins power in Quebec.
1977	200-mile marine limit declared.
1980	Quebec referendum on sovereignty-association.
1982	Constitution Act; 84 crew members lost on the *Ocean Ranger*.
1985	Atlantic Accord; Report of the Royal Commission on the Economic Union and Development Prospects for Canada (Macdonald Commission).
1987	Atlantic Canada Opportunities Agency established; Reform Party founded; Meech Lake Accord.
1988	Canada–US Free Trade Agreement signed.
1992	Cod moratorium; Charlottetown Accord; North American Free Trade Agreement signed; oil production begins off Sable Island.
1993	Westray Mine disaster kills 26 men.
1994	Voisey's Bay nickel deposit discovered.
1995	Second Quebec referendum; Spanish trawler *Estai* seized for fisheries violations.
1997	Confederation Bridge opens; oil production begins at the Hibernia field.
1999	Supreme Court decision in the Marshall case.
2002	Undersea boundary arbitration award between Newfoundland/Labrador and Nova Scotia

Federalism in Transition

Federal politics in the last two decades of the twentieth century were complicated by constitutional manoeuvres. With the defeat of sovereignty association in the 1980 Quebec referendum, Trudeau decided to move ahead with patriating the constitution, unilaterally if necessary. The concept of replacing the British North America Act with a Canadian statute was not controversial in itself, but earlier attempts to do so had been derailed by the challenge of finding an amending formula that would satisfy both the federal government and the provinces. In addition, Trudeau wanted the constitution to include a Charter of Rights and Freedoms, a proposal that Quebec and most other provinces believed would curtail provincial powers. Only Progressive Conservative premiers Richard Hatfield in New Brunswick and William Davis in Ontario, were initially prepared to support the legislation. Since most provincial governments thought unilateral federal action would be unconstitutional, they called in the lawyers.

The Supreme Court eventually ruled that the support of a majority of provinces was sufficient to move ahead with constitutional reform, and the premiers and the prime minister met in November 1981. A compromise agreement was reached during the night of 4 November, at an informal meeting attended by three Atlantic premiers—Brian Peckford of Newfoundland, John Buchanan of Nova Scotia, and J. Angus MacLean of Prince Edward Island. Peckford claimed, perhaps with some exaggeration, that they worked from a proposal developed by the Newfoundland delegation, and that with some amendments the compromise became the basis of the Constitution Act, 1982.[4] Whatever its origins it was accepted by all provinces except, significantly, Quebec.

In Atlantic Canada the new constitutional arrangements were welcomed. Most people in the region embraced the Charter of Rights and Freedoms, which enshrined the basic human rights to freedom and equality that had informed public policy in Canada since the UN Declaration of 1948. While controversial in some circles, the new constitution included a series of clauses entrenching New Brunswick's bilingual status and affirmed Aboriginal treaty rights. In addition, the Act included a section obliging the federal government to support equal opportunities and services across the country, and to respect "the principle of making equalization payments."

The rights of provinces large and small were carefully calibrated in the amending formula. For amendments other than those affecting representation in the House of Commons, Senate, and the Supreme Court, which required unanimous consent, the approval of the federal Parliament was necessary, plus two-thirds of the provinces representing 50 per cent of all Canadians. In addition, any province that considered its legislative or proprietary rights to be compromised by an amendment could declare it null and void within its boundaries.

Document

The Constitution and Equalization, 1982

The Atlantic provinces played a central role, along with Manitoba and Saskatchewan, in securing a clause in the Constitution Act, 1982, entrenching Ottawa's obligation to support equalization as a means of muting regional disparities. Part III, article 36 of the Act reads:

EQUALIZATION AND REGIONAL DISPARITIES

I. Commitment to promote equal opportunities

(1) Without altering the legislative authority of Parliament or of the provincial legislatures, or the rights of any of them with respect to the exercise of their legislative authority, Parliament and the legislatures, together with the government of Canada and the provincial governments, are committed to

  (a) promoting equal opportunities for the well-being of Canadians;

  (b) furthering economic development to reduce disparity in opportunities; and

  (c) providing essential public services of reasonable quality to all Canadians.

II. Commitment respecting public services

(1) Parliament and the government of Canada are committed to the principle of making equalization payments to ensure that provincial governments have sufficient revenues to provide reasonably comparable levels of public services at reasonably comparable levels of taxation.

To date there is little case law on this federal obligation, and wrangling over equalization remains a perennial feature of Canadian federalism.

Mulroney and Meech

Less confrontational than Trudeau, Brian Mulroney pursued a more conciliatory approach to provincial relations, especially with respect to his home province of Quebec, which he desperately wanted to "bring into the constitution." The result was a constitutional agreement, negotiated at Meech Lake in 1987, that reflected a set of basic demands formulated by a cautiously federalist Liberal government in Quebec led by Robert Bourassa. The accord recognized Quebec as "a distinct society" with special powers, and this provision was initially accepted by all the premiers, including those from Atlantic Canada, who had reason to fear the prospect of Quebec independence. The 1982 amending formula required each province to ratify the accord within three years—a long time in politics.

The governments of Nova Scotia and Prince Edward Island, led by Progressive Conservative premier John Buchanan and Liberal premier Joe Ghiz respectively, remained committed to the accord, but the governments changed in New Brunswick and Newfoundland before the 1990 ratification deadline. In New Brunswick, where Frank McKenna's Liberals took every seat in the fall 1987 election, the government came under intense pressure from a variety of directions but especially from Acadians, who were concerned that a special deal for Quebec would leave them out in the cold. Nevertheless, after proposing a "companion accord" that was rejected by Quebec, McKenna eventually supported ratification.

In Newfoundland, the legislature ratified the accord in 1988, but the next year Brian Peckford—haunted by the province's chronic economic difficulties and a foolhardy scheme to grow cucumbers in a huge hydroponic greenhouse—retired from politics. The Liberals, led by Clyde Wells, won the ensuing election. A strong federalist, Wells quickly emerged as an articulate opponent of the accord. He thought it would make future constitutional amendments almost impossible, impose restrictions on federal spending that could harm the "have-not" provinces, and give Quebec a special status that could undermine the Charter of Rights and Freedoms. Wells therefore rescinded his province's ratification and, since there was no time for a provincial referendum, announced a free vote on the accord in the legislature. In the end, the vote did not take place because the accord was rejected by the Manitoba legislature. Mulroney nevertheless laid much of the blame for the debacle on Wells.

Refusing to give up, Mulroney orchestrated a second attempt to reach a constitutional package that would satisfy both Quebec and the rest of the country. Negotiations were held in Charlottetown, where another agreement was reached in 1992. Although Wells accepted the Charlottetown Accord because it included a new definition of Quebec's "distinct society" status, he, like the western premiers, was disappointed that its proposals for Senate reform fell short of a "Triple-E Senate"—equal, elected, effective. In a national referendum held in October, the accord was narrowly defeated in Nova Scotia and approved only in New Brunswick, Newfoundland, Prince Edward Island, and Ontario. The Atlantic region's response seemed to reflect a general desire to finish the constitutional business so that policy-makers could turn their attention to more pressing matters.

Quebec's reaction to constitutional reform had major implications for the dynamics of federal politics. After the Meech Lake failure, Lucien Bouchard resigned from Mulroney's cabinet to lead the Bloc Québécois, a new party determined to seek independence for Quebec. The Bloc won 54 of Quebec's 75 seats in the 1993 federal election, becoming the official opposition with just two more seats than the Reform Party. The Parti Québécois was elected to power provincially the following year and in 1995 held a second referendum on sovereignty, which was defeated by the slimmest of margins.

The seemingly endless constitutional wrangling exasperated many voters who had become tired of Quebec's special pleading and had never been comfortable with bilingualism. The Confederation of Regions Party (CoR), founded in 1984, made opposition to bilingualism a central plank in its platform, but it received less than 1 per cent of the vote in the 1984 and 1988 federal elections. In the west, where the party received much of its support, CoR was quickly gobbled up by the Reform Party, but it took on new life in New Brunswick. A provincial branch of CoR was established in 1989 and two years later it won eight seats in the provincial election, becoming the official opposition to McKenna's Liberals. Soon racked by internal divisions, CoR never again won a seat in the province and was formally dissolved in 2002.[5] The party's brief success was a reflection of the resentment among a minority of anglophones that New Brunswick's bilingual status was now a constitutional reality accepted by both mainline parties.

The Liberal Party managed to retain power in Ottawa until 2006, largely because of support from Ontario. Conservative forces, meanwhile, became more purposeful in their strategies. In 1998, newspaper baron Conrad Black founded the *National Post* as a vehicle for "uniting the right," while the Reform Party, which had become the official opposition in 1997, morphed into the Canadian Reform Conservative Alliance Party (commonly called the Canadian Alliance) in 2000 in an effort to attract wider support. The Progressive Conservative Party, which remained popular in Atlantic Canada, limped along under the leadership of former Prime Minister Joe Clark from 1998 to 2003 and then under Nova Scotia MP Peter MacKay, but clearly the days of the "red Tories" were numbered.

More Adjustments

The Mulroney government failed to achieve its goal of eliminating the federal deficit, but it began the process of fiscal reform. Business taxes were reduced and federal estate taxes, disliked by wealthy citizens, were eliminated. In 1991 a Goods and Services Tax (GST) was implemented, a policy in line with the Macdonald Commission's recommendation that there should be a shift from direct to indirect taxation. Workers felt the pinch of the restructuring exercise when the unemployment insurance program, essential to seasonal industries, was scaled back. To the dismay of many Atlantic Canadians, Ottawa passed new regulations allowing Canadian National Railways to reduce the number of its lines in the region, close its repair shops in Moncton, and abandon rail service in Newfoundland altogether. Funding for the Atlantic Canada Opportunities Agency (ACOA), the regional successor to DREE, was cut, while several military bases were closed and others downsized. Against a backdrop of a national recession, high interest rates, and relentless cuts in federal expenditures, provincial resources were strained to the breaking point and lines at food banks and welfare offices lengthened.

By 1993 the country had had enough of the Mulroney government's neo-liberal nostrums; in the election of that year only two Progressive Conservative MPs survived, one of whom was Elsie Wayne from Saint John. The election of the Liberals under Jean Chrétien made little difference in the general thrust of national policy. Indeed, the Chrétien government was possibly more ruthless than its predecessor. Although international financial circles applauded when Finance Minister Paul Martin managed to rein in the deficit by the end of the 1990s, governments in the "have-not" provinces were less enthusiastic.

In the face of growing deficits, the governments of all four Atlantic provinces sought to balance their budgets by reducing costs in the areas that absorbed most of their funds: medical care, education, and social services. The numbers of public employees were reduced through layoffs and early retirement packages, and those who remained were handed either wage freezes or very limited increases. Collective agreements were typically ignored. Not surprisingly, there were angry demonstrations in front of provincial legislatures, but full employment was no longer a goal of government policy. Instead, departments and services were reorganized to save money and reduce taxes. As the numbers of teachers, medical workers, and civil servants declined, services suffered and so did the regional economy, which in the past had been buoyed by government spending.

Provincial reforms brought deep changes to the region. In Newfoundland, the Wells government began the contentious process of dismantling the denominational school system, and health care systems everywhere were downsized. Grants to universities fell, forcing steep rises in tuition fees. The amalgamation of municipalities was promoted, enabling cities such as Halifax and Saint John to expand their control over surrounding areas. In Nova Scotia and New Brunswick, school buildings were outsourced to private companies and toll highways were constructed. Taxes and fees increased for citizens but not for businesses, which were courted in every province in the hope of creating and retaining jobs. Under the resourceful Frank McKenna, New Brunswick capitalized on its bilingual status to attract call centres, which were criticized for their employment practices,[6] but welcomed by young people eager to work in their home province.

As the neo-liberal agenda worked its way through the regional economy, population growth in the Maritimes slowed to a crawl, with New Brunswick and Nova Scotia suffering slight declines between 1996 and 2001. Newfoundland's population fell by 10 per cent during the 1990s, the exodus prompted by a crisis in the fisheries. Long accustomed to roaming North America in search of work, Atlantic Canadians increasingly found it in Alberta. Fort McMurray, a sleepy town of less than 2,000 in 1961, expanded to nearly 45,000 by 1991 and its population would double again by 2011. Located near the huge reserves of the Alberta tar sands, Fort McMurray became home for some Atlantic Canadians, but many others commuted to their jobs by scheduled or chartered flights.

In Prince Edward Island, J. Angus MacLean, a veteran of the Diefenbaker government, led the Progressive Conservatives to victory on a platform of "rural renewal" in 1979. His efforts to slow the tide of modernity included placing a moratorium on new shopping malls, breaking a contract with New Brunswick to purchase energy from its Point Lepreau nuclear power plant, and the passage of a Land Protection Act that restricted individual and corporate land holdings. The restriction was in part aimed at another New Brunswick interest: the powerful Irvings, who were building up their landholdings to support their processing operations. Although Prince Edward Island seemed to weather the adjustment process better than its neighbours, the Liberal government led by Catherine Callbeck, elected in 1992, had little alternative but to impose a tough neo-liberal agenda in response to federal downsizing. Callbeck was Canada's first elected female premier, but this status did little to enhance her popularity in the face of swingeing cutbacks. She was forced to retire before the 1996 election, which was won by the Progressive Conservatives, led by Pat Binns. A native of Saskatchewan, he remained in office until 2007.

Nova Scotia voters increasingly warmed to the NDP, especially in the Halifax area, where party leader Alexa McDonough held a seat from 1980 until 1994, when she stepped down to become her party's national leader. The good-natured Progressive Conservative Premier John Buchanan won successive elections from 1978 to 1990, but his successor, Donald Cameron, quickly lost ground to Dr John Savage's Liberals. Although Savage won the 1993 election he too found it impossible to satisfy voter demands in an era of government restraint, and in 1998 the Liberals and NDP each won 19 seats, forcing another election the following year in which the Progressive Conservatives, led by another medical doctor, John Hamm, won a majority government. In New Brunswick, McKenna held on until 1997 before retiring to the private sector, leaving his successor to face defeat two years later by the Progressive Conservatives under the leadership of the 33-year-old Bernard Lord.

Clyde Wells resigned late in 1995 to be replaced as Newfoundland's premier by the energetic Brian Tobin, who was immensely popular in the province because of his handling of the foreign overfishing issue as federal fisheries minister. He easily defeated the Progressive Conservatives in February 1996. Tobin brought an end to the province's entrenched and expensive denominational school system, against strenuous opposition from the Pentecostal and Roman Catholic churches. In an attempt to appease the increasingly alienated people of Labrador, he arranged to change the province's name to "Newfoundland and Labrador." By the time the change took effect in 2001 Tobin had resigned to run in the federal election of 2000.

Crisis in the Fisheries

The challenges of neo-liberalism were compounded by the collapse of the east coast fisheries. With little regulation and unenforceable quotas, an international assault on the fish stocks off Canada's east coast had begun during the 1950s. Sophisticated fishing vessels from Canada, Western Europe, Iceland, the Soviet Union, and elsewhere fished indiscriminately and intensively, with little regard for the health of the stocks. Haddock and redfish were the first species to become commercially extinct. In the mid-1970s the Canadian government called for a reduction in cod fishing, but several countries refused to comply.

Faced with this intransigence, Canada declared a 200-mile (370-km) marine limit in 1977, a policy urged by New Brunswick MP Roméo LeBlanc, the minister of fisheries for most of the period between 1974 and 1982. Foreign vessels were allowed access only to so-called "surplus" fish and "underutilized species" in this zone, which represented a vast new frontier for fishermen in the Atlantic region. Between 1974 and 1980, the number of Atlantic Canadians engaged in the fishing industry rose from about 31,000 to nearly 55,000 and Canada emerged as the world's leading fish-exporting country, with the Atlantic provinces accounting for 65 per cent of the national total. LeBlanc's popularity soared, especially among the inshore fishermen, who were soon feeling the pinch of declining fish stocks and corporate competition. During his term of office, LeBlanc introduced a new licensing system, imposed quotas and zones to protect the fisheries from over-expansion and foreign operators, and established advisory committees to give fishermen a larger voice in the management of the resource. This was not enough to save the inshore fishery or the people who made a living from it.

After a restructuring in 1982, the fisheries were dominated by two large corporations, National Sea Products and Fishery Products International, which demanded and were granted access to more fish. Overly generous quotas, foreign overfishing, and a series of cold years in the 1980s put more pressure on the cod stocks than they could bear. By the end of the 1980s, quotas were cut—but too modestly—and fish processing operations began to close. In 1992 Fisheries Minister John Crosbie, now an MP from St John's, announced a two-year moratorium on fishing northern cod; he later imposed stringent quotas on other stocks. With 1,300

Atlantic communities almost entirely dependent on the fishery, its collapse precipitated a crisis of unprecedented proportions. In Newfoundland, where much of the expansion in the fishery had occurred, as many as 30,000 people were thrown out of work, and the survival of some communities became doubtful, especially as the moratorium (which remains in force) was renewed from year to year. Newfoundland's population dropped dramatically in the 1990s and still has not regained its pre-moratorium level.

The vision for the future was a much smaller, professional fishing industry without part-time operators. Downsizing was accomplished in part by voluntary departures and in part by the retraining of former fisheries workers for other occupations, a program made possible by a generous compensation package from the federal government. Licensing and professionalization became mandatory, each fisher being allocated an Individual Transferable Quota as part of a drive to create a self-regulating fish-harvesting market—a form of privatization and downloading that was very much in the neo-liberal spirit. In Newfoundland, the number of fish licences fell from 24,409 in 1991 to 14,385 in 2001, and the number of fishing vessels by more than 6,000. At the same time, the value of fish landings increased from about $262 million to $519 million as the industry began to concentrate on crab and shrimp.

Brian Tobin goes to war, 1995. After the Spanish fishing vessel *Estai* was towed to St John's, Fisheries Minister Brian Tobin showed off the illegal nets found on board at a press conference in New York City. He famously announced: "We're down now to one last, lonely, unloved, unattractive little turbot clinging on by its fingernails to the Grand Banks of Newfoundland." The publicity stunt brought international attention to the issue of over-fishing in the North Atlantic. CP PICTURE ARCHIVE, AP/Richard Drew.

In the region, much of the blame for the crisis was placed on the federal government, which had obviously mishandled fisheries conservation, but hostility was also expressed towards foreign (mainly European) vessels fishing just outside the 200-mile limit on the Nose and Tail of the Grand Banks and on the Flemish Cap. In 1992 the premiers of Newfoundland and Nova Scotia demanded naval intervention, but Ottawa refused to extend custodial management beyond the 200-mile limit, preferring diplomatic initiatives. The North Atlantic Fisheries Organization (NAFO)—which set voluntary quotas outside the 200-mile limit—and the countries it represented were reluctant to impose conservation measures.

NAFO set a reduced quota for turbot in 1995, but even that was rejected by Spain and Portugal, backed by the European Union. The Canadian government, in which Brian Tobin was fisheries minister, decided that aggressive action was needed. After an armed standoff early in March 1995, Canadian vessels arrested the Spanish trawler *Estai* just outside the 200-mile limit and escorted it to St John's. Officers found

The Confederation Bridge linked the mainland to Prince Edward Island in 1997. Barrett & Mackay Photography Inc.

nets with undersized mesh and false bulkheads to hide illegally caught fish. A brief and explosive diplomatic crisis followed, but eventually agreement was reached on measures to control fishing on the Grand Banks more effectively.[7]

The imposition of a 200-mile limit also escalated the long-standing dispute between Newfoundland and Nova Scotia over the undersea boundary between them. With both fish and petroleum resources in question, there was a lot at stake. An arbitration tribunal awarded most of the potentially rich area to Newfoundland and Labrador in 2002. Ottawa's distribution of scarce fish quotas in the Gulf of St Lawrence was another continuing source of tensions among competing fishers from Quebec, Newfoundland and Labrador, New Brunswick, and Prince Edward Island.

Rebuilding Economies

A few successes lifted the gloom that descended over the Atlantic region as the twentieth century came to a close. In 1993 work began on Prince Edward Island's "fixed link" to the mainland. The Confederation Bridge, build by a private consortium, was completed four years later. Its construction gave a welcome boost to PEI's economy, but an amendment to the Constitution was required in order to charge tolls for its use.

In New Brunswick, Saint John seemed to do well, in part because of the success of the Irving interests. The rural community of Florenceville on the upper St John River thrived as the headquarters of McCain Foods, which had emerged as a global player in the frozen food industry. Moncton reinvented itself as a new-age transportation and communications hub for the Maritime region, hosting call centres, trucking companies, and a busy international airport. Many of Moncton's new citizens were young Acadians from the rural northern regions of the province. In 2003 the nearby town of Dieppe achieved city status, with francophones making up nearly three-quarters of its population.

Halifax, meanwhile, was becoming a thriving metropolis, with port facilities to accommodate the expansion of seagoing commerce, numerous corporate headquarters, regional federal offices, military installations, educational institutions, and health care facilities. Salter Street Films, which by the 1990s was producing popular television programs such as *This Hour has 22 Minutes* and *Emily of New Moon*, drew talent to what everyone agreed was a prosperous, lively, and "happening" city. At the same time Halifax became a magnet for organized crime, including drug-running, gambling, gang warfare, prostitution, and smuggling.

Like Halifax, St John's also had a lively cultural scene, but it stagnated economically during the 1990s. Offshore petroleum reserves promised future prosperity, while the discovery of a huge nickel deposit at Voisey's Bay in Labrador in 1994 was another cause for optimism. In 1973 the province established a department of tourism and worked with Parks Canada to develop outstanding sites such as Gros Morne, Port au Choix, L'Anse aux Meadows, and Red Bay, which have had a significant impact on the economy of the island's west coast and south Labrador. The province also encouraged the restoration of rural towns and outports, and developed the tourist potential of archaeological sites such as those at Boyd's Cove and Ferryland.

Tourism was touted throughout the region as an alternative to resource exploitation as a source of employment. In 1995 Lunenburg was declared a UNESCO World Heritage Site for its unique architecture and civic culture that had thrived during the town's once prosperous fishery. Grand Pré, Nova Scotia, and St Andrews, New Brunswick, also received historical designations, while in PEI "Green Gables," declared a National Historic Site in 1985, became the centre of a flourishing tourist operation. In Newfoundland elaborate programs were mounted to mark the 500th anniversary of the "discovery" of Newfoundland by John Cabot in 1997, 50 years of Confederation in 1999, and the "Viking Millennium" in 2000.

It's Oil!

The most dramatic economic development in this period was the exploitation of the region's offshore oil and gas reserves. Exploration on the Scotian Shelf had begun in 1959, and the 1970s saw significant hydrocarbon discoveries in the Sable Island sub-basin, where the testing was focused. Since the water in the area is relatively shallow and the location near markets in the United States, it was attractive to oil companies. The exploration of the Grand Banks began in the mid-1960s and in 1979 there was a promising oil strike at the Hibernia field, located east of St John's about 20 km inside the 200-mile limit. These discoveries made it urgent to settle the question of which level of government owned and controlled offshore resources.

Although Nova Scotia had debated the jurisdictional issue with the federal government, it never directly contested Ottawa's management role. Newfoundland premier Brian Peckford, eager to see the benefits of offshore resources accrue to his province, decided to mount a challenge. His government argued that Newfoundland had entered Confederation as an independent state and had never surrendered ownership. Ottawa disagreed. The question therefore went to the courts, which ruled that ownership and control beyond 12 nautical miles (22.2 km) lay with the federal government. The Peckford government also lost court challenges intended to undermine the Churchill Falls contract, and got nowhere with demands for a share in fisheries management.

When Mulroney assumed office in 1984, his determination to make peace with the energy-producing western provinces also boded well for the eastern provinces with offshore oil and gas. His government negotiated accords with Newfoundland (1985) and Nova Scotia (1986), which provided that in each case development would be the joint responsibility of the provinces and the federal government; that the provinces could tax the resources; and that they would have some protection against any major decline in equalization payments once the oil and gas began to flow. The settlement gave the green light to negotiations that led to an agreement relating to Hibernia in 1990, and oil started to flow from the huge gravity-based platform in 1997. Oil was discovered off Sable Island in 1971 and Canada's first offshore oil development, the Cohasset–Panuke Project (COPAN), began producing in 1992. The oil was exhausted by 1999, but the production of natural gas began the same year, shipped by pipeline to a plant in Goldboro. By 2001 natural gas was Nova Scotia's leading export.

Historical Focus

Neo-Nationalism in Newfoundland

People who live on islands possess a strong sense of identity, and Newfoundlanders are no exception. Despite internal divisions—"townies" and "baymen," Protestants and Roman Catholics, upper class and lower, those of English and Irish descent—most have seen "the Rock" as a special place with a distinct identity, however frequently it has been romanticized, mythologized, and distorted. After 1949 the central issue was how to preserve that distinctiveness now that Newfoundland was a Canadian province, firmly part of the North American world and open to all its influences. A related question was what the new province's place might be in the Canadian federation. During the later 1960s, a consensus began to develop that the province needed to be more assertive on both counts.

The roots of Newfoundland's cultural nationalism go back to the 1940s, if not before, but a political edge became more apparent as Smallwood's seemingly perpetual government came under increasing criticism. The outport culture seen as crucial to the Newfoundland identity seemed to be under threat, and it was not clear what would replace it. Although modernization was welcomed, its impact on what was imagined to be the "traditional Newfoundland" was a matter of growing concern, and a new nationalism developed that celebrated and encouraged all aspects of Newfoundland culture. Labrador had to wait its turn.

Two important catalysts contributed to the upsurge of Newfoundland nationalism. First, Memorial University, which became a degree-granting institution in 1949, played a vital role in promoting the study of local history and culture. It also helped to produce the educated, urban middle class that supported the cultural revival in music, theatre, writing, and the visual arts. The second catalyst was the reaction against the international anti-sealing movement. The activities of Greenpeace and the International Fund for Animal Welfare caused deep offence, and prompted a spirited defence of the traditional outport economy. In this context, Cassie

Continued

Brown's *Death on the Ice* (1974), an account of the 1914 sealing disaster, was a bestseller, and David Blackwood's etchings of traditional life on the island's northeast coast, where sealing was deeply embedded, became highly sought after.

This cultural nationalism was an essential precondition for the new phase of provincial nationalism that emerged in the late 1970s. Symbolized by the provincial flag that the artist Christopher Pratt designed in 1980, it is associated with the government of Brian Peckford (1979–89), who campaigned for greater provincial autonomy and more control over natural resources, especially fisheries and offshore oil and gas. Newfoundland premiers since Peckford have emphasized similar themes, and some have followed his lead in borrowing phrases such as "distinct society" and "masters in our own house" from the lexicon of the Parti Québécois.

Fights with Ottawa have never harmed Newfoundland politicians; scapegoating is an entrenched feature of the political landscape. Gains have been won, though it can be argued that more important and divisive local issues have been obscured or neglected as a result.[8] While political nationalism tends to wax and wane according to the state of federal–provincial relations and the personalities involved, cultural nationalism remains an enduring feature of Newfoundland society.

The Costs of Development

As in previous periods, human lives in the region were sometimes sacrificed to the gods of corporate investment. In the winter of 1982, 84 crew members died when Mobil Oil's rig *Ocean Ranger* capsized in a fierce storm that swept through the Hibernia oil field. In the aftermath, a Canadian Royal Commission spent two years exploring the disaster and reached damning conclusions: the crew was improperly trained, safety equipment was inadequate, the rig had design flaws, and neither Canada nor the United States had effective regulations and inspection practices.

In Nova Scotia, similar failures resulted in yet another coal mining disaster. Toronto-based Curragh Resources had opened the Westray mine in Pictou County in September 1991. Workers reported rock slides, cave-ins, and dangerous levels of methane gas, but their complaints were largely ignored. When one miner complained to inspectors, he was fired. Losing his job may have saved his life. On 9 May 1992 an explosion destroyed the mine, killing 26 men. The mine owners were not held responsible for their negligence and the surviving 117 miners who had not been working that day endured six years of legal wrangling before they received 12 weeks' severance pay. In 2003, after years of intense lobbying, the United Steelworkers of America, which represented the miners, managed to secure an amendment to the Criminal Code of Canada to hold criminally liable the managers and directors of corporations who failed to take steps to protect the lives of their employees.

Most corporations also avoided the environmental costs of their enterprises. Both DEVCO and SYSCO had been decommissioned by the turn of the century, but their legacies lived on. Among the worst of those legacies are the Sydney Tar Ponds, Canada's largest industrial waste site. The size of three city blocks, the ponds are reservoirs for 700,000 tonnes of toxic sludge—benzene, kerosene, naphthalene, PCBs—produced as waste by the coke ovens and furnaces used in Sydney's steel processing operations for more than 80 years. The tar ponds are especially troubling to those living nearby, who have suffered a wide range of physical problems, including severe headaches, nosebleeds, breathing problems, birth defects, miscarriages, and cancer. In 2004 the federal and provincial governments agreed to spend up to $400 million on a 10-year plan to clean up the site.[9]

Aboriginal Claims

A new factor in resource development in Atlantic Canada was the assertion of Aboriginal claims both to land and to specific hunting and fishing rights. In the Maritimes such claims were based in part on treaties signed with the British in the eighteenth century and in part on the possession of Aboriginal rights that had never been extinguished. While the Mi'kmaq and Wolastoqiyik found the courts receptive, Ottawa continues to ignore the demands of the Passamaquoddy for recognition. The Inuit and Innu of Labrador have no treaty rights, and whether Newfoundland Mi'kmaq are covered by the eighteenth-century treaties remains in dispute.

All First Nations in Canada have been sustained in their resolve to redress past injustices by a series of Supreme Court decisions and by Section 35c of the Constitution, which recognizes and affirms existing Aboriginal rights. One of the most important Supreme Court rulings was brought down in 1990, in *R. v. Sparrow*, which declared that Aboriginal people had the right to fish for subsistence and ceremonial purposes unless the government could demonstrate why limitation was necessary. In response, Ottawa introduced an Aboriginal Fisheries Strategy whereby communal fishing licences were distributed to First Nations in Atlantic Canada and British Columbia. Two Mi'kmaq communities—Membertou and Afton—refused to sign licensing agreements, arguing that treaty rights secured in 1761 superseded federal fisheries legislation.

In 1993 the Department of Fisheries and Oceans (DFO) charged Donald Marshall Jr of Membertou with catching eels out of season and with fishing and selling eels without a licence. The case eventually reached the Supreme Court, which dismissed the charges in 1999. It was a landmark ruling, reaffirming the integrity of eighteenth-century treaties and confirming the Mi'kmaq right to make a moderate living from the fishery. By extension, the Mi'kmaq could claim access to other ocean resources and to hunting. The firestorm that followed this decision forced the Supreme Court to qualify its judgment to the extent of arguing that the federal government had the power to restrict even the right to a "moderate livelihood" if it could justify the regulation on the "grounds of public importance."[10]

Nevertheless, the DFO would now be obliged to negotiate fisheries agreements rather than impose them on the Mi'kmaq. Since it was slow to respond, the Mi'kmaq in some areas began fishing lobster out of season. In St Mary's Bay, Nova Scotia, Aboriginal and non-Aboriginal fishers negotiated an agreement to jointly manage the lobster fishery, but elsewhere conflict often prevailed. When the Mi'kmaq of Esgenoopetits (Burnt Church), New Brunswick, laid lobster traps in the fall of 1999, non-Aboriginals responded by destroying their traps, attacking their property, and vandalizing fish plants that accepted lobsters from Aboriginal fishers. The federal government tried to establish quotas for both sides, but tensions continued.

In 2005 the Supreme Court handed down rulings in two cases relating to logging rights that had dragged through the courts for years. The appeals by Stephen Frederick Marshall and 34 other Mi'kmaq in Nova Scotia and by Joshua Bernard in New Brunswick were denied on the grounds that there was no connection between the commercial cutting of timber and Aboriginal trading activities at the time the treaties were signed.

In Newfoundland, where the Conne River Mi'kmaq were recognized as Status Indians under the Indian Act in 1984, Conne River became a reserve (Miawpukek). In 1996 the Mi'kmaq launched a claim to about 20 per cent of the island of Newfoundland. The province's Supreme Court ruled in 2003 (in *R. vs. Drew*) that there was insufficient evidence of a Mi'kmaq presence in the area before the arrival of Europeans to sustain the claim. Although appealed, the decision was upheld, and permission to appeal to the Supreme Court of Canada denied.

With both Innu and Inuit advancing their claims, the situation in Labrador was especially complex, and negotiations proved long and difficult. The Innu Nation and the Labrador Inuit Association (LIA) filed overlapping land claims in 1977. Negotiations with the LIA began in 1988, but an agreement in principle was not reached until 2001. There were also long delays with the Innu claim, filed in 1990. It was resubmitted in 2001, when negotiations resumed. The process was no doubt encouraged by the Voisey's Bay discovery, and renewed interest in developing the hydro potential of the lower Churchill River. The Innu became Status Indians in 2002, with reserves at Natuashish (2003) and Sheshatshiu (2006).

A further complication in Labrador was the intervention of the Labrador Métis, known since 2010 as the NunatuKavut Community Council. Representing people of mixed Inuit–European ancestry (sometimes known as Inuit–Métis, or southern Inuit) living in central and southern Labrador, the organization filed a land claim in 1991, but there have been no negotiations because both the provincial and federal governments have rejected the Council's claim to distinct Aboriginal status. The community persists in its efforts, hoping that ongoing research into its history will change attitudes.

Meanwhile, Aboriginal women in the region struggled to overcome the discrimination they faced as a result of the Indian Act. Sandra Lovelace Nicholas, a member of the Tobique First Nation in New Brunswick, played an important role in this struggle. In 1970 she married an American and moved to California. When the marriage failed, she moved back to Tobique with her children, only to be denied access to housing and other rights provided under the Indian Act. Like all Aboriginal women subject to the Act, she had lost her Indian status when she married a non-Aboriginal man. In co-operation with both Aboriginal and non-Aboriginal women's organizations, Nicholas fought the case in the courts, and in 1979 she appealed to the United Nations. Two years later, when Canada was found in breach of the International Covenant on Civil and Political Rights, the government was slow to respond, in part because many First Nations men opposed giving women equal rights to scarce reserve resources.

Under the Charter of Rights and Freedoms, double standards such as those sanctioned by the Indian Act could no longer be condoned. The Act was finally revised in 1985 to ensure that Aboriginal women who marry non-Aboriginal men and their children would no longer lose their status, although complications remained for women and their children who wanted to reclaim their lost status. In 2005 Sandra Lovelace became the first Aboriginal person from Atlantic Canada to be appointed to the Canadian Senate.[11]

Social Struggles

The movements for human rights and social equality that had gained ground in the postwar period fought uphill battles in the age of neo-liberalism. As jobs vanished, union membership declined and politicians in mainline parties were no longer eager to be seen courting the votes of organized labour. Restructuring led to the proliferation of part-time and contract jobs in which workers had no union representation and few benefits. In the end, this trend produced the "flexible" work force that neo-liberals demanded, but at great cost to those at the bottom of the economic pyramid. The promised "trickle-down" effects of a more competitive economy failed to materialize, resulting in an ever-widening gap between rich and poor.

In this period women began to break through the glass ceiling in politics, but not consistently and not in large numbers. Politics continued to be dominated by men, though no more so in Atlantic Canada than elsewhere in Canada.[12] Although the abortion law of 1969, which required the approval of a three-doctor panel, was declared a violation of human rights by the Supreme Court in 1988, conservative forces (a coalition led by Roman Catholics and fundamentalist Protestants) prevented the governments of Prince Edward Island and New Brunswick from requiring hospitals to provide abortion services. Abortion rights activist Henry Morgentaler, who established a clinic in Fredericton, took the New Brunswick government to court to establish a woman's right to abortion on demand, but he died in 2013 before the case was resolved.[13] Voluntary organizations worked diligently to address violence against women, the lack of affordable day care, and the gender gap in remuneration for paid work, but governments now had the excuse that rising public debt meant that there was little money for new social programs.

While lesbian, gay, bisexual, and transgendered (LGBT) people in Atlantic Canada won some concessions in this period—including the right to be ordained as ministers in the United Church in 1988—the Roman Catholic Church and evangelical Protestants continued to denounce homosexuality, along with abortion and divorce, as a threat to the traditional family. Homophobia sometimes manifested itself in violence, forcing LGBT people to be cautious in expressing their sexuality. This caution largely disappeared when the Acquired Immune Deficiency Syndrome (AIDS) pandemic descended on the world in the 1980s. Since gay men initially formed the majority of the victims of the disease, they took the lead in developing support systems for people infected with the disease and in mounting education campaigns to slow its spread. No longer confined to the closet, LGBT people took part in gay pride parades and established organizations that focused on their lifestyles and concerns.

As elsewhere in Canada, regular church attendance in the Atlantic region declined precipitously in the postwar period. This trend was exacerbated for the Roman Catholic Church by revelations of physical abuse and sexual misconduct by priests. Canada's largest abuse scandal involved the residents of the Mount Cashel orphanage in St John's, run by the Christian Brothers. The sorry tale of abuse and cover-up became widely known in 1989, but compensation cases took more than two decades to wend their way through the courts. An apology from the Christian Brothers, finally issued in February 2014, was also agonizingly slow in coming. In the meantime, the orphanage was closed and the site razed to the ground.

At the same time Christian churches remained important institutions in many communities, and new religions gained converts. Evangelical traditions such as Pentecostalism continued to attract adherents, while the Anglican and United churches saw their followers drifting away. By 2001, 11.6 per cent of Nova Scotians were prepared to claim no religious affiliation at all, but people in the other provinces in the region were less likely to do so. Only 2.5 per cent of the people of Newfoundland and Labrador—superficially Canada's most Christian province—reported no religious affiliation, compared to 16.2 per cent of Canadians overall.[14] In 1978 some 500 Tibetan Buddhists moved from Boulder, Colorado, to Nova Scotia, attracted by its mix of basic amenities, traditional values, and pace of life.[15] They were among the many newcomers to the city who contributed to the growth of its cultural, business, and professional life.

Minorities, old and new, continued their efforts to achieve equality in a region where deeply rooted white communities formed the overwhelming majority. In the Halifax area, African Nova Scotians were buoyed by the election in 1993 of Wayne Adams, a long-time Halifax municipal councillor, to the Nova Scotia Assembly. He was defeated in 1998 by Yvonne Atwell, a native of Preston, who had served as the president of the Black United Front. When Joseph Atallah ("Joe") Ghiz, the son of a Lebanese-born shopkeeper in Charlottetown, led the Liberal Party to victory in Prince Edward Island in 1986, he became the first provincial premier in Canada of non-European descent. While these may have been small victories in the larger scheme of things, they signalled a new openness to diversity in what many people viewed as a hide-bound region.

The environmental movement rolled on, propelled by disasters around the world—Three Mile Island (1979), Bhopal (1984), Chernobyl (1986)—and concern about acid rain, global warming, nuclear winter, ozone depletion, and population growth. In 1987 a United Nations World Commission on the Environment and Development, chaired by Norway's Gro Harlem Brundtland, published a report (*Our Common Future*) calling for a global strategy of sustainable development rather than growth at any cost. The Brundtland Report provided the momentum for the Mulroney government to pursue a more ambitious environmental agenda, shaped with the help of environmental activist Elizabeth May, who had cut her activist teeth on budworm battles in Nova Scotia. In addition to adopting an Environmental Assessment Act and an Environmental Protection Act, Ottawa signed a bilateral acid rain treaty with the United States, and Canada was the first industrialized country

Biography   *Elizabeth May*

Elizabeth May was born in Hartford, Connecticut, in 1954, where her mother was a prominent peace activist and her father worked in the insurance business. In 1972 the family moved to Cape Breton Island, where they eked out a living by running a restaurant and gift-shop in the community of Margaree Harbour.

In 1975, Elizabeth May joined a local group opposed to the spraying of the now-banned chemical fenitrothion to combat a spruce budworm infestation in the region. An inspired activist, she stood up to the Swedish multinational Stora Kopparberg, which threatened to pull out of Nova Scotia if the government refused to conduct a spraying program. When the company launched a lawsuit against the protesters, May travelled to Sweden with Ryan Googoo, Grand Chief of the Mi'kmaq, to raise support for her cause. She also became involved in protests against both uranium mining in Nova Scotia and Scott Paper's plans to spray Agent Orange to kill hardwood trees and shrubs to facilitate the cutting of softwood for their pulp and paper operations.

Eager to see improvements in environmental policy, May agreed in 1986 to work as an advisor to Prince Edward Islander Tom MacMillan, minister of the environment in the Mulroney cabinet. She resigned two years later, when MacMillan granted permits for the Rafferty-Alameda Dams in Saskatchewan without an environmental assessment. In 1989 she became the founding Executive

to embrace the Climate Change Convention and Biodiversity Convention proposed by the United Nations Earth Summit in 1992. The Chrétien government signed the 1997 Kyoto protocol, agreeing to reduce emissions, but Canada's greenhouse gases actually rose in the following decade as economic growth continued to trump efforts to develop a new relationship between people and the planet.

Region and Culture

Cultural industries went from strength to strength as actors, artists, musicians, and writers found increasingly receptive audiences. Musical, literary, and theatrical events sprouted in all four provinces, many of them tied into the tourist season. Beginning in 1976, for example, the island of Lamèque in northeastern New Brunswick staged an annual International Baroque Music Festival, which drew audiences to concerts held in the island's Roman Catholic churches. Three New Brunswick sopranos—Measha Brueggergosman, Suzie LeBlanc, and Wendy Nielsen—earned wide international followings. Cape Bretoners combined local culture and spectacular autumn scenery in the Celtic Colours International Festival, first held in 1997. After a decade of hard organizational work, the East Coast Music Association began showcasing regional musicians at a high-profile gala held annually from 2000. With the proliferation of urban venues, it became possible for popular singers and bands to make a living from their music.

By the end of the century Atlantic Canada was also gaining recognition for its creative writers, many of whom drew on the region's rich history for inspiration. Literary scholar Herb Wyile has suggested that this focus may reflect a need to re-examine and validate the region's past, given its

Director of the Sierra Club of Canada. From this position she lobbied for a variety of environmental causes and continued to draw media attention. In 2001 she conducted a 17-day hunger strike on Parliament Hill to demand the relocation of families living next to the Sydney Tar Ponds.

With environmental issues continuing to trouble many voters, the Green Party, founded in 1983, gained a larger following. The Greens fielded candidates in every riding in the 2004 election and won 4.3 per cent of the popular vote. In 2006, Elizabeth May left her position with the Sierra Club to become leader of the Green Party, which increased its support to 6.8 per cent in the 2008 election. May herself won 32 per cent of the votes in the riding of Central Nova where she ran against Defence Minister Peter MacKay. In the 2011 election, May won the riding of Saanich–Gulf Islands in British Columbia, becoming the first Green Party member to sit in the House of Commons.[16]

Elizabeth May. THE CANADIAN PRESS/Adrian Wyld.

peripheral status in Canada and the tendency of the increasingly important tourist industry to commodify and airbrush historical developments.[17] Successful writers such as Wayne Johnston, Michael Winter, Lisa Moore, and Michael Crummey in Newfoundland and Labrador, and George Elliott Clarke, Ann-Marie MacDonald, Alistair MacLeod, and David Adams Richards in the Maritimes have no time for romanticizing the region's history. What they and others have presented is a raw and imaginative interpretation of events that effectively supplements our understanding of the Atlantic region's history and contributes to a lively historical memory.

Conclusion

As the new millennium dawned, Atlantic Canadians could look back on a quarter century of rapid change. Their provincial governments had adjusted to neo-liberalism, if often unwillingly, and tried to adapt to the challenges posed by the oil and gas industry, the collapse and restructuring of the fisheries, and new notions of federalism. Influences

Natalie MacMaster, a highly accomplished fiddler, is one of the most successful musicians to have emerged from the Celtic music revival in Cape Breton. Photo by James Fraher/Michael Ochs Archives/Getty Images.

from other parts of an intensely interconnected world fostered new attitudes and expectations. In 2000–1 speculative investment in information and communications technologies jolted the global economy when the so-called "dot-com bubble" burst. The future promised more shocks, but few people in the Atlantic region or anywhere else could have imagined what was to come.

Further Readings

Bavington, Dean. 2010. *Managed Annihilation: An Unnatural History of the Newfoundland Cod Collapse*. Vancouver: University of British Columbia Press.

Carbert, Louise. 2005. *Rural Women's Leadership in Atlantic Canada: First-Hand Perspectives on Local Political Life and Participation in Electoral Politics*. Toronto: University of Toronto.

Coates, Ken S. 2000. *The Marshall Decision and Native Rights*. Montreal: McGill-Queen's University Press.

Forbes, E.R., and D.A. Muise, eds. 1993. *The Atlantic Provinces in Confederation*. Toronto: University of Toronto Press. (Chapter 13 and Epilogue)

Griffiths, Naomi E.S. 2011. *The Golden Age of Liberalism: A Portrait of Roméo LeBlanc*. Toronto: James Lorimer.

House, J.D. 1999. *Against the Tide: Battling for Economic Renewal in Newfoundland and Labrador*. Toronto: University of Toronto Press.

Rose, George A. 2007. *The Ecological History of the North Atlantic Fisheries*. St John's: Breakwater Press.

Sandberg, Anders L., and Peter Clancy. 2000. *Against the Grain: Foresters and Politics in Nova Scotia*. Vancouver: University of British Columbia Press.

Savoie, Donald. 2001. *Pulling Against Gravity: Economic Development in New Brunswick During the McKenna Years*. Montreal: Institute for Research on Public Policy.

———. 2006. *Visiting Grandchildren: Economic Development in the Maritimes*. Toronto: University of Toronto Press.

———. 2013. *Harrison McCain: Single-Minded Purpose*. Montreal: McGill-Queen's University Press.

Thomsen, Robert C. 2010. *Nationalism in Stateless Nations. Selves and Others in Scotland and Newfoundland*. Edinburgh: John Donald.

Wadden, Marie. 2001. *Nitassinan: The Innu Struggle to Reclaim Their Homeland*. Rev. edn. Vancouver: Douglas and McIntyre.

Wicken, William C. 2002. *Mi'kmaq Treaties on Trial: History, Land, and Donald Marshall Junior*. Toronto: University of Toronto Press.

Wyile, Herb. 2011. *Anne of Tim Hortons: Globalization and the Reshaping of Atlantic Canadian Literature*. Waterloo, ON: Wilfrid Laurier University Press.

Historical Spotlight

Holmes, Jacqueline D., and Justine B. Hollander. 2013. "Regenerating Devastated Landscapes in Moncton, New Brunswick, and Sydney, Nova Scotia," in *Land and Sea: Environmental History in Atlantic Canada*, ed. Claire Campbell and Robert Summerby-Murray. Fredericton: Acadiensis Press.

Ommer, Rosemary, and Nancy J. Turner. 2004. "Informal Rural Economies in History," *Labour/Le Travail* 53 (Spring): 127–57.

Recommended Websites

Cod Moratorium
http://www.heritage.nf.ca/society/moratorium.html

Constitution Acts, 1867 to 1982
http://laws-lois.justice.gc.ca/eng/Const/Index.html

Mi'kmaq Rights Initiative
http://mikmaqrights.com/negotiations/treaties/

Sydney Tar Ponds Agency
http://www.tarpondscleanup.ca

Understanding the Past to Build the Future [Inuit Métis of Southen Labrador]
http://www.mun.ca/labmetis/

Chapter 16

Whither Tending? Atlantic Canada in the Twenty-First Century

The early years of the twenty-first century were punctuated by a series of crises that ushered in a new age of anxiety. On 11 September 2001, attacks on the United States by Muslim extremists set off an ongoing "war on terror." The following year, an outbreak of SARS (severe

Setting the Context

11 September 2001

On 11 September 2001 Muslim terrorists hijacked four planes. Two were used to destroy the twin towers of the World Trade Center in New York, one smashed into the Pentagon, and one crashed in a Pennsylvania field. Airports in the Atlantic region were immediately turned into reception points for flights in transit as the United States went into lockdown.

Driven by religious zeal, the suicide bombers were participants in a holy war intended to punish the United States for supporting anti-Islamic forces around the world and exploiting the resources of oil-producing Arab countries for financial gain. Six weeks after the attacks, US President George W. Bush, with the support of NATO, launched an invasion of Afghanistan on the pretext that its Islamic extremist rulers, the Taliban, were sheltering Osama bin Laden, the leader of the terrorist organization believed responsible for the 9/11 attacks. The Taliban were ousted from formal power, but their guerrilla forces continued to fight. Global tensions escalated further in 2003 when the United States led a coalition that included Great Britain in an invasion of Iraq. The aim was to remove its dictatorial leader Saddam Hussein, who was accused of stockpiling "weapons of mass destruction," although no such weapons were found. Like Afghanistan, Iraq remained in a state of constant guerrilla warfare after Hussein's government collapsed.

The immediate impact of 9/11 was to focus the attention of governments around the world on "the war on terror." In Western nations more funds were devoted to military preparedness, and physical security trumped civil rights whenever terrorism was suspected. Prime Minister Jean Chrétien refused to send Canadian troops to Iraq, but did agree to take part in the occupation and reconstruction of Afghanistan. Although the mission officially ended in 2011, Canadian soldiers remained in a training capacity until March 2014. A total of 158 military personnel died in the fighting, and many more were scarred both physically and mentally. As journalists and scholars have noted, Canada in the early twenty-first century abandoned its peacekeeping image and became a "warrior society."[1]

Airplanes parked at Halifax Stanfield International Airport during the 9/11 crisis. Following the terrorist attacks, airports in the Atlantic region became part of Operation Yellow Ribbon, in which flights heading to the United States from Europe were diverted to Canadian airports outside major urban centres. In May 2002, to honour two of the communities that provided shelter for nearly 14,000 stranded passengers, Lufthansa named a new Airbus A 340-300 "Gander-Halifax." Halifax International Airport Authority.

acute respiratory syndrome) in China quickly spread to Canada, a stark reminder that pandemics are oblivious to borders. And although the issue of global warming had been under discussion for decades, the United Nations Intergovernmental Panel on Climate Change confirmed in 2007 that the petroleum-addicted world is cruising toward ecological disaster. This news was followed by a financial meltdown in the United States, precipitated by loose mortgage-lending policies. In September 2008 the global economy, now integrated to a degree never before possible, collapsed into a recession equalled in magnitude only by the Great Depression of the 1930s. In these circumstances, Atlantic Canadians, like people everywhere, were obliged to establish priorities and hope they could weather the storms to come.

Coming Together?

By the beginning of the twenty-first century it was abundantly clear that the postwar liberal consensus had been laid to rest. Developments at the federal level provided a final confirmation. Jean Chrétien reluctantly stepped down in 2003, giving Paul Martin his long-awaited opportunity to become prime minister. After the June 2004 election, Martin emerged as the leader of a shaky minority government, and he had to return to the polls less than two years later after the NDP, led by Jack Layton, withdrew its support. The newly minted Conservative Party of Canada (CPC)—a merger of the Progressive Conservatives and the Canadian Alliance—formed a minority government under the leadership of the Alberta ideologue Stephen Harper after the January 2006 election. As the world financial system began to collapse, Harper called a snap election for October 2008 that

Table 16.1	**Timeline**
2000	Council of Atlantic Premiers established.
2001	Terrorists attack the World Trade Center and the Pentagon.
2002	Canadian troops arrive in Afghanistan.
2003	Report of the Newfoundland and Labrador Royal Commission on Renewing and Strengthening Our Place in Canada.
2005	Agreement on offshore royalties for oil and gas; creation of Nunatsiavut.
2008	Newfoundland and Labrador no longer receive equalization payments.
2009–13	Darrell Dexter leads NDP government in Nova Scotia.
2010	Muskrat Falls hydro development agreement.
2011	New Dawn agreement with Labrador Innu.
2014	Last Canadian troops leave Afghanistan.

yielded another minority government. He finally achieved a majority of seats with less than 40 per cent of the vote in May 2011.

Although his father had been raised in New Brunswick, Harper grew up in Toronto and had little sympathy for the Atlantic region. Indeed, he became notorious for commenting that Atlantic Canadians suffered from a "culture of defeat"—the reason, he implied, for their lack of success in the free-market economy. A lingering sympathy for "progressive" conservatism in the Atlantic provinces meant that Conservative Party candidates there tended to do poorly in federal elections, at least until New Brunswick awarded eight of its ten seats to them in 2011.

Meanwhile, political leaders in the region had regrouped in an effort to maintain a standard of living that seemed to be under constant threat. In May 2000 the Council of Maritime Premiers became the Council of Atlantic Premiers and set out to find "efficiencies" through regional co-operation. The Council's key initiatives involved energy and resource development, incentive programs to attract immigrants, and private investment to jump-start economic growth. Under its director Brian Lee Crowley, the Atlantic Institute for Market Studies (AIMS) encouraged business and political leaders to make the Atlantic provinces the transportation and energy hub of "Atlantica," a North Atlantic economic zone that would include northern New England and southern Quebec.[2]

This approach appealed to New Brunswick's political leaders, but proved difficult for Bernard Lord's Progressive Conservative government to implement. With his administration bogged down in complaints about cuts to medical services and the costs of automobile insurance, the Liberals won a majority of seats, though not of the popular vote, in the 2006 election. Making a virtue of necessity, Premier Shawn Graham launched a "self-sufficiency campaign" designed to position New Brunswickers to go it alone in the face of federal cutbacks. He also embraced an aggressive economic program that included building a second nuclear power plant, supporting an Irving-backed liquefied gas facility, and making Saint John a major player in an Atlantic Gateway strategy that would put the region at the centre of global trade. In the end it was not enough. The cost overruns incurred in refurbishing the nuclear power facility at Point Lepreau and the decision to sell New Brunswick Power to Hydro-Québec produced a backlash that led to a resounding victory for the Progressive Conservatives led by David Alward in 2010.

The new government limped along, promising to slay the deficit but unable to do so even under the careful guidance of Finance Minister Blaine Higgs, a former employee of J.D. Irving Limited (JDI). Determined to attract private capital, Alward moved full steam ahead with plans for a natural gas industry based on hydraulic fracking, a controversial process that prompted angry public protests by those who believed that the damaging environmental impact outweighed the prospect of jobs. As the 2014 election approached, Alward made more enemies when he decided to release 25 per cent of the remaining Crown forest reserves to JDI. The Liberals, led by Brian Gallant, emerged the victors on 22 September, and David Coon, leader of the provincial Green Party, became the second Green member of a provincial legislature anywhere in Canada when he won a seat in Fredericton.

In Prince Edward Island, Patrick Binns sought an unprecedented fourth-term majority in 2007, running on a policy of continued good governance and job creation, but he was trounced by the Liberals under Robert Ghiz (the son of former premier Joe Ghiz). More than other premiers in the Maritimes, Ghiz caught the new wave of thinking in his "Focus for Change" program, which included an emphasis on environmentally friendly energy sources. Given that rising sea levels threatened the very existence of his low-lying island province, it was a timely initiative. His popularity ensured his government another majority victory in 2011 but, after seven years in office, Ghiz decided to step down in 2015 to seek opportunities elsewhere.

Nova Scotia's Progressive Conservative premier John Hamm was succeeded in 2006 by Rodney MacDonald, a Cape Breton educator and an accomplished fiddler. In the ensuing election, he emerged as the leader of a minority government and, following the loss of a confidence vote in the assembly, called an election for June 2009. His lead in the polls quickly evaporated, permitting the NDP, led by Darrell Dexter, to break the stranglehold of the two mainline parties on the region's politics. While his government launched a series of progressive measures, it read from the same hymn book as other jurisdictions when it came to provincial finances. Dexter achieved his goal of balancing the provincial budget in 2011, but at the price of increasing the Harmonized Sales Tax (HST) by two percentage points, cutting the Yarmouth to Portland ferry, and pursuing other unpopular cost-saving measures. Although it launched a progressive environmental program and landed a multi-billion dollar naval shipbuilding contract for Halifax Shipyards (owned by the Irving interests), the Dexter government suffered a crushing defeat in the 2013 election, which returned the Liberals under Stephen McNeil.

Roger Grimes, who succeeded Brian Tobin as premier of Newfoundland and Labrador in 2001, decided to appoint a royal commission to explore how best to renew and strengthen the province's place in Canada. It was telling that the commissioners held hearings not only in the Atlantic region but also in Toronto and Fort McMurray, where so many of the province's citizens now worked. The commission's report, tabled in 2003, summarized the province's difficult economic situation and offered practical remedies, but Ottawa was not interested. Grimes lost a provincial election later that year to the Progressive Conservatives, led by Danny Williams, and the commission report was quietly buried.

Williams was more than just a new kid on the block. A Rhodes Scholar and self-made millionaire, he soon became a household name in Canada—something that could not be said of any other Atlantic premier of his generation. A Newfoundland nationalist in the Brian Peckford mould, he proved to be equally confrontational and flamboyant. Utterly fearless, he appeared on the CNN program *Larry King Live* in the late winter of 2006 to debate former Beatle Paul McCartney and his then wife Heather Mills, who were in the region to protest the seal hunt. By that time Williams was locked in a David and Goliath battle with Ottawa over equalization payments.

In the fall of 2004 Williams abruptly walked out of a federal–provincial conference on equalization policy, claiming that Paul Martin had reneged on his pre-election promise to give Newfoundland and Labrador and Nova Scotia a better deal on royalties from offshore development. After three months of posturing—Williams went so far as to have the Canadian flag removed from provincial government buildings—an agreement was finally reached in January 2005 that gave the two provinces most of what they wanted. Newfoundland and Labrador would receive $2 billion and Nova Scotia $830,000 over eight years to compensate them for equalization clawbacks, and the agreement could be extended for a further eight years if the provinces were still receiving equalization payments. When Harper later tried to reform equalization in a way that would penalize the Atlantic provinces, Williams objected and mobilized an effective "Anyone But Conservative" campaign in the 2008 federal election. As a result, six of the province's seven seats went to the Liberals, and the other to the NDP.

By that time significant expansion of the offshore oil industry meant that Newfoundland and Labrador no longer qualified for equalization payments. This was a major milestone in the province's history but, as in most resource economies, prosperity was unevenly shared and could be unstable. St John's and its hinterland have been the chief beneficiaries of offshore development; most other areas have done less well.

The Williams effect continued for a while after his resignation in 2010. His successor, Kathy Dunderdale, easily retained her seat in the provincial election of 2011, though the province returned

From the mid-nineteenth century, the Roman Catholic cathedral/basilica (right) dominated the downtown skyline of St John's. It now shares the hilltop with The Rooms (left), a striking building that has been the home of the province's museum, art gallery, and archives since 2005. Image taken by rebfoto of St John's, Newfoundland, Canada. ©rebfoto.

only a single Conservative in the federal election that year. She resigned early in 2014, and since then the Progressive Conservatives have faced leadership problems, increasing criticism, and a loss of popular support.

Trends, Old and New

Rural areas throughout the Atlantic region bore the brunt of continued restructuring. Between 1991 and 2011 Cape Breton Island's population dropped from 162,000 to 136,000 and seemed poised for further decline. Tourism remained an important source of income, but it could never generate the employment levels achieved by the coal and steel industries in their heyday. As young people moved to urban centres such as Moncton, Halifax, and Montreal, northeastern New Brunswick, the cradle of post-expulsion Acadia, also faced population decline. Unemployment levels remained high in rural areas, approaching 20 per cent or more, while cities grew dramatically, gobbling up the adjacent countryside, attracting the majority of new immigrants, and sustaining the bulk of provincial services. In the new economic climate, development no longer focused on assisting poor people and regions. Instead, the goal was to build on success, which meant focusing on metropolitan areas, the undisputed drivers of knowledge and power in the Information Age.

In the spirit of Atlantic co-operation (and provincial self-interest), Nova Scotia and Newfoundland and Labrador worked together to support the development of the hydro potential of the lower Churchill River. That development had been effectively blunted by the Quebec government, which insisted that electricity from Labrador could not be exported across Quebec to markets elsewhere, but had to be sold to Hydro-Québec at the provincial border. Although the situation was patently unfair, attempts to change it failed and Ottawa refused to intervene. The Williams government focused on sending power to the island of Newfoundland and other markets by a partly undersea route that avoided Quebec altogether—an idea first mooted in the Smallwood era.

Before this plan could be implemented, Labrador's Aboriginal peoples had to be consulted. Agreement with the Labrador Inuit Association was reached in 2005, with the creation of the semi-autonomous territory of Nunatsiavut. Negotiations with the Innu were more protracted, but a "New Dawn Agreement" was concluded in 2008 and finally ratified three years later. The Innu agreed to the proposed Lower Churchill hydro developments in return for a framework land-claim settlement, financial compensation for the damage done to ancestral lands by the Churchill Falls dam, and other payments and concessions related to the first stage of the power project at Muskrat Falls.

Williams abruptly resigned late in 2010, shortly after an agreement had been reached between Nalcor Energy, a provincial Crown corporation created in 2007, and the Halifax-based Emera 2000, which had emerged from the privatization of Nova Scotia Power. Jointly, these companies planned to build a generating station at Muskrat Falls, with transmission lines, partly undersea, to Nova Scotia and the island of Newfoundland. The federal government later agreed to guarantee the loan, which would be raised by Nalcor and the Newfoundland and Labrador government. Although the Inuit and the NunatuKavut Inuit–Métis expressed reservations about the project, as of 2015 their concerns have not been addressed. In addition, many consumers in Newfoundland and Labrador, still haunted by the Churchill Falls debacle, have yet to be persuaded of the wisdom and viability of this hugely expensive project.

Historical Focus

Nunatsiavut

Labrador boasts the first modern Native land claims settlement in Atlantic Canada. On 22 January 2005, after 30 years of negotiations, the Labrador Inuit signed an agreement with the federal and provincial governments covering 72,520 square kilometres of land, to be known as Nunatsiavut ("our beautiful land"). It includes Labrador north of Hamilton Inlet, land on both sides of Lake Melville, and 44,030 square kilometres of sea rights. Of the land area, the Inuit own 15,800 square kilometres designated as Labrador Inuit Lands and enjoy special rights related to traditional land use elsewhere. The agreement also established the Torngat Mountains National Park Reserve in the northern area of the land claim. The package included $130 million in compensation for the forced relocation of the Inuit from Hebron and other communities in the 1950s; provincial royalties for resources; land, mineral, and marine rights; and $120 million to establish self-government.

The Nunatsiavut Government represents not only the residents (Inuit and non-Inuit) of the land-claim area but also Labrador Inuit living elsewhere in Canada. Nunatsiavut remains part of Newfoundland and Labrador, but its government has authority over health, education, justice, cultural affairs, economic development, and natural resources. The government consists of an elected president (who appoints an executive council) and an assembly of 16 members representing seven constituencies. The assembly elects the first minister. In addition, there are elected municipal councils in each town, led by an "angajukKâk": the chief executive and mayor, who sits in the assembly.[3]

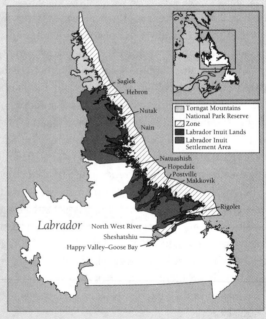

Map of Nunatsiavut.

The Muskrat Falls development was not the only ambitious project on the region's drawing boards in the second decade of the twenty-first century. With the United States dragging its heels on building a new pipeline to carry crude oil from Alberta, TransCanada proposed an extension of its east-west pipeline to Irving refineries in Saint John, which would expand its marine facilities to accommodate ever larger numbers of ocean-going vessels. In 2013 Calgary-based Pieridae Energy pushed forward with plans to build a liquefied natural gas terminal at Goldboro, Nova Scotia, while New Brunswick's Nashwaak watershed was poised to produce tungsten-molybdenum from a massive open-pit mine, and the Potash Corporation of Saskatchewan, which had been exploiting the area near Sussex since the 1980s, planned to double its output for markets in Brazil, the Caribbean, and the eastern United States. With new discoveries of oil off Newfoundland and Labrador, the petroleum industry remained a magnet for foreign capital.[4] In each case, critics expressed concern that such large-scale development would have dangerous environmental implications. Even Prince Edward Island's "wind farms," eight of which had been constructed by 2014, were unpopular among residents who lived near the noisy whooshing of the turbines. Ultimately, the Atlantic region was on the front lines of what was turning out to be the major question of the twenty-first century: what are the limits to growth?

Where Are We Now?

The political scientist Donald J. Savoie has suggested that governing in Atlantic Canada is like pulling against the forces of gravity.[5] No matter what strategies its political leaders tried in the first decade of this century, the region continued to face high unemployment, low wages, and uncertain prospects. Ballooning health-care costs (which absorbed 40 per cent or more of provincial revenues), an aging population, the hollowing out of rural areas, continuing outmigration, rising sea levels—all needed to be addressed by more than neo-liberal nostrums.

While the financial meltdown in 2008 offered a reminder that unregulated capitalism fails to address many of the large issues facing humankind, neo-liberal perspectives remained strong among corporate and political leaders. The ultimate irony for Atlantic Canadians, of course, is that as other areas of the country faced business collapses and job losses, Ottawa became more interested in providing stimulus packages for faltering industries. With Ontario increasingly a beneficiary of equalization, the grumbling about "handouts" abated somewhat, but this did little to improve the share of national resources coming to Atlantic Canada. People in the region adjusted as they had always done—by finding work elsewhere.

Most policy-makers concede that Confederation remains the preferred framework in which to help the Atlantic provinces close the gap between national and regional living standards. Although the gap has not disappeared, economic growth in the region has kept pace, if at a distance, with the spectacular growth of the nation as a whole since the 1950s, and that in itself is a major achievement. So too is the emergence of new industries, including high-tech operations to support offshore development, fish farming, and wineries whose products win international competitions. Whether they can maintain the pace in an increasingly competitive and uncertain global context is difficult to predict.

Table 16.2 Population Size by Province, 1991–2011

	1991	1996	2001	2006	2011
NL	568,474	551,792	512,930	505,469	514,536
PEI	129,765	134,557	135,290	135,851	140,204
NS	859,942	909,005	908,005	913,462	921,727
NB	723,900	738,133	729,500	729,997	751,171
Total	2,282,081	2,333,487	2,285,725	2,284,779	2,327,638

Regional population increase, 2.0%; Canada, 18%

Source: Statistics Canada. Reproduced and distributed on an "as is" basis with the permission of Statistics Canada.

Table 16.3 Population of selected census metropolitan areas (CMA) in the Atlantic region, 2011 (figures in thousands)

Halifax, Nova Scotia	409.7
St John's, Newfoundland and Labrador	197.5
Saint John, New Brunswick	127.8
Moncton, New Brunswick	104.7
Fredericton, New Brunswick	94.3
Charlottetown, Prince Edward Island	64.5
Sydney, Nova Scotia	31.6

Source: Statistics Canada. Reproduced and distributed on an "as is" basis with the permission of Statistics Canada.

Conclusion

Four centuries after the first permanent European settlements were established in the region, Atlantic Canada continues to respond to forces centred elsewhere. Reform, retrenchment, and restructuring have been the mantra of the new world order, but Atlantic Canadians have embraced them more out of necessity than conviction. While a few have been converted to the religion of the unshackled marketplace, many more regret the abandonment of the noble dream that made human welfare rather than corporate profits the measure of a civil society. "Where are we," asked the Newfoundland writer Moses Harvey in 1885, "and whither tending?"[6] The answer remains obscure, but the region is undeniably at another turning point in its long history.

Further Readings

Reid, John G., and Donald J. Savoie, eds. 2011. *Shaping and Agenda for Atlantic Canada*. Halifax: Fernwood Publishing.

Historical Spotlight

James Bickerton, 2011. "The New Federalism and Atlantic Canada," in *Shaping an Agenda for Atlantic Canada*, ed. John G. Reid and Donald J. Savoie. Halifax: Fernwood Publishing.
Locke, Wade. 2011. "Atlantic Canada: Myth or Reality?" in *Shaping an Agenda for Atlantic Canada*, ed. John G. Reid and Donald J. Savoie. Halifax: Fernwood Publishing.

Recommended Website

Nunatsiavut: Winds of Change
http://www.nunatsiavut.com/en/windsofchange.php

Bibliographic Note

The historical literature on Atlantic Canada is extensive, making a selection of sources difficult. Although published more than two decades ago, *Canadian History: A Readers' Guide*, 2 vols (Toronto: University of Toronto Press, 1994) is still useful for finding early works relating to the region. The Atlantic Canada Portal (http://atlanticportal.hil.unb.ca) includes a searchable database of the *Acadiensis* bibliographies and other publications to 2008. Sources on the history of Newfoundland and Labrador before 1869 can be found on a website maintained by Olaf Uwe Janzen (www2. grenfell.mun.ca/nfld_history/index.htm) and more generally on the Centre for Newfoundland Studies website (www.library.mun.ca/qeii/cns/index.php). See also Marguerite Maillet, *Bibliographie des publications de l'Acadie des provinces maritimes: livres et brochures, 1609–1996* (Moncton: les Éditions d'acadie, 1997) and Brian Douglas Tennyson, comp., *Cape Bretoniana: An Annotated Bibliography* (Toronto: University of Toronto Press, 2005). Articles on the region's history can be found in *Acadiensis*, *The Journal of New Brunswick Studies*, *Newfoundland and Labrador Studies*, *The Newfoundland Quarterly*, *Them Days*, *The Nova Scotia Historical Review*, *The Island Magazine*, *Les Cahiers de la Société historique acadienne*, and *The Cape Breton Magazine*.

For an extensive thematically organized selection of works on the history and culture of the Atlantic region, please visit http://www.oupcanada.com/AtlanticCanada3e.

Notes

Introduction: A Region in the Making

1. On the challenges of writing on Atlantic Canada, see Ian McKay, "A Note on 'Region' in Writing the History of Atlantic Canada," *Acadiensis* XXIX, 2 (Spring 2000): 89–101, and James K. Hiller, "Is Atlantic Canadian History Possible?" *Acadiensis* XXX, 1 (Autumn 2000): 16–22.

2. Alan Wilson, "Crosscurrents in Maritime Regionalism," in Bruce Hodgins et al., *Federalism in Canada and Australia: Historical Perspectives, 1920–1988* (Peterborough: Frost Centre for Canadian Heritage and Development Studies, 1989), 366.

3. Phillip A. Buckner and John G. Reid, eds., *The Atlantic Region to Confederation: A History* (Toronto and Fredericton: University of Toronto Press and Acadiensis Press, 1994); and E.R. Forbes and D.A. Muise, eds, *The Atlantic Provinces in Confederation* (Toronto and Fredericton: University of Toronto Press and Acadiensis Press, 1993).

4. Murray Beck, "An Atlantic Region Political Culture: A Chimera," in David Jay Bercuson and Phillip A. Buckner, eds., *Eastern and Western Perspectives: Papers from the Joint Atlantic Canada/Western Canadian Studies Conference* (Toronto: University of Toronto Press, 1981).

5. Janice Kulyk Keefer, *Under Eastern Eyes: A Critical Reading of Maritime Fiction* (Toronto: University of Toronto Press, 1987), 10.

6. Francis Bolger and Elizabeth R. Epperly, eds, *My Dear Mr. M: Letters to G.B. MacMillan from L.M. Montgomery* (Toronto: McGraw-Hill Ryerson, 1980), 65.

7. Patrick O'Flaherty, *The Rock Observed: Studies in the Literature of Newfoundland* (Toronto: University of Toronto Press, 1979), 100.

8. Edward MacDonald, *If You're Stronghearted: Prince Edward Island in the Twentieth Century* (Charlottetown: Prince Edward Island Museum & Heritage Foundation, 2000).

9. Ian McKay, "Of Karl Marx and the Bluenose: Colin Campbell McKay and the Legacy of Maritime Socialism," *Acadiensis* XXVII, 2 (Spring 1998), 3.

10. Barry Cooper, "Regionalism, Political Culture, and Canadian Political Myths," in *Regionalism and Party Politics in Canada*, ed. Lisa Young and Keith Archer, (Toronto: Oxford University Press, 2002), 97.

11. Ian McKay, *The Quest of the Folk: Antimodernism and Cultural Selection in Twentieth-Century Nova Scotia* (Montreal: McGill-Queen's University Press, 1994).

12. Margaret Conrad and David Northrup, "Fail Again, Fail Better: Atlantic Canadians and Their Pasts," in *Shaping and Agenda for Atlantic Canada*, ed. John G. Reid and Donald J. Savoie (Halifax: Fernwood, 2011). For the larger context, see Margaret Conrad et al., *Canadians and Their Pasts* (Toronto: University of Toronto Press, 2013).

13. Herb Wyile, *Anne of Tim Horton's: Globalization and the Reshaping of Atlantic-Canadian Literature* (Waterloo: Wilfrid Laurier University Press, 2011), 1.

14. Gary Burrill, *Away: Maritimers in Massachusetts, Ontario, and Alberta* (Montreal: McGill-Queen's University Press, 1992).

15. Stephen H. Ullman, "Nationalism and Regionalism in the Political Socialization of Cape Breton Whites and Indians," *American Review of Canadian Studies* 5, 1 (Spring 1975): 66–97.

16. Marilyn Porter, *Place and Persistence in the Lives of Newfoundland Women* (Aldershot: Avebury, 1993).

17. E.R. Forbes, *Challenging the Regional Stereotype: Essays on the 20th Century Maritimes* (Fredericton: Acadiensis Press, 1989) and Donald J. Savoie, *Visiting Grandchildren: Economic Development in the Maritimes* (Toronto: University of Toronto Press, 2006).

18. Sean T. Cadigan, "Regional Politics are Class Politics: A Newfoundland and Labrador Perspective on Region," *Acadiensis* XXXV, 2 (Spring 2006), 168.

19. Donald J. Savoie, *Regional Economic Development: Canada's Search for Solutions*, 2nd edn (Toronto: University of Toronto Press, 1992), 233–8.

20. Rosemary E. Ommer and Nancy J. Turner, "Informal Rural Economies in History," *Labour/Le Travail* 53 (Spring 2004): 127–57.

21. David Alexander, "New Notions of Happiness: Nationalism, Regionalism, and Atlantic Canada,"

Journal of Canadian Studies 15, 2 (Summer 1980): 29–42.

Chapter 1: Beginnings

1. Atlantic Geoscience Society, *The Last Billion Years: A Geological History of the Maritime Provinces* (Halifax: Nimbus Publishing, 2001).
2. A summary of scholarship on this period of the region's history can be found in Stephen A. Davis, "Early Societies: Sequences of Change," in *The Atlantic Region to Confederation*, ed. Phillip A. Buckner and John G. Reid (Toronto and Fredericton: University of Toronto and Acadiensis Press, 1994).
3. George F. MacDonald, "Debert: A Paleo-Indian Site in Central Nova Scotia," *Anthropology Papers* (Ottawa: National Museum of Man, 1968). For a brief outline of more recent archaeological developments in and around Debert, see Robyn Crook and Matthew Munro, "The Many Layers of Debert: Exploring Nova Scotia's Oldest Archaeological Site," in *Underground Nova Scotia: Stories of Archaeology*, ed. Paul Erikson and Jonathan Fowler (Halifax: Nimbus, 2010).
4. In recent years, some archaeologists have called this theory into question. They argue that the human occupation of the Americas dates back 30,000, even 50,000, years and that people perhaps came from multiple directions. See, for example, Dennis J. Stanford and Bruce Bradley, *Across Atlantic Ice: The Origins of America's Clovis Culture* (Berkeley: University of California Press, 2012), which argues that Clovis culture is European in origin.
5. Susan Blair, ed., *Wolastoqiyik Ajemseg: The People of Beautiful River at Jemseg*, vol 2: *Archaeological Results* (Fredericton: Archaeological Services, Heritage Branch, Culture and Sports Secretariat, 2004) and Susan Blair and Karen Perley, "'The People of the Beautiful River' at Jemseg," in *Underground New Brunswick: Stories of Archaeology*, ed. Paul Erickson and Jonathon Fowler (Halifax: Nimbus, 2013).
6. James A. Tuck, "The Archaic Period in the Maritime Provinces," in *Prehistoric Archaeology in the Maritime Provinces: Past and Present Research*, ed. Michael Deal and Susan Blair (Fredericton: Council of Maritime Premiers, 1991). There has been considerable debate on this issue. B.J. Bourque, for instance, maintains that the Late Archaic in the southwestern Maritimes and Maine represents a separate cultural tradition, which he calls the "Moorehead phase." Bruce J. Bourque, *Diversity and Complexity in Prehistoric Maritime Societies* (New York: Plenum Press, 1995).
7. Lisa Rankin, "Native Peoples from the Ice Age to the Extinction of the Beothuk," in *A Short History of Newfoundland and Labrador* (Portugal Cove–St Philip's: Bolder Publications, 2008) and Kevin McAleese, "Ancient Uses of Ramah Chert," http://www.heritage.nl.ca/environment/landscape_ramah.html.
8. Robert McGhee, *Ancient Peoples of the Arctic* (Vancouver: University of British Columbia Press, 1996).

Chapter 2: Aboriginal Peoples

1. Olive Patricia Dickason, *Canada's First Nations: A History of Founding Peoples from Earliest Times* (Toronto: McClelland and Stewart, 1992), 12.
2. The complicated evolution of naming conventions, territorial locations, and military alliances of Aboriginal peoples in the Maritime region are usefully summarized in John G. Reid, "Empire, the Maritime Colonies, and the Supplanting of Mi'kma'ki/Wulstukwik, 1780–1820," *Acadiensis* XXXVIII, 2 (Summer/Autumn 2009), note 4, 79–81.
3. For various perspectives on the numbers of Mi'kmaq at the time of contact, see Daniel N. Paul, *We Were Not the Savages*, 2nd edn (Halifax: Fernwood Publishing, 2000), 45–6; Virginia P. Miller, "Aboriginal Micmac Population: A Review of the Evidence," *Ethnohistory* 23, 2 (Spring 1976): 117–27, and "The Decline of the Nova Scotia Micmac Population, AD 1600–1850," *Culture* 2, 3 (1982): 107–20; Harald E.L. Prins, *The Mi'kmaq: Resistance, Accommodation, and Cultural Survival* (Fort Worth: Harcourt Brace College Publishers, 1996), 27; and Ralph Pastore, "The Sixteenth Century: Aboriginal Peoples and European Contact," in *The Atlantic Region to Confederation*, ed. Phillip A. Buckner and John G. Reid (Toronto: University of Toronto Press, 1994), 24.
4. Cole Harris, *The Reluctant Land: Space and Environment in Canada before Confederation* (Vancouver: University of British Columbia Press, 2008), 46–7.
5. Laurie Lacey, *Mi'kmaq Medicines*, 2nd edn (Halifax: Nimbus, 2012).
6. Cited in Ruth Holmes Whitehead, *The Old Man Told Us: Excerpts from Micmac History, 1500–1950* (Halifax: Nimbus, 1991), 11–12; translated by

Margaret Anne Hamelin from a "Lettre à Madame de Drucourt," n.d [c. 1750], in *Les Soirées canadiennes* (Quebec: Brousseau Frères, 1863), 300–1. Reprinted with permission from Nimbus Publishing Limited.

7. Father Chrestien Le Clercq, *New Relation of Gaspesia With the Customs and Religion of the Gaspesian Indians*, 2nd edn, ed. and trans. William F. Ganong (Toronto: Champlain Society, 1910), 239.

8. Ruth Holmes Whitehead, *Stories from the Six Worlds: Micmac Legends* (Halifax: Nimbus, 1988), 165–7, and Anne-Christine Hornborg, *Mi'kmaq Landscapes* (Aldershot: Ashgate, 2008).

9. Silas Tertius Rand, *Legends of the Micmac* (1894; New York: Longmans, Green and Com., 1894), 31–2. Available online through New Jersey: Invisible Book, 2005: http://www.invisiblebooks.com/Rand.pdf.

10. Prins, *The Mi'kmaq*, 39–41.

11. Vincent O. Erickson, "Maliseet-Passamaquoddy," in *Northeast*, ed. Bruce G. Trigger. Vol. 15, *Handbook of North American Indians*, ed. William C. Sturtevant (Washington, DC: Smithsonian Institution, 1978).

12. Donald H. Holly, "From Space to Place: An Archaeology and Historical Geography of the Recent Indian Period in Newfoundland," PhD dissertation, Brown University, 2002.

13. Nain station diary, 5 November 1772. Quoted in J.K. Hiller, "The Foundation and the Early Years of the Moravian Mission in Labrador, 1752–1805," MA thesis, Memorial University, 1967, 163.

14. Pastore, "The Sixteenth Century", 34–5.

15. Translation from W.C. Sturtevant, "The First Inuit Depiction by Europeans," *Études/Inuit/Studies* 4, 1–2 (1980): 47–9.

Chapter 3: European Encounters, 1000–1598

1. Josiah Jeremy to Silas Rand, 26 Sept. 1869. Cited in Ruth Holmes Whitehead, *The Old Man Told Us: Excerpts from Micmac History* (Halifax: Nimbus, 1991), 8.

2. David Armitage, "Three Concepts of Atlantic History," in *The British Atlantic World, 1500–1800*, ed. David Armitage and Michael J. Braddick (Basingstoke: Palgrave Macmillan, 2002).

3. See two articles by Birgitta Wallace: "The Norse in Newfoundland: L'Anse aux Meadows and Vinland," *Newfoundland Studies* 19, 1 (2003): 5–43, and

"Nova Scotia's Place in Vineland: On the Trail of the Elusive Norse," in *Underground Nova Scotia: Stories of Archaeology*, ed. Paul Erikson and Jonathan Fowler (Halifax: Nimbus, 2010).

4. R.A. Skelton, "Cabot, John," "Cabot, Sebastian," *Dictionary of Canadian Biography* (http://www.biography.ca); and Peter E. Pope, *The Many Landfalls of John Cabot* (Toronto: University of Toronto Press, 1997). For recent research on Cabot, see Evan T. Jones, "Alwyn Ruddock, John Cabot and the Discovery of America," *Historical Research*, LXXXI (2008): 224–54 (available online at: http://onlinelibrary.wiley.com/doi/10.1111/j.1468-2281.2007.00422.x/full) and "Henry VII and the Bristol Expeditions to North America: the Condon Documents," *Historical Research*, LXXXIII (2010): 444–54 (available online at: http://onlinelibrary.wiley.com/doi/10.1111/j.1468-2281.2009.00519.x/full). Following Ruddock's death in 2005, research on her claims was centred at the University of Bristol, where Evan Jones and Margaret Condon coordinate the Cabot Project: http://www.bristol.ac.uk/history/research/cabot.html.

5. James Axtell, "At the Water's Edge: Trading in the 16th Century," in *After Columbus: Essays in the Ethnohistory of Colonial North America* (New York: Oxford University Press, 1988), 145.

6. Luca Codignola, "Another Look at Verrazano's Voyage, 1524," *Acadiensis* XXIX, 1 (Autumn 1999): 29–42, and William F.E. Morley, "Verrazzano, Giovanni da," *Dictionary of Canadian Biography* (http://www.biography.ca).

7. Emily Burton, "Portuguese Settlement in Northeastern North America: The 1520s Fagundes Expedition," *Nashwaak Review* 22/23 (Spring/Summer 2009): 413–46.

8. In addition to Harold Innis's classic study *The Cod Fisheries: The History of an International Economy* (New Haven: Yale University P 1940), see David J. Starkey, Jon Thor, and Ingo Heidbrink, eds., *A History of the North Atlantic Fisheries*, vol. 1: *From Early Times to the Mid-Nineteenth Century* (Bremerhaven: German Maritime Museum, 2008) and D.J. Starkey and J.E. Candow, eds., *The North Atlantic Fisheries: Supply, Marketing and Consumption, 1560–1900* (Hull: Studia Atlantica Publications, 2006). See also Peter Pope, "Transformation of the Maritime Cultural Landscape of Atlantic Canada by Migratory European Fishers, 1500–1800," in *Beyond the Catch: Fisheries of the North Atlantic, the North Sea*

and the Baltic, 900–1850, ed. Louis Sicking and Darlene Abreu-Ferreira (Brill: The Hague, 2009).

9. Dan Conlin, Pirates of the Atlantic: Robbery, Murder and Mayhem off the Canadian East Coast (Halifax: Formac, 2009), 7–15.

10. As translated in Sally Ross and Alphonse Deveau, The Acadians of Nova Scotia, Past and Present (Halifax: Nimbus, 1992), 3–4.

11. D.B. Quinn, "The Voyage of Etienne Belanger to the Maritimes in 1583: A New Document," Canadian Historical Review, XLIII, 4 (December 1962): 328–43.

12. Cited in D.B. Quinn, North American World, vol. 4 (New York: Arno Press, 1979), 64–5.

13. Axtell, "At the Water's Edge," 177. On the linguistic development of the Mi'kmaq after contact, see Peter Bakker, "'The Language of the Coastal Tribes is Half-Basque': A Basque-American Indian Pidgin in Use Between Europeans and Native Americans in North America ca 1540–ca 1640," Anthropological Linguistics 31, 3–4 (1989): 117–47. The gulf of St Lawrence fishery is discussed in Laurier Turgeon, "French Fishers, Fur Traders, and Amerindians during the Sixteenth Century: History and Archaeology," William and Mary Quarterly, 3rd series, 55 (1998): 585–610.

Chapter 4: Colonial Experiments, 1598–1632

1. Cited in Patrick O'Flaherty, The Rock Observed: Studies in the Literature of Newfoundland (Toronto: University of Toronto Press, 1979), 10.

2. Elizabeth Jones, Gentlemen and Jesuits: Quests for Glory and Adventure in the Early Days of New France (Toronto: University of Toronto Press, 1986), 29. On the larger context in which Acadia's history unfolded, see John Reid, Acadia, Maine, and New Scotland: Marginal Colonies in the Seventeenth Century (Toronto: University of Toronto Press, 1981) and Jean Daigle, "Acadia from 1604 to 1763: An Historical Synthesis," in Acadia of the Maritimes, ed. Jean Daigle (Moncton: Chaire d'études acadiennes, 1995), 1–43.

3. Lucien Campeau, "Membertou, Henri," Dictionary of Canadian Biography (http://www.biography.ca).

4. George MacBeath, "Gravé du Pont, Robert," Dictionary of Canadian Biography (http://www.biography.ca).

5. M.A. MacDonald, Fortune and LaTour: The Civil War in Acadia (Halifax: Nimbus, 2000) and Brenda

Dunn, A History of Port-Royal/Annapolis Royal, 1605–1800 (Halifax: Nimbus, 2004), 33–45.

6. On the colonization efforts of the Alexanders, see John G. Reid, "Sir William Alexander and North American Colonization," and "The 'Lost Colony' of New Scotland and its Successors to 1670," in Essays on Northeastern North America: Seventeenth and Eighteenth Centuries (Toronto: University of Toronto Press, 2008), and Andrew D. Nicholls, "'The purpois is honorabill, and may conduce to the good of our service': Lord Ochiltree and the Cape Breton Colony, 1629–1631," Acadiensis XXXIV, 2 (Spring 2005): 109–23.

7. Richard Guthry, "A Relation of the Voyage and Plantation of the Scots Colony in New Scotland under the conduct of William Alexander Younger, 1629," republished in N.E.S. Griffiths and John G. Reid, "New Evidence on New Scotland, 1629," William and Mary Quarterly, 3rd Series, 49, 3 (July 1992): 500–8.

8. Peter Pope, "Six Letters from the Early Colony of Avalon," Avalon Chronicles 1 (1996), 6.

9. George Calvert to King Charles I, 19 Aug. 1629, quoted in Gillian Cell, Newfoundland Discovered: English Attempts at Colonization, 1610–1630 (London: Hakluyt Society, 1982), 295–6.

10. Ramsay Cook, "1492 and All That: Making a Garden out of a Wilderness," in Consuming Canada: Readings in Environmental History, ed. Chad Gaffield and Pam Gaffield (Toronto: Copp Clark, 1995). See also Heather L. MacLeod, "Responding to the Land: Experiencing Nature in Nova Scotia, 1607–1900," in Land and Sea: Environmental History in Atlantic Canada, ed. Claire Campbell and Robert Summerby-Murray (Fredericton: Acadiensis Press, 2013).

11. Cited in Ruth Holmes Whitehead, The Old Man Told Us: Excerpts from Micmac History, 1500–1950 (Halifax: Nimbus, 1991), 39.

12. Cited in Peter Neary and Patrick O'Flaherty, By Great Waters: A Newfoundland and Labrador Anthology (Toronto: University of Toronto Press, 1974), 10.

Chapter 5: Colonial Communities Take Root, 1632–1713

1. Joan Dawson, "Colonists or Birds of Passage? A Glimpse of the Inhabitants of LaHave, 1632–1636," Nova Scotia Historical Review 9, 1 (June 1989): 42–61.

2. Robert Le Blant, "Les compagnies du Cap-Breton,

1629–1647," *Revue d'histoire de l'Amérique française* XVI, 1 (juin 1962): 81–94.

3. The most comprehensive coverage can be found in M.A. MacDonald, *Fortune and LaTour: The Civil War in Acadia* (Halifax: Nimbus, 2000). See also Brenda Dunn, *A History of Port-Royal/Annapolis Royal, 1605–1800* (Halifax: Nimbus, 2004) and John G. Reid, *Acadia, Maine, and New Scotland: Marginal Colonies in the Seventeenth Century* (Toronto: University of Toronto Press, 1981).

4. George MacBeath, "Denys, Nicolas," *Dictionary of Canadian Biography* (http://www.biography.ca).

5. For a brief summary of these developments, see Alan Taylor, *Colonial America: A Very Short Introduction* (New York: Oxford University, Press 2013), Chapter 7.

6. Gregory Kennedy, "Marshland Colonization in Acadia and Poitou during the 17th Century," *Acadiensis* XLII, 1 (Winter/Spring 2013): 37–66. Reprinted with permission from Acadiensis.

7. N.E.S. Griffiths, "The Acadians," *Dictionary of Canadian Biography* (http://www.biography.ca). For a more detailed discussion, see Naomi E.S. Griffiths, *The Contexts of Acadian History, 1686–1784* (Montreal and Kingston: McGill-Queen's University Press, 1992) and *From Migrant to Acadian: A North American Border People, 1604–1755* (Montreal and Kingston: McGill-Queen's University Press, 2005).

8. Dunn, *A History of Port-Royal/Annapolis Royal, 1605–1800*, 77.

9. Geoffrey Plank, "New England and the Conquest," in *The "Conquest" of Acadia, 1710: Imperial, Colonial, and Aboriginal Constructions*, ed. John G. Reid et al. (Toronto: University of Toronto Press. 2004).

10. Gisa I. Hynes, "Some Aspects of the Demography of Port Royal, 1650–1755," *Acadiensis* 3, 1 (Autumn 1973): 3–17.

11. "Reply to the King in Council of the Merchants, Owners and Masters of Ships of the Western Parts . . .", 1668. Calendar of State Papers.

12. Gordon Handcock, *"Soe longe as there comes noe women": Origins of English Settlement in Newfoundland* (St John's: Breakwater Press, 1989), 37.

13. Peter E. Pope, *Fish into Wine: The Newfoundland Plantation in the Seventeenth Century* (Chapel Hill: University of North Carolina Press, 2004), 300.

14. Alan F. Williams, *Father Baudoin's War: D'Iberville's Campaigns in Acadia and Newfoundland, 1696, 1697* (St John's: Memorial University, 1987), 33, 48.

15. John G. Reid, "Unorthodox Warfare in the Northeast, 1703," *Canadian Historical Review* LXXIII, 2 (June 1992): 211–20, and Geoffrey Plank, "New England and the Conquest," in *The "Conquest" of Acadia, 1710*.

16. Brenda Dunn, "Lives of Women in Ancienne Acadie," in *Looking Into Acadie: Three Illustrated Lectures*, ed. Margaret Conrad (Halifax: Nova Scotia Museum, 1997), 43.

17. William Wicken, "Mi'kmaq Decisions: Antoine Tecouenemac, the Conquest, and the Treaty of Utrecht," in *The "Conquest" of Acadia, 1710*, 86–100.

Chapter 6: Renegotiating the Atlantic Region, 1713–1763

1. John G. Reid et al., eds., *The "Conquest" of Acadia, 1710: Imperial, Colonial, and Aboriginal Constructions* (Toronto: University of Toronto Press, 2004), 208.

2. Jerry Bannister, *The Rule of the Admirals: Laws, Custom, and Naval Government, 1699–1832* (Toronto: University of Toronto Press, 2003).

3. Dan Conlin, *Pirates of the Atlantic: Robbery, Murder and Mayhem off the Canadian East Coast* (Halifax: Formac, 2009), 21.

4. Louisbourg is the subject of three fine studies by A.J.B. Johnston: *Endgame 1758: The Promise, the Glory, and the Despair of Louisbourg's Last Decade* (Lincoln: University of Nebraska Press, 2007); *Control and Order in French Colonial Louisbourg, 1713–1758* (East Lansing: Michigan State University Press, 2001); and *Religion in Life at Louisbourg* (Montreal: McGill-Queen's University Press, 1984).

5. Brenda Dunn, *A History of Port-Royal/Annapolis Royal, 1605–1800* (Halifax: Nimbus, 2004), 106.

6. Kenneth Donovan, "Slaves and Their Owners in Île Royale, 1713–1760," *Acadiensis* 25, 1 (Autumn 1995): 3–32.

7. A.J.B. Johnston, *Storied Shores: St Peter's, Isle Madame, Chapel island in the 17th and 18th Centuries* (Sydney: UCCB Press, 2004), 102.

8. Thomas Garden Barnes, "'The Dayly Cry for Justice': The Judicial Failure of the Annapolis Royal Regime, 1713–1749," in *Essays in the History of Canadian Law*, vol. III, *Nova Scotia*, ed. Philip Gerard and Jim Phillips (Toronto: University of Toronto Press, 1990), 33.

9. N.E.S. Griffiths, "The Golden Age: Acadian Life, 1713–1748," *Histoire Sociale/Social History* 17, 33 (May 1984): 21–34.

10. John Grenier, *The Far Reaches of Empire: War in Nova Scotia, 1710–1760* (University of Oklahoma Press, 2008); Geoffrey Plank, *An Unsettled Conquest: The British Campaign Against the Peoples of Acadia* (Philadelphia: University of Pennsylvania Press, 2000); George F.G. Stanley, *New France: The Last Phase, 1744–1760* (Toronto: McClelland and Stewart, 1968); and J.B. Brebner, *New England's Outpost before the Conquest of Canada* (New York: Columbia University Press, 1927).

11. James Pritchard, *Anatomy of a Naval Disaster: The 1746 French Expedition to North America* (Montreal: McGill-Queen's University Press, 1995), 228–9.

12. Judith Fingard, Janet Guildford, and David Sutherland, *Halifax: The First 250 Years* (Halifax: Nimbus, 2004). 8–22.

13. Cited in Ruth Holmes Whitehead, *The Old Man Told Us: Excerpts from Micmac History, 1500–1950* (Halifax: Nimbus, 1991), 114.

14. Cited in Gérard Finn, "Le Loutre, Jean-Louis," *Dictionary of Canadian Biography* (http://www.biography.ca).

15. Thomas Aikins, ed., *Selections from the Public Documents of the Province of Nova Scotia* (Halifax: Public Archives of Nova Scotia, 1869), 582.

16. Stephen A. White, "The True Number of Acadians," in Ronnie-Gilles LeBlanc, dir., *Du Grand Dérangement à la Déportation: nouvelles perspectives historiques* (Moncton: Chaire d'études acadiennes, Université de Moncton, 2005), 21–56; and Earle Lockerby, "The Deportation of the Acadians from Ile St-Jean, 1758," *Acadiensis* 27, 2 (Spring 1998): 45–94.

17. Warren Perrin, *Acadian Redemption* (Erath, LA: Acadian Heritage and Cultural Foundation, Inc., 2004) and James Laxer, *The Acadians in Search of a Homeland* (Toronto: Doubleday Canada, 2006), 103–10.

18. John Mack Faragher, *A Great and Noble Scheme: The Tragic Story of the Expulsion of the French Acadians from Their American Homeland* (New York: W.W. Norton, 2005), 469. See also Ronnie-Gilles LeBlanc, dir. *Du Grand Dérangement à la Déportation: nouvelles perspectives historiques* (Moncton: Chaire d'études acadiennes, Université de Moncton, 2005); Dean Jobb, *The Acadians: A People's Story of Exile and Triumph* (Mississauga: Wiley and Sons, 2005); and Christopher Hodson, *The Acadian Diaspora: An Eighteenth-Century History* (Oxford: Oxford University Press, 2012).

19. Johnston, *Endgame 1758*, 274.

20. Cited in M.A. MacDonald, *Rebels and Royalists: The Lives and Material Culture of New Brunswick's Early English-Speaking Settlers, 1758–1783* (Fredericton: New Ireland Press, 1990), 21.

Chapter 7: Community Formation, 1749–1815

1. John Reid, "Pax Britannica or Pax Indigena? Planter Nova Scotia (1760–1782) and Competing Strategies of Pacification," *Canadian Historical Review* 85, 4 (December 2004): 669–93; and Julian Gwyn, *Excessive Expectations: Maritime Commerce and the Development of Nova Scotia, 1740–1870* (Montreal and Kingston: McGill-Queen's University Press, 1998).

2. Stephen J. Hornsby, *Surveyors of Empire: Samuel Holland, J.F.W. DesBarres, and the Making of the Atlantic Neptune* (Montreal: McGill-Queen's University Press, 2012).

3. J. Garth Taylor, "The Two Worlds of Mikak," *The Beaver* 314, 3 (1984): 4–13, and 314, 4 (1984): 18–25. See also Marianne P. Stopp, "Eighteenth Century Labrador Inuit in England," *Arctic* 62,1 (2009): 45–64, and the entries on Francis Lucas, Mikak, and Tuglavina in *Dictionary of Canadian Biography* (http://www.biography.ca).

4. This question was initially probed in great detail by J. B. Brebner, *The Neutral Yankees of Nova Scotia* (1937; Toronto: McClelland and Stewart, 1969). See also George Rawlyk, *Revolution Rejected, 1775–1776* (Scarborough, ON: Prentice-Hall, 1968) and Elizabeth Mancke, *The Fault Lines of Empire: Political Differentiation in Massachusetts and Nova Scotia, ca. 1760–1830* (London: Routledge, 2005). For the larger context of developments discussed in this chapter, see Julian Gwyn, *Excessive Expectations: Maritime Commerce and the Economic Development of Nova Scotia, 1740–1870* (Montreal: McGill-Queen's University Press, 1998) and Stephen J. Hornsby, *British Atlantic, American Frontier: Spaces of Power in Early Modern British America* (Hanover: University Press of New England, 2005).

5. For the background to the conflict, see Merrill Jensen, *The Founding of a Nation: A History of the American Revolution, 1763–1776* (Indianapolis: Hackett Publishing, 2004).

6. Captain John Stanton, "A Report of the State of the Province of Nova Scotia," 4 December 1775, CO 217, vol. 52, fol. 60, cited in Carol Campbell and

James F. Smith, *Necessaries and Sufficiencies: Planter Society in Londonderry, Onslow, and Truro Townships, 1761–1780* (Sydney: Cape Breton University Press, 2011), 216.

7. Julian Gwyn, *Frigates and Foremasts: The North American Squadron in Nova Scotia Waters, 1745–1815* (Vancouver: University of British Columbia Press, 2003), 56.

8. Stephen Hornsby, *British Atlantic, American Frontier: Spaces of Power in Early Modern British America* (Hanover: University Press of New England, 2005), Chapter 6.

9. "Extracts from the Record of a Conference of the St. John and Micmac Indians with the Americans: July 10–July 17, 1776," in *Source Materials Relating to the New Brunswick Indian*, ed. W.D. Hamilton and W.A. Spray (Fredericton: Centennial Print and Litho Ltd., 1976), 40–50. The details of the negotiations relating to the treaty and the responses to it are discussed in Ernest Clarke, *The Siege of Fort Cumberland, 1776: An Episode in the American Revolution* (Montreal: McGill-Queen's University Press, 1995), 58–66.

10. Jerry Bannister, "Canada as Counter-Revolution: The Loyalist Order Framework in Canadian History, 1750–1840," in *Liberalism and Hegemony: Debating the Canadian Liberal Revolution*, ed. Jean-François Constant and Michel Ducharme (Toronto: University of Toronto Press, 2009).

11. David Bell, *Loyalist Rebellion in New Brunswick: A Defining Conflict for Canada's Political Culture* (Halifax: Formac, 2013), 26. For the larger Loyalist experience, see Ruma Chopra, *Choosing Sides: Loyalists in Revolutionary America* (Lanham, MD: Rowman & Littlefield, 2013); Maya Jasanoff, *Liberty's Exiles: American Loyalists in the Revolutionary World* (New York: Alfred Knopf, 2011); and Wallace Brown, *The Good Americans: The Loyalists in the American Revolution* (New York: William Morrow, 1969).

12. Neil MacKinnon, *This Unfriendly Soil: The Loyalist Experience in Nova Scotia, 1783–1791* (Montreal: McGill-Queen's University Press, 1989), 96.

13. Ann Gorman Condon, "1783–1800. Loyalist Arrival, Acadian Return, Imperial Reform," in *The Atlantic Region to Confederation*, ed. Phillip A. Buckner and John G. Reid (Toronto: University of Toronto and Acadiensis Press, 1994), 192.

14. Cassandra Pybus, *Epic Journeys of Freedom: Runaway Slaves of the American Revolution and their Global Quest for Liberty* (Boston: Beacon Press, 2006) and James W. St. G. Walker, *The Black Loyalists: The Search for a Promised Land in Nova Scotia and Sierra Leone, 1783–1870* (Toronto: University of Toronto Press, 1992).

15. Bonnie Huskins, "'Remarks and Rough Memorandums': Social Sets, Sociability, and Community in the Journal of William Booth, Shelburne, 1787 and 1789," *Journal of the Royal Nova Scotia Historical Society* 13 (2010): 103–32, and Ann Gorman Condon, "The Family in Exile: Loyalist Social Values After the Revolution," in *Intimate Relations: Family and Community in Planter Nova Scotia, 1759–1800*, ed. Margaret Conrad (Fredericton: Acadiensis Press, 1995).

16. Edward Winslow to Ward Chipman, 7 July 1783, University of New Brunswick Archives, Harriet Irving Library, Winslow Family Papers, MG H2, Vol. 2, Part 2, p. 104 available in *The Edward Winslow Letters, 1783–1785*, Atlantic Canada Virtual Archives, http://atlanticportal.hil.unb.ca/acva.

17. Graeme Wynn, *Timber Colony: A Historical Geography of Early Nineteenth Century New Brunswick* (Toronto: University of Toronto Press, 1981).

18. Keith Mercer, "The Murder of Lieutenant Lawry: A Case Study of British Naval Impressment in Newfoundland, 1794," *Newfoundland and Labrador Studies* 21, 2 (Fall 2006): 255–89.

Chapter 8: Maturing Colonial Societies, 1815–1860

1. Joseph Howe, "The Blue Nose," in M.G. Parks, ed., *Joseph Howe: Poems and Essays* (Toronto: University of Toronto Press, 1973), 145–6.

2. Karl Polanyi, *The Great Transformation: The Political and Economic Origins of Our Times* (Boston: Beacon Press, 1957).

3. Jacques Poitras, *Imaginary Line: Life on an Unfinished Border* (Fredericton: Goose Lane, 2011).

4. Johnstone is cited in D.C. Harvey, ed., *Journeys to the Island of St. John* (Toronto: Macmillan, 1955), 105. On the Miramichi fire of 1825, see Alan MacEachern, "'Popular by our Misery': The International Response to the 1825 Miramichi Fire," in *Land and Sea: Environmental History in Atlantic Canada*, ed. Claire Campbell and Robert Summerby-Murray (Fredericton: Acadiensis Press, 2013).

5. Cited in Jennifer Reid, *Myth, Symbol, and Colonial Encounter: British and Mi'kmaq in Acadia,*

1700–1867 (Ottawa: University of Ottawa Press, 1995), 36.

6. "Statement of the Indian Delegation, 23 June 1842," in *Source Materials Relating to the New Brunswick Indian*, ed. W.D. Hamilton and W.A. Spray (Fredericton: Centennial Print and Litho Ltd., 1976), 112.

7. Eric W. Sager with Gerald E. Panting, *Maritime Capital: The Shipping Industry in Atlantic Canada, 1820–1914* (Montreal: McGill-Queen's University Press, 1990), 17.

8. Gwynneth C.D. Jones, "Gisborne, Frederic Newton," *Dictionary of Canadian Biography* (http://www.biography.ca)

9. T.W. Acheson, "The 1840s: Decade of Tribulation," in *The Atlantic Region to Confederation: A History*, ed. Phillip A. Buckner and John G. Reid (Toronto and Fredericton: University of Toronto and Acadiensis Press, 1994).

10. Sean T. Cadigan, *Hope and Deception in Conception Bay: Merchant–Settler Relations in Newfoundland, 1785–1855* (Toronto: University of Toronto Press, 1995).

11. A.J. Sandy Young, *Beyond Heroes: A Sport History of Nova Scotia*, vol. 2 (Hantsport: Lancelot Press, 1991), 15.

12. Patrick O'Flaherty, "Carson, William," *Dictionary of Canadian Biography* (http://www.biography.ca).

13. Rusty Bittermann and Margaret McCallum, "When Private Rights become Private Wrongs: Property and the State in Prince Edward Island in the 1830s," in *Despotic Dominion: Property Rights and British Settler Societies*, ed. John McLaren, A.R. Buck, and Nancy Wright (Vancouver: University of British Columbia Press, 2005).

14. Ian McKay, "The Liberal Order Framework: A Prospectus for a Reconnaissance of Canadian History," *Canadian Historical Review* 81, 4 (December 2000): 617–45.

15. Jerry Bannister, "Canada as Counter-Revolution: The Loyalist Order Framework in Canadian History," in *Liberalism and Hegemony: Debating the Canadian Liberal Revolution*, ed. Jean-François Constant and Michel Ducharme (Toronto: University of Toronto Press, 2008) and Ruth Sandwell, "The Limits of Liberalism: The Liberal Reconnaissance and the History of the Family in Canada," *Canadian Historical Review* 83, 3 (September 2003): 423–50.

Chapter 9: Confronting Confederation, 1860–1873

1. Greg Marquis, *In Armageddon's Shadow: The Civil War and Canada's Maritime Provinces* (Montreal: McGill-Queen's University Press, 1998), 35.

2. Ian Ross Robertson, ed., *The Prince Edward Island Land Commission of 1860* (Fredericton: Acadiensis Press, 1988), 69–70. Reprinted with permission from Acadiensis.

3. Andrew Smith, *British Businessmen and Canadian Confederation: Constitution Making in an Age of Anglo-Globalization* (Montreal: McGill-Queen's University Press, 2008), 3.

4. Phillip A. Buckner, "The 1860s: An End and a Beginning," in *The Atlantic Region to Confederation: A History*, ed. Phillip A. Buckner and John G. Reid (Toronto and Fredericton: University of Toronto Press and Acadiensis Press, 1994), 377.

5. Cited in J. Murray Beck, ed., *Joseph Howe: Voice of Nova Scotia* (Toronto: Carleton Library/McClelland & Stewart, 1964), 175.

6. Cited in Kenneth G. Pryke, *Nova Scotia and Confederation, 1864–74* (Toronto: University of Toronto Press, 1978), 41.

7. C.M. Wallace, "Tilley, Sir Samuel Leonard," *Dictionary of Canadian Biography* (http://www.biography.ca).

8. Donald Warner, *The Idea of Continental Union: Agitation for the Annexation of Canada to the United States, 1849–1893* (University of Kentucky Press, 1960), 814.

9. David G. Alexander, "Economic Growth in the Atlantic Region, 1880–1940," in *Atlantic Canada and Confederation: Essays in Canadian Political Economy*, comp. Eric W. Sager, Lewis R. Fischer, Stuart O. Pierson (St John's and Toronto: Memorial University and University of Toronto Press, 1983), 74.

10. James K. Hiller, "Confederation Defeated: The Newfoundland Election of 1869," in *Newfoundland in the Nineteenth and Twentieth Centuries: Essays in Interpretation*, ed. James K. Hiller and Peter Neary (Toronto: University of Toronto Press, 1980).

11. Ian Ross Robertson, *The Tenant League of Prince Edward Island, 1864–1867: Leasehold Tenure in the New World* (Toronto: University of Toronto Press, 1996), 273.

Chapter 10: The Industrial Challenge, 1873–1901

1. David G. Alexander, "Economic Growth in the Atlantic Region, 1880–1940," *Acadiensis* III:1 (Autumn 1978): 47–76. Harold A. Innis, *The Cod Fisheries. A History of an International Economy* (Toronto: University of Toronto Press, 1954), 425–43.

2. T.W. Acheson, "The National Policy and the Industrialization of the Maritimes, 1880–1910," *Acadiensis* 1, 2 (Spring 1972): 3–28.

3. D. Murray Young, "Gibson, Alexander," *Dictionary of Canadian Biography* (http://www.biography.ca).

4. L.D, McCann, "The Mercantile–Industrial Transition in the Metal Towns of Pictou County, 1857–1931," *Acadiensis* X, 2 (Spring 1981): 29–64, and Don Macgillivray, "Henry Melville Comes to Cape Breton: The Saga of the Gilded Age Entrepreneur," *Acadiensis* IX, 1 (Autumn 1979): 44–70.

5. Ken Cruikshank, "The People's Railway: The Intercolonial Railway and the Canadian Public Enterprise Experience," *Acadiensis*, XVI, 1 (Autumn 1986): 78–100.

6. Kealey, Greg, ed., *Canada Investigates Industrialism*, © University of Toronto Press 1973: pp. 395–6.

7. James Hiller, "The Railway and Local Politics in Newfoundland, 1870–1901," in *Newfoundland in the Nineteenth and Twentieth Centuries: Essays in Interpretation*, ed. James Hiller and Peter Neary (Toronto: University of Toronto Press, 1980).

8. On out-migration see Alan A. Brookes, "Out-Migration from the Maritime Provinces, 1860–1900: Some Preliminary Considerations," *Acadiensis* V, 2 (Spring 1976): 26–55, and Patricia A. Thornton, "The Problem of Out-Migration from Atlantic Canada, 1871–1921: A New Look," *Acadiensis* XV, 1 (Autumn 1985): 92–120.

9. Judith Fingard, "The 1880s: Paradoxes of Progress," in *The Atlantic Provinces in Confederation*, ed. E.R. Forbes and D.A. Muise (Toronto: University of Toronto Press, 1993), 97.

10. Margaret Conrad and Heather Steel, "They Come and They Go: Four Centuries of Immigration to New Brunswick," in *Rendez-Vous Immigration 2004*, ed. Hélène Destrempes and Joe Ruggieri (Fredericton: Policy Studies Centre, University of New Brunswick, 2005).

11. Martha Elizabeth Walls, *No Need of a Chief for this Band: The Maritime Mi'kmaq and Federal Electoral legislation, 1899–1951* (Vancouver: University of British Columbia Press, 2010).

12. Anne Hart, "Brooks, Lydia (Blake, Campbell)," *Dictionary of Canadian Biography* (http://www.biography.ca).

13. Colin D. Howell, "W.S. Fielding and the Repeal of Elections of 1886 and 1887 in Nova Scotia," *Acadiensis* VIII, 2 (Spring 1979): 28–46.

14. Ian McKay, "'By Wisdom, Wile or War': The Provincial Workmen's Association and the Struggle for Working-Class Independence in Nova Scotia, 1879–97," *Labour/Le Travail* 18 (Fall 1986): 18–62.

15. Robert MacIntosh, "The Boys in the Nova Scotia Coal Mines: 1873 to 1923," *Acadiensis* XVI, 2 (Spring 1987): 35–50.

16. Bridglal Pachai, *Beneath the Clouds of the Promised Land: The Survival of Nova Scotia's Blacks, Volume II: 1800–1989* (Halifax: Black Educators Association, 1990), 87.

17. Naomi Griffiths, "Evangeline: A Tale of Acadie," *The Canadian Encyclopedia*, 2nd edn (Edmonton: Hurtig, 1988), II, 729.

18. Denis Bourque et Chantal Richard, *Les Conventions Nationales Acadiennes, Tome 1* (1881-1890) Moncton: Institut d'études acadiennes, 2013. Reprinted with permission from Institut d'études acadiennes.

19. Colin Howell, "Reform and the Monopolistic Impulse: The Professionalization of Medicine," *Acadiensis* XI, 1 (Autumn 1981): 3–22, and Colin Howell and Michael Smith, "Orthodox Medicine and the Health Reform Movement in the Maritimes," *Acadiensis* XVIII, 2 (Spring 1989): 40–71.

20. E.R. Forbes, "Battles in Another War: Edith Archibald and the Halifax Feminist Movement," in *Challenging the Regional Stereotype: Essays on the 20th Century Maritimes* (Fredericton: Acadiensis Press, 1989).

21. Alan Brookes, ed., "The Provincials by Albert Kennedy," *Acadiensis* IV, 2 (Spring 1975), 94.

Chapter 11: The Promise and Peril of a New Century, 1901–1919

1. Anne Hart, Roberta Buchanan, and B.A. Green, *The Woman Who Mapped Labrador: The Life and Expedition Diary of Mina Hubbard* (Montreal: McGill-Queen's University Press, 2005); Mina Hubbard, *A Woman's Way through Unknown Labrador*, ed. Sherill Grace (1908; Montreal: McGill-Queen's University Press, 2008); Dillon Wallace, *The Lure of the Labrador*

Wild: The Story of the Exploring Expedition Conducted by Leonidas Hubbard Jr. (New York: Revell, 1905) and *The Long Labrador Trail* (London, Hodder and Stoughton, 1915).

2. David Frank, "The Cape Breton Coal Industry and the Rise and Fall of the British Empire Steel Corporation," in *Cape Breton Historical Essays*, ed. Don Macgillivray and Brian Tennyson (Sydney: College of Cape Breton Press, 1980), 114–15.

3. Gregory P. Marchildon, "John F. Stairs, Max Aitken and the Scotia Group: Finance Industrial Decline in the Maritimes, 1890–1914," in *Farm, Factory and Fortune: New Studies in the Economic History of the Maritime Provinces*, ed. Kris Inwood (Fredericton: Acadiensis, 1993).

4. Ian McKay, "Strikes in the Maritimes, 1900–1914." *Acadiensis* XIII, 1 (Autumn 1990): 3–46.

5. Fishermen's Advocate, 29 October 1910. Quoted in Ian D.H. McDonald, "To Each His Own." *William Coaker and the Fishermen's Protective Union in Newfoundland Politics, 1908–1925* (St John's, 1987), 21–2.

6. Ramsay Cook, *The Regenerators: Social Criticism in Late Victorian English Canada* (Toronto: University of Toronto Press, 1985).

7. Colin Howell, "The 1900s: Industry, Urbanization, and Reform," in *The Atlantic Provinces in Confederation*, ed. E.R. Forbes and D.A. Muise (Toronto: University of Toronto Press, 1993).

8. Mary Rubio and Elizabeth Waterston, eds, *The Selected Journals of L.M. Montgomery*, 5 vols (Toronto: Oxford University Press, 1987–2004).

9. Ian McKay, "The Five Ages of Nova Scotian Tourism," *New Maritimes* 5, 11–12 (1987), 8.

10. Gerald L. Pocius, "Tourists, Health Seekers and Sportsmen: Luring Americans to Newfoundland in the Early Twentieth Century," in *Twentieth-Century Newfoundland: Explorations*, ed. James K. Hiller and Peter Neary (St John's: Breakwater Press, 1994).

11. Quoted in Christopher Clark, *The Sleepwalkers. How Europe Went to War in 1914* (London: Penguin Books, 2013), xxi. See also Margaret MacMillan, *The War that Ended Peace: The Road to 1914* (Toronto: Random House, 2013).

12. James Robert Johnston, *Riding into War: The Memoir of a Horse Transport Driver, 1916–1919* ed. Brent Wilson (Fredericton: Goose Lane and the New Brunswick Military Heritage Project, 2004).

13. M. Olga McKenna, *Micmac by Choice: Elsie Sark—An Island Legend* (Halifax: Formac, 1990).

14. James W. St G. Walker, "Race and Recruitment in World War I: Enlistment of Visible Minorities in the Canadian Expeditionary Force," *Canadian Historical Review* 70, 1 (March 1989): 1–26.

15. Major A. Rayley, "Beaumont Hamel," *Veterans' Magazine* 1, 3 (1921), 37.

16. Janet F. Kitz, *Shattered City: The Halifax Explosion and the Road to Recovery* (Halifax: Nimbus, 1989), 82, 96–104.

17. Ian McKay, "The 1910s: The Stillborn Triumph of Progressive Reform," in *The Atlantic Provinces in Confederation*, ed. E.R. Forbes and D.A. Muise (Toronto and Fredericton: University of Toronto Press and Acadiensis Press, 1993), 229.

18. Mark Osborne Humphries, *The Last Plague: Spanish Influenza and the Politics of Public Health in Canada* (Toronto: University of Toronto Press, 2013).

19. Extract from Periodical Accounts relating to the Missions of the Church of the United Brethren, 1919, in Helge Kleivan, *The Eskimos of Northeast Labrador: A History of Eskimo–White Relations, 1771–1955* (Oslo: Norsk Polarinstitutt, 1966), 181.

20. Jane Jenkins, "Baptism of Fire: New Brunswick's Public Health Movement and the 1918 Influenza Epidemic," *Canadian Bulletin of Medical History* 24, 2 (2007): 317–43.

21. Sylvia Bashevkin, *Toeing the Lines: Women and Party Politics in English Canada*, 2nd edn (Toronto: University of Toronto Press, 1993), 5.

Chapter 12: Between the Wars, 1919–1939

1. Robert Skidelsky, "The Growth of a World Economy," in *The Twentieth Century*, ed. Michael Howard and William Roger Louis (Oxford and New York: Oxford University Press, 1998), 50–7, and Eric Hobsbawm, *The Age of Extremes. A History of the World, 1914–1991* (New York: Vintage Books, 1996), 85–108. The classic Canadian study is A.E. Safarian, *The Canadian Economy in the Great Depression* (1959; Ottawa: Carleton University Press, 1970).

2. Heidi MacDonald, "Olton, Robert Trenholm" *Dictionary of Canadian Biography* (http://www.biography.ca).

3. S.A. Saunders, *The Economic History of the Maritime Provinces*, ed. T.W. Acheson (Fredericton: Acadiensis Press, 1984), 38.

4. E.R. Forbes, *The Maritime Rights Movement, 1919–1927: A Study in Canadian Regionalism* (Montreal:

McGill-Queen's University Press, 1979), 176. See also Don Nebras. "Revisiting Maritime Rights: Bourgeois Saint John and Regional Protest in the 1920s," *Acadiensis* XXXVII, 1 (Winter/Spring 2008): 110–30, and David Frank "The 1920s: Class and Region, Resistance and Accommodation," in *The Atlantic Provinces in Confederation*, ed. E.R. Forbes and D.A. Muise (Toronto: University of Toronto Press, 1993).

5. Douglas O. Baldwin, *She Answered Every Call: The Life of Public Health Nurse, Mona Gordon Wilson (1894–1981)* (Charlottetown: Indigo Press, 1997), 299.

6. William C. Wicken, *The Colonization of Mi'kmaw Memory and History, 1794–1928* (Toronto: University of Toronto Press, 2012).

7. Daniel N. Paul, *We Were Not the Savages: A Mi'kmaq Perspective on the Collision between European and Native American Civilizations* (Halifax: Fernwood, 2000), 270–1.

8. Ruth Holmes Whitehead, *Tracking Doctor Lonecloud: Showman to Legend Keeper* (Fredericton: Goose Lane, 2002).

9. E.R. Forbes, "Cutting the Pie into Smaller Pieces: Matching Grants and Relief in the Maritime Provinces during the 1930s," in *Challenging the Regional Stereotype: Essays on the 20th Century Maritimes* (Fredericton: Acadiensis Press, 1989) and "The 1930s: Depression and Retrenchment," in *The Atlantic Provinces in Confederation*, ed. E.R. Forbes and D.A. Muise (Toronto: University of Toronto Press, 1993).

10. Quoted in William C. Gilmore, *Newfoundland and Dominion Status: The External Affairs Competence and International Law Status of Newfoundland, 1855–1934* (Toronto: Carswell, 1988), 102.

11. Neary, Peter, ed., *White Tie and Decorations: Sir John and Lady Hope Simpson in Newfoundland, 1934–1936*, © University of Toronto Press 1996: pp. 158–60.

12. Jim Lotz, *The Humble Giant: Moses Coady, Canada's Rural Revolutionary* (Toronto: Novalis, 2005) and Santo Dodaro and Leonard Pluta, *The Big Picture: The Antigonish Movement of Eastern Nova Scotia* (Montreal: McGill-Queen's University Press, 2012).

13. James Overton, "Brown Flour and Beri-beri: The Politics of Dietary and Health Reform in Newfoundland in the First Half of the Twentieth Century," *Newfoundland Studies* 14, 1 (1998), 15.

14. J.T. Jackson Lears, *No Place of Grace: Antimodernism and the Transformation of American Culture, 1880–1920* (New York: Pantheon Books, 1983. For a regional exploration of these developments, see Margaret Conrad, "'But Such is Life': Growing Up in Nova Scotia in the Interwar Years," *Journal of the Royal Nova Scotia Historical Society* 2 (1999): 1–26.

15. Suzanne Morton, *Ideal Surroundings: Domestic Life in a Working-Class Suburb in the 1920s* (Toronto: University of Toronto Press, 1995), 97.

16. Karen Balcom, *The Traffic in Babies: Cross-Border Adoption and Baby-Selling Between the United States and Canada, 1930–1972* (Toronto: University of Toronto Press, 2011).

17. Ian McKay, "Among the Fisherfolk: J.F.B. Livesay and the Invention of Peggy's Cove," *Journal of Canadian Studies* 23, 1–2 (1988): 23–45.

18. Edward MacDonald, "A Landscape . . . with Figures: Tourism and Environment in Prince Edward Island," in *Land and Sea: Environmental History in Atlantic Canada*, ed. Claire Campbell and Roberts Summerby-Murray (Fredericton: Acadiensis Press, 2013), 68.

19. Gwendolyn Davies, "Frank Parker Day's *Rockbound*," in *Studies in Maritime Literary History* (Fredericton: Acadiensis Press, 1991), 174.

20. Alan MacEachern, *Natural Selections: National Parks in Atlantic Canada, 1935–1970* (Montreal: McGill-Queen's University Press, 2001).

21. Kirk Niergarth, "'Missionary for Culture': Walter Abell, Maritime Art and Cultural Democracy, 1928–1944," *Acadiensis* XXXVI, 1 (Autumn 2006): 3–28, and Sandra Paikowsky, "'From Away': The Carnegie Corporation, Walter Abell, and American Strategies for Art in the Maritimes from the 1920s to the 1940s," *Journal of Canadian Art History* XXVII (2006): 36–72.

22. John Reid, "Health, Education, Economy: Philanthropic Foundations in the Atlantic Region in the 1920s and 1930s," *Acadiensis* XIV, 1 (Autumn 1984): 64–83.

Chapter 13: The Emergence of Atlantic Canada, 1939–1949

1. Reginald Whitaker and Gerald Marcuse, *Cold War Canada: The Making of a National Insecurity State, 1945–1957* (Toronto: University of Toronto Press, 1994) and Phillip Buckner, ed., *Canada and the End of Empire* (Vancouver: University of British Columbia Press, 2004).

2. The broad outlines of the impact of the war on the Maritimes can be found in E.R. Forbes, "Consolidating Disparity: The Maritimes and the

Industrializing of Canada during the Second World War," in *Challenging the Regional Stereotype: Essays on the 20th Century Maritimes* (Fredericton: Acadiensis Press, 1989).

3. Gerry Harrop, *Clarie: Clarence Gillis, M.P., 1940–1957* (Hantsport, NS: Lancelot, 1987) and Paul MacEwan, *Miners and Steelworkers: Labour in Cape Breton* (Toronto: Samuel Stevens Hakkert, 1976).

4. Georges Arsenault, *The Island Acadians, 1720–1980*, trans. Sally Ross (Charlottetown: Ragweed Press, 1989), 242.

5. John P. Humphrey, *Human Rights and the United Nations: A Great Adventure* (New York: Transnational Publishers, 1984) and Universal Declaration of Human Rights, http://www.un.org/Overview/rights.html.

6. Martha Walls, "Countering the 'Kingsclear blunder': Maliseet Resistance to the Kingsclear Relocation Plan, 1945–1949," *Acadiensis* XXXVII, 1 (Winter/Spring 2008): 3–30.

7. J.R. Smallwood, "An Appeal," 31 May 1948. Cited in Peter Neary, ed., *The Political Economy of Newfoundland, 1929–1972* (Toronto: Copp Clark, 1973), 142.

8. Bill McNeil and Morris Wolfe, *Signing on: The Birth of Radio in Canada* (Doubleday Canada, 1982).

9. Quoted in Jeff A. Webb, *The Voice of Newfoundland: A Social History of the Broadcasting Corporation of Newfoundland, 1939–1949* (Toronto: University of Toronto Press, 2008), 142.

10. Adrian Tanner, "The Aboriginal Peoples of Newfoundland and Labrador and Confederation," *Newfoundland Studies* 14, 2 (1998): 238–52

11. Cited in Corey Slumkoski, "The Maritime Reaction to Newfoundland's Entry into Confederation" (PhD dissertation, University of New Brunswick, 2009), 57.

Chapter 14: A Region Transformed, 1949–1975

1. Manfred B. Steger and Ravi K. Roy, *Neoliberalism: A Very Short Introduction* (Oxford: Oxford University Press, 2010), 1–20.

2. W.S. MacNutt, "The Atlantic Revolution," *Atlantic Advocate* (June 1957): 11–13. See also Margaret Conrad, "The Atlantic Revolution of the 1950s," in *Beyond Anger and Longing: Community and Development in Atlantic Canada*, ed. Berkeley Fleming (Fredericton: Acadiensis Press, 1988).

3. Excerpted from *Gentlemen, Players and Politicians* by Dalton Camp. Copyright © 1970 Dalton Camp.

Reprinted by permission of McClelland & Stewart, a division of Random House of Canada Limited, a Penguin Random House Company.

4. James P. Feehan and Melvin Baker, "The Origins of a Coming Crisis: Renewal of the Churchill Falls Contract," *Dalhousie Law Journal* 30, 1 (2007), 242.

5. Della M.M. Stanley, *Louis Robichaud: A Decade of Power* (Halifax: Nimbus, 1984), 93. See also Lisa Pasolli, "Bureaucratizing the Atlantic Revolution: The 'Saskatchewan Mafia' and the New Brunswick Civil Service, 1960–1970." *Acadiensis* XXXVIII, 1 (Winter/Spring 2009): 126–50.

6. Edward MacDonald, *If You're Stronghearted: Prince Edward Island in the Twentieth Century* (Charlottetown: Prince Edward Island Museum and Heritage Foundation, 2000), 297–307.

7. On the Canadian context of the 1960s, see Bryan D. Palmer, *Canada's 1960s: The Ironies of Identity in a Rebellious Era* (Toronto: University of Toronto Press, 2009).

8. Maureen Elgersman Lee, *Black Bangor: African Americans in a Maine Community, 1880–1950* (University of New Hampshire Press, 2005).

9. Africville Genealogical Society, *The Spirit of Africville* (Halifax: Formac, 1992), 70. See also Tina Loo, "Africville and the Dynamics of State power in Postwar Canada," *Acadiensis* XXXIX, 2 (Summer/Autumn 2010): 23–47.

10. Labrador Inuit Association, "Nunatsiavut News," accessed 15 July 2005 at www.nunatsiavut.com/en/windsofchange.php.

11. Elizabeth May (with Richard E.L. Rogers), *Budworm Battles: The Fight to Stop the Aerial Insecticide Spraying of Forests in Eastern Canada* (Halifax: Four East Publications, 1982) and Mark J. McLaughlin, "'Green Shoots': Aerial Insecticide Spraying and the Growth of Environmental Consciousness in New Brunswick, 1952–1973," *Acadiensis* XXXX, 1 (Winter/Spring 2011): 3–23.

12. Marie Thompson, "The Myth of the Vanishing Cape Breton Fiddler: The Role of a CBC Film in the Cape Breton Film Revival," *Acadiensis* XXXV, 2 (Spring 2006): 5–26.

13. For a perceptive analysis of outmigration in this period, see Greg Marquis, "Confederation's Casualties: The 'Maritimer' as a Problem in 1960s Toronto," *Acadiensis* XXXIX, 1 (Winter/Spring 2010): 83–107.

14. Robert Viau, *Antonine Maillet: 50 ans d'écriture* (Ottawa: Éditions David, 2008).

Chapter 15: Atlantic Canada in the Global Village, 1975–2001

1. Manfred B. Steger and Ravi K. Roy, *Neoliberalism: A Very Short Introduction* (Oxford: Oxford University Press, 2010), 1–20.
2. Bruce Mazlish and Akira Iriye, eds, *The Global History Reader* (New York: Routledge, 2005).
3. E.R. Forbes, "Atlantic Provinces, Free Trade and the Canadian Constitution," in *Challenging the Regional Stereotype: Essays on 20th Century Atlantic Canada* (Fredericton: Acadiensis Press, 1989).
4. Brian Peckford, *Some Day the Sun Will Shine and Have-Not Will Be No More* (St John's: Flanker Press, 2012), 173–7, 256–89.
5. Geoffrey Martin, "The Rise and Fall of the New Brunswick CoR Party, 1988–1995," http://www.revparl.ca/english/issue.asp?param=154&art=1051.
6. Joan McFarland, "Call Centres in New Brunswick: Maquiladoras of the North?," *Canadian Woman Studies* 21/22, 4/1 (2002), 65–70.
7. Dean Bavington, *Managed Annihilation: An Unnatural History of the Newfoundland Cod Collapse* (Vancouver: University of British Columbia Press, 2010), 1–39, 59, and George A. Rose, *Cod: An Ecological History of the North Atlantic Fisheries* (St John's: Breakwater Books, 2007), 379–477.
8. On this point, see Sean Cadigan, "Not a Nation! (Or Why Newfoundland Nationalism Doesn't Make Historical Sense)," *Newfoundland Quarterly* 102, 1 (2009): 40–3.
9. Susan Dodd, *The Ocean Ranger: Remaking the Promise of Oil* (Halifax: Fernwood, 2012) and Dean Jobb, *Calculated Risk: Greed, Politics and the Westray Tragedy* (Halifax: Nimbus, 1994).
10. See William Wicken, *Mi'kmaq Treaties on Trial: History, Land, and Donald Marshall Junior*. (Toronto: University of Toronto Press, 2002) and Ken S. Coates, *The Marshall Decision and Native Rights* (Montreal: McGill-Queen's University Press, 2000).
11. Sandra Lovelace v. Canada, Communication No. 24/1977: Canada 30/07/81, UN Doc. CCPR/C/13/D/24/1977, http://www.escr.net/docs/i/1307559.
12. Margaret Conrad, "Remembering Firsts: Female Politicians in the Atlantic Provinces in the 20th Century," in *Making Up the State: Women in 20th-Century Atlantic Canada*, ed. Janet Guildford and Suzanne Morton (Fredericton: Acadiensis Press, 2010).
13. Katrina R. Ackerman, "'Not in the Atlantic Provinces': The Abortion Debate in New Brunswick, 1980–1987," *Acadiensis* XLI, 1 (Winter/Spring 2012): 75–101.
14. Figures from Statistics Canada, Census of 2001.
15. Judith Fingard, Janet Guildford, and David Sutherland, *Halifax: The First 250 Years* (Halifax: Formac, 1999), 188–9.
16. Elizabeth May's biography has been compiled from her website (http://elizabethmaymp.ca) and her entry in *Wikipedia*.
17. Herb Wyile, *Anne of Tim Hortons: Globalization and the Reshaping of Atlantic Canadian Literature* (Waterloo, ON: Wilfrid Laurier University Press, 2011), 233–5.

Chapter 16: Whither Tending? Atlantic Canada in the Twenty-First Century

1. Michael Valpy, "Canada's Military: Invisible No More," *Globe and Mail*, 20 Nov. 2009, www.theglobeandmail.com/news/politics/canadas-military-invisible-no-more/article1372117/. See also Ian McKay and Jamie Swift, *Warrior Nation? Rebranding Canada in an Age of Anxiety* (Toronto: Between the Lines, 2012).
2. For reports by Brian Lee Crawley and others, see *Atlantic Institute for Market Studies* (AIMS), http://www.aims.ca/library/
3. Nunatsiavut Government, "The Path to Self-Government," undated, www.nunatsiavut.com/government/the-path-to-self-government/ "Labrador and Inuit Land Claims Agreement," undated, www.laa.gov.nl.ca/laa/land_claims/agreement.html.
4. Darren Campbell, "Big Builds," *Atlantic Business* 25, 2 (March/April, 2014): 20–31.
5. Donald J. Savoie, *Pulling Against Gravity: Economic Development in New Brunswick During the McKenna Years* (Montreal: Institute for Research on Public Policy, 2001). See also Savoie's *Visiting Grandchildren: Economic Development in the Maritimes* (Toronto: University of Toronto Press, 2006).
6. Moses Harvey, *Where Are We and Whither Tending? Three Lectures on the Reality and Worth of Human Progress* (Boston: Doyle and Whittle, 1886).

Index

Abbadie de Saint-Castin, Bernard-
  Anselme d', 62
Abell, Walter, 220
Abenaki: relations with Mi'kmaq, 19,
  100; relations with French, 56; attack
  on Pemaquid, 61; militia, 62; relations
  with English, 75
Aboriginal peoples: activism, 233, 250,
  255; artists, 18, 259; attitudes towards
  Europeans, 30, 37, 39, 48, 70, 75, 98;
  British and, 62, 68, 75–6, 78, 81, 88,
  89, 91, 92; chiefs and leaders, 16, 17,
  33, 39, 44, 56, 77, 82, 109, 120, 165,
  192, 209, 276, 278; Christianity and,
  38, 39, 69; creation stories, 2; crafts,
  119, 164; First World War, 192;
  franchise, 133, 242; French and, 51,
  56, 62, 68, 70, 73, 75–6, 78–80, 82,
  86; healing practices, 16; impact of
  contact with Europeans, ix, xii, 1, 17,
  22, 25, 33, 35, 67, 85, 87, 118–20,
  120; Indian Act, 164–5, 209; Indian
  Affairs, 145, 209, 233, 236; in
  Newfoundland and Labrador, 16, 165,
  236–7, 255, 287, 288; land, 88–9,
  108–9, 120, 255; language, 75; oral
  history, 19; population, 14, 19, 49,
  209, 255; reserves, 89, 102, 109, 126,
  164, 165, 209–10, 233, 237, 276;
  residential schools, 210; rights, 76,
  133, 233, 242, 255, 265, 275;
  settlements, 9; slavery, 21, 25, 30,
  73–4; Status Indian, 164, 255, 276;
  tools, 11; trade, 33–4, 92; traditions,
  18; treaties and proclamations, 76, 77,
  87, 237; treaty rights, 265, 275–6;
  United States and, 99–100, 110,
  values, 20; women, 120, 165, 276; see
  also specific groups
Aborigines' Protection Society, 119
abortion, 257, 277
Acadia/Acadie, ix; attacks on, 5, 53, 62,
  79; British and, 43, 53, 67; civil war,
  50–3; fishery, 54, 56, 59, 72; French
  settlement in, 39–42, 44, 48, 51,
  54–7, 58, 62; in 20th c., 185, 189, 219,
  253, 287; missionaries, 40, 56, 72;
  partitioned, 64; population, 43, 53,
  54, 56, 57, 75, 77, 78, 82–3, 95; trade,
  40, 50–1, 52–3, 56, 59; treaties, 38,
  44, 50, 51, 53, 72, 76
Acadians: Aboriginal peoples and, xii,
  40, 56, 61, 75, 85, 86–7; artists, 257,
  258; attacks by, 79–80, 81, 99; British
  and, 56, 61, 64, 67, 69, 70, 72, 76–7,
  78, 81–2, 98; conventions and

congresses, 15, 168, 170; diet, 57;
  dikes, 55; expulsion, 69, 82–5, 86, 91,
  130, 168; film, 253; flag, 168–9; First
  World War, 195–6; French authorities
  and, 57, 62, 67, 72, 74, 81; identity, xi,
  168–9, 170, 253; in 19th c., 115, 125,
  127, 130, 156, 167; language, 167–8;
  politics, 242, 247, 266; population,
  168, 169, 174, 271; post-war, 214;
  returning, 89, 92, 94, 102; Roman
  Catholic Church and, 69, 78, 102,
  127, 167, 174; see also francophones
Acorn, Milton, 258
acts: Abolish Slavery, 104, 118; British
  North America, 144, 145, 147, 148,
  150, 264; Common Schools, 167;
  Constitution, 264–5; Coercive, 97;
  Dominion Fuel, 207; Education, 167,
  253; Environmental Assessment, 278;
  Environmental Protections, 278; Free
  Schools, 133; Indian, 156, 164–5, 209,
  233, 236–7, 255, 276; King William's,
  51, 60, 70, 132; Land Protection, 268;
  Land Purchase, 142; Lands and Forests,
  209; Lord's Day, 178, 184; Maritime
  Freight Rates, 207; Navigation, 54, 107,
  109; Nova Scotia Trade Union, 202,
  215, 232; Official Languages, 253;
  Pesticides Control, 256; Quebec, 88;
  Scott, 156, 170; Stamp, 97, 98;
  Triennial Band Council Elections, 156;
  Union, 108; Wagner, 215
Adams, Wayne, 278
Afghanistan, 282, 284
African peoples, 1, 250; Americans, 102,
  117–18, 192; Canadians, 192; Nova
  Scotians, 254, 270, slaves and slave
  trade, 25, 73; see also black peoples
African United Baptist Association, 118,
  127
Africville, 126, 195, 242, 253–4
agriculture: Agricola and, 130;
  Confederation and, 144, 145, 147;
  European settlers and, 25, 30; in
  Acadia, 50, 55; in Maritimes, 155,
  160, 177, 192, 201, 203, 249; in
  Newfoundland, 44, 46, 131, 162, 196;
  mechanization, 116; organizations for,
  184, 249; see also farming
Aitken, Max (Lord Beaverbrook), 182,
  225
alcohol: Aboriginal peoples and, 33, 74,
  119, 165; changing attitudes towards,
  230; prohibition, 133, 159;
  temperance, 170; see also liquor
Alexander, Sir William, and the younger,

38, 43, 44, 53
Allan, Jonathan, 99,
Alline, Henry, 100
Alward, David, 284–5
Amalgamated Mine Workers of America,
  215, 228
American Civil War: in fiction, 172; trade,
  126, 138–9, 140, 144, 146, 150, 172
American Revolutionary War, 92, 97;
  British colonies and, 100, 101, 105–6,
  130; borders, 115; Loyalists, 91, 101;
  republicanism, 68; trade, 107
Amherst, NS, 100, 108, 123; business,
  159, 179, 180; railway, 180; strikes, 197
Amherst, Jeffrey, 85–6
Anne of Green Gables, xi, 178, 188, 193
Anglo-Newfoundland Development
  Company, 179, 244
Annapolis Royal, NS: 64, 67, 78, 80, 108;
  attacks on, 75, 79, 83, 100; garrison
  at, 70, 76–7; politicians, 147
Annexation League, 150
Anspach, Lewis, 130
Antigonish, NS, 108, 175, 214
Antigonish Movement, 202, 214
Arabella, 95
Arbuthnot, Mariot, 98
Archaic culture, 3, 7–9, 11
Archibald, Edith and Charles, 172
Arguimaut (L'kimu), 17
Arsenault, Angèle, 257
Arsenault, Joseph-Octave, 170
Atlantica, 284
Atlantic Accord, 264
Atlantic Canada/Atlantic Provinces: as a
  term, ix, x, 224, 238; history and
  historiography of, ix, xii–xiii, 1, 12,
  279, 291; identity, ix–xii, 238;
  Newfoundland and, 233–7, 273, 288
Atlantic Canada Opportunities Agency
  (ACOA), 264, 267
Atlantic Development Board, 242, 245
Atlantic Gateway, 284
Atlantic Institute for Market Studies, 284
Atlantic Provinces Adjustment Grant,
  242, 248
Atlantic Provinces Economic Council,
  241, 242
Atlantic realism, xi, 259
Atlantic Resolutions, 242, 243–4
Atlantic Revolution, 241– 3, 247
Atwell, Yvonne, 278
automobiles, 178, 189, 200, 216
Avalon, HMCS, 224
Avalon Peninsula, 8, 31-32, 44-47, 58,
  59, 61, 117, 164, 216

Baffin Island, 5, 11, 26
Baker, Carroll, 257
Baldwin, F.W., 186
Ball, John, 103
Baltimore, Lord, 45, 46
banks, 125, 156, 159, 161, 172, 175, 202;
  crashes, 163, 200; offshore, 250
Banks, Harold (Hal), 225, 231
Barrett, Sylbie, 215
Basques: boats, 31, 34; fishery, 26, 31,
  73; relations with the English, 82–3;
  traders, 35, 42; whaling, 32–5
Bates, Stewart, 228
battles: Atlantic, 225, 226; Beaumont
  Hamel, 178, 192, 193–4; Boyne, 128;
  Culloden, 81; Grand Pré, 69; Kars,
  147; Louisbourg, 79, 85, 88;
  Passchendale, 191; Restigouche, 69; St
  Lawrence, 225; Signal Hill, 87;
  Somme, 192; Vimy Ridge, 191;
  Waterloo, 112
Baxter, J.B.M., 206
Bear, Ned and Shirley, 259
Beaverbrook Art Gallery, 258
Beckwith, Julia Catherine, 118, 130
Bélanger, Étienne, 33
Belcher, Jonathan, 87
Belcourt, George-Antoine, 125
Bell, Alexander Graham, 186
Bengough, J.W., 151
Bennett, Charles Fox, 152
Bennett, R.B., 216
Beothuk: ancestors, 12; name, 16;
  culture, 19–20; last of, 20, 119–20;
  relations with the Europeans, 33, 44,
  95; see also Aboriginal peoples
Bernard, Joshua, 275
Biard, Pierre, 40, 48
Biencourt, Charles de, 39, 40, 41–2
Bill of Rights, 253
Binns, Patrick, 268, 285
birth control, 173–4, 217–18, 257
Black, Conrad, 267
Black Cultural Society, 254
Black Panthers, 253
black peoples: activism, 218, 233, 253;
  athletes, 187, 255; artists, 257;
  education, 167, 194, 218, 253; First
  World War, 192; in 19th c., 126, 127;
  Loyalists, 92, 103–4, 117;
  organizations, 202, 218, 242, 278;
  population, 254; religion, 127, 128;
  slavery, 73, 74, 103; women, 202, 218,
  278; see also African peoples
Black Power movement, 253
Black, William, Jr., 100
Black United Front, 242, 253, 278
Blackwood, David, 259, 274
Blair, Andrew G., 166
Bluenose, 202, 218
Bloc Québécois, 266
Bond, Robert, 166, 185
Bonaparte, Napoleon, 68, 109, 111, 112
Booth, John Wilkes, 140
Booth, William, 104
bootlegging, 204, 209, 230

Borden, PEI, 181, 249
Borden, Robert, 184, 185, 192, 195
Boscawen, Edward, 85–6
Boulton, Henry John, 131
Bourque, B.J., 293
Bowring, Benjamin, 125
Bradley, Gordon, 234, 237
Bradstreet, Simon and John, 78
Britain, see Great Britain
British Commonwealth, 212
British Empire: American Revolution
  and, 101; colonies of, 140,
  Confederation and, 144; emergence
  of, 37, 173; First World War, 189, 190;
  flight, 178, 186; Newfoundland and,
  155, 212; responsible government,
  115, 133; Roman Catholics in, 127;
  slavery, 104, 118; trade, 1, 125–6;
  women, 156, 175; see also England,
  Great Britain
British Empire Steel Corporation (BESCO),
  202, 204, 228
British Newfoundland Corporation
  (BRINCO), 245
British North America: business, 122,
  144, 147; colonies, 1, 2, 101, 105, 133;
  literature, 105, 130; population, 102,
  117, 142; responsible government,
  134; union, 139–40, 145–8
British North America Act, 144, 145, 147,
  148, 150, 264
British North American Association
  (BNAA), 144
Brittain, Miller, 220, 259
Broad Point (Susquehanna) people, 8
Broadcasting Corporation of
  Newfoundland (BCN), 215, 216
Brothers and Sisters of Cornelius Howatt,
  249
Brouillan, Jacques-François de, 61
Broussard, Joseph, 83
Brown, Cassie, 273–4
Brown, George, 140
Browne, Bill, 244
Brownists, 43
Brueggergosman, Measha, 279
Brundtland, Gro Harlem, 278
Brunel, I.K., 123
Buchanan, John, 264, 266, 268
Buckler, Ernest, 258
Burpee, Richard, 127
Bushell, John, 80
Butler, Edith, 257
Butler, Nat, 188
Byrne, Edward G., 242, 247
Byron, John, 86
Cabot, John (Zuan Caboto), 1, 24, 26,
  28–9, 30–1, 45; anniversary of
  voyage, 173, 272
Cabot, Sebastian, 26, 29
Cabot Strait, 4, 6, 10, 123, 175
Cabot Trail, 5, 219
Callbeck, Catherine, 268
Callbeck, Phillips, 98
Calvert, George, 38, 45, 46
Cameron, Donald, 268

Cameron, John Allan, 257
Camp, Dalton, 243–4
Campbell, Alexander, 247
Campbell, Lydia, 165
Campbell, Ted, 220
Campbellton, NB, 160
Campobello Island, 147
Canada Council, 258
Canada East/Canada West, 107, 117, 121,
  140
Canada–US Free Trade Agreement, 149,
  264
Canadian Broadcasting Corporation
  (CBC), 216, 217, 254
Canadian Coloured Cotton Company,
  161
Canadian Fishermen and Fish Handlers'
  Union, 232
Canadian Food and Allied Workers
  Union, 251
Canadian Manufacturers' Association, 215
Canadian National Railways, 202, 203,
  267
Canadian Reform Conservative Alliance
  Party, 267, 283
Canadian Seamen's Union, 231
Cape Bonavista, 28, 30, 45, 64, 173
Cape Breton Island, ix; Aboriginal peoples
  and, 8, 209, 233; Acadians and, 94;
  artists, 257, 280; attacks from and on,
  61, 86; annexation, 118; Britain and,
  88; budworm, 256; causeway, 237;
  coal, 124, 150, 158, 180, 204, 248;
  colonization, 26, 30, 38, 43, 91, 92,
  102, 107; exploration, 28, 30; fishery,
  31, 94; fortress Louisbourg,
  248; France and, 64, 68, 72; Gaelic/
  Celtic heritage, 219, 279, 280;
  geography of, 5, 6, 10, 108;
  government, 132, 214, 228, 251, 285;
  identity, xii; immigration, 126; iron ore,
  208; Loyalists and, 102; mapping of,
  93; out-migration, 248; parks, 219, 248;
  population, 179, 287; postwar decline,
  231, 248; railways, 181; steel industry,
  163, 180, 204, 248; strikes, 202; trade,
  33, 156, 158; unions, 204–5; wireless
  telegraphy, 186; see also Île Royale
Cape Breton Development Corporation,
  242, 248
Cape Breton Highlands National Park,
  219, 249
Cape Sable, 6, 76, 77
capitalism, industrial, 116, 161, 200,
  240, 289
Capuchins, 50, 53, 56
Carleton, Guy, 103
Carleton, Thomas, 104
Carmen, Bliss, 188
Carmichael, Stokeley, 253
Carson, Kenneth, 243
Carson, Rachel, 256
Carson, William, 120, 131, 132
Carter, Frederic, 151
Carter, Wilf, 217
Cartier, George-Étienne, 140

Cartier, Jacques, 24, 26, 30, 33, 39, 118
Cartwright, George, 92, 95, 100
Cartwright, John, 95
Carvery, Aaron, 254
Cashin, Richard, 251
Champlain, Samuel de, 21, 38, 39–40, 41, 50, 60, 115
Charitable Irish Society, 108
Charles I (England), 43, 46, 58, 60
Charles Robin and Company, 158
Charlottetown, PEI, 75, 108; armed forces, 224; attacks on, 98; boxing, 188; business, 219; education, 128, 171, 208; music, 217; name, 93; orphans, 194; politicians, 278; population, 117, 254, 290; protests, 249; railway, 181; trade, 124, 207
Charlottetown Accord, 264, 266
Charlottetown Conference, 139, 145–6, 258
Charlottetown Festival, 258
Charter of Rights and Freedoms, 264, 265, 266, 276
chert, 8
Chesapeake, 110, 111
Cheticamp, NS, 94, 108
children: Aboriginal, 17–18, 20, 21–2, 34, 96, 100, 119, 120, 165, 210, 276; Acadian, 52, 56, 62, 82, 86, 167, 180; as labour, 161, 167, 232; black, 167, 194; education, 122, 167–8, 183, 187, 194, 210, 217, 232, 251, 257; First World War, 192, 193–4; health and welfare, 207, 217; 'home', 164; Newfoundland, 60, 171, 183, 196, 213; in 19th c., 116, 117, 171, 172, 173–4; in 20th c., 255, 257; Loyalists, 106; Second World War, 230; slavery, 73
Children's Aid Society, 171
Chipman, Ward, 106
Chrétien, Jean, 263, 267, 279, 282, 283
Christianity: Aboriginal peoples and, 18, 38, 56–7; 'muscular', 171; *see also* religion and specific denominations
Church, Benjamin, 61, 62
Church of England, 43, 77, 78, 80, 91, 149; education, 103, 107, 128, 133, 167; literature, 105; relations with other denominations, 107; relations with government, 105, 128, 133
Churchill Falls, NL, 179, 242, 245–6, 255, 272, 287
Churchill, Winston, 225
Clark, Joe, 267
Clarke, George Elliott, 280
climate, 5, 7, 32; early settlement and, 38–9, 44–6, 83; first peoples and, 7; climate change, 278-79, 283
Coady, Moses Michael, 214
Coaker, William Ford, 178, 182–3, 202, 208
coal: deposits/formation, 2, 3, 7, 93; government, 242, 248; industry, 153, 156, 158, 177, 179, 180, 182, 192, 202, 204, 205, 207, 216, 227, 228, 249, 287; mines/mining, 100, 123,

124, 141, 148, 158, 167, 177, 192, 196; mining disasters, 167, 274; Second World War, 227; strikes, 167, 178, 205, 215, 225, 227; tariffs and duties, 147, 148, 158; trade, 138, 150, 161
Cochran, William, 105
Cochrane, Thomas, 131, 132
Cockburn, George, 111–12
Code Noir, 73
Colbourne, Tom, 191
Colville, Alex, 259
Cold War, 223, 240, 250, 251, 256
Coles, George, 133, 142
colleges, 107, 115, 128, 169, 171, 175, 183, 184, 189, 220
Collins, Enos, 111, 125
Colonial Office, 118, 132–3, 142, 146, 163
colonization: Aboriginal peoples and, 255; and Acadian identity, 170; in Newfoundland, 45; in 17th c., 38, 40, 43, 44–5, 48, 50, 54; in 16th c., 37
Colony of Avalon, 38, 45
Coloured Education Society, 218
Coloured Citizen's Improvement League, 218
Columbus, Christopher, 1, 26, 28, 29
Comingo, Joseph Brown, 105
Committee for Industrial Organization (CIO), 200
communication: in Atlantic Canada, 237, 271; in colonial era, 80, 98, 106, 149, 143, 166; systems, ix; technologies, 123, 137, 138, 173, 186, 261–2, 280; with United States, 141
Communist Party, 201, 214
Compagnie de la pêche sédantaire de l'Acadie, 54
Compagnie des Cent-Associés, 43–4, 50, 52
Compagnie du Cap-Breton, 50, 52
Company of Adventurers to Newfoundland, 58
Confederation: anniversary of, 272; attaining, 152; attitudes towards, 140, 146–8, 150–1, 153, 206; British financiers and, 144; Civil War and, 146; conferences on, 139, 146; impact of, 164, 171, 166, 185, 206, 289; New Brunswick and, 138, 139, 149; Newfoundland and, ix, x, 137, 138, 139, 150, 151, 152, 166, 213, 223, 225, 233–5, 237, 241, 243, 272; Nova Scotia and, 138, 139, 148–50, 166, 184; Prince Edward Island and, 138, 139, 152–3; poets, 188; proponents against, 147, 148, 150, 151, 235; proponents of, 140, 144, 147, 149
Confederation Bridge, 264, 271
Confederation Centre of the Arts, 258
Confederation of Regions Party, 267
Congress of Coloured Women, 202, 218
Connelly, T.L., 147
Connors, Stompin' Tom, 257
Conroy, Nicolas, 143
conscription, 178, 183, 192, 195–6
Conservative Party: in federal

government, 151, 152, 166, 184, 195, 284; in provincial government, 172, 185, 206, 211, 214; in 19th c., 134, 140, 141, 142; in 20th c., 197, 211; politicians, 107, 142, 145, 147, 151, 184, 185, 195, 206, 208–9, 216; *see also* Progressive Conservative Party
Conservative Party of Canada (CPC), 283, 286–7
Constitution Act (1982), 264, 265
Continental Congress, 97, 98
Cook, James, 92, 93
Coon, David, 285
Cooper, Barry, x
Cooper, William, 132
Co-operative Commonwealth Federation (CCF), 201, 214
Co-operative Union of Canada, 184
co-operatives, 171, 184, 204, 214; banking, 125; movement, 228
Cope, Jean-Baptiste, 82
Cormack, William, 118, 119, 124
Corne, Louis, de la, 79
Corner Brook, NL, 202, 203, 208, 209, 237
Cornwallis, NS, 224
Cornwallis, Edward, 80, 81–2
corporations, 175, 227, 269, 274
Corte-Real, Gaspar, 24, 26, 29
Coughlan, Laurence, 107
Council of Atlantic Premiers, 284
Council of Maritime Premiers, 242, 249, 284
Crawford, Julia, 220
Crimean War, 138, 147
Crosbie, John, 248, 269
Croucher, Victor, 157
Crowley, Brian Lee, 284
Crowne, William, 53
Crummey, Michael, 280
Cullen, Joseph, 259
culture: Aboriginal, 3, 7–9, 11, 12, 14, 15, 18, 20, 24, 119, 210; Acadian, 85; arts and, 188, 220, 258; British, 91, 112; civic, 272; colonial, 78; consumer, 200, 216, 257; culture of defeat, 284; European, 25; immigrant, 117; in 19th c., 173, 174; in 20th c., 206, 230; Irish, 108; Newfoundland, 256, 258, 273; North American, xi, 137; popular, 257; regional, x, 279; tradition and, 218
Cumberland Coal and Railway Company, 180
Cunard, Samuel, 118, 123, 125, 143, 153
Cupids Cove, NL, 38, 44–5, 47
Cuyler, Abraham, 102
Dale, Thomas, 41
d'Anville, Duc, 69, 79
d'Aprendestiguy, Martin, 42
d'Aulnay, Charles de Menou, 50–3
Davidson, Margaret, 192
Davidson, Walter, 190
Davidson, William, 94
Davies, Thomas, 87

Davis, William (miner), 205
Davis, William (politician), 264
Davis Inlet, 165, 255
Dawson, J. William, 2
Dawson, Robert McGregor, 231
Day, Frank Parker, 219
Day of Concern, 252
Debert, NS, 3, 7, 10, 224
Demasduit (Mary March), 119
Dennis, Agnes, 172
Dennis, Clara, 210
Dennis, William H., 218, 219
Denson, Henry Denny, 94
Denys, Nicolas, 50, 51, 52–3, 54,
Department of Regional Economic
   Expansion (DREE), 242, 245, 252, 267
Depression: see Great Depression
DesBarres, Joseph F.W., 93, 94, 102
Desmond, Viola, 233
Deutsch, John, 242, 249
Dexter, Darrell, 284, 285
Diamond Glass, 161
Diefenbaker, John, 228, 242–3, 244–5, 268
Dièreville, Sieur de, 55
disease: Aboriginal peoples and, 1, 16,
   22, 25, 33, 48, 79, 118–19; Acadians
   and, 82; AIDS, 277; immigrants and,
   117; Inuit and, 95, 165; regulations
   and, 197; Spanish flu 196; venereal,
   230
Dixon, George, 187
Dobbin, Craig, xiii
Doiron, François-E., 232
Dominion Coal Company, 156, 158
Dominion Cotton Mills, 161
Dominion Fuel Act, 207
Dominion Iron and Steel Company, 156,
   159, 180, 204
Dominion Status, 212
Dominion Steel and Coal Corporation
   (DOSCO), 215, 227, 231
Dominion Steel Company, 178, 180–1,
   182, 202
Dorset people, 3, 11
Douglas, Tommy, 251
Doyle, Gerald S., 219
Drucour, Augustin de Boschenry de, 85
Du Bois de la Motte, Comte, 85
Duchambon, Louis Du Pont, 79, 82
Duckworth, John, 131
Duncan, Andrew Rae, 202, 205, 206–7
Duncan, Norman, 189
Duncan Royal Commission on Maritime
   Claims, 202, 206
Dunderdale, Kathy, 286
Dunn, James, 258
Duquesnel, Jean Baptiste-Louis Le
   Prévost, 79
Dutch, 173; colonization, 102; conflict,
   51, 54, 56, 59, 60; exploration, 40, 52;
   fishery, 58; immigration, 251; trade,
   53–4

East Coast Music Association, 279
Easton, Peter, 44
Eaton, Cyrus, 256
Echaniz, Joanes, de, 32

economic crises, 183, 208, 214, 261
economy: Aboriginal, 16, 165; British,
   138; family, 127; global, 122, 240,
   280, 283; industrial, 160, 231;
   interwar, 200–1; in 19th c., 122;
   Maritimes, 125, 155, 175, 204;
   market, 126, 284; national, 182, 262,
   277; New Brunswick, 110, 156;
   Newfoundland, 73, 110, 124, 157,
   162–3, 171, 204, 215, 233, 273; North
   American, 232; Nova Scotia, 214, 272;
   Prince Edward Island, 247, 271;
   regional, 112, 126, 155, 204, 231,
   250, 268; rural, 256; Second World
   War, 227
Eddy, Jonathan, 99
Edmonds, Sara Emma, 140
education, 118, 120, 245; adult, 199;
   compulsory, 211; in 18th c., 156–7;
   golden age and, 228–9; public, 117–
   18; women and, 163
Eiriksson, Leif, 26
employment: Aboriginal, 164, 250;
   children, 161, 167; declines in, 204,
   209, 231, 287, 289; First World War,
   200; Great Depression, 139, 201, 210–
   11, 215; increases in, 227, 250, 268;
   legislation, 184, 225, 231, 233, 240,
   242, 250, 267; Newfoundland, 63,
   202; royal commission on, 161–2;
   Second World War, 224; tourism and,
   272, 287; women, 173, 250
Engels, Friedrich, and Karl Marx, 116
England: Aboriginal peoples and, 96,
   120, 180; exploration, 25, 28, 29, 30;
   colonization, 37, 38, 44, 83;
   immigrants, 94, 102, 107; merchants,
   32, 50, 53–4, 125; Newfoundland
   and, 58, 70; organizations in, 171;
   relations with France, 37, 43, 53, 60,
   62; transportation, 123; wars, 32, 60,
   62, 78; see also British Empire, Great
   Britain
English Civil War, 58, 60
entrepreneurs: colonial, 38, 61, 80, 95;
   from Atlantic Canada, xiii, 248, 258;
   19th c., 125, 159, 161; economic
   development and, 241, 247
environmental movement, 200, 249, 256,
   274, 278–279, 285, 289
equalization payments and policy, 231,
   242, 265, 273, 284, 285–6, 289
escheat, 95, 102, 132
Escheat Party, 132
Europe: Aboriginal people and, 21, 40;
   conflicts, 37, 43, 60, 63–4, 68, 85,
   101, 116, 138–9, 189–90, 196, 223–4,
   229, 255; exploitation, 49, 53;
   exploration, 14, 25, 26, 27, 28, 35;
   immigrants, xii, 164, 230, 251; trade,
   166, 178, 201, 204, 241, 245, 250,
   256, 269, 270
Europeans: Aboriginal peoples and, ix,
   9–10, 11, 12, 14, 15–22, 24–5, 33–5,
   48, 64, 70, 73, 95, 96, 118–19, 120–
   21, 179, 276; explorers, 1, 24–5, 26–7,

   28, 30, 41; population, 53, 57, 120;
   settlements and settlers, xii, 8, 30, 37,
   38, 44–6, 56, 67, 88, 118, 290; trade,
   16, 33–5, 53, 54, 60, 126, 157
Evangeline (poem), xi, 130, 168-9, 189
Fagundes, João Alvarez, 24, 30
Falkland Islands, 83, 84
Falkland, Lord, 45
family allowances, 225, 231, 232, 240, 250
Farmer–Labour coalition, 204
farming: Acadians and, 55, 62, 72, 74,
   82, 83; banks, 125; British settlers
   and, 94; fish/fox/fur, 203, 289; Dutch
   and, 251; in Maritimes, 112, 115, 117,
   126, 175, 203, 214, 216; in
   Newfoundland, 108, 155, 201;
   Loyalists and, 102, 103, 106; New
   England Planters and, 92, 94; political
   parties, 197, 204; postwar change,
   231, 232, 240, 247, 249, 250; reforms
   and rights, 132, 143, 182, 184, 195;
   Second World War, 227, 228; trade,
   141, 155; see also agriculture
federalism, 231, 235, 238, 264–5, 280
Fédération francophone de Terre-Neuve
   et du Labrador, 253
Federation of Newfoundland and
   Labrador Indians, 255
Fenerty, Charles, 130
Fenian Brotherhood, 139, 146, 147
Fergusson, Muriel McQueen, 256
Fernandes, João, 29
Ferryland, NL, 31, 34, 38, 45, 46–7, 51,
   58, 61, 121, 272
Field, Cyrus W., 123
Fielding, William S., 166, 184
films: 254; regional, 258–9; studios, 164,
   253, 272; first, 189
First World War, 172, 177, 182, 190, 200,
   207, 217, 223
Fisher, Charles, 141
fishery, see specific place (e.g.,
   Newfoundland)
Fisheries Products International, 269
Fishermen's Protective Union (FPU), 178,
   182–3, 202
fishing admirals, xi, 58, 70
Fléché, Jessé, 39, 40
Fleming, Michael, 128, 131
Fleming, Hugh John, 241, 242
folk artists, 259
foreign Protestants 69, 81
forestry industry, 115, 126, 144, 160,
   249, 250; see also pulp and paper
Forrestall, Tom, 259
Fort Beauséjour, 67, 69, 82, 83
Fort Cumberland, 92, 99
Fort Edward, 67, 69, 81
Fort Lawrence, 67, 69, 81–2, 83
Fort McMurray, xi, 268, 285
France: Aboriginal peoples and, 39;
   Acadians and, 83; American
   Revolution, 100, 101; Cape Breton, 68,
   72; colonization, 37, 38, 39, 40, 42,
   43, 44, 48, 50–1, 57; exploration and
   expansion, 25, 29–30, 37, 64; First

World War, 189, 190, 193; fishery, 31, 32, 59, 68, 73, 88, 101, 124, 162–3, 185; Great Britain and, xii, 1, 43, 53, 60, 62, 64, 70, 78–80, 81, 82, 85, 87–9, 162, 185; Second World War, 223; trade, 53–4; treaties, 63–4, 68, 80, 101; War of 1812, 110

franchise: Aboriginal peoples and, 133, 237, 255; men and, 133; Newfoundland and, 234; women and, 133, 172, 197, 209; *see also* vote

Francklin, Michael, 100

francophones, 94, 163, 169, 170, 228, 247, 249, 252–3, 271; *see also* Acadians

free trade, 242, 243–4; in colonial era, 68, 101; in 19th c., 115, 118, 126, 133, 138, 141, 149, 153, 166; in 20th c., 184, 261, 262, 263; *see also* reciprocity, trade

Free Trade Agreement (Canada-US), 149, 263, 264

Free Trade Agreement (North America), 262, 263, 264

freight rates, 196, 203, 204, 206, 207, 242

French Revolutionary and Napoleonic Wars, 1, 92, 109–10, 125; end of, 91, 112, 124, 131, 132

French Treaty Shore, 101, 121, 124, 133, 162

Friedman, Milton, 240

Frontenac, Comte de, 61

fur trade: Aboriginal peoples and, 33, 120, 225; French settlers and, 40, 42, 48, 50; in Newfoundland, 44; monopolies, 38–9

Gage Thomas, 97, 98, 99

Gagetown, NB, 87, 108, 149

Gagetown, CFB, 250

Galbraith, John Kenneth, 240

Gallagher, Del, 247

Gallant, Brian, 285

Galt, Alexander, 140

Gander, NL, 224, 225, 283

Gaulin, Antoine, 63, 69

Geddie, John, 127

gender: Aboriginal peoples and, 17, 18, 20; franchise and, 133; identity, xii; in colonial era, 57; in 19th c., 174; 20th c., 250, 277

General Mining Association, 118, 123, 124, 133

Geological Survey of Canada, 124, 162, 179

George, David, 103

Gesner, Abraham, 2, 119, 130

Ghiz, Joe, 266, 278, 285

Ghiz, Robert, 285

Gibson, Alexander (Boss), 159

Gilbert, Sir Humphrey, 37–8, 48

Gillis, Clarie, 228

Gisborne, Frederic Newton, 123

globalization, 25, 261

global warming, 278, 283

Glooscap (Klu'skap), xi, 18

Googoo, Ryan, 278

golden age, xi; 218; for Acadians, 78, 82; in Newfoundland, 189; in 19th c., 115; of piracy, 71–2

Gomes, Estévão, 26, 30

Goose Bay, NL, 224, 225, 229, 255, 288

Gordon, Arthur Hamilton, 147

Gordon, Walter, 242

Goreham, Joseph, 99

Graham, Shawn, 284

Grand Banks: disputes, 109; fishery, 32, 70, 101, 177, 270–1; oil exploration, 272; shipping, 72; weather, 6

Grandfontaine, Hector d'Antigné de, 54, 56

Grand Trunk Railway Company, 144, 147

Gray, John Hamilton, 142, 147

Great Britain: Acadia/Acadians and, 64, 83; American Civil War, 139–41; American Revolution, 97, 101; as a term, 62; colonials and, 129, 131, 134, 173; colonization/colonies, 80, 91, 108, 137; communications, 123; Confederation and, 144, 147, 150; economy, xii; First World War, 189–90; France and, 1, 64, 67, 78–9, 85–6, 88–9, 110, 223; geography, 6, 52; immigration, 117, 164, 251; imperialism, xii, 69, 173; kings, 43, 109; Loyalists, 101, 103, 105; navy, 109; neo-liberalism, 262; New Brunswick and, 109, 116–17, 141; Newfoundland and, 132, 185, 211–12, 235, 237; Nova Scotia and, 109; railways, 144; responsible government, 132–3; postwar, 200; Roman Catholics and, 108; Second World War, 223–5; trade, 115, 118, 124, 125–6, 138, 141, 153, 159, 177, 203; treaties, 63, 67, 76, 80, 88, 101; United States and, 105, 115, 139–40, 146, 148, 153, 200, 223, 282; War of 1812, 110–3; youth organizations, 187; *see also* British Empire, England

Great Depression, 200–1, 202, 210–13, 236, 283

Greenland, 5, 12, 26, 27, 29, 30, 52, 95, 152

Greenleaf, Elisabeth, 219

Green Party, 279, 285

Grenfell, Wilfred and Grenfell Mission, 156, 171, 180, 209, 255

Grimes, Roger, 285

Gros Morne National Park, 3, 5, 272

Guercheville, Antoinette de Pons, 40, 41

Gulf of St Lawrence, 4, 6, 10, 15, 24, 181; Aboriginal peoples and, 22; exploration of, 26, 27, 30, 93; fishery, 31, 34, 35, 101, 271; geology, 8; Second World War and, 223; settlement, 64

Guy, John, 44

Guysborough, NS, 54, 108, 210

Haliburton, Thomas Chandler, 130

Halifax, NS: Aboriginal peoples, 9, 119, 194, 209, 210; Acadians, 81; amalgamation, 268; American Revolution, 98–9; artists, 130, 258, 272; banks, 125, 161; black peoples, 126, 167, 194, 195, 202, 218, 233,

242, 253, 254, 278; British and, 97, 99, 100, 109, 146, 153, 173; communications, 123; education, 112, 171, 220, 237; explosion, 178, 192–5; First World War, 189, 192; fishery, 166, 178, 201; fortifications, 104, 109, 224; founding, 69, 80, 91; French and, 79, 81, 87; immigration, 164; industry, 126, 158, 159, 161, 207, 227, 248, 285; in late 20th c., 272, 287; Irish, 108, 117; labour, 161, 167, 197, 225, 227, 231; Loyalists, 99, 102, 104, 105, 106; newspapers, 80, 98, 148, 218; politics, 251, 268, 278; population, 229, 290; prohibition, 196; railways, 141, 144, 158, 160, 181; Second World War, 224, 225, 226, 227, 229; settlement, 69, 81; social reform, 171, 184, 196; sports, 187, 188; tourism, 219; trade, 80, 94, 99, 110, 124, 125, 158; War of 1812, 110, 111; women, 172, 173, 192, 202, 217, 218, 256

Halifax Relief Commission, 194

Halifax Shipyards Limited, 227, 285

Hamm, John, 269, 285

Hammonds Plains, NS, 117

Happy Valley, NL, 229, 288

Harmsworth, Harold and Alfred, 179

Harper, Stephen, 283–4, 286

Harris, Lawren S., 205

Harris, Robert, 168, 188

Harvey, NB, 217

Harvey, John, 133

Harvey, Moses, 290

Hatfield, Richard, 247, 248, 252, 253, 256, 264

Haven, Jens, 96

Hay, Gilbert, 259

Haythorne, Robert, 153

Hazen, J.D., 185

Hazen, Moses, 86

Hazen, William, 91

Hébert, Louis, 39

Heiser, Victor G., 195

Henri IV (France), 38

Henry VII (England), 20, 29

Henry VIII (England), 30

Henry, Anthony, 98

Herbert, Mary Eliza, 130

Herjolfsson, Bjarni, 26

Hibernia, 264, 272, 273, 274

Higgs, Blaine, 285

Historic Sites and Monuments Board of Canada, 219

Hitler, Adolf, 223

Holland, Samuel, 92, 93, 94

Hope Simpson, John and Quita, 213

Hopkins, Frances, 60

Hopson, Peregrine Thompson, 82

Horwood, Harold, 258

hospital insurance, 250

House of Commons, 145, 150, 151, 185, 228, 265, 279

How, Edward, 78

Howe, C.D., 245

Howe, John, 105

Howe, Joseph: Aboriginal peoples, 118–19; Civil War, 140–1; Confederation, 147, 148, 150; land tenure in PEI, 142; libel trial, 130; ode, 115; railways, 141, 144, 149; responsible government, 132

Howley, James P., 125

Hoyles, Hugh, 145, 147

Hubbard, Leonidas and Mina, 180

Hudson's Bay Company: colonial era and, 64, 101; in 19th c., 120, 122, 140, 144, 165; in 20th c., 196, 202, 206, 209, 229

Huguenots, 38, 75, 78, 102

human rights: in Canadian law, 265, 277; movement, 218, 232–3, 253, 254, 276; UN and, 223, 225, 240

Humphrey, Jack, 220

Humphrey, John Peters, 233

hunting: Aboriginal peoples and, 7, 8, 77, 88, 165, 209, 275; as tourism, 189; settlers, 41, 87

Hydro-Québec, 242, 245, 285, 287

Hynes, Ron, 258

Iberville, Pierre Le Moyne d', 51, 61

Ice Age: Last, 3, 4, 5; Little, 27, 32

Île Royale, 52, 67, 78; fishery, 88; settlement, 69, 72–4, 75, 82, 83; *see also* Cape Breton

Île Saint-Jean, 52, 64, 67, 69, 88; attacks on, 79; deportation of Acadian from, 86; settlement, 74–5, 78; *see also* Prince Edward Island

Iles de la Madeline, ix, 6, 42, 67; settlement, 74, 83, 88, 93, 101

illiteracy, 232

immigration, *see* specific place (e.g. Nova Scotia)

imperialism, 25, 163, 170 182

impressment, 100, 110; *see also* press gangs

Indian Act, 156, 164–5, 209, 233, 236–7, 255, 276

Indian Commissioners, 119

Industrial Revolution, 116, 126, 158–62

industrialization, 116, 138, 155, 159, 166, 248

Information Age, 261–2, 287

information and communication technologies (ICTs), 261, 280

Inglis, Charles, 105

Ingstad, Helge, 27

Innu: culture, 20, 120–1; colonization, 120, 165, 179; disease, 255; European contact, 22, 33, 60; name, 16, 255; origins, 12, 16, 20; population, 120; religion, 121; relocation, 255; rights and claims, 246, 275, 276, 284, 287; Second World War, 229; trade, 33, 120–1, 165; women, 20

Intercolonial Railway: construction of, 147, 150, 156, 158, 202, economic development and, 160, 164; Joseph Howe and, 141, 144; Samuel Tilley and, 149

International Fund for Animal Welfare, 273

International Power and Paper (IPP), 203

International Woodworkers of America (IWA), 244

Inuit: culture, 20–1; disease, 95, 165, 196; colonization and, 120, 165; education, 122; European contact, 21, 22, 33, 95; federal government and, 237, 255, 287, 288; missions, 95, 122, 196, 255; name, 16; origins, 11, 15, 20; population, 120, 165, 196; religion, 121–2; relocation, 255, 288; rights and claims, 275, 276; Second World War, 229; trade, 33, 95, 165; women, 21–2, 96, 165

Iraq, 282

Ireland, 26, 43, 52; famine, 118; fishery, 95; immigration from, 70–1,73, 94, 102, 107, 108, 110, 117, 126; organizations, 108, 109, 146; relations with Britain, 146, 147, 148; undersea cable from, 123; unrest in, 108

Iroquois, 61, 62

Irving, K.C., xiii, 248, 271

Janes, Percy, 258

J.D. Irving Ltd., 271, 284, 285, 288

Jeremy, Josiah, 24

Jesuits, 40, 41, 56

Joggins, NS, 2–3, 167

Johnson, Charles, 71

Johnston, James, 167

Johnston, James Robert, 191

Johnston, Wayne, 280

Johnstone, Walter, 117

Jones, Burnley (Rocky), 253

Jones, J. Harry, 214

Jones, John, 107

Jones, John Paul, 100

Jones, Leonard, 253

Jones, Walter, 232, 237

J. Rhodes, Curry, and Company, 159, 180

Judicial Committee of the Privy Council, 180, 209

Jukes, James, 124

Julian, John, 109

Karpeles, Maud, 219

Karslefni, Thorfinn, 26

Kavanagh, Lawrence, 127

Keefer, Janice Kulyk, x

Kent, Tom, 248

Keynesian economics, 215, 240, 261

Killam, Isaac Walton, 258

King, Boston, 103

King, William Lyon Mackenzie, 206, 231, 241

King's College, 107, 128, 133

King William's Act, 51, 60, 70, 132

King William's War, 51, 60

Kirke, David, 43, 51, 58, 60, 61

Kirke, Sara, 58, 60

Klu'skap (Glooscap), xi, 18

Ku Klux Klan, 214

Labour: legislation, 215, 248; movement, 167, 197, 229, 251; unrest, 166, 182–3, 195, 197, 201, 227

Labour Party, 204

Labrador, ix, x; Aboriginal peoples, 3, 7, 8, 11–12, 15, 20–1, 96, 120, 165, 236–7, 255, 275, 276, 284, 287, 288; artists, 280; boundaries, 202, 209, 264, 271; colonization, 64, 88–9, 95, 92, 120–2; Confederation (1949), 235, 236; exploration, 25, 26, 27, 29, 179–80; federal government and, 234, 284, 286; First World War, 192; fishery, 21, 32, 95, 101, 109, 112, 122, 124, 133, 171; forestry, 179, 180; francophones, 253; geography, 3, 4, 5–7, 10, 52, 121; hydro-power, 179, 245–6, 255, 287; mapping, 93; minerals, 7, 179, 245, 249, 272; missions, 92, 95, 121, 156, 17, 196, 209; Newfoundland and, ix, 92, 95, 133, 180, 211, 215, 225, 229, 269, 273; offshore resources, 286, 289; origin of name, 29; political parties, 248; population, 165, 290; Quebec and, 92, 95, 209, 245–6; railways, 245; religions, 277; royal commissions, 284, 285; Second World War, 223–5, 226, 228–9; tourism, 272; trade, 33, 10, 121, 202, 225; whaling, 32; women, 96, 165, 192

Labrador Inuit Association, 255, 276, 287

Laksi, Germain, 210

land grants, 91, 94, 102, 162, 163, 164

Lane, Michael, 93

L'Anse Armour, 8, 10

L'Anse aux Meadows, 27, 28, 272

La Hève, 50, 61, 67

Langford, Sam, 187

Larkins, Joseph, 161

la Roche de Mesgouez, Marquis de, 38

La Rochelle, 31, 42, 53

La Tour, Agathe de Saint-Étienne de, 78

La Tour, Charles, 39, 42, 44, 50, 51–3

La Tour, Claude de Saint-Étienne de, 39, 42, 43–4

La Tour, Françoise-Marie Jaquelin, 51–2

Lattimer, J.E., 231

Laurier, Wilfrid, 166, 170, 177, 184, 185

Lawrence, Charles, 81, 82, 85, 91, 92

League of Nations, 197, 212

Leased Bases Agreement, 225

LeBlanc, Roméo, 269

LeBlanc, Suzie, 279

Le Borgne, Alexandre, 60

Le Borgne, Emmanuel, 51, 53

Le Clercq, Chrestien, 17

Legge, Francis, 98

Le Loutre, Jean-Louis, 69, 79, 81–2

Le Loutre's War, 81, 83

Leonowens, Anna, 172

Lescarbot, Marc, 39, 48,

Levesque, René, 263

Lewis, Maud, 259

liberalism, 101, 134, 137, 240

Liberal Party, 134; as government, 133, 166, 177; federal, 166, 177, 184, 241, 244, 245, 251, 262–3, 267; First World

War, 195; New Brunswick, 166, 206, 232, 237, 247, 266, 267, 284, 285; Newfoundland, 142, 197, 208, 247, 248, 266, 286; Nova Scotia, 166, 204, 206, 214–15, 232, 237, 268–9, 285; Prince Edward Island, 152, 206, 232, 237, 241, 247, 266, 268, 278, 285; Quebec, 266
liquor: laws and regulations, 172, 209, 216, 228; Second World War, 229; trade, 204; *see also* alcohol
literacy, 68, 103, 116, 129, 138, 173, 175
literature: classical, 41; historical, 26, 291; immigration, 164, popular, 217; tourism, 189
Liverpool Packet, 111
Livingstone, 'Red' Dan, 205
lobster: canning, 157, 158; fishery, 158, 163, 216, 275
Lockhart, Grace Annie, 156, 174
London, Eng: Aboriginal peoples, 96, 119, 120; colonial involvement, 92, 98, 132, 134, 155; Confederation, 139, 147, 150; contact with, 77, 123, 129; financiers, 138, 141, 144, 182; immigrants from, 95; Newfoundland and, 180, 185, 196, 200, 211, 212, 215, 234; trade, 58, 64, 166
London and Bristol Company, 38, 44
London Conference on Confederation, 139
Londonderry, NS, 94, 108, 124, 228
Lonecloud, Jerry, 210
Longfellow, Henry Wadsworth, 130, 168
Longley, J.W., 172
Lord, Bernard, 269, 284
Lord's Day Act, 178, 184
Louis XIV (France), 54, 60, 61, 64
Louisbourg, 67, 181; attacks on, 69, 79–80, 83, 85, 86, 91; fishery, 72; founding of, 68, 69; 72; modern reconstruction, 181, 219, 248; population, 72–4, 85; relations with Aboriginal peoples, 81, 85; slavery at, 73, 80; trade, 78, 80
Low, Albert P., 179
Lowell, R.T.S., 130
Lower Canada, 92, 110, 115, 117, 132, 140
Loyalists: arrival, 91, 99; black, 92, 103, 117; impact, 101–2, 104–5, 106, 149
Lucas, Francis, 96
Lunenburg, NS, 108, 181; artists, 105; attacks on, 100; *Bluenose*, 218; fishery, 158, 201; founding, 69, 81; UNESCO World Heritage Site, 272
Lyell, Charles, 2
McCain Foods, 271
McCain, Harrison, xiii, 248
McCartney, Paul and Heather Mills, 285
McCulloch, Thomas, 108, 118, 130
McCurdy, J.A.D., 178, 186
Macdonald, Angus L., 214, 215, 219, 231, 232, 237, 241
MacDonald, Ann-Marie, 280
Macdonald Commission on Economic Union and Development Prospects for Canada, 262, 264, 267

Macdonald, Donald, 262
Macdonald, Douglas, 228
MacDonald, Edward, x
MacDonald, John, 95
Macdonald, John A., 140, 149, 150–1, 152, 153, 155, 166
MacDonald, Margaret, 192
MacDonald, Rodney, 285
McDonough, Alexa, 268
MacGregor, James, 108
MacIsaac, Ashley, 258
MacKay, Peter, 267, 279
McKenna, Frank, 266, 267, 268, 269
Mackenzie, Norman A.M., 231
McLachlan, James B., 182, 205, 228
McLean, A. Neil, 237
McLean, John, 179
Maclean Commission (1927), 201, 202
MacLean, J. Angus, 264, 268
MacLellan, Gene, 257
MacLeod, Alistair, 280
McLeod, Norman, 126
McLuhan, Marshall, 262
MacMaster, Natalie, 258, 280
McNair, J.B., 232, 243–4
McNeil, Rita, 257
McNutt, Alexander, 94
MacNutt, W.S., 241
Madokawando, 56
Maillard, Pierre-Antoine-Simon, 17, 69, 73, 81, 86
Maillet, Antonine, 258
Maliseet, *see* Wolastoqiyik
Malli, Joseph, 120
Map making, 29–30, 93
March, John, 62
Marconi, Guglielmo, 186
Marco Polo, 112, 124
Maritime Arts Association, 220
Maritime Freight Rates Act, 207
Maritime Provinces Amateur Athletic Association, 187
Maritime Provinces Board of Trade, 241, 241
Maritime Provinces Higher Education Commission, 251
Maritime Rights movement, 202, 206, 207
Maritime Union, 145, 150, 242
Markland, 26, 27
marriage: Aboriginal peoples, 17, 276; Acadians, 56; British, 77; in 19th c., 117, 173, 174; inter-marriage, 50, 56; slaves, 73; in 20th c., 217, 230
Marshall, Donald Jr., 264, 275
Marshall, Stephen Frederick, 275
Marshall, Teresa, 259
Martin, Paul, 267, 283, 286
Marysville, NB, 159
Mascarene, Paul, 75, 79
Massachusetts-Halifax Relief Committee, 193, 195
Massé, Énemond, 40
Mason, John, 43, 45
Matheson, Alexander, 241
Mauger, Joshua, 80, 91–2

May, Elizabeth, 256, 278–9
Mechanics' Institutes, 129
Medicare, 250, 251
Meech Lake Accord, 264, 266
Meighen, Arthur, 206
Membertou, 38, 39, 40
Membertou, NS, 275
mercantile system, 50, 53, 54, 99, 110, 115, 125–6, 158, 171
Métis, 179, 180, 276, 287
Mexico, 14, 30, 138, 250, 262
Micmack, *see* Mi'kmaq
Mikak, 96
Mi'kmaq, xii; creation story, 18; culture, 16–19, 119; disease, 79, 118; British and, 44, 69, 75, 79, 81–2, 86, 99–100; Cape Breton and, 102, 209, 233; colonization and, 108–9, 118–19; education, 201; European contact and, 19, 22, 24, 93; French and, 17, 33, 39, 41, 42, 48, 50, 56, 62, 63, 69, 72, 79, 81; Halifax Explosion, 194; impact of contact, 64, 79; in 19th c., 123, 165; leaders, 39, 44, 82, 109, 120, 209, 210, 278; name, 16; Newfoundland and, 95, 165, 236, 275; origins, 9, 16; population, 16, 75, 79, 95, 118, 165; relations with other Aboriginal peoples, 18–19, 56, 100; religion, 17–18, 42, 56, 57; relocation, 209, 233; rights and claims, 209, 233, 275–6; trade, 33, 48; treaties, 64, 69, 75, 81, 99, 209, 275; women, 42, 119; *see also* Aboriginal peoples
military bases: colonial, 51, 68, 72; closing of, 267; post-war, 250; Second World War, 224–5, 228
milling, 126, 179, 203, 249
Mirimachi, 182, 197; fire, 117, 118; geography, 42, 67, 108; river, 9, 27, 86, 109, 159; settlement, 94, 100; shipbuilding, 107,
Monckton, Robert, 82, 86, 87
Moncton, NB, 108; business, 179, 271, 241, 242; education, 247, 252; politicians, 243, 248, 253; population, 271, 287, 290; railway, 160, 181, 267; settlement, 94; World War I, 191; World War II, 224
Montagnais-Naskapi, *see* Innu, Inuit
Montgomery, James, 95, 109
Montgomery, Lucy Maud, x, 188
Monts, Pierre Du Gua, Sieur de, 38, 39–40, 48
Moore, Lisa, 280
Moores, Frank, 248
Moral and Social Reform Council of Canada, *see* Social Service Council of Canada
Moravians: disease, 122; missionaries, 96, 255; missions, 95, 121; settlement, 21; 92; trade, 196, 202, 209, 229
Morgentaler, Henry, 277
Morton, Suzanne, 217
Morris, Charles, 102
Morris, Christianne Paul, 119

Morris, Edward, 185, 190, 196
Morris, Maria, 130
Morris, Patrick, 131, 132
Morse, Samuel, 123
Motin, Jeanne, 52
Mulroney, Brian, 262, 266–7, 273, 278
mummering, 128–9, 256, 258
Munn, William A., 27
Murray, Alexander, 124
Murray, Anne, 257
Murray, George, 172, 184
Murray, L.W., 229
music: black people and, 257; Celtic, 257,
   280; colonial, 72; New Brunswick
   and, 279; Newfoundland and, 220,
   273
National Council of Women of Canada,
   172, 173
National Farmers Union, 249
nationalism, 163, 273–4
National Policy, 149, 155, 156, 158,
   162–3, 179, 180
National Sea Products Limited, 225, 228,
   269
navy: American, 111; British/Royal, 63,
   72, 80, 109, 111; Canadian, 224, 226;
   chaplains, 107; French, 79;
   impressment, 110; merchant, 224
neo-liberalism, 269, 276, 280
Neptune Theatre, 41, 258
New Brunswick (NB), ix; Aboriginal
   peoples, 8, 9, 10, 16, 18, 118–19, 120,
   233, 255, 275, 276; Acadians, xi, 94,
   168–70, 196, 214, 247, 252–3, 258,
   271; agriculture, 155; alcohol, 204;
   American Revolution, 111, 115;
   artists, 105, 217, 258, 259, 279;
   Atlantic Resolutions, 243; banks, 118,
   125; black peoples, 103, 117, 118,
   186, 253, 254; boundaries, 115, 117,
   123; Civil War, 140–1; coal, 7, 124,
   158; colonization, 52, 68, 91, 92;
   communications, 118, 123, 271;
   Confederation, 138, 139, 145, 147,
   148, 149; constitution, 264–7; Crown
   land, 133; Declaration of Human
   Rights, 233; economy, 140–1, 149,
   158, 160, 165, 166, 210, 214, 231–2,
   252, 268; education, 107, 128, 133,
   167, 168–9, 232, 268, 271;
   environment, 256; First World War,
   196; fishery, 271; forestry, 108, 109–
   10, 112, 156, 159, 249; geography, 5,
   6, 108, 152; histories of, 130; hydro-
   power, 203, 284; immigration, 164;
   imperialism, 173; Irish, 108, 128,
   138; Irvings, 268, 271; labour, 161;
   language, 168, 242, 247, 252, 265,
   267, 268; Loyalists, 102, 103;
   manufacturing, 158, 159, 241, 271;
   Maritime Rights, 206; military, 111
   141, 250; mining, 249, 252, 253, 288;
   municipal reform, 242, 247; nuclear
   energy, 268, 284; newspapers, 127;
   political parties, 197, 204, 267;
   politicians, 142, 147, 149, 185, 206,

216, 232, 237, 241, 243, 247, 252, 253,
   264, 266, 268, 269, 284; population,
   142, 168, 169, 177, 287, 290;
   prohibition, 118, 127, 133, 202; public
   health, 196, 207; pulp and paper, 203,
   249; railways, 141, 159, 160, 181;
   religion, 127, 128, 169, 277;
   shipbuilding, 110, 112, 122; sports,
   186, 187; tourism, 272; women, 140,
   167, 178, 197, 207, 277
New Democratic Party (NDP), 201, 251,
   262, 268–9, 283, 284, 285, 286
New England: Aboriginal peoples, 7, 9,
   14, 56, 60, 69, 75; Acadians and, 56,
   59, 62, 78, 79; American Revolution,
   98, 99, 107, 111; artists, 130; attacks
   from/on, 51, 57, 60–1, 62, 75, 79;
   boundaries, 101; colonization, 33, 43,
   50; fishery, 75, 78, 97, 99, 158, 177;
   immigration, 80, 83, 91, 98, 99;
   Loyalists, 106; militia/military, 62, 79;
   out-migration to, 163; piracy, 72;
   'Planters', 91, 92, 94, 100; privateers,
   79; religion, 80, 91, 100; trade, 107,
   110, 284; treaties, 76–7, 80
Newfoundland (NL), ix, x; Aboriginal
   peoples, 3, 8, 11, 12, 16, 19–22, 61,
   89, 95, 120, 165, 236–7, 255, 275,
   276, 288; agriculture, 130, 155–6,
   237; American Revolution, 97, 101;
   artists, 189, 219, 220, 258, 25, 280;
   Atlantic Provinces cooperation, 264,
   270, 287; auks, 118; automobiles, 216;
   banks, 156, 163; British Empire and,
   155, 173, 185, 197; boundaries, 88,
   180, 209, 264, 271; Civil War, 140;
   colonial government, 69, 70–1, 92,
   95, 118, 131, 132–4, 142, 185, 196,
   202, 208; colonization, 44–7, 48, 50,
   51, 58–60, 89, 61, 64, 91;
   communications, 123, 186, 216, 235;
   Confederation (1867), 137, 138, 139,
   145, 147, 151, 152, 153; Confederation
   (1949), 150, 166, 211–12, 215, 22,
   229, 233–7, 241, 245; courts, 92;
   economy, 124, 125, 132, 155, 157,
   177, 200, 208, 241, 245; education,
   128, 167, 268, 269; exploration, 25,
   26, 27. 29, 30, 38, 173, 272; federal
   government and, 242, 243, 266, 270,
   272–3, 284, 285; First World War,
   178, 189, 190, 192, 193–4, 196, 197;
   fishery, 31–2, 33, 44, 51, 58, 59, 68,
   70–1, 87–8, 89, 95, 101, 107, 109,
   110, 119, 122, 124, 132, 151, 157,
   162–3, 165, 166, 178, 201, 202, 208,
   215, 227, 251, 268, 269, 270, 271;
   forestry, 156; French-English
   relations, 51, 58, 59, 60, 61–2, 64, 82,
   87, 101, 109; geography, 3, 4, 5, 6, 10,
   52, 121, 152; Great Depression, 201,
   210–12; histories of, 130, 131; hydro-
   power, 287; immigration, 164, 210;
   Irish, 108, 109, 117, 147; Labrador
   and, 92, 95, 122, 133, 209, 225, 229,
   236, 269; labour, 182, 183, 195, 19,

210, 214, 242, 244, 248, 251;
   language, 253; Loyalists, 102;
   mapping/surveys, 74, 92, 93, 124;
   mining, 158, 208, 215; militia/
   military, 51, 61, 98, 109, 190, 193,
   194, 224–5, 228, 229; mummering,
   128, 258; national parks, 3; National
   Policy, 162–3; neo-nationalism, 273–
   4; newspapers, 102, 127, 131; offshore
   resources, 272–3, 286, 289; out-
   migration, 163–4; outports, xi, xii,
   130, 189, 207, 259; piracy, 72;
   population, 91, 95, 107, 108, 127, 14,
   163–4, 165, 268, 270, 290;
   prohibition, 202, 204; public health,
   207; pulp and paper, 178, 179, 208,
   209, 244; Quebec and, 246, 287;
   railways, 156, 175, 179, 181, 209, 267;
   religion, 105, 107, 109, 127–8, 131,
   142, 167, 171, 218, 268, 269, 277,
   286; royal commissions, 284, 285;
   seal fishery, 110, 124, 178, 189, 256,
   259, 285; Second World War, 223–5,
   227–8, 229, 230; settlement, 91, 92,
   95, 108, 117, 214, 242, 246;
   shipbuilding, 107, 157; songs, xi, 189,
   219; social reform, 171, 172;
   temperance, 170; tourism, 189, 219;
   trade, 33–4, 60, 107, 110, 125, 156,
   157, 166, 178, 210, 225, 241; treaties,
   51, 101, 166; whaling, 32; women, 60,
   172, 192, 197, 202, 207–8, 213, 217,
   218, 224, 230, 256
Newfoundland Fishermen, Food, and
   Allied Workers, 251
Newfoundland Lumbermen's
   Association, 244
Newfoundland Militia, see Royal
   Newfoundland Regiment
Newfoundland Outport Nursing and
   Industrial Association, 207
Newfoundland Ranger Force, 215
Newfoundland Renaissance, 235–6
New France: Acadians and, 84;
   colonization, 39, 42, 43, 50, 51;
   conflict, 82; geography, 52, 64; name,
   30; religion, 39; theatre, 41
New Labrador Party, 248
New Netherland, 40, 53, 54
New Scotland, 42, 43, 44
New York: 93; Acadians, 83–4; attacks
   on, 61; British in, 87, 99, 101;
   Loyalists, 102, 106; name, 54; 9/11,
   282; people, 102, 105, 129, 139, 172,
   180, 217, 220, 257; stock market, 200;
   trade, 80; UN, 223
New York, Newfoundland, and London
   Telegraph Company, 123
newspapers: Acadian, 169; agricultural,
   184; colonial, 68; 19th c., 115, 127,
   130, 134; 20th c., 261
Nicholas, Sandra Lovelace, 276
Nicholson, Francis, 62
Nielsen, Wendy, 279
Norse, 12, 25–6, 27, 28; Viking
   Millennium, 272

North Atlantic world: Aboriginal peoples, 12; 18th c., 68, 69, 80, 101, 104; exploration of, 29, 93, 48; fishery, 31, 270; geography, ix, 3; 19th c., 117, 129, 137, 153, 173; piracy, 33, 72; resources, xii; 20th c., 284; wars, 1, 226–7

North Atlantic Treaty Organization (NATO), 223

Northwest Atlantic Fisheries Organization (NAF), 270

Nova Scotia (NS), ix, xii; Aboriginal peoples, 7, 8, 9, 63, 75, 76, 79, 81, 118–19, 209–10, 233, 255, 275; Acadians in, 78, 83, 94, 169–70, 253; agriculture, 126, 130, 155, 184, 214; American Revolution, 97–100; artists, 105, 117, 257; banks, 156, 16, 172; black peoples, 103–4, 117–18, 126, 127, 167, 187, 194, 218, 233, 253–4, 278; boundaries, 68, 101, 264, 271; British dominance, 76–7, 80, 86–7; coal, 7, 124, 148, 158, 167, 179, 180, 182, 202, 215, 248, 274; Civil War, 140, 150; colonial government, 68–9, 70, 88–9, 91, 118, 127, 132; colonization, 38, 43–4; communications, 118, 123, 186; Confederation, 138, 139, 147–8, 15, 166; economy, 112, 140, 148, 165, 179, 210, 214, 242, 243–4, 268; education, 108, 130, 167, 194, 253, 268; environment, 256, 278; exploration, 26, 30, 31, 38; federal government and, 206, 214, 231, 243–4, 250, 264, 266; First World War, 172, 195; fishery, 112, 124, 166, 177, 178, 201, 228, 270; forestry, 179; French-British relations, 53, 63–64, 67, 68–9, 79, 80, 83, 87; geography, 1, 2, 5–6, 10, 52, 88, 108, 152; golden age myth, xi; Great Depression, 210; histories of, 130; hydro-power, 287; immigration, 91, 95, 107, 117; labour, 161, 167, 178, 204, 215, 228, 232, 248, 250; land grants, 95, 102, 126; Loyalists, 91, 101–4, 106; manufacturing, 158, 179, 247; mapping/surveys, 93; Maritime Rights, 201, 206; Maritime Union, 145, 166; mining, 118, 124, 133, 148, 167, 180, 202, 274, 278; natural history, 130; newspapers, 130, 169; offshore resources, 272, 27, 286, 288; piracy, 72; 'Planters', 91, 92; political parties, 197, 204, 241, 267, 268, 284, 285; population, 78, 81, 83, 91, 101–3, 107, 117, 142, 177, 203, 268, 290; prohibition, 178, 184, 202, 204; pulp and paper, 203; railways, 141, 181; religion, 100, 105, 107–8, 127, 133, 167, 277; responsible government, 132–3; royal commission, 231; Scots, 10, 117; secession movement, 139, 149–50, 166, 156; settlement, 63, 67, 81, 94; songs, xi; social reform, 184; sports, 129, 187; steel industry, 156, 158, 182, 204, 215, 248; tourism, 189, 218–19, 272; trade, 150–1, 184, 214; treaties, 101; unions, 13, 202, 215, 228, 232; women, 130, 156, 167, 172, 178, 184, 197, 217, 256; Yorkshire, 92, 94

Nova Scotia Home for Coloured Children, 194

Nova Scotia Steel and Coal Company, 156, 158, 180, 204

Nova Scotia Association for the Advancement of Coloured People (NSAACP), 233, 253

Nowlan, Aldan, 258

Nowlan, George, 243–4

Nunatsiavut, 284, 287, 288

Ocean Ranger, 264, 274

Ochiltree, Lord, 38, 43

O'Donnel, James, 107, 109

Official Languages Act, 253

O'Flaherty, Patrick, x

oil and gas, 124, 248, 272, 273, 274, 280, 284

oil crisis (1973), 241, 261, 263, 264

Oliver, Pearly and Pearleen, 253

Orange Order, 128, 235

Ordre de Bon Temps, 38, 39

O'Ree, Willie, 254

Osborne, Henry, 69, 70

out-migration: in late 20th c., 201, 232, 254, 259; in 19th c., 139, 163–4, 170; post-war, 197

overfishing, 32, 269

Paleo-Eskimos, 3, 11

Paleo-Indians, 3, 7–8, 12

Palliser, Hugh, 92, 95, 96

Palliser, Jonathan, *see* Tutauk

Palmer, Edward, 142

Parkhurst, Anthony, 32

Parkin, George, 173

Parmenius, Stephen, 48

Parr, John, 102, 104

Parti Acadien, 242, 253

Parti Québécois, 263, 264, 266, 274

Passamaquoddy people: 9, 16, 19; population, 118; relations with Europeans, 86; 99, 119; relations with Ottawa, 165, 275; territory, 56; treaties, 64, 69, 75, 81

Patriotic Association of Newfoundland, 190, 196

Paul, Leonard, 259

Pearson, Lester, 244, 245, 248

Peckford, Brian, 244, 264, 266, 272, 274, 285

Peggy's Cove, NS, 219

Penobscot people, 56, 76, 77

Penobscot River/Bay, 41, 43, 100

pensions: 210, 240, 250

Perkins, Simeon, 98

Perley, Moses, 119

Peters, Thomas, 103, 149

Petit, Louis, 56

Petit Nord, 31, 64, 133

Philadelphia plantation, 94

Philipps, Richard, 69, 70, 78

Phips, Sir William, 51, 61

Pickersgill, J.W., 241, 242

Piers, Harry, 210

Pinsent, Gordon, 259

piracy, 33, 37, 44, 71–2

Pitts, Herman H., 169–70

Placentia, NL, 32, 34, 62, 69, 70, 98

Placentia Bay, 45, 47, 121, 181

plantations, 44–6, 58–9, 60, 73, 94, 102, 110

Planters: New England, 91, 92, 94, 100; Newfoundland, 58–9, 62, 72

Point Lepreau nuclear power plant, 268, 284

Point Tupper Heavy Water plant, 248

Policy of Progress, 162, 163, 179

politics: colonial, 145; electoral, 197; federal, 184, 23, 264, 266; Maritime, 214; Newfoundland, 132, 19, 208, 266; Nova Scotia, 247; radical, 214; regional, 243, 285; religion and, 182, 183; women and, 197, 277

Poor, Joseph Alfred, 141

Pope, James, 152, 153

Pope, Peter, 60

Port-aux-Baleines colony, 43

Port-aux-Basques, NL, 162

Porter, Gladys, 256

Port-Royal, 67; Acadians, 55, 56, 62, 63, 83; attacks on, 5, 61, 62; education, 56; English settlement, 43–4, 64; French settlement, 38–42, 50–1, 53–4, 62; modern reconstruction, 219

Portugal, 25, 29, 31, 32, 110, 270

Portuguese, 21, 24, 25, 26, 27, 29, 30, 31, 52

Potash Corporation of Saskatchewan, 288

Poutrincourt et de Saint-Juste, Jean de, 39, 40–2

poverty: black people and, 103, 253; in Newfoundland, 171, 202, 213; in 19th c., 113, 126, 133, 164; in 20th c., 201, 231, 252; women and, 174

Pratt, Christopher, 259, 274

Pratt, E.J., 189

Pratt, Mary, 259

press gangs, 100, 110, *see also* impressment

primary industries, 133, 163, 230, 231, 259, *see also* specific industry

Prince Edward Agustus, 108

Prince Edward Island (PEI), ix; Aboriginal peoples, 9, 17, 18, 109, 119; Acadians, 125, 170, 253; agriculture, 112, 155, 203, 204, 237, 249; artists, 168, 188, 257, 259; automobiles, 178, 189; banks, 125; colonization, 107, 108; Civil War, 140; communications, 123; Confederation, 138, 139, 145, 147, 151, 152; Confederation Bridge, 271; economy, 165, 232, 242, 247; education, 118, 125, 127, 133, 167, 232; exploration, 30; ferries, 185, 207; federal government and, 241, 248, 264, 266; First World War, 193, 195; fishery, 271; fox farming, 177, 203; franchise, 133; Great Depression, 210; histories

of, x; immigration, 117; geography, 4,
5, 7, 108; Land Commission, 139, 142,
143; Maritime Rights, 206; Maritime
Union, 166; mills, 126; name, 92, 107;
national parks, 219; political parties,
132–3, 206, 268, 278, 285,
population, 10, 127, 132, 142, 163,
177, 203, 290; prohibition, 156, 170–
1, 184, 204; public health, 207;
railways, 141, 181; religion, 127, 167;
royal commissions, 231; songs, xi,
188, 257; tenant–landlord relations,
129, 132, 133; tourism, 189, 219, 247;
trade, 141–2; 'wind farms', 289;
women, 188, 197, 202, 207, 277; see
also Île Saint-Jean
Prince Edward Island Land Commission,
139, 142, 143
privateers, 45, 60, 61, 62, 71, 79, 92, 98,
111, 125
Progressive Conservative Partym, 241–4,
247–8, 251, 262–3, 264, 266, 267–9,
283, 284, 285, 287; see also
Conservative Party
Progressive Party, 197, 206
prohibition: alcohol 118, 127, 133, 169,
170–1, 178, 183, 184, 196;
automobiles, 189; bills, 149; end of,
202, 204, 209; Scott Act, 156, 170
prostitution, 272
Protestants: colonial era, 25, 38, 43, 45,
70; education, 128; 'Foreign', 69, 81;
Halifax, 80; settlers, 89, 91, 94, 95,
107, 108, 117, 128, 140; Labrador, 95;
newspapers, 127; navy and, 107; New
Brunswick, 169–70; Newfoundland,
107, 131, 142, 183, 273; values, 127,
169–70, 277
provincial governments, 173, 210, 215,
216, 253, 256, 264, 265, 275, 280, 288
Provincial Workmen's Association (PWA),
156, 167, 182
public health, 171, 195, 207
Pugwash Conference on Science and
World Affairs, 256
pulp and paper: environment and, 278;
industry, 208, 249, 256; mills, 178,
179, 203; see also forestry industry
Quakers, 91, 95
Quebec: Aboriginal peoples, 12, 20, 237;
Acadia and, 52, 54, 56, 59, 62, 67, 73,
80, 82; Acadians and, 83, 84, 168–70,
253; American Revolution, 97, 110;
attacks on, 43, 60, 61, 86, 93, 97, 99,
110; boundaries, 88, 180; British
control of, 101; colonization, 42; Civil
War, 141; Confederation, 139, 145,
147–8, 151, 155; constitution, 266–7;
exploration, 30; federal government,
185, 205, 206, 231, 242, 263; First
World War, 190, 195; fishery, 271;
fortification, 40; geography, 5, 10,
152; hydro-power, 204, 242, 245–6,
284, 287; immigration, 164; Labrador
and, 92, 95, 120, 245, 287, Louisbourg
and, 81; Loyalists, 102; Newfoundland

and, 209, 246, 287; population, 142,
150; prohibition, 170; railways, 141,
144, 181; referendum, 263, 264;
religion, 127; Second World War, 224;
trade, 158, 204, 263, 284
Quebec resolutions, 147, 148, 151
Queen Anne's War, 51, 62
radio, 189; Acadians and, 253;
broadcasting, 216, 234, 257;
Newfoundland and, 216, 234, 235;
use of, 200, 216–7, 257, 262
railways: financing and debt, 139, 144,
153, 212; first, 118, 123, 140;
industrial development and, 124; 157,
159, 162, 177, 179, 204; Intercolonial,
147, 150, 156, 158, 160, 164, 202,
203; Joseph Howe and, 140, 141, 149;
Labrador, 245; New Brunswick, 159–
6, 181; Newfoundland, 147, 156, 162–
3, 165, 175, 179, 181, 209; Prince
Edward Island, 141, 152–3, 181;
transcontinental, 141; 155, 156, 158,
161, 162, 164, 166, 177, 203, 267
Ramezay, Jean-Baptiste-Nicolas-Roch de,
79
Rand, Ivan, 248
Rand, Silas, 18, 119
rangers, 79, 86, 215
Razilly, Isaac de, 50–1
reciprocity, 126, 150, 155, 156, 166; see
also free trade
Reciprocity Treaty, 118, 126, 141, 142,
146, 158, 185
Récollets, 17, 42, 56, 73
Reconstruction Party, 201, 214
Red Cross, 172, 192, 193, 207, 210
Reeves, John, 131
reform movements, 131, 170, 172
Reform Party: in 19th c., 133, 140; in
20th c., 263, 264, 266, 267
regiments: Canadian Forestry Corps,
192; Canadian Machine Gun Corps,
191; 1st Essex, 194; militia, 189; No, 2
Construction Battalion, 192; 104th,
111; 40th, 75, 77; Provincial, 102;
Royal Artillery, 77; Royal Fencible
American, 99; Royal Newfoundland,
98, 109, 178, 190, 192, 193, 194, 224;
St John's Royal Volunteers, 131; Swiss,
74
regionalism, ix, xii, 243
Reid, Robert G., 163
Reid Newfoundland Company, 189, 195,
202, 209
religion, see specific denomination
Rhodes, E.N., 206
Richards, David Adams, 280
riots: Caraquet, 156, 167; colonial, 100;
labour, 129; political, 142, 197, 211;
race, 103; Second World War, 225, 229
Ritchie, Amelia, 172
Ritchie, J.W., 142
Roberts, Bartholomew, 71–2
Roberts, Charles G.D., 188
Roberts, William F., 196
Robertson, Thomas, 209

Robichaud, Louis J., 247, 249
Rogers, Malcolm, 246
Roma, Jean-Pierre, 75, 79
Roman Catholics: Aboriginal peoples, 38,
39; Acadians and, 78, 169; British and,
68, 69, 102, 108; churches, 128, 279,
286; colonization, 43, 45, 50, 54, 56,
59; education, 127, 128, 167, 168, 175,
269; franchise, 107, 118, 127; Labrador,
121; missionaries, 17, 56; New
Brunswick, 147, 167; Newfoundland,
87, 107–8, 128, 131, 142, 145, 182–3,
235, 269, 273; newspapers, 127; Nova
Scotia, 214; population, 127, 169;
practices, 30, 127, 174, 217, 277; Prince
Edward Island, 152; Protestants and,
25, 38, 127–8, 277; settlers, 95, 107;
slaves and, 73
Ronde, Louis Denys de la, 62
Roosevelt, Franklin D., 215
Royal Canadian Air Force (RCAF), 224
Royal Canadian Navy, 224
Royal Commissions: 236; Canada's
Economic Prospects, 242; Coal
(1960), 248; Coal Mining Industry
(1925), 202, 205; Dominion-
Provincial Relations (Rowell-Sirois),
215; Economic Union and
Development Prospects for Canada,
262, 264; Fisheries (Maclean), 201,
202; Fiscal and Trade Policies, 214;
Labour and Capital, 161; Maritime
Claims, 202, 206; Municipal Finance
and Taxation, 247; Newfoundland
(Amulree), 202, 212; Ocean Ranger,
274; Provincial Development, 231;
Reconstruction, 228; Renewing and
Strengthening Our Place in Canada
(NL), 284, 285; Terms of Union
(Newfoundland), 243; Status of
Women, 242, 256
Royal Newfoundland Regiment, 98, 109;
First World War, 178, 190, 192, 193–
4; Second World War, 224
Royal Proclamation, 1763, 89, 92
Rupert's Land, 52, 64, 88, 144, 151
Russell, Earl, 148
Russell, John, 96, 132
Russell, Ted, 258
Rut, John, 30
Rutherford, Erica, 259
Sable Island, 5; exploration of, 93; oil
exploration, 264, 272, 273;
settlement, 38
sack trade, 58, 60
Saint-Castin, Vincent de, 56, 61, 62
St Croix River, 19, 38, 101, 115,
Saint John, NB, 108; artists, 217, 220;
British and, 110; economy, 207, 248,
268, 271; education, 171; fires, 156;
First World War, 196; founding, 102,
104, 105; government, 178;
immigration, 164; industry, 159, 227,
248, 284, 288; labour, 167;
newspapers, 102; politicians, 149;
politics, 173, 267; population, 156,

290; railways, 123, 141, 181; religion, 128; Second World War, 224, 229; settlers, 108; ships and shipbuilding, 122, 124, 126; social reform, 171; sports, 186; tourism, 219; trade, 124, 133, 156, 158

St John River, NB, 67, 93; Aboriginal peoples, 16, 19, 87, 92, 233; Acadians, 83, 87; boundaries, 115; colonization, 42, 44, 51, 61, 80, 86, 92, 94, 98, 99–100; hydro-power, 241; immigration, 117, 164; industry, 271; Loyalists, 102, 106; railways, 159; shipbuilding, 110

St John's, NL, Aboriginal peoples, 96, 119; Acadians and, 83; airport, 224, 229; American navy, 225; artists, 189, 220, 256, 258; attacks on, 51, 59, 61–3, 69, 87, 109; banks, 163; colonization, 110; communications, 123, 186, 216; Confederation (1949), 234–5; co-operatives, 214; education, 171; exploration, 37, 173; fire, 156; fishery, 46, 87, 269, 270; fortifications, 62, 98, 109; geography, 47, 88, 121; immigration, 164; industry, 125, 162, 178, 208; Irish, 108, 131; labour, 178, 182, 183; 202, 209, 214; Loyalists, 102; name, 31; newspapers, 127; offshore resources, 272, 286; piracy, 72; population, 229, 290; politicians, 131, 132, 208, 209, 269; politics, 142, 173, 190, 208, 211–12; religion, 107, 128–9, 277, 286; regatta, 129; roads, 216; seal fishery, 124, 178, 189; social reform, 171; tourism, 219, 272; trade, 178, 202; War of 1812, 111; women, 171, 172

St John's Island, 91–5, 97, 101, 102, 107, 109; see also Île St Jean, Prince Edward Island

St Lawrence River, 6, 10, 15, 152, 181; Aboriginal peoples and, 33; defense of, 68; development, 155; exploration, 30, 32; Seaway, 241; Second World War, 225, 226; settlement around, 40, 42, 50, 115; transportation, 140, 141, 158

St-Laurent, Julie, 109

St Laurent, Louis, 241

St Lawrence Seaway, 241

Saint-Ovide, Governor, 72, 75

Saint-Pierre, Comte de, 69, 74, 75

Saint-Pierre and Miquelon, ix, 84, 88, 89, 101, 112, 121, 204

Saint-Sauveur colony, 38, 41

Salt Codfish Board, 202

Sark, Elsie, 192

Sark, John J., 192

Sark, Jonathan, 259

Saskatchewan, 190, 206, 232, 247, 251, 265, 268, 278

Saskatchewan mafia, 247

Saunders, Margaret Marshall, 188

Saunders, S.A., 204

Savage, John, 268

schools: Aboriginal, 122, 210; Acadian, 125, 168–9; acts, 133, 167; attendance, 217, 232, 250; blacks, 167, 253; charity, 127; colonial, 56, 78, 107, 129; construction of, 268; denominational, 147, 152, 167, 183, 268, 269; discipline, 129; French-language, 253; Grenfell, 171; in 19th c., 115, 147; inspections, 197, 207–8; Newfoundland, 213, 269; nursing, 171; post secondary, 256; postwar, 230; Prince Edward Island, 232; public, 118, 127, 129, 141, 167, 174, 232; Second World War, 229; segregated/separate, 103, 147, 167, 253; Sunday, 127, 149; vocational, 250; see also education

Scotland, 43, 62, 81, 129, 148; immigration from, 94, 108; trade, 107

secession movement, 139, 149–51, 156, 166

Second World War: begins, 202, 225; convoys, 226; impact of 139, 200, 215, 220, 223, 235; origins, 223; postwar, 241; prohibition, 204; women, 207

Segipt, 44

Sedgwick, Robert, 51, 53

Selkirk, Earl of, 107

Senate: American, 166, 185; Canadian, 145, 265, 266, 276; women and, 256

Seven Years' War, 1, 69, 85–7, 92, 97

Seward, William, 146

Shaheen, John, 248

Shanawdithit, 20, 118, 119

Shannon, 111

Shebib, Don, 259

Shelburne, NS, 102–4, 108, 110, 224

Sherbrooke, John, 112

Sheshatshiu, 255, 276, 288

shipbuilding: decline of, 156, 166; in 18th c., 94, 107; in 19th c., 110, 112, 115, 122, 124, 126, 142; in 20th c., 285

Shirley, William, 79

Sierra Leone, 92, 103–4

Simonds, Charles, 133

Simonds, James, 91

Sinclair, Prince Henry, 26

slavery: abolition of, 68, 116, 118; at Louisbourg, 73; black people and, 103–4; in America, 138

Smallwood, Joseph: as premier, 237, 241, 242, 243, 244–6, 247, 248, 249, 273, 287; assessment of Newfoundland, 208; career, 220, 234; Confederation, 234–5, 237

Smith, Albert J., 147

Smith, Titus, 130

Snow, Hank, 217

Sobey, Frank, xiii, 248

social assistance plans, 240, 250

social gospel movement, 170

social justice, 232, 253

social reform, 171, 173, 175, 218, 251

Social Service Council of Canada, 184

social unrest, 166–73, 196, 215

Société Nationale l'Assomption/de l'Acadie, 169

Society for the Propagation of the Gospel, 78, 107

Sons of Temperance, 170

South Africa, 173, 212

South African War, 156, 173, 187

Southack, Cyprian, 61

Spain: colonization, 32; conflicts, 85, 100, 101; exploration, 25, 29, 30; fishery, 31, 32, 110, 270; merchants, 53; treaties, 63–4

Spanish influenza pandemic, 137, 177, 178, 196

sports, 129, 164, 165, 186–8, 254–5

Springhill, NS: business, 180; mining disasters, 249–50; railways, 180, 281; strikes, 167, 178, 182

Squires, Helena, 256

Squires, Richard, 183, 208–9, 211, 216, 234

Stanfield, Robert L., 241, 244, 247, 248

Stanton, John, 98

Status Indians, see Aboriginal peoples

Statute of Westminster, 144, 202, 212

steamships, 118, 123, 125, 262

steel industry, 161, 177, 179, 182, 192, 203–5, 207, 216, 231, 248, 287; beginnings of 153, 156; companies, 156, 158, 159, 163, 178, 180, 182, 202, 204, 215, 227, 228, 248; consolidation, 180–1, 202, 204; railways, 158, 248; strikes and unrest, 182, 202, 205, 215; tar ponds, 274; wartime expansion, 196, 227

Steele, Harry, xiii, 248

Stern, Fritz, 190

Stewart, James, see Ochiltree, Lord

Stewart, J.D., 206

Stewart, Robert, 80

Stine, Anne, 27

strikes: coal industry, 167, 178, 182, 202, 225; fishery, 182, 197, 232, 242, 251; forestry, 242, 244; in 19th c., 129, 167; in 20th c., 177, 182, 195, 197, 215, 229; offshore oil industry, 272; steel industry, 202, 205, 227

Subercase, Daniel d'Auger de, 62, 63

Sullivan, Laurence, 153

Supreme Court: in Newfoundland, 92, 107; in Nova Scotia, 233; in the US, 253; of Canada, 255, 264, 265, 275–6, 277

Sydney, NS: 204, 210; tar ponds,

Sydney Steel Corporation (SYSCO), 248, 274

Syliboy, Alan, 259

Sylliboy, Gabriel, 209

Taliban, 282

Tansley, Donald, 247

technology: Aboriginal, 7, 9; colonial, 37, 109; industrial, 116, 124, 157, 159; seagoing, 25

Tecouenemac, Antoine, 63

telegraph, 118, 123, 163, 186, 262

temperance, 116, 127, 149, 170, 175

Temple, Sir Thomas, 53, 54
Tenant League, 139, 142, 153
terms of union, 62, 148, 234, 236–7, 243
Testard de Montigny, Jacques, 62
Ternay, Charles-Henry d'Arsac de, 87
Théâtre de Neptune, Le, 41 Theatre New
    Brunswick, 258
Thompson, John, 184
Thompson, Stanley, 219
Thule people, 3, 11–12, 20
Tilley, Samuel Leonard, 141, 147, 149
Tobin, Brian, 269, 270, 285
Tompkins, Jimmy, 220
Torngat Mountains National Park
    Reserve, 5, 288
tourism, 189, 219, 247, 272, 287
trade, *see* specific place
Trade Union Act (1937), 202, 215
Trade Union Act (1947), 232
Trans-Canada Airlines, 229
transportation, 116, 123, 145, 175, 186,
    214, 241, 248, 271, 284
trawlers: construction of, 228, 250;
    fleets, 177–8, 201; Spanish, 264, 270;
    strikes, 242, 251
treaties: acid rain, 278; Aix-la-Chapelle,
    69, 80; Breda, 51, 53; Ghent, 92, 112;
    Paris, 1, 69, 88, 92, 101; Peace and
    Friendship, 69; Reciprocity, 118, 126,
    141, 146, 150, 158,166; Ryswick, 51,
    62; Saint-Germain-en-Laye, 38, 44,
    50, 60; 1726, 76; Tordesillas, 29, 33;
    Utrecht, 51, 63–4, 68, 69, 72, 80, 88;
    Versailles, 197, 212, 223; Washington,
    139, 150, 156, 157; Webster-
    Ashburton, 115, 118
Treworgie, John, 58
truck system, 126, 213
Trudeau, Pierre Elliott, 245, 255, 262,
    263, 264, 266
Tupper, Charles, 141, 145, 147–8, 150,
    184
Tutauk, 96
unemployment insurance, 225, 231, 240,
    242, 250, 267
Uniacke, James Boyle, 133
Union government, 195
Union of New Brunswick Indians, 255
Union of Nova Scotia Indians, 255
unions: breaking of, 231; credit, 214;
    militancy of, 204, 215; trade, 133,
    182, 232, 251; *see also* strikes
Unitas Fratrum, *see* Moravians
United Farmers, 204
United Fishermen and Allied Workers'
    Union, 251
United Mineworkers of America (UMW),
    215, 228
United Nations: 83, 223, 232, 240, 276,
    278, 279, 283; UNESCO World Heritage
    Site, 3, 27, 272
United Nations Intergovernmental Panel
    on Climate Change, 283
United States, xii; black people and, 253;
    boundaries, 115; Civil War, 138, 140,
    146; Cold War, 256; dominance of,

139, 146, 155, 217, 223; education,
    129; environment, 278; exploration,
    14; financial crisis of 2008, 283; First
    World War, 197; fishery, 124, 157,
    166, 185, 201; hydro-power, 245;
    immigration from, 117, 215, 256;
    independence, 1, 91, 100, 101;
    industrialization, 116, 123, 124;
    influenza, 196; Labrador, 224;
    Loyalists, 102, 105; military bases,
    225; 9/11, 282; Nova Scotia and, 150;
    oil, 272, 274, 288; out-migration to,
    156, 164, 169, 217; sports,
    187;prohibition, 204; Second World
    War, 229, 230; trade, 101, 107, 124,
    126, 141, 142, 150, 158, 159, 166,
    178, 184, 185, 200, 203, 256, 262–3,
    289; War of 1812, 110–11, 118
universities, 172, 187, 220, 231, 250–1,
    268; Acadia, 175, 220; Dalhousie, 175,
    188, 220; McGill, 231; Memorial, 220,
    273; Mount Allison, 128, 156, 174–5,
    259; Mount Saint Vincent, 128, 237;
    Queen's, 249; St Francis Xavier, 128,
    175, 214; Saint Mary's; Université de
    Moncton, 252, 253; University of New
    Brunswick, 133, 167, 231
Upper Canada, 111, 115, 140
Valdmanis, Alfred, 245
Van Horne, William, 181
Vaughan, William, 44–5
Verrazzano, Giovanni da, 24, 26, 29–30
veterans, 197, 231
Vikings, *see* Norse
Villiers, Louis Coulon de, 79
Vinland, 26, 27
Voisey's Bay, NL, 264, 272, 276
voluntarism, 116
vote, right to, 70, 133, 165, 172, 197, 202,
    236, 242, 255; *see also* franchise
Wabanaki ('Dawnland') Confederacy, 56,
    60–1, 62, 63
Wabanaki-New England War, 69, 75, 85
Wabush, NL, 245
wages: and working conditions, 129, 194,
    215, 244; decreases in, 72, 204, 205,
    216, 262, 289; earners, xiii, 103, 126,
    162, 164, 191, 210, 250, 268;
    minimum, 183, 227, 240
wage and price controls, 261
Wagner Act (US), 215
Wallace, Dillon, 180
Wallace, F.W., 218
War of the Austrian Succession, 69, 75,
    78–80
War of 1812, 92, 110–12, 117
War of the League of Augsburg, *see* King
    William's War
War of the Spanish Succession, *see* Queen
    Anne's War
Warren, Peter, 79
Washington, DC, 112, 123, 146, 234
Washington, George, 97, 99
Watt, Isasc, 77
Wedderburn, Gus, 253
welfare state, 231, 240, 250, 262

Wells, Clyde, 248, 266, 268, 269
Wentworth, John, 104
Western Charter, 51, 58, 59
Westray mine disaster, 264, 274
whaling, 11, 12, 20, 21, 26, 31, 32, 33,
    34, 35
Whitbourne, Richard, 33, 45
White House, 112
White, James, 91
White, Portia, 257
White, William, 192
White Paper on Indian Policy, 242, 255
Whiteway, William, 162
Whitney, Henry M., 158–9, 180
Whitney Pier, NS, 164, 205
Wilkinson, Moses, 103
William of Orange, 60
Williams, Arch, 259
Williams, Danny, 255, 285–6, 287
Williams, William Fenwick, 147
Wilson, Mona, 207–8
Winslow, Edward, 106
Winslow, Mary Mathilda, 167
Winter, Michael, 280
Winton, Henry, 128
Wolastoqiyik (Maliseet): Acadians and,
    92, 102; British and, 99–100; culture,
    18–19, 210; European contact, 119,
    165; name, 16; origins, 9, 15, 16;
    Mi'kmaq and, 44, 56, 63, 64, 75–6,
    86, 99, 100, 108, 209, 275;
    Passamaquoddy and, 81, 86;
    population, 118; religion, 201;
    relocation, 233; rights and claims,
    275; treaties, 69; *see also* Aboriginal
    peoples
Wolfe, James, 86, 93
women: Aboriginal, 16, 17, 20, 96, 120,
    165, 196, 255, 276; birth control,
    173–4, 217–18, 230, 257; blacks, 103,
    195, 202, 218; education, ix, 167, 171,
    174–5, 255, 256; employment, 158,
    173, 174, 224, 227, 250; exploration
    and, 27, 34, 44; First World War, 182,
    192, 195; franchise, 133, 156, 172–3,
    178, 195, 197, 202, 209, 255;
    missionaries, 175; organizations, 171,
    172, 175, 184, 192, 202, 208, 218,
    256, 276, 277; out-migration, 163,
    224; politics, 172, 277; popular
    culture, xi, 217; population, 117, 246,
    255; pregnancy, 217; prostitution, 217,
    230; religion, 128, 174, 175, 218;
    rights, 68, 171, 172, 174, 184, 218,
    255–6, 276; royal commissions, 242,
    256; Second World War, 224, 228,
    230; settlement and, 54, 56, 57, 60,
    62, 71, 82, 85, 86, 100; sports, 187
Women's Christian Temperance Union
    (WTCU), 170, 172
Women's Patriotic Association, 192
Wyile, Herb, 279
Wynne, Edward, 46
Young, John, 118, 130
Young Men's/Women's Christian
    Association (YMCA/YWCA), 171, 187